EXAM C] G000114432

The Server+ Cram Sheet

This Cram Sheet contains key facts about the Server+ exam that you should review before you enter the testing center, paying special attention to those areas in which you feel you need the most review. You can transfer any of these facts from your head onto a blank sheet of paper immediately before you begin the exam.

SERVER TYPES

1. General-purpose servers are employed in most small businesses for multiple purposes such as handling departmental email and providing file, print, and web services running on standard NOSes.

2. Appliance servers provide single services such as handling departmental email or providing file, print, and web services that run on standard NOSes.

3. Application servers run programs accessed by multiple users, and often handle large information databases.

4. Mail servers are client/server types of application servers used to receive and store electronic mail messages in private mailboxes, even when users are not actually logged directly on to the network.

5. Firewall servers control the connections between two networks, such as acting as an Internet gateway, where access control blocks unwanted traffic, while allowing acceptable communications.

6. Proxy servers act as intermediaries between client workstations and the Internet.

7. Web servers host web pages for intranet and/or Internet access, and can be configured to host more than one site depending on the server's underlying OS.

8. Database servers are utilized to store and sort through data in response to client queries, where organizations must manage large quantities of data.

9. Terminal servers are special-purpose computers fitted with multi-ported asynchronous modem connections, as well as ports designed to interface with a LAN, or some other host machine.

10. DNS servers contain database listings used to resolve computer names to IP addresses.

11. Gateway servers interface between different types of networks, protocols, or mechanisms to provide access to another system.

12. Router servers manage the shared resources of all other routers in the network, as well as the various transmission speeds and different protocols being used within an organization's network.

13. Bridge servers use multi-NICs to connect groups of computers and reduce network traffic. They translate between protocols and help to reduce network traffic.

14. FTP servers transfer files across the Internet, an extranet, or an intranet through the use of FTP client software.

15. NAS servers move storage out from behind the file server, and put it directly on the transport network, permitting any network user with access rights to directly access stored NAS data.

16. SAN servers operate in enterprise storage environments with disk array controllers and tape libraries attached.

17. RAS servers allow clients to dial in to a computer from a remote site, even if they are not connected to a LAN.

18. DHCP servers are used to temporarily assign dynamic IP addresses to both network workstations and Internet clients.

SERVER POWER PROBLEMS AND REQUIREMENTS

19. When determining server installation power requirements, maximum load ratings for all hardware must be calculated, including overhead lighting, UP equipment, rack-mounted fans, and air-conditioning units.

20. Electrical line noise is either chronic or intermittent high-frequency interference triggered by RFI or EMI from transmitters, printers, generators, welding devices, lightning, or nearby high-voltage lines.

21. Frequency variations in the stability of the 60-cycle AC generation occur when generators are switched between online or offline operations, potentially damaging sensitive electronic equipment.

22. Harmonic distortions are deformations of the power waveform from nonlinear loads such as variable-speed drives, copiers, and fax machines. They can cause overheating, hardware damage, and data errors.

SERVER COMPONENTS AND DEVICES

23. The common unit of measurement in rack systems is the Unit, or U. At 1.75 inches in height, the U is considered the smallest unit that can be placed into a rack. A full rack is 42 Us in height. Rack-mount cases and components typically come in 1U, 2U, 4U, or 5U sizes.

24. Pedestal-mount systems are used in smaller networks and are less expensive than rack-mounted systems.

25. Server boards are designed to support multiple microprocessors and large quantities of installed RAM. Built-in sensors are used to monitor performance and environmental conditions.

26. Redundant power supplies are used to provide the system's fault tolerance. If one unit fails, another remains operational.

27. RAID arrays employ multiple disk drives for high-speed fault tolerance. Error detection and correction features permit the system to regenerate missing data if one of the drives in the array fails.

28. Multiple network cards are used to provide fault tolerance for the network connection. If one card fails, the other will keep the network available.

SERVER NETWORK PROTOCOLS

29. Subnet masks employ the decimal number 255 to hide the network portion of an IP address, while still showing the host portions. The default subnet mask for Class A IP addresses is 255.0.0.0. Class B is 255.255.0.0, and Class C is 255.255.255.0.

30. The POP3 protocol is used for receiving incoming email.

31. The SMTP protocol is used for sending outgoing email.

32. The SNMP protocol provides network management services for TCP/IP networks. It is the Internet standard protocol developed to manage IP network servers, as well as other nodes such as workstations, routers, switches, and hubs.

33. The TCP/IP protocol suite is used by all major operating systems and is routable.

34. The NNTP protocol is used to post, distribute, and retrieve USENET messages.

35. The PPP protocol provides a method of connecting servers to the Internet. PPP employs error checking, dynamic assignment of IP addresses, and data compression.

36. The PPTP protocol works specifically with VPNs to ensure that messages transmitted from one VPN node to another are secure.

37. The L2TP protocol is an extension to the PPP protocol that enables ISPs to operate VPNs. It merges the best features of Microsoft's PPTP with Cisco's L2F, and requires support from an ISP's routers.

38. The IPSec protocol was developed to support secure packet exchanges at the IP layer. Its wide deployment is meant to support VPN implementations.

39. The FTP protocol is used to transfer files across the Internet, an extranet, or an intranet. It is a viable alternative to using email for transferring extremely large files.

40. The SNA protocol was developed for telecommunications networks to permit clients to access IBM mainframe and mid-level data facilities.

41. The DHCP protocol is used to temporarily assign dynamic IP addresses to both network workstations and Internet clients.

42. The ICMP protocol is an extension to the IP that supports data packets containing error, control, and informational messages. ICMP is used by the PING command to test an Internet connection.

43. The Ethernet protocol is a LAN architecture that uses a bus or star topology supporting data transfer rates of 10Mbps.

44. The FCIP protocol is a Fibre Channel format using an FCIP gateway connected to a specified MAN/WAN network that enables the merging of geographically remote Fibre Channel SANs.

45. The iFCP protocol is a Fibre Channel format that delivers FC traffic over TCP/IP between various iFCP gateways.

46. The PCI-X protocol utilizes an enhanced PCI bus that is backward-compatible with previous PCI cards. It improves upon the speed of PCI from 133MBps to as much as 1GBps.

47. The PCI-X 2.0 protocol is a more efficient version of PCI technology, which operates at higher clock frequencies and transfers more bits of data per clock cycle.

48. SAS is a point-to-point serial communication protocol linking controllers directly to disk drives and enabling the simultaneous connections of up to 128 full-duplex devices, including hot-pluggable drives.

49. The SMP protocol communicates management information to SAS expanders.

50. The STP protocol is used by SAS hosts to communicate with SATA devices, including disk drives.

51. The SSP protocol is used by SAS hosts to communicate with standard SAS devices, such as disk drives and interface cards, using SCSI commands.

52. The iSCSI protocol is an IP-based technology for connecting data storage devices and facilities across a network and distributing data using SCSI commands over IP networks.

53. The HIPPI protocol permits the physical connections of devices over short distances and high speeds. Basic HIPPI transfers 32 bits in parallel at 0.8Gbps. The wide version of HIPPI can transfer 64 bits in parallel, providing speeds of 1.6Gbps.

54. The SMB protocol is used by DOS and Windows to enable the sharing of files, directories, and devices.

EXAM CRAM™ 2

CompTIA Server+

Charles J. Brooks

Marcraft International

CERTIFICATION

Server+ Certification Exam Cram 2 (Exam SK0-002)

International Standard Book Number: 0-7897-3368-4

Library of Congress Catalog Card Number: 2004118399

Printed in the United States of America

First Printing: November 2005

08   07   06   05   4   3   2   1

Trademarks

Warning and Disclaimer

Bulk Sales

Que Publishing offers excellent discounts on this book when ordered in quantity for bulk purchases or special sales. For more information, please contact

U.S. Corporate and Government Sales
1-800-382-3419
corpsales@pearsontechgroup.com

For sales outside the United States, please contact

International Sales
international@pearsoned.com

Publisher
Paul Boger

Executive Editor
Jeff Riley

Development Editor
Ginny Bess

Managing Editor
Charlotte Clapp

Project Editors
Dan Knott
Elizabeth R. Finney
Gregory Sorvig

Copy Editor
Margaret Berson

Indexer
Chris Barrick

Proofreader
Juli Cook

Technical Editor
Rob Shimonski

Publishing Coordinator
Cindy Teeters

Multimedia Developer
Dan Scherf

Interior Designer
Gary Adair

Cover Designer
Ann Jones

Page Layout
Nonie Ratcliff

CERTIFICATION

Que Certification • 800 East 96th Street • Indianapolis, Indiana 46240

A Note from Series Editor Ed Tittel

You know better than to trust your certification preparation to just anybody. That's why you, and more than 2 million others, have purchased an Exam Cram book. As Series Editor for the new and improved Exam Cram 2 Series, I have worked with the staff at Que Certification to ensure you won't be disappointed. That's why we've taken the world's best-selling certification product—a two-time finalist for "Best Study Guide" in CertCities' reader polls—and made it even better.

As a two-time finalist for the "Favorite Study Guide Author" award as selected by CertCities readers, I know the value of good books. You'll be impressed with Que Certification's stringent review process, which ensures the books are high quality, relevant, and technically accurate. Rest assured that several industry experts have reviewed this material, helping us deliver an excellent solution to your exam preparation needs.

Exam Cram 2 books also feature a preview edition of MeasureUp's powerful, full-featured test engine, which is trusted by certification students throughout the world.

As a 20-year-plus veteran of the computing industry and the original creator and editor of the Exam Cram Series, I've brought my IT experience to bear on these books. During my tenure at Novell from 1989 to 1994, I worked with and around its excellent education and certification department. At Novell, I witnessed the growth and development of the first really big, successful IT certification program—one that was to shape the industry forever afterward. This experience helped push my writing and teaching activities heavily in the certification direction. Since then, I've worked on nearly 100 certification related books, and I write about certification topics for numerous Web sites and for *Certification* magazine.

In 1996, while studying for various MCP exams, I became frustrated with the huge, unwieldy study guides that were the only preparation tools available. As an experienced IT professional and former instructor, I wanted "nothing but the facts" necessary to prepare for the exams. From this impetus, Exam Cram emerged: short, focused books that explain exam topics, detail exam skills and activities, and get IT professionals ready to take and pass their exams.

In 1997 when Exam Cram debuted, it quickly became the best-selling computer book series since "...For Dummies," and the best-selling certification book series ever. By maintaining an intense focus on subject matter, tracking errata and updates quickly, and following the certification market closely, Exam Cram established the dominant position in cert prep books.

You will not be disappointed in your decision to purchase this book. If you are, please contact me at etittel@jump.net. All suggestions, ideas, input, or constructive criticism are welcome!

Contents at a Glance

Table of Contents

. . . .

Chapter 18

Chapter 19

Chapter 20

About the Authors

. . . .

Charles J. Brooks is currently the President of Marcraft International Corporation, located in Kennewick, Washington, and is in charge of research and development. In addition to authoring the *A+ Training Guide, A+ Concepts and Practices*, and *Microcomputer Systems—Theory and Service* publications, he has authored numerous other books, including *Speech Synthesis, Pneumatic Instrumentation, The Complete Introductory Computer Course, Radio-Controlled Car Project Manual*, and *IBM PC Peripheral Troubleshooting and Repair*. A former electronics instructor and technical writer with the National Education Corporation, Charles has taught and written on postsecondary EET curriculum, including introductory electronics, transistor theory, linear integrated circuits, basic digital theory, industrial electronics, microprocessors, and computer peripherals. His experience in the electronics field also includes high-voltage distribution systems, relay logic control circuits, and totally automated microprocessor control systems.

Whitney G. Freeman, President of Free Man International, is a curriculum developer with 20 years of experience in the creation of technical education courses. He has worked with Marcraft International Corporation in the development of their innovative Knowledge Transfer Projects, including the *Sonic Rover Project Manual*, which combined the excitement of kit building with the exposure to, and learning of, technical innovation and development. Whitney also was instrumental in developing several of Marcraft's popular Technology Education Modules, including *Introduction to Electronics, Introduction to Flight, Introduction to Computer Aided Design, Introduction to Manufacturing, Introduction to Mechanisms, Introduction to Electronic Music, Introduction to Graphic Design, Introduction to Radio Production, Introduction to PC Communications, Intermediate Computer Construction*, and *Intermediate Desktop Publishing*. Mr. Freeman edited Marcraft's *Classroom Management System* manual and more recently was involved with developing its *Enhanced Data Cabling Installers Certification* and *Fiber Optic Cable Installers Certification* textbooks. Whitney previously developed three training courses for the employees at Framatome ANP, designed to keep workers aware of their safety responsibilities while working around nuclear materials. He created the training material used by the Spokane School District in preparing their employees and students for emergency response situations. Other safety materials developed by Mr. Freeman include those designed to keep employees at the Department of Energy current regarding safety issues and qualifications at various nuclear and non-nuclear workstations. As an electronics instructor and curriculum developer with the National Education Corporation, Whitney created and taught courses in digital electronics and computer electronics.

Jason T. Ho is currently the network administrator for Marcraft International Corporation and also assists in the technical dissemination of new ideas, pertaining primarily to networking and operation systems. He has assisted in the technical support of Marcraft's various products, and in the writing of lab exercises for A+, Network+, and other courseware published by Marcraft. Jason graduated from the University of Washington with a bachelor's degree in Economics. He carries certifications in A+, Network+, Server+, and i-Net+.

Daniel S. Smith is a technical researcher and developer for Marcraft International Corporation and is currently specializing in the computer sciences, attending college, and working toward a Network Administration degree. Daniel earned a Computer Electronics degree in 1995 from Centralia College, in Washington State, and has been working with computers and electronics equipment for the past 10 years. While assisting Marcraft's project coordinators in the gathering of technical information, he has been instrumental in writing and proofreading sample test questions for the A+ and Network+ certification courses and their accompanying lab guides. Daniel's knowledge and experience with fiber optic tools and equipment have been extremely valuable in the development of labs for fiber splicing, fiber testing, and the assembly of ST and SC hot melt and/or epoxy connectors. He is also the co-author of Marcraft's *Introduction to Networking* textbook.

Dedication

Once again, I want to thank my wife, Robbie, for her support throughout another book campaign. Without her support and help, I'm sure there would be no books by Charles Brooks. I also want to mention Robert, Jamaica, Michael, and Joshua for adding to my life.

—Charles J. Brooks

I would like to thank my parents for giving me the support and the inspiration throughout my life. I both appreciate and thank them for all that they've done for me. And to all my coworkers at Marcraft; this was truly a collaborative effort, from editing, to brainstorming ideas.

—Jason T. Ho

I would like to give a special thanks to my wife Shelley Smith and my 4 wonderful kids Danielle, D' Anna, Dustin and Dakota for all their help and support. This book is the result of many contributions and collaborative efforts. I would also like to thank the Marcraft staff for all their help and support and send a special thanks to Charles Brooks for this opportunity.

—Daniel S. Smith

My contributions to this book are dedicated to my loving wife Judi, and my son James, both of whom kept me going throughout its creation with fine preparations from the perpetual barbecue, day and night, summer, fall, winter, and spring. Thanks also to my beloved mother, Maybelle Elizabeth, who never accepted anything on my report card following the first letter of the alphabet.

—Whitney G. Freeman

Acknowledgments

As usual, the production of a technical book requires the dedicated efforts of many gifted individuals. Fortunately for me, several of my co-workers here at Marcraft International Corporation, Kennewick, Washington, were within arms' reach at various points along the way. It would have been very foolish of me not to take advantage of their close proximity.

Counting the copies of certification books written by my boss, Charles J. Brooks, that are spread across the technical bookshelves and study desks of qualified A+ and Network+ technicians would be an impossible task. The organization of the material in this book would also have been impossible without his guiding hand and experience in such matters. Our relationship also served to keep me focused on the importance of observing schedules and meeting deadlines.

Hats off to Daniel S. Smith for the researching intensity he brought to this project. Thanks to his efforts, information about late-breaking server technology was available for consideration and inclusion. Contributions by Jason T. Ho made possible the definitive explanations of various technical aspects of server technology, while Grigoriy Ter-Oganov helped to keep the practical facts from being confused with future postulations.

A great deal of credit must go to Michael R. Hall for the original graphics provided for this book, and to Cathy Boulay for keeping this book's organization on track and for the ongoing communications between Marcraft and the fine folks at Que Publishing.

When mentioning Que Publishing, the dedication, cooperation, and honest effort provided by their entire staff cannot be overemphasized. Many thanks go out to Jeffery A. Riley, Elizabeth R. Finney, Margaret Berson, Ginny Bess, Robert J. Shimonski, and Gregory Sorvig for their much-needed guidance and contributions. Certified Server+ technicians will soon be grateful to you all for your sincere efforts.

—Whitney G. Freeman

We Want to Hear from You!

. . . .

As the reader of this book, *you* are our most important critic and commentator. We value your opinion and want to know what we're doing right, what we could do better, what areas you'd like to see us publish in, and any other words of wisdom you're willing to pass our way.

As an executive editor for Que Publishing, I welcome your comments. You can email or write me directly to let me know what you did or didn't like about this book—as well as what we can do to make our books better.

Please note that I cannot help you with technical problems related to the topic of this book. We do have a User Services group, however, where I will forward specific technical questions related to the book.

When you write, please be sure to include this book's title and author as well as your name, email address, and phone number. I will carefully review your comments and share them with the author and editors who worked on the book.

Email: feedback@quepublishing.com

Mail: Jeff Riley
         Executive Editor
         Que Publishing
         800 East 96th Street
         Indianapolis, IN 46240 USA

For more information about this book or another Que Certification title, visit our website at www.examcram2.com. Type the ISBN (excluding hyphens) or the title of a book in the Search field to find the page you're looking for.

Introduction

. . . .

Welcome to *Server+ Certification Exam Cram 2*! This book is dedicated to helping you pass the Computing Technology Industry Association (CompTIA) certification exam SKO-002, the CompTIA Server+ Certification. We explain some facts about CompTIA's certifications in this introduction, along with how this series of Exam Cram 2 publications can help you to prepare for not only SKO-002, but for other CompTIA certifications as well.

By carefully following the prescribed technological objectives provided by CompTIA throughout the specified domains, you will be empowered with the necessary understanding for taking and passing the exam. Obviously, no Exam Cram 2 book can teach you everything that you may be asked on a given exam. However, if you focus on the physical products, industry standards, terminology, and installation guidelines, the questions you encounter on the Server+ Certification exam will not surprise or stump you.

The production staff here at *Exam Cram 2* has worked diligently to prepare a study guide that will provide you with the knowledge and confidence needed to pass the exam with a superior grade. Although other prerequisite certifications are not required, holding an A+ or Network + certification is beneficial in preparing for the issues involved in implementing, operating, and maintaining a commercial server network, the topic of this exam.

For those who have limited knowledge and experience with server networking technology or the hardware referenced in the Server+ Examination Objectives, it may be necessary to seek additional classroom training or to study various server technology tutorials that are offered. CompTIA and its affiliated testing centers can provide assistance regarding the availability of related courseware.

This *Server+ Certification Exam Cram 2* publication presents an up-to-date look at current server networking strategies from both the installation and servicing perspectives. It thoroughly examines the areas of general server hardware including bus architectures, server types and functions, and their various memory requirements. The advantages and limitations of Small Computer System Interface (SCSI) and Advanced Technology Attachment (ATA) solutions are discussed and contrasted with Fibre Channel hardware. From pre-installation planning to hardware installation, the development of the server management plan is stressed. Server software and hardware configurations are examined along with the use of Simple Network Management Protocol (SNMP), system monitors, and event logs. The importance of baselining is detailed, especially with respect to performing server upgrades. Various backup procedures are examined in connection with making adjustments of SNMP thresholds, performing server room physical housekeeping, and maintaining both physical and environmental security. Troubleshooting skills are also stressed, including sections on problem determination and the use of hardware and software diagnostic tools. In the context of running performance tools, the systematic identification and removal of system bottlenecks is examined in detail. The idea of establishing an early disaster recovery plan is also explained, as well as the various backup hardware and media used to make disaster recovery possible.

Taking a Certification Exam

When your preparations for the Server+ exam have been finalized, the registration for taking the exam must be completed. You will need to contact a certified testing center to schedule a specified date and time to report. The Server+ Certification Exam costs $164 for non-CompTIA members, and $143 for CompTIA members, but these prices are subject to periodic changes. You must pass this exam in order to obtain the Server+ certification. This test is currently being administered by Pearson VUE:

➤ *Virtual University Enterprises (VUE)*—Registration for the exam can be accomplished through the VUE website at http://www.vue.com.

You may apply for an exam using a valid credit card, or by contacting one of these companies for instructions on mailing them a check in the United States. After the check has cleared, or payment has been verified, registration can take place. To schedule for testing, you must either visit the website or call an appropriate telephone number. When a test has been scheduled, any cancellation or rescheduling must occur before 7 p.m. Pacific Standard Time on the day before the test is scheduled. During the summer months, Pacific Daylight Time (PDT) is applicable. Failure to observe this requirement will result in an examination charge regardless of your actual attendance. When it's time to schedule the test, be prepared with the following information:

➤ Your name, organization (if any), and mailing address

➤ Your test ID number (for United States citizens, this is your Social Security number)

➤ The name of the exam and its identification number(s)

➤ The method of payment

After the registration and payment method have been completed, you will be contacted with details concerning the date, time, and location for taking the exam. Normally, two separate forms of identification are required, including a photo ID, prior to admission to the testing room. You will want to arrive at the testing facility at least 15 minutes before the start time shown on your examination schedule.

Understand that all certification examinations are closed-book types, and no study materials will be permitted within the test area. You will, however, be permitted to use a blank sheet of paper and a pen/pencil to write down any memorized information prior to beginning the exam. This type of information is printed on the tear-out Cram Sheet located in the inside front cover of your *Exam Cram 2* book, and should be reviewed completely just before taking the test. At the completion of the exam, the administration software will let you know if you have passed or failed. You can retake a failed exam at a later time, but you must repeat the registration process and submit another exam fee.

How to Prepare for an Exam

There is no way to prepare for a CompTIA exam without first obtaining the necessary study materials focusing on the subject matter being tested. For Server+ certification candidates, these materials should provide information emphasizing the topics associated with the exam alerts and practice questions presented in this book. In addition, certified training companies can be located by checking the http://www.comptia.org/sections/cla/training_Providers.aspx website.

About This Book

Don't forget about the Cram Sheet inside the front cover containing key points, definitions, and terms that should be reviewed just before going into the examination facility. Those topics needing the most attention can be transferred to scratch paper after you enter the exam area. The *Exam Cram 2* study guide for Server+ follows the general objective outline fairly closely. Pay particular attention to the following study aids provided in each chapter:

➤ *Terms you'll need to understand*—At the beginning of each chapter is a list of terms, abbreviations, and acronyms that you'll need to know in order to get the most out of the chapter.

➤ *Concepts and techniques you'll need to master*—When it comes to running a server installation, various tasks are highlighted at the beginning of each chapter because of their importance. Try memorizing as many of these tasks as you can during your chapter reviews.

➤ *Exam alerts*—These flags appear next to material that should be focused on closely. They provide an extra warning that the material being covered will most likely appear somewhere in the exam. Be sure to remember these points and pay special attention whenever they are displayed.

➤ *Tips*—Closely related background information that may or may not appear on the exam is included when the possibility of confusion over terminology exists, or when a controversial technical issue requires further explanation.

➤ *Exam prep questions*—To help you prepare for the Server+ exam, questions covering the main topics are included at the end of each chapter along with explanations about both the correct and incorrect answers.

➤ *Details and resources*—Each chapter ends with a section titled "Need to Know More?" which provides suggestions for locating additional sources of relevant information. Various publications, tutorials, and related websites are listed to provide optional research possibilities. They are not provided as "must read" sources, but merely as suggestions for gaining additional related information.

Using This Book

The topical structure in this book closely follows the eight technological domains making up the Server+ examination objectives. Because these topics tend to build on one another, those appearing in later chapters are easier to understand after the material in earlier chapters has been digested. After initially reading this book from front to back, use the index or table of contents to locate specific topics or questions that you feel you need to brush up on.

Don't neglect the Self-Assessment that follows this introduction. It will help you to identify exactly what you need to know in order to properly prepare yourself for taking the Server+ examination. Answer the questions presented to you honestly in order to accurately determine your readiness to take the exam.

This book is an important tool for use in preparing to take the Server+ exam, and we at *Exam Cram 2* are determined to continue improving it for future test-takers. To that end, please feel free to share your thoughts about this book with us. Your comments and input will be carefully considered for later publications.

Self-Assessment

· ·

Most *Exam Cram 2* study books include a Self-Assessment section in order to help the potential test-taker evaluate his or her potential for gaining the specified certification. In this case, the target exam is the CompTIA Server+ Certification SKO-002, and the following pages are designed to help you understand whether you are indeed ready to take it. You will undoubtedly want to pass this examination with an exceptional score, rather than a minimal one. Use the following information as a guide in identifying areas of concern that you may have in securing your Server+ certification.

Server Technology in the Real World

CompTIA certifications are designed to validate the holder's technical knowledge in a selected discipline. They serve to inform the personnel who work in various industrial employment departments that a prospective employee possesses the basic skill sets associated with a specified job title or description. Many currently employed individuals are ideal candidates for taking the SKO-002 exam because they already perform the duties specified in one or more of the following job titles:

➤ Small or office computer network technician

➤ Computer backup tape librarian

➤ Internet website technician

➤ Corporate network administrator

➤ Computer operations supervisor

➤ Corporate network support technician

➤ Corporate network operator

The Ideal Server+ Certification Candidate

To get an idea of what activities or qualifications are involved with being a server-certified employee, examine the following list. These qualifications are not meant to discourage you, but to indicate the types of work experience and/or training that correspond to the attainment of this certification. If any of the descriptions fall outside your sphere of experience, your subsequent research and study should concentrate on these areas. Please understand that at least one or two years of academic training and work experience in the following technological areas, or extensive understanding not necessarily associated with active employment, will place you on the right track.

➤ Experience maintaining, troubleshooting, and administering local area networks (LANs) or wide area networks (WANs)

➤ Work experience with mainframe networks, computer workstations, and peripheral equipment

➤ Knowledge or experience evaluating and/or installing computer hardware, networking software, and NOS software

➤ Experience in the operation of a master console, for performance monitoring of a computer network system and the control of computer network system access

➤ Holding of current A+ or Network+ certifications

➤ Knowledge about loading computer backup tapes/disks, and installing application software

➤ Experience using and networking computer peripheral equipment, as well as loading printer paper and forms

➤ Problem-solving experience with network client and user services

➤ Knowledge and/or experience implementing data, software, and hardware security procedures

➤ Ability to perform routine network startup and shutdown procedures and to maintain control records/logs

➤ Ability to perform data backups and disaster recovery operations

Putting Yourself to the Test

The following series of questions and suggestions are included to help you identify the areas that may need further attention before you actually take the exam. They are fairly specific in nature, rather than designed to provoke a right or wrong answer. The idea here is to prevent you from wasting the time and expense of taking an examination for which you may not yet be fully prepared. Do not become discouraged when the answer to a question is "no." This merely identifies a weak area in your background and provides a target for improvement.

It is possible that you as an individual possess the resourcefulness to train yourself in certain technological areas. Only you can make the determination as to how much additional knowledge, training, and on-the-job experience you may still need in addition to what you already have. However, keep the following points in mind when considering the required background of candidates suited to take the Server+ certification exam:

➤ Knowledge of computer networking fundamentals and experience working with computer systems would be helpful.

➤ Work experience with a server system, either as a paid technician, or through the installation and administration of a home server network using recognized industry best practices, would make you an ideal test candidate.

Educational Background

1. Are you familiar with basic electrical circuits or electronic fundamentals? (Yes or No)

2. Have you ever taken any classes related to digital circuits or computer electronics? (Yes or No)

3. Have you taken any courses related to computer networking or server operations? (Yes or No)

If you answered "Yes" to these three questions, you are on track toward gaining a Server+ certification. The administration and technical servicing aspects of server networking require a familiarity with digital electronic circuits and computer operations. The fundamental concepts of computer networking are also necessary for understanding how server networks function.

If you answered "No" to questions 1 or 2, you may want to read about the fundamentals of digital electronics with emphasis on basic computer circuitry. The following books may be useful in exploring these important topics:

➤ *Digital Computer Electronics*, 3rd edition, by Albert P. Malvino and Jerald A. Brown, McGraw-Hill (ISBN: 0028005945)

➤ *Computer Architecture: A Quantitative Approach* by John L. Hennessey, Morgan Kaufmann Publications (ISBN: 1558605967)

If you answered "No" to question 3, you may want to examine server networks more closely by reading the following books:

➤ *Sams Teach Yourself Microsoft Windows Server 2003 in 24 Hours* by Joe Habraken, Pearson Education, Sams Publishing (ISBN: 0672324946)

➤ *Microsoft Windows Server 2003 Delta Guide*, 2nd edition, by Don Jones and Mark Rouse, Pearson Education, Sams Publishing (ISBN: 0672326639)

Work or Hands-on Experience

One of the more important considerations in preparing for the Server+ Certification Exam is to take advantage of any and all related experience you may have with server network operating systems, including Windows 2000 Server, Windows Server 2003, Novell NetWare 6.5, IBM OS/2 Warp Server, UNIX, and Linux. Knowledge about and experience with any of these systems should put you in a favorable position for seeking a Server+ certification. There is simply no substitution for the experience gained through installing, configuring, and maintaining these types of server network operating systems. Think about what experience you might have with these products as you answer the following questions:

1. Have you ever installed, configured, or maintained any of the server-based network operating systems listed in the preceding paragraph?

2. Have you ever participated in the hardware or software upgrade of an existing server network?

3. Have you ever participated in a company-wide server system backup operation for the protection of vital company data?

4. Have you ever been involved in any troubleshooting scenarios involving a commercial server network system?

5. For a given server network installation, have you ever been involved with a major environmental improvement, change, or disaster that directly affected the well-being of a server network?

6. For a given server network installation, have you ever performed a full, differential, or incremental backup of a commercial server network?

7. For a given server network installation, have you ever been involved in a disaster recovery procedure that directly affected the continued profitability of a commercial enterprise?

If you were able to answer "yes" to all seven of these questions, you are definitely a candidate for earning your Server+ certification. Where "no" answers were given, realize that these are the areas that will require additional attention, through the research of related articles or publications. Good places to begin are the "Need To Know More?" sections at the end of each chapter.

Assessing Readiness for Exam SKO-002

Some very important tools are available to you for improving your chances of successfully passing the exam. An exam costing more than $160 is worth passing the first time! No one wants to spend that much merely to satisfy some misplaced curiosity about whether or not he or she can pass the exam, because an exam retake will require an equal sum. The reading material listed in this self-assessment section is ideal for added preparation, as are the books and articles listed at the end of each chapter in the "Need to Know More?" sections. In addition to the two practice exams contained in this book, its accompanying CD contains a practice exam that will help you to identify those areas that require additional preparation.

More Resources for Assessing Your Exam Readiness

Although this self-assessment section contains many useful sources of information, you will find it worthwhile to go to the CompTIA website at http://www.comptia.org/ for the latest news about the Server+ certification exam. Among the postings there are the test objectives for the exam along with a Server+ Exam Study Guide, which includes a detailed overview of new and updated server technologies, key practical information, reference websites, and sample exam questions for each objective.

Onward, Through the Fog

After you have earnestly assessed your preparation for the Server+ certification exam, researched the latest information about server technology, products, or systems, and acquired enough practical experience in the operation of server networks to master their basic concepts, you'll be ready to take some practice exams. They will definitely help you to become familiar with the related terminology, and together with the accompanying assessment steps will thoroughly prepare you for the day when you finalize your examination appointment. Don't be reluctant to repeat the practice exams until the terminology related to server technology seems familiar. Good luck to you!

1

1.0—Server Basics

. . . .

Terms you'll need to understand:

✓ Server
✓ Client
✓ Proxy
✓ Firewall
✓ Gateway
✓ Router
✓ Bridge
✓ Remote Access Service (RAS)
✓ Domain Name System (DNS)
✓ Windows Internet Naming Service (WINS)
✓ Dynamic Host Configuration Protocol (DHCP)

Techniques you'll need to master:

✓ Differentiating between various server types and functions
✓ Knowing which networks use rack-mount or pedestal equipment housings
✓ Understanding the advantages of rack-mount server equipment over consumer computers
✓ Moving equipment racks from one location to another correctly
✓ Identifying typical components found in server rack-mount cabinets
✓ Knowing the purpose of a keyboard, video, mouse (KVM) switch

✓ Listing which components promote fault tolerance through redundancy

✓ Recognizing unauthorized intruder and environmental alerts

✓ Listing the three major server types and describing their general applications

✓ Identifying what types of businesses use general-purpose servers

✓ Reviewing the types of services best suited for the use of appliance servers

✓ Describing the three application server models

✓ Defining the two distinct services provided by mail server applications

✓ Detailing how firewall servers protect a network

✓ Explaining the job of a demilitarized zone

✓ Differentiating between two types of proxy server cache requests

✓ Describing how and why network personnel use management services

✓ Identifying why messaging, scheduling, and calendar services are considered useful

✓ Knowing how collaboration services are used to share business information

✓ Defining how a news server can be used to receive, store, and distribute news articles

✓ Listing the ways in which a web server can be used and configured

✓ Explaining why database servers are necessary

✓ Describing the main purpose behind the use of a terminal server

✓ Identifying why DNS servers are necessary

✓ Recognizing what gateway and router servers do, and why they are important

✓ Identifying the minimum requirements of a bridge server computer

✓ Detailing the proper use of a File Transfer Protocol (FTP) server

✓ Tracing the development of the Systems Network Architecture (SNA) server

✓ Explaining how Network-Attached Storage (NAS) servers alleviate common slowdowns and service interruptions

✓ Describing how Storage Area Network (SAN) servers access their data

✓ Identifying which types of clients are taken care of by RAS servers

✓ Listing the reasons for file and print servers

✓ Explaining why fax servers are ideal for business organizations

✓ Knowing what WINS servers do

✓ Outlining the advantages for using DHCP

✓ Defining a multi-tiered server structure

✓ Learning when back-end and front-end servers are required

✓ Describing how mid-tier machines are backed up in a larger company

Introduction

The Server+ Exam Objective 1.3 states that the test taker should know the basic purpose and function of various types of servers. This chapter discusses server types and their functions:

➤ Servers used as gateways, routers, and bridges

➤ Firewall servers

➤ Proxy servers

➤ Database servers

➤ Client servers

➤ Application servers

➤ Mail and FTP servers

➤ SNA, NAS, SAN, and RAS servers

➤ File and print servers

➤ Fax servers

➤ DNS, WINS, and DHCP servers

➤ Web servers

The test taker should also be able to describe the hardware types (blade servers, tower servers, and rack-mount servers), including their module classifications, basic specifications, limitations, and requirements (especially with regard to power and cooling). Each of these types is also discussed in this chapter.

Comparing Server Systems

Consumer and commercial computers both exist in the form of desktop or notebook PC configurations. Many can be used as workstations attached to a network, but they cannot perform the controlling function of a network server.

Server computers supporting commercial networks are based on physical configurations that are different from common consumer units, often employing multiple processors with disk drive arrays.

Server Cases

Servers are housed in one of two different case types: *rack-mounts* (rack-mount chassis) or *pedestals*. The most popular is the rack-mount chassis because rack-mount components can be slid in and out of the cabinet easily for inspection and maintenance.

The *Unit*, simply designated as *U*, is a common unit of measurement in rack systems. Rack-mount cases typically come in 1U, 2U, 4U, or 5U sizes. One U is 1.75 inches high and is the smallest unit that can be placed into a rack. A full rack is 42 Us in height. The server case may be any size, but is measured in multiples of the U size designation.

Remember that a 1U server chassis is 1.75 inches high.

Know how to calculate the space that will be taken up by a server rack component of multiple Us in height.

Rack-Mount Systems

Differences between servers and desktops include the concept of rack-mounted components. These racks allow service personnel easy access to troubleshoot, repair, or replace server components. Pullout rails and easy access panels facilitate maintenance procedures. They serve in business client/server environments to limit or eliminate downtime due to maintenance or component replacement.

Most racks have wheels on the bottom for ease of movement, but they are not designed to be moved with components in them. Be sure to move the rack empty and then install (or reinstall) the components later. This prevents damage to the rack components.

 Know the correct procedure for moving a rack-mounted server system.

Typical rack-mount cabinets contain many different server system component types. A single cabinet may contain several servers, a backup tape system, a high-speed Redundant Array of Independent Disks (RAID), and an Uninterruptible Power Supply (UPS).

Servers do not tend to include a wide array of peripheral devices. When several servers are housed in a single cabinet, typically only one monitor, one keyboard, and one mouse is used. A KVM switch is used to share these resources among the various servers in the rack. The KVM switch enables both administrator and users to operate multiple servers by using the same keyboard, mouse, and monitor.

 Know what a KVM switch does.

Inside a typical rack-mount chassis, some components are similar to those in desktop system units, whereas others are different. Server systems include familiar system boards, disk drives, power supplies, and adapter cards. However, they are less likely to possess individual monitors, keyboards, or mice because they tend to share these peripherals between several units.

Because other computers rely on servers to get their work done, the biggest requirement for a server installation is reliability. Therefore, servers use components and configurations that provide fault tolerance for the system. This is provided using redundant components, where two components work in tandem so that if one fails, the other will continue working and no loss of data or service will be incurred. A typical server chassis will house the following:

➤ *A server board* (AT- or ATX-style system board)—Uses multiple microprocessors (from 2 to 32), large quantities of installed Random Access Memory (RAM), and built-in sensors.

➤ *Multiple redundant power supplies*—Used to provide fault tolerance for the system's power and to preclude server shutdown due to a power supply failure.

➤ *Multiple disk drives*—Arranged in a RAID disk array, they provide high-speed fault tolerance for the disk drive subsystem.

➤ *Multiple network interface cards (NICs)*—Used to provide fault tolerance for the network connection.

 Know the difference between improving the fault tolerance of a server, and improving the capability of a server.

Some of the special server-related advantages to be aware of include

➤ Hinged front panels that incorporate locks to prevent access to control buttons and switches

➤ Low-friction rails that allow the chassis to slide in and out of the cabinet for easy access

➤ Slide-off lids for quick access after the security locks have been opened

➤ Cabinet and chassis access alarms to provide unauthorized intruder and environmental condition alerts

➤ Multiple cooling fans (cabinet fans, chassis fans, processor fans, and power supply fans) to prevent overheating

 Know the advantages of the various specialty features associated with a server rack.

Pedestal-Mount Systems

The pedestal design is similar in appearance to an extra-wide full-tower desktop case. However, the inside of the case is designed to incorporate typical server functions. Pedestal cases are used in smaller networks because they tend to be less expensive.

Pedestal servers feature integrated Ethernet controllers, redundant hot-swap power supplies, hot-swap Small Computer System Interface (SCSI) drive bays, Peripheral Component Interconnect (PCI) hot-plug support, and redundant hot-swap fans. A pedestal server's durability and availability is further enhanced by using RAID controllers within a server platform specifically designed to respond to changing business environments. Pedestal servers are designed to grow along with the size of the business they support. They typically support from one to four processors, service up to 10 hard drives, are equipped with eight PCI slots, and operate PCI hot-plug peripherals for growth without interruption.

Blade Server Centers

Enterprise networks often include server types that perform different network functions. In rack-mount server environments, multiple-server chassis are mounted in a rack enclosure with their support systems. They can be managed at a single location and interconnected through peripheral port and control interfaces.

To squeeze more servers into less space, *blade servers* are used. An independent server blade is a server, mounted on a card that fits in a special chassis, or shell, approximately 3U in height. These blades are modular, hot-swappable, and independent. Modular arrangements provide a computing architecture that improves operational efficiencies. Blade server environments offer a convenient alternative to conventional rack systems. Several single-board servers mount inside an enclosure known as the blade center, where they plug into a common backplane. The backplane allows devices within the enclosure to communicate without additional cabling, reducing the required amount by nearly 90%, and providing shared power and interconnection to other enclosures within the rack.

Blade enclosures require special interconnect cards that slide into the blade center and collect network and storage signals from the server blades. Included within the custom-built chassis is the power and I/O connectivity circuitry. Each blade typically utilizes one or two processors, 512MB of RAM, three 20GB hard drives, and one or two network connections.

Blade servers increase the capacity of a standard enterprise data-center rack, and are best suited for working in Tier 1 service delivery networking environments, as a front-end system for email, web hosting, directory services, firewalls, and network management. Although several manufacturers have recently released multiprocessor, higher-performance blade servers designed to handle Tier 2 application server environments, and Tier 3 database operations, questions remain as to whether blades are a suitable platform for these more demanding workloads, given their existing performance, heat generation, and cost-efficiency problems.

Know what purpose each environment blade server is best suited for.

Blade management systems monitor the contents of all enclosures, remember physical device locations, and reallocate resources as needed, to facilitate hot-plug operations. In addition, they simultaneously enable multiple administrators to service multiple servers, at the server facility or remotely.

Server Types

Although all servers perform the basic functions we've described so far, in practice they tend to vary significantly in their physical appearance and purpose. Servers can be divided into three major types: general-purpose, appliance, and multi-tier, and defined by the primary applications they are designed to perform.

 Ensure that you understand each server type and its general application.

The *multi-tier server* category is subdivided into three groups: front-end, mid-tier, and back-end. These subgroups are defined by the position in the network structure where they are employed, and by their assigned tasks. Servers falling into these subdivisions have unique characteristics.

General-Purpose Servers

General-purpose servers are intended to provide a wide variety of services, such as handling departmental email or providing file, print, and web services that run on an industry-standard network operating system (NOS).

As the most common server products in use today, general-purpose servers are typically configured with multiple processors.

They are employed in most small businesses because they can be used for multiple purposes and are designed to do many functions fairly well. In small businesses, the server must have redundancy to keep its resources available without undue cost. Redundancy is the practice of devoting extra hardware to maintain network resources and is the primary form of fault tolerance used in server systems. It is created inside a server chassis with backup power supplies, hard drives, and network cards, and on a system-wide basis by adding more servers to the network.

Typical redundant items used in general-purpose servers include multiple hot-swap power supplies, multiple hot-swappable hard drives, and specialized hot-swap PCI slots.

Although these items do not individually prevent the server from failing, they allow components to be exchanged with the system still running. Combined with the use of redundant components, the effects of hardware failures are minimized or eliminated entirely.

Powerful processors are selected for use in general-purpose servers to perform multiple functions. Such servers utilize two or more Pentium III, Xeon, Pentium 4, or Itanium processors from the Intel group.

The amount of installed RAM in a general-purpose server is medium to high, depending on the server's intended use. Hard drive configuration depends on whether the client will use it as a file server or not. If so, it will usually include a RAID 5 array for redundancy, speed, and capacity.

Appliance Servers

Appliance servers provide a single service, such as web serving, or multi-services such as providing Internet caching and firewall protection. This server is usually treated as a *Field-Replaceable Unit (FRU)*, so that when it crashes, it is simply replaced by a comparable unit as quickly as possible. No attempt is made to repair the unit while it is still connected to the network. When a company installs an appliance server, two of them will normally be placed in the network together. If one server fails, the other will guarantee that network resources remain up and running.

Appliance servers tend to employ middle-level processors and various other hardware. If the appliance server was intended to provide web services, large quantities of RAM would be required to enable the caching of whole web pages into memory. For use as a file server, it would include an advanced RAID controller to provide improved disk access times, and the amount of installed RAM wouldn't be a critical consideration. Appliance servers come as specifically preconfigured units and are simply connected to the network and turned on to perform the prescribed function.

Appliance servers are generally in the middle range in terms of cost, and tend to be less expensive than general-purpose servers. They are typically found in medium-sized businesses, where using specialized servers to provide specific functions can be justified.

Application Servers and Services

Server+ Exam Objective 1.4 states that the test taker should know the function of dedicated application servers, distributed application servers, and peer-to-peer application servers:

➤ A *dedicated application* is reserved for a specific need, such as a dedicated channel (leased line). A *dedicated server* is a single PC set up in a reserved network to serve the needs of the PCs within that network. A dedicated server in some networks will manage communications, and in others it may manage printer resources.

➤ A *distributed application* is a single application or group of applications designed for specified end users. For example, email providers use a distribution server to distribute the email data to end users who participate in their mail service.

➤ A *peer-to-peer application* is the sharing of computer goods and services by directly exchanging information between users. For example, Napster is a peer-to-peer server that enables an Internet user to share files with other users and exchange information stored on their computers. The resources and services that are generally exchanged include information, data cycles, and storage for files on disk.

Application servers are configured to run programs that can be accessed by multiple users, and can be implemented for handling large information databases. Also called an *appserver*, these machines manage application programs running between client computers and the organization's database.

Among the many types of application servers or services in use today are:

➤ Mail servers

➤ Firewall servers

➤ Proxy servers

➤ Management services

➤ Messaging services

➤ Scheduling and calendar services

➤ Collaboration services

➤ News servers

➤ Web servers

➤ Database servers

➤ Terminal servers

➤ Domain Name System servers

The following list describes the ways in which flow performances are improved when application servers are used to deliver information:

➤ Security algorithms are applied to both the data and all user traffic.

➤ Client programs are reduced in size and complexity.

➤ The flow of data is cached, and effectively controlled.

Mail Servers

Mail servers send and receive email. These application servers receive and store electronic mail messages in private mailboxes. seen as folders on the network mail server. When a user invokes his or her mail client software, the main mail folder is queried, and the mail server sorts through the account folders retrieving the mail messages that belong exclusively to the user. The mailbox processing is performed on the server side, and the results are then passed to the client.

Mail server applications are actually two distinct services, receiving incoming email and distributing outgoing email. The normal protocols used are Post Office Protocol (POP3) for receiving incoming email, and Simple Mail Transfer Protocol (SMTP) for sending outgoing email.

Firewall Servers

Firewall servers control the connections between two networks, commonly acting as gateways to the Internet. They protect the network by implementing access control to block unwanted traffic, while allowing acceptable communications. Firewall servers come in both the hardware and software variety.

Hardware firewalls are suitable for co-location duties and for use with partitioned networking environments using demilitarized zones (DMZs). When a hardware firewall is said to be performing co-location duties, this means that the firewall resides in a rack belonging to a service provider that may house other firewalls or equipment used by other companies. A DMZ is a useful safety feature when hosting a server, in order to separate the corporate Local Area Network (LAN) from any simultaneous public server activity. It permits the separation of the administrative and main website traffic.

Although software firewall products may be provided for various server platforms, some are designed to protect mission-critical applications and data hosted on Windows servers. They employ intrusion prevention systems capable of stopping active and/or date-oriented attacks, and also use application-hardening techniques. They are designed to be easily deployed, and to integrate seamlessly into various network infrastructures.

Proxy Servers

Proxy servers are similar to firewalls, and they act as an intermediary between a client's workstation and the Internet. Over time, they cache frequently visited websites. This saves Internet bandwidth and increases access speeds by allowing the internal network to access these sites from the proxy server. This type of arrangement works well only for Internet downloading chores. When both uploading and downloading activities are required, a firewall server will be used.

Anonymous proxy servers conceal the Internet Protocol (IP) addresses of users on the network side of the Internet connection. This shields clients from having their personal IP addresses recorded by hackers trying to gain unauthorized Internet access to their computers. Client IP addresses are secure, as are their browsing interests. Anonymous proxy servers don't reveal that clients are using them to browse the Internet, and are commonly used for web-based email, web chat rooms, and FTP transfers.

Websites can gather personal information about visitors through their unique IP addresses. This activity is actually a form of spying, and can reveal personal reading interests. Revealed personal information can make that person a target for marketing and advertising agencies, through the use of unwanted email or spam. Although proxy servers can help to prevent this, they can also be used by employers to filter outgoing web requests, or to prevent company employees from accessing a specific set of websites.

Remember that a proxy server is capable of two types of cache requests:

➤ *Reverse proxy cache*—The cache is configured to act as the original server from which the client requests the data.

➤ *Forward proxy cache*—The client requests the Internet data and this request is forwarded through the cache on the way to the original server.

If the cache does not currently contain the requested information, the proxy server requests the information from the original server, and stores a copy in its cache for any future requests. If the cache already contains the requested data, it is sent to the client without contacting the original server.

Management Services

Management services are special tools and protocols used for remote system management. The Simple Network Management Protocol (SNMP) is the

Internet standard protocol to manage IP network servers, workstations, routers, switches, and hubs. Such protocols enable network administrators to handle network problems, manage network performance, and plan for network growth. They can automatically notify a system administrator when specific changes and/or circumstances affect the server.

Messaging Services

Messaging services provide the capability to send instant messages throughout the network and are usually included in the operating system. The Windows, Unix, and Linux operating systems include their own messaging service utilities.

Scheduling and Calendar Services

Scheduling and calendar services help to organize a company's schedule, or to document various departmental meetings. These products range from basic calendars that list important events, to programs that notify employees via email, pager, or cell phone of group meetings or report deadlines. They also permit the tracking of product timelines and workgroup projects.

Collaboration Services

Collaboration services allow multiple users to communicate using text, graphics, video, or voice. Whiteboard applications allow the client to communicate in a text chat box, and draw diagrams to clarify subjects discussed.

Email messages are sent and received through what is commonly referred to as a *client device*. Client devices can include personal computers, company workstations, mobile phones, and Pocket PCs. Centralized computer systems are made up of servers or mainframe computers, where the enterprise email-boxes are stored as part of the business network. The email client typically connects to a network of centralized email servers, which in turn connects to both the Internet, and any number of private networks. What makes a collaboration tool so useful is its family of protective controls that make sending and receiving electronic information a secure experience for company-wide operations.

News Servers

A *news server* is a computer with software installed to receive, store, and distribute news articles to and from newsgroups on a specific network, or on the Internet. The most recognizable example of a news server is USENET, an Internet-based network using the Network News Transfer Protocol (NNTP).

USENET consists of numerous global bulletin boards divided into a variety of discussion group categories, called newsgroups.

To connect to a news server, a user needs to know the appropriate server name, and the port number to be accessed, normally 119. In the corporate environment, a news server is an extremely useful tool because various company branch-specific bulletin boards can be organized to focus on a variety of workplace topics. This enables company employees to pool their resources and share ideas.

Web Servers

A *web server* hosts web pages for intranet and/or Internet access, and can host more than one site depending on its underlying operating system. Web servers are used to share information and often replace old-fashioned file and print servers. Today we access websites using browser software, including Microsoft Internet Explorer and Netscape Communicator.

When configuring a web server with Microsoft Windows 2000, security can be applied by using

➤ *User authentication*—The ability to control who can access data on a website, by forcing a user logon.

➤ *Data encryption*—The scrambling of data so that it will not transfer across the network in a readable format.

➤ *Web permissions*—The granting of access to resources by assigning specific permission levels to the data, or the folders in which the data resides.

During a browse, the web application server links a database server with the client. The application server determines if the required information is already in the database. If so, it is quickly located and transferred to the client in much less time than it would take to reload the specified web page from scratch.

Database Servers

Database servers store and sort through data in response to client queries. Servers of this type are necessary for organizations that must manage large quantities of data. All data processing is performed on the server using server-side application software. The client's software defines the query and is called the client-side application.

Terminal Servers

Terminal servers are special-purpose computers fitted with multi-ported asynchronous modem connections, and a number of LAN ports. A terminal server allows serial line devices to connect to the network, with basic arrangements permitting access only to dumb terminals via modems and telephone lines. The terminal server answers modem-based phone calls and completes the connections to the appropriate node(s). Sophisticated terminal servers permit intelligent terminals such as PCs to connect to the network using higher-level protocols such as Point-to-Point Protocol (PPP). If network connections are solely obtained through the use of modems, the terminal server is referred to as a modem server.

At a minimum, the terminal server serves these functions:

➤ A remote control solution for remote users

➤ A multi-session operating system, similar to Unix, which allows multiple user sessions

➤ A centralized management of the networked environment

➤ A solution for lowering the network's total cost of ownership (TCO)

When connected to the Internet, terminal servers provide either PPP or Serial Line IP (SLIP) services, and terminals connect to the LAN through one network connection. The terminal server performs host Telnet services to all terminals connected to the network, becoming, in effect, a Telnet server.

Part of the Transmission Control Protocol/Internet Protocol (TCP/IP) suite of protocols is the Telnet protocol. It enables network clients to connect to Telnet servers and run character-based applications from any remote location. In Unix systems, Telnet has historically been the primary method of enabling clients to access Unix servers and run various applications. In Windows systems, the primary use of the Telnet utility is by administrators, to facilitate remote access and remote administration from Telnet clients.

Domain Name System Servers

A *Domain Name System (DNS)* server contains a database listing, called the DNS database, used to resolve computer names to IP addresses. These servers contain mappings between TCP/IP names such as www.mic-inc.com, and the IP addresses they represent, such as 207.45.4.12. DNS caching shortens the time taken to perform name resolution and decreases traffic on the network. Whenever a DNS server receives address information for another host, or domain, it stores it for a limited time in order to service similar DNS requests. These repeated requests are not forwarded across the Internet because the DNS server already has the required information.

Know what type of server resolves TCP/IP names into IP addresses.

People deal better with alphanumeric names than they do with numbered sequences. Conversely, to a digital computer, everything is a number. TCP/IP networks, such as the Internet, can use human-readable host names corresponding to unique numbers called IP addresses that have been assigned to computers. The IP addresses being resolved are usually of the static variety. For residential Internet users, websites are reached using modem, DSL, or cable connections through dynamic IP addressing. The local Internet Service Provider (ISP) temporarily assigns the client an IP address used only for the duration of that specific connection. A different IP address will be assigned for the next Internet connection. DSL or cable Internet services allow the use of a static IP address. A dynamic IP operation does not affect the typical Internet user because the flow of information is all incoming. It does present a problem for any client hosting a personal website. A web server using a dynamic IP will be impossible to link to, because there is no direct relationship between it and its domain name!

Dynamic DNS (DDNS) solves this dilemma through the use of special DDNS service providers. DDNS is a method of keeping a domain name linked to a changing, or dynamic, IP address. It allows dynamic IP Internet addresses to be able to use applications that require static IP addresses by mapping a third-level domain name to the client's DDNS IP address. When the client's ISP-assigned IP address changes, the DDNS client program will forward the new IP address to the DDNS.

 Know what types of servers are capable of caching and forwarding requests.

Servers Used As Gateways

A *gateway* interfaces between different types of networks, or protocols. It's a special-purpose device that performs conversions between various protocols, at the application layer. Either a hardware or a software arrangement translates between these dissimilar protocols. In an enterprise environment, gateway servers route traffic from individual PCs to the network serving the specified web page. They also act as proxy servers and a firewalls. A residential gateway acts as an ISP, connecting the client to the Internet.

Gateways can exist at the intersection of two networks, such as a business LAN and the Internet. The end result is the successful transfer of data between them. Gateways close the gap between two otherwise incompatible applications, or networks, so that data can be successfully transferred.

Large corporate gateways can perform translations between internal, proprietary email formats and the Internet email format. Often the gateway conceals the IP address of the sending client, while those accessing the information from outside the network only see the gateway's IP address.

TCP/IP host gateways can access two or more different Ethernet networks, forwarding messages between them, whereas other hosts cannot. These hosts are fitted with multiple IP addresses, one for each network being accessed. Such a gateway might exist at addresses 192.0.1.8 and 196.0.1.8, as shown in Figure 1.1. Host computers forwarding messages between these networks would first address them to their local gateway. The gateway would then pass them on to the other network. If a server at address 192.0.1.33 had to communicate with a host at address 196.0.1.58, it would first have to contact the gateway machine on its local network. When contacted, the local gateway would forward the message between networks 192.0.1 and 196.0.1.

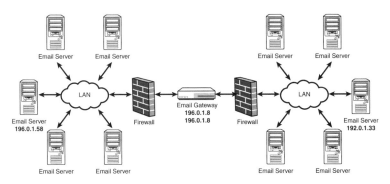

Figure 1.1   A gateway for network-to-network messaging.

Servers Used As Routers

Not long ago, using a server as a router was a very bad idea, and provided hackers with unfettered opportunities for compromising a system's security. Newer products now secure combined server/router operations by keeping the routing chores separated from other critical server duties. Terminal router cards plug into the server and provide the connectivity, performance, and expandability of a selectable four-port RS-232 terminal server/TBOS port, or a 10/100BASE-TX Ethernet switch with dedicated routing functionality.

Servers used as *routers* manage the shared resources of all other routers in the network, including the various transmission speeds and protocols used. Routing advertising packets are sent every three seconds or so when the protocol process is first started, and then about every 10 minutes thereafter.

Servers Used As Bridges

A server *bridge* requires at least two NICs to connect two groups of computers. The bridge will act as a server by isolating MAC addresses, managing network traffic, and translating from one protocol to another. It reduces network traffic by determining whether a data frame should remain in its originating network or be forwarded to another.

A bridge contains a list of which computers are on each side, and passes only packets that must transfer from one side to the other. Network activity is significantly reduced when individual groups have heavy internal traffic, but much less between each other. Computer servers being used as bridges should have their server software set up first. Then the bridge software should be installed and configured. Windows XP can be configured as a software bridge to permit two or more networks to be tied together to act like a single network. Software-based bridging requires that the server computer operating the software bridge be turned on in order for the networks to communicate.

FTP Servers

An *FTP server* transfers files across the Internet, an extranet, or an intranet. To access an FTP server, the client computer must have an FTP client program installed. Modern web browsers include a minimal FTP client that allows files to be sent and received using the FTP protocol.

Many companies utilize an FTP server for software downloads, such as free, beta, or demo versions, or patches and upgrades. By segregating software download operations from a company's web server, the overall level of network traffic is reduced.

FTP is also a viable alternative to using email for transferring extremely large files. Experienced email users know that large files included as attachments take considerably longer to send or download with an email server than when transferred to or from an FTP server.

Most users think about FTP from the perspective of uploading or downloading operations, rather than the way in which an FTP server is set up. FTP software programs are intended to reside on the FTP server itself, and permit the site operator to control settings that dictate how the FTP server will operate. FTP server software is used to set limitations on transfer speeds and maximum users allowed. In addition, specific security measures can be adjusted, for blocking bounce attacks, hammering, and FXP (server-to-server copying, or FXP mode, which is built into FTP).

In a *bounce attack*, the hacker misuses the PORT command on an FTP server to indirectly access arbitrary ports on other machines, or systems, not directly accessible by other means. When the hacker is connected, he or she is free to bypass any access controls that would otherwise apply.

Hammering is the repeated attempt to connect with an unavailable FTP server without permitting a normal delay time between attempts. FTP servers cannot process an unlimited number of requests, and when running at full capacity, they deny further access until capacity is freed. Hammering causes a server that is already working at capacity to send a busy response to any device trying to connect every time a connection is attempted, further depleting server resources. FTP sites normally require their clients to set retry times at specific intervals, commonly at least 120 seconds between each attempt. They also monitor for hammering devices, banning access to offending IP addresses temporarily, or permanently.

Properly used, FXP is a useful function. However, hackers with bad intentions can also misuse it. An FTP client connects to two servers at the same time, with one server directed to receive an incoming file, and the other instructed to send it. The sending and receiving servers connect to each other, and transfer the requested file without it first being copied to the originating FTP client. Because this function can cause great damage if improperly used (bounce attacks), it is normally disabled on most FTP servers. FTP administrators usually enable FXP functions for specific reasons, at specific times, for specific customers.

SNA Servers

SNA was developed in 1970 as a proprietary protocol for telecommunications networks, primarily because large corporations demanded more throughput and better security from their existing networks.

An *SNA server* allows client access to mainframe (IBM) and mid-range data facilities, and also permits print facilities to be located on the host computer. SNA server load-balanced configurations work well with high-priority situations because the failure of any one server is transparent to a connected client machine. When one server fails, the client is automatically switched to the next available server.

Microsoft SNA Server was developed in order to share IBM data in the PC environment, resulting in seamless mainframe-to-desktop file transfers. Further refinements in this type of system interoperability resulted in the introduction of Host Integration Server (HIS) 2000, which has succeeded SNA Server.

NAS Servers

Because of slowdowns and service interruptions that commonly occur in conventional file servers, Network-Attached Storage (NAS) is one alternative. *NAS servers* effectively move storage out from behind the file server, and put it directly on the transport network. Whereas file servers normally use SCSI and LAN adapters, an NAS appliance uses an NIC to transmit both LAN and storage communications. Because NAS servers operate independently from the file server, any client with access rights, anywhere on the network, can directly access stored NAS data.

NAS servers are also optimized for faster processing of I/O storage transactions, avoiding inherent delays from file server hardware or operating systems.

NAS server arrays can be housed within a 3U rack-mount chassis, equipped with a redundant power supply featuring an audible alarm. They often use Serial ATA (SATA) hard drives specifically designed for enterprise operations featuring 100% duty cycles. NAS server rack-mounts can be fitted with PCI RAID cards, with each running on its own dedicated PCI bus. Each unit includes two 2.8GHz CPUs and 4GB of RAM. A dedicated internal hard drive keeps the operating system separated from the RAID operating system. Each chassis also comes with an internal CD-ROM drive. These arrays can be centralized within racks to form systems that are considerably more robust, as shown in Figure 1.2.

Common rack-mount features include improved manageability, high-end performance at low acquisition cost, and up to 56TB of data storage per cabinet. Easy-to-use GUI or command-line interfaces provide for rapid system deployment and maintenance. Cross-platform file support is also provided for any combination of Linux, Unix, Windows, or MacOS environments, and compatibility exists for leading data backup and replication software. When a rack-mount system is connected to smart UPS battery backup equipment, a controlled automatic shutdown can be performed during any power failure.

To process requests from networks running multiple types of operating systems, NAS servers and appliances use a common file server access protocol. The physical complexity associated with using parallel SCSI buses to connect storage disks to file servers is alleviated.

The main disadvantage of an NAS server is that it shifts storage transactions from parallel SCSI connections to the production network, forcing the local area network to handle its normal end-user traffic plus storage disk operations, including backup. Although file server backups have always resulted in large bandwidth consumption, NAS does not resolve this issue by using the production network for backup and recovery. However, an alternate file-handling strategy called a SAN does remove backup traffic from the LAN.

Figure 1.2   An NAS server rack system.

Although comparisons between network-attached storage and a storage-area network are inevitable, each type of system has its proper use. Remember that as the name NAS implies, its data storage can be accessed via a network, using the TCP/IP protocol. The NAS system is usually configured with multiple hard drives, and uses RAID for redundancy. One important advantage of NAS servers over SAN servers involves improved scalability.

SAN Servers

A SAN is a network designed to attach such computer storage devices as disk array controllers and tape libraries to servers. *SAN servers* are common in enterprise storage, which focuses not only on storage, but also on data protection and retrieval within large-scale environments.

SAN servers access their data using low-level block storage methods, as opposed to the file storage access method, similar to the way in which data is identified on ATA and SCSI internal disk drives. To access network data, most SANs use the SCSI communications protocol, without the lower-level physical interface structure. Over a shared network, a SAN permits many computers to access many storage devices.

SAN server racks combine the SAN fabric with RAID disk redundancy to create an extremely robust and high-performing file system. Multiple computers with different operating systems are enabled for direct access to the shared file system. If any server connected to the SAN fails, all data is still accessible by all other servers. In addition, all systems connected to this SAN server have simultaneous access to the same files, at local disk speeds.

RAS Servers

A Remote Access Service (RAS) allows the client to dial in to a computer from a remote site. Therefore, an *RAS server* is devoted to taking care of these clients, even though they are not connected to the LAN but do require remote access to it. If a home-based office PC is connected to the main office LAN via an RAS server's modem port, the RAS server enables this client to access files and/or printer services on the targeted LAN. It provides connectivity into a private or corporate network for the remote modem user, necessitating the running of the TCP/IP network protocol encapsulated inside PPP. The remote machine has access to the targeted network as though it were directly plugged into it.

For example, when a client dials into the office network from his or her home PC, the analog modem will dial into an RAS server at the office, and the client will then be authenticated and granted access. Following this identification process, printers and shared drives can be accessed just as if the client were actually at the office and connected directly to the network. In addition, the server could be configured to only allow access during certain periods for a particular group of users.

Remember that an RAS server can also be attacked in a similar fashion as described with FTP servers.

When a suitable RAS server becomes the target, there are techniques hackers can use to try to break in, such as using common usernames and passwords like "Administrator" or "root." To secure the server from this type of attack, a callback system can be implemented, where even if a would-be hacker is armed with the correct username and password, the callback goes only to an authorized client.

For sales or technical personnel out on the road, preventing a hack becomes harder. In these cases, a token-based security system can be implemented, where clients log in by using a PIN and a digital "token."

Because the token changes at least once every minute, only the token generator and the server will know what it is.

Callback systems are also implemented for the purpose of reverse charging, so that the commercial site picks up the employee's connection charges.

File and Print Servers

The *print server* decreases the administrative and management workload by streamlining both local and remote printer control. A client's print job is spooled much more quickly by a print server than by sending it directly to a traditional printer. When using the print server, a client does not have to wait for the print job to finish before continuing other work. A print server is often a small box equipped with at least two connectors: one for a printer, and another that attaches directly to the network cabling. Other print servers can be equipped with two, three, or four printers, all being operated simultaneously.

A *file server* helps manage access to data files and other network-related applications. It's a computer dedicated to specifically storing files, and enables any network client to store files on it. When a system administrator plans to use disk space to store, manage, and share files and network-accessible applications, the system should be equipped with a file server.

In large client/server environments, files are stored on centralized, high-speed file servers that are accessible to client PCs, making network access speeds much faster than those found on peer-to-peer networks. In order to permit the tracking of networking tasks, network services such as printing and email transfers are routed through the file server. Not only can users' activities be closely monitored, but also inefficient network segments can be reconfigured to make them faster. Any messages from one client to another are sent to the file server first. From the file server, they are then routed to their destination. When dealing with networks comprising tens or hundreds of client PCs, a file server makes the management of complex and simultaneous operations of large networks possible.

Fax Servers

Fax servers help to reduce the amount of telephone infrastructure, while providing the ability to quickly transport required documents. The authenticity of printed faxes as legal and official documents, as well as their use for information exchange and data confirmation within the corporate environment is well established. Although fax servers are often standalone operations, they are sometimes combined with email services.

Most fax server products are software-based, where the administrator is free to choose the accompanying hardware, such as a network-ready server, a fax modem, an Integrated Services Digital Network (ISDN) adapter, or a dedicated fax board.

WINS Servers

The Windows Internet Naming Service (WINS) server is a Microsoft NetBIOS name server that permits the client to search for resources by computer name, instead of by IP address. It provides a distributed database for registering and prompting for dynamic mappings of NetBIOS names over TCP/IP for networked groups. WINS maps NetBIOS names by their actual IP addresses, providing NetBIOS name resolution in routed environments.

NetBIOS names were used by earlier versions of Windows to locate, identify, register, and resolve names for shared or grouped network resources. Although the NetBIOS naming protocol established networking services in earlier Microsoft OSs, it is also used with network protocols other than TCP/IP. WINS was designed specifically for use over TCP/IP-based networks in order to simplify the management of NetBIOS namespace.

The order of the events for a typical WINS operation is as follows:

1. The WINS client registers any of its local NetBIOS names with its configured WINS server.

2. Another WINS client prompts the WINS server to locate the IP address for the first WINS client on the network.

3. The WINS server replies with the IP address for the first WINS client (192.168.1.20 for example).

WINS eliminates the need to use local IP broadcasts for NetBIOS name resolution, permitting users to locate remote systems on the network more easily. When a client first joins the network, the WINS registrations are done automatically and the database is automatically updated. When a DHCP server issues a new or changed IP address to a WINS-enabled client computer, client WINS information is updated without requiring clients or administrators to make any manual changes.

When managing a name-to-address database, or mapping NetBIOS names to IP addresses, a *WINS* server is required. Microsoft Windows 2000, Windows XP, and Windows Server 2003 are configured with WINS server addresses either manually, or automatically (DHCP), for name resolution.

DHCP Servers

The *Dynamic Host Configuration Protocol (DHCP)* temporarily assigns dynamic IP addresses to network workstations and Internet clients each time they are detected. When these units power down, or disconnect, their IP addresses become available for reassignment to another client. A group of dynamic IP addresses, called a *scope*, will be maintained at the DHCP server. The scope must be identified during the DHCP server's configuration procedure.

Temporarily assigned IP addresses from DHCP permit the efficient management of the entire IP addressing scheme. Software tracks the IP addresses of additional computers rather than requiring an administrator to manually assign them.

Dynamic addressing provides each networked device with a different IP address every time it connects to the network, sometimes changing them during a connected session. DHCP also supports a mix of static and dynamic IP addresses, and Internet Service Providers (ISPs) often reserve dynamic IP addressing for dial-up users. When the *DHCP server* assigns IP addresses to clients using DHCP, it automatically uses leased IP addresses. A standard DHCP lease is the total amount of time permitted by that server for a client to use one of its IP addresses, and the DHCP server normally permits the network administrator to set its lease time.

Multi-Tiered Server Architectures

In large organizations with complex networks, the concept of using specialized servers to perform specific functions is further refined by organizing groups of servers into a tiered structure. These tiers optimize the use of different server types for performing related functions. A *multi-tiered server* structure combines these server types into clusters for seamless client access.

The major server tiers include

➤ Front-end servers

➤ Mid-tier servers

➤ Back-end servers

Understand the name and function of each tier of a multi-tiered server.

Front-End Servers

Front-end servers function similarly to appliance servers. They can be configured to perform one function, or a multiple of related functions, and are
treated as field-replaceable units. Typical front-end servers are used for

➤ Mail servers

➤ Proxy servers

➤ Firewall servers

➤ Web services

Front-end servers are specifically configured to pull information from the
organization's mid-tier and back-end servers, such as data being presented by
the front-end server's web services. To quickly retrieve and display the data
from the other tiers on the web page, the front-end server is configured with
a large amount of installed RAM to accommodate the necessary volume of
data efficiently.

Front-end servers also provide and control the external or remote access to
the company network. This is normally accomplished through the telephone
system using dial-up connections. Windows server OSs manage this function
through a Remote Access Service (RAS) utility, the client portion of which is
sometimes called Dial-up Networking.

Before adding a dial-up connection to a network, additional hardware and
configuration effort must be applied to the server. An even greater concern
in adding dial-up access to the network is the security exposure from opening the network to access by outsiders.

The network administrator must balance the advantages of granting access
to trusted remote users—such as outside sales people, traveling personnel,
and work-at-home personnel—against the risks posed by intruders and
hackers. Additional security-related hardware and server configuration settings are required to compensate for these possibilities.

 Be aware of factors that should be considered before adding a dial-up connection to a network.

Remote access can also be provided through an Internet connection using a
Virtual Private Network (VPN). Secure VPN communications are provided
through a tunneling protocol that encrypts the data, so that only the intended receiver can decrypt and read it.

Mid-Tier Servers

Mid-tier servers are used to process and relay information between front-end and back-end servers. Using hardware very similar to that described for general-purpose servers, most mid-tier servers are designed to perform more than one function. They may act as both a file server and as a mail server, or designed to act as a back-end or a front-end server. A mid-tier server is normally too powerful to be used simply as a front-end server, and not powerful enough to perform as a reliable back-end server.

In larger companies, the mid-tier is usually made up of network servers. In very large organizations, the middle tier may include database and web servers that pull data from back-end servers Fault tolerance is provided by including redundant components inside the chassis, and using redundant machines throughout the tier.

Mid-tier machines are more expensive than front-end servers, and the purchase of offline backup machines is not cost-effective. Instead, larger companies often install a second machine to perform the identical function. If one mid-tier machine fails, the redundancy from the online backup guards against losing the resource. By adding the second machine online, the overall performance of the middle tier for that function is increased.

Back-End Servers

Back-end servers typically are large, expensive units used to store vast volumes of data in archive and data farms. A typical back-end server used in a data warehouse operation may have 30 or more disk drives connected to it. Because they hold the data required by working mid-tier and front-end servers, back-end servers are usually required to be up and running 99.99% of the time.

A *data warehouse* is a computer storage system containing a wide variety of data. Information is combined from many different databases across an entire organization. These storage structures are used to track business conditions at any single point in time. Systems for extracting data from large databases provide IT managers with flexible methods of access. Keep in mind that a data farm is synonymous with a data warehouse.

An archive server holds all of the data that has previously been backed up and archived. This differs from a traditional backup where data is transferred to some type and then stored in a secure area. Retrieving traditional data backups requires physically going to the secure area and inserting the media into the backup server. An archive server will store all the data to some type of media, and will allow the archived data to be accessed without manual intervention. For tape backups, the server would access the specific tape containing the required data using a mechanical arm to retrieve and insert the tape into the server.

Back-end machines are so expensive that procuring an additional standby machine is not a cost–effective solution. Instead, a high level of redundancy is built into the chassis of a back-end server, including power-on fault tolerance, in order to keep the system up and running even when replacing failed components.

 Large network systems often provide multiple levels of data backup. The first, and most efficient, backup level is directly on a local hard disk drive. The second level of archival storage is reserved for data that is not used immediately. The first level of backup data may periodically be archived on a secondary storage device, such as a tape drive. In large networks, the archival storage function may be performed and controlled by a server, or a cluster of servers, referred to as archival servers.

Back-end servers do not require large amounts of RAM, but they do require fast disk access, plenty of processing power, and high storage capacities. In data farms, the servers may be organized into Storage Area Networks (SANs). SANs are specialized, high-speed fiber optic networks that extract data from the servers without using the main network's bandwidth. They are connected directly to the back-end servers, and pull the data up to the main network.

Implementing Server Tiers

How servers are implemented in an organization is usually determined by the size of the organization and what resources are required. Smaller companies may not implement a fully tiered front-end, mid-tier, and back-end server network. They are more likely to build their network structure around a cluster of general-purpose servers, where each server performs many tasks. One server might be designated as a proxy server providing all network users with Internet access. It may also perform as the mail server, and also take on the intranet server chores. The company may also have another general-purpose server, configured and designated to provide database and file services.

Large organizations design their networks with all three tiers of the multi-tier server model. The construction and function of each server tier are based on the applications they are to provide in the network structure. The front-end machines are used to provide the interface between the network and the users, such as customers and employees. This tier is typically made up of multiple servers and redundant machines, to ensure that the required resources are always available.

As indicated earlier, the middle tier is made up of servers that act as intermediates between the front-end and back-end tiers. Like the front-end tier, the middle tier normally consists of multiple machines and redundant machines. However, the servers in this tier also tend to include a high level of redundancy inside the chassis itself.

The back-end tier is made up of large, expensive machines that typically rely on redundancy inside the system to keep them available. Their high cost tends to make using separate redundant units unrealistic. As you can see, the reasoning behind the types of redundancy employed at each level is driven primarily by cost.

Some mid-sized companies may skip either the back-end or front-end server tiers depending on their current needs. Other medium-sized companies may configure a portion of their multi-tiered servers to perform at more than one level. For example, a company might use what would be considered mid-tiered machines to perform front-end and mid-tier tasks, while their back-end servers simply perform back-end functions. This arrangement, as depicted in Figure 1.3, would save the company money without totally compromising their resources. In addition, the structure could later be expanded into a fully tiered network as the company's needs grow.

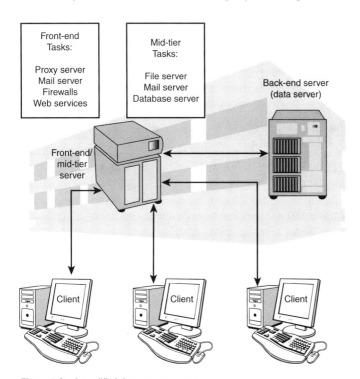

Figure 1.3 A modified tier server structure.

Exam Prep Questions

1. Which of the following types of servers is designed to provide client access to mainframe (IBM) and mid-range data facilities?
   - ❏ A. DNS server
   - ❏ B. SNA server
   - ❏ C. NAS server
   - ❏ D. Mail server

2. How many inches of rack space are provided in a full rack?
   - ❏ A. 52.5 inches
   - ❏ B. 56 inches
   - ❏ C. 70 inches
   - ❏ D. 73.5 inches

3. What type of server is used to store vast volumes of data in archive and data farms?
   - ❏ A. Application server
   - ❏ B. General-purpose server
   - ❏ C. Back-end server
   - ❏ D. Front-end server

4. In a multi-tiered server system, which tier is typically used to pass information between front-end and back-end servers?
   - ❏ A. Back-end servers
   - ❏ B. Mid-tier servers
   - ❏ C. Web-tier servers
   - ❏ D. Front-end servers

5. Which of the following could be a major disadvantage for a server rack?
   - ❏ A. Racks exhibiting poor airflow characteristics
   - ❏ B. Multiple rack-mounted UPS units
   - ❏ C. Low-friction rails for easy access
   - ❏ D. Moderate server room environmental conditions

6. Which of the following can act as the intermediary between a workstation and the Internet, and cache frequently visited websites?
   - ❏ A. Management services
   - ❏ B. Web server
   - ❏ C. Proxy server
   - ❏ D. Messaging services

7. Which of the following application servers are primarily used to answer modem-based phone calls and complete connections to the requested node(s)?

  ❑ A. Terminal server
  ❑ B. Proxy server
  ❑ C. News server
  ❑ D. Mail server

8. In which tier environment would blade servers be considered unsuitable?

  ❑ A. Tier 3, as a database server
  ❑ B. Tier 1, as a front-end server
  ❑ C. Tier 4, as a back-end server
  ❑ D. Tier 0, as an edge server

9. Which type of server is used by a client when searching for resources by computer name, instead of by IP address?

  ❑ A. DNS server
  ❑ B. Proxy server
  ❑ C. WINS server
  ❑ D. DHCP server

10. Which type of server is capable of permitting clients to dial in to a computer from a remote site?

  ❑ A. DNS server
  ❑ B. RAS server
  ❑ C. DHCP server
  ❑ D. Proxy server

11. Which of the following uses would be suitable for an edge server?

  ❑ A. Back-end system for web hosting
  ❑ B. Middle-end email reader
  ❑ C. To cache and/or mirror web multimedia content
  ❑ D. Front-end system for web hosting

12. When moving a full server rack, what procedure should you always follow?

  ❑ A. Remove the components before moving the rack.
  ❑ B. Make sure that all components are securely plugged in before moving the rack.
  ❑ C. Allow the rack to clear everything in its path as it is moved to its new destination.
  ❑ D. Move the server rack to its new destination without removing its components.

13. It is necessary to reroute some cables, requiring a server rack to be moved. What is the least sensible option in the following list for moving an established server rack?

- ❏ A. Place the server on a gurney and move it to the new location.
- ❏ B. Take the lighter components off the rack and move it with the heavier equipment to the new location.
- ❏ C. Take the heavier components off the rack and move it with the lighter equipment to the new location.
- ❏ D. Remove all equipment from the rack before moving it to its new location.

Answers to Exam Prep Questions

1. Answer B is the correct answer. An SNA server is designed to provide client access to mainframe (IBM) and mid-range data facilities. Answer A is incorrect because a Domain Name System (DNS) server is designed to resolve TCP/IP names to IP addresses. Answer C is incorrect because an NAS server is designed to effectively move storage out from behind a file server and put it directly on the transport network. Answer D is incorrect because a mail server is used to receive and store electronic mail messages in private mailboxes.

2. Answer D is the correct answer. If the height of one U is equal to 1.75 inches, the height of a full rack is 42×1.75, or 73.5 inches. Answer A is incorrect because 52.5 inches of rack space would provide a rack height of only 30U. Answer B is incorrect because 56 inches of rack space would provide a rack height of only 32U. Answer C is incorrect because 70 inches of rack space would provide a rack height of only 40U.

3. Answer C is the correct answer. A back-end server is large, expensive, and used to store vast volumes of data in archive and data farms. Answer A is incorrect because application servers manage application programs running between client computers and the organization's database. Answer B is incorrect because a general-purpose server is intended to provide a wide variety of services, such as handling departmental email, or providing file, print, and web services. Answer D is incorrect because a front-end server is usually configured to perform one function, or a multiple of related functions.

4. Answer B is the correct answer. Mid-tier servers are designed to pass information between front-end and back-end servers. Answer A is incorrect because large pools of information used by the front-end and mid-tier servers are stored in the back-end servers. Answer C is incorrect because there is no such thing as a web-tier server. Answer D is incorrect because a front-end server is configured to perform one function, or a multiple of related functions.

5. Answer A is the correct answer. Depending on a server rack's design and compliment of equipment, not having adequate airflow could become a fatal flaw. Answer B is incorrect because server racks having multiple UPS units are well protected against power fluctuations or loss. Answer C is incorrect because having rack equipment chassis that slide smoothly in and out on low-friction rails for easy access is an advantage. Answer D is incorrect because moderate environmental conditions are always a good thing when using server racks.

6. Answer C is the correct answer. Proxy servers act as the intermediary between a workstation and the Internet, and can cache frequently visited websites. Answer A is incorrect because management services are special tools and protocols used for remote system management by administrators. Answer B is incorrect because web servers host web pages for intranet and/or Internet access. Answer D is incorrect because messaging services provide the capability to send instant messages throughout the network.

7. Answer A is the correct answer. Terminal servers are primarily used to answer modem-based phone calls and complete connections to the requested node(s). Answer B is incorrect because proxy servers act as the intermediary between a workstation and the Internet and can also cache frequently visited websites. Answer C is incorrect because news servers receive, store, and distribute strictly news articles to and from newsgroups on a specific network, or on the Internet. Answer D is incorrect because mail servers have nothing to do with caching web pages.

8. Answer A is the correct answer. Blade servers have performance, heat-generation, and cost-efficiency problems making them unsuitable for more demanding Tier 2 or Tier 3 operations. Answer B is incorrect because blade servers are best suited for Tier 1 environments, as a front-end system for service delivery networks such as web hosting, email, directory services, firewalls, and network management. Answer C is incorrect because no such thing as a Tier 4 environment was discussed in this chapter. Answer D is incorrect because there is no such thing as a Tier 0 environment.

9. Answer C is the correct answer. A WINS server is used by a client when searching for resources by computer name, instead of by IP address. Answer A is incorrect because a DNS server receives host or domain address information and stores it for a short time. Answer B is incorrect because a client's request for Internet data is forwarded through a proxy's cache on the way to the original server. Answer D is incorrect because DHCP is used to temporarily assign dynamic IP addresses to network workstations and Internet clients.

10. Answer B is the correct answer. RAS servers are used primarily to permit clients to dial in to a computer from a remote site. Answer A is incorrect because a DNS server is used to cache client requests for a limited amount of time. Answer C is incorrect because DHCP is concerned with IP address assignments rather than with client requests. Answer D is incorrect because a proxy server can store client requests indefinitely, until they are needed again.

11. Answer C is the correct answer. An edge server is used to cache and/or mirror multimedia content otherwise stored on the WWW. Answer A is incorrect because an edge server is not powerful enough to assume back-end responsibilities. Answer B is incorrect because there is no such server category as middle-end. Answer D is incorrect because web hosting is a Tier 1 operation suitable for a blade server, but not for an edge server.

12. Answer A is the correct answer. Be sure to move the rack empty and then install the components later. This will prevent damage occurring to the components installed in the rack. Always remember that racks are not designed to be moved with components still mounted in them. Answers B and D are incorrect because the components should already be removed before the rack is repositioned. Answer C is incorrect because the rack should not impact any obstructions while being moved.

13. Answer A is the correct answer. Moving the rack to a new location fully loaded, regardless of the method used, is totally unacceptable. Answer B is incorrect because even though all of the equipment was not removed prior to moving the rack, at least the lighter items were. Answer C is incorrect because the lighter components can still be damaged. In fact, a lighter rack will vibrate even more than a fully loaded one, shaking the lighter components vigorously! Answer D is incorrect because removing all components from the rack before moving it is the most sensible option listed.

2.0—Server Availability

Terms you'll need to understand:

✓ Clustering
✓ Scalability
✓ High availability
✓ Fault tolerance
✓ Failover

Techniques you'll need to master:

✓ Keeping a network running smoothly
✓ Maintaining high levels of reliability
✓ Selecting the proper server software
✓ Associating alarms with specific server subsystems
✓ Activating alert notifications
✓ Using validated components
✓ Using three primary factors to determine scale-up or scale-out upgrades
✓ Explaining clustered resources and what they do
✓ Knowing the minimum number of required nodes to configure a cluster
✓ Identifying single points of server network failure
✓ Understanding how network load balancing (NLB) helps to achieve high server availability
✓ Describing a quorum and how it is used
✓ Explaining the weaknesses of a single-quorum-device server cluster

✓ Describing how a majority node set works

✓ Understanding scalability and how to recognize its limits

✓ Contrasting differences between centralized and client/server system architectures

✓ Defining a program thread

✓ Describing why modern server operating systems support Symmetrical Multiprocessing (SMP)

✓ Relating high availability to downtime

✓ Identifying the industry standard rating for network availability and how to calculate it

✓ Learning how general-purpose servers use hot-swappable components

✓ Explaining how back-end servers achieve high availability

✓ Understanding the conceptual arrangement of computer load balancing

✓ Knowing what fault tolerance is

✓ Describing how a redundant network interface card (NIC) makes a server more fault-tolerant

✓ Examining how critical systems use failover for fault tolerance

✓ Defining how transparency works throughout the duration of a server outage

✓ Explaining how failover server systems communicate using a heartbeat

Introduction

Server+ Exam Objective 1.13 states that the test taker should know the attributes, purposes, functions, and advantages of server clustering, scalability, high availability, and fault tolerance. Examples of these server attributes, purposes, functions, and advantages include

➤ Rapid switching

➤ Redundancy

➤ Failover mode

➤ Subsystem alarm circuitry

➤ Component validations

➤ System expansion

➤ Continuously available data storage

➤ Network load balancing

➤ Majority node set

➤ Query/response strategy

➤ Threads

➤ Parallel processing operations

➤ Business continuity plan

➤ Remote configuration

➤ Field-replaceable components

➤ Hot-swappable Peripheral Component Interconnect (PCI) slots

➤ Load balancing

➤ Uninterruptible power supplies

➤ Identical shared disks

➤ Heartbeat communications

The Impact of Server Failures

Server failures directly impact a company's revenues, financial performance, productivity, and reputation. The severity of a failure can range from not being able to back up data for a couple of days, to being out of business while the server is down. The ultimate impact of server failure depends on how critical the application is to the organization.

Some businesses can suffer a catastrophic loss if systems fail, such as those that rely heavily on a productive sales website. Even if a failed server only causes company websites to run slow, Internet customers will tend to go elsewhere.

Even in a non-sales environment, such as a publishing production room, poor server reliability will result in costs associated with lost business opportunities, reduced productivity, and idle personnel. For these reasons, administrators strive to maintain high levels of reliability for all servers.

The emphasis on reliability should initially focus on the server software. Only 20% of the downtime incurred on business servers is caused by hardware failures. The balance is directly attributable to application and operator errors.

Designing Reliable Server Networks

Good server network design is based on two concepts: redundancy and monitoring.

We already mentioned the use of redundant components inside the chassis and additional servers in the network to provide for various levels of fault tolerance.

A major consideration in designing reliable server operations is the importance of *failover mode*. Having additional machines located on the network that can assume the duties of a failed server provides failover. During implementation, the network administrator must have an operational strategy for keeping server resources available to the network in the event of a failure.

We now discuss techniques used to monitor server components and the immediate environment surrounding the servers, including temperature and supply voltage levels. In a well-designed server network, there should be alarms associated with

➤ RAID system failures

➤ CPU failures

➤ Hard disk drive failures

These subsystems should have built-in alarms to alert technicians and administrators when trouble occurs.

Even if a reliable server has redundant subsystems that allow the network to continue running when one component fails, it's important to realize that this server has now become more vulnerable to failure because its system is not running at full capacity. Initially, the administrator and/or technician should receive an alert, giving him or her an opportunity to troubleshoot and repair the problem before the occurrence of a full system failure.

Such alerts are normally provided through email, pager, or other signaling method, and are an essential element of reliable server design. Tools for notifying system administrators of problems must be applied while the server is still running. Alert notifications include environmental changes that could adversely affect the server's performance, such as air conditioning failures. Although such situations would initially cause server degradation, they would inevitably cause component or system failure if not corrected. Timely alert notifications can be provided by temperature sensors built into the server's main board, including temperature alarm routines in its BIOS.

Alarms are also provided for supply voltage monitoring, and activated when values exceed preset minimums or maximums. If supply voltage drops below 90 volts, effective operation of the server is in jeopardy and associated components could be damaged. Whenever blackouts or brownouts occur, the servers will be initially unaffected, because the UPS battery backup system is equipped to protect them. By applying a steady, expected voltage to the system, the UPS would permit the servers to run for a prescribed period of time before system shutdown. If configured to do so, the UPS will power itself down after issuing an alert to the server's network operating system (NOS).

Another way to ensure server reliability is to use *validated components* that have been rigorously tested by the supplier and guaranteed to effectively work together.

Know that to ensure hardware component reliability, all server components should be validated before installation.

Scaling Up and Scaling Out

When designing server systems for reliability, administrators must also consider the future of their systems. When expansion time comes, consideration must be given to how the upgrade might proceed. Two common methods are used to upgrade servers. They are referred to as either *scale up* or *scale out*.

In a scale-up operation, components are added to the server computer, making it more powerful.

In this scenario, the technicians expand the system by adding components, or by upgrading the existing components inside the case. Scale-up operations continue throughout the life of a server until either

➤ The operational limit of the server computer is met, or

➤ External redundancy is added to ensure protection against system failure.

When scale-up operations are no longer possible, server network administrators begin scaling out their systems.

In scale-out operations, additional servers are installed, load-balancing techniques are implemented, and increased out-of-chassis redundancy is also employed. These concepts are used widely in the enterprise networking industry. Administrators must consider short-term and long-term solutions. Scaling up will bring the current server closer to its maximum capacity. Scaling out will extend the maximum capacity of the network permitting further expansion in the future.

Three primary factors that server system administrators take into account when deciding between scale-up or scale-out scenarios are capacity, reliability, and cost.

When companies need something immediately, they tend to scale up, to save time and money. Complete server systems are costly, whereas adding internal components is less expensive. Companies tend to scale out when additional server capacity is needed in the future. Scaling out provides administrators with greater flexibility, and expands their server capacity by providing additional server redundancy. Over time, scaling up, scaling out, upgrades, and repair operations should always be documented. Documentation is one of the key tools in system troubleshooting and administering server facilities.

Clustering

Businesses require that their data be available at all times. *Clustering* provides a way of configuring server data storage so that it is continuously available.

Basically, a cluster is two or more servers (also known as nodes when referring to clustering) that act as one and are managed as one. This way, when a node fails, another is there to take over the load, increasing data availability and uptime. Clustering eliminates single points of failure because if one server fails, another server within that cluster will take over and deliver the requested data.

 Know the advantages of clustering and the minimum number of nodes required to configure a clustered server environment.

The following are examples of single points of failure that clustering can avoid to prevent system downtime:

➤ PC power failure

➤ Adapter failure

➤ Cable failure

➤ Motherboard failure

➤ Processor failure

➤ NIC failure

Compared to using a single computer, a two-node (or greater) cluster can eliminate nearly all single-point hardware failures and increase the availability of data.

 | Know the advantages of a two-node cluster.

Clustering has had its share of problems to overcome, such as the high cost of server redundancy. Although keeping a commercial network up and running is obviously good for business, if it costs more to deploy a cluster than the improved uptime saves, clustering will not be considered worth the money. On the other hand, if ongoing maintenance costs are dwarfing the upfront hardware and software costs of a cluster, the situation needs to be rectified.

In the past, significant administration time was required for monitoring, managing, and troubleshooting the added complexity of clusters. Deployment of additional software besides the base operating system was required, and administrators had to be trained to use it.

Server Clustering

Modern clustering technology has simplified former administration chores. Server software divides the clustering philosophy into two technologies: server clustering and *network load balancing (NLB)*. Depending on which type is being provided, the servers can be configured for high availability (HA).

Server clustering is used with application services such as databases, Enterprise Resource Planning (ERP) software packages, Customer Relationship Management (CRM) software packages, On-Line Transaction Processing (OLTP), file and print management, and email and other messaging applications. These applications are frequently considered critical enough to employ server clustering with high availability through failover.

Server software permits the deployment of clustering by configuring a minimum of two servers that will act as *nodes* in the cluster.

After cluster identification, the resources are configured according to the requirements of a specified application. Clustered resources are the required network names, IP addresses, software applications, network services, and disk drives necessary to process the anticipated client requests. The finalized cluster then goes online to begin interfacing with the clients.

Clustered applications are usually assigned to one cluster node at a time, along with their associated resources. When clustering software detects the failure of a clustered application's primary node, or if that node is temporarily taken offline for maintenance, a backup cluster node is selected to start up the clustered application. The impact of the failure is minimized because client requests are immediately redirected to the backup cluster node. To optimize hardware utilization, a cluster can run many services simultaneously, although most clustered services run on only one node at a time. Certain clustered applications can also run on multiple server cluster nodes simultaneously.

A *quorum* is the storage device that must be controlled by the primary node for a clustered application. Nodes in the specified cluster use the quorum to determine which node owns a clustered application. Because only one node at a time may own the quorum, the backup cluster node takes ownership of the quorum only when an application fails over to a backup node. When the cluster nodes are all attached to a single storage device, the quorum is created on the storage device. This type of cluster is referred to as a *single-quorum-device* server cluster in Windows Server 2003.

A single-quorum server cluster simplifies the job of transferring data control to a backup node. However, a server architecture that connects all nodes to a single storage device has serious weaknesses. The entire cluster becomes unuseable if the single storage device fails. In addition, if the entire storage area network (SAN) fails, the cluster fails. Some protection is possible using complete redundancy with both the storage device, and the SAN. All the redundancy in the world will fail if the facility itself goes down, and the facility could be subject to floods, fires, earthquakes, and extended power failures, causing the entire cluster to fail. When commercial operations must continue regardless of a single facility's online status, a single-quorum-device server cluster is not the ideal solution.

Another solution stores the quorum on locally attached storage devices, with one connected directly to each of the cluster nodes. This arrangement is called a *majority node set (MNS)*, requiring the backup node to contain a copy of the quorum data before assuming control. Server clustering software ensures that this requirement is met by replicating quorum data across the network. The basic requirement for MNS clusters is that their nodes be connected to a local area network (LAN), a wide area network (WAN), or a virtual private network (VPN) connecting cluster nodes in different buildings or cities. They overcome the geographic restrictions otherwise imposed by the storage connections.

MNS clusters must have at least three nodes, although this is not a concern for single-quorum-device server clusters. To ensure an effective failover between nodes on a MNS cluster, more than half of the cluster nodes must be continually active. For a cluster of three nodes, two of them must be active to maintain functionality. For a cluster of eight nodes, five nodes must be active to keep it online. Single-quorum-device server clusters can continue to function even with only a single node.

Network Load Balancing
The alternate clustering technology, NLB, doesn't use a quorum. NLB is used to provide high availability for applications that scale out horizontally, such as web servers, proxy servers, and similar networked services requiring the distribution of client requests across various nodes in a cluster. Examine Table 2.1 to compare the features of server clustering with NLB.

Table 2.1 Comparing Server Clustering with NLB	
Server Clustering	**Network Load Balancing**
Used for databases, email services, line of business (LOB) applications, and custom applications	Used for web servers, firewalls, and proxy servers
Included with Windows Server 2003 Enterprise Edition, and Windows Server 2003 Data Center Edition	Included with all four versions of Windows Server 2003
Provides high availability and server consolidation	Provides high availability and scalability
Can be deployed on a single network or geographically distributed	Generally deployed on a single network, but can span multiple networks if properly configured
Supports clusters up to 8 nodes	Supports clusters up to 32 nodes
Requires the use of shared or replicated storage	Requires no special hardware or software; works out of the box

Because neither storage nor network requirements are imposed on the cluster nodes, NLB automatically redirects incoming requests to the remaining nodes if a node in the cluster fails. When a node in the cluster must be taken offline, NLB permits existing client sessions to be completed first, eliminating end-user impact during planned downtimes. High-powered and legacy servers can be mixed for efficient hardware utilization because NLB is capable of weighting requests.

Although NLB clusters can scale up to 32 nodes, they are most often used to build redundancy and scalability for firewalls, proxy servers, Internet Security and Acceleration servers (ISAs), or Internet Information Servers (IISs).

Other applications commonly clustered with NLB include endpoints for virtual private networks, streaming media servers, and terminal services. NLB is provided with all versions of Windows Server 2003, including the Web Edition.

Scalability

Scalability involves how well the server system's software, hardware, and components will adapt to the increasing demand for more network growth. Can the additional loading be resolved by making minor modifications to the system? Suppose a networked server system started out with only a few clients and then suddenly expanded to several hundred. If this network system is truly scalable, and capable of continued operation, it must be able to handle the increasing load requirements of these new clients.

 Know what scalability is and how to describe it.

Planning for future growth is every system administrator's job. Capital is conserved by initially designing small, inexpensive systems to last several years. Proper planning for future scaling permits this initial system to grow as demand dictates. The cost and risk of system deployment is reduced and tied directly to company growth. The philosophy of starting small and scaling capacity as needed permits the administrator to make conservative utilization estimates for new services. These estimates can be accurately scaled after a real demand is established. The deployment of a new web service requires detailed answers to several questions in order to accurately estimate the network's anticipated capacity. These questions include

➤ How many users must the web service support?

➤ How busy will each user's connection be?

➤ What will be the peak load capacity required by the system?

➤ What computing resources will the web service require to service the anticipated web traffic?

A client/server network has good scalability when additional users can be integrated into the system without response times being lengthened considerably. Centralized server architectures using mainframe file-sharing systems can improve scalability by installing faster processors and disk drives. The server is the source of both operational software and/or the data, and running programs have exclusive access to its CPU and disk drives.

However, running the server faster cannot solve scalability problems with client/server network architectures, which are based on the query/response strategy. This reduces network traffic by not blindly demanding a total file transfer for every operation. The overall speed of the server is not the main concern. Instead, the workload is divided between the client and the server.

Although the server provides database management, it also serves multiple clients. Any network client request submitted to the server must be queued until the server is free to respond. After all prior requests have been performed, the server can then proceed to the next request in the queue. If the queue is empty, the server rests until the next request arrives.

Performance characteristics between a centralized system and a client/server architecture differ dramatically. The performance of the client/server network degrades exponentially with an increasing number of requests. At some point, the response of the server may become too slow to tolerate. This is where a server's scalability comes into play.

Server operating systems are capable of dividing programs into multiple *tasks*, and dividing tasks into multiple *threads* for processing on multiple microprocessors. A thread is a separate part of a program that can be time-sliced by the operating system to execute simultaneously with other threads. This processing format is impossible if a server is running a simple MS-DOS OS on a multiple-processor system board. Because a basic DOS operating system can use only one processor at a time, a significant amount of computing power would simply be wasted, especially if dual processors were installed. Remember that a single-process operating system cannot simultaneously process multiple threads.

Symmetrical Multiprocessing

Even though desktop operating systems such as Windows 98, Windows ME, and Windows XP include support for multiple processor operations, they cannot offer the high-volume processing power expected of servers. Software operating systems must be specifically written to support multiple processor operations.

Virtually all of the major server operating systems available today provide high-volume, multiprocessor capabilities by supporting *Symmetrical*

Multiprocessing (SMP) parallel processing operations. SMP permits multiple processors to work on single tasks simultaneously. This means that if an application is properly coded, it can allow different parts of its operation to be handled by multiple processors at the same time. The difference between symmetric multiprocessing and asymmetric processing is that an asymmetric processor is assigned to perform an individual task on its own.

 Know the definition and advantages of SMP.

SMP permits improved scalability in machines that are specifically designed to use it, and more will be covered on this subject in a later section.

High Availability

The greatest fear for a network administrator is *downtime*. When it occurs, something or someone must be blamed. For example, the hardware is responsible when a memory chip fails. Nature is responsible when heavy rains flood the data center. The cleaning personnel are responsible when they unplug the server in order to plug in a vacuum machine. Having someone or something to blame does not, however, make up for losses suffered by the company when a critical service is offline. Regardless of the cause, a failure is ultimately the responsibility of the server network administrator.

Therefore, the administrator must plan for all of these types of "unpredictable" events ahead of time. Modern server operating systems include tools to meet the most demanding network availability and scalability requirements.

The term *high availability* refers to the capability of a server system to endure a software or hardware disaster, and still function. Some form of system duplication must be incorporated to remove any single point of failure. Consequently, server clusters are equipped with high-availability resolve for systems that require read and write admittance to information such as email, file servers, and databases.

This requires the use of programs that monitor network errors, and alert network administrators before the network takes a serious hit. Naturally, administration notifications are issued immediately when a server actually goes down, and a detailed log file of the incident is created. The system administrator can monitor servers in either a LAN or WAN arrangement, and these program tools maintain a list of servers organized by logical name,

IP address, and port. This list is checked repeatedly, and the log file is updated with each server monitoring report.

Multiple server lists are maintained with capabilities to add or remove servers to/from each list, set up servers to be checked automatically, edit listed servers manually, or permit a client to examine a server upon request. Administrators can also build network maps in order to visually control the network's behavior.

A variety of protocols and services are supported, including

➤ Internet Control Message Protocol (ICMP) network monitoring (ping)

➤ NT Event Log computer monitoring

➤ HTTP(S)/FTP URL Internet monitor (with or without content filters)

➤ Free Disk Space hardware monitor

➤ NT Service State server monitor

➤ Oracle Server network monitor

➤ MS SQL Server monitor

➤ SQL query result monitor

➤ SQL Server monitoring through Open DataBase Connectivity (ODBC)

➤ External application execution system monitor

➤ File existence file monitor

➤ NetBIOS LAN monitor

➤ SMTP/POP3 mail server monitor

➤ IPX/SPX file server monitor

➤ Remote Access Service (RAS) server dial-up monitor

➤ VBScript program

➤ Telnet Server monitor

➤ Network News Transfer Protocol (NNTP) Server monitor

➤ Internet Message Access Protocol (IMAP) mail server monitor

➤ Borland Database Engine (BDE) servers monitoring

➤ Lightweight Directory Access Protocol (LDAP) servers monitoring

➤ TCP/IP monitor

➤ Various plug-ins and add-ons

Availability Ratings

Companies make the effort to determine the amount of time required for shared server resources to be available on the network. This requirement is called *availability*, and it's expressed as a percentage. The more critical a resource component is, the higher its availability must be. The resource must be there (available) when clients need to use it, and their needs and response times differ. Although payroll clerks may require access to the payroll service between 8 a.m. and 5 p.m. on business days, a customer service representative (CSR) may require access to an order entry service 24 hours a day, 7 days a week. Response times for a CSR may have to occur within 2 seconds, whereas a marketing analyst may accept a transaction time of 30 seconds for retrieving and formatting product sales histories.

When the availability requirement has been quantified, it directly impacts the network's design. This includes the level of built-in redundancy, as well as the components selected for use. For 24/7 business models, system designers need to determine realistically how much server downtime for maintenance or repair can be tolerated. At this point, the server's availability will be expressed as a percentage.

The industry standard rating for availability is called *five 9's*, and signifies that the rated resource is available for 99.999% of the time. A five-9's rating is the standard requirement for back-end servers, and provides for only 5.265 minutes per year of downtime. Various 9's ratings are used to express the availability of other server applications. For example, *four 9's* represents an availability of 99.99%, which provides for an annual downtime maximum of 52.26 minutes.

The data for analyzing the availability of multipurpose server networks already exists in the form of Simple Network Management Protocol (SNMP), ping, trap, and trouble ticket reports already collected by most network administrators. Published statistics by the vendors of network devices are also freely available. Software exists to put this data together in useful ways so that network managers can observe the availability levels that their clients experience. Hopefully, potential problems can be identified and corrected before those clients become negatively affected. Although the idea of having a five-9's availability rating has been the traditional aim for service-provider network administrators, availability often has more to do with having that highly available network where you need it most—for mission-critical applications.

Availability Calculations

Examine the following equation, which attempts to describe the basic concepts of availability:

$$\text{Availability} = 1-(\text{total network downtime})/$$
$$(\text{total network uptime})$$

or

$$= 1-\text{downtime/uptime}$$

Here, a connection is defined as the successful data transfer from one end device to another. The connectivity itself would involve physical connectivity, link-layer protocol connectivity, and network-layer protocol connectivity. The specified commercial organization might choose to include a time factor in the definition of high availability. Although trouble ticket reports about the network might be used to derive the actual numbers, the overall availability of the network provides little detail about specific devices, communications paths, or applications operations. These parameters would have to be individually charted for availability in order to get a true picture.

The availability for individual devices must be expressed using a more focused equation. Notice the two additional parameters being utilized, *Mean Time Between Failure (MTBF)* and *Mean Time To Repair (MTTR)*.

$$\text{Availability} = \text{MTBF}/(\text{MTBF} + \text{MTTR})$$

Consider an individual networked device with an MTBF of 38,830 hours, and an MTTR of only 6 hours. For the device specified, its availability would be equal to

$$\text{Availability} = 38{,}830/(38{,}830 + 6)$$

$$= 38{,}830/38{,}836$$

$$= .998455$$

$$= 99.98455 \text{ percent}$$

Essentially, this equation states that the availability of a device equals the MTBF for that device slightly lessened by the small value of MTTR. Using this approach to determine the availability for paths results in the expression:

$$\text{Availability} = \text{MTBF}(x)/(\text{MTBF}(x) + \text{MTTR}(x))$$

where x equals a failure due to software, hardware, power, human error, or path convergence time in redundant systems.

Network managers and administrators calculate network availability by using equations such as these. Of course, they must be able to identify which factors must be tracked to produce the calculation. The calculations are often executed by network management software that incorporates the proper equations and can be customized for individual companies. The critical data points are the values for MTBF and MTTR. These data categories should be collected and analyzed for each device type in the network, as well as from every path.

To gather data on both devices and paths, organizations typically use

➤ Trouble tickets to derive Impacted User Minutes (IUMs)

➤ Polling and traps using SNMP, to derive the status of links and devices

➤ Testing ping packets using ICMP, to determine reachability

Appliance Server Availability

The criticality of the provided service determines the availability criteria for appliance servers. If the appliance server providing email service crashes, it's reasonable to expect that the business will continue to operate without interruption. Although the email service should be in operation almost all of the time, treating this server as a field-replaceable unit would permit the network to achieve a high availability rating. However, if the appliance server controlling an airport's tower communications system went down, the problem would be much more serious. To achieve a high level of availability, it might be necessary to employ three or four appliance servers to simultaneously perform the communications function, with two of them operating 24 hours a day.

For locally managed Internet connections (LMICs), appliance servers are the easiest solution considering maintenance and configuration. They provide

➤ Access to the Internet using various connection methods

➤ Firewall security for the internal private network

➤ Web caching for the faster retrieval of web pages

➤ Web access control categorized by user, group, date, and time

➤ Support for Virtual Private Network (VPN), Point-to-Point Tunneling Protocol (PPTP), and Internet Protocol Security (IPSec)

➤ Website and File Transfer Protocol (FTP) support

➤ Secure remote administration with 128-bit security

➤ Wireless network support for the LAN

➤ Dial-in access for remote users

➤ Fault-tolerant data storage

➤ User security and file sharing dependent upon login

➤ Backup to an external device

➤ Out-of-the-box functionality as a turnkey solution

An LMIC usually consists of a single system unit, fitted with one or more LAN ports connecting to the local private network through a hub or switch. Its WAN port will connect to the Internet using a router or modem. Appliance servers do not require a keyboard, monitor, or a mouse, making them somewhat more secure. Therefore, after being connected to the local network, the appliance server is remotely configured and administered from another computer, using an Internet browser or a software wizard.

Local users pass their network traffic and requests to the appliance server across its LAN port, and the appliance server acts as a proxy or gateway to the Internet. Traffic passes through the server's internal cache, firewall, and other systems before being sent to the WAN port for forwarding to the Internet. Of course, information from the Internet will flow in the opposite direction.

An email originating from a computer is normally passed to an email server, through the proxy server, out to the firewall, and finally to a router for transmission out to the Internet. This situation works well until some type of fault develops. Because email is dependent on all parts of the chain working properly, one broken or impassable link will bring the entire process to a halt.

If email can be sent directly from the user's computer, to the appliance server, and right out to the Internet, several links are removed from the chain and all processing can be conducted within the appliance server. From the standpoint of availability, the network's email rating will be high.

Although an appliance server can be configured to provide basic and reliable selective functionality, for advanced functions, dedicated units are always required.

General-Purpose Server Availability

In small business networks, general-purpose servers are commonly the primary, and often the only, servers used. Hot-swappable components such as power supplies and hard disks are used to achieve availability, along with integrated management tools. Another feature of general-purpose servers is hot-swappable PCI slots designed to hold redundant network PCI cards, to ensure that the server will not be disconnected from the network if one of the NIC cards becomes inoperable. Special circuitry, built into hot-swappable PCI slots, permits power to be selectively disabled to the specified slot without cutting power to the server. The suspected PCI card can then be exchanged while the server is still running the network.

Front-End Server Availability

High-service availability is achieved using a front-end server just as with an appliance server. There will most likely be another server waiting on the shelf ready to take over a front-end server's functions if they are not considered critical. The server administrator or technician merely has to plug it into the network, as if it were a field-replaceable unit. When front-end servers are running critical applications, large businesses achieve their high availability ratings by implementing failover servers. In the event of a critical server failure, the network can switch over to the failover machine.

Mid-Tier Server Availability

Because a mid-tier server has a high level of redundancy built inside its chassis, it is closely related to the general-purpose server mentioned earlier. However, a mid-tier server typically shares its processing load with another computer, in an arrangement referred to as load balancing.

Application software designed for use with mid-tier load-balanced servers achieves high system-level availability, permitting the use of lower-cost hardware. Traditional monolithic mid-tier applications are run on back-end servers in some organizations, to take advantage of their high single-system availability and scaling capability.

Back-End Server Availability

Because of their high costs, back-end servers generate higher demands for single-server availability. An expensive back-end server must continue to run, even if any of the hardware it contains fails and needs replacement. Load balancing is not an option here, because the back-end server is usually the most expensive machine in the network.

Back-end servers must have a high level of redundancy inside the chassis, in order to achieve five-9's availability, and must exhibit greater fault resilience than other server types. Their subsystems must be replaceable without requiring the entire system to be shut down. This necessitates the use of more costly technologies, including hardware items such as

➤ Multiple power supplies

➤ An Uninterruptible Power Supply (UPS)

➤ Hot-swappable PCI slots

➤ Hot-swappable hard disks

➤ Multiple network cards

Various server types are listed and summarized in Table 2.2, along with explanations as to how they achieve their expected high availability ratings.

Table 2.2 Achieving High Availability Ratings with Servers	
Server Type	**Method of Achieving High Availability Ratings**
Appliance server	Scale out by having multiple appliance servers to balance the load and to make sure that at least two are up at all times.
General-purpose server	Hot-swappable components, integrated management tools, as well as redundant PCI cards for added fault tolerance.
Front-end server	Use failover servers that automatically begin operations when the other server goes down.
Mid-tier server	Availability reached by having hot-swappable components and integrated management tools, as well as multiple PCI cards of the same type for added tolerance. Multiple mid-tier servers are usually utilized for load balancing.
Back-end server	Multiple power supplies, hot-swappable PCI slots, and RAID array of hard disks, as well as multiple PCI cards of the same type for added fault tolerance, will be utilized.

Fault Tolerance

Networking hardware such as Ethernet switches, routers, servers, and network cards can be configured to provide fault-tolerant services. *Fault tolerance* involves a server system's capability to successfully respond to a sudden software or hardware failure.

Know what fault tolerance is and how to describe it.

Modern fault-tolerant systems duplicate operations to ensure that if one or several component(s) fail to operate, others will continue to work with no loss of data or downtime. These capabilities are achieved through load-balancing applications, or through features within the network device firmware or operating system. An example of configuring a server for fault tolerance is the way in which redundant NICs are used. Redundant NICs allow the server to maintain a network connection even if one NIC fails to operate, ensuring that less data is lost when transferring packets to client computers.

Know that a redundant NIC can make a server more fault-tolerant.

Software applications help to achieve more robust redundant network card configurations. For example, NIC array software helps to bind a single network address to multiple NICs, for high throughput and increased fault tolerance. Client/server communications can fail over from one NIC to another, in the event of a breakdown. Other configurations provide the means to balance network requests across all the NICs in one server array, simultaneously.

An NIC software array driver can be placed between the NIC drivers and the protocol stack, within the OS, combining multiple network interfaces together into an array, and assigning connections to various adapters in a round-robin fashion, maintaining access to the server. All traffic must pass from the protocol stack through the software array driver on its way to the network interface cards. In this way, network traffic bottlenecks are intelligently identified as faults across the storage network, while data transfers are transparently rerouted around those faults.

Even a resting network is monitored periodically through the transmission of watchdog packets that loop throughout the data storage areas. If a watchdog packet does not return, triangulation algorithms are employed to pinpoint the problem area. Traffic is then rerouted with nearly zero packet loss while maintaining high availability. Keep in mind that eventually, any faulty equipment must be identified and replaced on a regular basis.

Failover

As mentioned previously in this chapter, *failover* is basically a backup operation that automatically redirects a user request from a failed system to the backup system for continued operation. Services being offered on one device are moved to another upon device failure, to maintain high availability. Critical systems that rely on continuous availability use failover as an important fault-tolerant function. One requirement to ensure data consistency and rapid recovery in a failover situation is to connect the servers to the identical shared disks.

Know the importance of failover.

At a minimum, the migration of services during a failover should include

➤ Transparency

➤ Rapid switching

➤ Minimal manual intervention

➤ Guaranteed data access

During migration from a failed server to a backup machine, the intrusiveness detected by actively working clients should be nonexistent. Throughout the outage, the network itself must not reflect any problem. If any intrusiveness is detected, it should be reflected only after a full restoration, when clients attempt to get back to work. At most, a simple reboot should be all that is necessary for clients accessing server applications following a failover.

For work with databases, the client may have to log back in to the user application. However, logging back in should not be required for non-authenticated web and file services. Login sessions originally connected to the server that failed will still require a repeat login at the failover server.

Failover should require less than two minutes to complete, and certainly no more than five minutes. This goal assumes that the takeover server is already booted and actively running many of the underlying system processes. Failover times will increase dramatically if a full reboot is required, sometimes taking an hour or more!

During a failover, most applications, except databases, can be up and running within two to five minutes. Databases can only be restarted following the caching and rerunning of all outstanding transactions. Then they must be updated. Caching of transactions is done to speed up routine database performance. However, data recovery is a time-consuming process. There is no practical way to predict how long it might take a database to run through all outstanding transactions, unless someone has gone through this experience before. During transaction review, the database remains inaccessible from a user's perspective.

During failover, the ideal situation is one in which no human intervention is required. Although some server sites or applications may require a manual initiation during a failover, this is not a desirable approach. The host machine receiving the failover should already be running, rather than requiring a reboot.

Following a failover the receiving host should see exactly the same data as the original host. Simply copying data to a host computer not actually sharing its disks adds unnecessary security risk and increases the network's complexity.

Such duplication is definitely not recommended for host computers located physically near each other. Any area-related disaster would probably compromise both machines and the duplicated data.

Server systems networked in a failover configuration should communicate with each other continuously. This type of communication, called a *heartbeat*, ensures that each system is kept aware of its partner's state.

Exam Prep Questions

1. Which of the following scaling options should be implemented for an SMP-capable NOS and server board for a web server that is failing to meet its performance requirements? The server board is currently configured with a Pentium IV 2.3GHz microprocessor, and the maximum amount of RAM.
   - ❏ A. Upgrade the CPU to a Pentium 5
   - ❏ B. Install an additional server to help carry the load
   - ❏ C. Install more memory
   - ❏ D. Install a second Pentium IV 2.3GHz CPU

2. Why should all server components be validated before installation?
   - ❏ A. To ensure that all hardware has been updated
   - ❏ B. To ensure hardware reliability
   - ❏ C. To ensure that they have been burn-in tested
   - ❏ D. So that the components counted match the components ordered

3. Which of the following component installations will make the server more fault-tolerant?
   - ❏ A. An additional floppy drive
   - ❏ B. A larger power supply
   - ❏ C. An additional stick of RAM
   - ❏ D. A redundant NIC

4. Which of the following is not a feature of fault-tolerant server networks?
   - ❏ A. The prevention of data loss
   - ❏ B. A high downtime percentage
   - ❏ C. RAID configurations
   - ❏ D. Immunity from component failure

5. The ease with which server boards and processors can be added to the system to increase network performance is called
   - ❏ A. Availability
   - ❏ B. Functionality
   - ❏ C. Scalability
   - ❏ D. Reliability

6. A clustered server environment can be configured with as few as _____ computers.
   - ❏ A. Eight
   - ❏ B. Four
   - ❏ C. Three
   - ❏ D. Two

7. Which of the following are not true advantages of clustering services? (Select two.)
   - ❏ A. Data is continuously available.
   - ❏ B. RAM can be replaced without shutting the server down.
   - ❏ C. Single points of failure are eliminated.
   - ❏ D. ESD cannot affect any data.

8. What are redundant NICs used for in a server?
   - ❏ A. To reduce network traffic
   - ❏ B. To increase the speed of the server
   - ❏ C. To keep the network available in the event that one NIC fails
   - ❏ D. To reduce the amount of data loss when transferring packets to client computers

9. How can single points of failure in a cluster be eliminated?
   - ❏ A. By configuring the cluster with two nodes
   - ❏ B. By doubling the possibilities for single points of failure
   - ❏ C. By downloading data twice as fast
   - ❏ D. By eliminating the possibility of virus attacks

10. Why do system administrators consider using failover strategies?
   - ❏ A. Because virus software is automatically updated
   - ❏ B. Because RAM failures are handled through the use of redundancy
   - ❏ C. Because the switchover to redundant server equipment requires no human intervention
   - ❏ D. Because switching UPS equipment protects servers against power surges

11. What should be checked when a failover server system sees the secondary server attempt to take over the system prematurely?
   - ❏ A. The timeout settings in the primary server
   - ❏ B. Sufficient hard disk space in the primary server
   - ❏ C. Sufficient RAM in the primary server
   - ❏ D. Symmetric multiprocessing in the primary server

Exam Prep Answers

1. Answer D is the correct answer. SMP-capable server boards are designed to use more than one CPU. The board can be scaled up significantly by installing a second matching CPU. Answer A is incorrect because a server board is designed to use one type of CPU only. Besides, there is no such thing as a P5 CPU. Answer B is incorrect because adding an additional server would be more expensive than adding another CPU. Answer C is incorrect because the maximum amount of RAM is already installed.

2. Answer B is the correct answer. Validating all server components before installing them helps to ensure hardware component compatibility and reliability. Answer A is incorrect because updated components are not necessarily compatible with the other server components. Answer C is incorrect because burn-in testing is performed only after validated components are assembled into a working system. Answer D is incorrect because having the proper component count does not ensure validity or reliability.

3. Answer D is the correct answer. Even if one of the NICs fails, the server can maintain a network connection if a redundant NIC is installed. Answer A is incorrect because floppy drives are usually not installed in servers. Answer B is incorrect because the size of the power supply is not directly related to the server's fault tolerance. Answer C is incorrect because more memory will not improve the fault-tolerance status of the server.

4. Answer B is the correct answer. Fault tolerance protects the server network so that when a component fails, another is ready to assume its responsibilities, and no downtime will be incurred. Answer A is incorrect because the prevention of data loss is one of the main features of fault-tolerant systems. Answer C is incorrect because RAID configurations serve to improve fault tolerance in servers. Answer D is incorrect because immunity from component failure is one of the major aspects of fault-tolerant systems.

5. Answer C is the correct answer. Scalability is the ease with which additional load can be added to a network system or component without causing problems. Answer A is incorrect because availability is a percentage measurement of how much time a network or a connection is actually running. Answer B is incorrect because functionality has to do with the capabilities or behaviors of server or network systems. Answer D is incorrect because reliability is the ability of the server or network system to consistently produce the expected results, either meeting or exceeding its specifications.

6. Answer D is the correct answer. A minimum of two servers is required when configuring a clustered environment. Therefore, Answers A, B, and C are incorrect by definition.

7. Answers B and D are the correct answers. In order to replace any RAM, the associated computer server must be powered down regardless of its location in the cluster. ESD remains capable of causing data failure regardless of cluster configuration. However, clustering can protect against the complete loss of that data. Answer A is incorrect because having data continuously available is definitely an advantage of clustering. Answer C is also incorrect because clustering does eliminate single points of failure.

8. Answer C is the correct answer. Redundant NICs are used to provide fault tolerance for the network connection. If one card fails, the other will still keep the network available. Answer A is incorrect because the number of NICs being used in the server does not directly relate to the amount of server data traffic. Answer B is incorrect because the presence of redundant NICs is unrelated to a server's speed capabilities. Answer D is incorrect because the amount of data loss is not dependent upon the network's continued availability.

9. Answer A is the correct answer. Single points of failure can be eliminated in a cluster by configuring the cluster with two nodes. If one fails, the other takes over. Answer B is incorrect because doubling the number of possibilities for single points of failure does nothing to eliminate them. Answer C is incorrect because cluster failures do not directly relate to the data download speeds. Answer D is incorrect because clusters are just as vulnerable to virus attack as any other server configurations.

10. Answer C is the correct answer. Continuous availability and fault tolerance are maintained through the use of failover, especially in the absence of the administrator. Answer A is incorrect because failover is not a strategy designed to deal with virus threats. Answer B is incorrect because the use of redundancy is not feasible in preventing RAM failures. Answer D is incorrect because failover only relates to power problems in the case of a node going down with a bad power supply. Failover would simply switch to an alternate node.

11. Answer A is the correct answer. The primary's timeout parameter settings could be set too low, causing failover to be initiated in spite of the fact that the primary server is working correctly. Answer B is incorrect because the primary server apparently has enough hard disk space to run the system properly. Answer C is incorrect because insufficient RAM in the primary server would reveal itself prior to any failover attempts. Answer D is incorrect because SMP is not directly related to the failover operation.

3.0—Multiprocessing

Terms you'll need to understand:

- ✓ Multiprocessing
- ✓ Internal register
- ✓ Network operating system (NOS)
- ✓ Loose coupling
- ✓ Tight coupling
- ✓ High-level cache
- ✓ Shared memory
- ✓ Symmetrical multiprocessing (SMP)
- ✓ Asymmetrical multiprocessing (ASMP)
- ✓ Scalable system architecture
- ✓ Coherent system
- ✓ Spinlock mode
- ✓ Microkernel architecture
- ✓ Process programming
- ✓ Multithreading
- ✓ Bus snooping
- ✓ Massively parallel processing (MPP)
- ✓ Overhead
- ✓ Latency
- ✓ Determinism
- ✓ Skew
- ✓ Steppings
- ✓ Bit ratings

Techniques you'll need to master:

- ✓ Increasing the overall processing power of a single node
- ✓ Allocating resources
- ✓ Increasing the overall processing power of a system
- ✓ Differentiating between level 2 and level 3 cache
- ✓ Using multiple threads
- ✓ Flushing the cache
- ✓ Configuring network operating systems
- ✓ Preventing the system bus from becoming a bottleneck
- ✓ Determining the bit rating of a specified processor
- ✓ Tuning a server network's performance

Introduction

Server+ Exam Objective 1.12 states that the test taker should know the features, advantages, and disadvantages of multiprocessing. This information includes knowledge about:

➤ Unix

➤ OS/2

➤ Windows NT/2000/XP

➤ Program kernel

➤ Xeon

➤ Pentium

➤ Node

➤ Embedded space

➤ Linux

➤ System bus

➤ Feedback loop

➤ Digital content creation (DCC)

➤ Windows XP Professional x64 Edition

➤ Windows on Windows 64 (WOW64) x86

Multiprocessing Systems

A computer's capability to process more than one task simultaneously is called *multiprocessing*. A multiprocessing operating system is capable of running many programs simultaneously, and most modern network operating systems (NOSs) support multiprocessing. These operating systems include Windows NT, 2000, XP, and Unix.

Although Unix is one of the most widely used multiprocessing systems, there are others. For many years, OS/2 has been the choice for high-end workstations. OS/2 has been a standard operating system for businesses running complex computer programs from IBM. It is a powerful system, employs a nice graphical interface, and can also run programs written for DOS and Windows. However, OS/2 never really caught on for PCs.

The main reason why multiprocessing is more complicated than single-processing is that their operating systems are responsible for allocating resources to competing processes in a controlled environment.

With the growth of commercial networks, the practice of using multiple processors in embedded motherboard designs has become almost universal. Not too long ago, clients or network administrators constructed most multi-processing configurations at the board or system level themselves. Today, motherboards are available incorporating multiple microprocessors on the same die.

A multiprocessing system uses more than one processor to process any given workload, increasing the performance of a system's application environment beyond that of a single processor's capability. This permits tuning of the server network's performance, to yield the required functionality. As described in Chapter 2, "Server Availability," this feature is known as *scalability*, and is the most important aspect of multiprocessing system architectures. Scalable system architecture allows network administrators to tune a server network's performance based on the number of processing nodes required.

Collections of processors arranged in a loosely coupled configuration and interacting with each other over a communication channel have been the most common multiprocessor architecture.

This communication channel might not necessarily consist of a conventional serial or parallel arrangement. Instead, it can be composed of shared memory, used by processors on the same board, or even over a backplane. These interacting processors operate as independent nodes, using their own memory subsystems.

Recently, the embedded server board space has been arranged to accommodate tightly coupled processors, either as a pair, or as an array. These processors share a common bus and addressable memory space. A switch connects them, and interprocessor communications is accomplished through message passing. In the overall system configuration, the processors operate as a single node, and appear as a single processing element. Additional loosely coupled processing nodes increase the overall processing power of the system. When more tightly coupled processors are added, the overall processing power of a single node increases.

These processors have undergone many stages of refinement over the years. For example, the Xeon processors were designed for either network servers or high-end workstations. Similarly, Pentium 4 microprocessors were intended solely for desktop deployment, although Xeon chips had also been called "Pentiums" to denote their family ancestry. Pentium and Xeon processors are currently named separately. The Xeon family consists of two main branches: the Xeon dual-processor (DP) chip, and the Xeon multiprocessor (MP).

Multiprocessing Features

Dual-processor systems are designed for use exclusively with dual-processor motherboards, fitted with either one or two sockets. Multiprocessor systems usually have room on the board for four or more processors, although no minimum requirement exists. Xeon MPs are not designed for dual-processor environments due to specific features of their architecture, and as such, are more expensive.

Dual processors were developed to function at higher clock speeds than multiprocessors, making them more efficient at handling high-speed mathematical computations. Multiprocessors are designed to work together in handling large databases and business transactions. When several multiprocessors are working as a group, even at slower clock speeds, they outperform their DP cousins. Although the NOS is capable of running multiprocessor systems using Symmetrical Multi-Processing (SMP), it must be configured to do so. Simply adding another processor to the motherboard without properly configuring the NOS may result in the system ignoring the additional processor altogether.

Types of MPs

Various categories of multiprocessing systems can be identified. They include

➤ Shared nothing (pure cluster)

➤ Shared disks

➤ Shared memory cluster (SMC)

➤ Shared memory

In *shared nothing* MP systems, each processor is a complete standalone machine, running its own copy of the OS. The processors do not share memory, caches, or disks, but are interconnected loosely, through a LAN. Although such systems enjoy the advantages of good scalability and high availability, they have the disadvantage of using an uncommon message-passing programming model.

Shared disk MP system processors also have their own memory and cache, but they do run in parallel and can share disks. They are loosely coupled through a LAN, with each one running a copy of the OS. Again, communication between processors is done through message passing. The advantages of shared disks are that disk data is addressable and coherent, whereas high availability is more easily obtained than with shared-memory systems. The disadvantage is that only limited scalability is possible, due to physical and logical access bottlenecks to shared data.

In a *shared memory cluster (SMC)*, all processors have their own memory, disks, and I/O resources, while each processor runs a copy of the OS. However, the processors are tightly coupled through a switch, and communications between the processors are accomplished through the shared memory.

In a strictly *shared memory* arrangement, all of the processors are tightly coupled through a high-speed bus (or switch) on the same motherboard. They share the same global memory, disks, and I/O devices. Because the OS is designed to exploit this architecture, only one copy runs across all of the processors, making this a multithreaded memory configuration.

Importance of SMP

The explosion of bandwidth for networking servers has placed unreasonable demands on single-processor systems, which cannot handle the workload! It must be distributed across multiple processors, using SMP. The main differences between an SMP system and every other system are that it utilizes more than one processor, and operates from a somewhat specialized motherboard. The main advantages to using SMP have to do with network speed and expense. Surprisingly, not only is an SMP solution faster than a single-processor solution, but also less expensive. Its higher performance is due to the fact that a multiprocessor motherboard can deliver multiple paths of data processing, whereas a single-processor motherboard can only harness the single processor's capabilities. Compare it to moving 20 students to a server networking class using either a turbo-charged Ferrari or four Volkswagen Beetles. Even though the Beetles are cheaper, they will also get the job done faster. Of course, driving to class in a Ferrari would be more fun!

Hardware performance can be improved easily and inexpensively by placing more than one processor on the motherboard. One approach is called asymmetrical multiprocessing (ASMP), where specific jobs are assigned to specific processors. Doing ASMP effectively requires specialized knowledge about the tasks the computer should do, which is unavailable in a general-purpose operating system such as Linux.

The second approach is the one mentioned often in this book, called *symmetrical multiprocessing (SMP)*, where all of the processors run in parallel, doing the same job. SMP is a specific implementation of multiprocessing whereby multiple CPUs share the same board, memory, peripherals, resources, and operating system (OS), physically connected via a common high-speed bus.

Compared to ASMP, SMP is relatively easy to implement because a single copy of the operating system is in charge of all the processors.

In early SMP environments, programmers had to remain aware that because the processors shared the same resources, including memory, it was possible for program code running in one CPU to affect the memory being used by another. Programming for these types of situations required special protection. Often, process programming was normally only run on one processor at a time, keeping the process safe from intrusion. However, the program kernel was still subject to call by various codes running on different processors. One solution involved running the kernel in spinlock mode, where only one CPU at a time was serviced. Other processors seeking entry had to wait until the first CPU was finished. Although the system was protected from competing processors, it operated inefficiently.

SMP systems do not usually exceed 16 processors, although newer machines released by Unix vendors support up to 64. Modern SMP software permits several CPUs to access the kernel simultaneously. Threaded processes can run on several CPUs at once, yet without suffering from kernel intrusion. Recall that a thread is a section of programming that has been time-sliced by the NOS in order to run simultaneously with other threads being executed in an SMP operation.

Know that the main idea behind symmetrical multiprocessing is the use of multiple threads.

The benefits of properly using SMP server networking power are

➤ Multithreading—Unless communicating with another process, single-threaded programs do not gain from SMP.

➤ Instruction safety—Programs do not rely on unsafe non-SMP instructions, or improper thread priorities.

➤ Processor utilization—Subtasks are divided so that all CPU-bound instructions take no longer than 30 milliseconds.

Symmetric Multiprocessing Environments

Symmetric multiprocessing environments require that each CPU in the system have access to the same physical memory using the same system bus. Otherwise, the execution of a program cannot be switched between processors. All CPUs sharing the same physical memory must also share a single logical image of that memory to achieve a *coherent* system. In a coherent system, all of the SMP CPUs see and read the identical data byte from the same memory address. SMP does not permit running of a unique copy of the OS on each CPU, nor does it permit each CPU to build its own unique logical memory image. A completely distinct image for each CPU would be chaos! Figure 3.1 depicts a simple SMP system.

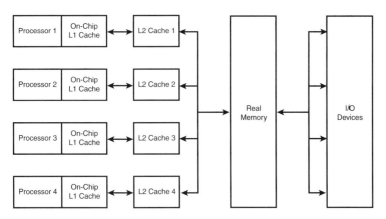

Figure 3.1   A simple SMP environment.

Four boxes represent four individual processors, each with its own on-chip level 1 cache. Data is transferred between a processor's level 1 cache to a separate level 2 cache that is assigned to that processor. Data can be transferred to and from the L2 cache and real memory, or I/O devices for processing.

Memory coherence and shared memory are a great challenge to designers of multiprocessing architectures, further complicated by the existence of on-chip, high-speed cache memory. This high-speed cache is used to store values read by the CPU from system-memory locations. In a system that does not utilize high-speed cache, the processor repeatedly reads these memory locations during program execution. High-speed cache relieves the CPU from having to read this memory using the slower system bus. This reduces the drain on the system bus, and improves performance.

More processing time is saved during write caching because of the thousands of times that cache values might change before the processor either flushes the cache or writes its contents to the system memory. Between cache flushes, the main system memory actually becomes incoherent, because each CPU still has its own private copy of small portions of it. As time passes, these copies may slightly deviate from one another due to cache memory writes. Until the next cache flush or the next system memory write, the most recent data values reside in the cache memories of the individual CPUs.

This creates a memory coherence problem. How can a system memory access (access to outdated data) be prevented from some other system device before it is correctly updated? One solution is called *bus snooping*. Bus snooping permits a processor to monitor the memory addresses placed on the system bus by other devices. The snooping processor is looking for memory addresses on the system bus that it has cached. When it finds a match, it writes the values of those memory addresses from its cache to the system memory prior to completion of the current bus cycle. Bus snooping is considered to be a critical mechanism in maintaining data coherency. While one processor is accessing memory, another processor snoops on bus activity. If current memory access operations are related to its memory space, the appropriate measures are taken to ensure that all affected processors and bus-masters have the most recent data.

Is maintaining a coherent memory more easily accomplished by removing the cache from multiprocessors and eliminating the need for bus snooping? A close examination of this idea reveals that the implementation of bus snooping and the use of CPU cache are more efficient, allowing SMP systems to realize the full potential of all their processors. In a single-CPU machine, a superfast CPU cache is used primarily as an inexpensive performance booster. However, in a multiprocessing architecture, the main priority is preventing the system bus from becoming a bottleneck, not improving a single CPU's memory performance. When the system relies primarily on the system bus, each additional CPU in the multiprocessing system increases its strain. Therefore, cache memory and bus snooping are considered more important for multiprocessing than for single-processing systems. Well-engineered multiprocessor technology implements a snooping mechanism that is sensitive to the system's performance. The snooping channel must be capable of providing a processor with snoop information even while that processor transfers data. A processor should also be able to broadcast snoop information even while simultaneously receiving data, providing data concurrency and enhanced system performance. This is superior to non-split shared-bus formats, where snooping is limited to the current access on the system bus. In such situations, concurrent data transfers must somehow be related to current snoop activity. If a processor performs a memory transaction, the following questions must be answered:

➤ Is the requested data contained in the requestor's cache, and if so, is it stale or accurate data?

➤ If the data is stale, is the accurate data in main memory, or in another processor's cache?

➤ If the data is in another processor's cache, has the other processor recently changed the data?

The analysis and actions that move and update the data to maintain coherency are part of the bus-snooping process. Bus snooping and the maintenance of data coherency are shared responsibilities of the system processors, core logic, and participating bus-masters. For example, observe the bus-snooping arrangement for an AMD-760 processor in Figure 3.2.

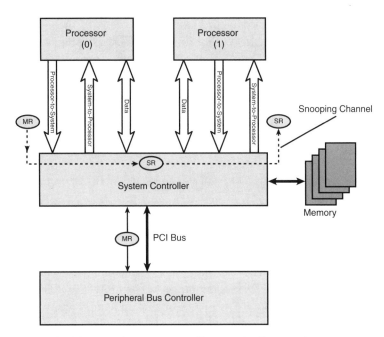

Figure 3.2   A bus-snooping arrangement—Processor 0 to Processor 1.

A memory request (MR) is launched by processor 0 to the system controller to obtain data or instructions that are not currently in its cache. The system controller interprets this as a snoop request (SR) and then queries processor 1 to determine if it has the requested data. Using its processor-to-system bus, processor 1 will respond to the request. Processor 1 will return the data to processor 0 if it has it. Otherwise, the system controller will have to fetch the data from main memory. While this *virtual snooping channel* has been created between processor 0, processor 1, and the system controller, processor 0 can concurrently receive messaging on its system-to-processor bus and data on its data bus. Processor 1 can concurrently transmit messaging and data over its processor-to-system and data buses. Notice that transfers unrelated to the current snoop activity can be concurrently performed by both processors. This concurrency plays a significant role in improved performance over less robust multiprocessing architectures. The reverse snooping procedure is shown in Figure 3.3.

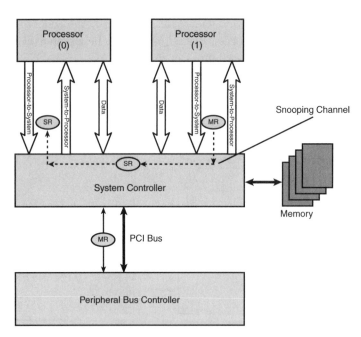

Figure 3.3 A bus-snooping arrangement—Processor 1 to Processor 0.

The system controller also needs to monitor any transactions occurring across the PCI bus as part of the snooping process. Therefore, the PCI bus-masters also have the power to access processor cache memory areas. The system controller then is responsible for snooping PCI traffic and generating snoop requests to the processors. The virtual snooping channel created between the PCI bus and processor 0 is illustrated in Figure 3.4.

Although maintaining coherent memory remains an important consideration, caching reads and writes prevents the system bus from becoming overloaded. The standard coherent multiprocessing architecture for systems that share the same system buses among multi-CPUs is the shared memory architecture. Although the shared-bus design provides better performance at less expense than other multiprocessing architectures, it only scales well up to 32 CPUs, depending on the system and the particular CPU being utilized.

Not all OSs can take full advantage of the concurrency offered by SMP hardware. A suitable NOS must be capable of functioning with components naturally suited to SMP environments. The high degree of parallelism used in these systems permits many different components to run concurrently, effectively utilizing the benefits derived from having many processors available.

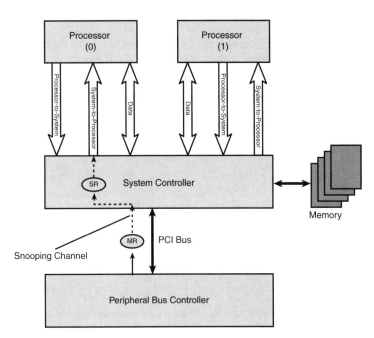

Figure 3.4   A PCI bus virtual snooping channel to Processor 0.

SMP processor cores lie in close proximity to each another, being physically connected by a high-speed bus. Although resources such as memory and peripherals are shared by all CPUs, the NOS coordinates the execution of simultaneous threads among them, scheduling each CPU with independent tasks for true concurrency. This permits the simultaneous execution of multiple applications and system services. The only incremental hardware requirements for a true symmetric multiprocessing environment are the additional CPUs, as shown in Figure 3.5. Because the SMP hardware transparently maintains a coherent view of the data distributed among the processors, software program executions do not inherit any additional overhead related to this.

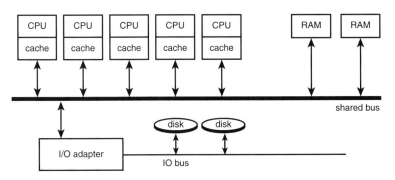

Figure 3.5   A simple SMP arrangement.

SMP is more than just multiple processors and memory systems design because the NOS can schedule pending code for execution on the first available CPU. This is accomplished by using a self-correcting feedback loop that ensures all CPUs an equal opportunity to execute an specified amount of code; hence, the term symmetric multiprocessing. Only one queue runs in an SMP operating system, with the dumping of all work into a common funnel. Commands are distributed to multiple CPUs on the basis of availability in a symmetric fashion.

Although SMP can potentially use CPU resources more efficiently than asymmetric multiprocessing architectures, poor programming can nullify this potential. Therefore, process scheduling for SMP requires a fairly complex set of algorithms, along with synchronization devices as spin locks, semaphores, and handles. In using all of the available CPU resources, SMP pays a price for the scheduling overhead and complexity, resulting in less than perfect scaling. A system with two CPUs cannot double the overall performance of a single processor. Typically, the second CPU improves the overall performance by about 95 to 99%. With increased overhead for each additional processor, the efficiency goes down, moreso when multiple nodes are involved, as shown in Figure 3.6.

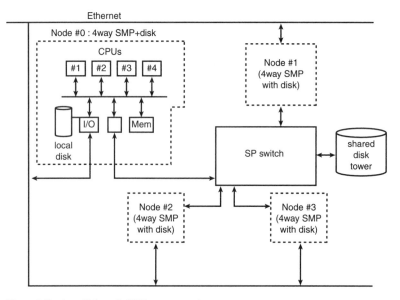

Figure 3.6   A multiple-node SMP arrangement.

SMP Derivatives

Two major derivatives of SMP exist: clustering and *massively parallel processing (MPP)*.

Although the overall goal of both SMP derivatives is speed, each format solves a number of additional problems. Recall how clustering links individual computers, or nodes, to provide parallel processing within a robust, scalable, and fault-tolerant system. These clustered nodes communicate using high-speed connections to provide access to all CPUs, disks, and shared memory to a single application. The clustering applications are distributed among multiple nodes, so that when one machine in the cluster fails, its applications are moved to one of the remaining nodes.

The downside of pure clustering involves the overhead required to coordinate CPU and disk drive access from one machine to the next. This overhead prevents clusters from scaling as efficiently as pure SMP, which maintains closer ties between the processors, memory, and disks. System management is greatly simplified with clustering, however, due to the flexibility of merely adding another node to the cluster for additional processing power. If one machine fails, it's replaced without affecting the other nodes in the cluster.

Massively parallel processing, where tightly coupled processors reside within one machine, provides scalability far beyond that of basic SMP. Basic SMP suffers from decreasing performance as more processors are added to the mix, whereas MPP performance increases almost uniformly as more processors are introduced. In the MPP arrangement, the processors do not share a single logical memory image and, therefore, do not have the overhead required to maintain memory coherency or move processes between processors. Special applications are needed to tap the power of MPP systems, though, capable of making heavy use of threads, and able to partition the workload among many independent processors. The application must then reassemble the results from each processor. Consider Figure 3.7.

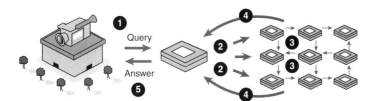

Figure 3.7   An MPP solution.

Early MPP systems were built as single computers, with many processors. A recent trend in computer research, however, is to tap the power of individual machines to build large distributed MPP networks. Examples include the Search for Extraterrestrial Intelligence (SETI), and several Internet cryptography projects. These projects centrally manage and distribute the processing load across multiple machines around the world, and collect the results to build a final answer.

Multiprocessing Advantages

Because multiprocessing targets database and transactional systems, its typical deployment occurs on server boards carrying 4 to 8 processors. Often, high-end systems will feature up to 32 processors working together to scale the workload. Using multiple threads with multiple transactions, multiprocessing systems manage large data-intensive workloads without executing demanding mathematical calculations. An interesting fact regarding the MP's capability to manage large amounts of data emerges as the amounts of data increase. For example, Table 3.1 indicates the results of testing a multiprocessor configuration against a dual-processor arrangement using a 3GB database.

Table 3.1 A 3GB Benchmark Database Multiprocessor Test	
System Configuration	Transactions/second
2 x Intel Xeon processor (2.8MHz)	1260
2 x Intel Xeon processor MP (2.0MHz)	1102
4 x Intel Xeon processor MP (2.0MHz)	2070

Observe that although the dual processors are running 40% faster that the multiprocessors, their results are only 14% faster than when pitted against the two MP processors. This is attributed to the level 3 caches being utilized in the two MPs. When the scalability factors come into play using four MP processors, throughput for the multiprocessor design increases by 88% over the two-chip operation. Because the multiprocessor is designed for use with much larger databases than used in Table 3.1, this test can be repeated on a larger system, with even more convincing results. In Table 3.2, the test is repeated using much greater volumes of data.

Table 3.2 A 25.2GB Benchmark Database Multiprocessor Test	
System Configuration	Transactions/second
2 x Intel Xeon processor (2.8MHz)	1433
2 x Intel Xeon processor MP (2.0MHz)	1485
4 x Intel Xeon processor MP (2.0MHz)	2497

With a larger database to handle, even the two slower MP processors handle a greater number of transactions than the two DP processors running at 2.8GHz. When using four MP processors, the scalability is maintained.

SMP Commercial Advantages

The commercial advantages to the use of symmetrical multiprocessing include

➤ Increased scalability to support new network services, without the need for major system upgrades

➤ Support for improved system density

➤ Increased processing power minus the incremental costs of support chips, chassis slots, or upgraded peripherals

➤ True concurrency with simultaneous execution of multiple applications and system services

For network operating systems running many different processes operating in parallel, SMP technology is ideal. This includes multithreaded server systems, used for either storage area networking, or online transaction processing.

Multiprocessing Disadvantages

Multiprocessing systems deal with four problem types associated with control processes, or with the transmission of message packets to synchronize events between processors. These types are

➤ *Overhead*—The time wasted in achieving the required communications and control status prior to actually beginning the client's processing request

➤ *Latency*—The time delay between initiating a control command, or sending the command message, and when the processors receive it and begin initiating the appropriate actions

➤ *Determinism*—The degree to which the processing events are precisely executed

➤ *Skew*—A measurement of how far apart events occur in different processors, when they should occur simultaneously

The various ways in which these problems arise in multiprocessing systems become more understandable when considering how a simple message is interpreted within such architecture. If a message-passing protocol sends packets from one of the processors to the data chain linking the others, each individual processor must interpret the message header, and then pass it along if the packet is not intended for it. Plainly, latency and skew will increase with each pause for interpretation and retransmission of the packet.

When additional processors are added to the system chain (scaling out), determinism is adversely impacted.

A custom hardware implementation is required on circuit boards designed for multiprocessing systems whereby a dedicated bus, apart from a general-purpose data bus, is provided for command-and-control functions. In this way, determinism can be maintained regardless of the scaling size.

In multiprocessing systems using a simple locking kernel design, it is possible for two CPUs to simultaneously enter a test and set loop on the same flag. These two processors can continue to spin forever, with the read of each causing the store of the other to fail. To prevent this, a different latency must be purposely introduced for each processor. To provide good scaling, SMP operating systems are provided with separate locks for different kernel subsystems. One solution is called *fine-grained kernel locking*. It is designed to allow individual kernel subsystems to run as separate threads on different processors simultaneously, permitting a greater degree of parallelism among various application tasks.

A fine-grained kernel-locking architecture must permit tasks running on different processors to execute kernel-mode operations simultaneously, producing a *threaded kernel*. If different kernel subsystems can be assigned separate spin locks, tasks trying to access these individual subsystems can run concurrently. The quality of the locking mechanism, called its *granularity*, determines the maximum number of kernel threads that can be run concurrently. If the NOS is designed with independent kernel services for the core scheduler and the file system, two different spin locks can be utilized to protect these two subsystems. Accordingly, a task involving a large and time-consuming file read/write operation does not necessarily have to block another task attempting to access the scheduler. Having separate spin locks assigned for these two subsystems would result in a threaded kernel. Both tasks can execute in kernel mode at the same time, as shown in Figure 3.8.

Notice that while Task 1 is busy conducting its disk I/O, Task 2 is permitted to activate the high-priority Task 3. This permits Task 2 and Task 3 to conduct useful operations simultaneously, rather than spinning idly and wasting time. Observe that Task 3's spin lock is released prior to its task disabling itself. If this were not done, any other task trying to acquire the same lock would idly spin forever. Using a fine-grained kernel-locking mechanism enables a greater degree of parallelism in the execution of such user tasks, boosting processor utilization and overall application throughput. Why use multiple processors together instead of simply using a single, more powerful processor to increase the capability of a single node? The reason is that various roadblocks currently exist limiting the speeds to which a single processor can be exposed. Faster CPU clock speeds require wider buses for board-level signal paths. Supporting chips on the motherboard must be developed to accommodate the throughput improvement. Increasing clock speeds will not always be enough to handle growing network traffic.

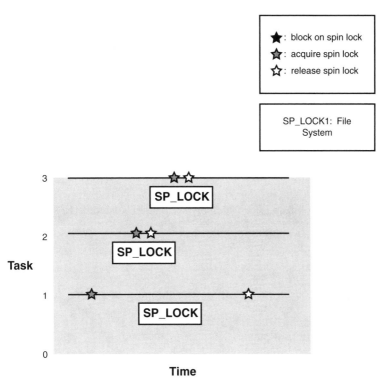

Figure 3.8   A spin lock using a threaded kernel.

Installing Multiple Processors

Normally, processor manufacturers issue minor revisions to their devices over their manufacturing life cycle. These revisions are called *steppings*, and are identified by special numbers printed on the body of the device. More recent steppings have higher version numbers and fewer bugs. Hardware steppings are not provided in the same manner as software patches that can be used to update a version 1.0 of a program to a 1.01 or 1.02 version. When new steppings come out having fewer bugs than their predecessors, processor manufacturers do not normally volunteer to exchange the older processor for the newer one. Clients are normally stuck with the original stepping unless the updated processor version is purchased separately.

Know that processor revisions are known as steppings.

When using multiple processors, always ensure that the stepping numbers on each one match. A significant gap in stepping numbers between different processors running on the same server board greatly increases the chances of a system failure. The server network administrator should make certain that all processors on a server board are within at least three stepping numbers of other processors in the system. Within this safety range, the BIOS should be able to handle small variances that occur between the processors. However, if these variances are more significant, the BIOS may not be capable of handling the resulting problems.

Know that all of the processors utilized on one server board should be within three steppings in order to avoid system problems.

Two methods can be used to determine the stepping of a given Intel processor:

➤ The CPUID utility program

➤ The S-spec number

The *Frequency ID utility* identifies a genuine Intel processor, and determines the processor's family, model, and stepping. For a given processor, the Frequency ID utility and its installation instructions can be downloaded from Intel's website at: http://support.intel.com/support/processors/tools/frequencyid/.

The *S-spec number* is located on the top edge of the specified Intel processor, as shown in Figure 3.9. It identifies the specific characteristics of that processor, including the stepping. The S-spec number can be referenced in the specification update for the selected processor, and downloaded from Intel's website.

Another common but avoidable problem occurs with multiprocessor server boards when processors are installed that are designed to use different clocking speeds. To expect multiprocessors to work properly together, they should have identical speed ratings. Although it's possible that in some cases a faster processor can be clocked down in order to work in the system, problems normally occurring between mismatched processors will cause operational glitches beyond the tolerance of server networks. The safest approach with multiprocessor server boards is to install processors that are guaranteed by their manufacturer to work together. These will generally be matched according to their family, model, and stepping versions.

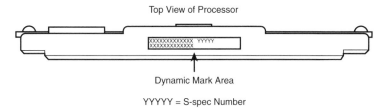

Top View of Processor

XXXXXXXXXXXXX YYYYY
XXXXXXXXXXXXX

Dynamic Mark Area

YYYYY = S-spec Number

Figure 3.9   The S-spec number location for an Intel processor.

Server Processor Subsystems

Server+ Exam Objective 1.14 states that the test taker should understand the processor subsystem of a server. This understanding includes being able to describe

➤ Multiprocessing systems

➤What are they?

➤How do they differ from dual-processor systems?

➤ 64-bit server environments

➤What are they?

➤Why and when are they important?

➤ What are the different architectures?

In determining when and why 64-bit server environments are important, the test taker should consider:

➤ Microprocessor bit ratings

➤ Database management software

➤ WOW64

➤ Windows Server 2003

➤ Redhat Linux

➤ Windows XP Professional x64 Edition

> Internal registers

> 64-bit architecture

Know that Redhat Linux and Windows Server 2003 operating systems are available in 64-bit versions.

Server Environments for 64-Bit Processors

When examining information about PCs and servers, their applicable micro-processors are usually rated according to a number of bits, such as *32-bit* or *64-bit*. This rating is a tipoff as to how powerful or capable its associated computer system is, because a bit represents the smallest unit of information that can exist in a digital environment. A 32-bit rating means that 32 bits of digital data can be processed or transmitted in parallel, for each clock cycle. This rating can also refer to the number of bits used for a single element in the server's internal data structure.

When used in conjunction with a processor, this term indicates the width of its internal registers, which compose a special, high-speed storage area. All data must be represented in a register before being processed in any way. In order to multiply two numbers, both of the numbers must first reside in specified registers. After multiplication, the result must also be placed in a register. These registers can alternately contain specified memory address locations, where the actual data is stored. The number and size of a given microprocessor's registers determine its power and its speed. For a 32-bit microprocessor, each internal register is 32 bits wide and each program instruction manipulates 32 bits of data. Obviously, such a processor would also process data and memory addresses represented by 32 bits. The Intel 486 microprocessor, shown in Figure 3.10, is a well-known example of a 32-bit CPU.

Figure 3.10   The Intel 486 microprocessor.

A 64-bit rating refers to a processor containing registers that store 64-bit numbers, indicating that a 64-bit server board architecture would process double the amount of data processed for each clock cycle, compared to a 32-bit system. Clients experience a noticeable performance increase due to the ability of the 64-bit microprocessor to handle more memory and larger files. One of the most important benefits of using 64-bit processors is the amount of memory supported by the accompanying system architecture, which is capable of addressing an impressive 1 terabyte (1,000GB) of memory. Compare this with a contemporary 32-bit desktop system, where the maximum amount of RAM supported is 4GB. Many commercial motherboards cannot support even that much RAM, which is shared between any running applications and the operating system (OS) software.

It should be noted that the majority of desktop computers today do not contain as much as 4GB of installed memory. Such amounts are not required to properly use most small business and home desktop computer software. In residential systems, 32-bit operations provide more than adequate processing power, although it is possible in the near future that 4GB of RAM could become a limitation, as more complex software and animated graphical games evolve. However, in scientific and data management industries, the 4GB memory limitations of the 32-bit system have already been reached. Because the need for 64-bit processing has become apparent, major database management software developers, such as Oracle and Microsoft, currently offer 64-bit versions of their database management systems.

The momentum for developing 64-bit systems has come from the commercial networking environment, where larger, faster, more capable servers are in constant demand. The development of 64-bit processors, such as the Intel Itanium has been paralleled by the development of other key components, such as 64-bit operating systems, software, and drivers capable of taking advantage of 64-bit processor features.

These developments provide real benefits to demanding applications such as video encoding, scientific research, and massive database management, where being able to load massive amounts of data into the network server's RAM memory is required. AMD has also developed a 64-bit microprocessor capable of handling these heavy-duty applications.

In supercomputing and in database management systems, 64-bit architecture has been used for many years. Having to access huge amounts of data, many companies and organizations have already made the transition to 64-bit servers. They support a greater number of larger files, and are capable of effectively loading large enterprise databases into RAM memory for faster searches and data retrieval. By using 64-bit servers, these organizations are capable of supporting many more clients simultaneously on each server. Replacing several 32-bit servers with one 64-bit network server greatly reduces the overall hardware requirements.

The ever-expanding data and performance needs of business, academic, engineering, and scientific organizations push the limits and the capabilities of existing information technology (IT) platforms. Accordingly, advances in processor technology by AMD and Intel have brought the power of 64-bit computing to these PC users.

The capabilities of the x86 architecture have been extended, enabling customers using a 64-bit operating system to seamlessly run 32-bit and cutting edge 64-bit applications. The newer hardware can also be used with today's standard 32-bit operating systems and applications. Microsoft has developed a new 64-bit version of Windows XP Professional called Windows XP Professional x64 Edition.

Windows XP Professional x64 Edition permits users to take advantage of the new 64-bit technology to improve PC or workstation performances. It provides a rich platform on which to integrate both new 64-bit applications and current 32-bit applications using what is called the *Windows on Windows 64 (WOW64) x86* emulation layer. The WOW64 subsystem isolates 32-bit applications from 64-bit applications, in order to prevent file and registry collisions. The unique feature about Windows XP Professional x64 Edition processor architecture is its ability to run both 32-bit and 64-bit applications equally well.

Server Software Architectures for 64-Bit Processors

Windows XP Professional x64 Edition is designed to address the most demanding business needs of technical workstation users who require large amounts of memory and floating-point performance in areas such as mechanical design and analysis, digital content creation, and scientific and high-performance computing applications. The following business segments should benefit from Windows XP Professional x64 Edition.

➤ Engineering (CAD/CAM)—Automotive or aerospace design engineers conceptualize designs while meeting stringent design safety requirements. Designers and engineers who use *computer-aided design (CAD)* and engineering applications will benefit from the large memory support, fast memory throughput, and improved floating-point speeds provided by 64-bit systems. They need these applications to work with larger models in a shorter period of time.

➤ Digital Content Creation—Two-dimensional (2D) and three-dimensional (3D) animation and rendering, video editing, and game development are its three major areas. It allows game developers and animators to save time in rendering models or scenes. The ability to view completely rendered models during the development process gives animators and developers the freedom to work at their peak level of creativity.

➤ 3D Gaming—Video game developers are at work building exciting 64-bit native games to help them push these limits even further because they hold the potential for significantly accelerated graphics rendering. Game makers build today's most sophisticated 3D titles around extremely complicated database engines that enable the use of artificial intelligence, and the play of massive-level 3D games, in ways that were not formerly possible.

➤ Video Editing—Professional and amateur photographers, web designers, and home PC enthusiasts are increasingly using PCs to do sophisticated video editing and photo manipulation, especially with 64-bit workstations.

Exam Prep Questions

1. Which of the following items is not considered important when matching characteristics for additional Intel microprocessors on SMP-capable server boards?

   ❏ A. Family
   ❏ B. Stepping
   ❏ C. Model
   ❏ D. Cache

2. The NOS is capable of running multiple CPUs. However, following the installation of the newest processor, the system boots up without recognizing it. What is the most sensible action to take at this point?

   ❏ A. Configure the NOS for SMP.
   ❏ B. Replace the bad CPU.
   ❏ C. Examine the stepping of the new CPU.
   ❏ D. Perform a BIOS upgrade.

3. Select the most accurate statement:

   ❏ A. SMP systems are more expensive to implement than ASMP.
   ❏ B. SMP is easier to implement than ASMP.
   ❏ C. SMP is a slower implementation than ASMP.
   ❏ D. In an SMP server system, all CPUs share the same board, but require their own memory, peripherals, and NOS.

4. What is the most important functional aspect of SMP?

   ❏ A. The running of multiple threads simultaneously on multiple processors
   ❏ B. The division of tasks between multiple processors being executed one at a time
   ❏ C. The running of multiple NOSes by multiple processors
   ❏ D. The composition of multiple threads into a single thread prior to execution

5. Which of the following is not a 16-bit or a 32-bit operating system?

   ❏ A. Panther
   ❏ B. Windows 2000 Server
   ❏ C. Windows Server 2003
   ❏ D. Windows 98

Exam Prep Answers

1. Answer D is the correct answer. The cache memory is not considered when matching characteristics between processors on SMP server boards. The important characteristics for matching include the family, model, and stepping. In addition, if these characteristics match, it's likely the cache will also. Answers A, B, and C are therefore all incorrect.

2. Answer A is the correct answer. Although Answer D might be necessary in some situations, the most likely cause of the problem is that the NOS is not properly configured to provide SMP support. Answer B is incorrect because not enough information is known to assume that the new CPU is bad. Answer C would usually be considered before selecting the new CPU to ensure compatible stepping values.

3. Answer B is the correct answer. ASMP requires specialized knowledge to implement its computer, whereas symmetrical multi-processing is relatively easy to implement. Answer A is incorrect because an SMP solution is less expensive to implement. Answer C is incorrect because SMP is faster than a single-processor solution. Answer D is incorrect because SMP processors share not only the same board, but the NOS, memory, and peripherals as well.

4. Answer A is the correct answer. SMP time-slices its operations into multiple threads for simultaneous execution by multiple processors. Answer B is incorrect because nothing is gained by having multiple processors that can only execute one task at a time. Answer C is incorrect because running multiple NOSes by multiple processors does not describe SMP. Answer D is incorrect because SMP does just the opposite.

5. Answer C is the correct answer. The Windows Server 2003 OS package provides 64-bit computing for business and home use. Answer A is incorrect because Apple's Panther OS uses a 32-bit platform. Answer B is incorrect because Windows 2000 Server is also a 32-bit system. Answer D is incorrect because Windows 98 is a 16-bit platform capable of running some 32-bit software.

4.0—Server Memory

Terms you'll need to understand:

- ✓ Static RAM (SRAM)
- ✓ Dynamic RAM (DRAM)
- ✓ Volatile
- ✓ Enhanced DRAM (EDRAM)
- ✓ Synchronous DRAM (SDRAM)
- ✓ Internal interleaving
- ✓ Single Data Rate SDRAM (SDR-SDRAM)
- ✓ Synchronous Graphics RAM (SGRAM)
- ✓ Enhanced SDRAM (ESDRAM)
- ✓ Virtual Channel Memory SDRAM (VCM-SDRAM)
- ✓ Double Data Rate SDRAM (DDR-SDRAM)
- ✓ Enhanced DDR SDRAM (EDDR-SDRAM)
- ✓ Extended Data Out (EDO)
- ✓ Double Data Rate-2 SDRAM (DDR-2 SDRAM)
- ✓ Rambus DRAM (RDRAM)
- ✓ Error Checking and Correction (ECC)
- ✓ Unbuffered registered memory
- ✓ Buffered registered memory
- ✓ Registered memory
- ✓ Latency
- ✓ Checksum
- ✓ Dual-Inline Memory Module (DIMM)
- ✓ Cache

Techniques you'll need to master:

✓ Identifying and differentiating between various types of RAM

✓ Explaining why dynamic RAM devices require periodic data refreshing

✓ Discussing how SRAM stores its data

✓ Listing the uses for SRAM

✓ Describing the use of refresh circuitry

✓ Identifying which memory type is used primarily in L2 cache

✓ Explaining how high-speed burst mode works

✓ Demonstrating how internal interleaving is employed

✓ Defining the two versions of SDRAM

✓ Describing how Extended Data Out (EDO) memory increases the speed of RAM operations

✓ Contrasting the differences between DDR-2 SDRAM and the original DDR SDRAM

✓ Explaining the features of Rambus technology

✓ Showing how memory interleaving improves processor performance

✓ Differentiating between ECC, non-ECC, and extended ECC memory formats

✓ Describing the advantages of buffered memory

✓ Identifying a manufacturer's hardware compatibility list

✓ Differentiating between L1 and L2 cache

✓ Explaining how the cache controller circuitry monitors all memory-access instructions

Introduction

Server+ Exam Objective 1.5 states that the test taker should know the characteristics and server requirements of the following types of memory:

➤ EDO memory

➤ Random Access Memory (RAM)

➤ DDR memory

➤ DDR-2 memory

➤ RAMBUS memory

➤ Memory interleaving

➤ ECC vs. non-ECC vs. extended ECC memory

➤ Unbuffered vs. buffered vs. registered memory

➤ Hardware compatibility listing

➤ Memory caching

Selecting Server Memory

When planning to build a server, familiarity with the various types of Random Access Memory (RAM) suitable for use with its motherboard is pivotal. Some processors require specific types of RAM to be used. For example, certain versions of the Pentium 4 processor require a special type of memory to be installed, known as Rambus RAM.

Similar to the situation with desktop motherboards, server boards use predominantly two types of semiconductor RAM: *Static RAM (SRAM)* and *Dynamic RAM (DRAM)*. Although they both perform similar memory storage functions, they use completely different methods. Whereas SRAM stores information bits as long as power to the memory chips is not interrupted, DRAM requires periodic refreshing to maintain its data, even when electrical power is continuously available.

DRAM stores data bits in rows and columns of IC capacitors that lose their charge over time, and require periodic data-refreshing operations. SRAM uses IC transistors to store data, and is capable of maintaining it as long as power is supplied to the chip. By virtue of its transistorized structure, SRAM performs much faster than DRAM. However, because SRAM can store only roughly 25% as much data as DRAM for a given device size, it tends to be more expensive.

Know that SRAM performs much faster than DRAM.

RAM has the disadvantage of being volatile, regardless of whether static or dynamic devices are used. This means that if power to the computer is disrupted for any reason, all data stored in RAM will be lost. However, both types of RAM perform their read and write operations quickly and with equal ease.

Generally, SRAM is used in smaller memory systems, such as cache and video, where the added cost of refresh circuitry would raise the cost-per-bit of storage beyond reason.

Cache memory is a special memory structure that works directly with the microprocessor, and video memory is also specialized memory that contains the information to be displayed on the monitor. In larger memory systems, such as the server system's main memory, DRAM is selected. Here, the added cost of refresh circuitry is distributed over a greater number of bits and is offset by the reduced operating cost associated with DRAM chips.

Advanced DRAM

If both types of RAM (SRAM and DRAM) are brought together to create an improved memory device, the result is referred to as *Enhanced DRAM or EDRAM.*

The integration of an SRAM component into a DRAM device provides a performance improvement of 40%. An independent write path allows the system to input new data without affecting the operation of the rest of the chip. EDRAM devices are used primarily in L2 (secondary) cache memories.

Advanced SDRAM

Another modified DRAM type, referred to as *Synchronous DRAM (SDRAM)*, employs special internal registers and clock signals to organize and synchronize all data memory requests. Unlike asynchronous memory modules, SDRAM devices operate in step with the system clock. After an initial read or write access has been performed on an SDRAM memory device, subsequent accesses are conducted using a high-speed burst mode, operating at 1 access per clock cycle. Burst mode allows the processor to perform other tasks while the data in memory is being manipulated.

Special internal configurations also speed up SDRAM memory operations. For example, internal interleaving is employed, permitting one side of the SDRAM memory device to be accessed while the other half is completing an operation. Be aware that there are two versions of SDRAM (2-clock and 4-clock) available. Therefore, the motherboard's chipset must be examined to be sure that the SDRAM type being used is supported.

Several advanced versions of SDRAM include

➤ *Single Data Rate SDRAM (SDR-SDRAM)*—This SDRAM version transfers data on one edge of the system clock signal.

➤ *Synchronous Graphics RAM (SGRAM)*—This SDRAM version handles high-performance graphics operations, featuring dual-bank operations that permit two memory pages to be open simultaneously.

➤ *Enhanced SDRAM (ESDRAM)*—This advanced SDRAM version, used in L2 cache applications, employs small cache buffers to provide high data access rates.

➤ *Virtual Channel Memory SDRAM (VCM-SDRAM)*—This SDRAM version requires a special support chipset with onboard cache buffers to improve multiple access times and provide I/O transfers on each clock cycle.

➤ *Double Data Rate SDRAM (DDR-SDRAM)*—This SDR-SDRAM version transfers data on both the leading and falling edges of each clock cycle, doubling the data transfer rate of traditional SDR-DRAM, and is available in various standard formats, including SODIMMs for portable computers.

➤ *Enhanced DDR SDRAM (EDDR-SDRAM)*—This advanced DDR SRAM employs onboard cache registers to deliver improved performance.

Table 4.1 summarizes the characteristics and usages of various types of SDRAM.

Table 4.1	Memory Specifications				
Memory Type	Configuration	Voltage	Density	Frequency (MHz)	Package
RDRAM RIMM	32 × 16 32 × 18 64 × 16 64 × 18 128 × 16	2.5V	64 MB 72 MB 96 MB 108 MB 128 MB 144 MB	300, 356, 400	184-pin RIMMs
DDR SRAM DIMMs (unbuffered)	16 × 64 32 × 64	2.5V	128 MB 256 MB	200, 266	184-pin DIMMs
DDR SRAM DIMMs (registered)	32 × 72	2.5V	256 MB	200, 266	184-pin DIMMs
SDRAM AIMM	1 × 32	3.3V	4 MB	166	66-pin AIMM

(continued)

Table 4.1   Memory Specifications (continued)

Memory Type	Configuration	Voltage	Density	Frequency (MHz)	Package
168-Pin DIMMs	4 × 64 8 × 64 16 × 64	3.3V	32 MB 64 MB 128 MB	166 66,100, 133	168-pin SDRAM DIMMs
168-Pin DIMMs	8 × 64 16 × 64	3.3V	64 MB 128 MB	66,100, 133	168-pin DIMMs
168-Pin DIMMs	16 × 64 32 × 64	3.3V	128 MB 256 MB	 100, 133	168-pin DIMMs
168-Pin DIMMS	4 × 72 8 × 72 16 × 72	3.3V	32 MB 64 MB 128 MB	66,100, 133	168-pin DIMMs
168-Pin DIMMS	8 × 72 16 × 72	3.3V	64 MB 128 MB	66,100, 133	168-pin DIMMs
168-Pin DIMMS	8 × 72 16 × 72	3.3V	64 MB 128 MB	100, 133	168-pin DIMMs
168-Pin DIMMS	16 × 72 32 × 72	3.3V	128 MB 256 MB	100, 133	168-pin DIMMs
168-Pin DIMMS	16 × 72 32 × 72 64 × 72	3.3V	128 MB 256 MB 512 MB	100, 133	168-pin DIMMs
168-Pin DIMMS	32 × 72 64 × 72	3.3V	256 MB 512 MB	100, 133	168-pin DIMMs
168-Pin DIMMS	64 × 72	3.3V	512 MB	100, 133	168-pin DIMMs
168-Pin DIMMS	64 × 72 128 × 72	3.3V	512 MB 1 GB	100, 133	168-pin DIMMs

EDO Memory

Extended Data Out (EDO) memory increases the speed at which RAM operations are conducted. This is accomplished by not disabling the data bus pins between bus cycles, effectively eliminating the 10-nanosecond (ns) wait time normally required between memory addressing commands. EDO is an advanced type of fast page-mode RAM, also referred to as hyper page-mode RAM. EDO's advantage occurs when multiple sequential memory accesses are performed. By not turning the data pin off after the first access, each successive access is accomplished in two clock cycles rather than three.

DDR SDRAM

Double Data Rate SDRAM (DDR-SDRAM) is a form of SDRAM that can transfer data on both the leading and falling edges of each clock cycle. Obviously, having this capability effectively doubles the data transfer rate of traditional Single Data Rate SDRAM (SDR-SDRAM). It is available in a number of standard formats, including *Small Outline Dual Inline Memory Modules (SODIMMs)* for portable computers. DDR SDRAM has various categories of speed, including DDR-266, DDR-333, and DDR-400. DDR SDRAM uses 184 pins.

 Know that DDR-SDRAM can transfer data on both the leading and falling edges of each clock cycle.

DDR-2 SDRAM is the successor to DDR SDRAM. DDR-2 boasts a larger maximum bandwidth over DDR SDRAM. In addition, DDR-2 memory uses less voltage than DDR SDRAM, resulting in lower power consumption. However, DDR-2 SDRAM is not totally backward compatible with DDR SDRAM because it uses 240 pins per module.

RAMBUS RAM

An organization named Rambus designed a proprietary DRAM memory technology that provides high data delivery speeds. The technology has been given a variety of different names, including *Rambus DRAM (RDRAM)*, *Direct Rambus DRAM (DRDRAM)*, and *Rambus Inline Memory Module (RIMM)*. The RIMM reference applies to a special 184-pin memory module specifically designed to hold the Rambus devices.

The Rambus technology employs a special, internal 16-bit data channel that operates in conjunction with a 400MHz clock. The 16-bit channel permits the device to operate at much higher speeds than more conventional 64-bit buses.

 One special requirement concerning server motherboards utilizing Rambus RAM is that all memory slots must be filled. Continuity modules are substituted when there are not enough memory modules to fill the available slots.

Memory Interleaving

To improve performance, server memory can be logically divided into multiple sections. This permits the processor to quickly access data held in memory from multiple sources, thus improving and increasing memory speed. Typical interleaving schemes divide the memory into two banks of RAM, with one bank storing even addresses and the other storing odd addresses. The reason this increases speed is that with separate memory banks for odd and even addresses, the next byte of memory can be accessed while the current byte refreshes.

 Know how to define memory interleaving and why it is used.

ECC, Non-ECC, and Extended ECC RAM

Error Checking and Correction (ECC) RAM is a type of RAM that includes a fault detection/correction circuit that can detect and fix memory errors on the fly. Occasionally, the information in a single memory bit can flip or change states (logic 0 to logic 1, or logic 1 to logic 0), which causes a memory error to occur when the data is read. Using a parity memory scheme, the system can detect that a bit has been flipped during the memory read process, but it can only display a "Parity Error" message and discontinue further processing.

Although this prevents the bad data from being written, it also erases all of the current data. However, an ECC memory module can detect and correct a single-bit error (1 flipped bit in 64), or it can detect errors in two bits. The latter condition causes a parity error shutdown to occur, similar to the parity checking operation. ECC memory is important in applications in which data integrity is the major concern.

Non-ECC RAM is normally found in client workstations and in the consumer computer market, where data integrity is not such a major concern. Obviously, there is usually a lower performance associated with the requirement to fix memory errors.

Some high-end computer ECC memory chips use extended nine-bit bytes, often called *extended ECC*. This scheme examines each byte (8 bits) individually for errors. The ninth bit is called the *check bit*, and is assigned to each 8-bit byte to ensure that the total number of ones in the extended byte is even (even parity). This overall operation is referred to as the *checksum*, and will declare a parity error whenever an even number of ones for each nine bits is not detected.

 Know what a checksum is, and what it is used for.

Even though the computer hardware will signal an error whenever it reads an extended byte containing an odd number of ones, the running software does not even detect the ninth bit. ECC modules cannot be mixed with non-ECC (non-parity) memory on server boards designed specifically for use with ECC. It is possible that server boards designed for non-ECC modules may work properly using ECC modules. However, mixing ECC and non-ECC module types should always be avoided.

 Know that ECC and non-ECC memory modules should not be used interchangeably because the chipset installed on the server board usually dictates the use of one or the other.

Buffered, Unbuffered, and Registered Memory

RAM is classified according to its buffering status, divided between unbuffered, buffered, and registered. For example, EDO memory is available in buffered and unbuffered categories. RAM designed specifically for consumer purposes tends to be *unbuffered*, and is used in the vast majority of PCs. With unbuffered memory, the processing chipset communicates directly with the memory itself, with nothing in between. *Buffered* memory is designed to protect the memory with respect to electrical load by providing a temporary and protective data storage area (called a *buffer*). The use of buffered memory is necessary with systems using a large quantity of RAM.

 Know that buffering is a method of protecting large amounts of memory data with respect to electrical loading.

Buffer registers hold and retransmit data signals in cooperation with the memory chips. Various types of SDRAM and DDR memory modules contain buffer registers directly on the module. Buffered memory permits a memory module to function properly, without being affected by the delays imposed by other devices.

Registered SDRAM is also considered buffered, and these terms are interchangeable when describing SDRAM intended for use in workstations and servers. Buffering the address and control inputs helps to reduce system loading and permits the connection of up to eight DIMMs to a memory controller. Registered and unbuffered memory modules cannot be mixed together.

Hardware Compatibility List

When building a server system, RAM components, the operating system being used, and the system board selected must all be compatible. RAM manufacturers and/or their resellers normally provide the necessary *hardware compatibility list*, or *HCL* on their websites. A server administrator or technician should be suspicious if the specified system board and processor do not appear on the HCL for the selected RAM.

Know what a hardware compatibility list is and how to use it.

Cache Memory

A small, fast section of SRAM, called *cache memory*, is normally reserved for local, temporary data storage by the microprocessor. To provide for fast access, the cache is located logically and physically as close to the microprocessor as possible. A cache controller monitors all memory-access instructions from the processor to determine if the specified data is stored in the cache. If the cache controller scores a hit, the control circuitry can present the specified data to the processor without the delay of wasted clock pulses (wait states). If the specified data cannot be located in the cache, the controller declares a miss, and the access request is passed on to the system's RAM.

The cache controller's primary objective is to maximize the ratio of hits to total accesses. The higher the hit rate, the fewer the wait states encountered during memory accesses. By making the cache memory area as large as possible, the possibility of having the desired information in the cache is increased. The size of the cache is limited, however, due to the relative costs, energy consumption, and the physical size of SRAM devices. Cache memory sizes for server boards run between 128kB and 1MB.

Pentium microprocessors have a built-in first-level cache, also known as L1, used for both instructions and data. This internal cache is divided into four 2kB blocks, each containing 128 sets of 16-byte lines. Adding an external, second level of memory cache on the system board often extends this caching capability. As might be expected, the second-level cache is also referred to as the L2 cache.

Know that cache memory is reserved for local, temporary data storage by the microprocessor.

Exam Prep Questions

1. Why is RAM that works properly in a workstation often incompatible with RAM used in the server?
   - ❏ A. The RAM is DDR-2, and the server supports DDR.
   - ❏ B. The RAM is designed for a faster machine.
   - ❏ C. The workstation RAM is defective.
   - ❏ D. The workstation RAM may not be ECC-compatible.

2. Select the RAM types usually found on server boards from the following choices. (Select two.)
   - ❏ A. Static RAM (SRAM)
   - ❏ B. Dynamic RAM (DRAM)
   - ❏ C. Distributed RAM (DRAM)
   - ❏ D. Stable RAM (SRAM)

3. When comparing SRAM with DRAM:
   - ❏ A. SRAM memory is slower and less expensive than DRAM.
   - ❏ B. DRAM memory is slower and more expensive than SRAM.
   - ❏ C. SRAM memory is faster and more expensive than DRAM.
   - ❏ D. DRAM memory is faster and less expensive than SRAM.

4. What term describes the loss of RAM data when power is discontinued?
   - ❏ A. Swappability
   - ❏ B. Compatibility
   - ❏ C. Scalability
   - ❏ D. Volatility

5. What makes DDR-SDRAM so important?
   - ❏ A. The ability to transfer data on the falling edge of each clock cycle
   - ❏ B. The ability to transfer data only during the most stable portion of each clock cycle
   - ❏ C. The ability to transfer data on both the leading and falling edges of each clock cycle
   - ❏ D. The ability to transfer data on the leading edge of each clock cycle

6. During its internal operations, where does the processor store its temporary data?
   - ❏ A. In its cache memory
   - ❏ B. In the video memory area
   - ❏ C. In the buffered memory
   - ❏ D. In the registered memory area

7. Which of the following should the network administrator consult when determining the compatibility between the operating system, the system board, and the RAM memory?

❑ A. The system compatibility list
❑ B. The hardware compatibility list
❑ C. The memory compatibility list
❑ D. The software compatibility list

8. Why is buffered memory so important?

❑ A. It protects memory data with respect to electrical snooping.
❑ B. It protects memory data with respect to electrical interference.
❑ C. It protects memory data with respect to electrical failure.
❑ D. It protects memory data with respect to electrical loading.

9. Which of the following memory types can perform the checksum operation?

❑ A. Extended ECC
❑ B. Expanded ECC
❑ C. ECC
❑ D. Non ECC

10. What does the memory interleaving scheme permit?

❑ A. It permits the assignment of a numerical location for each byte of computer memory.
❑ B. It permits the processor to use a private area of memory for its internal operations.
❑ C. It permits the processor to quickly access data held in memory from multiple sources.
❑ D. It permits the protection of memory data with respect to electrical loading.

Exam Prep Answers

1. Answer D is the correct answer. Servers usually use ECC RAM, and will not operate properly if non-ECC RAM is installed or mixed with ECC. Answer A is incorrect because DDR-2 cannot be physically installed on boards designed for DDR RAM. Answer B is incorrect because RAM that is capable of working on a faster server will also operate properly at a lower speed. Answer C is incorrect because the workstation would not have operated properly with defective RAM.

2. Answers A and B are the correct answers. The two types of RAM used predominantly on server boards are Static RAM (SRAM) and Dynamic RAM (DRAM). Answers C and D are incorrect because there are no such known RAM types as Distributed RAM or Stable RAM.

3. Answer C is the correct answer. SRAM memory performs much faster than DRAM, but is also more expensive. For its size, SRAM stores only 25% as much data as DRAM. By association, answers A, B, and D are all incorrect.

4. Answer D is the correct answer. RAM memory is volatile because a loss of power will also cause a loss of the data stored there. Answer A is incorrect because swapping various components, including RAM modules, is not related to the data-loss characteristic of RAM when power is discontinued. Answer B is incorrect because although RAM must be compatible in order to work properly in a given board, this term has nothing to do with data loss. Answer C is incorrect because scalability describes the ability of a network to grow in size without degrading in performance.

5. Answer C is the correct answer. DDR-SDRAM can transfer data on both the leading and falling edges of each clock cycle. Answer A is incorrect because only the falling edge of each clock cycle is mentioned. Answer B is incorrect because the leading and falling portions of a waveform, where DDR-SDRAM transfers its data, are not the most stable. Answer D is incorrect because only the leading edge of each clock cycle is mentioned.

6. Answer A is the correct answer. Cache memory is used by the processor for temporary data storage during its internal operations. Answer B is incorrect because the memory area reserved for video data is unavailable for use by the microprocessor. Answer C is incorrect because buffered memory is a temporary and protective data storage area used to electrically isolate user data. Answer D is incorrect because registered and buffered memory are synonymous.

7. Answer B is the correct answer. Various hardware and software manufacturers and/or their resellers provide hardware compatibility lists on their websites to verify that their products are compatible with various NOSes, server boards, and memory types. Microsoft now uses Windows Catalogs to maintain this type of information. Answers A, C, and D are fictitious and are therefore incorrect.

8. Answer D is the correct answer. Buffered memory is not subject to the delays imposed by other devices. It provides a temporary and protective data storage area free from the effects of varying electrical load. Answer A is incorrect because buffered memory is totally unrelated to electrical snooping. Answer B is incorrect because electrical interference could be strong enough to affect the data stored in buffer memory. Answer C is incorrect because no RAM memory scheme can protect data from loss caused by electrical failure.

9. Answer A is the correct answer. Each 8-bit byte is individually examined for errors. The ninth check bit is assigned to each 8-bit byte to
ensure that the total number of ones in the extended byte is even. An
ECC memory module can detect and correct a single-bit error.
Answer B is incorrect because there is no such thing as expanded
ECC. Answer C is incorrect because ECC memory without the ninth
"extended" bit cannot make the necessary corrections to an erroneous
bit. Answer D is incorrect because non-ECC RAM is normally found
in client workstations and in the consumer computer market, and does
not provide error detection or correction.

10. Answer C is the correct answer. Memory interleaving permits server
memory to be logically divided into multiple sections, for quick access
to data by many sources. Answer A is incorrect because memory
addressing permits the assignment of a numerical location for each
byte of computer memory containing either data or instructions.
Answer B is incorrect because memory caching permits the processor
to use a private area of memory for its internal operations. Answer D
is incorrect because memory buffering is used to protect memory data
with respect to electrical loading.

5.0—Server Bus Architectures

Terms you'll need to understand:

- ✓ Peripheral Component Interconnect (PCI)
- ✓ Industry Standard Architecture (ISA)
- ✓ MicroChannel Architecture (MCA)
- ✓ Extended Industry Standard Architecture (EISA)
- ✓ VESA Local Bus (VLB)
- ✓ Accelerated Graphics Port (AGP)
- ✓ Universal Serial Bus (USB)
- ✓ Northbridge and Southbridge
- ✓ Advanced Configuration Power Interface (ACPI)
- ✓ Super-I/O
- ✓ Front Side Bus (FSB) and Back Side Bus (BSB)
- ✓ Expansion slot
- ✓ Data bus and Address bus
- ✓ Bus-master
- ✓ Plug-and-play (PnP)
- ✓ Hot swap
- ✓ Bandwidth
- ✓ Interrupt lines
- ✓ Signaling levels
- ✓ Hot-Plug PCI
- ✓ PCI Extended (PCI-X)
- ✓ Throughput

✓ Double Data Rate (DDR) and Quad Data Rate (QDR)

✓ Error Correcting Code (ECC)

✓ PCI Express (PCIe)

✓ Arapahoe

✓ Isochronous data transfer

✓ Form factor

✓ Server I/O Module (SIOM)

✓ Bottleneck

✓ Fault tolerance

✓ Hierarchical and Peer PCI buses

✓ Intelligent Input/Output (I2O)

Techniques you'll need to master:

✓ Using software utility programs

✓ Recognizing various bus interfaces, the reasons they were developed, and the differences between them

✓ Explaining the use and technique of bus-mastering

✓ Calculating the data throughput for a given processor

✓ Explaining the development of the AGP port

✓ Listing the features of the super-I/O controller

✓ Understanding how ISA cards disrupt the plug-and-play process

✓ Knowing the operating parameters of all proposed server components

✓ Knowing which factors limit the maximum number of server board slots

✓ Understanding how dual-voltage PCI expansion cards operate

✓ Plugging hot-swap cards into the PCI system

✓ Defining the hot-plug PCI hardware standard

✓ Identifying the PCI-X 2.0 standard

✓ Explaining PCI-X 266 and PCI-X 533 voltage signals

✓ Listing PCI Express implementations

✓ Describing the hierarchical PCI bus

Introduction

Server+ Exam Objective 1.1 says that the test taker should know the characteristics, purpose, function, limitations, and performance of the following system bus architectures:

➤ PCI Bus Mastering

➤ PCI Hot swap

➤ PCI-Express

➤ PCI-X

➤ Hierarchical PCI Bus

➤ Peer PCI Bus

➤ I2O—Intelligent Input-Output

➤ Hot-Plug PCI

➤ PCI Expansion Slots

➤ PCI Interrupts

➤ EISA

Server boards are designed around particular types of microprocessors. However, the microprocessor is not the only integrated circuit (IC) device on the board.

Additional intelligent devices are required to support the processor's operation making up the server board's chipset. IC manufacturers have developed chipsets to support Pentium processors and their clones. Most chipset designs feature a basic three-chip arrangement that supports a combination of *Peripheral Component Interconnect (PCI)* and *Industry Standard Architecture (ISA)* bus interfacing.

Industry Standard Architecture

The Industry Standard Architecture (ISA) bus originated at an IBM lab in Boca Raton, Florida in the early 1980s, and an 8-bit subset of the ISA bus was included with the original IBM Personal Computer (PC). Then, in 1984, IBM began shipping the PC-AT, which included the ISA bus's first full 16-bit implementation, then called the AT bus. The CPU, memory, and I/O bus all shared a common 8MHz clock. This bus arrangement became the basis for all subsequent clone computers, but because the term "AT" was a registered trademark of IBM, this I/O bus became known as the ISA bus.

For some time, every PC supported ISA interface slots as system extender interfaces. The bus and its matching adapter cards were relatively simple and cost-effective. However, because the ISA bus is a 16-bit interface, data can be transferred only two bytes at a time. Other limiting factors include its maximum clock speed of only 8MHz, and the two or three clock ticks required to transfer those two bytes of data. For the inherently slower devices at the time, such as modems, printers, sound cards, or CD-ROMs, this was not a major problem. But the ISA bus remains much too slow for modern high-performance disk access, and is therefore not acceptable for server use or for modern Windows display adapter circuits.

MicroChannel Architecture

In 1987, IBM introduced the *MicroChannel Architecture (MCA)* bus, which improved the maximum clock speed to 10MHz. MCA cards are automatically configured using a software utility program, rather than by manipulating physical switches and jumpers. The MCA bus also transfers four bytes of data at a time, with the possibility of conducting one data transfer for every clock pulse for certain configurations with specific interface cards. The MicroChannel system, including the necessary adapter cards was expensive, and the hassle with IBM licensing also encumbered the technology.

Extended Industry Standard Architecture

Another short-lived bus architecture called the *Extended Industry Standard Architecture (EISA)* is worth mentioning. Designed by a group of IBM competitors called the "gang of nine," the EISA bus was aimed at PCs using the Intel 80386, 80486, or Pentium microprocessor families. It was 32 bits wide, supported multiprocessing, and could transfer four bytes of data per clock operation. Essentially an extension of the older ISA interface, the EISA slot added an extra socket with additional connections. This design permitted clients to plug either older ISA cards or the newer EISA cards into the slots.

MicroChannel Architecture

The principal difference between EISA and MCA is that EISA was backward compatible with the ISA bus, whereas MCA was not. PCs using the MCA were limited to using only MCA expansion cards. This situation meant that the type of bus in the computer determined which expansion cards could be installed, dooming both technologies to failure. In addition, although EISA cards supported a 32-bit data interface, the need to remain compatible with older ISA cards limited EISA to running at 8MHz. As the 486 CPU chip became popular, the need to run I/O devices at 8 or 10MHz collided with a motherboard that ran everything else at 33MHz. At $500, the cost of the EISA system, the adapter cards, and the required extra logic was too expensive. The final blow came when the newer PCI technology was developed for the local bus and was successfully used in combination with the older ISA bus.

VESA Local Bus

The *Video Electronics Standards Association (VESA)* is a consortium of companies that manufacture video displays and display adapters. Prior to the development of PCI, they attempted to solve the EISA/MCA battle with the *VESA Local Bus (VLB)*, introduced in 1992, and which became popular in 1993. Computer systems that connect a video expansion card to the VLB can add extra graphics capabilities through an interface that supports 32-bit data flow at up to 50MHz.

Desktop machines began to include one or two VLB slots to support the features included with high-speed video cards, as well as other high-speed computer devices that were being marketed, such as VESA SCSI adapter cards and VLB LAN adapters. Because the VESA bus was able to utilize the 33MHz clock speeds provided by the motherboard for the 486 CPU, SCSI and LAN manufacturers eagerly sought to take advantage of the VESA bus. However, in spite of these additional products, VLB has remained largely a display standard.

Peripheral Component Interconnect

PCI is a 64-bit local bus standard developed by the Intel Corporation, although normally implemented as a 32-bit interface running at clock speeds of 33 or 66MHz.

PCI appears as a 64-bit interface within a 32-bit package. When using a 32-bit bus at a speed of 33MHz, it yields a throughput rate of 133 megabytes-per-second (MBps). A bit of mathematical computation is required to determine how this operates. Keep in mind that a PCI bus running at 33MHz can transfer 32 bits of data (four bytes) during every clock tick, similar to what would be expected on a 32-bit bus. However, a clock tick at 33MHz consumes 30 nanoseconds, whereas the fastest memory at the time had a speed of only 70 nanoseconds. While fetching data from RAM, the processor had to wait at least three clock ticks to receive the requested data.

By transferring data every clock tick, the PCI bus delivers the same through-put on a 32-bit interface that other parts of the machine deliver through a 64-bit path. Most modern PC motherboards include the PCI bus in addition to the general ISA expansion bus. It is also used on newer versions of Macintosh computers.

The PCI bus is designed to contain all the signals of the old ISA bus, allow-ing a PCI adapter card to properly interface with older equipment. For example, a PCI disk controller can respond to the same addresses and gen-erate the same interrupts as an older disk controller for compatibility with the BIOS. However, these same PCI devices can also be self-configuring and operate in a plug-and-play mode. The PCI bus is inserted between the CPU/memory bus at one end, and the older traditional I/O bus at the other. The PCI interface chip is capable of supporting the video adapter, the EIDE disk controller chip, and possibly two external adapter cards.

Desktop machines used only one PCI chip, and featured a number of extra ISA-only expansion slots. Servers could contain additional PCI chips, although extra server expansion slots were usually EISA-compatible. Although ISA and EISA interfaces are exclusively PC-oriented, the PCI bus is also used in Power Macintosh and PowerPC computer environments, minicomputers, and other RISC workstations.

PCI and AGP

Although the original PCI bus was designed to support two-dimensional graphics, local area networking, and higher-performance disk drives, the increasing bandwidth requirements of 3D graphics subsystems soon out-stripped its 32-bit, 33MHz bandwidth. As a result, Intel and several graphics suppliers created the *Accelerated Graphics Port (AGP)*. Its specification defines a high-speed PCI bus dedicated solely to graphics operations in client sys-tems, rather than server environments. AGP bus development freed up bandwidth for other communications and I/O operations as graphics traffic was offloaded from the PCI system bus. I/O demands on the PCI bus were reduced further when Intel added a dedicated *Universal Serial Bus (USB)* interface and Serial ATA links to the PCI chipsets.

Video performance requirements have doubled every two years since the introduction of PCI. Various incarnations of the graphics bus have come and gone during this time, starting with the first transition from PCI to AGP. The industry then saw movements from AGP through AGP2X, AGP4X, and finally to AGP8X, which operates at 2.134GBps. Yet progressive perform-ance demands continue to put design and cost pressures on the AGP bus. Like the PCI bus, extending the AGP bus becomes more difficult and expen-sive as frequencies increase.

Server Bus Management

The primary difference between a standard PCI motherboard chipset and a PCI system designed for server operations is the presence of additional, server management–related devices. These devices are added to the chipset specifically to handle the server's additional instrumentation and management functions.

In addition to the PCI and ISA bus interfaces, server board architectures typically include another chipset component to handle server-specific management functions. This component is referred to as the *server management controller*.

A typical Pentium chipset consists of a memory controller (called the *Northbridge*), a PCI-to-ISA host bridge (referred to as the *Southbridge*), and an enhanced I/O controller. The memory controller provides the interface between the system's microprocessor, its various memory sections, and the PCI bus. The host bridge provides the interface between the PCI bus, the IDE bus, and the ISA bus. The enhanced I/O controller chip interfaces the standard PC peripherals (LPT, COM, and FDD interfaces) to the ISA bus. These typical chipset arrangements vary due to specialized functions such as an AGP bus or a USB interface, or to accommodate changes in bus specifications.

The Northbridge and Southbridge are jointly responsible for interfacing the PCI slots, depending on the direction and speed of the data involved. However, these responsibilities may not always be required for every type of server board because manufacturers arrange these bridges differently to achieve control over various board functions.

A recent change is the *Intel Hub Architecture (IHA)*, which has replaced the Northbridge/Southbridge chipset. Also composed of two parts, the IHA chipset contains the *Graphics and AGP Memory Controller Hub (GMCH)*, and the *I/O Controller Hub (ICH)*. The IHA architecture is incorporated into the Intel 800 chipset series, which is the first chipset architecture to change from the Northbridge/Southbridge design.

As with other types of motherboards, server boards are defined by the capabilities of their chipsets. For example, if a processor is designed to operate at 133MHz, combining it with a chipset that operates at a maximum of 100MHz will severely limit its performance. Although these microprocessors are usually mounted to the motherboards in sockets, and can be changed or replaced relatively easily, their related chipset components are typically soldered onto the board permanently. As a result, when constructing a server computer, it is important to become familiar with the operating parameters of all the components involved.

In spite of the recent developments, the majority of server chipsets still in operation are primarily of the Northbridge and Southbridge variety. The Northbridge memory controller is usually responsible for handling communication requests between the processor bus, memory bus, and the 64/32-bit PCI slots operating at 66 MHz. It's responsible for accepting requests from the host (processor) bus and directing them either to memory, or to one of the PCI buses, and for controlling all data transfers to and from the memory.

The Southbridge provides the interface bus for all the system's legacy devices, the 32-bit PCI slots that operate at 33MHz, the IDE controller, the USB controller, and the *Advanced Configuration Power Interface (ACPI)* controller. An ACPI-compliant *super-I/O* device has also been developed utilizing both the ACPI controller and extender capabilities. Using plug-and-play (PnP) capabilities, these chips permit desktops and notebooks to take advantage of the power savings inherent with ACPI use, and comply with the PC97 design guide standard defining power management and standard system configurations. The super-I/O controller provides increased system flexibility, utilizes either ACPI or non-ACPI logic chipsets, and is highly integrated, featuring

➤ A floppy disk controller

➤ A keyboard and mouse controller

➤ A super-I/O ACPI controller/extender

➤ A real-time clock

➤ Enhanced Advanced Power Control (APC)

➤ Two enhanced Universal Asynchronous Receiver-Transmitters (UARTs) with infrared support

➤ A full IEEE 1284 parallel port

➤ Twenty-four general-purpose I/O ports

Microprocessor and chipset manufacturers continually strive to speed up the operation of their systems. One way to do this is speeding up the movement of data across the system's data buses. Data buses operating directly between the microprocessor and Northbridge run at one speed, while the PCI bus runs at a different speed. In addition, the ISA/MIO devices are running at still another speed. Chipset devices must take responsibility for coordinating the movement of control and data signals between all buses and devices.

Buses that run between the microprocessor and the Northbridge are collectively referred to as the *Front Side Bus (FSB)*, whereas the PCI and ISA buses are collectively referred to as the *Back Side Bus (BSB)*. Historically, Pentium processors have operated at various speeds ranging between 50MHz and 2.4GHz, whereas their front side buses have been operating at speeds of 66MHz, 100MHz, and 133MHz. Likewise, the PCI bus has operated at standard speeds of 33MHz, 44MHz, and 66MHz. Although the speeds associated with these buses have steadily improved, the operational speed of the ISA bus has remained constant at 8MHz. For example, suppose a specified Pentium system board is using a processor running at 1.1 GHz internally. It's probable that this board's front side bus is running at 133 MHz, its PCI bus is running at 44.3 MHz, and its IDE bus is running at 100MHz. Meanwhile, the ISA bus is straggling along at 8MHz. Chipset components are responsible for coordinating the movement of data and commands between all buses. To synchronize the movement of data between faster to slower buses, the bridges incorporate time-matching protocols and buffer registers.

Expansion Slots

Although server boards use expansion slots to provide access for peripheral interface cards, they do not include the numbers and types of slots found in desktop units. Because server boards hold multiple processors and large quantities of RAM, they don't have room for older slot types that support only single functions. Although many server board designs still include a single ISA expansion slot for compatibility purposes, this feature is disappearing. Recent server board designs incorporate several 32-bit expansion slots (typically PCI) and a couple of 64-bit PCI expansion slots. Although AGP slots are typically found on desktop motherboards, they do not appear on server board designs.

PCI Local Buses

First released in 1992, the design of the PCI local bus incorporated three elements, including

1. A low-cost, high-performance local bus

2. Automatic configuration of installed expansion cards (plug-and-play)

3. The ability to expand functionality with the introduction of improved microprocessors and peripherals

The PCI bus platform rapidly evolved into a viable replacement for the ISA bus, and became the most commonly used system for upgrading a PC. It eventually comprised the I/O backbone of nearly every computing platform. It solved many of the problems with older architectures, while simultaneously delivering substantial increases in processing speed. PCI provided a simplified method for connecting peripherals to the processor and to the system memory. Problems associated with interrupt requests (IRQs) and address conflicts were alleviated, especially when installing new cards. The longevity of the bus was ensured by making newer PCI specifications backward compatible with older designs. Although PCI boards were originally installed in systems still using ISA bus devices, this practice is no longer prevalent as ISA operations have become obsolete.

The performance of the PCI standard made it the bus of choice for most early Pentium-based server boards, incorporating specifications that included slot-addressing capabilities and reserve memory space to permit plug-and-play (PnP) reconfiguration of each device installed in the system. Unfortunately, server boards that also employ an ISA-compatible slot can experience PnP configuration problems because ISA cards have no identification or reconfiguration capabilities, and can seriously disrupt the plug-and-play process.

The host bridge routes 32-bit PCI data directly to the PCI expansion slots through the local bus at speeds compatible with the microprocessor. However, it must route non-PCI data to the PCI-to-ISA bridge for conversion into a format compatible with the ISA slot. During this process, the data is converted from the 32-bit PCI format to the 16-bit ISA format. These transfers occur at the 8MHz maximum speed capabilities of the ISA bus.

PCI uses multiplexed address and data lines to conserve the pins of its basic 124-pin connector, which contains signals for control, interrupt, cache support, error reporting, and arbitration. It also uses 32-bit address and data buses (AD0–AD31). However, its specification defines 64-bit multiplexed address and data buses for use with 64-bit processors such as the Pentium. Its clock (CLK) line, although originally defined for a maximum frequency of 33MHz and a 132MBps transfer rate, can be implemented with microprocessors operating at higher clock frequencies (66MHz) under the PCI 2.1 specification.

The Request (REQ) and Grant (GNT) control lines provide arbitration conventions for bus-mastering operations using logic contained in the host bridge. For faster access, a bus master can request use of the bus while the current bus cycle is in progress. When the current bus cycle ends, the master can immediately begin to transfer data, assuming the request has been granted.

PCI Configuration

Because the PCI standard is part of the plug-and-play hardware standard, any server using it must also be equipped with a system BIOS and system software that specifically supports it. Although the PCI function is self-configuring, many of its settings can be viewed and altered through the server's CMOS Setup utility.

During a portion of the boot-up known as the detection phase, a PnP-compatible BIOS checks the system for devices installed in the expansion slots to see what types they are, how they are configured, and which slots they are in. On PnP-compatible I/O cards, this information is held in a ROM device.

The BIOS reads the information from all of the cards, assigns each adapter a handle (logical name), and stores this configuration information in the registry. Next, the BIOS compares the adapter information with the system's basic configuration to detect any resource conflicts. After evaluating the requirements of the cards against the system's resources, the PnP routine assigns system resources to the cards as required. Warning messages might be displayed when requirements exceed the available resources.

Because the PnP process has no method to reconfigure legacy devices during the resource assignment phase, it begins by assigning resources, such as IRQ assignments, to legacy devices before servicing the system's PnP devices. If and when the BIOS detects the presence of new devices during the detection phase, it disables the resource settings for its existing cards, checks to see what resources are required and available, and then reallocates the system's resources as necessary.

Depending on the CMOS settings available with a particular PCI chipset, the startup procedure might be instructed to configure and activate all PnP devices at startup. With other chipsets, it might also be possible to check all cards, but only enable those actually needed for startup. Some CMOS routines contain several user-definable PCI configuration settings. Typically, these settings should be left in their default positions. The rare occasion for changing a PCI setting occurs when directed to do so by a product's installation guide.

PCI Interrupts

Systems can theoretically contain an unlimited number of PCI slots. However, a maximum of four slots are normally included on a system board due to signal loading considerations. The PCI bus includes four internal interrupt lines (INTa through INTd, or INT1 through INT4) that allow each PCI slot to activate up to four different interrupts. PCI interrupts should not be confused with the system's IRQ channels, although they can be associated with them if required by a particular device. In these cases, IRQ9 and IRQ10 are typically used.

 Know that PCI interrupts are not the same as the system's IRQ channels.

Server PCI Slot Considerations

When a server technician must configure a server, the characteristics of the server board's PCI slots must be considered. The three main items to be concerned with when selecting the server board and its PCI components are

➤ Bandwidth

➤ Voltage

➤ Combination limitations

When determining the bandwidth of the PCI slot, remember that the normal data transfer performance of the PCI local bus is 132MBps when using a 32-bit bus at a speed of 33MHz. When the operation of the 64-bit PCI bus must be considered, the additional bandwidth increases the data transfer performance to 264MBps, while still using the 33MHz clock. The latest PCI slot incorporates a 64-bit PCI bus operating at a clock speed of 66MHz. This increases the total bandwidth of the bus to 528MBps.

 Know into which slots a 64-bit 66MHz adapter can be installed.

Determining data transfer rates for the PCI bus is fairly simple. When the bus width is known, simply multiply it by the bus speed. For example, if the bus width is 32-bits and the bus speed is 33MHz, then

PCI data transfer rate = bus width × bus speed

PCI data transfer rate = 32 × 33,000,000

PCI data transfer rate = 1,056,000,000 bps

PCI data transfer rate = 1,056,000,000 bps/8

PCI data transfer rate = 132MBps

This roughly equals 1Gbps. Because there are 8 bits in each data byte, the data transfer speed in bits-per-second must be divided by 8. At this point, the data transfer rate turns out to be 132 megabytes per second (MBps).

Suppose the width of the PCI data bus is 64 bits and the speed of the bus is 66MHz. The data transfer rate would then be

PCI data transfer rate = bus width × bus speed

PCI data transfer rate = 64 × 66,000,000

PCI data transfer rate = 4,224,000,000 bps

PCI data transfer rate = 4,224,000,000/8

PCI data transfer rate = 528,000,000 bytes or 528MBps

Obviously, by increasing the width and operating speed of the bus, the amount of transferred data is multiplied accordingly.

Know how to calculate the total bandwidth for a PCI slot.

The various bandwidths of PCI, PCI-X, and PCI Express (PCIe) are shown in Table 5.1.

Table 5.1 Bandwidth Comparisons for PCI, PCI-X, and PCI Express Buses				
PCI Bandwidth Table				
			Bandwidth	
PCI Type	**Data Bus**	**Frequency**	**Single**	**Dual**
PCI 32/33	32 bit	33 MHz	133.3 MBps	n/a
PCI 32/66	32 bit	66 MHz	266.7 MBps	n/a
PCI 64/33	64 bit	33 MHz	266.7 MBps	n/a
PCI 64/66	64 bit	66 MHz	533.3 MBps	n/a
PCIx 64/66	64 bit	66 MHz	533.3 MBps	n/a
PCIx 64/100	64 bit	100 MHz	800 MBps	n/a
PCIx 64/133	4 bit	133 MHz	1066 MBps	n/a
PCIx 64/266	64 bit	266 MHz	2132 MBps	n/a

(continued)

Table 5.1 Bandwidth Comparisons for PCI, PCI-X, and PCI Express Buses *(continued)*				
PCI Bandwidth Table				
			Bandwidth	
PCI Type	**Data Bus**	**Frequency**	**Single**	**Dual**
PCIx 64/533	64 bit	533 MHz	4264 MBps	n/a
PCIe x 1	8 bit/serial	2.5 GHz	250 MBps	500 MBps
PCIe x 2	8 bit/serial	2.5 GHz	500 MBps	1000 MBps
PCIe x 4	8 bit/serial	2.5 GHz	1000 MBps	2000 MBps
PCIe x 8	8 bit/serial	2.5 GHz	2000 MBps	4000 MBps
PCIe x 12	8 bit/serial	2.5 GHz	3000 MBps	6000 MBps
PCIe x 16	8 bit/serial	2.5 GHz	4000 MBps	8000 MBps

PCI bus slot technologies employ PCI chips that can be operated at either a 3.3V or a 5V signaling level. For compatibility between PCI cards and PCI chips, they must match the signaling levels. Accordingly, these cards are universally designed to support either, or both, the 3.3V and 5V specifications. To ensure the proper assembly of a system, the adapter card's connector is keyed to permit only compatible devices to be installed. Universal PCI cards are keyed so that they will fit into either type of slot, where they can detect the correct voltage being used through special voltage-in pins.

Even though the keyed connectors will not permit the intermixing of 5V and 3.3V cards, they will permit a mixture of 32-bit and 64-bit cards. PCI bus technology is intelligent enough to determine which type of card is inserted, and to handle each properly. For example, when a 64-bit card is inserted into a 32-bit slot, only the lower half of the data bus is used to perform transfers.

 Know under which voltages a Universal 32-bit PCI card operates.

Server board manufacturers often impose expansion limitations in order to avoid the inevitable problems of incompatibility that occur using various combinations of adapter cards. One technique that has been resorted to is the placement of only one adapter slot on the board period, especially for mini server boards. Such a simple arrangement seems ridiculous to a multi-server administrator with each unit running a number of RAID controllers.

For technical reasons, the PCI bus is limited to a maximum of four slots per bus. Two of these slots must accommodate a busmastering device, and be labeled accordingly, either on the board or in its user manual. In situations where additional PCI slots are required, then a PCI-to-PCI bridge must be incorporated into the board. Some PCI chipset implementations do not support the *byte-merging* feature, in which writes to sequential memory addresses are merged into one PCI-to-memory operation. In slower server boards, data buses must wait for the processor to catch up before completing the current transfer. Beware of motherboards that do not automatically configure the PCI bus, requiring instead the outdated need to fiddle with various jumpers.

Server boards fitted solely with PCI slots avoid many of the incompatibilities of earlier models that attempted to 'play ball' with ISA and PCI slots simultaneously. The speed limitations imposed by the ISA bus made this approach a nightmare for server administrators. Even in a server board fitted with fully compatible expansion slots, the use of any expansion card should be viewed with suspicion, regardless of compatibility claims, in the event that the server will not boot, the server fails the POSTs, or a parity error message appears. Although moving the expansion card to a different slot may solve the problem, not using the expansion card is a better solution.

PCI Bus Mastering

Bus mastering is a technique, first popularized by the PCI bus, allowing peripheral devices to transfer data to and from each other without using or interfering with the CPU or the system memory. It permits non-chipset devices to take control over the bus and carry out transfers directly. Bus mastering permits multiple devices to run simultaneously without locking each other out. Maximum throughput is given to any solely running device. Bus mastering greatly increases the speed of a computer or server network.

Such an arrangement transforms the PCI bus into a tiny local area network (LAN) inside the server. In order to implement bus mastering, several pins on the PCI bus have been reserved. PCI devices may take control of the bus at any time, including the ability to shut out the CPU during an important data or control transfer, and using whatever bandwidth is available.

The initiating device sends request signals to the central resource circuitry on the server board shared by all bus devices. When the device receives a grant signal, the transfer is conducted, subject to any future bus activity. Unlike the way arbitration and control signals were combined on both the MicroChannel and the ISA architectures, PCI permits greater flexibility over the bus arbitration process.

Interrupt sharing can be implemented using four level-sensitive interrupts, located on the bus at pins A6, B7, A7, and B8. Each interrupt can be assigned to any of 16 separate devices. These interrupts can be activated at any time because they are not synchronized with the other bus signals. The PCI specification leaves the implementation of interrupt sharing to the server board manufacturer. For example, one company's board might provide up to eight serial ports from one PCI slot. An interrupt status register is used to recognize which of the ports triggered the interrupt. Other motherboards might provide serial operations through dedicated port connections.

Before the PCI standard, access to memory data was performed by an operation called direct memory access (DMA), which used special controllers and signals to operate various hardware devices correctly and efficiently. This increased the workload on the processor. There are no DMA channels on the PCI bus, because bus mastering performs similar functions formerly assigned to DMA channels. Special controller operations pass control of the bus to the PCI adapters. CPU workload is minimized because data is delivered directly to RAM, while the bus master keeps track of all transactions.

To make effective use of a bus-mastering scheme, two requirements must be met. First, the server must be capable of conducting other operations during the time in which I/O transfers are occurring. Second, the operating system must permit I/O operations to run in the background, as on server machines being run on a multitasking operating system.

PCI Hot-Swap Technology

Hot-swap technology permits server administrators to insert or remove various PCI modules from within a host system without shutting down the system's power. This increases system availability by reducing downtime, simplifying repairs, and promoting system upgrades. Networking operations that have been positively influenced by the use of hot-swap designs include telecom systems, RAID arrays, hot-plug PCI connections, servers, USB ports, and CompactPCI interfacing. Hot-swap techniques permit these operations to be scalable, upgradeable, and repairable without disrupting any other part of a networked server system.

Know that hot-swap technology allows server administrators to insert or remove cards, cables, PC boards, drives, and modules from a host system without shutting the power off.

In a high-availability system, hot-swap power management is often used to maintain 100% uptime. Often, power is not applied to the specified card socket until after the card is plugged in. Even at that point, the system may examine the card's requirements before actually applying the power.

Insertion and Removal of Hot-Swap Components

The status of the hot-swap system should be recognized before an event is undertaken, as the host system's backplane is fully powered. Because all bulk and bypass capacitors are fully charged in a live system, the insertion of an uncharged card into the system will quickly charge the card. Unfortunately, the live system itself will be discharged because the act of uncontrolled card charging demands a large inrush of current. This in turn results in an uncontrolled system current discharge, significant enough to reduce the backplane voltage.

A viable hot-swap solution must therefore control the power-up of uncharged cards and properly manage the response of the system. Any card being mated into a live system connector may bounce the power ON and OFF as the card is rocked into the connector, taking several milliseconds for the card to connect properly. The capacitors on the card initially begin to charge, drawing current from the live system as soon as the card is inserted. The charging capacitors make the card appear as a short while a large amount of current is drawn. Such a large current demand on the system may cause its capacitors to discharge and the system voltage to drop.

Controlling a Hot-Swap Event

Implementing an effective hot-swap design involves four basic methods:

➤ The utilization of simple, low-cost discrete components

➤ The addition of a discrete MOSFET

➤ The combination of a MOSFET and a hot-swap IC

➤ The combination of a hot-swap switch IC and a hot-swap power manager (HSPM) IC

There are advantages and disadvantages to each of these solutions, including cost and application availability trade-off considerations.

Hot-Swap Solutions with Discrete Components

Basic discrete or mechanical hot-swap solutions often implement Positive Temperature Coefficient (PTC) or Negative Temperature Coefficient (NTC) resistors and capacitors, often combined with staggered pins to manage the hot-swap power event. In the staggered-pin solution, the connector has a combination of long and short pins. The longer pins mate first and start charging the board capacitance through a series of resistors. When the board is fully seated, the shorter pins mate, bypassing the resistors connected to the longer pins and creating a low-impedance path for powering the inserted card. This solution requires a specialized connector, which can be expensive. Other drawbacks include the fact that the card's capacitance charge rate and its rate of insertion are both impossible to control. This means that the simple discrete solution is relegated to exhibiting large inrush currents.

In older systems, two popular and simple discrete solutions involve the use of those PTCs or NTCs mentioned earlier, where a standard connector is used. The most glaring limitations for PTC/NTC solutions are

➤ The presence of additional impedance in the power path

➤ The lack of fault management features

➤ The fact that power management is dependent on temperature

Although PTCs have been used in some hot-swap designs, they are not suited for high-availability applications. The PTC circuit changes from a low-impedance circuit to a high-impedance circuit during high current situations, effectively turning off the card. However, this change in load must exist for some time before the PTC effectively responds to it because the PTC reacts to temperature, not current. It cannot respond rapidly enough to suppress the large inrush currents that occur during a hot-swap insert event, making it incapable of sensing over-current activities, or responding to serious fault conditions.

Each simple discrete solution also requires some type of fuse or other rapidly acting fault protection device, adding a voltage drop to the power path, and increasing the service costs for board repair.

Hot-Plug PCI Technology

Hot-Plug PCI is a special hardware standard that enables individual PCI slots to be powered on and off independently, allowing PCI adapters to be inserted, or removed, without having to power down the computer system. Hot-Plug PCI is particularly important to the administrators of mission-critical server systems, who may find it necessary to swap out various PCI devices on a running system. However, Hot-Plug PCI technology should not be confused with the failover functionality, which automatically switches operations to a redundant device whenever a primary device fails. Instead, Hot-Plug PCI involves only the inserting and removing of PCI devices in a running system. Unrelated to Hot-Plug PCI is CompactPCI, which is a completely different hardware technology also providing hot-plug and failover functionality.

Know that Hot-Plug PCI enables individual PCI slots to be powered on and off independently, which in turn allows PCI adapters to be added or removed without having to power down the computer system.

The *PCI Special Interest Group (PCI SIG)* publishes the PCI Hot-Plug Specification, describing the hardware requirements and interfaces used. Although it describes hardware requirements, it currently does not define a complete software interface for handling insertion and removal events. Microsoft Windows 2000, Windows XP, and Windows Server 2003 operating systems all support Hot-Plug PCI technology through the Advanced Configuration and Power Interface (ACPI).

This makes ACPI the de facto software interface standard for Windows support of the Hot-Plug PCI standard. It defines how to implement standard plug-and-play drivers for various manufacturers' hot-pluggable devices and controllers. These drivers should also correctly implement insertion and removal notifications as specified by ACPI.

Connecting General-Purpose Events

ACPI discovers hardware events when a general purpose event (GPE) is asserted and a *System Control Interrupt (SCI)* is raised. Hot-Plug PCI controllers must therefore be wired to the GPE bits of the core chipset. Because of the flexibility of GPEs, there are a number of implementations. For example, a single GPE bit could be used for all Hot-Plug PCI events in the system. Or, the selected implementation could wire up a GPE bit for each event on each slot. However, regardless of how the events are shared on GPEs, the standard rules for ACPI events must be followed.

Event Flow for Hot-Plug Insertion

When a device is inserted into the system, the following events take place:

1. The user inserts the hardware in the slot.

2. The Hot-Plug PCI controller (HPPC) asserts a GPE.

3. The core chipset raises a System Control Interrupt (SCI).

4. The ACPI driver clears the GPE event, and runs the _Lxx control method associated with the GPE.

5. The selected _Lxx method reads the status bits from the HPPC, identifies the event as an insertion event, and determines which slot the event took place on.

6. The selected _Lxx method executes a Notify command on the PCI bus signaling that the slot is on.

7. An ACPI driver executes the appropriate _STA method for the device(s) specified in the previous Notify command.

8. The appropriate _STA returns a code indicating that the specified device is present, but not yet enabled.

9. The ACPI driver now signals the PCI driver to enumerate the bus.

10. The PCI driver then reads the configuration space to identify the specified device.

11. The driver subsystem for PCI/plug-and-play loads and executes the appropriate drivers for all functions of the device.

12. The appropriate device drivers request that the device functions be turned on.

13. The ACPI driver executes the applicable _PS0 power control methods to the selected slot, if present.

14. The PCI driver then writes to the configuration space, activating the device according to PCI Power Management specifications.

15. Finally, the device driver begins to use the hot-plug device normally.

Event Flow for Hot-Plug Removal

When the user requests to eject a device, the following steps take place. Keep in mind that these steps assume that the hardware is equipped with an eject button associated with each device. If the specified device does not implement a hardware eject button, the user must use the Add/Remove Hardware Wizard to control the ejection activity. In this case, the removal process would start at step 8 in the following list:

1. The user presses the eject button for the slot.

2. The Hot-Plug PCI Controller (HPPC) asserts a General Purpose Event (GPE).

3. The core chipset raises a System Control Interrupt (SCI).

4. The ACPI driver clears the GPE event and then runs the _Lxx method associated with the GPE.

5. The _Lxx method reads the status bits from the HPPC to identify that the specified event was an eject request. It also determines at which slot the event occurred.

6. The `_Lxx` method then executes the appropriate `Notify` function for the slot requesting the eject event.

7. The ACPI driver then requests that the plug-and-play system perform an eject action on the specified device.

8. The driver subsystem for PCI/plug-and-play queries all drivers for all functions of the device. If successful, it instructs the drivers to unload.

9. The specified PCI driver writes to the configuration space deactivating the device according to PCI Power Management specifications.

10. The ACPI driver executes the applicable `_PS3` power control methods to the selected slot, if present.

11. The ACPI driver executes the required `_EJ0` command.

12. The `_EJ0` command engages the necessary motors, solenoids, and lights required to eject the device. When the device has been ejected, and status bits have been updated accordingly, it returns the appropriate signal.

13. The ACPI driver now executes `_STA` in order to verify that the device performed the eject command successfully.

14. The `_STA` function returns a Device Not Present status report, indicating a successful ejection process. Had the device not ejected successfully, `_STA` would have returned a Device Present But Not Functioning status report.

15. The ACPI driver now executes a complete cleanup. Had `_STA` returned a Device Present But Not Functioning status report, the ACPI driver would have reported a problem to the operating system, and an error dialog message would pop up on the user's screen.

PCI-X

The success of the PCI architecture resulted in the development of numerous PCI adapter cards running the application gamut. As technology pressed on, the need for higher-performance I/O interfaces became increasingly evident.

This momentum set the stage for the introduction of the *PCI-X* specification, also known as the PCI-Extended bus, a high-performance enhancement to the conventional PCI bus. PCI-X's first incarnation provided an immediate doubling of the maximum PCI clock frequency from 66MHz to 132MHz, and quickly enabled communication speeds greater than 1GBps!

Split transactions and transaction byte counts vastly improved the efficiency of the PCI bus and its attached devices. Server operations were greatly improved through the incorporation of Gigabit Ethernet, Fibre Channel, and other data transfer protocols. The PCI-X architecture accelerated the performance of high-bandwidth devices, and was very successful.

Server systems originally fitted with 32-bit/33MHz PCI buses were immediately extended to 64-bit/66MHz buses. With the demand for more bandwidth continually growing, PCI-X introduced a 64-bit/133MHz bus with a peak bandwidth of 1GBps, providing adequate bandwidth for the server I/O requirements of Gigabit Ethernet, Fibre Channel, and Ultra320 SCSI. PCI-X, like its predecessor, incorporated a shared bus with backward compatibility with older PCI devices.

PCI-X 2.0

Emerging, ultrahigh-bandwidth technologies such as 10Gigabit Ethernet and 10Gigabit FibreChannel, forced the creation of a standard meeting the PCI SIG's performance objectives, while still maintaining backward compatibility with previous generations of PCI-based machines.

The *PCI-X 2.0* standard introduced two improved 64-bit speed grades offering bandwidths two to four times that of PCI-X 133:

➤ PCI-X 266

➤ PCI-X 533

These speed grades ultimately resulted in bandwidths more than 32 times faster than the original PCI standard. Data transmission through a 64-bit bus at either two or four times the base clock frequency was achieved through *Double Data Rate (DDR)* and *Quad Data Rate (QDR)* techniques. Throughputs were provided at rates of either 266MHz or 533MHz.

PCI-X 2.0 preserved many elements from previous PCI generations, including the original PCI operating systems, connectors, device drivers, form factors, protocols, BIOSes, and electrical signaling. Many new and previous-generation PCI adapter cards were already on the market and capable of being utilized by every PCI-X 266 and PCI-X 533 slot. The backward compatibility of PCI-X 2.0 extended to the legacy 32-bit/33MHz PCI adapter cards keyed for 3.3V, or universal signaling. They could also be plugged into the higher-performance PCI-X 2.0 slots and operate seamlessly. Alternatively, the highest-performance PCI-X 2.0 adapter cards could also operate in 3.3V PCI slots from past-generation computers, making every interface slot on the server board useable.

Because signaling adjustments were executed automatically and transparently, the need for clients to reset jumpers, modify BIOS settings, upgrade software, or install new drivers was nullified. Although the PCI-X 2.0 technology is applicable to any computer platform, its reason for existence has to do mostly with its high-performance I/O interface for use in systems requiring the high bandwidth offered by PCI-X 266 and PCI-X 533, including enterprise servers, professional workstations, high-end Unix servers, mainframes, networking, and communication applications.

The main reason behind the ability of PCI technologies to provide such high operational bandwidth is their efficient pin use, especially when compared to serial I/O technologies, requiring one-fourth the number of data pins. One wire is required for both transmit and receive operations per bit.

At the very high data rates of PCI-X 266 and PCI-X 533, a new 1.5V signalling system has been devised. The I/O buffers are carefully designed to support both 1.5V and 3.3V PCI signaling technologies.

Another improvement with PCI-X 2.0 is the addition of *Error Correcting Code (ECC)* to provide additional fault tolerance. Even though the bit error rates are already extremely low, ECC provides PCI-X 2.0 the robustness needs for use with the most error-sensitive applications, protecting not only the data, but also the header. Using eight check bits, the protocol corrects single-bit errors, and detects dual-bit errors, which are tagged for retransmission. These ECC functions take the same amount of time to execute, as did the simple parity error detection of previous PCI generations.

New configuration registers specific to PCI-X 2.0 are defined in order to support ECC functionality, which automatically defaults to the functional values for earlier PCI generations to maintain backward compatibility.

The PCI-X 2.0 protocol transfers more bits of data per clock cycle, saving significant bandwidth and improving bus utilization.

PCI Express

High-bandwidth expansion can be provided through a proprietary interface between the Northbridge and PCI-X bridge chips, using multiple PCI-X buses for service to the high-speed expansion slots, 10Gigabit Ethernet, and SAS/SATA drives. However, there are several problems with this arrangement.

The PCI-X bridge chips and their serial interconnects are strictly proprietary. Latency is introduced between the Northbridge and the I/O devices. It's also expensive and inefficient to attempt connecting a serial 10Gbps fabric to a point-to-point, 64-bit parallel bus and interfacing the bus with a proprietary PCI-X bridge chip. Connecting the PCI-X bridge chip through a proprietary serial interconnect into the Northbridge is another chore.

The demand for more I/O bandwidth from new technologies such as 10GHz networking, high-end graphics, and high-speed storage interfaces has led to the development of the data transfer standard called *PCI Express (PCIe)*. PCI Express delivers greater bandwidth scalability combined with lower-cost implementation. Formerly known as Third Generation I/O (3GIO), PCI Express was also referred to as *Arapahoe*, after the IEEE work group that first created it as a shared project with the Intel Corporation.

The immediate advantages of PCI Express over the previous incarnations of PCI include

➤ Scalable performance using serial technology

➤ Possible bandwidth implementations between 5 to 80Gbps

➤ Dedicated point-to-point links for each device, rather than PCI bus sharing

➤ A direct chipset connection to the controller for lower server latency

➤ Easier system implementation using small connectors

➤ Guaranteed bandwidth through use of isochronous data channels

The term *isochronous* refers to data transfer processes where data must be delivered within certain time constraints. For example, an isochronous transport mechanism is required for multimedia data streams to ensure that its delivery occurs as fast as it is displayed. This transfer process must also ensure that the audio is synchronized with the video. Two related terms can be compared with isochronous for contrast. Transfer processes in which data streams can be broken by random intervals are referred to as *asynchronous*. Transfer processes in which data streams can be delivered only at specific intervals are called *synchronous* processes. Isochronous processes are not as rigid as synchronous processes, and not as lenient as asynchronous processes.

PCI Express is a general I/O technology for workstations, desktops, and servers to speed up internal chip-to-chip data movement as well as graphic adapter operations.

Unlike PCI and PCI-X technologies, which depend on 32-bit and 64-bit parallel buses, PCIe uses high-speed serial technology similar to that employed with Gigabit Ethernet, Serial-Attached SCSI (SAS), and Serial ATA (SATA). PCI Express is replacing shared parallel buses with high-speed, point-to-point serial buses to keep up with new I/O advances and processor speeds over the next decade. During the last half of 2004, PCI Express began replacing the PCI-X bus in various server systems, and was expected to eventually assume the duties of AGP parallel graphics buses in systems providing high bandwidth and multimedia traffic support. Attributes offered by PCI Express include

➤ Compatibility with current PCI software, facilitating smooth transitions to new hardware

➤ Useability, while still allowing time for software to develop that takes advantage of its features

➤ Interfacing with low-pin counts, offering more bandwidth per pin

➤ Enabling the use of smaller form factors, minimizing the overall cost of design and development

➤ Support for interconnect widths of 1-, 2-, 4-, 8-, 12-, 16-, and 32-line assemblies to match required performance bandwidths

➤ A 16GBps scalable bandwidth using a 2.5GHz signaling rate, producing higher transfer rates for future technologies

➤ New features supporting advanced power management, data integrity, error handling, and real-time data traffic

➤ Support for new hot-plug and hot-swap devices

Because the AGP standard, like PCI, has run out of available bandwidth needed for new emerging software applications, early PCI Express devices obviously include graphics cards for desktops. Current 16x PCI Express technology is double the speed of AGP 8x. Also, AGP uses a half-duplex interface while PCI Express uses full-duplex, moving data in both directions simultaneously. PCI Express significantly impacts both server and desktop operations, and replaces existing PCMCIA and CardBus standards with ExpressCard technology. ExpressCard combines PCI Express with USB 2.0, providing a higher bandwidth and modular expansion architecture for notebook PCs. Adapter cards are allocated additional power draw maximums up to three times what was formerly possible.

One PCIe link is composed of dual simplex channels, with each channel implemented as a transmit/receive pair for bidirectional simultaneous transmissions. Data signals are composed of two low-voltage, differentially driven pairs, with the data clock embedded in each pair, utilizing a clock-encoding scheme achieving very high data rates.

As shown earlier in Table 5.1, the bandwidth of the PCIe link is scalable. If required, signal pairs can be added to form multiple lanes between the two devices. Lane widths of x1, x4, x8, and x16 are supported with data bytes being striped across the links accordingly. Following the negotiation of lane widths and operational frequency between the connected agents, the striped data bytes are transmitted with 8b/10b encoding. Because the basic x1 data link can handle a peak raw bandwidth of 2.5Gbps, the effective raw data transfer rate is 5Gbps due to the bidirectional nature of the bus.

Form Factors for PCI Express

Various form factors have been devised for the PCIe standard depending on the selected computer platform. These form factors include

➤ Standard-size and low-profile expansion cards for desktops, workstations, and servers

➤ Mini-cards for portable computers

➤ ExpressCards for both portable and desktop computers

➤ Newly defined Server I/O Modules (SIOMs)

PCI Express Expansion Cards and Slots

PCIe expansion cards are similar in size to existing PCI cards now used in server, workstation, and desktop platforms. They can replace or coexist with legacy PCI cards, as they have the same dimensions and are equipped with rear brackets to accommodate external cable connections.

Differences between legacy and PCIe cards become apparent when their I/O connectors are observed. For example, an x1 PCI Express connector reveals a complement of 36 pins, while a standard PCI connector hosts 120 pins. Observe the comparisons between the legacy PCI and PCI Express low-profile cards in Figure 5.1. The contact area between the pins and the x1 PCI Express card connector is much smaller than that for the PCI card. The small tab next to the PCIe connector prevents it from being inserted into a legacy PCI slot. Both standard and low-profile form factors also support x4, x8, and x16 PCI Express implementations.

Use Figure 5.2 to compare the sizes of various PCI Express motherboard connector implementations to the PCI, AGP8X, and PCI-X connectors they are designed to replace.

Workstation motherboards designed for PCI Express utilization are gradually migrating from legacy PCI slot connectors to the x1 PCI Express connector, as shown in Figure 5.3. For PCI-X workstations, the migration moves to x4 PCI Express connectors. Notice that the AGP8X connectors are being replaced by the x16 PCI Express connector. Although the AGP connector was specifically designed for graphics, the x16 PCI Express connector is used for other applications when a PCIe graphics card is not specified.

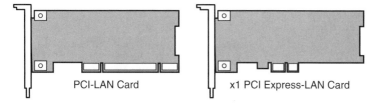

Figure 5.1 PCI Express and legacy PCI comparisons.

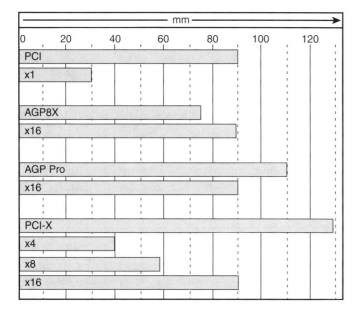

Figure 5.2 PCI Express and legacy PCI connectors.

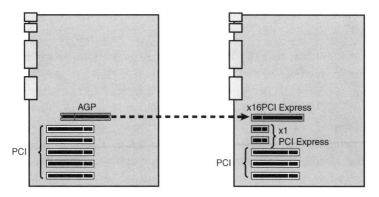

Figure 5.3 PCI to PCI Express x1 migration.

Servers are migrating from PCI-X connectors to primarily x4 and x8 PCIe connectors. Administrators began to see a mix of PCI Express and PCI/PCI-X slots in their server systems, beginning in 2004. This permits system administrators to adopt the new technology, while maintaining support for legacy equipment still being utilized. When comparing the I/O connectors on a typical legacy PCI client motherboard to those found on a transitional PCI Express system, notice that the PCI board contains five standard PCI slots and one AGP slot. Although the PCI Express system board also contains six I/O slots, only three of them are legacy PCI slots. Two slots are x1 PCI Express connectors, and one is an x16 PCI Express connector replacing the AGP8X slot. To distinguish them from off-white PCI slots and brown AGP slots, the PCI Express connectors on the system board are black. Systems mixing both PCI and PCI Express equipment are expected to exist for many years, similar to the transition experienced from the ISA to PCI bus.

Server I/O Modules for PCI Express

The *Server I/O Module (SIOM)* specification is the most recent PCI Express specification to be defined. Slated for inclusion with the second generation of PCIe technology, SIOMs provide a robust form factor that can be easily installed or replaced in a running server system without opening the chassis. This makes it a more radical component design than other PCI Express form factors.

Designed for use in data center environments where many people handle them, SIOMs are hot-pluggable. Their reliability is enhanced through the use of covers designed to protect their internal components. Because high-speed server devices tend to generate a lot of heat, these modules are also designed with forced-air cooling, originating from the back, top, or bottom of the module. Network administrators now have more thermal solutions for rack-mounted systems equipped with SIOMs. The largest SIOM form factors accommodate relatively complicated functions and are capable of handling the entire range of PCIe server interfaces.

The industry's first networking SIOM known as the Yukon II dual-port controller, is specifically designed to deliver reliable multi-gigabit bandwidth for the PCI Express server architecture. It is based on a proprietary *Concurrent Data Streaming (CDS)* structure specifically designed to reduce the impact of system and peripheral latencies on PCI Express throughput. The SIOM's form factor demonstrates a modular I/O adapter design that is both hot-pluggable and closed-chassis, capable of coupling the large PCI Express bandwidth with new levels of system design flexibility. The Yukon II, shown in Figure 5.4, includes a comprehensive suite of drivers capable of supporting Windows, Linux, Netware, and Unix.

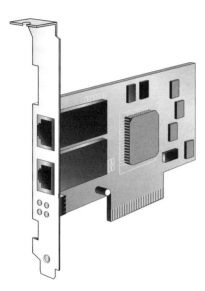

Figure 5.4   A PCIe x4 server I/O module.

PCI Express Architectures

PCIe architectures vary somewhat depending on whether the computer performs as a network client or as a server.

To replace the AGP bus between the graphics subsystem and the Northbridge memory controller, an x16 PCI Express link will be used. The link between the Northbridge and Southbridge will also be replaced with a PCIe variant path, relieving the troublesome bottleneck between the Northbridge and peripheral I/O devices. The Southbridge will feature various PCIe links to the NIC, 1394 devices, and other peripheral units, while continuing to support legacy PCI slots. This indicates that desktop systems will continue to simultaneously carry both PCI and PCIe buses for some time. Design specifications will ensure that PCI cards will not be inserted into PCIe slots, nor will PCIe cards find their way into legacy PCI slots. PCI Express will enable a rapid migration to high-speed Gigabit Ethernet, 10Gigabit Ethernet, and 1394b devices in client systems. The increasing bandwidth requirements of graphics subsystems will also be supported.

Similar to the desktop system, PCI Express technology replaces the AGP bus and the Northbridge/Southbridge link in portable computer systems. PCI buses running between the Southbridge and the customized equipment interface sockets are replaced with PCI Express technology, such as PCI Express Mini Cards.

The PCI bus between the Northbridge and the docking station has also migrated to a PCI Express pathway. Replacing the PC card slot is an x1 ExpressCard slot designed for such things as a USB 2.0 link. Supporting integrated peripheral devices such as audio generators, graphics engines, and Gigabit Ethernet interfaces are individual PCI Express links, instead of the former PCI bus.

Server systems are greatly simplified using architectures similar to that shown in Figure 5.5. In this arrangement, PCIe is implemented with dual processors in a way that significantly reduces server system complexity. Notice how the Northbridge connects directly to the PCI Express links for I/O devices and slots.

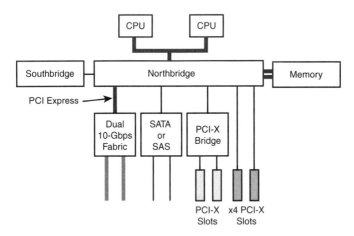

Figure 5.5 A PCIe server architecture.

Advantages to using PCI Express architectures in server environments include

➤ Higher available bandwidth for next-generation I/O, such as 10Gbps Ethernet and x4 InfiniBand. For example, an x8 PCI Express link can accommodate the peak bandwidth required for a dual-ported 10Gbps controller.

➤ Lower server board implementation costs, with more slots and embedded I/O devices connected directly to the system chipset, rather than bridging chips.

➤ The elimination of PCI-X bridges, lowering data transfer latencies between I/O devices, processors, and memory.

Once again, however, the first PCI Express servers also include PCI-X slots, so that legacy PCI-X cards can still be used during early upgrades.

One remaining consideration is the adoption of a PCI Express cable specification. In a client and server system, PCI Express is used with high-speed interconnects between components having high data rates and low-pin-count connectors. Designers envision modular systems, using separate high-speed components and being connected with specially formulated PCI Express cables.

These split systems would serve to separate heat-generating components such as processors, memory, and graphics engines from other components such as removable storage, display devices, and I/O ports. For example, high-end graphics subsystems, which require more power and generate heat, are separated from the main processor chassis. Appropriate power and cooling is then more easily delivered to the graphics subsystem.

Hierarchical PCI Bus

A hierarchical PCI bus is a two-layered system bus that has a primary and secondary I/O. It is used because of the load-related noise phenomenon associated with PCI's shared bus scenario. The PCI system bus also suffers from clock-skewing issues, limiting its use to no more than five card-based devices. An extremely clean communication path, perhaps achieved by directly soldering all PCI devices directly onto the motherboard, would probably permit slightly more than five devices on a single PCI bus. These types of bus-loading limitations resulted in early motherboards providing only three PCI expansion slots. In order to operate more than five PCI devices on a given system, PCI-to-PCI (P2P) bridging chips must be utilized.

The original PCI bus structure was distinguished from next-generation peer-to-peer and point-to-point interconnect formats by the hierarchical tree. The master controller stood at the top of the arrangement, initializing and configuring all of the system's PCI devices during boot-up. With one master controlling them, all PCI devices became slaves. Because the master controller had to configure the entire system and name all of the devices during boot-up, no hot-plugging or hot-swapping techniques were available. This led to the development of next-generation interconnects like HyperTransport and InfiniBand.

Peer PCI Bus

Increasing data throughput was soon achieved by having two peer PCI buses joined together with a host processor. This created a distributed PCI bus, enabling more than four PCI slots to be used. The splitting of devices between both buses increased the system's overall performance.

Intelligent Input/Output

Specifically designed for use with PCI, Intelligent I/O (I2O) became available in 1998. Since its successful development, this technology was incorporated by high-performance I/O architectures for various processors. I2O facilitated a standard, low-cost networking approach complementing existing I/O device drivers, while generating the development of portable I/O solutions for high-end workstations. I2O architecture provided various I/O device drivers not directly related to their host operating systems or the devices they controlled.

I2O also works with intelligent I/O subsystems supporting message passing for multiple processors, where high-bandwidth applications such as networked video, client-server processing, and groupware are enabled to deliver I/O throughput more effectively. Although not intended to replace existing driver architectures, I2O provides a complementary approach to these drivers by creating a framework for future generations of intelligent, portable I/O devices. It provides extremely high-performance I/O by offloading its related processing from the CPU, similarly to the way mainframes handle I/O processes.

Special I/O processors (IOPs) eliminate I/O bottlenecks, such as interrupt handling, buffering, and data transfer. Accompanying I2O drivers consist of OS-specific modules (OSMs) and hardware device modules (HDMs). Whereas OSMs deal with high-level operating system details such as accessing files, HDMs communicate with specific devices. Most importantly, OSMs and HDMs are autonomous, capable of performing their tasks independently, without having to send any data over the I/O bus.

In data flow for traditional I/O processing, various problems encountered include

➤ Host CPUs must interrupt normal processing to perform the I/O. Processing in progress must be interrupted by the host's operating system every time a peripheral device makes an I/O request. Computing resources are used inefficiently.

➤ Clients are responsible for manually installing and managing all specified device drivers. Drivers must be reinstalled following system upgrading, system maintenance, or whenever the drivers themselves are upgraded.

➤ Device drivers must be written and supplied by equipment vendors/
manufacturers for every peripheral device, and for each OS the device
runs on. OS manufacturers must ensure that the operating system is
compatible with each device driver.

➤ I/O processing statistics are limited by the OS on the host computer.
Depending on the platform, I/O data from a host OS may be incomplete or inconsistent. One OS may report the number of empty queue
buffers, but another may not.

Intelligent I/O (I2O) processing defines three software layers.

➤ The OS Services Module (OSM) handles the communication between
the host processor's operating system and the I2O messaging layer. The
OSM is unique for each class of device and each operating system.

➤ The I2O messaging layer uses standard protocols for handling communication between the OSM and HDM, eliminating the need for original
equipment manufacturers to develop multiple drivers for a single device.

➤ The hardware device module (HDM) handles communication chores
between the peripheral device and the messaging layer, and is also
unique for each device class. Although traditional device drivers are
specifically written according to the host processor's OS, only one HDM
is required due to its OS independence.

Intelligent I/O makes wide-scale deployment of modern hardware and
software technologies quicker and simpler, and provides a detailed review of
networking I/O statistics, unencumbered by the limited perspective of any
particular processor, OS, or device driver.

Exam Prep Questions

1. Which of the following bus slots will accept a 64-bit, 68MHz PCI adapter? (Select two.)
   - ❑ A. 64-bit 33MHz PCI
   - ❑ B. 32-bit 33MHz PCI
   - ❑ C. EISA
   - ❑ D. 64-bit 66MHz PCI

2. A 32-bit PCI bus is operating at a clock speed of 66MHz. What is the total bandwidth of the bus?
   - ❑ A. 264MBps
   - ❑ B. 512MBps
   - ❑ C. 528MBps
   - ❑ D. 544MBps

3. How do universal 32-bit PCI cards detect the correct voltage?
   - ❑ A. Through the use of tank circuits
   - ❑ B. Through the use of a voltage divider network
   - ❑ C. Through parallel charging capacitors
   - ❑ D. Through special voltage-in sensing pins

4. When PCI hot-swap technology is being used, what is the server administrator doing?
   - ❑ A. Inserting or removing RAM memory on a powered PCI-equipped server board
   - ❑ B. Inserting or removing a PCI card or device module to/from a powered host system
   - ❑ C. Inserting or removing RAM memory on an unpowered PCI-equipped server board
   - ❑ D. Inserting or removing a PCI card or device module to/from an unpowered host system

5. How can PCI adapter cards that are not equipped with hot-swap technology be added to or removed from a powered server system?
   - ❑ A. Through the use of hot-plug PCI technology, where individual PCI slots can be powered on and off independently
   - ❑ B. Through the use of cold-plug PCI technology, where individual PCI slots can be powered on and off independently
   - ❑ C. Through the use of hot-swap PCI technology, where individual PCI slots can be powered on and off independently
   - ❑ D. Through the use of cold-swap PCI technology, where individual PCI slots can be powered on and off independently

6. What is the first troubleshooting step to perform when a replacement hot-plug NIC is not recognized by the system?

❑ A. Consider the replacement NIC to be faulty.

❑ B. Configure the NIC to transmit both LAN and storage communications.

❑ C. Check to be sure that the hot-plug PCI slot has been reactivated.

❑ D. Use the Windows configuration tools to define the NIC as a software bridge.

Exam Prep Answers

1. Answers A and D are the correct answers. If its bus width is identical, and its clock speed equal to or less than that provided by the slot, an adapter will be accepted. In the case of answer B, the given adapter would only run at half its normal speed capability. Answer B is incorrect because the bus width of the slot is only half of that required. Answer C is incorrect because an EISA slot will not accept a PCI adapter.

2. Answer A is the correct answer. At a clock speed of 66MHz, a 32-bit PCI bus will provide a total bandwidth of 264MBps. Answer B is incorrect unless the bus is 64 bits wide and the clock speed is 64MHz. Answer C is incorrect unless the bus is 64 bits wide. Answer D is incorrect unless the bus is 64 bits wide and the clock is running at 68MHz.

3. Answer D is the correct answer. Universal PCI cards are keyed so that they will fit into either type of slot. These cards can detect the correct voltage through special voltage-in sensing pins. Answer A is incorrect because tank circuits are used in amplifiers rather than voltage sensors. Answer B is incorrect because voltage dividers are used in power supplies rather than voltage sensors. Answer C is incorrect because charging capacitors involve the use of hot-swap adapters.

4. Answer B is the correct answer. The administrator can insert or remove PCI cards and device modules from a host system without shutting the power off through the use of hot-swap technology. Answer A is incorrect because RAM memory is never installed to or removed from a powered system. Answer C is incorrect because hot-swap technology has nothing to do with RAM. Answer D is incorrect because there is no need for hot-swap technology when PCI cards or device modules are inserted on an unpowered host.

5. Answer A is the correct answer. The hot-plug PCI standard enables individual PCI slots to be powered on and off independently so that PCI adapters can be added to or removed from a powered server system. Answer B is incorrect because there is no such thing as cold-plug technology. Answer C is incorrect because hot-swap technology does not require a PCI slot to be powered off. Answer D is incorrect because there is no such thing as cold-swap technology. A cold swap is merely the normal replacement of an adapter to an unpowered system.

6. Answer C is the correct answer. If power was initially switched off to the slot before removing and replacing it, the slot must be reactivated after the replacement NIC is securely inserted and tightened. Answer A is incorrect because not enough is known about the replacement NIC to assume that it is bad. Answer B is incorrect because it would be impossible to configure any hardware not recognized by the system. Answer D is incorrect because the question did not indicate that the NIC was being used for bridging purposes.

6.0—SCSI Systems

Terms you'll need to understand:

✓ Small Computer System Interface (SCSI)

✓ Wide SCSI

✓ Fast SCSI

✓ Ultra SCSI

✓ Ultra Wide SCSI

✓ Ultra2 SCSI

✓ Wide Ultra2 SCSI

✓ Low-Voltage Differential (LVD) and High-Voltage Differential (HVD)

✓ Single-Ended (SE)

✓ Ultra160 SCSI, Ultra320 SCSI, and Ultra640 SCSI

✓ Serial Attached SCSI (SAS)

✓ Parallel SCSI

✓ Fanout expanders and edge expanders

✓ Initiator

✓ Extender

✓ Regenerator

✓ Repeater

✓ Converter

✓ Segment

✓ Domain

✓ Controller

✓ Expander connection manager (ECM) and Expander connection router (ECR)

✓ Broadcast Primitive Processor (BPP)

✓ A-cable, B-cable, P-cable, and Q-cable

✓ Centronics

✓ D-shell

✓ BERG connector

✓ Logical Unit Number (LUN)

✓ Fibre Channel

✓ Passive, active, and forced perfect termination

✓ Internet SCSI (iSCSI)

✓ Fibre Channel over IP (FCIP)

✓ Fibre Channel Tunneling

✓ Storage Tunneling

✓ Internet Fibre Channel Protocol (iFCP)

✓ Quality-of-Service (QoS)

Techniques you'll need to master:

✓ Describing a SCSI host adapter and identifying the SCSI host computer

✓ Explaining how to daisy-chain SCSI devices

✓ Differentiating between various SCSI connectors and bus widths

✓ Summarizing the characteristics of various SCSI versions

✓ Identifying a Wide SCSI interface cable

✓ Describing the improved features of Wide Fast SCSI

✓ Explaining why the Ultra SCSI standard limited the number of attached devices

✓ Detailing how the Ultra Wide SCSI standard improved data throughput

✓ Examining why longer cable lengths for LVD devices are permitted

✓ Identifying the maximum throughput for a Wide Ultra2 SCSI adapter

✓ Describing the multimode capabilities of LVD SCSI devices

✓ Defining the Double Transition (DT) clocking technique for improving SCSI throughput

✓ Explaining the need for quality cables using Ultra160 and Ultra320 SCSI technology

✓ Identifying the clock speed for Ultra320 SCSI operations

✓ Enumerating the advantages of SAS over parallel SCSI technology

✓ Listing the three transport protocols defined for SAS

✓ Differentiating between edge expanders and fanout expanders

✓ Defining an SAS domain

✓ Illustrating how extenders work

✓ Distinguishing between the characteristics of regenerators and repeaters

✓ Demonstrating how converters can improve the capabilities of the SCSI bus

✓ Contrasting the use of expanders and bridges

✓ Describing the advantages of directly addressing either SAS or Serial ATA (SATA) drives in the same network

✓ Listing the various components of an expander

✓ Understanding the end-of-line termination requirements for physical SCSI connections

✓ Knowing how to determine the maximum number of devices available for a given SCSI system

✓ Explaining why and how Logical Unit Number (LUN) expanders are employed

✓ Differentiating between passive, active, and forced perfect terminations

✓ Comparing iSCSI data storage techniques with FCIP and iFCP systems

Introduction

Server+ Exam Objective 1.6 states that the test taker should know the differences between various SCSI solutions, their advantages, and their specifications, including the following:

➤ SCSI 1, 2, and 3

➤ SCSI bus width (Narrow and Wide)

➤ SCSI bus speed (Fast and Ultra, Ultra Wide, Ultra 2, Ultra 160, Ultra 320, iSCSI, SAS)

➤ SCSI connectors, cables, and terminations (passive, active, and multimode)

➤ SCSI IDs and LUNs

➤ Single-Ended Devices

➤ Low-Voltage Differential (LVD)

➤ High-Voltage Differential (HVD)

➤ BUS lengths

➤ Multitasking

➤ Multithreading

➤ Disconnect and reconnect

The Small Computer System Interface (SCSI)

For mass storage functions, desktop PCs tend to employ Integrated Drive Electronics (IDE) drives. Servers, however, are more likely to use SCSI-based drive arrays for storage and backup. The *Small Computer System Interface (SCSI)* is often referred to as the "skuzzy" standard and provides a true system-level interface for a hard drive. Most of the drive's controller electronics are located on the peripheral itself, whereas some server boards provide an integrated SCSI connection. Other systems require that an adapter card be placed in one of the expansion slots. Even when the server provides its own integrated SCSI connector for the disk drive function, it may require a separate SCSI host adapter for attaching RAID configurations.

The SCSI adapter card is referred to as a host adapter because it provides the physical connection to one of the system's expansion slots. Using this arrangement, data arrives at the system interface in a form that is already useable by the host computer. This can be seen through the original SCSI interface illustrated in Figure 6.1.

An important feature of the SCSI interface is that it can be used to connect different types of peripherals to the server system. Additional SCSI devices can be added to the system by daisy-chaining them together.

The original SCSI interface makes provision only for 8-bit parallel data transfers.

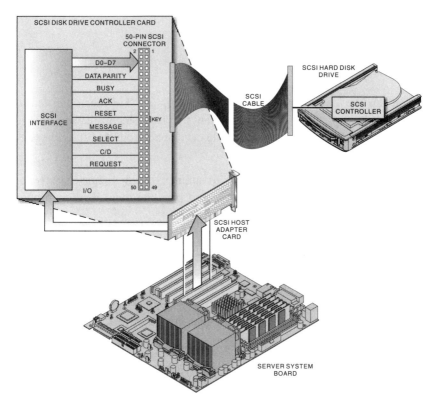

Figure 6.1 The original SCSI interface.

SCSI is an intelligent I/O parallel peripheral bus using a standard, device-independent protocol, and permitting many peripheral devices to be connected to one SCSI port. The original SCSI bus could drive up to eight devices, with one of these units being the host adapter or controller. Each device was assigned a different SCSI ID number, ranging from 0 to 7.

SCSI Development

The following list shows the sequence in which specific SCSI standards were introduced during the period from 1981 to 2004:

➤ SCSI 1

➤ SCSI 2

➤ SCSI 3

➤ Ultra SCSI

➤ Ultra2 SCSI

➤ ULTRA160

➤ ULTRA320

➤ ULTRA640

As you can see, development has progressed rapidly. This has often led to frustration in implementation because new standard versions have routinely appeared before manufacturers have fully developed products fitting the previous specifications.

Take a moment to examine Table 6.1. It summarizes the major characteristics of several SCSI standard versions, and presents them in their proper chronological order.

Table 6.1 A Chronology of Various SCSI Standards						
Interface	Bus Size	Devices (w/controller)	Max Cable Length	Bus Speed (MHz)	Max MBs per sec	Pins
SCSI (SCSI-1)	8 bits	8	6m (20 ft)	5	5	50
Wide SCSI (SCSI-2)	16 bits	16	6m (20 ft)	5	10	50
Fast SCSI (SCSI-1)	8 bits	8	3m (10 ft)	10	10	50
Wide Fast SCSI (SCSI-2)	16 bits	16	3m (10 ft)	10	20	50
Ultra SCSI	8 bits	8	1.5m (5 ft)	20	20	50
Ultra Wide SCSI (SCSI-3)	16 bits	16	1.5m (5 ft)	20	40	68
Ultra2 SCSI	8 bits	8	12m (40 ft)	40	40	68
Wide Ultra2 SCSI	16 bits	16	12m (40 ft)	40	80	68
Ultra160 SCSI	16 bits	16	12m (40 ft)	40	160	68
Ultra320 SCSI	16 bits	16	12m (40 ft)	80	320	68

Because much of the exam involves differentiating between the different versions of SCSI, it's a good idea to become familiar with all of them.

For each version, know the number of devices that can be connected, the connector types, their speeds, their data bus widths, and their maximum lengths. Try to memorize the SCSI specifications given in Table 6.1, including the interface specifications and their associated connectors.

SCSI 1 and Wide SCSI 2

SCSI 1 has a data bus width of 8 bits, and supports up to eight devices, including the controller. The maximum transmission speed of the SCSI-1 bus, 5MBps (1 byte × 5MHz = 5MBps), is also important to remember. The next version developed by the industry increases the width of the bus to 16 bits (2 bytes), and is suitably called Wide SCSI 2. This SCSI bus can transfer data at twice the former speed (2 bytes × 5MHz = 10MBps).

Fast SCSI

The Fast SCSI standard increases the clock speed of the original SCSI-1 bus from 5MHz to 10MHz. This provides a maximum transfer rate of 10MBps (1 byte × 10MHz = 10MBps) to the SCSI-1 bus, increasing the speed of the bus and its vulnerability to crosstalk. Because crosstalk occurs earlier with increased clock speeds, the useable cable length is cut from 6 meters to 3 meters.

Wide Fast SCSI

SCSI 2 is also given the higher 10MBps clock speed. The combination of a faster bus speed and the wider bus is called Wide Fast SCSI. It transfers 16 bits of data at a speed of 10MHz, giving it a total transfer rate of 20MBps (2 bytes × 10MHz = 20MBps). However, the cable length remains at three meters due to the crosstalk inherent with the 10MHz clock.

Ultra SCSI

The next 16-bit standard involves speeding the bus clock up again. The Ultra SCSI standard pushes the bus speed up from 10MHz to 20MHz, using the original SCSI-1 interface. Although this increases the maximum transfer rate of the original SCSI-1 interface from 5MBps to 20MBps (1 byte × 20MHz), it also results in an additional reduction in the maximum useful cable length to 1.5 meters. Although still suitable for most applications, the 1.5m cable length physically limits the number of attached devices.

Ultra Wide SCSI 3

The next advancement for the SCSI standard increases the data bus width and is appropriately called Ultra Wide SCSI (SCSI 3). Although this bus width increases the overall throughput from 20MBps to 40MBps (2 bytes × 20MHz = 40MBps), it still keeps the cable length at 1.5 meters and supports seven devices.

Ultra2 SCSI and Wide Ultra2 SCSI

At this point, the existing hardware interface could not support any further increase in bus speed. The maximum allowable cable length would be too short to use. Efforts to increase the bus speed to 40MHz produced the Low-Voltage Differential SCSI specification. LVD operates on 3-volt logic levels instead of the older, TTL-compatible 5-volt logic levels. By employing LVD technology, the Ultra2 SCSI specification doubled the data throughput of the 8-bit SCSI bus (1 byte × 40MHz = 40MBps), and increased the maximum allowable cable length to 12 meters. In situations where a single LVD device is connected to a single controller, cable lengths up to 25 meters are possible.

Combining LVD technology with the Wide SCSI specification produced Wide Ultra2 SCSI. Although the cable length remained at 12 meters, Wide Ultra2 SCSI increased the maximum data throughput to 80MBps (2 bytes × 40MHz = 80MBps).

Know that LVD operates on 3-volt logic levels instead of the older, TTL-compatible 5-volt logic levels.

Although LVD SCSI devices operate in multimode, they are backward compatible with single-ended SCSI. When connecting one single-ended peripheral to a multimode LVD bus, the entire bus switches to the single-ended mode, complete with the single-ended data throughput and cable length limitations.

Know what happens when you plug a single-ended connector into an LVD system.

To preserve the data throughput and cable length of the LVD bus when adding a single-ended peripheral to it, a SCSI expander unit, called a converter, is utilized. The converter can translate between the various SCSI interfaces, such as

➤ LVD to SE

➤ LVD/MSE to LVD/MSE

➤ SE to HVD

➤ HVD to LVD

It divides the SCSI domain into two bus segments, one operating at the LVD data throughput rate and cable length, and the other operating at the single-ended data throughput and cable length ratings. LVD controllers usually employ a single-ended connector for connecting to slower tape drives, while simultaneously preserving the speed and cable length of the LVD segment.

 Know what happens when an Ultra2 SCSI controller is connected to a Fast SCSI device.

Ultra160 SCSI and Ultra320 SCSI

DT clocking techniques enable an Ultra160 SCSI controller to send data on both the rising and falling edges of each clock cycle. Although the bus width remains at 16 bits, and the clock frequency still operates at 40MHz, DT clocking techniques increase the maximum throughput to 160MBps (2 bytes × 40MHz × 2 = 160MBps). The maximum cable length remains at 12 meters, but the cable itself is manufactured to more stringent specifications, for reliability.

The latest Ultra320 SCSI specification increases the clock speed from 40MHz to 80MHz. Using the DT clocking scheme, Ultra320 SCSI provides a maximum throughput of 320MBps (2 bytes × 80MHz × 2 = 320Mbps).

Ultra640 SCSI

A newly proposed parallel SCSI specification is currently slated for development, called *Ultra640 SCSI*. The Ultra640 SCSI standard proposes to increase the throughput of the interface to 640MBps.

Although the details of Ultra640 cabling have not yet been determined, it is possible that the industry itself will choose a different direction. Industry experts now believe that the Serial Attached SCSI standard, which is initially reaching speeds of 1.5Gbps, is the next logical evolution from its currently deployed counterpart, parallel SCSI. Because the parallel SCSI technology transmits multiple bits down the wire simultaneously, they must all be clocked simultaneously as well. At greater transfer speeds, it becomes impossible to line these multiple bits up properly.

Serial Attached SCSI

Serial Attached SCSI (SAS) holds the promise of the future, where enterprise networks will eventually require more power, easier connectivity, and greater scalability. Compared with the problems just discussed with parallel SCSI technology, the methodology employed with Serial Attached SCSI transmits only one bit of data at a time. This eliminates the headaches associated with clocking and skew compensation, and permits the attainment of those high data-transfer speeds often required by modern networks.

In addition to providing greater data bandwidths, Serial Attached SCSI devices are capable of transmitting their data over larger geographic distances than parallel SCSI devices. Because Serial Attached SCSI technology uses point-to-point communication, its disk drives can be attached, or fanned out, to many devices with each device having a dedicated link. However, due to the use of a shared bus, parallel SCSI drive attachments are limited to a maximum of 15 devices. The theoretical fanning limit according to the Serial Attached SCSI specification is in the tens of thousands. Practically, this limit is probably between 120 to 256 devices. Also, the reliability and backward compatibility to which clients have historically become accustomed with regard to parallel SCSI continues to be maintained with SAS.

The SAS protocol not only links the controller directly to the disk drives, but it also enables multiple devices of various types and sizes to be connected simultaneously. In fact, SAS supports up to 16,256 addressable devices, supporting full-duplex data transfers at speeds up to 3Gbps in its initial implementation. SAS drives are also hot-pluggable and their form factors are compatible with SATA drives, allowing SCSI enterprise class drives to coexist with lower cost/gigabyte SATA drives.

The SAS protocol can be multi-interfaced using cards called initiators, featuring dual-ported capabilities not typically found using desktop hard drives. Through the use of a point-to-point serial interface, the imposed physical addressing limits of parallel SCSI are removed. Yet SAS preserves compatibility with legacy SCSI software developed over the last 20 years.

To support communications between, and co-existence of, various device types such as Serial ATA and SAS drives, SAS defines three transport protocols as follows:

➤ Serial Management Protocol (SMP)—This is a protocol or mechanism that communicates management information to the SAS expanders. Without the SMP, communication to the SAS expanders would be impossible. Through the use of SMP, interface initiators are able to access information about the specified expander, such as the number of physical connections in the expander, the type of device connected to a particular expander phys (physical connection), and information about the expander's manufacturer.

➤ Serial ATA Tunneling Protocol (STP)—STP is the method used by an SAS host to communicate with SATA devices, including disk drives. This is accomplished through the use of the SAS expanders.

➤ Serial SCSI Protocol (SSP)—SSP is used to communicate with standard SAS devices, such as disk drives and interface cards, using SCSI commands. The communication routes between these so-called initiators and targets are mapped.

SAS Expander Types

SAS expanders can be connected to other expanders, SATA target devices, SAS target devices, or SAS initiators, with each expander theoretically capable of being directly connected to 128 end devices. Two types of expanders predominate: edge expanders and fanout expanders.

There are a few minor differences between them, but the primary difference is the way in which they enable devices to be connected, for example

➤ Fanout expanders are capable of being connected to two or more edge expander devices.

➤ Edge expanders can be directly connected to a maximum of one other expander, whether it is an edge or a fanout.

Cost-sensitive edge expanders are implemented without using internal memory to buffer their SCSI payloads. In addition, they limit the number of devices that can be addressed, constraining the size of their associated routing tables and reducing their complexity. Edge expanders are a low-cost way of expanding SAS architecture. They may be combined to form an edge expander device set. An edge expander device set may be attached to no more than one other edge expander device set, or one fanout expander device. Each edge expander device set may address up to 128 devices.

Expander Developments

In a complete SCSI system, peripherals other than mass storage devices also need to be incorporated, including high-speed scanners, printers, data acquisition systems, and video recorders using SCSI interface hardware. When connected to the system, they all have access to the standardized, high-speed communications that SCSI provides. Recall the 1.5- to 6-meter maximum cable lengths permitted for single-ended SCSI attachments, as well as the 25-meter maximums for differential (HVD) SCSI. These restrictions place such devices far from their useful physical locations. Cable length restrictions even impact many SCSI network system RAID packages, backup devices, and other mass storage arrangements negatively.

The solution comes in the form of expanders, a device class that enhances the capabilities of the SCSI bus. First used with the physical parallel SCSI bus, various classifications of expanders were soon recognized. Among SCSI enhancement devices classified as expanders were

➤ Extenders

➤ Regenerators

➤ Converters

Physically locating peripheral devices exactly where they are needed is solved through the use of SCSI bus *extenders*, which separate the bus into two segments, in either fiber optic or coaxial systems. Although each segment has its own set of physical terminations, the extenders are not assigned a bus ID and are logically transparent to the rest of the system.

The extender allows the connected devices to be accessed as if they were connected within a single segment. SCSI signals are converted for transport by fiber, coax, or differential medium over a point-to-point extension. On the other side of the extension, these signals are converted back to their original SCSI format. Although SCSI bus extenders have been commercially available since 1989, their major design issue concerns the arbitration and disconnect/reconnect timing associated with various multithreaded SCSI applications.

Cable length problems are also solved through the use of SCSI bus *regenerators*. Regenerators receive and transmit all of the signal lines between two completely isolated bus segments. The placement of a regenerator can be independently determined for each segment.

SCSI *repeaters* have been implemented in various forms for many years, supporting longer distances by reshaping the REQ and ACK signal lines, and fully regenerating/isolating bus signals and terminations. As the SCSI bus has increased in performance, repeaters no longer can be relied on to fully regenerate the bus traffic. At Fast or Ultra SCSI transmission rates, they may not operate properly. Differences in functionality between regenerators and repeaters warrant the name distinction between the two.

SCSI *converters* are an older form of expander, used since the early 1980s. Currently supporting system upgrades, they are taking an increasing role in new system implementations. Early parallel physical implementations of the SCSI bus caused a demand for the use of converters, permitting various SCSI bus types to communicate with each other, converting between single-ended and differential SCSI systems, and improving the capabilities of the SCSI bus.

To clarify what these expanders do, it's necessary to understand that a valid SCSI bus *segment* must have a single, electrical path of devices terminated at each end. A valid SCSI *domain* must contain one or more SCSI bus segments. Within a SCSI domain, expanders provide the glue between the various segments by allowing all of the devices within the domain to communicate, just as if there were no segmentation.

It's important not to confuse expanders with bridges, which are used to connect two domains together. An expander remains within the specifications of a domain, whereas a bridge provides the communications window between two domains. The bridge itself appears as a network device to both of the domains it connects. The expander operates within a domain, but does not appear as a network device.

This new generation of SCSI SAS expanders is designed to either enable or enhance the capabilities of the Serial Attached SCSI systems already described. SAS expanders connect initiators to various targets, thereby constituting an SAS domain. As such, they are an indispensable component of the SAS architecture. SAS ports physically connected to an SAS host controller may directly address either SAS or SATA drives. However, the number of drives addressed is limited by the number of physical ports actually integrated into the host SAS controller. Obviously, not providing enough SAS ports would dramatically limit the utility of certain systems. In an effort to solve this dilemma, serial attached SCSI deploys SAS expanders to extend the addressing throughout the complete range of 16,256 devices specified in the SAS standard. As additional expanders provide redundancy, and the capability of addressing large numbers of devices, they also incrementally expand internal and external storage capabilities in those systems requiring greater bandwidth and more connections.

Expanders, in general, offer the capability for a host port to establish an operating connection with the desired device, be it a SAS device, a SATA device, or another expander. In order to accomplish these connections, all expanders support an addressing mechanism for routing requests, a means for managing the connections between devices or other expanders, and the capability to broadcast primitive commands across all of the expanded connections supported.

An expander device contains the following components:

➤ An expander connection manager (ECM)—An object within an expander function that manages routing

➤ An expander connection router (ECR)—The portion of an expander function that routes messages between expander object devices

➤ A Broadcast Primitive Processor (BPP)—An object within an expander function that manages broadcast primitives

➤ Two or more physical expander links—Two or more differential signal pairs, one pair in each direction, that connect two physical object devices

➤ An expander port available per physical connection—An expander device object that interfaces to the service delivery subsystem and to SAS ports in other devices.

➤ An SMP, SSP, or STP target port—A SAS target device object in a SAS domain that interfaces to the service delivery subsystem with SMP, SSP, or STP

SCSI Cables and Connectors

Over the years, the SCSI standard has been implemented using a number of cable types. For SCSI-1 systems, the SCSI interface uses a 50-pin signal cable arrangement. Internally the cable is a 50-pin flat ribbon cable, examples of which were shown in a previous section. However, 50-pin shielded cables equipped with the Centronics-type connectors shown in Figure 6.2 are used for external SCSI connections. SCSI cables fitted with 50-pin SCSI connections are referred to as A-cables.

Figure 6.2 Male and female 50-pin SCSI connectors.

Advanced SCSI specifications have created additional cabling requirements. For example, a 50-conductor alternative cable using the 50-pin D-shell connectors shown in Figure 6.3 has been added to the *A-cable* specification for SCSI-2 devices.

Figure 6.3 Male and female 50-Pin SCSI A-cable connectors.

A second cable type, referred to as *B-cable*, was added to the SCSI-2 specification to provide 16- and 32-bit parallel data transfers. However, this arrangement employed multiple connectors at each end of the cable, and never received widespread acceptance in the market. A revised 68-pin *P-cable* format using D-shell connectors, as shown in Figure 6.4, was introduced to support 16-bit transfers in the SCSI-3 specification. A 68-pin *Q-cable* version was also adopted in SCSI for 32-bit transfers. The P and Q cables must be used in parallel to conduct 32-bit transfers.

Figure 6.4   Male and female 68-Pin SCSI P-cable connectors.

For some PS/2 models, IBM used a special 60-pin Centronics-like connector for their SCSI connections. The version of the SCSI interface used in the Apple Macintosh employs a variation of the standard that features a proprietary, miniature 25-pin D-shell connector, similar to that shown in Figure 6.5. These cabling variations create a hardware incompatibility between different types of SCSI devices. Likewise, there are SCSI devices that will not work with each other due to software incompatibilities.

Figure 6.5   Male and female 25-Pin D-shell SCSI cable connectors.

SCSI devices may be classified as either internal or external devices. An *internal SCSI device* has no power supply of its own, and must be connected to one of the system's options power connectors. *External SCSI devices* come with built-in or plug-in power supplies that need to be connected to a commercial AC outlet. Therefore when choosing a SCSI device, always inquire about compatibility between it and any other SCSI devices installed in the system. Figure 6.6 depicts a 25-pin D-shell, a 50-pin Centronics type SCSI connector, and a 68-pin D-shell connector used for external SCSI connections.

As you already know, inside the computer, the SCSI specification uses a 50-pin ribbon cable, fitted with the type of BERG pin connectors shown in Figure 6.7.

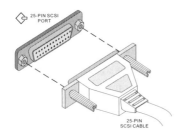

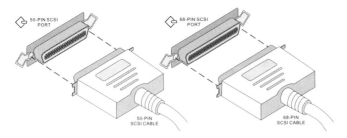

Figure 6.6 SCSI external connectors.

Figure 6.7 SCSI 50-pin internal connectors.

SCSI Addressing

The SCSI specification permits up to eight SCSI devices to be connected, while counting the SCSI controller as one device. The controller may be located on an interface card, or mounted right on the server motherboard. Another SCSI device counted among the eight permitted is the hard drive communicating with the remaining internal or external devices. Where no other internal SCSI devices are present, the interface can be daisy-chained to permit the connection of up to six external peripherals. Within a SCSI-1 arrangement, each device in the chain is automatically assigned a unique ID number, with the SCSI controller referred to as device number seven. The default assignment for the first internal hard drive is device zero. Out of eight possible SCSI ID controller numbers, only six remain available for use with other devices.

It is possible to use multiple SCSI host adapters to increase the number of supported devices. The system's first SCSI controller can handle up to

7 devices (minus the first hard drive, of course), while the additional SCSI controller can boost the system support up to 14 SCSI devices.

To physically connect multiple SCSI devices to a SCSI host, each device except the last, must have two interchangeable SCSI connectors, applying one as SCSI-In, and the other as SCSI-Out. The last device in the chain must be self-terminating with only one connector, or have a terminator installed on the SCSI-Out connector. If two devices are set to the same ID number, one or both of them will appear invisible to the system.

Because a PC can support four SCSI buses, the devices attached to them can share the same address. However, distinct interrupt request (IRQ) settings may be required for each SCSI bus adapter. Although internal devices can usually be addressed with jumpers, external devices are equipped with switches that greatly simplify this chore. Modern SCSI devices are equipped with plug-and-play features for automatic address configuration. They can coexist on the bus with standard SCSI devices without problems. Whenever a SCSI adapter is connected to all internal or all external devices, the adapter itself is the end of the line and must be terminated. This situation does not hold true whenever the adapter is connected to a combination of internal and external devices.

 Know what problems may occur when adding an external SCSI device.

The same type of identification used for SCSI-1 is also used for the Wide SCSI specification, except that the SCSI 2 bus can support up to 16 devices. The addressing scheme is enlarged, whereby SCSI devices can be assigned ID numbers ranging from 0 to 15. Using this approach, the number of SCSI devices that could be connected to a three-channel, SCSI-3 RAID 5 controller would be 45.

 Know the maximum number of drives available on multiple channel SCSI controllers.

Large server-based SCSI configurations view the number of devices addressable by a single SCSI port as a limitation. These servers must access large banks of devices, and SCSI buses are viewed as limiting factors. *Logical Unit Number (LUN)* expanders are employed to increase the number of devices on one bus domain, through a single SCSI port. Each LUN can address up to 8 devices at each SCSI ID, with the maximum allowable bit size for a SCSI 3 ID LUN of 64 bits. Targets of 64 bits are common in iSCSI and Fibre Channel, whereas 64-bit LUNS can be repartitioned into four subdevice levels if necessary.

SCSI Terminations

Electrical signals traveling along an unterminated SCSI bus cause unintended results by reflecting back and forth and interfering with more recent signals. To eliminate these reflections, terminating resistors are installed at each end of the line, especially with SCSI daisy chains. Single-connector SCSI devices usually provide the necessary terminations internally. Poor or improper terminations can be a major source of SCSI-related problems, including:

➤ Failed system startups

➤ Hard drive crashes

➤ Random system failures

 Know that improper termination of a SCSI system can result in intermittent and unpredictable failures.

Several termination types are commonly used with SCSI buses. Quality bus terminations result in quality signal transfers and reliable networks. For servers, reliability is everything. Slower buses are less particular in the termination method used, whereas faster buses must be more precise. Buses using HVD and LVD devices require special termination.

Termination types include

➤ Passive Termination—The simplest and least reliable termination mode, it uses resistors to terminate the bus, similar to the way terminators are used on coaxial Ethernet networks. This is fine for short, low-speed SCSI-1 buses but is not suitable for modern SCSI buses.

➤ Active Termination—Involves adding voltage regulators to the resistors of a passively terminated SCSI bus, allowing for more reliable and consistent termination. This is the minimum requirement for faster-speed, single-ended SCSI buses.

➤ Forced Perfect Termination (FPT)—A more advanced form of active termination where diode clamps are added to the circuitry in order to force its termination to the correct voltage. This is the most reliable form of termination for a single-ended SCSI bus, and eliminates SCSI termination problems.

Three signaling systems are used by SCSI devices:

➤ High-Voltage Differential (HVD)—Also known as Differential (DIFF), HVD was originally used with SCSI-1 buses, running on 5 volts DC.

➤ Single-Ended (SE)—Uses half the wires in the cable for a ground point, and the remaining lines for data transferring/control mechanisms. This type of connector was also heavily used in SCSI-1 buses.

➤ Low-Voltage Differential (LVD)—Used on newer buses requiring a unique type of terminator. In addition, special LVD/SE terminators are used with multimode LVD devices that function in either LVD or SE modes. In a bus running in single-ended mode, LVD/SEs behave like active terminators. LVDs are currently more popular than HVDs because LVDs can support the Ultra 2 Wide SCSI standard, doubling the bandwidth from 80 to 160 MB/sec.

Adapters are used to permit different SCSI connectors to work together. For example, an appropriate adapter would permit an HVD connector to be used with a LVD SCSI card.

Know the different types of SCSI signaling systems (HVD, LVD, and SE). In spite of the fact that LVD is the most popular SCSI server signaling system used today, knowledge about the other types is very beneficial to the server technician.

A SCSI device paired with a single-ended connector will function properly. However, the device will run at SE speeds, and the effective data bandwidth halved for all devices on the bus, not just for the SE-connected device itself.

When troubleshooting the cables and connectors on a SCSI bus, the HTI+ technician should remember to do the following:

➤ Properly terminate the bus, with a terminator installed on the very extreme ends of the bus, rather than in the middle or somewhat near the end. It's best to use an active terminator, rather than relying on the termination features of storage devices.

➤ Ensure that every device has a unique SCSI ID, with devices numbered in the identical sequence in which they are attached on the bus, if possible. Alternately if the numbers are unique between devices, it does not matter which ID numbers are assigned.

➤ Ensure that no loose connectors, improper terminations, or inferior cable quality is permitted to create intermittent bus problems.

iSCSI

Internet SCSI (iSCSI) is an IP-based technology for connecting data storage devices and facilities across a network. By transporting SCSI commands over IP networks, iSCSI is used to facilitate data transfers over intranets and to manage storage over long distances. At the physical layer, iSCSI supports the Gigabit Ethernet interface, permitting direct connection to any standard Gigabit Ethernet switch, or IP router. The iSCSI specification maps SCSI into the TCP/IP protocol, allowing clients to directly connect with SCSI devices across a network, and conduct block transfers, rather than file-level transfers. The communication between an initiator and target occurs over one or more TCP connections. A similar technology has been developed for Fibre Channel as well, permitting the use of modern, high-speed Metropolitan Area Network (MAN)/Wide Area Network (WAN) communications.

The iSCSI protocol is expected to spur rapid development in the use of SANs, by increasing the capabilities and performance of storage data transmission. Because of the universal reach of IP networks, iSCSI can be used to transmit data over LANs, WANs, and the Internet, enabling location-independent data storage and retrieval.

The following steps occur when a client or a server application sends a data transfer request:

1. The OS generates the appropriate SCSI commands and the specified data request.

2. The SCSI commands/requests are encapsulated and encrypted.

3. A packet header is added before transmission of the IP packets over an Ethernet connection.

At the receiving end, when a packet is received, the following occurs:

1. If a packet was encrypted prior to transmission, it is decrypted.

2. The packet is disassembled, and the SCSI commands are separated from the data request.

3. The SCSI commands are sent on to the SCSI controller.

4. The controller relays the specified commands to the SCSI storage device.

5. Due to the bidirectional nature of iSCSI, data can be selected and retrieved from the SCSI storage device, if requested.

Considering iSCSI as suitable for transmission over existing Ethernet networks, Cisco, IBM, and McDATA Corporation have introduced iSCSI-based products, including switches and routers. Alternatively, Sun Microsystems considers TCP/IP to be impractical for use in storage area networks, due to the enormous processing latency involved with reading and forwarding data packets.

Note that iSCSI is one of two main approaches to storage data transmission over IP networks. The second method includes the use of Fibre Channel technology. The Fibre channel approach is divided between two formats: *Fibre Channel over IP (FCIP)*, and *Internet Fibre Channel Protocol (iFCP)*.

FCIP

Fibre Channel over IP (FCIP) is a revolutionary protocol that doesn't bring any changes into the basic SAN storage structure. It's concerned with functionally integrating a number of geographically remote storage networks.

The problem of geographical distribution is effectively solved with FCIP, by integrating various SANs distributed across large distances. For existing SANs running over Fibre Channel, the protocol is transparent across modern MAN/WAN network infrastructures. One FCIP gateway connected to a specified MAN/WAN network enables the merging of geographically remote Fibre Channel SANs. An FCIP-based geographically distributed SAN links devices connected to a MAN/WAN network so that the resulting IP traffic appears to belong to a usual FC network. The FCIP standard specifies the following:

➤ The rules of FC frame encapsulation for TCP/IP delivery

➤ The encapsulation rules for the creation of a virtual connection between FC devices and network elements

➤ The TCP/IP environment supporting creation of a virtual connection

➤ The TCP/IP environment supporting FC traffic tunneling through an IP network, including data safety, integrity, and rates

Following are some operations that can be successfully accomplished using the FCIP protocol:

➤ Remote backup

➤ Data recovery

➤ Shared data access

FCIP translates FC control codes and data into IP packets for transmission between geographically distant FC SANs. FCIP is also known as *Fibre Channel Tunneling* and *Storage Tunneling*. However, it can be used only in conjunction with FC technology.

iFCP

Internet Fibre Channel Protocol (iFCP) delivers FC traffic over TCP/IP between various iFCP gateways. The FC transport level is replaced with the IP network transport. Traffic between various FC devices is routed and switched using TCP/IP. The iFCP protocol allows the connection of existing FC data storage systems to an IP network, which provides the network services for supporting these devices.

The iFCP specification does the following:

➤ Overlays FC frames for their delivery to a predetermined TCP connection

➤ Overlaps FC message delivery and routing services in the iFCP gateway

➤ Manages FC network structures and components using TCP/IP rather than mixing them in one FC SAN

➤ Dynamically creates IP tunnels for FC frames

The iFCP protocol uses an IP network to provide FC device-to-device connections. This is a more flexible arrangement than SAN-to-SAN connections. For example, suppose that an iFCP system is supporting a TCP connection between two FC devices. The connection benefits from its own quality-of-service connection level, independent from any other QoS level between other pairs of FC devices also communicating.

Exam Prep Questions

1. Which of the following is not a SCSI signaling system?

   ❏ A. SE
   ❏ B. DSSS
   ❏ C. LVD
   ❏ D. HVD

2. An external SCSI tape drive is installed on a system that previously was configured with a SCSI card and an internal SCSI hard drive. What should be done if the system fails to recognize the new tape drive during the bootup process?

   ❏ A. On the internal hard drive, enable its termination.
   ❏ B. On the SCSI controller card, enable its termination.
   ❏ C. On the SCSI tape drive, disable its termination.
   ❏ D. On the SCSI controller card, disable its termination.

3. A newly installed server communicates properly with its SCSI drives for six hours before requiring a reboot to continue communicating with them. Where does the problem lie?

   ❏ A. The NOS drivers need to be updated.
   ❏ B. The server's power supply is too small.
   ❏ C. The SCSI drives are improperly terminated.
   ❏ D. The system is operating normally.

4. When the first SCSI standard appeared, what was its bus size and speed?

   ❏ A. 8 bits wide at 5MHz
   ❏ B. 8 bits wide at 7MHz
   ❏ C. 16 bits wide at 7MHz
   ❏ D. 8 bits wide at 8MHz

5. Ultra Wide SCSI (SCSI-3) permits which of the following features?

   ❏ A. A maximum of 8 connected components using 1.5m (5 ft) cables
   ❏ B. A maximum of 16 components using 1.5m (5 ft) cables
   ❏ C. A maximum of 8 components using 3m (10 ft) cables
   ❏ D. A maximum of 16 components using 3m (10 ft) cables

6. An Ultra2 SCSI system can support up to how many devices?

   ❏ A. 16
   ❏ B. 12
   ❏ C. 10
   ❏ D. 8

7. What would be the results of plugging a single-ended connector into an LVD SCSI system?

 ❑ A. Data throughput is limited to multimode parameters.

 ❑ B. The SCSI bus will switch to multimode.

 ❑ C. The entire bus will switch to the single-ended mode.

 ❑ D. The single-ended device will begin to function incorrectly.

8. Why are most LVD controllers fitted with a single-ended connector?

 ❑ A. To decrease the system transfer speed and to limit the interface cables to single-ended mode.

 ❑ B. To decrease the system transfer speed to single-ended limitations, but keep the cable lengths as they are.

 ❑ C. To keep the system transfer speed high, but limit the cable lengths to single-ended limitations.

 ❑ D. To preserve the speed and cable length of the main LVD segment.

9. What signaling systems operate on the older 5-volt logic levels? (Select two.)

 ❑ A. LVD

 ❑ B. HVD

 ❑ C. TTL

 ❑ D. DT clocking

10. A SCSI system is using a three-channel SCSI-3 RAID 5 controller. How many SCSI devices can be connected?

 ❑ A. 30

 ❑ B. 40

 ❑ C. 45

 ❑ D. 55

11. When adding external SCSI devices to a poorly terminated server, which of the following problems would not occur?

 ❑ A. Power outages

 ❑ B. Hard drive crashes

 ❑ C. Random system failures

 ❑ D. Failed system startups

12. Which SCSI interface uses half the wires in the cable for data transferring and control mechanisms, and the remaining wires for a ground point?

 ❑ A. LVD

 ❑ B. FPT

 ❑ C. HVD

 ❑ D. SE

13. SCSI-1 networks normally use which type of termination?
- ❏ A. Passive
- ❏ B. Active
- ❏ C. HVD
- ❏ D. LVD

14. A SCSI scanner is added to a system that was formerly operating correctly with all internal SCSI devices. If the system now refuses to boot properly, what could the problem be?
- ❏ A. A physical connection between the network and the scanner does not exist.
- ❏ B. No power is reaching the server.
- ❏ C. Termination for the scanner has yet to be configured.
- ❏ D. The server is no longer recognized by the network.

15. What are Logical Unit Number (LUN) expanders used for?
- ❏ A. To decrease the number of devices that can be placed on one bus domain, through a dual SCSI port
- ❏ B. To increase the number of devices that can be placed on one bus domain, through a dual SCSI port
- ❏ C. To decrease the number of devices that can be placed on one bus domain, through a single SCSI port
- ❏ D. To increase the number of devices that can be placed on one bus domain, through a single SCSI port

Exam Prep Answers

1. Answer B is the correct answer. DSSS is not a SCSI signalling system. Instead, it is an acronym for Direct-Sequence Spread Spectrum, one of two types of spread spectrum radio. Answer A is incorrect because SE (Single-Ended) is a legitimate SCSI signalling system. Answer C is incorrect because LVD (Low-Voltage Differential) is a legitimate SCSI signalling system. Answer D is incorrect because HVD (High-Voltage Differential), also known as DIFF (Differential), is a well-known SCSI signalling system used by SCSI devices.

2. Answer D is the correct answer. The original configuration used termination at the controller (SCSI ID 0) and the internal drive (SCSI ID 7). With the new configuration, the channel must be extended to the external device, and termination at the SCSI controller must be disabled. Answer A is incorrect because termination is already enabled on the internal hard drive. Answer B is incorrect because the system is failing to recognize the tape drive even though termination is already

enabled on the SCSI controller card. Answer C is incorrect because disabling the tape drive's termination would make it invisible to the system.

3. Answer C is the correct answer. When a SCSI system is improperly terminated, intermittent and unpredictable failures will occur. Answer A is incorrect because the existing NOS drivers do not base their SCSI operations on time limits. Answer B is incorrect because an insufficient amount of power would result in many more symptoms besides the ones described. Answer D is obviously incorrect because a server should not normally require a reboot every six hours.

4. Answer A is the correct answer. SCSI-1 operated with a maximum speed of 5MBps and a data bus width of 8 bits. Answer C is incorrect because SCSI-1 used an 8-bit bus. Answers B and D are incorrect because the clock speeds are too great.

5. Answer B is the correct answer. The SCSI-3 standard permits the connection of up to 16 devices (including the controller) using a maximum cable length of 1.5 meters. Answer A is incorrect because a maximum of 16 components can be connected. Answer C is incorrect because a maximum of 16 components can be connected, and the cable length is restricted to 1.5m (5 ft). Answer D is incorrect because the cable length cannot exceed 1.5m (5 ft).

6. Answer D is the correct answer. An Ultra2 SCSI system can support 8 devices, including the controller. Answer A is incorrect because the bus being discussed is not a Wide Ultra2 SCSI. Answers B and C are incorrect because no existing SCSI buses have been designed to support a maximum of 10 or 12 devices.

7. Answer C is the correct answer. Connecting one single-ended peripheral to a multimode LVD bus will cause the entire bus to switch to the single-ended mode with applicable limitations on data throughput and cable length. Answer A is incorrect because single-ended data throughput parameters are limited, not multimode parameters. Answer B is incorrect because the bus cannot run in multimode with a single-ended connector attached. Answer D is incorrect because the connected single-ended device will function properly.

8. Answer D is the correct answer. Most LVD controllers employ a single-ended connector for connecting to slower tape drives in order to preserve the speed and cable length of the main LVD segment. Answer A is incorrect because it mentions limitations that are not imposed. Answer B is incorrect because the system transfer speed is

preserved, not decreased. Answer C is incorrect because the interface cables on the main LVD segment are not limited to single-ended mode.

9. Answers B and C are the correct answers. TTL and HVD both operate on the older, 5-volt logic levels. Answer A is incorrect because LVD operates on the new 3-volt logic levels. Answer D is incorrect because DT clocking pulses are not considered to be signal data. It operates with LVD systems, permitting the data transfer twice per clock cycle, on both the rising and falling edges.

10. Answer C is the correct answer. The number of SCSI devices that can be connected to a three-channel SCSI-3 RAID 5 controller would be 45 (3 * 15 = 45), considering the fact that each channel of the controller will accommodate 15 devices. Answers A, B, and D are therefore all incorrect.

11. Answer A is the correct answer. Power outages have no direct relationship to improperly terminated server connections. However, poor terminations could cause a variety of other system problems, including hard drive crashes (answer B), random system failures (answer C), and failed system startups (answer D).

12. Answer D is the correct answer. Single-ended connectors, especially in SCSI-1 buses, use only half the wires in the cable for data transferring and control mechanisms. The remaining wires are all used to establish a ground point. Answer A is not correct because only 7 grounding wires are used in a 68-wire LVD cable. Answer B is incorrect because Fast Processing Technology (FPT) is used for high-speed, high-resolution MIDI data transmission on USB. Answer C is not correct because a 50-wire HVD cable uses only 7 wires for grounding purposes, whereas a 68-wire HVD cable only uses 6 ground wires.

13. Answer A is the correct answer. Short, low-speed SCSI-1 buses do well using passive termination techniques. Answer B is incorrect because active termination is the minimum requirement for faster-speed, single-ended SCSI buses. Answer C is incorrect because HVD terminations require their own termination types, and cannot be mixed with others. Answer D is incorrect because LVD buses require a unique type of terminator.

14. Answer C is the correct answer. In order for the system to boot properly, the scanner must be terminated because it's the only external device at the end of the line. If the scanner had been terminated internally, the system would have booted correctly. Now, it will have to be

terminated externally. Answer A is incorrect because the question states that the scanner has been added to the system. Answer B is incorrect because not plugging in the server would result in a dead system, with no valid indication of a server boot failure to observe. Answer D is incorrect because the system has not even booted yet. It would have to at least boot in order to indicate that it does not recognize the server.

15. Answer D is the correct answer. Logical unit number expanders increase the number of devices that can be placed on one bus domain, through a single SCSI port. Each LUN can address up to eight devices at each SCSI ID. This makes answers A, B, and C incorrect by definition.

7.0—IDE Systems

Terms you'll need to understand:

- ✓ Advanced Technology Attachment (ATA)
- ✓ Integrated Drive Electronics (IDE)
- ✓ Small Form Factor (SFF)
- ✓ Master and Slave
- ✓ Jumper block
- ✓ Cable select (CSEL)
- ✓ IDE/ATA specification
- ✓ Enhanced IDE (EIDE)
- ✓ ATA-2/EIDE/ATAPI specification
- ✓ Primary and Secondary
- ✓ IDE1 and IDE2
- ✓ AT Attachment Packet Interface (ATAPI)
- ✓ ATA-3/Ultra ATA 33 specification
- ✓ Ultra DMA (UDMA)
- ✓ Terminations
- ✓ Ringing
- ✓ Parallel ATA
- ✓ Serial ATA
- ✓ Serial ATA International Organization (SATA-IO)
- ✓ Low-voltage differential signaling
- ✓ Port multipliers and selectors
- ✓ Native command queuing

✓ Online, offline, and nearline storage

✓ Mean Time Between Failure (MTBF)

✓ Input/Output (I/O)

Techniques you'll need to master:

✓ Identifying an IDE drive's low-level formatting information

✓ Describing a standard IDE interface

✓ Differentiating between host adapter cards and controller cards

✓ Detailing the differences between various ATA versions

✓ Configuring IDE disk drives

✓ Selecting a master or a slave drive

✓ Identifying hard drive partitions and logical drives

✓ Listing the maximum throughput for a standard 40-pin IDE signal cable

✓ Knowing which IDE standard doubles the maximum throughput to 16.7MBps

✓ Explaining the IDE improvements provided by the AT Attachment Packet Interface (ATAPI)

✓ Contrasting a Primary and a Secondary IDE interface

✓ Identifying which specifications boost IDE throughput to 33.3MBps

✓ Stating which specification doubles the number of conductors in the IDE signal cable to 80

✓ Reviewing the structure of an IDE controller

✓ Describing source termination configurations and implementations

✓ Contrasting the differences between parallel and serial ATA

✓ Differentiating between the two types of SATA cables

✓ Defining low-voltage differential signaling

✓ Identifying three important features of SATA II that make it more suited for enterprise environments

✓ Comparing online, offline, and nearline storage

Introduction

Server+ Exam Objective 1.7 says that the test taker should know the differences between various ATA (IDE) solutions, their advantages, limitations, and specifications. These solutions include

➤ ATA 33

➤ ATA 66

➤ ATA 100

➤ ATA 133

➤ Serial ATA (SATA)

➤ SATA II (SATA II v1.2)

➤ Ultra DMA

➤ Cabling and connectors

➤ Jumper settings

Integrated Drive Electronics Interfacing

Also referred to as the *Advanced Technology Attachment (ATA)*, the *Integrated Drive Electronics (IDE)* interface is a system-level connection scheme that places most of the necessary controller electronics on the hard drive unit itself.

IDE interfaces transport data in a parallel format between the computer system and the hard disk drive. The drive's controller circuitry processes all of the parallel-to-serial and serial-to-parallel conversions, permitting the use of an interface completely independent of the host computer. The disk geometry is invisible to the host. Instead, it sees only the pattern presented to it by the IDE controller.

 Remember that ATA is an acronym for Advanced Technology Attachment, and it is a disk drive implementation that integrates the controller on the drive.

The manufacturing process includes the placement of an IDE drive's low-level formatting information, which is used by the controller for alignment and sector-sizing purposes. The IDE controller extracts the raw data, including the formatting, from the drive's read/write (R/W) heads, and converts this into signal data applied to the computer's buses.

The standard IDE interface uses a single, 40-pin cable to connect the hard drive(s) to an adapter card, or directly to the system board. When an adapter card is used in conjunction with a system-level IDE interface, it is referred to as a host. Host adapter cards are not the same as controller cards because they contain no intelligent control devices. They simply extend the physical system bus to the specified Input/Output (I/O) device. There are several versions of the ATA, all developed by the *Small Form Factor (SFF)* Committee. These include:

➤ ATA—Also known as IDE, this version supports one or two hard drives, a 16-bit interface, and Programmed Input/Output (PIO) modes 0, 1, and 2.

➤ ATA-2—This version supports PIO modes 3 and 4, and multiword direct memory access (DMA) modes 1 and 2. It also supports logical block addressing (LBA) and block transfers, and is marketed as Fast ATA and Enhanced IDE (EIDE).

➤ ATA-3—This version constitutes a minor revision to ATA-2.

➤ Ultra-ATA—This version supports multiword DMA mode 3, running at 33MBps. It is also called Ultra-DMA, ATA-33, and DMA-33.

➤ ATA/66—This is a version of ATA by Quantum Corporation, supported by Intel, that doubles throughput to 66MBps.

➤ ATA/100—This is an updated version of ATA/66 that increases data transfer rates to 100MBps.

Configuring IDE Drives

The host adapter provides bus-level interfacing between the system and the IDE devices, and includes the required buffering of the system's address and data buses. To differentiate between a single drive, or master and slave drives in a multiple-drive system, the host adapter provides the necessary select signals.

IDE drives arrive from the manufacturer configured as a single drive, or as the *master* drive in a multidrive system. To install the drive as a second, or *slave* drive, it is usually necessary to install, remove, or reposition one or more jumpers on the drive's *jumper block*, as illustrated in Figure 7.1. Some hosts can disable the interface's *cable select* (*CSEL*) pin on any drive identified as a slave. To cooperate with this type of host, it is necessary to install a jumper enabling the drive's cable select option.

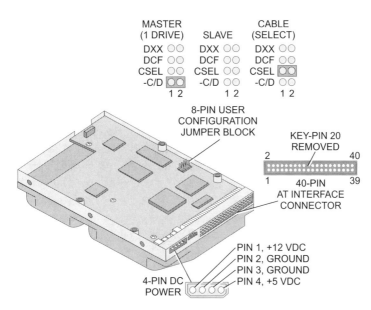

Figure 7.1 IDE master/slave settings.

 Remember the three configurations that can be set on an IDE drive: master, slave, and cable select.

In Microsoft operating systems, the primary partitions of multiple IDE hard drives are assigned the first logical drive identifiers. This means that if an IDE drive is partitioned into two logical drives, the system will identify them as the C: drive and the D: drive. If a second IDE drive is installed as a slave drive and is also partitioned into two additional logical drives, the partitions on the first drive will be reassigned as logical drives C: and E:, whereas the partitions on the slave drive will be assigned as D: and F:.

Advanced EIDE Specifications

With the passage of time, a variety of IDE-related specifications have arisen. The initial IDE standard was called the *IDE/ATA* specification, identifying IDE and ATA as the same standard. It supported a maximum throughput of 8.3MBps using the standard 40-pin IDE signal cable. To permit more than two drives to coexist on the interface, updated IDE specifications were developed.

The second IDE standard included the ATA-2/EIDE/ATAPI specifications, with the *ATAPI* standard being a derivative of ATA-2. It doubled the maximum throughput to 16.7MBps through the familiar 40-pin IDE signal cable. Called *Enhanced IDE (EIDE)* or simply *ATA-2*, it permitted up to four IDE devices to operate in a single system. The host supplied two IDE interfaces with each handling a master and a slave device, in a daisy-chained configuration. The first interface was called the *Primary* IDE interface, and was typically labeled *IDE1*. The second IDE interface was likewise called the *Secondary* IDE interface, and labeled *IDE2*, as illustrated in Figure 7.2.

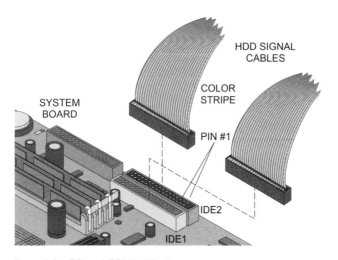

Figure 7.2   IDE1 and IDE2 identification.

EIDE increased the number of drives that could be accommodated by the system and provided for improved IDE drivers, collectively known as the *AT Attachment Packet Interface (ATAPI)*. ATAPI drivers designed for use with CD-ROM drives introduced new DMA data transfer methods. Development of the ATA standard continued, with the *ATA-3/Ultra ATA 33* specifications boosting IDE throughput to 33.3MBps. This standard retained the 40-pin IDE signal cable and relied on the system to support its 33.3MBps burst-mode transfer operation using the *Ultra DMA (UDMA)* protocol.

The fastest IDE enhancements, referred to as ATA-4/Ultra ATA 66 and Ultra ATA 100, extend the throughput capabilities of the bus by doubling the number of conductors in the IDE signal cable to 80. Although the number of wires has doubled, the connector remains compatible with the 40-pin connection, and each pin has its own ground conductor in the cable. The Ultra ATA 66 specification provides 66MBps, whereas the Ultra ATA 100 connection provides 100MBps. Using an older 40-wire IDE cable in conjunction with a newer UDMA EIDE drive will severely limit the new drive's performance.

Remember how the Ultra ATA 66 interface cable can be identified.

The IDE/EIDE interface has served for quite some time as the standard PC disk drive interface, becoming an integrated portion of most PC system boards, including BIOS and chipset support for the board's specified IDE version, and host connections.

Remember that IDE bus driver support is built into the BIOS of system boards that have integrated IDE host adapters.

Ultra ATA Termination Strategy

Ultra ATA configurations implement source *terminations* in order to minimize *ringing*. Using the source termination scheme, a series resistor is placed at the driver's transmit output. The amount of resistance is selected so that when added to the transmitter's output impedance, it matches the impedance of the controlled trace and/or the cable. However, if the termination resistor is improperly chosen, some of this reflected signal would be re-reflected, causing ringing in the received signal. If the ringing is strong enough, settling time of the received signal may be adversely affected.

This termination scheme is effective when using a single driver and receiving device at opposite ends of the connecting cable. However, the standard ATA cable allows for a second device to be attached some distance from the end of the signal path, making control more difficult. Although limiting the output slew rate can help to control ringing, the problem will grow worse as greater bus speeds are implemented.

Serial ATA (SATA)

All standard ATA interfaces are called *parallel ATA*. They stand in sharp contrast to the *serial ATA (SATA)* interface standard, which signifies a radical evolution away from parallel ATA. The *Serial ATA International Organization (SATA-IO)* is responsible for developing, managing, and pushing for adoption of the serial ATA specifications. Serial ATA operates over a serial data link, composed of a single cable with a minimum of four wires, creating a point-to-point connection between devices. SATA data transfer rates begin at 150MBps, and SATA's thinner serial cables facilitate more efficient airflow inside the server chassis. Smaller form factors allow for smaller chassis designs, giving SATA powerful advantages over parallel ATA systems. IDE cables used in parallel ATA systems are bulkier, and can extend only to 40cm. In contrast, SATA cables can extend up to 1 meter.

The serial ATA interface has been positioned to compete with other interface types employing serial data transmission, such as the USB bus, the IEEE-1394 bus, the serial ATA interface, and the latest SCSI interface, which is covered in Chapter 6, "SCSI Systems."

These modern serial transmission modes are fast, and they provide high performance. The initial SATA specification conducts transfers at up to 150MBps using 250mV differential signaling techniques. In addition, only two data channels are required: one for sending and one for receiving. Seven-wire ATA connection data cables include three independent ground return paths, varying considerably from the ribbon cables used with parallel interfaces. They are thin and flexible, and their connectors are merely 8mm wide. Because these cables can range up to a meter in length, there is no inherent problem connecting a serial ATA disk drive mounted in the top bay of a large tower case to the server board.

Early SATA interfaces used only PCI cards, restricting their maximum data transfer rate of 150MBps to the 133MBps provided by the PCI bus. Their performance was no better than that of the more established Ultra ATA/100 and Ultra ATA/133 interfaces. Although the original SATA roadmap called for speed enhancements culminating to 600MBps, the SATA II implementation is already providing speeds of 300MBps for use with specifically designed motherboards. This momentum will continue to build as serial ATA gradually replaces parallel ATA technology. Although serial ATA will not be able to directly interface with legacy Ultra ATA hardware, it is fully compliant with the ATA protocol and thus is software compatible, supporting all ATA and ATAPI devices.

SATA Cabling

SATA cabling consists of a minimum four-wire cable containing two differential pairs for data transmission and reception. Functioning similarly to the 40 interspersed grounds making up the 80-pin Ultra ATA cable, the serial ATA cabling supports three independent ground return lines that are used to minimize impedance and crosstalk. The maximum length specified for SATA cables is 1 meter.

SATA Connectors

The SATA signal connector is only half an inch wide, directly connecting the four signal wires and three ground lines to the receiving terminal in a single row, as shown in Figure 7.3. Very little crosstalk is introduced because the connector includes the shielding ground pins. Observe that the receiving terminal uses an extended connector pin for the grounding chores to ensure a sharing of the ground reference between the device and host prior to the application of signals to the input.

Figure 7.3   A serial ATA connector.

A similar connection sequence is enforced with the new 7/8-inch wide, 15-pin single row power connector. This is a necessary feature in situations where hot plugging must be accommodated. Again, several pins are extended for grounding.

 Know how to differentiate between a serial ATA signal and power connectors.

SATA Impedance Specifications

Achieving proper termination for all lines is less expensive, in both dollars and design complexity, because serial ATA uses only four signal lines per channel. This is fortunate because all devices are required to provide precision termination impedances. Exact matching to any cable or device is ensured through the use of active impedance matching circuits. Although serial ATA utilizes the same source termination scheme as parallel ATA, the use of near-perfect terminations along with point-to-point connection topology eliminates problems. The only receiving device is guaranteed to reside only at the endpoint of the transmission line.

SATA's Low-Voltage Differential (LVD) Signaling

Because of the noise rejection capabilities of SATA's wire pairs, *low-voltage differential signaling* can be achieved. Voltage swings of plus or minus 0.125V from its minimum common-mode voltage of 0.25V remove the 5V tolerance constraint previously imposed by older ATA specifications. This means that serial ATA does not maintain hardware compatibility with parallel ATA.

Additional SATA Capabilities

Serial ATA includes 32-bit CRC error correction for all transmitted bits, rather than just the data packets, as was the case with Ultra ATA. In addition, the design of the SATA connector supports hot-swapping featuring

➤ Variable-length pins

➤ Minimal insertion force designs

➤ Specified locations on device back plates

Specific software drivers have been developed to permit serial ATA devices to be internally hot-plugged or blindly mated to a server's backplane or device bay. Serial ATA also provides built-in support for bus-mastering DMA operations, eliminating the data delays associated with on-board DMA controllers. Bus-mastering DMA is made possible by building the DMA controller chip right onto the drive controller, enabling the controller to directly transfer data to and from system RAM without intervention by the host system's CPU or a third-party DMA controller. Only half as many bus cycles are required to perform the data transfer.

SATA I Versus SATA II

As already mentioned, SATA has been designed and marketed as the replacement for parallel ATA, and SATA I drives and controllers currently reside in many new desktop machines. However, the recent excitement involving SATA has more to do with improvements to its specification, making it suitable in enterprise server environments. This improved specification is called SATA II, and products built for it are currently shipping. Three important features about SATA II that make it better suited for enterprise environments are

➤ Port multipliers

➤ Port selectors

➤ Native command queuing

Port Multipliers

In SATA I, parallel ATA drives had to be configured as masters and slaves, with daisy chaining required from each controller. The port multiplier specification for SATA II allows up to 15 drives to be connected to the SATA controller, through the use of a *port multiplier*. Although this number is far less than the number of drives that can be connected using either Fibre Channel, or Serial Attached SCSI (SAS), this improvement will make it much easier for network administrators to build server disk enclosures using SATA drives.

Port Selectors

Port selectors permit two hosts to be connected to one drive. This capability creates a redundant connection to the specified disk drive. If one of the hosts suffers a failure, the second host, acting as a spare, can assume network operations and maintain access to the storage. This type of redundancy is essential for enterprise environments.

Native Command Queuing

Native command queuing improves the performance and efficiency of SATA II drives. As commands arrive at the hard drive specifying reads or writes from or to different locations on the disk, they are executed in the order they arrive. This causes a great deal of mechanical overhead through the constant repositioning of the read/write heads. SATA II drives use an algorithm to determine the most efficient sequence in which to execute commands, substantially reducing the amount of mechanical overhead and greatly improving performance.

Nearline Storage

Although SATA improvements make it much more useful to enterprise data centers, they will not of and by themselves cause server administrators to forget about SCSI, Fibre Channel, or SAS. SCSI, Fibre Channel, and SAS will remain the primary candidates for mission-critical storage. However, SATA II can be utilized to solve other enterprise storage problems, such as *nearline storage*.

In the past, network storage was considered to be either online or offline. *Online storage* refers to a data center that operates 24 hours a day, 7 days a week. Usually such an operation is configured with high-performance Fibre Channel and SCSI server arrays. *Offline storage* refers to data that is not immediately accessible, because it's formatted as backup data, usually located offsite, either on tape or on CDs. As modern ideas about the information management lifecycle gained widespread acceptance, it became clear that data storage should exist in more than two states.

Data loses its business value as it ages, and is therefore accessed less and less as time goes on. Therefore, it doesn't make sense to store that older data on expensive, high-performance server drives. Instead, it makes more sense to move the aging data onto lower-cost SATA drives, and take the performance hit that this data shift entails. As the data grows even older, it can later be moved to tape or CD storage. In this way, data stored on SATA drives becomes more accessible than it would be if it were only stored on tape. At the same time, valuable space at the main data center can be reserved for more frequently accessed data.

Current SATA drives are designed for 24/7 availability, capable of longer *Mean Time Between Failure (MTBF)* rates. However, they are not yet designed to be as durable as enterprise-class SCSI or Fibre Channel drives. Remember that enterprise hard drives must be running and available at all times, usually in high *input/output (I/O)* environments. These newer SATA drives must also be available continuously, but won't necessarily get as much traffic in the low I/O environments for which they are selected. Because SATA II drives experience less wear and tear, they don't need to be as robust as enterprise drives, and can be priced similarly to parallel ATA drives, and significantly less than higher-end storage. Improved SATA II drives are showing up in many data centers, and are proving to be a cost-effective tool in managing and storing data information.

Exam Prep Questions

1. How many conductors are provided by the ATA-66 IDE cable specification?
   - ❏ A. 20
   - ❏ B. 40
   - ❏ C. 60
   - ❏ D. 80

2. Server boards equipped with integrated IDE host adapters specifically support which one of the following items through their BIOS programs?
   - ❏ A. Printers
   - ❏ B. Mice
   - ❏ C. IDE hard drives
   - ❏ D. Scanners

3. When installing an IDE drive in a system, which of the following jumper settings does not apply?
   - ❏ A. Terminal
   - ❏ B. Master
   - ❏ C. Cable Select (CS)
   - ❏ D. Slave

4. An Ultra ATA-66 hard disk drive is connected to the server board using a 40-pin IDE cable. What will be the maximum data throughput expected for this drive?
   - ❏ A. 10MBps
   - ❏ B. 33MBps
   - ❏ C. 66MBps
   - ❏ D. zero MBps

5. How do server boards with integrated IDE controllers provide IDE support?
   - ❏ A. Using the operating system
   - ❏ B. Using the installed applications
   - ❏ C. Using the installed drivers
   - ❏ D. Using the BIOS firmware

6. How are IDE drives assigned their drive letters?
   - ❏ A. Through the BIOS settings
   - ❏ B. Through assignments from the operating system
   - ❏ C. Through user programming
   - ❏ D. Through the IDE controller

7. An older computer has only one IDE controller and another IDE device must be added. The system already has a hard drive and a CD-ROM drive connected. How can the additional IDE device be added?

❑ A. Add an IDE controller card to the system.

❑ B. Obtain an additional IDE cable.

❑ C. Connect the hard drive to the remaining connector on the floppy disk cable.

❑ D. Add a SCSI controller to the system.

8. Which of the following features describe a SATA signal connector? (Select two.)

❑ A. A width of seven-eighths of an inch

❑ B. A single row of 7 lines

❑ C. A double row totaling 15 lines

❑ D. A width of half an inch

Exam Prep Answers

1. Answer D is the correct answer. The ATA-66 specification provides greater data throughput by doubling the number of conductors in the IDE cable to 80. Answer B is incorrect because the ATA-33 specification provides for an IDE cable having 40 conductors. Answers A and C are incorrect because no ATA specification exists for IDE cables having 20 or 60 conductors respectively.

2. Answer C is the correct answer. IDE bus driver support is usually built into the BIOS of system boards equipped with integrated IDE host adapters. Driver support for the devices listed in answers A, B, and D are provided by the NOS software or by third-party vendors.

3. Answer A is the correct answer because there is no such IDE jumper setting as "Terminal." Answer B is incorrect because in a multi-drive system, the "Master" jumper setting is valid for an IDE drive. Answer C is incorrect because the Cable Select (CS) setting is valid where the system itself determines the drive configuration settings. Answer D is incorrect because in a multi-drive system, the Slave jumper setting is valid for a secondary drive in a multi-drive IDE system.

4. Answer B is the correct answer. Connecting an Ultra ATA-66 hard drive to the system with a 40-pin IDE cable forces it to operate according to the ATA-33 standard, with a maximum data throughput of 33MBps. Answer A is incorrect because a Fast SCSI system is not

being used. Answer C is incorrect because an 80-pin IDE cable is not being used. Answer D is incorrect because enough compatibility exists with this combination to provide at least ATA-33 standard throughput.

5. Answer D is the correct answer. Depending on the board's IDE version and host connections, the IDE controller is an integrated section of the server board, including its BIOS and chipset support. Answer A is incorrect because the server board's firmware settings override the operating system. Answer B is incorrect because the interaction between IDE components and the installed applications is determined by the system setup. Answer C is incorrect because the integrated IDE controller contains the required driver support.

6. Answer B is the correct answer. Drive assignments are carried out within the operating system environment. Identifications include letters for each logical drive, such as C, D, E, and so on. Answer A is incorrect because the authority of the BIOS is limited, and it usually lists the drives according to the way in which the operating system determines. Answer C is incorrect because OS assignments cannot be overridden by the user. Answer D is incorrect because the hardware interface determines where the IDE controller's authority ends. The controller must use whatever drive names or letters the operating system determines.

7. Answer A is the correct answer. Because each IDE controller can handle only two IDE devices, at least two controllers are required for this situation. Older system boards have only one onboard controller and another must be added to the system to support the additional IDE drive. Answer B is incorrect because without another controller, an additional IDE cable is useless. Answer C is incorrect because a floppy disk cable cannot be connected to a hard disk drive. Answer D is incorrect because IDE devices cannot be interfaced with a SCSI controller.

8. Answers B and D are the correct answers. The SATA signal connector directly connects four signal wires and three ground lines to the receiving terminal in a single row. It is only half an inch wide. Answer A is incorrect because the SATA power connector is seven-eighths of an inch wide. Answer C is incorrect because the SATA power connector is a 15-pin, single-row arrangement.

8.0—RAID Systems

Terms you'll need to understand:

- ✓ Redundant Arrays of Independent Disks (RAID)
- ✓ Single Large Expensive Disk (SLED)
- ✓ Striped drive array
- ✓ Mirrored drive array
- ✓ Redundancy
- ✓ Error correction
- ✓ Disk duplexing
- ✓ Parallel transfers
- ✓ Parity striping
- ✓ Hot swapping
- ✓ Automatic rebuild
- ✓ Dual-parity operation
- ✓ Dual-level RAID
- ✓ Distributed parity
- ✓ Fault tolerance
- ✓ Availability
- ✓ Hot spare

Techniques you'll need to master:

- ✓ Listing RAID advantages
- ✓ Explaining how disk drives are shared
- ✓ Describing how striped drive arrays and mirrored arrays work
- ✓ Identifying various RAID systems
- ✓ Differentiating between disk mirroring and disk duplexing
- ✓ Calculating RAID 10 drive array space
- ✓ Explaining why RAID 3 uses low-efficiency error correction
- ✓ Describing RAID 5 data regeneration and the major drawback of Raid 5 arrays
- ✓ Identifying the pros and cons of various RAID configurations
- ✓ Describing the operation of a hot spare
- ✓ Explaining how zero-channel RAID is used
- ✓ Differentiating between software and hardware RAID implementations

Introduction

Server+ Exam Objective 1.10 states that the test taker should know the features and capabilities of the following RAID levels, when they apply, and how each relates to fault tolerance or high availability (non-proprietary):

➤ RAID 0

➤ RAID 1

➤ RAID 3

➤ RAID 5

➤ RAID 5+1

➤ RAID 0+1

➤ RAID 0+5

➤ RAID 1+0

➤ RAID 5+0

➤ Zero Channel RAID

➤ Hardware vs. software RAID

RAID Development

Every minute of downtime can potentially cost money, with the amount lost dependent on the server's role and the length of time it remains unuseable. Statistics about server component failures indicate that 50% of server downtime can be attributed to disk drive failures.

In 1988, three researchers from the University of California introduced a paper titled "A Case for Redundant Arrays of Inexpensive Disks (RAID)," proposing a strategy to address this problem. It described the use of multiple, inexpensive disk drives combined to outperform a *Single Large Expensive Disk (SLED)* drive. Advantages included data availability, data protection, and increased performance over a single disk drive. The many benefits offered by RAID (now called Redundant Arrays of Independent Disks), popularized this strategy in server environments.

Server storage requirements have surpassed what is available on single hard drives, making it logical to combine several drives together. For desktop units, this amounts to adding an additional physical hard drive to the system. Wide

Area and Local Area Networks (WANs and LANs) connect computers together so that resources such as disk drives, printers, and files can be shared. When shared physical disk drives operate under the direction of a single controller, the result is a drive array!

The evolution of disk drive arrays parallels the growing storage requirements of server-based local area networks. Drive arrays prove particularly useful in client/server networks.

Where multiple drives are located within a single unit, or scattered across a network, they all assume a unique letter designation. Yet, during the Power On Self Test (POST), a stack of drives can appear as a single large hard drive, and can deliver data to the controller in a parallel format. A system controller simultaneously handling data from eight drives can conduct data transfers eight times faster than with one hard drive. This parallel technique is referred to as a *striped drive array*, and requires a specialized RAID controller and software.

Small arrays are useful as data backup systems and when so configured, are referred to as *mirrored drive arrays*. In a mirrored array, each drive in the array holds identical data. If data from one drive is corrupted, or unreadable, the data remains available from one of the other drives. The mirrored drive array must be composed of at least two hard drives, both storing identical data. Operating a mirrored drive array also requires a specialized RAID controller and accompanying software.

Know which RAID system uses redundancy to improve fault tolerance.

The current version of the Server+ exam only asks questions associated with single RAID levels 0, 1, and 5; however, levels 2, 3, and 4 are included as possible answers to each question. Therefore, it is important in studying for the Server+ exam to recognize the difference between each single RAID level.

RAID systems can simultaneously protect data and provide immediate online access to it, even when a single disk fails. Some RAID systems can withstand up to two concurrent disk failures, while still providing uncorrupted data access. They also allow online reconstruction of the failed disk's data to a replacement disk.

RAID Levels

The following section presents each level of RAID, explaining which type of array it is and where it would be used.

RAID 0 is the simplest level, and uses disk striping without parity. It requires less time for disk access, but provides no redundancy or error correction. This type of RAID is used only when reliability is not vital, and should never be used in a server environment. At least two identical hard drives are required, so as not to waste any drive space. If the drives are not identical, the array's data capacity equals the number of drives times the smallest drive's capacity. For example, if one 1GB and three 1.2GB drives are set up using RAID 0, the result will consist of a 4GB (4×1GB) disk array.

Striping involves the interleaving of read and write sectors between the multiple drives. Data is broken down into blocks, which are written to alternating drives in the array.

Giving up redundancy allows this RAID level the best overall performance characteristics of the single RAID levels, especially for its cost. If one of the drives in the array fails, however, all data is lost.

RAID 1 uses disk mirroring, and/or disk duplexing, where duplicate information is stored on both drives. *Disk mirroring* duplicates identical data on more than one drive, effectively increasing reliability of the system by protecting data through redundancy. It uses the same controller to operate both hard drives, making it a single point of failure. If and when the controller card fails, both drives will fail.

When retrieving a file from the array, the controller reads alternate sectors from each drive, effectively reducing the read time by half. When considering RAID 1, people usually think only of mirroring, because mirroring is more often implemented than duplexing.

Disk duplexing is a form of RAID 1 that eliminates the controller as a single point of failure by using a separate controller for each of the hard disks. Disk duplexing is more often found in software RAID solutions because of high hardware costs. Although mirroring is more widely used due to having two drives using a single controller, disk duplexing is growing in popularity as the costs of controller cards fall.

Duplexing is superior to mirroring in terms of availability because it provides protection against both drive and controller failures. Although duplexing costs more due to the additional hardware, it is becoming more popular for RAID 1 configurations.

Because hardware RAID configurations assume that the RAID controller will handle all drives in the array, the duplexing option is not supported in most PC hardware RAID solutions, including the most expensive ones. More often, duplexing is found in software RAID solutions managed by the operating system. In high-level operating systems, the data can easily be split between the host adapters.

Expensive external RAID servers have been fitted with hardware RAID duplexing solutions, where separate drive controllers speed up the otherwise slow write operations. Because RAID 1 must write twice as much data in order to operate effectively, the client receives only half the storage space he or she might initially expect.

Know the differences between disk mirroring and disk duplexing.

RAID 2 uses data striping with error recovery, and is designed for use where high data-transfer rates are required.

Bits or blocks of data are striped across the disks in a parallel format providing extremely fast data transfers. In large RAID 2 arrays, complete bytes, words, or double words can be simultaneously written and read.

The RAID 2 specification employs multiple disks for error detection and correction, reserving large portions of the array for non-data-storage overhead, depending on the error detection and correction algorithms used. However, when an error is detected, time-consuming corrective read operations are unnecessary, and the data delivered to the system is reliable.

Large server systems using RAID 2 use between three and seven drives for error correction purposes. RAID 2 employs a complex error detection and correction algorithm by the controller's circuitry that detects, locates, and corrects the error without having to retransmit any data. The expense of the controller hardware and the additional hard drives required for RAID 2 make it a rarely used solution today.

The *RAID 3* specification uses parallel transfers similar to RAID 2, along with byte-level parity striping. By using parity checking for error detection and correction, only one additional drive is required. To verify an error, the controller rereads the array and consumes additional time.

Because parity information is written by the hardware controller to a dedicated drive for each write operation, software RAID 3 implementations are not practical. Therefore, RAID 3 is considered to be a low-efficiency error correction method.

RAID 4 uses independent data disks along with a shared parity disk. Its block level striping can be adjusted for different applications. Because the hardware controller interleaves sectors across the drives in the array, the appearance of one very large drive is created. Although RAID 4 can be used for larger arrays, it is generally reserved for use with smaller ones due to its slow performance. One parity-checking drive is allocated for error control, and is updated after each read. This extra write activity makes RAID 4 slow.

RAID 5 distributes its parity blocks among its independent data disks. It differs from the RAID 4 specification by allowing the parity function to rotate throughout the various drives, removing the bottleneck of a dedicated parity drive. With RAID 5, error checking and correction is a function of all the drives.

When a single drive fails, the system is able to regenerate its data from the parity information on the remaining drives. Parity blocks are kept separate from data blocks to maintain fault tolerance, but they require time to be calculated and written during writes. Because it can be used on small arrays with a high level of built-in error recovery, RAID 5 is usually the most popular array deployed. Its drawback is that an extra drive is required for its redundancy. The minimum number of drives necessary to operate a RAID 5 array is three.

 Know that the total disk space for a RAID 5 array is the number of drives minus 1, multiplied by an individual drive's size.

One basic problem exists when using RAID 3, 4, and 5 systems. In the event that there is more than one missing bit/byte/block in a row, the system's algorithms will no longer be capable of reconstructing the missing data.

RAID 6 uses independent data disk arrays with two distributed parity blocks. It stripes blocks of data and parity across an array of drives similar to RAID 5, and calculates *two* sets of parity information for each parcel of data, requiring two drives to do so. This improves fault tolerance to the point that RAID 6 can handle the failure of any two drives in the array.

Preventing RAID 6 from being widely used in the industry are the complicated and expensive controllers required to accomplish the dual-parity operation. RAID 6 is generally slower than RAID 5 with writes due to the added overhead of more parity calculations. Random reads are faster, however, due to the spreading of data over one more disk. Similar to RAID levels 4 and 5, its performance can be adjusted by experimenting with different stripe sizes.

RAID 6 appears ideally suited to RAID 5 applications, where additional fault tolerance is required. However, few companies can justify paying so much more to insure against the relatively rare simultaneous failure of two drives.

RAID 6 becomes an even less viable solution when compared to the inclusion of hot swapping and automatic rebuild features with RAID 5, which permit recovery from a single drive failure in a matter of hours.

However, without these features RAID 5 would require downtime for rebuilding, thereby giving RAID 6 an attractive advantage. Dual-level RAID solutions also beat RAID 6 by offering attractive and less expensive feature combinations. For example, RAID 10 provides improved performance combined with some degree of multiple-drive fault tolerance, as described in the following section.

Dual-Level RAID Systems

Because single RAID levels don't always address the administrator's specific server situation, combinations exist to provide more comprehensive protection and greater performance. Multi-level RAID operations are complex enough to require hardware controllers, and software solutions to these situations remain impractical. Although RAID combinations are often referred to using only numerical digits, the Server+ Exam will indicate these multi-level RAID categories using the "+" sign between them. This is because the order of digits is directly related to the amount of fault tolerance provided by the specified system. For example, although RAID 0+1 is slightly different from RAID 1+0, they are the most commonly found combinations in use and they both require at least four drives to implement. However, not all combinations of RAID levels exist!

The *RAID 0+1* combination uses RAID 0 strictly because of its high performance and RAID 1 for its high fault tolerance. A server running eight hard drives is split into two arrays of four drives each. Then, RAID 0 is applied to each array, resulting in two striped arrays. RAID 1 is then applied to the two striped arrays with one array mirrored on the other. In this scenario, when a hard drive in one striped array fails, the entire array is lost. Although the other striped array remains, it contains no fault tolerance for protection against the failure of one of its drives.

The *RAID 1+0* combination applies RAID 1 first, after splitting the eight drives into four sets of two drives each. Now each set is individually mirrored with duplicate information. RAID 0 is now applied by individually striping across all four sets. This combination has better fault tolerance than RAID 0+1 because as long as one drive in a mirrored set remains active, the array still functions properly. Theoretically, up to half the drives can fail before everything is lost, as opposed to RAID 0+1, where the failure of two drives can lose the entire array.

Either RAID 0+1 or 1+0 provides increased performance to a RAID 1 installation. The benefits of this arrangement include the striping performance of a RAID 0 array with the mirroring redundancy of a RAID 1 array. Its conceptual drawback is the fact that half the drive space is taken for purposes of redundancy. This would require the use of eight 10GB hard drives to produce an array providing 40GB of storage space. The remaining 40GBs would be used solely for backup purposes.

 Know which RAID arrays will protect against two drives failing at the same time.

Remember that RAID 1+0 is a striped array, containing segments bearing the same fault tolerance as RAID 1. Again, by striping RAID 1 segments, high I/O rates are achieved. Although an expensive solution, it's excellent when the write performance of RAID 1 is required.

 Be able to calculate RAID 0+1 or RAID 1+0 drive array space.

 Know the differences between RAID 0+1 and RAID 1+0.

RAID 0+5 is used to form large arrays by combining the block striping and parity features of RAID 5 with the straight block striping of RAID 0. It is a RAID 5 array composed of a number of striped RAID 0 arrays, and is less common than RAID 5+0.

RAID 5+0 is a RAID 0 array striped across RAID 5 elements. It also provides better fault tolerance than the single RAID 5 level does.

RAID 5+0 and RAID 0+5 both improve upon the performance of RAID 5 through the addition of RAID 0, particularly during writes. As dual-level arrays that utilize multiple RAID 5 sets into a single array, a single hard drive failure can occur in each of the RAID 5 sets without any loss of data on the entire array. Keep in mind that, as the number of hard drives increases in an array, so does the increased possibility of a single hard drive failure. Although there is an increased write performance in both RAID 0+5 and RAID 5+0, once a hard drive fails and reconstruction takes place, there is a noticeable decrease in performance. Subsequent data and/or program accesses will be slower, as will data transfer speeds.

 Know the differences between RAID 0+5 and RAID 5+0.

RAID 5+1 includes mirroring, combined with block striping with distributed parity. RAID 5+1 is the only configuration using both mirroring and parity redundancy methods, to maximize fault tolerance and availability. Its arrays are composed of striped sets with parity using multiple mirrored pair components. Although similar in concept to RAID 1+0, the striping includes parity. RAID 5+1 mirrors the entire RAID 5 array, similar to RAID 1+0, except that the sets include the parity protection of RAID 5.

RAID 5+1 fault tolerance is such that an eight-drive array can tolerate the failure of any three drives simultaneously, and can handle the failure of as many as five, as long as one mirrored RAID 5 set has no more than one failure. RAID 5+1 storage efficiency is very low, its operation is complex, and the implementation is expensive. The RAID 1 component of this multi-level is capable of using duplexing, rather than mirroring, to provide increased fault tolerance. RAID 5+1 performs well, but not well enough to justify its high cost.

RAID 5+3 is a combination of RAID 0 and RAID 3. This configuration is a striped array (RAID 0) whose segments are essentially RAID 3 arrays. It has the same fault tolerance and high data-transfer rates of RAID 3, with the high I/O rates associated with RAID 0, plus some added performance. This configuration is expensive, requiring at least five drives.

 Know which RAID configurations actually provide redundancy and not just improved drive performance.

The RAID 5+3 specification is implemented as striped RAID 0 arrays whose segments are RAID 3. RAID 5+3 contains the same fault tolerance and overhead as RAID 3, but provides additional write performance. It's an expensive solution, requiring all drives to have the same synchronization.

Hot Spare

Hot spare refers to a standby drive that sits idle in an array until such time as a drive in the array fails. The hot spare then automatically assumes the role of the failed drive. Immediately, the RAID system begins to reconstruct the data onto the hot spare from the remaining drives. On completion, the system will return to its normal operating mode. Hot spares only make sense on RAID levels 5, 5+0, 0+5, 1+5, and 5+1 and are most often seen in RAID 5 arrays.

Zero-Channel RAID

A zero-channel RAID adapter is a PCI RAID controller card without any onboard SCSI channels. It is designed to use the internal SCSI channels of the server board for implementation of an effective, low-cost hardware RAID solution. Important requirements regarding zero-channel RAID implementations on Intel server boards include

➤ The card must be installed in a specified PCI slot.

➤ The SCSI ROM scanning option in the BIOS setup must be disabled.

➤ The Symbios SCSI drivers for the loaded operating system must not be used. (The Symbios name comes from the Colorado-based company Symbios, Inc., a leader in the storage components and storage subsystems markets, which was purchased in 1998 by LSI Logic Corporation.)

Software Versus Hardware RAID

RAID systems can be implemented using either dedicated hardware, or software running on the server. Software RAID is run by the OS, which manages all disks using an IDE, SCSI, or Fibre Channel controller. Although the software RAID option is slower, it doesn't require extra hardware to manage. Newer technologies now provide software RAID systems that run faster than most hardware systems.

Hardware RAID systems require a special RAID controller adapter. Modern desktop systems use a PCI expansion card for this chore, whereas other systems feature RAID interfacing built into the server board.

Exam Prep Questions

1. Which of the following RAID configurations does not provide data fault-tolerance?
   - ❑ A. RAID 0
   - ❑ B. RAID 1
   - ❑ C. RAID 3
   - ❑ D. RAID 5

2. The administrator is configuring a hardware-based mirror array designed to provide 160GB of storage capacity using 20GB SCSI drives similar to the seven units now on hand. In order to do this and still maintain redundancy, how many additional drives are required, and what type of RAID arrangement will succeed?
   - ❑ A. RAID 3 adding 7 drives
   - ❑ B. RAID 51 adding 1 drive
   - ❑ C. RAID 10 adding 9 drives
   - ❑ D. RAID 5 adding 13 drives

3. If two HDDs fail at the same time in a RAID array, which of the following RAID levels will not provide the required protection?
   - ❑ A. RAID 1
   - ❑ B. RAID 5
   - ❑ C. RAID 51
   - ❑ D. RAID 10

4. Which of the following is not a requirement for a zero-channel RAID implementation on an Intel server board?
   - ❑ A. The card must be installed in a specified PCI slot.
   - ❑ B. The SCSI ROM scanning option in the BIOS setup must be disabled.
   - ❑ C. The Symbios* SCSI drivers for the loaded operating system must not be used.
   - ❑ D. The onboard SCSI channels of the server's motherboard must not be used.

5. Drive A is 6GB in size and drive B is 10GB in size. If these two drives compose a RAID 1 array, how much available space remains on drive B if drive A holds 3GB of data?
   - ❑ A. 7GB
   - ❑ B. 5GB
   - ❑ C. 3GB
   - ❑ D. 1GB

6. What is the total available disk space for seven 10GB drives running in a RAID 5 array?

❑ A. 20GB

❑ B. 40GB

❑ C. 60GB

❑ D. 80GB

7. If two hard drives simultaneously fail in a RAID system, which of the following array configurations offers the required protection?

❑ A. RAID 10

❑ B. RAID 4

❑ C. RAID 5

❑ D. RAID 53

8. What is the job expected of a hot spare drive in a RAID configuration after a primary drive has failed?

❑ A. To continually sit by idly in the array

❑ B. To assume the role of a failed drive

❑ C. To return the system to its normal operational mode

❑ D. To reconstruct the lost data

9. Under what circumstances does the server see the RAID array as composed of only one drive?

❑ A. When the operating system is being booted

❑ B. When the Linux OS is mounting each drive to the root directory

❑ C. When the server is configured with multiple operating systems

❑ D. During the POST

10. What is the difference between disk mirroring and disk duplexing?

❑ A. Disk mirroring strips data and disk duplexing shares data parity disks.

❑ B. Disk duplexing uses one controller for both drives and disk mirroring uses one controller for each drive.

❑ C. Disk mirroring uses a minimum of three drives and disk duplexing uses two.

❑ D. Disk mirroring uses one controller for both drives and disk duplexing uses one controller for each drive.

11. In order to operate a RAID 5 array properly, what is the minimum number of drives required?

❑ A. 4

❑ B. 3

❑ C. 2

❑ D. 1

Exam Prep Answers

1. Answer A is the correct answer. RAID 0 does not provide any fault tolerance. Answer B is incorrect because RAID 1 provides fault tolerance through duplication of the data. Answers C and D are incorrect because RAID levels 3 and 5 use "parity" information to provide fault tolerance.

2. Answer C is the correct answer. It requires eight 20GB hard drives in order to reach a storage capacity of 160GB. Mirroring will be required to maintain redundancy. The solution will require an additional nine 20GB drives arranged in a RAID 10 array. Answer A is incorrect because RAID 3 does not provide mirroring, and even if it did, adding seven more drives would be insufficient. Answer B is incorrect because although RAID 51 does provide the necessary mirroring, adding only one additional drive will leave the array eight drives short. Answer D is incorrect because although enough drives are included for the mirroring requirement, RAID 5 does not provide mirroring.

3. Answer B is the correct answer. If two or more drives fail simultaneously, the array must include RAID 1 to provide mirrored drives in order to rebuild the lost data. RAID 5 alone cannot meet this requirement. Answers A, C, and D all include RAID 1 so that disk mirroring is available.

4. Answer D is the correct answer. Zero-channel RAID implementations are designed to use the onboard SCSI channels of the server's motherboard. Answers A, B, and C are all legitimate requirements for using a zero-channel RAID adapter.

5. Answer A is the correct answer. RAID 1 uses disk mirroring, where duplicate information is stored on both drives. Answers B, C, and D are all incorrect because drive B is 10GB in size. Subtracting the 3GB of data already stored on drive A leaves 7GB of space on drive B.

6. Answer C is the correct answer. In a RAID 5 array, the total disk space is the number of drives minus 1, multiplied by the size of an individual drive. Answers A and B are incorrect because the numbers given are not large enough. Answer D is incorrect because there is no way for seven 10GB hard drives to provide 80GB of storage space.

7. Answer A is the correct answer. Two drives can fail at the same time without losing any data provided that RAID 10 is being used. This arrangement would combine the performance of RAID 0 (striping) with the redundancy of RAID 1 (mirroring). Answer B is incorrect

because no mirroring is provided by RAID 4. Answer C is incorrect because although RAID 5 can regenerate corrupt data from its parity information, the simultaneous failure of two drives cannot be overcome. Answer D is incorrect because in spite of its superior speed considerations, a simultaneous failure of two RAID 53 drives dooms the array to failure.

8. Answer B is the correct answer. After the RAID system has rebuilt the data from the failed drive onto the hot spare, the hot spare will assume the role of the failed drive. Answer A is incorrect because the failure of another drive removes the hot spare from its idle state. Answers C and D are incorrect because these tasks are the responsibility of the RAID controller.

9. Answer D is the correct answer. The RAID drive array appears to the server as only a single drive during the POST procedure. Answer A is incorrect because the POST tests have already been completed by the time the OS is being booted. Answer B is incorrect because the Linux OS is already differentiating between the drives during the mounting procedure. Answer C is incorrect because all server operating systems differentiate among all components under their control.

10. Answer D is the correct answer. Disk mirroring uses one controller for both drives, whereas disk duplexing uses one controller for each drive. If the controller fails with disk mirroring, both hard drives will fail. Disk duplexing eliminates the controller as a point of failure by having a controller for each drive. Answer A is incorrect because disk mirroring and duplexing are not directly related to parity chores. Answer B is incorrect because disk mirroring and duplexing are described in reverse. Answer C is incorrect because the number of drives being used is irrelevant.

11. Answer B is the correct answer. To properly operate a RAID 5 array, a minimum of three hard drives is required. By the process of elimination, answers A, C, and D are all incorrect.

9.0—Advanced Storage Arrays

Terms you'll need to understand:

- ✓ Fibre Channel
- ✓ Small Computer System Interface (SCSI)
- ✓ High Performance Parallel Interface (HIPPI)
- ✓ Fiber Distributed Data Interface (FDDI)
- ✓ Host Bus Adapter (HBA)
- ✓ Direct Attached Storage (DAS)
- ✓ Arbitrated loop
- ✓ External storage arrays
- ✓ Storage Area Network (SAN) and Network Attached Storage (NAS)
- ✓ Serial Storage Architecture (SSA)
- ✓ GigaBit Interface Converters (GBIC)
- ✓ Small Form Pluggable GigaBit Interface Converter (SFP GBIC)
- ✓ High Speed Serial Data Connector (HSSDC)
- ✓ Small Form Factor Pluggable (XFP)
- ✓ Multimode Fiber (MMF) and Single-Mode Fiber (SMF)
- ✓ Gigabit Fibre Channel (GFC)
- ✓ Point-To-Point (FC-P2P)
- ✓ Arbitrated Loop (FC-AL)
- ✓ Fabric Switching (FC-SW)
- ✓ N, NL, F, FL, E, and G Ports
- ✓ Exchange

✓ Originator and responder

✓ Sequence

✓ Fibre Channel Standard (FCS)

✓ Dual looping

✓ Single Connector Attachment (SCA)

✓ Network File System (NFS)

✓ Common Internet File System (CIFS)

✓ Internet SCSI (iSCSI)

✓ Fibre Channel Over IP (FCIP)

Techniques you'll need to master:

✓ Explaining the spelling, and describing the benefits of Fibre Channel

✓ Comparing Fibre Channel to traditional SCSI and Wide SCSI Low Voltage Differential (LVD)

✓ Defining a server backplane and identifying its features

✓ Explaining what a DAS solution is

✓ Implementing an external storage array

✓ Revealing how SAN and NAS networks are managed

✓ Specifying the required standards for FC hard drives

✓ Describing the composition of an optical fiber

✓ Identifying the most common fiber core diameters

✓ Differentiating between LC and SC Fibre Channel connectors

✓ Listing the advantages to using XFP transceivers

✓ Identifying the maximum recommended length of copper Fibre Channel cable connections

✓ Knowing how many devices FC-AL will support on a single network

✓ Contrasting an originator port with a responder port

✓ Describing how FCS achieves data flow control

✓ Contrasting single and dual arbitrated loops

✓ Describing the philosophy behind the use of a SAN

✓ Differentiating between a NAS device and a common file server

✓ Identifying why iSCSI is an important development

✓ Describing the FCIP network storage technology in terms of features and advantages

✓ Connecting an FCIP adapter to a SAN switch

Fibre Channel Hardware

Server+ Exam Objective 1.8 states that the test taker should know the features and benefits of Fibre Channel hardware, including

➤ Storage arrays

➤ Disk drives

➤ Adapters

➤ Cables, connectors, GBICs, SFP GBICs

➤ Single- and multimode

➤ 1Gbit, 2Gbit, 10Gbit

➤ Bus lengths

➤ Point-to-point vs. switched vs. LOOP

Fibre Channel

Fibre Channel is the general name assigned to an integrated set of standards developed by the American National Standards Institute (ANSI). As mentioned in Chapter 8, "RAID Systems," *Fibre Channel (FC)* is a high-performance interface designed to bring speed and flexibility to multiple-drive data storage and transfer systems. It combines the benefits of both channel and network technologies. An *interface* is the point at which independent or unrelated systems connect together and interact. Computer interfacing permits one hardware device to interact and/or communicate with another. For multiple-drive systems, the Fibre Channel interface speeds up these necessary communications.

 NOTE Because the Fibre Channel specification is suitable for operation over both copper and fiber-optic lines, the French spelling was selected to avoid the idea that the standard operates only over fiber-optic cable.

A *channel* is defined as a closed, direct, structured, and predictable mechanism for the transmission of data between a limited number of devices. After a channel is established, little decision making is required. The desired result is the establishment of a high-speed environment that basically depends on the hardware being used. Established channels connect disk drives, printers, tape drives, and other equipment to a server or a workstation computer.

Common channel protocols include the *Small Computer System Interface (SCSI)* and the *High Performance Parallel Interface (HIPPI)*.

However, computer networks are not structured this reliably and are more unpredictable. Although networks are adaptable to changing environments and can support a larger number of connected nodes, additional software is required to successfully route data from one point to another. This complexity makes common networks such as Ethernet, Token Ring, and *Fiber Distributed Data Interface (FDDI)* inherently slower than channels.

Fibre Channel is making a substantial impact in the storage arena, particularly when SCSI is being used.

Compared to traditional SCSI, the mapping of the SCSI command set onto the Fibre Channel provides such benefits as greater data transfer speed, increased device connectivity, and greater distances between devices.

Fibre Channel is currently used in large networks as a replacement for traditional SCSI, connecting hundreds of networked drive arrays for data storage purposes. When considering the basic storage and backup needs of servers, the idea of gaining access to greater numbers of mass storage devices, from greater distances, and at greater speeds is bound to attract the attention of network administrators. For example, Fibre Channel can help in disaster recovery situations because storage devices can be networked remotely, up to 2 kilometers away.

 Know which cable technology is used to connect hundreds of drive arrays.

Fibre Channel is ideal for the following applications:

➤ High-performance storage, workgroups, and tape/disk I/O

➤ Server clusters

➤ Network-based storage (SANs)

➤ Campus backbones

➤ Digital audio/video networks

Fibre Channel Storage Arrays

Fibre Channel drives are specifically designed for use in multiple-drive system environments, and usually find their way into servers. Configurations normally consist of an external enclosure, called a *backplane*, which houses a specialized printed circuit board (PCB), multiple drive receptacles, and a Fibre Channel *Host Bus Adapter (HBA)*.

The backplane allows direct connections to the drives without the use of cables. It supplies power to all the drives, and controls their data input and output. Fibre Channel's benefits come from effectively handling multidrive data, rather than single-drive environments. In single-drive environments, substituting Fibre Channel for Wide SCSI LVD derives no significant performance enhancement. However, when compared side by side for multiple-drive environments, Fibre Channel wins every time, as shown in Table 9.1.

Table 9.1 Fibre Channel Versus Wide SCSI LVD

Feature	SCSI Wide (LVD)	Fibre Channel
Bandwidth	40–80MBps	100MBps
Connectivity	15 devices	126 devices
Attachment	Ribbon cable, jumpers, power	SCA backplane: no jumpers, switches, or power connections
Distance	1.5 meters total length SE (single ended), 12 meters total length (LVD)	30 meters device to device (copper), 10 kilometers device to device (optical)
Redundancy	Parity and running disparity	CRC protected frames
Interface	Wide, Narrow, SCA, Fast, Ultra, Single-Ended, LVD, HVD	Single version

Fibre Channel's scalability and availability features allow administrators to implement *Direct Attached Storage (DAS)* solutions to servers for immediate capacity relief. DAS is the term used to describe a storage device or array that is directly attached to a host system. The simplest example of DAS is the internal hard drive of a server computer. Storage devices housed in an external case can also be considered as direct attached storage. Although more robust storage methods are gaining wide acceptance, DAS remains the most common method of storing data for computer systems.

Enterprise storage arrays become almost mind-boggling in their complexity and capability. Through the addition of Fibre Channel switches and host bus adapters, a system supporting up to 256 redundantly connected servers is possible.

There are three basic hardware models for Fibre Channel disk storage: just a bunch of disks (JBODs), external storage arrays, and storage networks.

Fibre Channel JBODs

With the exception of DAS, the least complex and cheapest storage array option is achieved through internal or external configurations in peripheral bays. Disks are attached to an I/O channel, usually a SCSI bus. The server OS then addresses and manages each disk separately in a storage model called *just a bunch of disks (JBODs)*. Although most JBODs usually consist of 8 to 10 drives, larger and smaller groupings are also used.

JBODs use a common backplane within an enclosure to which a number of Fibre Channel disks are attached. For redundancy, this backplane often provides dual-ported connectivity to the outside world. Internally, the disks are configured in an *arbitrated loop* setup, with each drive physically addressable from the outside. Arbitrated loops often include their own controllers for more advanced management of the drives and the enclosure. The volume manager permits the drives to be accessed as a single disk, rather than individually. By grouping them within a JBOD into a single volume, they are treated as a pool of storage units to be carved up or combined. Although the OS will permit the volume manager to implement software Redundant Array of Independent Disks (RAID) at levels 0 and 1, performance might not be much improved due to operation of the arbitrated loop. This is because media access to the drives on the loop is shared, limiting the possibility of writing to multiple drives simultaneously.

Fibre Channel RAID

The second storage model is composed of *external storage arrays*, which are managed internally and connect to the server through an I/O channel as a single unit. In fact, the server typically does not even address individual disks, or manage the placement of data on those disks. The usual arrangement makes use of a hardware controller to manage multiple levels of RAID within the array. Although the RAID controller can be implemented in software, the preferred method is the hardware installation within a RAID disk enclosure. Recall that the possibility of flooding a single drive with data is avoided, while throughput of the storage system is increased through the use of striping to spread the data over multiple disks.

RAID enclosures also feature redundant, hot-swappable power supplies, automated diagnostics, and redundant fans for high-reliability operations and a degree of data integrity where no server downtime is tolerated. The RAID controller simplifies network operation because the Storage Area Network (SAN) can address it as a single logical unit.

Fibre Channel Storage Networks

The third storage model permits the centralization of storage for multiple servers on a special type of network called either a Storage Area Network (SAN), or Network Attached Storage (NAS). Modular server units can connect to a larger network, forming a centralized storage complex accessible by the individual servers, yet managed from a central point. Storage arrays and serial interfaces, known as *Serial Storage Architecture (SSA)*, using Fibre Channel in particular, are the enabling technologies for this storage complex.

Fibre Channel Disk Drives

Fibre Channel is an integrated set of standards developed by the American National Standards Institute (ANSI). Obviously, hard drives designed for use under Fibre Channel standards must be equipped with high-performance interfacing to bring the necessary speed and flexibility to their intended multiple-drive server systems. Disk drives capable of meeting the required FC standards must provide

➤ *Hot-plug capability*—Fibre Channel hard drives can be installed or removed within operational host systems, where little or no downtime can be tolerated.

➤ *ANSI serial port interface compliance*—Fibre Channel hard drives do not require expensive or customized adapters.

➤ *Speed capability*—Fibre Channel is the fastest hard drive option available for its intended environment.

➤ *Cost-effectiveness*—Because it does not require proprietary adapters, Fibre Channel is inexpensive when compared to other high-end solutions.

➤ *Loop resiliency*—For multiple-drive systems, Fibre Channel provides high data integrity, including FC RAID.

➤ *Reliable operations over longer cable lengths*—Configuring multiple devices is simplified through the use of longer cable lengths when compared to LVD, maintaining data integrity.

Fibre Channel Adapters

Host bus adapters (HBAs) provide the necessary interfacing between the server's internal bus, such as PCI, and the external Fibre Channel network. HBA manufacturers bundle enough software drivers to configure the server with a number of operating systems, including Windows NT, Solaris, and Linux.

Although a majority of HBAs are equipped with single transmit and receive connectors, some include multiple connectors for redundancy. Redundancy is also achieved using multiple host bus adapter cards in a single server, with each tied to a different switch. If one HBA fails, the server will remain accessible.

Fibre Channel Cables, Connectors, GBICs, and SFP GBICs

Server networking now includes a large number of Fibre Channel products from many vendors. In addition to drives and adapters, Fibre Channel products also include cables, connectors, *gigabit interface converters (GBICs)*, *small form pluggable gigabit interface converters (SFP GBICs)*, switches, hubs, and various interfaces providing FC interconnections. Most of these products feature compatibility with 1Gbit transfer speeds, and many provide operations at the 2Gbit levels. Review the main types of equipment discussed in the following section, as well as how they are used.

Fibre Channel Cables

Only the highest quality cables can be used on either 1Gbit or 2Gbit Fibre Channel buses to ensure maximum error-free performance. These requirements limit acceptable specifications to those shown in Table 9.2.

Table 9.2 Fibre Channel Cable Specifications		
Cable	Insertion Loss	Return Loss
Single-mode	0.2dB max; 0.1dB typical	55dB at PC endface
Multimode	0.1dB typical	20dB

Although Fibre Channel can utilize copper cabling, similar to Ethernet, this limits Fibre Channel to a maximum recommended reach of 30 meters.

An optical fiber is composed of a core, cladding, and the surrounding protective coating. The core and the cladding are manufactured as a single piece of glass; however, each section has its own *index of refraction*. A mirrored surface around the core causes light entering the core to ricochet off the surface of the cladding and propagate down the fiber. The most important parameters to be concerned with when specifying a fiber cable type are

➤ Multimode—Multimode cables are the more commonly seen Fibre Channel cables. They are used for short distance connections spanning over few meters.

➤ Single-mode—Single-mode cables are used for longer-distance applications that span miles rather than meters.

➤ Duplex—Duplex cables allow for simultaneous, bidirectional data transfers, and they permit devices to simultaneously send and receive data.

➤ Simplex—Simplex cables consist of one fiber that allows only one-way data transfer. Most common fiber applications utilize multimode duplex cables.

➤ Core size—Fiber cable descriptions often include references such as 50/125, or 62.5/125. These parameters refer to the diameter sizes of the fiber's core and its cladding. The most common fiber core diameters are 62.5 microns and 50 microns. However, a 9-micron core diameter is planned for several future fiber technologies. The most common diameter for the cladding is still 125 microns.

Fibre Channel Connectors

Because Fibre Channel allows for a variety of cabling solutions, different types of connectors are required. Connections to Fibre Channel switches and hubs are often accomplished using Gigabit Interface Converters (GBICs). GBICs provide SC-type connectors for their interfacing chores. GBICs are the most common transceivers used for optical cabling, including multimode fiber for short distances, and single-mode fiber for distances of up to 10km. For copper, the DB9 connector is the most commonly used type.

SFF GBICs provide LC-type connectors for their interfacing chores. Fibre Channel connectors are typically interchangeable, for reconfiguring a switch or hub to a different type of connection if needed. The technical specifications for an FC adapter card, or device, will always specify the type of connector it supports. Therefore, the Fibre Channel cable used for interconnection should always be selected based on the connector type being used by the devices at either end of the line.

Fibre Channel Gigabit Interface Converters

Fibre Channel *Gigabit Interface Converters (GBICs)* are small, hot-swappable, pluggable interface modules. They provide physical layer (copper or fiber) signaling for data, voice, storage, and video transport networks, including generic, modular interfacing for the optical transceivers in Gigabit Ethernet devices. Optical transceivers connected to circuits from varying distances can be plugged directly into the same slot blade manually switching the card out.

Before GBICs, Gigabit Ethernet switch vendors provided a port blade with between four to eight ports of Gigabit service. All the ports were fitted with an identical optical interface, usually multimode. Connecting to a single-mode optic port required the use of a media converter or a separate card.

These options were expensive and wasted resources. With GBIC, clients were provided with a blade mechanism of GBIC slots, which permitted the selection of optical or copper-based parameters for each individual slot.

GBIC devices have recently been upgraded to *Small Form Pluggable Gigabit Interface Converters (SFP GBICs)*. SFP optical interfaces are less than half the size of their GBIC predecessors, and their use has been expanded to additional protocols and applications.

The 10Gigabit *Small Form Factor Pluggable (XFP)* optical transceiver modules combine transmitter and receiver functions in one compact, flexible, low-cost package. Their small size permits up to 16 XFP modules on a typical rack card. They are protocol-independent, and can be used to support OC-192/STM-64, 10Gigabit Ethernet, 10Gigabit Fibre Channel, and G.709 data streams in routers, switches, and network cards. The XFP transceiver format will become dominant for 10Gbps applications by 2007.

Fibre Channel Specifications

Various specifications used with Fibre Channel are designed specifically for this technology, although others are more widespread in their application. The specific optical fiber link determines whether single-mode or multimode fiber will be used. Transmission speeds are continually being upgraded towards the lofty goal of 10GFC and beyond. Bus lengths for both copper and fiber connections represent considerable improvements over previous technologies.

Single-Mode and Multimode Fiber

Multimode fiber (MMF) optic cabling is more commonly used than *single-mode fiber (SMF)* optic cabling. The main reason for this is that MMF is less expensive than SMF, making it much more attractive for use with short-distance applications. SMF cable is capable of supporting longer distances because it uses a smaller diameter modal dispersion technique that is more expensive to produce. Although SMF is sometimes used for relatively short-distance applications as well, it is primarily used for long-distance applications such as between buildings in campus or industrial environments, or between widely separated cities. In fact, the fiber-optic cabling utilized for long-range and ultra-long-range applications spanning oceans and continents is always SMF-based.

Alternatively, the fiber-optic cabling located inside a storage subsystem or stretching between servers, switches, and other devices is typically MMF. MMF fiber cabling operates over shorter distances, and does not require such rigid fabrication standards. Keep in mind that as server systems migrate to faster interfaces including 10Gbit Fibre Channel, and 10Gbit Ethernet, future investments may be best placed with SMF. This includes those systems where MMF used to be adequate for extended campus and data center distances. Another cost factor to consider regarding fiber for Fibre Channel, Ethernet, and other optics-based networks is the cost of their transceivers, such as GBICs, SFPs, and XFPs.

Fibre Channel Transmission Speeds

In June 2003, the Fibre Channel Industry Association (FCIA) and its sister association, the Fibre Channel Industry Association–Japan (FCIA-J) decided to extend the 4Gbit Fibre Channel (4GFC) from an intracabinet storage device interconnect into switched SAN fabrics. The result of this action was the creation of a cost-effective migration for 2GFC technology. In addition, the industry saw a 4Gbit high-speed interface complementary to 10GFC.

The 4GFC specification represented a cost-effective migration for 2GFC applications because 2GFC dominated the SAN infrastructure in 2003. Previous infrastructure investments were preserved during the migration to 4GFC, including complete backward compatibility and interoperability with 1GFC and 2GFC products, enclosures, and cables. Newer 4GFC products used Fibre Channel's "autonegotiation" feature to automatically sense the data rate capability of products they were connected to without user intervention. For example, when 2GFC products were attached, 4GFC products automatically ran at 2GFC speeds. The same compatibility existed for use with 1GFC equipment, and ensured a smooth, affordable migration to 4GFC products. In addition, the 4GFC specification complemented the currently referenced 10GFC on FCIA's Fibre Channel roadmap. With twice the bandwidth of 2GFC, 4GFC drove the need for 10GFC in the network core. Fabric networks running 4GFC were matched perfectly with storage enclosures already utilizing 4GFC disk drives.

Then, in August 2004, the FCIA and FCIA-J similarly announced the extension of the Fibre Channel roadmap to 8Gbit Fibre Channel (8GFC) for storage device interconnections to switched SAN fabrics. As expected, previous 2Gbit Fibre Channel (2GFC) and 4Gbit Fibre Channel (4GFC) infrastructure investments are protected for both electrical copper and optical interfaces. Table 9.3 illustrates the FCIA's speed roadmap for Fibre Channel.

Table 9.3   The Fibre Channel Speed Chart for Base2 and Base10

Base2*				
Product Naming	Throughput (MBps)	Line Rate (Gbaud)	T11 Spec Completed (Year)	Market Availability (Year)
1GFC	200	1.065	1996	1997
2GFC	400	2.125	2000	2001
4GFC	800	4.25	2003	2005
8GFC	1,600	8.5	2006	2008
16GFC	3200	17	2009	2011
32GFC	6400	34	2012	Market Demand
64GFC	12800	68	2016	Market Demand
128GFC	25600	136	2020	Market Demand
Base10**				
10GFC	2400	10.52	2003	2004

*Base2 used throughout all applications for *Gigabit Fibre Channel (GFC)* infrastructure and devices. Each speed maintains backward compatibility with at least two previous generations. For example, 4GFC remains backward compatible to 2GFC and 1GFC.

**Base10 is commonly used for *Inter Switch Link (ISL)*, core connections, and other high-speed applications demanding maximum bandwidth. All speeds are single-lane serial streams, and the future dates are estimated.

Fibre Channel Hardware Bus Lengths

Although the maximum copper cable length recommended between Fibre Channel devices is 30 meters, keep in mind that this is significantly longer than the maximum LVD cable length of 12 meters. As might be expected, any installation that exceeds the recommended maximum cable lengths can significantly impact data integrity. Although they are more expensive, fiber-optic cables permit Fibre Channel distances to stretch up to 10 kilometers (6 miles). The Fibre Channel Infrastructure Application Matrix shown in Table 9.4 lists various suggested bus lengths for specific Fibre Channel markets. Important considerations to achieve these distances include the various fiber-optic cables used to interconnect Fibre Channel adapters, switches, hubs, and other devices.

Table 9.4	The Fibre Channel Infrastructure Application Matrix	
Market	**Connection***	**Length**
Metro [Optical]	ISL >= 5km	
Multiple Buildings (campus) [Optical]	ISL	300m–5km
Single Building (Local) [Optical]	ISL	30m–5km
Datacenter or Rack [Optical]	ISL/SEL/BEL	0m–100m
Datacenter or Rack [Copper]	ISL/SEL/BEL	0m–15m
Backplane [Copper]	IDL	0.6m

*ISL = Inter Switch Link
SEL = SAN Edge Link
BEL = Back End Link
IDL = Inter Device Link

Fibre Channel Hardware Topologies

Fibre Channel uses three different hardware topologies: Point-To-Point (FC-P2P), Arbitrated Loop (FC-AL), and Fabric Switching (FC-SW).

Each of these topologies are accomplished through the use of Fibre Channel ports, connected as point-to-point links, in a loop, or through a switch. Various port connections are accomplished through both optical and electrical media, working from 133Mbps up to 2.124Gbps, across distances up to 10 kilometers.

To successfully interface with a Fibre Channel network, the connecting device must be equipped with a minimum of one available Fibre Channel port. The following port types are available:

➤ *Node (N) Port*—A port linked to either a single F port or N port using a switch on a point-to-point connection. N ports are implemented on all devices such as servers and storage units.

➤ *NodeLoop (NL) Port*—An N port that has additional capabilities allowing it to participate with an arbitrated loop.

➤ *Fabric (F) Port*—A port used for connecting N-ported nodes through a Fibre Channel switch.

➤ *FabricLoop (FL) Port*—A port located on a switch that allows the switch to engage in an arbitrated loop. This basically means that all devices on the loop are able to access all devices connected to that switch.

➤ *Expansion (E) Port*—A port used for connecting one switch to another. Its primary function is to connect with larger fabric switch configurations.

➤ *Generic (G) Port*—A port that is often located on a switch and is capable of functioning as an F port, E port, or an FL port, depending on which type of port it's connected to.

 Know what port types are used when configuring a Fibre Channel network.

Using two Fibre Channels, information can flow between them in both directions simultaneously. The mechanism for sharing information between two N Ports is called the *Exchange*. The initiating Fibre Channel port is called the *Originator*, and the answering port is called the *Responder*. The data is transmitted in *frames* up to 2148 bytes long. Each frame has a *header* and a *checksum*, and a set of related frames for one operation is called a *sequence*. The Fibre Channel Standard (FCS) uses a look-ahead, sliding-window scheme for flow control and guaranteed data delivery. FCS can transport multiple existing protocols, including IP and SCSI.

Point-To-Point Fibre Channel

In a point-to-point (FC-P2P) topology, only two devices are directly connected together. The Fibre Channel port manages a simple connection between itself and one other device or to a switching fabric. Because the Fibre Channel system relies on ports logging in with each other and the fabric, it is irrelevant whether the fabric is a point-to-point connection, a circuit switch, an active hub, or a loop. A simple *point-to-point* Fibre Channel topology connects two FC devices that communicate at full bandwidth.

Arbitrated Loop Fibre Channel

In an *arbitrated loop* (FC-AL) topology, up to 127 devices are supported on a single network, including the hub, without having to use a switch. However, each device must arbitrate to gain access to the loop. Although only two devices can communicate with each other at the same time, they must all share the available bandwidth. During loop communications, each node device repeats its data to the adjacent node. All activity is interrupted whenever a device is either added to, or removed from, the loop. An arbitrated loop with only two devices degenerates into a point-to-point topology.

Although the failure of only one device will cause a break in the loop, Fibre Channel hubs can keep the connected devices together. They implement the arbitrated loop as a physical star topology, which provides a cost-effective storage sharing solution for small to medium-sized SANs. Fibre Channel hubs are fitted with 6 to 32 ports and offer loop bypass circuitry to help navigate around failing units and unconnected ports. Their major drawback is that their connected devices must share the bandwidth. Fixed hub connectors offer low-cost solutions; however, GBICs offer more flexibility.

Managed hubs are more expensive but come fitted with additional hardware and capabilities. The medium-priced FC hubs provide temperature and port status diagnostics using external connections through serial or Ethernet operations, or by using proprietary applications software. Operational parameters such as port statistics and loop status are provided by more advanced managed hubs.

The server technician must also be aware of dual arbitrated loops. *Dual looping* permits Fibre Channel drives to be simultaneously connected to two separate server environments, although only one loop can access the drive at any given moment.

The most significant dual loop advantage is the improved performance gained by the data sharing. Data can be stored in a central location, and accessed by both looped systems, eliminating the need for duplicate or synchronized data. Fibre Channel drives can simultaneously connect to two independent loops, with each loop transferring data up to 100Mbps! Such a dual-looped system could theoretically transfer data up to 200Mbps. On the other hand, a controller in a traditional Fibre Channel system can access only one loop at a time, in which case the maximum transfer rate remains at 100Mbps. Maximum transfer rates increase significantly for Fibre Channel RAID systems, depending on the number of drives available. The greater the number of available drives, the faster the data transfer rate will be.

Fibre Channel drives use a *Single Connector Attachment (SCA)* that combines the data signals and power supply lines, making it possible for up to 126 Fibre Channel drives to simultaneously connect to a single loop. A dual-loop system can have 126 drives connected to each loop, for a maximum of 252 drives. Shared drives subtract from the maximum number.

Switched Hubs

Switched hubs are the most advanced type of Fibre Channel hubs, providing for high-performance bandwidths. They offer several fabric-style features, while maintaining a lower cost per port. However, they do not implement arbitrated loops or possess the operational capabilities necessary for providing connections to scalable fabrics. Therefore, switched hubs are not as popular as fabric-aware switches, and are finding less relevance in the Fibre Channel market. Yet, for small, private networks running high transfer levels, switched hubs can still offer a viable solution.

Switched Fabric Fibre Channel

The fabric switching (FC-SW) topology uses a switch to interconnect its devices. A configuration of switches and devices is referred to as the *fabric*, and the most flexible Fibre Channel topology is the *switched fabric*. In this arrangement, all devices are connected to Fibre Channel switches in an arrangement similar to Ethernet. All servers and storage devices are permitted to communicate with each other. If a server or disk array ceases to operate properly, failover architecture permits continued operation of the fabric. The switches manage the state of the fabric, providing optimized interconnections and security.

This flexibility promotes the implementation of Storage Area Networks (SANs). Switches can directly route data from one port to another on the same server, or redirect traffic to other paths within the switch. Robust switches implement a fully connected backbone between all connected ports, whereas less expensive models offer lesser connectivity. Although port counts range from 8 to 16 on standard switches, the port counts on enterprise-level director switches vary from 32 to 64. Cascading switches through these ports create large fabrics, ensuring relatively painless expansion as storage requirements grow. Switches provide multiple interconnecting links to load balance server traffic and avoid network congestion.

Similar to hubs, switches are usually equipped with advanced management features, including port statistics, switch diagnostics, and port-zoning parameters. Port zoning permits the assigning of a device or switch port to a specified group of ports, so that only ports or devices in the specified group gain access to each other. Management software refines the zoning levels using either addresses or names as the group identifier rather than a specified port. When devices and switches on a SAN belong to different parts of an organization, zoning becomes very useful, especially for data and devices that are not intended for sharing. Zoning is also helpful in SANs connecting networks running different OSs where devices that share the same OS can be zoned into groups.

The main drawback to switches compared to hubs is the cost per port. However, because switches can be easily interconnected, it is possible to start with a low port-count switch, and add more switches to the fabric as needed.

Fibre Channel Bridges

If a SAN is composed of many competing network technologies, including Fibre Channel, another standard component likely to be running is a Fibre Channel *bridge*. An FC bridge permits devices from other network technologies to coexist with Fibre Channel devices on the SAN.

For example, because only a limited number of Fibre Channel tape drives are currently marketed, *serverless backup* is one of the most important applications enabled by SANs. In this scenario, CPU cycles normally burned during network backups are offloaded to intelligent SAN components such as SCSI/Fibre Channel bridge units. On a SAN using serverless backup, a specified physical disk can self-initiate a backup, during which time it makes itself unavailable to other SAN devices. Any modifications made to its files must be temporarily recorded elsewhere until the backup is complete. Although this takes place alongside regular user activities, the high bandwidths of typical SAN networks shorten the time required to run the backup and then merge changes made to the disk during its backup activity.

Other serverless tasks that can be performed on data besides backup include the ability of storage devices to transfer their own data without having to wait for a server to initiate migration. Archival storage can be initiated by a RAID system across Fibre Channel bridges to relocate seldom-used files or data. When the tape library controller detects specified data being heavily used, the data is moved to faster storage without interrupting administrators, servers, or clients.

The SAN no longer depends on servers to perform housekeeping tasks. Instead, servers are free to concentrate on SAN storage resource access points for clients and administrators.

To permit these backup operations to be conducted across Fibre Channel servers, FC-to-SCSI bridges are commonly employed. They allow the use of legacy SCSI tape drives, as well as other devices, to participate in the Fibre Channel framework. Other types of FC bridges are used as well, including FC-to-ATM and FC-to-Ethernet units.

SAN and NAS Specifications

Server+ Exam Objective 1.15 states that the test taker should know the basic specifications of, and the differences between, SAN and NAS, including block and file.

Storage Area Network (SAN)

A *Storage Area Network (SAN)* is a high-speed subnetwork of shared storage devices, often nothing more complicated than a system unit containing a disk drive, or a number of disk drives, for storing data. The SAN is connected through a server, or a cluster of servers, acting as access points for the clients. SAN architecture makes all included storage devices available to all servers, either on a limited LAN or on a WAN. As more storage devices are added, they are also accessible from any server throughout the larger network. The servers merely complete the pathways between clients and the stored data, which does not reside directly on any of the network servers. Server power is utilized strictly for business applications, and the full capacity of the network is available for client use.

A SAN is equipped with special switch mechanisms used for making various connections only between SAN devices. These switches make it possible for SAN devices to communicate with each other on a separate network, providing the ability to back up all network data outside of standard network infrastructure. This advantage is one reason why SANs currently account for more than 75% of all network storage.

Although a SAN is strictly a storage arrangement, it can also be configured as part of a much wider network in either Fibre Channel or iSCSI (discussed in the section "iSCSI and FCIP Features and Benefits") arrangements. Block data transfers over a SAN enjoy inherent performance advantages, and many commercial enterprises use SAN-attached disks for their mass storage requirements. Gigabit transport of data blocks over a SAN enhances throughput and enables Network Attached Storage (NAS) processors to more quickly retrieve raw data for file assembly/disassembly. High-performance applications such as streaming high-definition video are better supported by the block transfer characteristic of Fibre Channel SANs.

Network Attached Storage (NAS)

NAS is a data storage strategy utilizing specialized hardware devices that connect directly to the network media and are assigned their own IP addresses. They are accessible by clients through a server acting as a gateway to the data. In some cases, direct access to various storage devices is permitted without the need to go through the gateway. The main attraction of NAS is its networking environment, composed of multiple servers running different operating systems. This centralizes data storage, data security, management, and backup operations. Commercial networks utilize NAS technology to run large CD-ROM towers (standalone computer chassis containing multiple CD-ROM drives) directly connected to the network.

Another NAS advantage is its simplicity of expansion. Additional storage space is achieved by simply adding another NAS device. An additional level of fault tolerance is presented by a NAS storage strategy. Recall that in a DAS environment, the failure of a server ends the availability of its data. With NAS, the required data will still be available and accessible by clients throughout the network. Fault-tolerant measures (such as RAID) can be used to ensure that a NAS device does not become a point of failure. From a purely technical standpoint, a NAS device is not data storage attached to a network at all! The SCSI block I/O characteristics of its storage devices occur between the NAS processor and its attached storage arrays, not between the storage disks and the client's network. The network-attached portion of a NAS device is actually network-attached "file serving." When the NAS processor receives a file request, it must query the file system's metadata for that file, identify the data blocks on disk composing the file, sequentially reassemble the appropriate data blocks, and format the file content in TCP/IP for transmission onto the network. The "heavy lifting" of writing and reading blocks of data to disk, therefore, occurs behind the scenes within the specialized hardware, rather than on the network.

The difference between the NAS device and a common file server is that the server OS has been stripped of unrelated functions and optimized for sending and receiving files. These transfers occur through the use of IP protocols such as Network File System (NFS) or Common Internet File System (CIFS). The server OS can be a streamlined version of Unix or a streamlined version of Windows according to Microsoft's NAS initiative. In either case, the NAS processor serves files onto the network for clients, similar to traditional file servers, while back-ending its block SCSI I/O transfers.

NAS is better suited to provide cross-platform support for Windows, Solaris, Unix, and other operating systems because it uses common file-system protocols, such as NFS and CIFS. This capability permits an engineering department to share files between both Windows and Unix-based workstations having both NFS and CIFS client software loaded on each workstation.

iSCSI and FCIP Features and Benefits

Server+ Exam Objective 1.9 states that the test taker should know the features and benefits of iSCSI and FCIP, including storage arrays, adapters, cables and connectors, transfer speeds, and bus lengths.

Internet SCSI

Another example of successful network storage is *Internet SCSI (iSCSI)*. iSCSI is an IP-based technology that permits data to be transported, carrying SCSI commands, to and from storage devices over an IP network. Starting with a SCSI connection, the data is serialized and transported to a machine connected to the Internet. iSCSI supports a Gigabit Ethernet interface at the physical layer, which allows systems supporting iSCSI interfaces to connect directly to standard Gigabit Ethernet switches and/or IP routers. When requested, the OS generates the appropriate SCSI command followed by an IP packet over an Ethernet connection. On reception, the SCSI command is separated from the request, and both are sent to the SCSI controller. After reception by the SCSI storage device, iSCSI also returns a response to the requesting end using the same protocol.

iSCSI is an important development for SAN technology because it enables SAN deployment in either a LAN, WAN, or MAN.

 iSCSI was developed by the Internet Engineering Task Force (IETF) and became an official standard in February 2003.

As a block storage protocol, similar to Fibre Channel, iSCSI encapsulates SCSI commands within TCP/IP framing, whereas Fibre Channel encapsulates SCSI commands, status info, and data in Fibre Channel framing. In a pristine iSCSI environment, both hosts and storage targets have Ethernet or Gigabit Ethernet interfaces, and the IP network serves as the SAN infrastructure. Although modern iSCSI device drivers and network adapters provide host connectivity, mainstream SAN storage targets are connected to the Fibre Channel. To bring iSCSI hosts to Fibre Channel targets, a high-performance protocol gateway storage switch is required.

Similarities also exist between iSCSI and NAS in that both use TCP/IP as a transport protocol and Ethernet for their LAN infrastructure. Although it might appear that NAS and iSCSI are simply two ways of performing the same task, in reality, NAS and iSCSI each perform unique tasks. The decision to use a NAS solution for file access or an iSCSI solution for direct data block access depends entirely on the network's specific application requirements.

Similar to the Fibre Channel before it, iSCSI offers another means to access network storage. Unlike the situation with Fibre Channel, however, iSCSI and NAS operate over the same network types and appear to be competitors for the same storage market. Most vendors however, simply provide both NAS and iSCSI as customer options, without addressing the basic question as to when to use NAS and when to use SAN.

Database systems expect direct access to block storage, and are therefore not easily supported using NAS. For example, an SQL server directly reads and writes database records using the SCSI protocol, accessing its storage using DAS, Fibre Channel, or iSCSI. Other applications simply access files through volume managers, also directly accessing the storage through DAS or from an IP SAN. If necessary, file retrieval can be accomplished using a NAS processor. In addition, the moderate performance and capacity requirements of print serving can be supported using NAS. The question of whether to use file (NAS) or block (iSCSI) access for various applications is largely a matter of convenience.

Storage Arrays for iSCSI

High-density iSCSI storage arrays are cost-effective, shared-storage solutions designed for small businesses and/or remote offices. They are configurable for Ethernet-based SANs using existing software and/or high-performance hardware initiators. They provide flexible point-to-point configurations, including

➤ High availability

➤ Enhanced data protection

➤ Automated storage provisioning

➤ Dynamic volume expansion

➤ Snapshot scheduling

➤ Synchronous volume mirroring

➤ Management software

Adapters for iSCSI

Although iSCSI-based SANs provide benefits similar to Fibre Channel SANs, they also use the more familiar TCP/IP protocol. Their ability to seamlessly integrate with WANs has led to the wholesale adoption of iSCSI devices for the construction of remote storage applications.

iSCSI adapters are designed to implement the complete protocol stack, while simultaneously offloading all I/0 TCP/IP protocol processing from the host system. Ethernet, TCP/IP, and iSCSI protocols are all contained on a single chip, eliminating the processing load and reducing CPU interruptions. These protocols place significant burdens on the host system, especially at 1Gbit speeds. Without this offloading, the bandwidth available to other applications running on the host is seriously reduced.

iSCSI Cables and Connectors

One of the most powerful benefits of iSCSI is its cabling simplicity. There are virtually no new connectors or cable types to learn about when getting around to connecting the servers and switches. CAT5e or CAT6 cabling is used, and the connectors are the familiar RJ-45s that have been used for net-working purposes for years!

iSCSI Transfer Speeds

Because iSCSI operates across existing Ethernet networks, it must contend with higher latencies than Fibre Channel. When hundreds of files must be accessed simultaneously, latency becomes a major problem. For this reason, iSCSI is currently considered strictly as a mid-level solution. However, they are suitable for mid-sized businesses that do not require such high-speed access. When Fibre Channel was attaining speeds of up to 2Gbps, iSCSI systems were maxing out at about 1Gbps. However, as Fibre Channel speeds moved up to 4Gbps, improvements were also being made to Ethernet-based iSCSI. Industry experts see no reason why iSCSI won't soon be touching 10Gbps!

iSCSI latency revolves around TCP/IP demands for a significant portion of the host processor's resources. By offloading protocol stack processing tasks to other devices, or layers, significant throughput can be gained. One approach is processing TCP/IP and SCSI protocol stacks in the physical layer using host bus adapters and/or network interface cards. Data processing is significantly accelerated when the command stack operates above iSCSI.

iSCSI is an Ethernet-based storage solution, so bus lengths generally match those projected for Ethernet distances.

Fibre Channel Over IP

Fibre Channel Over IP (FCIP) is a network storage technology that combines the features of Fibre Channel and the Internet Protocol (IP) to connect distributed SANs over large distances. FCIP encapsulates Fibre Channel data and transports it over a TCP socket. FCIP is considered a tunneling protocol, because it completes transparent point-to-point connections between geographically separated SANs over IP networks. It depends on TCP/IP services to establish connectivity between remote SANs across LANs, MANs, or WANs. Responsibilities for congestion control, circuit management, error detection, and data recovery are all borne by TCP/IP. FCIP keeps Fibre Channel fabric services intact while using TCP/IP as the transport mechanism.

Storage Arrays for FCIP

Although FCIP is not envisioned as a storage array format in and of itself, it does provide a tunneling mechanism for Fibre Channel connectivity over IP-based networks. Various Fibre Channel SANs can be interconnected with TCP/IP used as the underlying transport. Benefits include both congestion control and the delivery of data in a FIFO sequence. The switching and routing chores are handled by standard Fibre Channel fabric services.

Adapters for FCIP

Data center consolidation is driving the demand for the deployment of business applications such as disk mirroring and remote tape backup over geographically dispersed sites. FCIP port adapter interfaces deliver connectivity between these data centers using SANs over a WAN infrastructure. Transfer speeds between fractional T1 to OC3 (155Mbps) are common.

Replicating data resources involves a variety of applications including disk mirroring, system snapshots, or remote tape backups. FCIP interface adapters permit SAN administrators to extend such mission-critical storage backup services over a WAN or MAN.

FCIP Cables and Connectors

Appropriate fiber-optic cables suitable for the connection of FCIP adapters, must be fitted with an appropriate LC connector, and plugged into a small form-factor pluggable (SFP) interface. If the SAN switch being used is fitted with an SFP module, an LC-to-LC fiber-optic cable is recommended. An LC-to-SC fiber-optic cable is recommended if the SAN switch is using a GBIC module. Table 9.5 provides sample FCIP cabling specifications for multimode operations at 850 nanometers (nm).

Table 9.5 Sample FCIP Port Cabling Specifications				
Wave-length (nm)	Fiber Type	Core Size (micron)	Modal Bandwidth (MHz/km)	Maximum Cable Distance
850	MMF	62.5	160	722 ft (220 m)
		62.5	200	902 ft (275 m)
		50.0	400	1640 ft (500 m)
		50.0	500	1804 ft (550 m)

FCIP Transfer Speeds

Using TCP/IP to extend the Fibre Channel by way of a tunnel established between two nodes in a TCP/IP network offers the longest possible reach in

SAN-to-SAN connections, up to thousands of kilometers. As explained earlier, the Fibre Channel frames are encapsulated into IP frames and transported through the tunnel. Although the FCIP scheme will soon become increasingly compelling as its performance improves in the near future, a breakthrough to 10Gbit technologies from the current 4Gbit standard would undoubtedly speed the process. With vendors issuing hybrid products, single devices are currently supporting multiple transport standards, such as FCIP and iSCSI.

FCIP Bus Lengths

FCIP cannot be thought of in terms of a rigid data bus delivery system. It's a tunneling protocol that connects geographically distributed Fibre Channel SANs transparently over LANs, MANs, and WANs. Control and management of FCIP's data congestion, error recovery, and data loss are conducted by TCP. Although TCP/IP handles FCIP transportation chores, it also maintains Fibre Channel services. Fiber connections running from FCIP-capable routers to the Fibre Channel switches are limited in length only by whatever wavelengths or fiber types are selected for the system operations.

Exam Prep Questions

1. Which data technology would best support an array composed of six servers handling 300 hard drives?
   - ❏ A. IEEE 1394
   - ❏ B. Fibre Channel
   - ❏ C. Ultra ATA-3
   - ❏ D. Ultra320 SCSI-3

2. In order to connect hundreds of drive arrays to a data storage network, which of the following technologies is best suited?
   - ❏ A. Ethernet
   - ❏ B. HIPPI
   - ❏ C. Fibre Channel
   - ❏ D. SCSI

3. Using a switch on a point-to-point connection, which Fibre Channel port should be used to link to either a single F port or N port?
   - ❏ A. An SS port
   - ❏ B. An FL port
   - ❏ C. An E port
   - ❏ D. An N port

4. What is the major difference between NAS and SAN server architectures?
   - ❏ A. Their data addressing schemes
   - ❏ B. The speeds of their systems
   - ❏ C. The cost of their systems
   - ❏ D. Their drive identification schemes

5. How can the same host bus adapter be used to run multiple operating systems?
   - ❏ A. By reformatting the server's hard drive with a different OS
   - ❏ B. By removing an HBA from one server and installing it in another
   - ❏ C. By networking the host bus adapter to a server running a different OS
   - ❏ D. By configuring a server for multiple OSs using the HBA manufacturer's drivers

6. A dual-looped Fibre Channel drive system is theoretically capable of transferring data at a rate of _____.
   - ❏ A. 1200MBps
   - ❏ B. 800Mbps
   - ❏ C. 400Mbps
   - ❏ D. 200MBps

7. Why should multiple connectors be placed on a host bus adapter?

❑ A. For the purpose of redundancy

❑ B. To connect peripheral equipment directly

❑ C. For simultaneously sending identical print jobs to multiple printers

❑ D. For use as replacement connectors

8. When multiple server HBAs are used, each tied through a different switch, what is gained?

❑ A. If one HBA fails, the network administrator will be notified immediately.

❑ B. If one server fails, an HBA will remain accessible.

❑ C. If one HBA fails, server accessibility is maintained.

❑ D. Multiple HBAs help to achieve low availability.

Exam Prep Answers

1. Answer B is the correct answer. Arrays composed of many hundreds of drives are possible through the use of the external Fibre Channel bus, at data speeds of up to 2Gbps using fiber optic cable. Answer A is incorrect because the maximum data transfer rate of Firewire (IEEE 1394) is only 400Mbps. Answer C is incorrect because Ultra ATA-3 is suitable only for midrange server storage tasks. Answer D is incorrect because the proposed problem is too large even for Ultra320 SCSI-3 technology.

2. Answer C is the correct answer. Fibre Channel technology has the advantage of having access to the greatest numbers of mass storage devices, at longer distances, and at faster speeds than the more traditional data transport systems. Answer A is incorrect because Ethernet has both distance and device limitations for the task described. Answer B is incorrect because HIPPI is mainly concerned with high-speed connections at short distances. Answer D is incorrect because compared with Fibre Channel, SCSI systems are limited in bandwidth and geographical connectivity.

3. Answer D is the correct answer. When using a switch on a point-to-point connection, use an N port to link to either a single F port, or another N port.. Answer A is incorrect because Fibre Channel technology does not incorporate an SS port type. Answer B is incorrect because switches that engage in arbitrated loops are equipped with FL ports. Answer C is incorrect because E ports are used primarily for interconnecting switches.

4. Answer A is the correct answer. NAS hardware devices are accessible on the Internet through a gateway server by clients who have been assigned their own IP addresses. Although the SAN architecture makes all network storage devices available to all servers, the data itself is not contained directly on any networked servers. Answer B is incorrect because neither data delivery system holds a speed advantage over the other. Answer C is incorrect although SAN is somewhat more expensive than NAS implementations. Answer D is incorrect because drive identification schemes are not used by either NAS or SAN systems to locate the required data.

5. Answer D is the correct answer. The server can be configured with a number of operating systems because the major HBA manufacturers bundle a number of software drivers with their products. Answers A and B are incorrect because too much work would be involved to justify the outcome. Answer C is incorrect because only the operating system installed on its own server can be used by a host bus adapter.

6. Answer D is the correct answer. Fibre Channel loops can transfer data at speeds of 100MBps. When FC drives are connected to two independent loops simultaneously, the dual-looped system could theoretically transfer data up to 200MBps. Answer A is incorrect due to the physical impossibility of transferring the data to or from the drives that quickly. Answers B and C are incorrect because their rates are listed in Mbps, which are too slow for Fibre Channel operations.

7. Answer A is the correct answer. For redundancy purposes, multiple HBA connectors provide alternate access paths to the same server. Answers B and C are incorrect because peripheral devices do not connect to HBAs. Answer D is incorrect because HBA connectors are not removable and are not cannibalized.

8. Answer C is the correct answer. Redundancy is achieved through the use of multiple host bus adapter cards in a single server. If one HBA fails, another takes its place through a different switch to provide continued server accessibility. Answer A is incorrect because an HBA is not used to provide notification to the network administrator. Answer B is incorrect because the accessibility of the HBA is irrelevant for a failed server. Answer D is incorrect because no administrator considers low availability as an "achievement."

10.0—Pre-Installation Planning

Terms you'll need to understand:

✓ Compatibility
✓ Windows catalog
✓ Robust
✓ Upgrades
✓ Validated
✓ Controllers
✓ Surges, spikes, and sags
✓ Continuity
✓ Amperage and supply voltage
✓ Surge protector
✓ Load ratings and power rating
✓ Power fluctuations
✓ Electromagnetic interference (EMI)
✓ Blackout or Brownout
✓ Switching transient
✓ Harmonic distortion
✓ Uninterruptible Power Supply (UPS)
✓ Standby or Online UPS
✓ Application Service Providers (ASPs)
✓ Internet Service Providers (ISPs)
✓ British Thermal Unit (BTU)

✓ Backup generator

✓ Protocol

✓ Domain

✓ Shielded Twisted Pair (STP)

✓ Unshielded Twisted Pair (UTP)

✓ Patch cables and crossover cables

✓ Ethernet

✓ Backbones

✓ UTP-to-Fiber converters

✓ SC, FDDI, ST, and MT-RJ connectors

Techniques you'll need to master:

✓ Verifying the installation plan

✓ Establishing compatibility between hardware components, RAM, and the NOS

✓ Securing and installing driver and BIOS updates

✓ Knowing how to take down a server

✓ Using only validated drivers

✓ Recognizing blackouts, brownouts, sags, surges, and spikes

✓ Checking ground connections for continuity

✓ Verifying server AC current ratings

✓ Monitoring server supply voltages

✓ Installing various surge protectors

✓ Knowing equipment load ratings

✓ Preventing server power fluctuations and blocking EMI

✓ Examining the quality of commercial electrical power

✓ Using uninterruptible power supplies

✓ Understanding how to use BTUs

✓ Explaining how UPS systems work with backup generators

✓ Identifying the L2TP and IPSec protocols

✓ Knowing the domain naming conventions

✓ Differentiating between server cables

✓ Listing the advantages of fiber over copper cabling

✓ Recognizing SC, ST, FDDI, and MT-RJ fiber connectors

✓ Moving a large server rack

✓ Naming the three major types of servers

Introduction

Server+ Exam Objective 2.1 states that the test taker should be able to conduct pre-installation planning activities. These activities include

➤ Planning the installation

➤ Verifying the installation plan

➤ Verifying hardware compatibility with the operating system

➤ Verifying power sources, space, UPS, and network availability

➤ Verifying network protocols, naming conventions, and domain names

➤ Verifying that all correct components and cables have been delivered

Supporting knowledge for this objective includes

➤ How to get drivers and BIOS updates

➤ Cables and connectors required

➤ UPS sizes and types

➤ Server power requirements

➤ Power issues (stability, spikes, and so on)

➤ BTUs for the UPS and associated equipment

➤ Server storage issues (rack requirements, rack sizes)

➤ Uses of the common server types (desk server, rack mount server, vs. blade server) and the pros and cons of each

Installation Planning

Careful planning is needed to have a successful server installation or upgrade. Depending on the size and complexity of the server(s) needed, planning the installation can take days or even months to complete. Before implementing any work, a detailed plan of the installation should come first, regardless of size and complexity. This eliminates the amount of time spent correcting oversights and fixing compatibility errors. In the following paragraphs we discuss the most common objectives for planning a server installation.

Securing the Plan's Verification

After completing the installation plan, verify it with the project manager and the customer. This ensures that the job is being planned correctly and that the client is getting a network that performs the required tasks. If any last-minute changes in the planning are required during the review, adjustments can be made before any money is actually spent.

Hardware and OS Compatibility

Before installing or upgrading the OS, it's important for the server technician to verify that *compatibility* exists between all initial hardware and any associated add-on components planned for the network. One of the best ways to ensure compatibility is to check the OS manufacturer's Hardware Compatibility List (HCL). The HCL is basically a list of hardware that has been tested and verified to work with the manufacturer's OS. Checking the HCL is an important consideration when purchasing server hardware.

Although Microsoft used to rely heavily on a hardware compatibility list to identify which equipment was known to be compatible with their operating systems, this reference is now called the "Windows Catalog." For more information about using the Windows Catalog, go to http://www.microsoft.com/whdc/hcl/default.mspx.

 Know where to find the list of compatible hardware for a specified operating system.

After compatibility, the minimum system requirements must also be met. No OS will function to its full capabilities without hardware capable of using it. Although it's always possible to squeak a robust OS onto a system with less than minimum hardware requirements, the performance will suffer.

Windows 2000 Server or Advanced Server OS software requires at least 256MB of RAM. OS software is usually built for tomorrow's hardware, rather than the models currently available. A successful server network is equipped with workstations or servers using processors that operate at speeds of 500MHz or better. In addition, the server boards should be loaded with as much high-speed RAM as the budget permits. Whatever type of RAM is purchased must be compatible with the server board. Incompatible RAM will in all likelihood prevent the system from booting properly.

 Know that the first thing to do when server components arrive is to verify that all parts are accounted for and that they are the correct types.

After you order the server components and they arrive, the first thing to do is examine all of the components carefully. Ensure that everything is exactly as ordered. Regardless of whether the server will be running a Microsoft, Linux, or Unix OS, go to the manufacturer's website for the latest hardware compatibility information. Do not trust substitutes that might or might not work properly, even if it appears likely that an erroneous substitute will probably work fine.

Know that for a Linux server you must go to the manufacturer's website for the latest hardware compatibility information.

Driver and BIOS Updates

Following the verification of component delivery, the latest validated drivers and BIOS updates should be obtained before preparing the chassis and the server board for assembly. BIOS updates are usually bundled with a proprietary installer program.

The term *validated* means that the drivers in question have been successfully tested on their specified hardware types. Most software companies include disclaimers in their product documentation regarding any problems encountered when using non-validated drivers, including no support provided.

Know that after component delivery has been verified, the latest validated drivers can be obtained for components making up the server assembly.

An important aspect of using the manufacturer's hardware documentation is the need for immediate recognition of when *driver updates* are available. A quick check of the documentation will reveal whether the available driver updates are newer than the drivers originally included with the hardware. Of course, downloading driver and BIOS updates must be accomplished by first connecting to the manufacturer's website and checking for the most recent versions. One important caution in this regard concerns beta drivers. UNDER NO CIRCUMSTANCES should a beta driver be downloaded for use with server components! Instead, download the latest confirmed gold driver.

Know what to implement first when installing multiple devices on a server.

However, drivers can be secured on a machine not directly connected to the network being actively configured. Whatever the situation is, be sure to download any new driver and/or BIOS updates before the installation is begun. At the very least, gather the latest drivers for any Small Computer System Interface (SCSI), video, network, and modem cards going into the system. After these devices are running properly, download any other necessary drivers. During an installation, the technician should always use the latest drivers for the system's devices.

Know how to locate and obtain the latest drivers when installing a server.

Even on a server system that has been operating successfully for some time, periodic updates and servicing are still required. Serious servicing might even require that the server be taken down for short periods. When this situation develops, the server technician must be certain that enough service personnel are available to handle the necessary tasks. Additional time should be allocated for unexpected situations, as well. These activities should never be planned for periods of peak network server usage.

Know that the first step when taking down the server is to ensure sufficient personnel are available to implement the required upgrade or repairs.

Hard Drives and Controllers

Hard drive controllers must be properly matched to the types of drives they support. A SCSI host adapter or the IDE/ATA controller normally interfaces between the system and the hard disk drives. ATA controllers are designed to work with IDE drives and SCSI controllers are designed to work with SCSI drives. They do not mix! Although high-volume servers typically use SCSI drives, they obviously require SCSI controllers in order to function properly.

Know what components to use when building a high-capacity server.

Power Source, Space, UPS, and Network Availability Verifications

All digital devices are susceptible to variations in power supply voltage. In fact, power variations are the source of many server problems, causing computers to shut down and reboot, and resulting in a loss of the data not saved to disk. More severe power problems can make computer components fail and completely disrupt the operation of the network.

When the power supply drops below normal levels, sags and brownouts occur. Sags are short periods of time when the supply voltage is low. Brownouts occur over longer periods of time (several seconds or longer). Overvoltage conditions are known as surges and spikes. A *spike* is a very high voltage level—usually twice the normal voltage—that is supplied for an instant (usually in the millisecond range), and can be deadly for servers. A *surge* is a voltage increase (10 or 20 volts above normal) that occurs over a longer period of time, such as for one or two seconds, and capable of damaging a chip.

These types of power supply variations frequently occur. It is important to understand that the commercial power supply system does not always deliver a clean voltage supply to the server facility.

There are small surges, spikes, and sags in the supply all the time. Fortunately, most of these variations occur in thousandths of a second, and commercial server installations simply ignore them. Of greater concern are the abnormal variations that occur over a longer time frame, or that are very large in scale.

Server Power Requirements

Server installations require dependable power sources to function properly and continually. Determining how much power will be required for a specific installation involves consultations with an electrician. The maximum *load rating* for every piece of hardware has to be taken into account. A typical rating of at least 45 to 60 watts per square foot of power consumption should be expected. However, a densely packed server room can require 80 to 100 watts or more per square foot, considering overhead lighting, UPS equipment, rack-mounted fans, and air-conditioning units.

The required number and placement of power outlets must also be planned. To allow for flexibility in moving server racks, floor-mounted outlets should be attached to flexible cabling rather than fixed plates. Be sure to evenly distribute the server's electrical load across all circuits for both current operations as well as future requirements. Isolating the cooling and ventilation circuits helps to prevent server *power fluctuations*. Because *electromagnetic interference (EMI)* must not reach the network cables and equipment, flexible steel conduit encased in a copper shield should be used for all power cable installation.

The power redundancy capabilities of the server room are mostly determined by the uptime requirements of the overall installation. Mission-critical data center systems running domain controllers, DNS servers, and web servers require backup generators and UPS units. Decisions about which servers or circuits will be connected to generator power, and which will be tied to uninterruptible power supplies must be made. The quality of commercial electrical power coming into the building must be examined and compared with the *American National Standards Institute (ANSI)* specifications. Additional power-conditioning devices may have to be installed.

Server room power testing and monitoring occurs before any computer equipment is installed to determine its stability under no load conditions. In the United States the AC voltage level should be 120 volts, while systems modeled after European designs should indicate an AC voltage level of 230 volts. Power system ground connections should also be checked for *continuity* back to the facility's main ground connection.

The AC current (*amperage*) ratings of all server room circuits should be verified to ensure their capability of delivering the power required to run the servers, printers, monitors, and peripheral equipment that will be installed. The facilities manager or an electrician can provide verification of this by reviewing amperage ratings of the breakers for branches supplying the server room. It may be necessary to distribute specific pieces of equipment across several available circuits.

When problems occur, it must be possible to examine the *supply voltage* data for the specified times of failure to rule it out as a cause. This makes the ability to monitor the level of commercial power supplied to the server room an important tool. The incoming line voltage must be logged so that it can be checked over a period of time, even when personnel are not present.

Know which power-related ratings should be checked in the server room before any equipment is installed.

Power Spikes and Instability

Modern server networks operate 24/7! Definitive steps must be taken to protect these data systems, networks, and the data itself, from vulnerability to power disruptions that can seriously cripple them. These disruptions can take the form of

➤ *Power failure (blackout)*—A blackout is a complete loss of utility power, which can be caused by grid over-demand, lightning strikes, downed or iced power lines, natural disasters, or accidents. These power failures trigger hard drive crashes and loss of active data.

➤ *Power spikes and surges*—Spikes and surges, also called impulses, are short-term power conditions that push voltage above 110 percent of nominal. A recent IBM study indicates that a surge of 100 to 1,000 volts occurs in all electrical environments daily!

➤ *Power sag*—Power sags are short-term, low-voltage conditions, produced by power utilities unable to meet demand, utility equipment failure, utility switching, lightning strikes, or the startup of large power loads.

➤ *Undervoltage (brownout)*—A brownout is a reduction in line voltage for an extended time period, ranging from a few minutes to a few days. Undervoltages are responsible for malfunctions and unexpected shutdowns of computer and process control equipment. They effectively reduce the life span of electrical gear, particularly motors.

➤ *Overvoltage*—Overvoltage consists of an increase in line voltage for an extended time period, from a few minutes to as long as a few days. Overvoltage created by lightning strikes can force line voltages above 6,000 volts.

➤ *Electrical line noise*—Electrical line noise is either chronic or intermittent high-frequency interference with the smooth sine wave expected from utility power. It can be triggered by radio frequency or electromagnetic interference from transmitters, SCR-driven printers, generators, welding devices, lightning, or nearby high-voltage lines.

➤ *Frequency variation*—Any change in the frequency stability of the 60-cycle AC generation is potentially damaging to sensitive electronic equipment. It can occur when electrical generating equipment, or small cogenerator sites are loaded and unloaded, or switched between online or offline operations.

➤ *Switching transient*—A switching transient is a very brief undervoltage, shorter than a spike, and generally measured in nanoseconds.

➤ *Harmonic distortion*—Harmonic distortion is a deformation of the normal electrical power waveform. It's produced by variable-speed motors and drives, copiers, fax machines, switch-mode power supplies, and other kinds of nonlinear loads. Harmonic distortions can cause overheating, hardware damage, and communication errors.

The simplest power protection device is a *surge protector*. It prevents spikes of electrical power from reaching the company's computer equipment. Surge protectors are designed for use with personal computers, not for servers, and do not protect from small surges, which are very dangerous to server equipment. They will only protect equipment from very large spikes in power, and may fail to cut power fast enough to protect the electronic system. When a surge protector detects the maximum allowable voltage (clamping voltage), it blocks any further current flow into its related computer or electronic system.

Uninterruptible Power Supplies

Most servers rely on an *Uninterruptible Power Supply (UPS)* to provide protection from small surges, and to supply power for short times during emergencies to prevent data loss when power goes out.

In a typical UPS, commercial power comes in and the same power goes out. This UPS is simply a battery backup system that will keep the system running, and permit the system to shut down normally in case of a power failure. Its only purpose is to prevent data loss in the event of a major power failure. If there is a surge or a sag in the power supply, this type of UPS will pass it right on through to the server.

Most UPS units feature power-line monitoring capabilities, which permit the incoming voltage level to be logged by the system. They can activate system alerts and alarms when the input voltage deviates outside of prescribed levels. The most important thing to consider when purchasing a UPS is its *power rating*, which is measured in Volt-Amps (VA). This indicates if the unit has the required capacity to support the server(s) in the event of a power outage.

Although a UPS is supposed to protect its server from disasters, it can also become a source of system failure because a UPS is a machine with major parts that can fail. More importantly, if there is no other form of protection, when any part of a UPS breaks down, the server(s) it supplies will lose power protection. If a power failure occurs while the UPS is damaged, the entire system could crash and severe data loss could occur.

 Know what is the most important thing to be considered before purchasing a UPS.

UPS Types and Sizes

After the power requirements have been determined for a specified server environment, a properly sized UPS can be selected for the system. A chart can be devised, similar to the one shown in Table 10.1, to help determine the size of the required UPS.

Table 10.1 UPS Calculations										
1.			**2.**			**3.**			**4.**	
Equipment	:	**Amps**	×	**Volts**	=	**VA**	×	**Quantity**	=	**VAnSubtotal**
	:		×		=		×		=	
	:		×		=		×		=	
	:		×		=		×		=	
	:		×		=		×		=	
	:		×		=		×		=	
	:		×		=		×		=	
	:		×		=		×		=	
	:		×		=		×		=	
	:		×		=		×		=	
							5. Total			

To determine the size of the required UPS:

1. List all equipment to be protected by the UPS. (Remember to include all monitors, terminals, external hard drives, hubs, modems, routers, and any other critical equipment.)

2. List the amps and volts. These figures can be found on a plate on the back of the equipment. Multiply amps by volts to determine VoltAmps (VA). Some devices list their power requirements in watts (W). To convert watts to VA, multiply watts by 1.4.

3. Multiply the VA by the number of pieces of equipment in the Quantity column to get VA Subtotals.

4. Add the VA Subtotals to get a Total.

5. Use the Total figure to select a UPS. When choosing a UPS, be sure that the total VA requirement of supported equipment does not exceed the UPS VA rating.

Know how to calculate the load on the specified UPS by multiplying the voltage by the amperes to derive the VA rating.

Standby UPS devices consist of a battery, a power sensor, and a fast switch. Generally, if utility power drops below about 104 volts, the UPS senses the drop, switches its battery on within 10 milliseconds, and beeps to indicate that power has failed. Its switching time is less than the several hundred milliseconds a server microprocessor can function without power. These devices add undervoltage and overvoltage protection and are effective against the first five power problems listed in the preceding section. Standby UPSs are recommended for small, medium, and large network systems that support enterprise networking environments.

More expensive UPS devices are called *online interactives*, which provide some power conditioning along with battery backup. They add filters to smooth any power spikes and to boost low voltages. They are always recommended for mission-critical applications such as server farms, *Application Service Providers (ASPs)*, *Internet Service Providers (ISPs)*, telecommunications facilities, manufacturing plants, and medical operations, and they offer the highest level of server power protection available.

UPS and Associated Equipment BTUs

The *British Thermal Unit (BTU)* is the standard unit for measuring the heat produced by electronic devices such as servers, and is usually expressed as the number of BTUs generated in an hour (BTU/hr). A fully loaded rack of server equipment generates about 15,000 BTUs per hour. Any UPS system expected to permit continued operations during a commercial power failure, or to provide an orderly shutdown sequence, must consider these requirements during the initial system-designing phase.

When expressing heat output or cooling requirements, the watt (W) is used. In terms of BTU/hrs, one watt is equal to 3.412 BTU/hr. Although air conditioning capacity is also measured in BTU/hrs or watts, the air conditioning requirements for buildings are rated in tons. A unit of cooling equal to 12,000 BTU/hr, (3517 watts) provides one ton of air conditioning. These relationships help to estimate how much air conditioning a server room will require.

Backup Generators

When the power goes out for extended periods of time, a backup generator is needed to keep power supplied to the system. Backup generators are normally powered by diesel fuel and they normally work together with the UPS, because they take time to start up and come online. The UPS must be responsible for keeping the computer running while the generator powers up. Small generators take from 5 to 10 seconds to come up, provided they are supplying power only to the servers. A generator large enough to supply power to an entire organization, or building, can take 10 minutes or longer to reach a stable 60Hz and 110V. In the meantime, a correctly sized UPS that can function throughout the time period required for the generator to sta-bilize, must protect the server.

In the past, many server installations did not include backup generators, and network administrators simply installed a UPS, gambling that the power would come back on before the server needed to shut down. However, with the increased number of recent power failures and rolling power blackouts, this might not be the trend of the future. Backup generators are becoming a normal part of the server industry. Lost revenue due to a downed website can far exceed the cost of installing and running the generator.

Network Protocols and Domain Naming Conventions

Often, a network administrator would like to implement secure remote access to servers for which he or she is responsible. Protocols such as L2TP over IPSec can be used to accomplish this. Whereas L2TP is a standard for layer 2 tunneling, IPSec is a standard for encryption and security.

Although these protocols are independent, they complement each other. The strengths of L2TP include per-user authentication and dynamic address allocation. Strengths of IPSec include secure encryption and data confiden-tiality. These are exactly the features required to provide server administra-tors with secure remote server access.

Domain naming conventions help to specify the Internet address of each host computer in an understandable way. The unique address of each host is specified as several layers of domain names separated by dots. For example, the address `lewis.ucs.ed.ac.uk` represents the host computer that acts as the anonymous `ftp` server (`lewis`) for the `university computing services (ucs)` at `Edinburgh (ed)`. Because this host computer is located at a British university, it resides in the `academic (ac)` domain for the `United Kingdom (uk)`. Its numer-ical address equivalent would be `129.215.70.239`.

It might not be necessary to enter the full address depending on the location of the connecting site. In the preceding example, someone at another UK academic site may only need to type in the `lewis.ucs.ed` part of the domain name because their local host is located in the same academic domain as the host to which they are connecting.

Web addresses can also be expressed as a series of dot-separated numbers. For example, 128.148.32.121 can be used instead of dns.cs.brown.edu. In this case the numbers identifying the various domain names are reversed, so 121 represents dns, 32 represents cs, 148 represents brown, and 128 represents edu. Unlike domain names, the leftmost number is the most significant, as it represents the top domain.

Component and Cable Verifications

Differentiating between various types of server cables, and the components they are designed to connect, is an important aspect of network server installation and administration. A server technician should easily recognize the types of connectors that appear on system components as well as the cable types required to integrate them into the network.

Required Cables and Connectors

The cable types most often used with servers and their associated equipment include *Shielded Twisted Pair (STP)* and *Unshielded Twisted Pair (UTP)*. IBM originally developed STP cable for Token Ring networks. It consists of two individual wires wrapped in a foil shielding to help provide protection against electrical interference. Lower-cost UTP cable consists of two unshielded wires twisted around each other and is used extensively for local-area networks (LANs) and telephone connections. It is less expensive and easier to work with than coaxial or fiber optic cable, but does not offer as much bandwidth or protection from interference.

These cable types are usually used in 4- or 16Mbps Token Ring systems, and 10Mbps 10BaseT Ethernet systems. UTP is often installed in buildings prior to network installations and is easy to terminate. However, it is prone to interference, serves low- to medium-capacity networks, and suffers from medium to high signal losses.

Older category 3 cabling has been all but phased out. Category 5e Ethernet systems running at 100Mbps are considered the minimum acceptable standard today. Connectors used with CAT5e and CAT6 cabling terminations include 8-pin RJ-45 plugs and sockets. Critical parameters include the length of the exposed wires, which is limited to less than 1/2 an inch. Table 10.2 reveals the standard twisted-pair wiring scheme.

Table 10.2	Twisted Pair Ethernet Horizontal Wiring	
Pin	Color	Signal
1	White/Orange	Tx* data +
2	Orange/White	Tx* data −
3	White/Green	Rx** data +
4	Blue/White	—
5	White/Blue	—
6	Green/White	Rx** data −
7	White/Brown	—
8	Brown/White	—

*Tx = transmit
**Rx = receive

 Know the UTP cable and connector types for server installations.

Patch cables come in two varieties, straight-through or reversed. Straight-through patch cable applications are used between modular patch panels within server system centers. When connecting workstation equipment to various wall jacks, the wiring could be either straight-through or reversed, depending upon the manufacturer. As a rule, reversed cables are normally used for voice systems. Determining which type is being used is easily accomplished by aligning the ends of the cable side by side. With the contacts facing you, compare the colors from left to right. If the colors appear in identical order on both plugs, the cable is straight-through. If the colors appear in the opposite order, the cable is reversed.

Crossover cables are useful when direct connections are required between two network devices, such as connecting two switches or hubs together, or connecting two servers or workstations together without a hub or switch. However, the straight-through wiring required for *Ethernet* nodes precludes the use of crossover cables. Medium capacity (RJ-58AU) coaxial cables are also used in Ethernet systems; however, they are somewhat more difficult to terminate. RJ-58A coaxial cable is terminated with resistors at each end. T connectors are used to join the cables together and attach them to various LAN workstations. They are not as subject to interference as UTP but require care when bending during installation.

Fiber-optic cable systems are fairly expensive, but they are necessary for use in *backbones* at speeds of 100Mbps or more. These systems are mostly high capacity and long distance in nature, and are immune to electromagnetic interference. Although joining various segments together is somewhat more difficult than with other formats, fiber systems exhibit low loss characteristics, making them suitable for overcoming distance limitations. As such, fiber links can be used to join two hubs or switches together in situations that were previously not possible due to distance limitations. When fiber systems were first installed, *UTP-to-Fiber converters* were required to interface at the local level. Currently, however, incoming fiber terminates in fiber optic patch panels that contain the necessary patching of fiber interconnections. Today, fiber connectors and patch cables are fairly common in modern server networking systems.

For fiber installations, consider the various connectors currently being used. The squarish *SC connector* is primarily used for networking applications, is keyed, and uses a 2.5mm push-pull mating. Its ferrule is furnished with a molded housing for protection. The cylindrical *ST connector* is also used for networking applications and uses a twist-lock coupling with a 2.5mm keyed ferrule. This connector is suitable for both short-distance applications and long-line systems. The *FDDI connector* is used for networking applications in a keyed, duplex configuration with a fixed shroud. The *MT-RJ connector* is also used for networking applications but is half the size of the SC connector it was designed to replace. Somewhat smaller than a standard phone jack, it is just as easy to connect and disconnect.

Server Racks

Recall that larger data warehouses use racks to house their numerous server farms. Occasionally, these racks may need to be moved to new locations. The proper order of events for moving a large server rack from one office or floor level to another is first to create an accurate wiring diagram, remove all racked components, move the rack to its new location, replace all of the components to their original rack locations, and finally to rewire the components according to the guidelines noted in the diagram.

Common Server Types

Servers are commonly divided into three major types, each having strengths and weaknesses that should be recognized. As reviewed in previous chapters, these server types include desk servers, rackmount servers, and blade servers.

Exam Prep Questions

1. Where can hardware compatibility lists for a given network operating system be found?
   - ❏ A. On the hardware vendor's website
   - ❏ B. On the installation CD for the specified hardware
   - ❏ C. On the installation CD for the network operating system
   - ❏ D. On the network operating system vendor's website

2. When selecting a UPS for server operations, which specification is the most critical?
   - ❏ A. Volt-Amps
   - ❏ B. Clamping voltage
   - ❏ C. Watts
   - ❏ D. Downtime

3. After checking all of the proposed hardware components against the NOS catalogs and compatibility lists, a technician performs a server installation, only to discover an NIC malfunction. What might have been done to prevent this problem?
   - ❏ A. Verifying all UTP cable connections
   - ❏ B. Planning the system resource designations
   - ❏ C. Locating and obtaining the latest OEM drivers before the installation
   - ❏ D. Checking the OEM hardware compatibility listings

4. The technician is building a high-capacity server and checks the supplied components. Among them are four SCSI hard drives, an Ultra100 RAID 5 controller, and cables fitted with SCA80 connectors. What will the technician report to the administrator?
   - ❏ A. The hard drives are not the correct type.
   - ❏ B. All of the required components are accounted for and building can begin.
   - ❏ C. The cable types are incorrect.
   - ❏ D. The wrong type of controller has arrived.

5. Which of the following steps comes first when assembling or upgrading a server system?
   - ❏ A. Implement ESD best practices
   - ❏ B. Verify compatibility
   - ❏ C. Perform firmware upgrade
   - ❏ D. Check system resources

6. When the components making up the proposed server installation are first received, what is the first thing to do?

   ❑ A. Test the assembled server system under networking conditions to learn about any unforeseen problems.

   ❑ B. Use the delivered components to assemble the server system.

   ❑ C. Download the latest validated drivers for all server components to preclude incompatibilities with new software.

   ❑ D. Conduct a component verification to ensure that delivered components exactly match the ordered components.

7. The ordered components for building the server have arrived. While matching the received items against those on the order list, the technician discovers that one of the adapter cards is a substitute. Although the substitute adapter will probably perform satisfactorily, what should the technician do?

   ❑ A. Send the substitute adapter card back and insist on receiving the originally requested component.

   ❑ B. Use the Internet to verify the substitute card's compatibility before building the server system.

   ❑ C. Ensure that the latest validated drivers for the substitute adapter are on hand. Then, build the server.

   ❑ D. Run the substitute adapter through various test procedures before beginning to build the server.

8. What is the most obvious symptom of a server board having incompatible RAM installed?

   ❑ A. The RAM modules are destroyed when power is applied to the server board.

   ❑ B. The network operating system becomes corrupted.

   ❑ C. The server computer refuses to boot properly.

   ❑ D. The server board overheats and components begin smoking.

9. Assuming that all server components have been delivered and verified, what should the server assembly technician's next step be?

   ❑ A. The server's chassis should be prepared.

   ❑ B. The most recent validated drivers should be obtained.

   ❑ C. The assembly of the server should begin.

   ❑ D. The server board should be installed in the case.

10. A suitable size for the proposed server's UPS can best be determined through the use of which of the following formulas?

   ❑ A. Ohms+Amps

   ❑ B. Amps–Volts

   ❑ C. Volts+Amps

   ❑ D. Volts*Amps

11. Which procedure best ensures the reliability of all server hardware components before installation?
    - ❏ A. Validation testing
    - ❏ B. Deferred testing
    - ❏ C. Isolated testing
    - ❏ D. Processor-based testing

12. When CAT5e cabling is being installed, what type of connector is used to perform terminations?
    - ❏ A. RJ-11 connectors
    - ❏ B. RJ-12 connectors
    - ❏ C. RJ-35 connectors
    - ❏ D. RJ-45 connectors

13. A crossover cable would be used incorrectly to connect which devices?
    - ❏ A. Two switches
    - ❏ B. Two servers
    - ❏ C. Ethernet networked devices
    - ❏ D. Computers in a two-workstation network

14. When selecting the UPS for a given server installation, what should the administrator consider as the highest priority?
    - ❏ A. That the current and wattage ratings are sufficient for the server's requirements
    - ❏ B. That its VA rating is higher than that required by the server system
    - ❏ C. That the batteries attached to the UPS are not too heavy
    - ❏ D. That the UPS includes protection from sags and spikes

15. When configuring a Linux server, where can a technician check for hardware compatibility between components?
    - ❏ A. The Windows Catalog listing on Microsoft's website
    - ❏ B. Microsoft's Software Compatibility List (SCL)
    - ❏ C. Websites run by manufacturers of the specified hardware components
    - ❏ D. Various Internet sites dealing with hardware compatibility

16. An older NIC is being configured for a server system. Where should the server technician look to obtain its latest validated driver?
    - ❏ A. The OS manufacturer's driver download site
    - ❏ B. Any driver download site on the Internet
    - ❏ C. The website providing Microsoft's Windows Catalog
    - ❏ D. The NIC manufacturer's website

17. When configuring Windows 2000 Server, where can the latest list of compatible hardware be located?
    - ❏ A. On the server manufacturer's website
    - ❏ B. On Microsoft's Windows Catalog website
    - ❏ C. On Microsoft's Windows Update page
    - ❏ D. On a comprehensive hardware compatibility website

18. When the administrator is planning to take the server down, what should his or her first step be?
    - ❏ A. To schedule the necessary upgrades or repairs in the early morning hours.
    - ❏ B. To schedule the upgrades or repairs during times of peak network usage.
    - ❏ C. To ensure that enough company personnel will be on hand to implement the required upgrades or repairs.
    - ❏ D. To inform all users and clients a few minutes in advance that the server will be going down.

19. What is the proper order of events for moving a large server rack between floors or offices?
    - ❏ A. Create an accurate rack wiring diagram, remove all components, move the rack, replace components, rewire components
    - ❏ B. Create an accurate rack wiring diagram, replace components, remove all components, move the rack, rewire components
    - ❏ C. Rewire the components, create an accurate rack wiring diagram, remove all components, move the rack
    - ❏ D. Remove all components, create an accurate rack wiring diagram, move the rack, rewire components, replace components

20. The network administrator wants secure remote server access. What protocols should be used?
    - ❏ A. WWW and ISP protocols
    - ❏ B. HTTP and FTP protocols
    - ❏ C. L2TP on IPSec protocols
    - ❏ D. STP and UTP protocols

Exam Prep Answers

1. Answer D is the correct answer. The network operating system vendor's website will supply hardware information in various catalogs or compatibility listings as to which items have been tested to work properly. Answers A and B are incorrect because hardware vendors never provide details about systems or conditions under which their products will not function. Answer C is incorrect, although the NOS installation

CD may mention certain products that are known to have specific problems with the NOS.

2. Answer A is the correct answer. The UPS power rating, specified in Volt-Amps (VA), is the most critical specification to consider. The unit must be capable of supporting all system servers during a power outage. Answer B is incorrect because surge protector data is more likely to specify clamping voltage information than UPS data. Answer C is incorrect because watts is not the correct parameter with which to rate the capability of a specific UPS. Answer D is incorrect because product specifications never mention downtime.

3. Answer C is the correct answer. The latest device drivers, including those for the NIC, should be obtained prior to conducting the installation. Answer A is incorrect because disconnected UTP cables would be evidence of a negligent technician at work. Answer B is incorrect because system resource planning would be more meaningful if you have the latest OEM drivers beforehand. Answer D is incorrect because hardware manufacturers do not normally provide HCLs.

4. Answer D is the correct answer. When SCSI hard drives are being configured for RAID operations in a high-capacity server, a SCSI RAID controller is necessary for the system to function properly. The Ultra100 ATA controller must therefore be replaced with an Ultra3 SCSI RAID controller. Answer A is incorrect because the SCSI drives are the required types. Answer B is incorrect because the Ultra100 controller is designed for ATA systems. Answer C is incorrect because the cables supplied are the right ones.

5. Answer B is the correct answer. Without establishing compatibility, any other installation steps may turn out to be a waste of time. Therefore, answers A, C, and D are incorrect because compatibility must be established first.

6. Answer D is the correct answer. Delivered server components must exactly match the ordered server components. If any substitutes are discovered, the server technician may risk constructing a server network that does not work properly. Answers A, B, and C are all important. However, they should not be performed before conducting the component verification.

7. Answer A is the correct answer. Any components that turn out to be compatibles should be returned and replaced with the components originally ordered prior to building the server. Answer B is incorrect because the substitute card's compatibility is not the issue. Answer C is

incorrect because having the latest validated drivers for the substitute card does not help in procuring the originally ordered component. Answer D is incorrect because testing the wrong adapter gains nothing. The compatibility or non-compatibility of the substitute must remain irrelevant to the installing technician.

8. Answer C is the correct answer. The main symptom of incompatible RAM being installed is the failure to boot properly. This problem can be prevented by always verifying that the RAM specified for the server board is installed. Answer A is incorrect because the technician will not be able to insert voltage-mismatched RAM into its designated slot(s). Answer B is incorrect because the operation or non-operation of system RAM cannot corrupt the NOS. Answer D is incorrect because the server board is in no danger from incompatible RAM being inserted.

9. Answer B is the correct answer. After the delivery of the required components has been verified, the latest validated drivers should be obtained. Answer A is incorrect because chassis preparation does not begin until all validated drivers are in-house. Answers C and D are incorrect because these steps cannot occur until the chassis preparation has been completed.

10. Answer D is the correct answer. UPS loads are rated in volt-amperes (VA), which can be calculated by multiplying the operational voltage by the number of supplied amps. By the process of elimination, answers A, B, and C are all incorrect.

11. Answer A is the correct answer. When components have been rigorously tested before installation by the supplier and guaranteed (validated) to work together effectively, the reliability of server hardware components is ensured. Answer B is incorrect because waiting until after installation to begin testing can result in wasted time and effort. Answer C is incorrect because unless the components are tested together, no proof of their compatibility can be established. Answer D is incorrect because as important as it is for components to work with the specified processor, other possible incompatibilities may exist.

12. Answer D is the correct answer. Terminations for CAT5e UTP network cables are performed using 8-pin RJ-45 plugs. Answer A is incorrect because RJ-11 connectors are fitted with 6 pins (4 wired). Answer B is incorrect because RJ-12 connectors are fitted with 6 pins, and all of them are wired. They are used primarily in situations that require three-line phone capabilities. Answer C is incorrect because RJ-35 connectors are rarely seen.

13. Answer C is the correct answer. The crossover cable allows for the direct connection of two devices without necessarily being part of a network, or using network hardware. Even within a network, a crossover cable can connect two switches or hubs together, or two servers or workstations together without the use of a hub or switch. Answers A, B, and D are all legitimate uses for a crossover cable.

14. Answer B is the correct answer. When selecting a UPS, make sure that the VA rating of the UPS is higher than that required by the computer system. Answer A is incorrect because wattage is not a valid parameter with which to rate a UPS. Answer C is incorrect because the battery weight is not a major consideration. Answer D is incorrect because a UPS may or may not provide power conditioning and filtering. Although desirable features, they are not the highest priority when selecting a UPS.

15. Answer C is the correct answer. Regardless of the OS being used, decisions about which hardware components to purchase should only be finalized after checking for hardware compatibility on a website run by the hardware manufacturer. If support for the selected operating system is not specified, the component may be useless for the application. Answer A is incorrect because Linux compatibility issues do not concern Microsoft. Answer B is incorrect because Microsoft does not provide an SCL on its website. Answer D is incorrect because Internet sites dealing with hardware compatibility may not have specific info about a particular component.

16. Answer D is the correct answer. To obtain the latest validated driver, go to the NIC manufacturer's website and download the latest confirmed gold driver. Do not use a beta driver, regardless of its release date. Answer A is incorrect because even if the OS manufacturer can provide some drivers, they will not be the latest versions. Answer C is incorrect because the Windows Catalog is not related to supplying drivers. Answer B is incorrect, especially when looking for the latest drivers.

17. Answer B is the correct answer. The Windows Catalog on Microsoft's website will contain the latest list of compatible hardware for Windows 2000 Server. Answer A is incorrect regardless of a server equipment manufacturer's claim of universal compatibility. Answer C is incorrect because the Windows Update page provides updates for many Microsoft products, rather than listings of compatible hardware. Answer D is incorrect because any given hardware compatibility list may not relate to Windows 2000 Server.

18. Answer C is the correct answer. During server downtime, enough personnel must be available to implement the planned upgrades or repairs in order to bring the server back online as quickly as possible. Answer A is incorrect because if something goes wrong, the server system could be out of operation for most of the day. Answer B is incorrect because maximum disruption of the workplace would occur. Answer D is incorrect because company personnel may need more notice in order to avoid serious work interruptions.

19. Answer A is the correct answer. The proper order of events for moving a large server rack between floors or offices is to create an accurate rack wiring diagram, remove all components, move the rack to its new location, replace all components, and finally to rewire components. Answers B, C, and D are all incorrect by the process of elimination.

20. Answer C is the correct answer. Although L2TP provides per-user authentication, and dynamic address allocation, IPSec provides secure encryption and data confidentiality. Answer A is incorrect because WWW and ISP are merely acronyms for World Wide Web and Internet Service Provider. Answer B is incorrect because neither the FTP nor the HTTP protocols can provide secure remote server access. Answer D is incorrect because STP and UTP are types of twisted-pair cabling, not network protocols.

11.0—Installing Hardware

Terms you'll need to understand:

✓ Grounding strap
✓ Heatsink fan
✓ Microfractures
✓ Split power cable
✓ Chassis exhaust blower
✓ Front panel LEDs
✓ IDE signal cables
✓ RAID card
✓ Burn-in
✓ Network patch cables
✓ RJ-45 connectors and crimping tools
✓ Uplink
✓ SCSI bus and SCSI ID
✓ Equipment rack
✓ Keyboard Video Mouse (KVM) switch
✓ Space optimization
✓ Cost-effectiveness
✓ Straight Tip (ST)
✓ Cable management
✓ Direct connect, interconnect, and cross-connect
✓ IEEE-802.3
✓ Fast Ethernet
✓ IEEE 802.3u
✓ Gigabit Ethernet

✓ IEEE 802.3ab

✓ IEEE 802.3z standard

✓ Fiber Distributed Data Interface (FDDI)

Techniques you'll need to master:

✓ Using an electrostatic discharge strap

✓ Installing a microprocessor

✓ Orienting and mounting a heatsink fan

✓ Matching the screw holes in the server board with the chassis mounting points

✓ Installing expansion cards

✓ Mounting CD-ROM, hard, and floppy disk drives

✓ Wiring the front panel LEDs

✓ Connecting various IDE, SCSI, and RAID signal cables

✓ Using cable ties to organize internal server chassis wiring

✓ Conducting a server system burn-in

✓ Selecting the proper height for the installation of a racked monitor and keyboard

✓ Differentiating between patch cable and crossover cable wire ordering

✓ Knowing the function of an uplink port on a switch or router

✓ Identifying the maximum length of a CAT5e or CAT6 cable run

✓ Explaining how to set operational SCSI IDs

✓ Making the proper checks before powering up a new server installation

✓ Enabling client control and software management of all server systems from a single console

✓ Designing rack solutions for fan-free environments

✓ Recognizing the critical aspects of a complex server network environment

✓ Differentiating between UTP and STP cabling formats

✓ Explaining how a crossover cable is used

✓ Preventing airflow obstruction

✓ Calculating available cabling space for a rack

✓ Comparing direct connect, interconnect, and cross-connect cable connections

✓ Implementing a KVM switch

✓ Understanding various network access protocols

✓ Listing the benefits of fiber-optic cabling
✓ Differentiating between various fiber Ethernet standards
✓ Comparing FDDI with Token Ring networks

Introduction

Server+ Exam Objective 2.2 suggests that the test taker should be able to install hardware using best practices.

This hardware includes

➤ Boards

➤ Drives

➤ Processors and power modules

➤ Memory

➤ Internal cable

➤ Internal fans

Installation activities associated with this objective include

➤ Mounting the rack installation (if appropriate)

➤ Cutting and crimping network cabling

➤ Installing a UPS (depending on environment)

➤ Verifying SCSI ID configuration and termination

➤ Installing external devices (for example keyboards, monitors, subsystems, modem rack, and so on)

➤ Verifying power-on via power-on sequence

Supporting knowledge for this objective includes

➤ Physical infrastructure requirements (for example, proper layout of equipment in the rack, adequate airflow, and so on)

➤ SCSI cabling, termination, and hot plug configuration

➤ Basic understanding of network cabling and connector types

➤ Cable management

➤ KVM implementation

➤ Rack mount security

Common network interface protocols whose characteristics should be known include

➤ Ethernet

➤ Fast Ethernet

➤ Gigabit Ethernet

Server Hardware Installation Practices

As with any computer hardware installation or service procedure, technicians should always wear an electrostatic discharge (ESD) strap to maintain proper grounding and avoid the destruction of electrostatically sensitive components caused by improper handling. If a *grounding strap* is not available, always touch a grounded object prior to handling sensitive server components. In addition, keep in mind that specific components should be securely mounted to server boards before the boards themselves are mounted in the server chassis. These include the heatsink retainer bracket, the processor, the heatsink, and the memory module(s).

 Know how to protect damage to electrostatically sensitive components.

Server Boards, Processor, and Memory

Begin by mounting tthe *heatsink retainer bracket* to the server board. First, check to ensure that the server board does not reveal protruding solder points near the heatsink area. These points can short-circuit and burn out the board and the processor if they contact the bottom of the retention bracket. If the bottom retainer bracket is not equipped with proper insulation, a nonconductive lining can be inserted between the bottom plate and the motherboard. Then mount the heatsink retention bracket included with the heatsink, by following the installation instructions in the server board's manual. Next, observe proper grounding precautions and install the processor and the memory module(s) as instructed in the manual. Don't neglect the application of thermal grease on the processor to prevent it from overheating.

Know how to prevent a microprocessor from overheating.

Orient the *heatsink fan* so as to direct the airflow toward the rear blower in the chassis. The rear blower is usually located next to the keyboard and mouse ports on the server board. Normally, the heatsink fan will mount in only two possible orientations. With the fan properly mounted, lock the retainer arms of the heatsink retention bracket into place. Check carefully to ensure that the retainer arms are securely locked in place! If they release, the processor will overheat. In some cases, the blower mounts next to the heatsink by clamping onto the metal edge between the retainer arm and heatsink. Plug the heatsink fan's power cable into the appropriate power supply pins on the server board. Repeat these steps for dual-processor boards.

The server board should now be ready for installation on the chassis. However, prior to mounting the server board, take a moment to count the mounting holes and note their locations. Compare these hole locations with the mounting points on the chassis. Make sure that the mounting holes in the server board match the mounting points located on the chassis. If they match up, proceed with the mounting. However, if an extra mounting point is discovered on the chassis beneath the server board, it must be covered with electrical tape or a pad of certified nonconductive material. Otherwise, it might be possible to short-circuit the server board when it contacts the chassis.

Carefully insert the server board into its I/O shield and gently align it to the chassis. After it is aligned, loosely fasten the board to the chassis using the screws provided by the manufacturer. Server boards usually have six mounting holes and they should all be properly aligned before tightening the screws. As you tighten the screws, begin at the center of the board and work your way to the edges. This technique helps to prevent *microfractures* in the server board and ensures the best fit. Sometimes boards that are manufactured with poor quality tstandards reveal a curved structure. When mounting such a board, it might be necessary to place plastic spacers between the board and the appropriate mounting points to prevent further bending.

Accessory Cards or Modules

Locate any required or optional PCI cards that must be installed into the server board. Older boards might require video cards and some printers require their own interface cards as well. Install any specified PCI expansion card into the system at this time. A good rule of thumb considers any video card as the most important, and therefore it is inserted in the first slot. Align the PCI card's faceplate with its rear slot bracket and use the appropriate hole in the back of the chassis to secure the PCI card with a screw. Repeat this procedure for any other expansion cards, including any RAID products, as required.

Drives

Select the desired 5 1/4-inch drive bay for mounting a CD-ROM, CD-R/RW, or DVD drive if applicable. This bay provides a snug fit but does not require brute strength to force a drive into its fitting. Secure the drive into place using either thumbscrews or Phillips screws on either side.

If an internal Zip drive is to be installed, ensure that it is first properly attached to its 5 1/4-inch caddy. Then, mount the caddy into an available 5 1/4-inch bay as with other drives. If the server is to perform tape backup duties using an internal solution, reserve a 5 1/4-inch bay for its installation as well.

Next, carefully mount the master hard drive into one of the closed 3 1/2-inch slots or caddies, using appropriately sized Phillips screws for tightening. If any slave hard drives are to be added, install them at this time. Remember that hard drives are both fragile and electrically sensitive devices. Proper precautions should be taken when handling them.

Be aware that newer solid-state disk (SSD) solutions for servers are gaining widespread acceptance for use in storage arrays. Internal units designed for location in 3 1/2-inch bays should also be installed at this time, if applicable.

After all hard drives have been installed, mount the 3 1/2-inch floppy drive(s) into the open drive bays or caddies provided.

Internal Cabling

The various components must now connect to the power cables and plugs running from the system power supply. Examine the cable/connector types running from the power supply into the vicinity of the server board. Locate the main power plug for the server board and slightly bend the connector's wiring toward a right angle to ensure a better fit, and then plug it into its mated connector on the board. Do not attempt to bend these wires with this connector plugged into the server board or the board will be damaged! Repeat this procedure for other proprietary power headers, such as the four-pin 12V auxiliary power cable that mates to onboard connectors.

Next, route an accessory power cable to each CDR, Zip, tape, hard, SSD, and floppy drive in the system. If enough power connectors are not available to adequately run all devices, including any exhaust fans mounted in the chassis, locate an accessory Y *split power cable* and plug it into one of the power leads. When using these splitter cables, check to be sure that the power supply is rated high enough to handle the additional load. Connect the *chassis exhaust blower*'s power cable to the special lead provided by the power supply for this purpose. On some server boards, headers are provided when power supplies do not provide the proper power leads.

Locate and unwrap the wiring for the *front panel LED* indicators. Carefully examine the user manual for the server board's front panel wiring. Follow the manual's diagram to connect the power switch and LED display cables to the proper pins on the server board. Most chassis and board manufacturers mark the pins and the wire plugs for proper identity. A recommended practice is to connect the red LED to indicate master hard drive activity.

After all power cables are connected, it's time to connect the flat *IDE signal cables* to all appropriate drives. Make sure that the pin 1s are matched on all board sockets and cable headers. For SCSI drives, connect the appropriate SCSI cable between the drives and the *RAID card*. After all cabling has been connected, use cable ties to properly organize and bundle the wiring. This step is essential to minimize airflow resistance. Finally, flip the internal switch on the power supply unit to its ON position. Remember that 1 corresponds to ON, and 0 corresponds to OFF.

Server Installation Activities

Most faulty electronic components, including motherboards and memory, fail during their first 72 hours of operation, so you should run the system at maximum operational capacity for at least this amount of time to reveal these problems and properly burn it in. Following a successful *burn-in*, rack equipment can be mounted and cabled to the network.

Rack Mounting

Most *server rack-mounting kits* include two sets of rail assemblies, two rail-mounting brackets, and the required mounting screws needed to install the equipment into the rack. It's always a good idea to read through the manufacturer's instructions before proceeding with the installation. Each rail assembly consists of two sections:

➤ An inner fixed chassis rail that secures to the server

➤ An outer fixed rack rail that attaches directly to the rack itself

A sliding rail guide sandwiched between the two should remain attached to the inner fixed rack rail. Prior to beginning the installation, both sets of inner and outer rails must be separated by pulling the fixed chassis rail out as far as possible, until the locking tab clicks as it emerges from inside of the rail assembly, locking the inner rail. Then depress the locking tab to pull the inner rail completely out.

First, attach the chassis rails to the server by performing the following steps:

1. Note that the rails are left- and right-specific.

2. Position the appropriate inner fixed chassis rail sections along the corresponding side of the server, and align the screw holes.

3. Screw the rail securely to the proper side of the server chassis.

4. Repeat this procedure for the remaining rail on the opposite side of the server chassis.

5. Attach the rail brackets for server installation into a two-post rack.

Next, perform the following steps to connect the rack rails to the rack:

1. Determine where the server will be placed in the rack.

2. Position one of the fixed rack rail/sliding rail guide assemblies at its desired rack location and face the sliding rail guide toward the inside of the rack.

3. Screw the assembly securely to the rack, using the brackets provided.

Repeat this procedure for the other rack rail/sliding rail guide assembly at the same height on the other side of the rack. After the rails are attached to both the server and the rack unit, the server is ready to be installed into the rack. To install the server in a four-post rack, perform the following steps:

1. Line up the rear of the chassis rails with the front of the rack rails.

2. Depress the locking tabs while inserting the chassis rails into the rack rails.

3. Slide the chassis rails into the rack rails, keeping the pressure even on both sides.

4. Push the server completely into the rack until the locking tabs audibly click.

5. Insert and tighten the thumbscrews to hold the front of the server to the rack.

To install the server into a two-post telco rack, you can also follow the preceding instructions. The main difference in the installation procedure is the positioning of the rack brackets in the rack. They should be spaced only as far apart as necessary to accommodate the width of the telco rack.

Network Cable Cutting and Crimping

Network patch cables can be purchased ready-made when necessary unless a custom length is needed. This is not the case, however, for outdoor/indoor premise wiring. As a result, a server installation technician needs to develop some expertise in cable cutting, terminations, and testing (verification).

The majority of network cabling today involves the use of CAT5e and CAT6 Ethernet cable along with RJ-45 terminating connectors and a high-quality *crimping tool* designed to install the connectors. Here are the main points to remember:

➤ Before going out to a job, be sure to have a larger quantity of *RJ-45 connectors* than actually needed. Nothing makes an installer look more foolish than to run out of them while in the field.

➤ Select from CAT5, CAT5e, or CAT6 cable, but keep in mind that plain old CAT5 is no longer certified for use by the TIA/EIA. For installations where clients are known to continually upgrade, go with CAT6.

➤When working at each end of the cable, leave enough slack for wire harnesses, routing to a patch panel, and/or retries before cutting the cable and installing the connector.

➤ Strip 1/2 to 3/4 inches of the outer shielding on one end of the cable, being sure not to cut the insulation or the stranded wires inside. This is an easy task when performed using a good quality crimping tool. Otherwise more skill is required to gently strip the shielding using a knife or a pair of wire cutters.

➤ Untwist the twisted-pair wires just enough to line them up properly in the connector, but no further.

➤ After they are untwisted, there is no need to try retwisting the wires, nor is it necessary to strip the insulation from the individual wires.

➤ Arrange the wires in the following order from left to right: white/orange, solid orange, white/green, solid blue, white/blue, solid green, white/brown, and solid brown. This corresponds to the T-568B wiring standard shown in Figure 11.1.

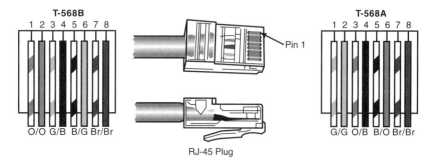

Figure 11.1 RJ-45 UTP Cable Wiring Schemes

➤ Clip the ends of the wires so that they are all equal in length.

➤ Slide the wires into the RJ-45 connector with the prong facing away.

➤ Ensure that all the wires are lined up in the proper order, and that they are pushed all the way into the end of the plug.

➤ Insert the plug in the crimping tool, and slowly squeeze its handle until a click is heard.

➤ Press the release lever on the crimping tool and examine the connection carefully. If observation reveals an incomplete or erroneous crimp, cut the connector off at its base and try again.

➤ Repeat the procedure at the other end of the cable if it will be inserted into a patch panel. Otherwise, follow terminal block wiring procedures.

This technique also works for creating patch cables to run from a switch or router to a PC. For direct PC-to-PC or hub-to-hub connections, the connectors must be prepared for a *crossover cable*, which reorders the wires at one end. Prepare one end of the crossover cable as stated in the preceding list, and then arrange the wires on the other end in the following order, from left to right: white/green, solid green, white/orange, solid blue, white/blue, solid orange, white/brown, and solid brown. This corresponds to the T-568A wiring standard shown in Figure 11.1.

Know what devices are normally connected with a crossover cable.

Keep in mind that connectorized CAT5e or CAT6 cables should run no longer than 100 meters (325 feet) in length. A hub does not provide any signal boosting, but switches and routers do. In addition, modern high-quality switches and routers automatically detect whether a specific cable is a patch or a crossover, and automatically perform the appropriate adjustment internally, permitting the use of either cable type. They often are also equipped with a specialized port called an *uplink*, which functions as a crossover connection even when a regular patch cable is plugged into it.

UPS Installations

An *Uninterruptible Power Supply (UPS)* is a necessity for network servers used for mission-critical applications. In fact, many network administrators consider the UPS as a necessity for every computer in the network, even on machines that don't shut down the entire company when they go down. For these managers, the danger of corrupted data is much more than an annoyance; it's an unacceptable revenue risk!

UPS units belong to two main classes:

➤ *Always-on*—This type of UPS supplies continuous power to the computer, and charges itself with the power coming from the commercially sourced wall outlet. The server does not see the power from the wall outlet. Instead, it runs totally and completely from the UPS unit, receiving a steady and safe level of power. Always-on UPS units are extremely expensive, large, and heavy. In addition, they require fresh batteries to be installed every couple of years. On the other hand, they are often considered worth the price when used with minicomputers, or large network servers that have many attached users. This is especially true in work environments that need 24/7 user access, not merely weekday work hours.

➤ *On-when-needed*—This type of UPS uses a battery that kicks in when the power actually fails. In addition, these batteries often kick in when the voltage merely drops sufficiently to warn the UPS that the power might be failing. This philosophy helps to prevent the network from ever experiencing the shock of a complete shutdown. This type of UPS includes two important features worth considering. These are

➤ Line conditioning features in addition to the battery backup.

➤ Software operations that initiate an orderly system shutdown whenever the battery kicks in. Data cabling between one of the computer's serial ports and the UPS handles the necessary communications.

On-when-needed UPS units are generally found attached to PC servers. The physical installation is quite simple. The UPS plugs directly into the wall, and the server and its monitor are plugged into outlets provided on the UPS. The UPS manufacturer provides instructions for connecting the cable between the UPS and one of the server's serial ports.

One thing to keep in mind after a UPS is physically connected to a server is that subsequent Windows installations risk toggling the serial port detector. If a UPS is actively connected to a serial port during such a toggle, it will interpret this as a power failure. To avoid such a problem, disconnect the UPS before beginning a reinstallation.

SCSI Server ID Verifications

SCSI devices must be correctly configured and terminated in any networking environment. Each device on the *SCSI bus*, including the server controller, must have a unique *SCSI ID* to uniquely define each SCSI device on the bus. SCSI IDs also determine which device gets priority whenever two or more devices attempt to use the SCSI bus simultaneously. In multichannel configurations, SCSI IDs on one channel do not interfere with IDs on another. Allowable SCSI IDs are 0 through 7 for devices with ID 7 having the highest priority and ID 0 the lowest. For SCSI II devices, allowable IDs are 0 through 15 with ID 7 still having the highest priority. The priority of the remaining IDs in descending order, is 6 to 0, then 15 to 8.

To set operational SCSI IDs, complete the following process:

1. Determine which ID number is currently assigned for each device on the SCSI bus. The default ID for the controller is usually ID 7. The IDs of the other SCSI devices must be determined by reading their documentation and examining their switch or jumper settings.

2. Set the appropriate number for each device, remembering that no two devices can be set to the same ID number. Leave the host adapter's ID at its default of SCSI ID 7. If an additional SCSI host adapter shares the same SCSI bus, make sure its ID is not also 7. If necessary, change either adapter ID to 6.

3. To boot the server from an array connected to the host bus adapter, assign SCSI ID 0 to the booting drive for that array and connect it to

whichever channel is specified for the server by the user's manual. To boot the server from a standalone SCSI drive, assign SCSI ID 0 to that drive. When two or more host bus adapters are used, be sure the boot drive or array is connected to the first scanned host adapter.

External Device Installations

External devices such as keyboards, monitors, modem racks, and others are often installed in server systems. These components can be connected in such a way as to permit the use of one set of devices in one location to control a number of servers. Such installations are usually found in, or as part of, an *equipment rack*.

 The prior removal of rack doors and side panels often makes these types of installations easier.

Power-On Sequence Verifications

Check the following before powering up a server installation for the first time.

➤ Check to be sure that the server is currently powered OFF (the O side of the power switch depressed).

➤ Verify that the power cord is plugged securely into the power supply module.

➤ Verify that the power cord is connected to an outlet.

➤ Ensure that power is available at the outlet you are using.

➤ Inspect the server's fuse and replace it, if necessary.

Supporting Hardware Knowledge

As a server installation technician, you must understand the basic requirements of the physical networking infrastructure. The following sections include information about:

➤ Rack equipment layouts

➤ SCSI cabling and terminations

➤ Network cable and connectors

➤ Cable management

➤ Using KVMs

➤ Security for racked equipment

Physical Infrastructure Requirements

Rack equipment must be selected and installed on the basis of

➤ *Scalability*—Because server installations expand in size over time, rack installations should be modular and planned in such a way as to readily accommodate future data center growth.

➤ *Flexibility*—Budget constraints should not serve as a hindrance when the client selects a rack solution. Both standard and enterprise rack offerings should permit mixing and matching of EIA-compatible equipment.

➤ *Availability* and *Reliability*—Power distribution units (PDUs) should be selected that enable connectivity to redundant, diverse power sources, including UPS options.

➤ *Manageability*—Clients appreciate the ability to control all of their racked systems from a single console, using appropriate management software. This type of software often comes with rack configuration tools that help plan and validate a given installation.

➤ *Rapid implementation*—Well-designed rack systems can be pre-installed prior to shipment following the submission of a validated installation plan. The rack arrives at the data center fully equipped and ready to run.

➤ *Security*—Well-designed racks are manufactured with lockable doors to provide a more secure environment for the protection of hardware, media, and data.

➤ *Space optimization*—Clients want easy access to crucial components in addition to the flexibility of consolidating server space when possible.

➤ *Cost-effectiveness*—Rack solutions must be competitively priced, deliver operational cost savings, simplify management, provide ease of configuration, offer simplified cabling, and consume no unnecessary office real estate.

Other important points to keep in mind when considering rack solutions include the following:

➤ Options included with any rack solution must be tested/rated for compatibility, so that clients can configure their server solutions with the confidence that all components will work well together out of the box.

➤ Fan installations are often touted as effective add-ons for handling thermal loads. However, well-designed racks offer exceptional cooling performance in fan-free environments. This is an advantage considering that fans are mechanical devices prone to failure.

➤ Carefully study the features, specs, and options. Look at what standard features are included in the base price. Some vendors consider such standard features as expensive add-ons, thus inflating the costs of their products.

➤ Data center space is expensive. Preconfigured racks containing servers and storage components can pack an amazing amount of processing power and terabytes of data storage capacity into a very compact space. This helps to reduce the amount of air conditioning and power consumption required.

➤ Small businesses that deploy tower units at several locations can consolidate their IT operations in a standard rack providing up to 11U of rack space. This is enough capacity for a small business to centralize its IT operations.

➤ The more complex a server network becomes, the more important the rack solution becomes. Clients requiring large-scale server solutions do not consider racks simply as convenient shelving systems to organize equipment and save space. In such complex environments, a rack solution is a critical tool for data handling and protection.

Network Cabling and Connector Types

Generally, four types of media are used to transmit data between computers and their associated hardware. The following sections discuss each type in more detail.

Copper Cabling

Copper coaxial cable (coax) is already familiar to most people as the type of conductor that brings cable TV signals into their homes. Coaxial cable consists of a single copper conductor surrounded by an insulating layer. A protective braided copper shield is placed around this layer of insulation. The outer protective jacket is commonly composed of polyvinyl chloride (PVC), suitable for either indoor or outdoor applications, and is available in black, white, tan, and gray.

As you already know, the twisted pair copper cabling used with data networks is generally divided into two basic formats: *Unshielded Twisted Pair (UTP)* and

Shielded Twisted Pair (STP). UTP networking cable contains four pairs of individually insulated wires, whereas STP cable is similar except that it also contains a foil shield surrounding the four-pair wire bundle. This shielding provides extended protection from induced electrical noise and crosstalk through the inclusion of a grounded conduction path to carry the induced electrical signals away from the cable conductors carrying the communications signals.

UTP Cable

UTP cable specifications have been established jointly by two standards organizations: the *Telecommunications Industry Association (TIA)* and the *Electronic Industry Association (EIA)*. They have categorized various grades of cable along with their connector, distance, and installation specifications to produce the TIA/EIA UTP wiring category ratings for the cabling industry, such as CAT3, CAT5, CAT5e, and CAT6. Table 11.1 lists the industry's various CAT cable ratings that apply to UTP data communications cabling. CAT5e cabling is currently the most widely used specification for data communication wiring, with CAT6 undergoing widespread deployment. UTP cabling is terminated in an eight-pin RJ-45 plug.

Table 11.1   UTP Cable Category Ratings

Category	Maximum Bandwidth	Wiring Types	Applications
3	16MHz	100μ UTP Rated Category 3	10Mbps Ethernet 4Mbps Token Ring
4	20MHz	100μ UTP Rated Category 4	10Mbps Ethernet 16Mbps Token Ring
5	100MHz	100μ UTP Rated Category 5	100Mbps TPDD 155Mbps ATM
5e	160MHz	100μ UTP Rated Category 5e	1.2Gbps 1000BASE-T High-Speed ATM
6	200-250MHz	100μ UTP Rated Category 6	1.2Gbps 1000BASE-T High-Speed ATM and beyond
7 Proposed	600-862MHz	100μ UTP Rated Category 7	1.2Gbps 1000BASE-T High-Speed ATM and beyond

Know the type of connectors used with CAT5 cabling.

The idea of using a crossover cable to connect two devices without the need for any extra hardware was discussed in the preceding chapter. The crossover cable has pair 2 and pair 3 reversed on the RJ-45 connector. This switches the transfer bit on the cable to the receive bit on the other end, permitting the direct connection of two switches or hubs together. The connection of two servers or workstations together, without the need for a hub or switch, is also possible.

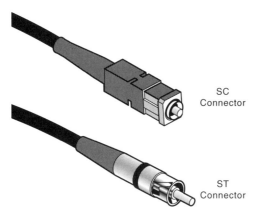

SC Connector

ST Connector

Figure 11.2 Fiber-optic ST and SC cable connectors.

Fiber-Optic Cabling

Fiber-optic cable is designed to carry voice or digital data in the form of light pulses through plastic or glass cable strands. The communication signals are introduced into the cable by a laser diode, and bounced along its interior until reaching the cable's end point. Here, a light-detecting circuit receives the light signals and converts them back into usable information. Fiber cabling offers potential signaling rates in excess of 200,000Mbps; however, current access protocols still limit fiber-optic LAN speeds to somewhat less than that. Modern 62.5/125-micron multimode fiber, the predominant fiber used in premises applications for more than a decade, is now being used to support Gigabit Ethernet applications at speeds up to 1Gbps. In addition, 50/125-micron fiber is gaining in popularity for applications that require high transmit speeds over longer distances, such as backbones transmitting at 10Gbps!

Because light moving through a fiber-optic cable does not attenuate (lose energy) as quickly as electrical signals moving along a copper conductor, segment lengths between transmitters and receivers can be much longer with fiber-optic cabling. In some fiber-optic applications, the maximum cable length can range up to 2 kilometers. Fiber-optic cable also provides a much more secure data transmission medium than copper cable because it cannot be tapped without physically breaking the conductor. Basically, light introduced into the cable at one end does not leave the cable except through the other end. In addition, it electrically isolates the transmitter and receiver so that no signal level matching normally needs to be performed between the two ends.

In Figure 11.2, the connector on the left is a *Straight Tip (ST)* connector and the one on the right is a *Subscriber Channel (SC)* connector. In both cases, the connectors are designed so that they correctly align the end of the cable with the receiver.

Newer connector types offering the benefits of SC and ST terminations and packaged in *Small Form Factor (SFF)*, high-density designs include the LC and MT-RJ connectors, shown in Figure 11.3. LC connectors can be terminated in about 2 minutes on 1.6mm jacketed fiber cables using the manufacturer's proprietary termination kit. The MT-RJ connectors offer innovative push-button fiber termination.

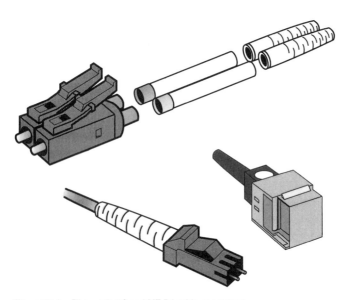

Figure 11.3   Fiber-optic LC and MT-RJ cable connectors.

Cable Management

The lack of proper *cable management* in modern server systems includes a number of serious mistakes. These include poor scalability planning for system upgrading, disregard for the impact of bend radius on network performance, disorganized cable routing in high port-density applications, and disregard for relationships between air flow and the amount of space consumed by cabling. Cable management begins within server racks and cabinets, which should provide ample vertical and horizontal organization. Although well-organized, efficient cabling offers an aesthetically pleasing appearance, the more important benefit is that it helps to keep equipment cool by removing obstacles to air movement.

The cabling space in racks or cabinets should not be more than 70% occupied to provide adequate cable management capacity. For example, for CAT6 UTP cable, currently the most widely used type of network cabling, you can calculate how much space is required by multiplying the number of cables by the cable diameter (0.0625 inches) and then multiplying that result by 1.30. For 350 cables, this is equal to 28.44 square inches for cable management purposes.

One way to simplify rack assembly and provide unified cable management is to use common rack frames and provide enough vertical and horizontal cable management hardware within and between rack frames. To provide for orderly growth, the installation should include overhead and under-floor cable pathways. The under-floor pathways should be reserved for permanent cabling, whereas overhead runs can be used for temporary cabling, or connections that might be moved from time to time. Depending on the growth potential of a specific installation, under-floor cabling might not be used at all. Some companies prefer to have all data and power cables routed above their racks for ease of identification and service.

The basics of cable management are covered in standards developed by the Telecommunications Industry Association (TIA) in their TIA 942. This standard provides an excellent model for network cabling infrastructure in data centers. Key server network components are identified in TIA 606, where compliant labeling helps to improve both cable management and traceability. Another area of concern in these publications is the need for proper grounding of racks and active equipment.

Another area of cable management often taken for granted is the consideration of various cabling connection methods. Equipment can be connected in three different ways within the data center environment, including

➤ Direct connect

➤ Interconnect

➤ Cross-connect

Although many IT departments opt for the simple direct connection, this is often a lazy and unwise choice that forces administrators to hunt for cables whenever any change is made, in addition to pulling the cables to the new location. A better option is to use the interconnection method through the use of a patch panel, which reduces the required reroutes to only the end cables. This is far more efficient than the direct connection. However, the interconnection method is not as easy or reliable as the cross-connection method. All network elements can be provided with permanent equipment cable connections that are terminated once and never handled again. This desirable situation can be realized by using a centralized cross-connect patching system. Required changes can be accomplished using semipermanent patch cord connections on the front of the cross-connect system, or distribution frame. The backplanes of sensitive routing and switching equipment remain undisturbed, while the necessary moves, additions, and changes are carried out on the patching frame. This greatly reduces the required time to add cards, move circuits, upgrade software, and perform maintenance. This approach saves time, money, and trouble while improving server network reliability.

KVM Implementation

A hardware switching device that enables a single keyboard, video monitor, and mouse to control more than one computer one at a time is called a *keyboard video mouse (KVM)*. KVM switches are used by businesses to save money when one employee must use more than one computer, or in server farms where it is only necessary to individually access each separate server in the farm, periodically.

The KVM is the switchbox through which these multiple servers are attached using a single keyboard, mouse, and monitor. KVM switches are commonly available to handle two, four, or eight separate servers. An important consideration when dealing with multiple servers on a rack mount system is to ensure that enough KVM ports are available for the existing servers, as well as any future servers that might be later installed.

 Know what a KVM switch is used for in a rack mount server system.

Rackmount Security

Several methods of providing rack security have been developed. One of these incorporates a keylocked, 3/16-inch thick smoke-gray Plexiglass door mounted in a steel frame. These locking, see-through security covers come in 2U, 4U, and 8U sizes. The 17.688-inch-wide opening and 1.5-inch front depth easily clear the front controls on most server equipment.

Keylocked rackmount security doors allow front access only to the uncovered portions of server equipment and are available in Plexiglass, vented, and solid steel styles. Racked equipment can be completely protected from tampering by unauthorized users. Equipment requiring client access can be installed in the open portion of the rack.

For visible but inaccessible requirements, 1-inch-deep security covers are available in 1U, 2U, and 3U sizes that feature permanent Plexiglass windows for easy equipment viewing. To completely conceal specified rack equipment, solid, 1-inch deep covers are also available in large or fine perforation styles. These opaque covers include installed rubber edgings that won't mar the server equipment being protected. Security rack screws can be used to enhance the level of security.

Network Access Protocols

In a network, some method must be used to determine which node is permitted to use the network's communications paths, and for how long. The network's hardware protocol handles these functions, and prevents more than one user from accessing the data bus at any given time. If two sets of data are simultaneously placed on the network, a collision and loss of data occurs. Through the development of computer networks, two basic networking protocols became the most often used: Ethernet and Token Ring. Today, versions of early Ethernet protocols continue to dominate the networking world, including Fast Ethernet, and Gigabit Ethernet. A network specification standard similar to Token Ring, called FDDI, uses fiber-optic cabling to achieve impressive results.

Ethernet

The standard specification for *Ethernet* has been published by the *International Electrical and Electronic Association (IEEE)* as the IEEE-802.3 Ethernet protocol. Its methodology for control is referred to as *Carrier Sense Multiple Access with Collision Detection (CSMA/CD)*. Using this protocol, a node first listens to the LAN to determine whether it is in use. If the LAN is not in use, the node begins transmitting its data. If the network is busy, the node waits for the LAN to clear for a predetermined time, and then takes control.

If two nodes are waiting to use the LAN, they will periodically attempt to access the LAN at the same time. When this happens, a data collision occurs, and the data from both nodes is rendered useless. The receiver portion of the Ethernet controller monitors the transmission to detect collisions. When the controller senses that the data bits are overlapping, it halts the transmission, as does the other node. The transmitting controller generates an abort pattern code that is transmitted to all the nodes on the LAN, telling them that a collision has occurred. This alerts any nodes that might be waiting to access the LAN that there is a problem.

The receiving node dumps any data that it might have received before the collision occurred. Other nodes waiting to send data generate a random timing number and go into a holding pattern. The timing number is a waiting time that the node sits out before it tries to transmit. Because the number is randomly generated, the odds against two of the nodes trying to transmit again at the same time are very low. The Ethernet strategy allows up to 1,024 users to share the LAN. From the description of its collision-recovery technique, however, it should be clear that with more users on an Ethernet LAN, more collisions are likely to occur, and the average time to complete an actual data transfer will be longer.

Ethernet Specifications

Ethernet is classified as a bus topology. The original Ethernet scheme was classified as a 10Mbps transmission protocol. The maximum length specified for Ethernet is 1.55 miles (2.5 km), with a maximum segment length between nodes of 500 meters. This type of LAN is referred to as a 10BASE-5 LAN by the IEEE organization.

The XXBaseYY IEEE nomenclature designates that the maximum data rate across the LAN is 10Mbps, that it is a baseband LAN (versus broadband), and that its maximum segment length is 500 meters. One exception to this method is the 10BASE-2 implementation, where the maximum segment length is 185 meters.

Newer Ethernet implementations produce LAN speeds of up to 100Mbps using UTP copper cabling. Their IEEE adopted 10BASE-T, 100BASE-T, and 100BASE-TX designations indicate that they operate on twisted-pair cabling and depend on its specifications for the maximum segment length.

The 100BASE designation is referred to as Fast Ethernet. Its TX version employs two pairs of twisted cable to conduct high-speed, full-duplex transmissions. TX cables can be CAT5 UTP or STP. There is also a 100BASE-FX Fast Ethernet designation that uses fiber-optic cabling.

Network cards capable of supporting both transmission rates are classified as 10/100 Ethernet cards. The recommended maximum length of a 10/100BASE-T segment is 100 meters. One problem with using 10/100BASE-T cards in a system is that the presence of a single 10BASE-T card in the network can slow the entire network down.

Ethernet Connections

Ethernet connections can be made through 50-ohm coaxial cable (10BASE-5), thinnet coaxial cable (10BASE-2), or UTP cabling (10BASE-T). The original UTP LAN specification had a transmission rate that was stated as 1Mbps. Using UTP cable, a LAN containing up to 64 nodes can be constructed with the maximum distance between nodes set at 250 meters.

Coaxial cables are attached to equipment through BNC (British Naval Connector) connectors. This connector type is also known as the BayoNet Connector, the Baby N Connector, or the Bayonet Neill-Concelman, after its inventors Paul Neill and Carl Concelman.

In a 10BASE-2 LAN, the node's LAN adapter card is usually connected directly to the LAN cabling, using a T-connector (for peer-to-peer networks), or by a BNC connector (in a client/server LAN).

UTP LAN connections are made through modular RJ-45 registered jacks and plugs. RJ-45 connectors are very similar in appearance to the RJ-11 connectors used with telephones and modems; however, the RJ-45 connectors are considerably larger than the RJ-11 connectors. Some Ethernet adapters include 15-pin sockets that allow special systems, such as fiber-optic cabling, to be interfaced to them. Other cards provide specialized ST connectors for fiber-optic connections.

Table 11.2 summarizes the different Ethernet specifications.

Table 11.2 Ethernet Specifications					
Classification	Conductor	Maximum Segment Length	Nodes	Maximum Length	Transfer Rate
10BASE-2	RG-58	185m	30/1024	250m	10Mbps
10BASE-5	RG-8	500m	100/1024	2.5km	10Mbps
10BASE-T	UTP/STP	100m/200m	2/1024	2.5km	10Mbps
100BASE-T	UTP	100m	2/1024	2.5km	100Mbps
100BASE-FX	FO	412m	1024	5km	100Mbps

Fast Ethernet

100BASE-T is a networking standard that supports data transfer rates up to 100Mbps (100 megabits per second). Based on the older Ethernet standard, 100BASE-T is 10 times faster than Ethernet and is often referred to as *Fast Ethernet*. The 100BASE-T standard is officially called *IEEE 802.3u*, and like Ethernet, it is based on the CSMA/CD LAN access method. Several different cabling schemes can be used with 100BASE-T, including

➤ 100BASE-TX—Two pairs of high-quality twisted-pair wires

➤ 100BASE-T4—Four pairs of normal-quality twisted-pair wires

➤ 100BASE-FX—Fiber optic cables

Gigabit Ethernet

Gigabit Ethernet is abbreviated *GbE*, and is an Ethernet version that supports data transfer rates of 1 Gigabit (1,000 megabits) per second, which is 100 times faster than the original Ethernet standard. Compatible with existing Ethernets, GbE uses the same CSMA/CD and MAC protocols. The first Gigabit Ethernet standard (802.3z) was ratified by the IEEE 802.3 Committee in 1998. There are two main cabling schemes that can be used with Gigabit Ethernet, including

➤ 1000BASE-T—With twisted-pair specifications described in the IEEE 802.3ab standard

➤ 1000BASE-X—With fiber-optic specifications described in the IEEE 802.3z standard

Fiber-Optic LANs

As indicated earlier in this chapter, fiber-optic cabling offers the prospect of very high-performance links for LAN implementation. It can handle much higher data-transfer rates than copper conductors, and can use longer distances between stations before signal deterioration becomes a problem. In addition, fiber-optic cable offers a high degree of security for data communications. It does not radiate EMI signal information that can be detected outside the conductor, it does not tap easily, and it shows a decided signal loss when it is tapped into.

Fiber Ethernet Standards

The IEEE organization has created several fiber-optic variations of the Ethernet protocol. They classify these variations under the IEEE-803 standard. These standards are referenced as the 10/100BASE-F specification. Variations of this standard include

➤ 10BASE-FP—This specification is used for passive star networks running at 10Mbps. It employs a special hub that uses mirrors to channel the light signals to the desired node.

➤ 10BASE-FL—This specification is used between devices on the network. It operates in full-duplex mode and runs at 10Mbps. Cable lengths under this specification can range up to 2 kilometers.

➤ 100BASE-FX. This protocol is identical to the 10Base-FL specification except that it runs at 100Mbps. This particular version of the specification is referred to as Fast Ethernet because it can easily run at the 100Mbps rate.

The FDDI Ring Standard

A Token Ring-like network standard has been developed around fiber-optic cabling. This standard is the *Fiber Distributed Data Interface (FDDI)* specification. The FDDI network was designed to work almost exactly like a Token Ring network, except that it works on two counter-rotating rings of fiber-optic cable.

FDDI employs token passing access control and provides data transfer rates of 100Mbps. Using the second ring, FDDI can easily handle multiple frames of data moving across the network at any given time. Of course, the dual-ring implementation provides additional network dependability because it can shift over to a single ring operation if the network controller senses that a break has occurred in one of the rings.

Exam Prep Questions

1. Terminations for CAT5e or CAT6 UTP cable are typically performed with what type of connector?

   ❑ A. ST

   ❑ B. BNC

   ❑ C. RJ-11

   ❑ D. RJ-45

2. A crossover cable would be used to make which of the following connections?

   ❑ A. A connection from an uplink port to a hub port

   ❑ B. A connection from an AUI to a hub port

   ❑ C. A connection from one hub port to another hub port

   ❑ D. A connection from an NIC to a hub port

3. When configuring a rackmount system, what is the purpose of a KVM switch?

   ❑ A. To enable the viewing of multiple servers using the same keyboard, mouse, and monitor

   ❑ B. To enable multiple network servers to be powered down

   ❑ C. To permit the disabling of memory banks during troubleshooting procedures

   ❑ D. To allow the use of multiple monitors, mice, and keyboards by one server

4. What is the full name for the acronym CSMA/CD?

   ❑ A. Carrier Sense Monolithic Access with CAT6 Detection

   ❑ B. Carrier Sense Multiple Access with CAT6 Detection

   ❑ C. Carrier Sense Monolithic Access with Carrier Detection

   ❑ D. Carrier Sense Multiple Access with Collision Detection

5. In addition to the multiple servers, which peripheral devices are connected to a KVM switch?

   ❑ A. A keyswitch, video, and monitor

   ❑ B. A keyboard, video monitor, and a mouse

   ❑ C. A keypad, vacuum tube, and a mouse

   ❑ D. A keylock, VCR, and a mouse

6. In the SCSI-1 protocol, the highest priority is always assigned to which SCSI ID?

   ❑ A. SCSI ID 0

   ❑ B. SCSI ID 3

   ❑ C. SCSI ID 7

   ❑ D. SCSI ID 8

7. What is the biggest difference between UTP and STP networking cables?

❏ A. An additional foil shield surrounds the four-pair wire bundle in STP cables.

❏ B. An additional layer of insulation surrounds the four-pair wire bundle in STP cables.

❏ C. An additional layer of insulation surrounds the four-pair wire bundle in UTP cables.

❏ D. An additional foil shield surrounds the four-pair wire bundle in UTP cables.

8. The new administrator walks into the server room and observes a dozen servers connected to a 24-port hub. The equipment is displayed on folding tables, behind which are displayed the routed cables. Which of the following steps will not help to improve the situation?

❏ A. The installation of racks to house the server equipment

❏ B. The rerouting of all communications cables

❏ C. The installation of a switch

❏ D. The installation of one or more KVMs

Exam Prep Answers

1. Answer D is the correct answer. RJ-45 connectors are used to terminate CAT5e or CAT6 UTP cables. Answer A is incorrect because ST connectors are used to terminate fiber optic cables. Answer B is incorrect because BNC connectors are used to terminate coaxial cables. Answer C is incorrect because RJ-11 connectors are used to terminate the flat, untwisted wire primarily used in telephone wiring.

2. Answer C is the correct answer. When a hub or a concentrator is not equipped with an uplink port, connecting one hub port to another must be accomplished through the use of a crossover cable. Answer A is incorrect because when a crossover connection is required, an uplink port can automatically reconfigure as needed. Answer B is incorrect because coaxial connections to an NIC are determined by the Attachment Unit Interface (AUI) Ethernet specification. Answer D is incorrect because a straight-through cable is used to accomplish an NIC-to-hub-port connection.

3. Answer A is the correct answer. The same keyboard, mouse, and monitor can be used through a KVM switch to view and operate multiple servers. Answer B is incorrect because permitting servers to be powered down through keyboard command would place the network at risk needlessly. Answer C is incorrect because KVM switches are not related to memory problems. Answer D is incorrect because a KVM performs just the opposite operation, using one monitor, keyboard, and mouse on different servers.

4. Answer D is the correct answer. The full name for the acronym CSMA/CD is Carrier Sense Multiple Access with Collision Detection. This makes answers A, B, and C incorrect by the process of elimination.

5. Answer B is the correct answer. Peripheral devices connected to the KVM switch include a keyboard, a monitor (video), and a mouse. Answer A is incorrect because no keyboard or mouse is listed. Answers C and D are incorrect because no keyboard or video monitor is listed.

6. Answer C is the correct answer. SCSI ID 7 is always assigned the highest priority regardless of which SCSI protocol is being used. Answer A is incorrect because SCSI ID 0 is reserved for the lowest priority. Answer B is incorrect because SCSI ID 3 is located in the middle of the priority rankings. Answer D is incorrect because there is no SCSI ID 8 in the SCSI-1 protocol.

7. Answer A is the correct answer. UTP contains four pairs of individually insulated wires, whereas STP cable is similar except that it contains an additional foil shield surrounding the four-pair wire bundle. Therefore, answers B, C, and D are incorrect by comparison.

8. Answer C is the correct answer. Installing a switch does nothing to improve the situation. Answer A is incorrect because the installation of racks for mounting the equipment would greatly improve the server organizational aspect. Answer B is incorrect because the reorganization of the server room cabling is long overdue. Answer D is incorrect because the use of KVMs will greatly ease the management of these servers.

12.0—Server Management Plans

Terms you'll need to understand:

✓ Manageability
✓ Security
✓ Environment
✓ Storage Area Network (SAN)
✓ Network-Attached Storage (NAS)
✓ Application Programming Interface (API)
✓ Storage virtualization
✓ Resource map
✓ Out-of-band or in-band
✓ Metadata
✓ Latency
✓ Fabric
✓ Logical Unit Number (LUN)
✓ Trunking

Techniques you'll need to master:

✓ Knowing the difference between storage networks and data networks
✓ Knowing the three areas of focus for network storage security
✓ Defining the Public-Key Infrastructure (PKI) protocol
✓ Detailing the authentication process between two switched devices

✓ Explaining how data encryption protects server data storage

✓ Delegating the administration of an effective network security plan

✓ Understanding the use of virtualization storage solutions

✓ Reading a consolidated resource map of all disks connected to a server

✓ Describing the two basic approaches taken by virtualization appliances

✓ Defining what metadata is and how it is used

✓ Identifying the pros and cons of in-band versus out-of-band virtualization

✓ Understanding how the TCO helps to determine administrative decisions regarding virtual storage

✓ Listing the characteristics of the out-of-band telecom storage network model

✓ Listing the characteristics of the in-band telecom storage networking model

✓ Explaining the benefit of using trunking

Introduction

Server+ Exam Objective 2.3 states that the test taker should be able to develop a server management plan, including in-band and out-of-band management.

As mentioned in previous chapters, a network's design and application determine the chief factors that affect the types of servers required by the network as well as the software programs that must be installed. The network administrator or the server manager is responsible for making these determinations. The primary administrative considerations associated with server networks include

➤ Manageability

➤ Security

➤ Environment

Manageability

Server hardware must be easy to manage. Manufacturers have focused on designing system components with options that make them easy to install, configure, or remove. Common features that help successfully manage server hardware include

➤ Rack-mounted components that slide in and out of the cabinet on rails for ease of maintenance.

➤ Exterior covers that are easy to remove, for quick access when trouble-shooting.

➤ Hot-swappable power supplies with handles, for quick and easy removal/insertion from/to the chassis.

➤ Hot-swappable drives that employ slide rails and multi-connectors. Multi-connectors include both power and communication connections to the controller.

➤ Cables that are labeled clearly and correctly.

➤ Administrative software tools that control computer access and permissions.

➤ Software tools that implement and track security policies.

➤ Information monitoring tools that track.

  ➤ System server temperatures

  ➤ Access to I/O ports

  ➤ Network usage

Modern *storage networks* have a limited number of existing architectures and two definitive concepts that underpin them.

The first concept involves the way in which data communications occur. Keep in mind that storage networks enable computers to communicate directly with individual storage devices. This differs sharply from *data networks*, where the communications are managed between two or more computers. Both storage networks and data networks resemble each other in that they both use network protocols to move the data. However, the nature of the data transfer differs somewhat between them. Storage networks transfer the *one and only copy* of the targeted data, whereas data networks usually transmit only a copy of the data and retain the original.

This distinction might seem minor; however, in actual practice the difference is critical. For example, in the data network architecture, Computer A is instructed to send some specified information to Computer B. If for some reason Computer B never receives the data, the original data is still available because Computer A still owns a copy, and Computer B can request a retransmission of the data.

This is not true in the operation of a storage network. If Computer A in a storage network sends the data to another storage device that never receives it, the data might be lost. The receiving device cannot determine that it never received the transferred data. All the responsibility for successfully sending the data to, and storing the data on, Computer B rests solely upon Computer A. This concept is inherently incorporated into the design of a storage network.

The second concept underpinning the operation of a storage network involves its data management. The only management concern of a data network is the transfer flight of a data copy between the communicating computers. Storage networks, however, must concern themselves with the following three items:

➤ Direct management of the data on the various storage devices in the network

➤ Which computer owns a particular piece of data

➤ Which storage device currently contains the specified data

Most modern data networks cannot successfully handle this level of data management. Yet a thorough understanding of storage network architectures dictates that these two concepts be mastered. In storage networks, computers communicate with storage devices, rather than with other computers. In addition, storage networks manage the data at a higher level than that found in modern data networks.

 Know that storage networks permit the communications between computers and individual storage devices.

Security Management

Although keeping data secure is an ever-increasing priority for network managers and administrators, these individuals have begun to realize that the typical network security measures used in past configurations might not be adequate. The ironclad protection required of data held in storage area networks (SANs) and network-attached storage (NAS) infrastructures is being eroded through its increased exposure to unauthorized or non-authenticated employees.

Although storage security has always been synonymous with network security, system analysts now contend that current network security measures are failing to protect this data. A typical server network is normally secured through the use of intrusion detection systems and other methods of access control. However, current systems analysis suggests that up to 85% of all security violations come from within the given enterprise. As a result, security measures that focus on external intrusion detection do not provide the required data security protection. The approach to network storage security management should focus on three specific areas: forensic security, management consoles, and encryption.

Forensic storage security technologies are designed to provide audit trails of storage configuration changes, whereby security violations can be profiled and corrected. Not only can the numbers of violations be tabulated, but the individual perpetrators can be profiled and identified. The administrator scrutinizes this information at regular intervals.

Several manufacturers produce storage security appliances that incorporate both encryption technologies and management tools. These hardware appliances authenticate any networked product that is attached to the SAN. For example, a 2U security appliance sits just outside of the SAN fabric and uses a software agent to communicate with switches, host bus adapters (HBAs), and other SAN components. This software agent can be a stripped-down version of the *Public-Key Infrastructure (PKI)*, which is a familiar authentication standard. The appliance architecture uses PKI to authenticate devices, rather than people. An alternate version of the security appliance works within NAS environments.

In the case of a network switch, the agent uses various *Application Programming Interfaces (APIs)* to determine whether the two specified devices should communicate with each other. The two devices are required to exchange digital certificates originally issued, managed, and validated by the security appliance for authentication of devices in the SAN. After authentication, the two devices are permitted to communicate and transport data. Complete or selective data encryption occurs within the host server through a PCI card. Therefore, data is never unprotected as it travels to and from the SAN. It is stored in its encrypted format so that any client trying to access the data must first be authenticated prior to any decryption activities. No encryption or decryption software is loaded onto hosts, clients, or servers so that random access to data is not slowed.

Environmental Impacts

Anything that impacts the environment of a server network also affects the management of its security. A secure server network environment is the result of careful planning from its initial deployment through times when new features or services are added. Server network managers know that ensuring a secure environment involves careful planning across such diverse areas as

➤ Directory services

➤ Networking

➤ Client configurations

Unless security is an essential element of an organization's operating environment, the best security plans and designs in the world cannot provide the necessary protection. Obviously, planning a comprehensive, secure data environment is a major challenge because each organization includes a unique blend of servers, clients, and user requirements. An inconsistent approach to security will result in certain areas of the network receiving extremely rigorous scrutiny, while others are granted only minimal attention.

An effective security planning process is based on two organizing principles:

1. Clients must be able to reach their data resources quickly. Although this access can be as simple as a desktop logon, with resources provided through the use of *Access Control Lists (ACLs)*, it can also provide external business partners/customers with optional services such as remote network logons and wireless network access.

2. The shared server environment requires security boundaries, secure servers, and secure services. To provide continuous network security, an effective plan for delegating its administration must also be formulated.

When a server environment is properly constructed, the required trust and integrity of the organization's storage network can be achieved. However, establishing a secure environmental framework requires a careful analysis of the specified organization's particular requirements, which is an important aspect of server management and administration.

Storage Virtualization Management

Data storage requirements for the typical commercial enterprise are doubling every one or two years. Although network-attached storage (NAS) and storage area networks (SANs) are evolving to meet this demand, administrators continue to add more storage servers and disks. Rising management complexity, escalating costs, and user disruptions are the new realities for scaling up capacity with these solutions.

The latest approach to the unification of storage management issues is called *storage virtualization*. Mostly oriented toward SANs, virtualization storage solutions help administrators properly manage large individual storage pools. The ultimate goal for virtualization is the creation of a single storage pool capable of being managed seamlessly across various platform types and widely dispersed geographic locations.

Although many SANs consist of heterogeneous collections of storage servers and disk arrays, virtualization creates a logical view of these numerous disks quite distinct from their physical makeup. A storage administrator using virtualization is presented with a consolidated *resource map* of all disks connected to a server, which appears as a single server resource. The individual physical disk drives are basically decoupled from their normal operations, and reconfigured into a "logical" and consolidated storage picture.

Virtual storage solutions are currently deployed through the use of a separate hardware appliance, although many SAN equipment vendors are contemplating the idea of incorporating virtualization features into their products. Virtualization appliances currently use two broad approaches, with each having its advantages and disadvantages. These approaches are called

➤ Out-of-band (asymmetrical)

➤ In-band (symmetrical)

Out-of-Band

The term *out-of-band* is a fairly simple concept to understand. For example, when you use a file management program such as Windows Explorer, the C: drive's logical screen representation is an out-of-band experience. The visible C: icon logically represents the actual physical path to the underlying disk. This seems simple enough. Yet such a concept can become complicated very quickly in a networked storage environment. Although the C: prompt/icon represents the logical path to the disk, it neither maps out its physical path, nor does it specifically identify on which physical storage device the data resides.

An effective storage administrator must know not only on which storage devices specific data resides, but also which path it follows through the storage network. Out-of-band servers, which reside outside of the data path, provide the administrator with control over, and information about, all critical storage components, as shown in the left half of Figure 12.1. An out-of-band appliance enables virtualization of multiple disk farms involving multiple storage servers on the SAN. The virtualization appliance supplies volume *metadata*, which the server uses to translate I/O addresses for the appropriate disk, by way of the appliance.

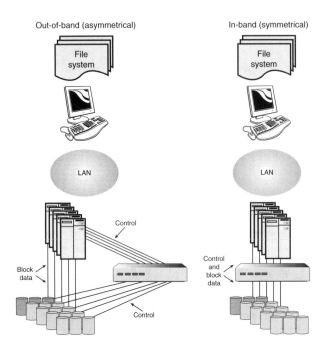

Figure 12.1 Two approaches to virtualization.

Although virtualization is capable of introducing latency into the storage access process, most such problems are alleviated using out-of-band configurations. This is because out-of-band virtualization appliances preserve near-native performance of the storage server by working outside of the data path.

To achieve out-of-band virtualization, network administrators must install appliance-related software on every server included in the map. This software must often be present on some host bus adapters (HBAs) as well, for certain out-of-band virtualization solutions. For each server added to the SAN, the administrator must add virtualization software. In addition, the virtualization appliance must also be reconfigured. As a result, the continuous cycle of reconfiguration for a growing server map can seem endless.

In-Band

Take a moment to contrast the out-of-band configuration with the example of in-band virtualization shown in the right half of Figure 12.1. In this configuration, the appliance is located in a direct path between the storage servers and the disk farm, eliminating the need to install appliance-related software on each server. Self-contained, in-band virtualization appliances are easier to manage and deploy, which lowers the *total cost of ownership (TCO)* when compared with out-of-band solutions. Administrators are not required to install or reconfigure server software every time new storage servers are added.

The tradeoff is that because the in-band solution resides directly in the data path between the server and the disk farm, storage performance can be affected and latency and availability issues can appear. Additional *latency* is created within the data path because the data must traverse the additional hardware located between the server and its disks. More time is consumed while the virtualization software performs its various translations. Another in-band weakness is that the appliance itself represents a single point of failure.

However, because many applications aren't affected by its additional latency, in-band virtualization has gained some market attention. Although applications that support many users can issue a continuous stream of I/O requests to a storage server, their traffic characteristics often vary in such a way as to not be affected by virtualization latency. For example, some applications have large volumes of small reads or writes, whereas others have smaller volumes of large reads or writes. In-band virtualization latencies are more likely to affect high-volume database applications that have more writes than reads. Higher processor speeds and new technologies will soon negate the potential for in-band virtualization-induced I/O delays.

The management of enterprise storage is usually the most expensive element of in-band virtualization. However, with the successful addressing of its latency and availability issues, in-band virtualization often emerges as the most cost-effective solution. In fact, in-band technology is really nothing new. Many computer connectivity devices are already configured for in-band operations. For example, Internet routers send data traffic around the world utilizing a form of in-band virtualization.

Know the pros and cons of in-band vs. out-of-band virtualization.

Out-of-Band ESCON

The term *Enterprise Systems Connection (ESCON)* comes from the IBM mainframe marketing world. It refers to the highly available, though relatively simple to configure, ESCON switches (also called black boxes or directors) that first connected servers and storage devices. ESCON products originally networked mainframe computers, attached storage, locally attached workstations, and other devices together within local channels.

These local channels governed the interconnection of hardware units throughout early IBM server networks, and were distinguished from remote or telecommunication connections. Nevertheless, they combined the use of optical fiber technology along with chains of dynamically modifiable ESCON switches to permit network extensions from the mainframe up to 37.3 miles (60 kilometers). Data rates over these links could reach up to 200Mbps (million bits per second) depending on the specific channel interface equipment.

The out-of-band and ESCON strategies were combined to create the earliest storage-networking model, called *out-of-band ESCON*. The out-of-band server manages the data paths by utilizing agents placed on the networked servers as well as the APIs of the respective storage networking components. The storage administrator can use this technology to configure all the storage networking components, such as the server, the ESCON switch, or the various storage devices. This architecture lends itself well to environments of 40 servers or less, where the administrator has control over all aspects of the storage-networking environment.

These elementary ESCON switches lack the advanced intelligence required for features such as routing, or *Quality of Service (QoS)*. However, they provide high availability and reliability combined with a relative ease of management.

The out-of-band telecom ESCON switch model is found in a significant segment of modern storage networking environments. The term *telecom* itself comes from those networking models that handle Internet and phone-line switching. ESCON switches designed for use in out-of-band telecom networks possess three distinct characteristics:

➤ They manage and report on where data lies on the storage devices.

➤ They remain outside the data path of the storage network itself.

➤ They contain more intelligence than early ESCON switches.

Telecom ESCON switches (also called simply telecom switches) support advanced features such as

➤ Quality of Service (QoS), which permits switches to prioritize traffic on the network, based on information contained in the data packets themselves

➤ Trunking between switches, enabling multiple physical switch paths to function as one logical path

➤ Security authentications for logging of devices into or out of the fabric

As already mentioned, out-of-band technology permits storage administrators to gather information about the data, and to manage its various paths throughout the storage network. Yet it accomplishes this from outside of the data path. Administration is performed from a central management server communicating with various server agents to learn how much storage each server has and to provide additional storage for those servers that need it. Although the out-of-band telecom model is suitable for organizations having either small or large SANs linked together to maximize storage utilization, two potential stumbling blocks exist with this approach:

1. Designing a *fabric* that interconnects many switches requires far more skill and forethought than that required to deploy only one or two switches.

2. The complexity of the switching software requires the use of more advanced skills following its initial deployment in order to manage and grow the fabric.

If an out-of-band telecom server storage model can be appropriately designed before construction, and adequately staffed after deployment, it merits due consideration. On the surface, the telecom model appears to offer a scalable and flexible model, and up to a certain size this is true. Keep in mind, however, that in large deployment, its out-of-band storage management component is so complex as to severely reduce much of its desirability. Developers of intelligent switches are well aware of these complexities, and have explored the possibilities of another storage management model to help reduce them.

In-Band ESCON, Telecom, and ESCOM

The terms "in-band" and "ESCON" combine to create the second storage-networking model, *in-band ESCON*. In-band refers to the fact that the storage intelligence has been moved into the network appliance. This methodology provides a central console to report on and manage data within the storage network itself. It also delivers this functionality without using server agents or APIs. Storage arrays from different vendors can be managed from one location. However, the end-to-end performance management solution required for some environments is not natively offered.

The in-band ESCON model also possesses three distinct characteristics:

➤ It reports in great detail which data resides where on the network of storage devices.

➤ It resides directly within the data path of the storage network itself.

➤ It utilizes a relatively simple switching technology.

The *in-band ESCON* model can be found more frequently in newer storage networking environments. In fact, the storage community already extensively uses in-band technology solutions in various forms.

Storage array vendors have placed in-band virtualization on the front end of their storage arrays for *Logical Unit Number (LUN)* management. An LUN is the logical representation of the physical data storage. LUN management configurations differ somewhat between various types of SANs, so the overall management of a server network may be somewhat limited in certain areas. Management scenarios include LUN masking, zoning, or some combination of these methods, and are normally hardware-configured at the switch, storage subsystem, or Host Bus Adapter (HBA) and not within the OS. In fact, Windows NOSs do not provide any capabilities for mapping LUNs.

Administrators can determine whether an LUN refers to a disk drive, a number of disk drives, or a specific partition on a disk drive, depending on the RAID configuration. This technology is so well accepted that it is used extensively in high-availability data centers, providing much of the SAN connectivity being used today. This architecture lends itself well to storage environments of 40 servers or less, including multiple servers, different operating systems, and/or storage arrays from different vendors. It also permits the limited management of the server environment without providing total control over all aspects of the storage network.

The *in-band telecom* model also represents an emerging segment of modern storage networking environments. It possesses three distinct characteristics:

➤ It manages the location of data on the storage devices.

➤ It performs its management within the storage network's data path.

➤ The switch itself can perform advanced functions such as routing and quality of service.

Because in-band technology enables the discovery and assignment of LUNs on any storage array it manages, its central console can be used to provide reports about, and manage data within, the storage network itself. As might be expected, it delivers this functionality without requiring the deployment of server agents, or the use of APIs. In-band telecom switches contain more intelligence than their ESCON counterparts and are capable of enabling advanced features such as Quality of Service (QoS), security, and trunking. The security function is used to authenticate servers logging into the network. *Trunking* enables multiple physical paths between switches to function as one logical path.

The in-band telecom model makes sense for organizations seeking to link larger SANs together, while simplifying the storage management problem created by the out-of-band telecom model. The tedious tasks of LUN masking and zoning are removed, while an important new storage network management layer is created. It is due to this storage management simplification that the industry has shifted toward the implementation of this solution.

However, although the in-band telecom model merits serious consideration for enterprises looking to deploy a mixed bag of SANs using multiple vendors, operating systems, and storage arrays, caution should still be exercised. Storage management might not be tied to any specific host or storage array, but it inevitably connects the network directly into the switch vendor that implements the technology.

Because the switch resides directly in the data path between the server and the disk farm, it is the most significant point of failure. If it goes, the network goes! The larger a server network becomes, the more dependent on the switch vendor the administrator becomes. Switches are designed to get along with each other, as long as the same manufacturer makes them. Therefore, once the in-band network is running, it is locked into the switch vendor.

Although the vendors of in-band switches might be eager to exploit their locking potential, administrators should be aware of in-band storage model derivatives that can circumvent the potential of vendor lock-in at the switch level. One of these derivatives combines components of the telecom, ESCON, and in-band models to form a new model. This new model is called the *in-band ESCOM* model, combining the terms ESCON and telecom.

The outer layer of the ESCOM model is formed from its telecom architecture. Servers connected to this model draw upon the strengths of the latest networking architectures, including Quality of Service (QoS), advanced routing protocols, management consoles, and advanced networking protocols. In addition, ESCOM provides reliable security schemes that will become more important with the spread of enterprise storage infrastructures.

ESCOM's in-band appliance creates a new interconnecting layer between the telecom and ESCON architectures, providing three important functions:

➤ It minimizes the drawback of routing tables, because all storage traffic is routed to, and all storage devices are controlled by, the appliance. This minimizes the complexity found in a large telecom model.

➤ The in-band appliance is permitted to configure and discover all storage. SAN administrators no longer face the current masking and zoning headaches presented by LUNs.

➤ It permits the organization to retain its existing infrastructure and gradually grow into the new environment.

In-band ESCOM represents a powerful new model for the connection of unrelated storage devices, networking protocols, and operating systems. At different points in the SAN infrastructure, ESCOM offers appropriate levels of

➤ Scalability

➤ Flexibility

➤ Simplicity

➤ Security

More importantly, it allows the server administrator to separately consider the highly technical computing disciplines of storage administration, network administration, and performance monitoring. All this permits data storage professionals to use the tools at their disposal to lower costs and make the best use of their existing resources.

Know that ESCOM in-band appliances remove the possibility of vendor lock at the switch level.

Exam Prep Questions

1. When considering the administration of server networks, what are the three primary areas of concern?
   - ❑ A. Networkability, configurability, and serviceability
   - ❑ B. Manageability, security, and environment
   - ❑ C. Quality of service, switch trunking, and authentication
   - ❑ D. Scalability, flexibility, and simplicity

2. When using storage virtualization appliances, what two methods are applied?
   - ❑ A. Out-of-band (musical) and in-band (non-musical) virtualization
   - ❑ B. Out-of-band (non-musical) and in-band (musical) virtualization
   - ❑ C. Out-of-band (symmetrical) and in-band (asymmetrical) virtualization
   - ❑ D. Out-of-band (asymmetrical) and in-band (symmetrical) virtualization

3. Which of the following represents a type of authentication standard?
   - ❑ A. Public-Key Infrastructure (PKI)
   - ❑ B. Total Cost of Ownership (TCO)
   - ❑ C. Logical Unit Number (LUN)
   - ❑ D. Quality of Service (QoS)

4. What are the main areas of focus for network storage security?
   - ❑ A. Scalability, flexibility, simplicity, and security
   - ❑ B. Directory services, networking, and client configurations
   - ❑ C. Encryption, management consoles, and forensics
   - ❑ D. Quick-access exterior covers, accurate cable identifications, and rack-mounted components

5. What is the main advantage to the use of ESCOM in-band appliances?
   - ❑ A. The increased scalability at the server level
   - ❑ B. The lack of vendor lock at the switch level
   - ❑ C. The minimization of large telecom complexity
   - ❑ D. The ability to configure and locate all storage

6. Which of the following features were not included in early ESCON switches? (Select two.)
   - ❑ A. High availability
   - ❑ B. Routing
   - ❑ C. Ease of management
   - ❑ D. Quality of Service (QoS)

Exam Prep Answers

1. Answer B is the correct answer. Primary administrative considerations associated with server networks are manageability, security, and the server environment. Answer A is incorrect because none of these terms were used in the chapter. Answer C is incorrect because authentication is a security function rather than an administrative function. Answer D is incorrect because these terms actually describe the attributes of in-band ESCOM.

2. Answer D is the correct answer. Answers A and B are incorrect because virtualization involves server network configurations rather than having anything to do with music. Answer C is incorrect because it provides opposite meanings to these two terms.

3. Answer A is the correct answer. PKI is a traditional authentication standard that is difficult and expensive to implement. Answer B is incorrect because when determining which system or product to implement, the TCO is merely one factor to consider. Answer C is incorrect because physical data storage can be represented logically through the use of LUNs. Answer D is incorrect because QoS uses information contained in the data packets to permit switches to prioritize network traffic.

4. Answer C is the correct answer. The main areas of focus for network storage security include encryption, management consoles, and forensics. Answer A is incorrect because these terms represent features of in-band ESCOM. Answer B is incorrect because these are areas of planning by server network managers for ensuring secure environments. Answer D is incorrect because these are features associated with the management of server hardware.

5. Answer B is the correct answer. Because ESCOM in-band appliances will work with any suitable switch, administrators maintain control over which switch vendor to use. Answers A, C, and D all list features that are permitted by ESCOM in-band appliances, none of which is considered the main advantage.

6. Answers B and D are the correct answers. Routing and QoS were not features available with the early ESCON switches. Answers A and C are incorrect because they list features that these ESCON switches did offer.

13.0—Configuration

Terms you'll need to understand:

✓ BIOS
✓ Drivers
✓ Firmware
✓ Updates
✓ Flash utilities
✓ Service partition
✓ Linux loader (LILO)
✓ NT loader
✓ Standard, beta, and bilingual FireWire
✓ USB 1.1, USB 2.0, and USB On-The-Go (OTG)
✓ Serial ATA (SATA)
✓ Release versions
✓ Patches
✓ Service packs
✓ Device drivers
✓ Upgrades
✓ Top-level directory
✓ Fragmentation

Techniques you'll need to master:

✓ Checking and upgrading BIOS and firmware levels
✓ Avoiding or dealing with major disruptions to data and clients
✓ Understanding update procedures and establishing update
  schedules

✓ Handling bundled update packages

✓ Using flash utility programs

✓ Updating RAID controller firmware and configuring RAID arrays

✓ Installing hard drive firmware updates

✓ Managing a service partition and running its software

✓ Understanding how to remotely boot a server

✓ Installing a boot loader

✓ Configuring communications protocols

✓ Performing external peripheral configurations

✓ Configuring UPS management software

✓ Understanding various cable types

✓ Updating network operating systems and drivers

✓ Testing the restore function following the current backup

✓ Installing new OS components

✓ Recognizing the Unix hierarchical file system

✓ Using the Unix installation CD

✓ Dealing with fragmentation problems between various Linux versions

Introduction

Server+ Exam Objective 3.1 states that the test taker should be able to check and upgrade BIOS and firmware levels, including those located on system boards, RAID controllers, and hard drives.

Preplanning the Update

Before a server system is updated, you need to carefully review the company's update strategy plan. This plan is normally based on specified conditions that govern when, where, and how updates to the server network are permitted. Valid reasons to update the server network include

➤ The existence of a security concern that requires correction

➤ The verification of a system problem, based on network support personnel recommendations

➤ An application's minimum requirements exceed the current system configuration

➤ Access to a new system feature or the gaining of improved system performance

➤ The periodic update of all company system components due to a scheduled maintenance process

Although these types of update pressures vary in intensity, they all require some type of preplanning to avoid major disruptions to data and clients. Company policies and procedures must be followed explicitly to make proper use of the system tools available. Update procedures will differ according to the current server-networking situation, and whether the update is classified as planned or unplanned.

Many organizations implement an established schedule for planned updates that occur as a part of the normal maintenance cycle of providing company systems with up-to-date *BIOS*, *drivers*, and *firmware*. Planned maintenance functions permit the organization to adopt quarterly or semiannual update schedules that all clients are familiar with. The plan might also call for an update to occur on an irregular basis when a new application is added to the system, or when the OS is upgraded or altered. A planned outage provides an opportunity to consider upgrading other system software components as well.

On the other hand, unplanned *updates* typically occur when data loss, service interruptions, or security threats become an immediate or critical threat. Unscheduled updates might be advised by company security personnel or by support professionals at various hardware or application software companies. To handle such possible situations successfully, a well-planned strategy should already be in place. Regardless of the urgency level involved, careful thought and consideration must be applied to ensure minimal disruption to clients during the update.

Obtaining and Installing Updates

For server systems purchased from single suppliers, update packages might already be prepared as bundled files that contain hardware updates organized by system component categories such as Embedded Server Management, FlashBIOS Updates, SCSI RAID, and so on. After the specific system model type is identified, a download category is selected. Alternately, all available updates for the specified system can be reviewed by OS and language.

When server system hardware has been purchased from many different vendors, system firmware updates must be obtained on a component-by-component basis. Consult the specific hardware documentation for specific instructions on how to obtain them, and from whom.

When websites provide the system updates, they generally offer summary information about each one, describing the issues a specified update is designed to resolve, the system for which it is designed, and other information. You should read this summary information to determine whether or not to download the update and apply it to the system. Some server administrator software can be used to help determine the suitability for a particular update package and identify the versions of system software currently installed. Of course, the most current version of the server administrator software should be used for this purpose.

After the selected update package has been downloaded, execute it by performing the following steps:

1. Double-click the filename in the Windows Explorer screen.

2. Read the update information displayed in the package window.

3. Click on the Install button to begin the installation.

4. Reboot the system, as required.

Server Boards

Server board manufacturers continually offer BIOS and driver updates for their boards to allow them to work properly with newer peripheral cards, increased memory, and OS upgrades. Often these updates are intended to fix known problems with the server board itself, to take advantage of the built-in features of their chipsets, or to provide increased compatibility with a specific OS. Some manufacturers offer live, automated update capabilities from their websites.

Often, a *flash utility* program can be used to reprogram the server board's BIOS chip directly after downloading the compressed file update package. However, these types of BIOS updates are often finicky as to which flash utility will load them successfully. To avoid BIOS update failures, most BIOS update packages include the correct flash utility program to be used.

Board manufacturers also offer software utility programs, usually available for download at no cost, designed specifically for their server boards. For example, a utility program might be available that can detect certain types of hardware status conditions during real-time operations, including the following:

➤ CPU and system temperatures

➤ Fan speed(s)

➤ System voltage

➤ Chassis intrusion

Because declining hardware status conditions accurately indicate the likelihood of future problems, they are frequently monitored in an effort to alert administrators of impending trouble. The utility programs designed for such monitoring can be configured to issue visual and/or audible warnings when specified parameters are exceeded. They can also send text messages to the administrator with details as to the nature of the specified hardware condition.

RAID Controllers

From time to time, RAID controller firmware can be updated in a similar fashion to server board BIOS chips, depending on the system hardware and OS being used. For example, if a RAID controller card is already operational and using an outdated driver on a server running on Windows 2000, 2003, or XP, the RAID driver can be updated with the following steps:

1. Right-click on My Computer and select Properties.

2. Click on the Hardware tab under the System Properties section.

3. Click on Device Manager, then on SCSI and RAID Controller.

4. Right-click on the specified RAID controller for the system (Silicon Image SATA Raid Controller, for example).

5. Click on Driver, then on Update Driver.

6. Select Search for a Suitable Driver for My Device[Recommended].

7. Insert the driver diskette or CD into the appropriate drive, or locate the driver on the hard disk.

8. Click on Next to execute the driver installation.

9. Click on Yes to reboot the system as necessary following the driver installation

After the driver has been installed, you can verify the installation by completing the following steps:

10. Right-click on the My Computer icon.

11. Select Properties, left-click on the Hardware tab, and then on the Device Manager button.

12. Double-click on SCSI and RAID Controllers.

13. Locate the specified RAID controller in the listing.

If no yellow *!* or *?* is indicated in front of the specified RAID controller, the driver is running properly.

Hard Drives

Hard disk drive manufacturers also produce their own utility programs to help determine when a system is configured with a drive that requires a firmware update. Certain utility programs even indicate the exact firmware level required. The manufacturer's web page will normally indicate which link to follow for the appropriate firmware update code needed by the hard drive.

These utility programs usually support a specific type of drive, such as an ATA hard drive connected to an IDE port on the server board. They search for every hard disk drive connected to the system to identify any hard drives that require the specified firmware update. Some provide the model, manufacturer, capacity, serial number, and current firmware level information for each drive detected.

RAID Configurations

Server+ Exam Objective 3.2 states that the test taker should be able to configure RAID arrays. These activities include using the manufacturer's tools to configure the array and testing the array by simulating a failure. Supporting knowledge required to successfully configure a RAID array includes the following:

➤ Familiarity with online capacity expansion (OCE)

➤ Familiarity with the characteristics of failover and spare drive types (cold, hot, warm, dedicated, and global)

➤ Familiarity with the characteristics, purpose, and function of the RAID cache, including when to turn off write caching

➤ Knowledge of how to calculate storage capacity

➤ Familiarity with the functionality of RAID controller battery

Network Operating System Installations

Server+ Exam Objective 3.3 states that the test taker should be able to install a *Network Operating System (NOS)*. Although network operating systems vary greatly, the steps required to plan and implement their installations are fairly similar.

Create and Implement a Pre-Installation Plan

A *pre-installation plan* that includes the following must be created and implemented:

➤ The installation plan itself

➤ The installation plan's verification

➤ Hardware compatibility verifications between the server and the NOS

➤ Disk drive preparation

➤ Service partition creation

Service Partition

When installing operating systems, the required hard drive partitions must be determined. For management purposes, a *service partition* should be created first, and configured on a small portion of the primary hard drive. The service partition permits management, backup, and recovery operations independent of any other action in the installation process. After the service partition is successfully installed, the network operating system can be installed on the drive's remaining portions.

A service partition hosts diagnostic agents and tests necessary to support the operating system. The partition is a DOS-based operating system configured with TCP/IP, PPP, and FTP protocols that support a redirection of a text-based console over supported communication paths, such as modems and network cards. A client service is used to communicate with the system and with various diagnostic agents from a remote console.

The server board manufacturer supplies the service partition software. You need to follow the instructions provided with each server board manufacturer. This usually involves booting the server with a utility CD-ROM that enables you to run the service partition manager. After creating the partition, it needs to be formatted before installing the service boot partition software.

Boot Loader Installations

After installing the service partition, a boot loader or an operating system that automatically installs a boot loader must be installed. This allows the selection of the proper boot partition upon system startup, before the server can be used. As a boot loader, Linux uses the *Linux loader (LILO)* utility, whereas Windows 2003 uses the *boot loader* utility. Each of these loaders can be modified to enable the selection of multiple operating systems. Figure 13.1 illustrates how the service partition works with the network operating system.

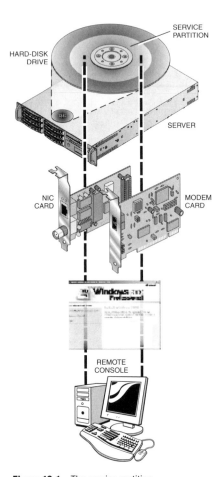

Figure 13.1 The service partition.

The following components allow remote booting of the server:

➤ Firmware running on the server

➤ BIOS console redirection for remote access to preboot BIOS setup

➤ BIOS support on the server for booting from a service partition

➤ A service operating system installed on the service partition at the server

If something detrimental happens to the bootable partition of the server's operating system, booting to the service partition and running the system diagnostic and management tools can help in attempting to recover the system. The bootable service partition can be used to perform an emergency server boot instead of using a CD-ROM or a floppy disk. Of course, this partition should be used only in an emergency situation or when booting the computer for operating system repairs.

Install the Network Operating System

The server version of the operating system must then be installed on all network servers. The NOS versions typically used in server applications include

➤ Windows Server 2003

➤ Novell NetWare

➤ Linux distributions

➤ Unix distributions

➤ Windows XP

Workstation versions of the operating system must be installed on the network's client computers, including client OS versions such as

➤ Windows NT 4.0 Workstation

➤ Windows 2000 Professional/XP Professional

➤ Windows Server 2003 Client Access License (CAL)

➤ Novell NetWare

➤ Linux distributions

➤ Unix distributions

Install Communications Protocols

As you already know, server networks can include computers running various server and client operating systems. To ensure communications between all servers and clients, the required communications protocols must be properly configured. These communications protocols might include

➤ TCP/IP (universal)

➤ NetBEUI (Microsoft only)

➤ IPX/SPX (Novell)

➤ AppleTalk (Apple)

Both hardware and software manufacturers include the necessary configuration information in their product documentation, or on their websites. Opportunities for the correct configurations of detected hardware devices are often provided by OS software.

Know where to look for checking the latest hardware compatibility.

External Peripheral Configurations

Server+ Exam Objective 3.4 states that the test taker should be able to configure external peripherals, such as uninterruptible power supplies, backup devices, and data storage subsystems. Supporting knowledge includes proper equipment layout, while meeting server UPS, space, power, and network availability requirements.

Cabling knowledge should include SCSI terminations, Fibre Channel requirements, and peripheral device cabling types such as FireWire, USB, and serial ATA.

UPS Configuration

A server must be properly configured to communicate with an *Uninterruptible Power Supply (UPS)* system. The most common physical connection between a server and a UPS is a direct cable connection. In the past, 9-pin serial cables were commonly used; today USB connections are becoming more popular.

After the cable is connected and secured, it is time to configure the management software that communicates with the UPS system. The software is important because it allows the system to send alerts to client machines regarding power outages and times when it is necessary to shut the server down. The software either comes with the operating system or is supplied by the manufacturer of the UPS system. Normally the software that comes with the operating system is more limited than what is supplied by the UPS manufacturer.

When configuring the UPS, you should configure it to allow maximum runtime within its limits. Properly calculating the power load allows you to tell what your runtimes are. After you finish configuring the UPS system, you are then ready to test it. If you boot up the system and the server can't recognize the UPS, your management software is most likely not properly configured, so be sure to double-check your work to avoid problems.

> Know that if the UPS management software is not properly configured the server might not recognize it.

Cable Types for Peripheral Devices

Like other computer types, servers connect to various peripheral devices through the use of specific cable types. Modern connectivity standards, USB for example, make it incredibly easy to add peripherals to servers. These connections can be accomplished on the outside of the computer without having to remove the covers. However, the need for security precludes the use of these device types with proprietary server storage networks that contain sensitive data. For example, the hot-swapping capabilities of USB and FireWire ports make them undesirable in the server environment because nonauthorized individuals could plug a USB or FireWire device into the system and gain immediate access to the server. On the other hand, for server systems designed for general purposes rather than the storage of sensitive data, the situation might not be so critical.

> Know why USB and FireWire devices are considered a security risk in the server industry.

A recent development in USB and FireWire technology has resulted in the use of smart card based security tokens containing 16-bit crypto-coprocessors.

These processors can perform fast encryption or authentication functions for use with secured USB or FireWire ports, or with specific USB or FireWire components. Unless an employee can unlock the USB or FireWire port using the security token, it remains inaccessible to any connected peripheral. An alternate strategy places the lock on the component itself, such as a hard drive.

FireWire

The IEEE 1394 (FireWire) standard is a fast, scalable, low-cost, all-digital interface that requires no DAC or ADC data conversion for transmission purposes. This makes it a perfect digital interface for consumer electronics and AV peripherals. It also enables multiple computers to share a given peripheral without requiring any special support in either the peripheral or the computers. Compared to bulky and expensive SCSI cables, FireWire is lightweight, flexible, and inexpensive. In addition, device IDs, jumpers, DIP switches, screws, latches, and terminating resistors are not required.

FireWire supports data rates of 100, 200, and 400Mbps, for up to 63 devices with a maximum cable length of 4.5 meters between devices. The maximum number of hops in a single chain is 16, permitting a total maximum end-to-end distance of 72 meters. The standard supports daisy chaining, branching, or peer-to-peer connections.

FireWire's high-speed operations support isochronous, as well as asynchronous, data delivery. It guarantees delivery of time-critical data at high data rates without lags or slowdowns, enabling applications to use smaller buffers, which reduces costs.

Standard FireWire interconnect cables are fitted with silver braid shielding and are rated to support 400Mbps in various combinations of 4-pin and 6-pin arrangements. Designed specifically for use with FireWire peripherals, they are available in lengths of 3, 6, 10, 15, and 25 feet. The 3-foot version is suitable for mobile users not enamored with cable clutter. The 25-foot special application version supports 100Mbps for use with most A/V applications. When using a device such as a camcorder with a PC, a 6-pin-to-4-pin cable is used to convert the interface.

The 6-pin connector, usually found on computers, provides two wire pairs for signals, and one pair to provide power to external equipment. Many FireWire computer peripherals draw their power directly from the interface. Computer peripherals using 6-pin FireWire connectors generally feature at least two, and often three, FireWire connectors for daisy chaining. The 4-wire FireWire connector is usually found on consumer electronics such as camcorders, VCRs, and video game systems. It provides four signal wires but no power wires. Accordingly, devices using the 4-pin FireWire connection generally have only one connector, and cannot be daisy-chained.

Premium 6-pin FireWire interconnect cables are rated to 400Mbps in lengths of 6, 10, and 15 feet. Intended for use with FireWire peripherals, these cables are fitted with internal LEDs that light up to indicate a completed connection using blue, green, white, or red LEDs. High-performance 9-pin FireWire 800 (IEEE-1394b) cables are rated to 800Mbps and represent the fastest serial technology yet developed for connecting peripheral devices together, or to a computer. Available in 3-, 6-, and 10-foot lengths, these cables come in both *Beta* and *Bilingual* versions. Beta cables have 9-pin connectors mounted on both ends. Bilingual cables connect FireWire 800 and FireWire 400 devices together. As might be expected, bilingual versions have the 9-pin connector on one end and the standard 6- or 4-pin connector on the other.

USB

In an effort to eliminate the guesswork in connecting peripheral devices to computers, the *Universal Serial Bus (USB)* standard was created. USB cables are suitable for connections between servers and printers, scanners, and hubs. They are commonly available in various lengths between 10 inches and 25 feet, with three connector combinations, and two standards. The cabled connector combinations include

➤ A to B—This is a male-to-male type connection, with two types of male connectors.

➤ A to A—This is also a male-to-male type connection, with type A male connectors only. Typical applications for this cable are to connect from a computer to a USB hub, or between a hub and another USB device.

➤ B to B—This is a B-male to B-female type connection. Typical applications for this cable are to extend an existing connection between a computer and a USB hub, or between a hub and a USB device.

USB devices are completely hot-swappable, so a computer can keep running while connections are made. Many USB devices don't require a separate power supply because the USB also distributes power, normally from a host computer or a powered hub. USB host controllers automatically detect peripherals being connected to or disconnected from a port, and the necessary configuration is conducted automatically (no drivers or software installations). USB peripherals simply plug into their respective ports and begin working, so interface cards become more and more unnecessary. The controllers manage the driver software, bandwidth, and electrical power required by each peripheral.

Using a tiered star topology, a single USB port can support up to 127 devices. It does this through the use of USB hubs, which serve as connection ports for other USB devices. Using standalone or embedded hubs (which are often included in devices such as a keyboard or disk drive), only one device need be physically plugged into the computer.

USB 1.1 originally specified the Type A and Type B connectors. As of 2002, USB 2.0 specification gained wide industry acceptance. Peripheral-to-PC connection speeds were increased from 12Mbps to 480Mbps, a 40-fold improvement over USB 1.1. Consequently, the adoption of USB 2.0 led to the increased use of high-throughput external peripherals, such as CD/DVD burners, scanners, digital cameras, and various other video devices. USB 2.0 supports both USB 2.0 and USB 1.1 peripherals, continues with the Type A and Type B connectors, and uses the newer Mini B connector. Various USB connector types are depicted in Figure 13.2.

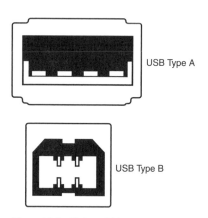

Figure 13.2 Various USB connectors.

➤ The newest USB standard called *USB On-The-Go (USB OTG)* enables devices other than a computer to act as the host. This permits connections between portable devices, such as PDAs, cell phones, and digital cameras, without the use of a PC host. The Mini A connector was developed as part of the USB OTG specification.

Serial ATA

The *Serial ATA (SATA)* final 1.0a specification was released on February 4, 2003. Shortly afterward, the industry began transitioning from the legacy 40-pin Parallel ATA interface to the 7-pin Serial ATA interface. The Serial ATA specification uses a thin, flexible point-to-point connection that allows for easy cable routing within a system. It also increases the allowable cable length from an 18-inch parallel ribbon cable to a very thin and flexible serial cable that can be as long as 1 meter internally, and 2 meters externally, avoiding the master/slave, daisy chain, and termination issues. Airflow is improved dramatically, compared to systems using the wider parallel ribbon cables.

Serial ATA technology supports all ATA and ATAPI devices and delivers 150MBps of throughput to each drive within a disk drive array. The performance gain over Parallel ATA is due to Serial ATA's point-to-point topology. The traditional ATA master/slave topology is required to share the ATA bus, with a best-case throughput of 100MBps for most modern drives. Parallel ATA implementations force pairs of devices to share a common cable in a master-slave relationship, cutting the available bandwidth shared between the devices in half. Parallel ATA devices interact with each other and must be capable of getting along. This complicates the design of system integration, and the controller must comprehend all possible device combinations.

Serial ATA uses a point-to-point interface, directly connecting each device to the host using a dedicated link that provides the entire interface bandwidth with no interaction required between devices. Its dedicated 150MBps maximum performance is guaranteed for each device. Coordination of access between master and slave devices sharing the same cable is eliminated, permitting the streamlining of software. Unlike Parallel ATA, Serial ATA also offers hot-plug connectivity.

Manufacturers are providing internal Serial ATA cables in various UV-sensitive and translucent formats and with connectors at 180-degree and 90-degree orientations. Angled connectors deliver the cable at a natural angle and are strengthened to force the cable to straighten within the enclosure.

Updating the NOS and Hardware Drivers

Server+ Exam Objective 3.5 states that the test taker should be able to install NOS and driver updates to design specifications. The following activities are associated with this objective:

➤ Obtaining an update

➤ Ensuring that there is a backup and recovery plan

➤ Making sure that old drivers are available for reinstallation

➤ Lab testing

➤ Installations

➤ System testing

Installing Operating System Updates

In the Windows environment, there are actually three parts of the operating system that you must address when installing a new version or upgrade:

➤ The network operating system and its *release version*

➤ The OS *patches* and *service packs*

➤ Third-party *device drivers*

An operating system release is a version of the installation media produced and distributed as a complete unit. However, due to the nature of product development and the pressures on software producers to bring new products to the market, new releases never seem to be complete or perfect. Therefore, manufacturers continue to develop and upgrade their operating systems after they have been released.

Rather than providing customers with a new version of the operating system when new features are added, or major problems are corrected, original equipment manufacturers (OEMs) provide patches for their products. Microsoft typically provides their patches in the form of updates, or in collections called service packs that include additional functionality, security enhancements, or new device drivers. Patches and service packs are not typically required to run an operating system release because a release is a complete OS package in its own right. However, installing a recent patch will probably correct a previous shortcoming and result in a more robust OS.

Situations can require that a completely fresh OS installation be conducted rather than using an update package. The current OS may contain problems that no current updates can correct. It's also possible that the system worked better before certain update packages were installed. A newer, more robust version of the OS may now be available containing features vital to continued server operations. Before you begin a fresh install of the NOS, be certain to back up your current system so that you can do a system restore if necessary. Be aware that creating a current backup and testing the restore function is especially vital when upgrading servers to a new version of the NOS. This procedure assumes the existence of a test network with which to simulate a restore scenario. Unless a backup can be successfully restored, it cannot be trusted.

Know the essentials when upgrading the NOS to a newer version.

When you install a fresh copy of an operating system that has been on the market for some time, or when you upgrade an existing operating system to a new version, there is a definite order for installing the new components, as follows:

1. Install the NOS release.

2. Install the OEM patches or the latest service pack.

3. Install the best device driver choices.

As a general rule, newer versions of NOS files should not be overwritten with older file versions.

 Know the correct order in which to install network operating systems, OEM patches, and drivers.

New or upgrade OS installations should automatically install their own drivers for the devices they detect. In most cases, these drivers are the best choices for installed devices because they have been tested to work with the operating system and should provide fewer problems. OEM drivers may not be written as well nor tested as thoroughly as those supplied with the operating system.

 Know the advantages of using the NOS-supplied drivers for peripheral devices.

For devices not listed in the operating system's hardware compatibility list, OEM drivers offer the only alternative. An OEM driver is also used when the device does not operate correctly with the OS-supplied driver. New service pack drivers might offer a better choice than using the original OEM drivers. However, if they do not produce the desired results, the OEM drivers must be reinstalled.

Unix Distributions

The Unix operating system uses a hierarchical file system with directories and subdirectories to maintain and organize files into logical units. Each file and directory in the Unix system has access privileges as defined by the user, group, and world settings for that file.

Remember that filenames in Unix are case sensitive, meaning that an A is not the same as an a. The delimiting character for a Unix directory is the forward slash character /. For example, a Unix directory path may appear as: /usr/local/bin. The Unix file system structure uses the / character to define the top-level, or root, directory of the file system.

When any problems occur reading or writing to the / partition, it is possible that the computer will no longer boot properly. Under such circumstances, the Unix installation CD must be used to correct the situation. When an update is performed on a Unix operating system, you must follow its accompanying instructions explicitly.

Linux Distributions

The Linux file system also works differently from the Windows-based file system. Whereas the Windows system has multiple top-level directories (C:, D:, and so on), the Linux file system has only one top-level directory, as represented by the symbol / (pronounced root). Instead of segregating partitions of a hard drive into various drive letters, Linux has a single entry point, the root directory. Similar to the situation in Unix, the root directory for Linux is designated with a single forward slash, which is also the path separator.

 Know that the Unix and Linux file systems use the symbol / (which stands for root) to define the *top-level directory* of the file system.

One of the main problems with updates to the Linux OS has been *fragmentation*. This can prevent an application developed for one version of Linux from working on another version. The Free Standards Group (FSG) has released the Linux Standards Base (LSB) 2.0 specification in an effort to keep this fragmentation to a minimum. The specification addresses application software that runs on Linux, as well as the distribution mechanisms. The certification authority consists of a vendor-neutral consortium.

With the release of LSB 2.0, commercial companies with an interest in shipping Linux-compatible software now have an enhanced standard on which to base their software. This will help vendors deliver software that is LSB-compliant and ensure interoperability.

Exam Prep Questions

1. If a Unix server will not boot properly, what software will the administrator need to solve the problem?

   ❑ A. The installation CD for the OS/2 server software
   ❑ B. The installation CD for the Windows 2000 server software
   ❑ C. The installation CD for the Unix server software
   ❑ D. The installation CD for the NetWare server software

2. Unlike Windows-based file systems, some network operating systems use only one top-level directory represented by the symbol /. Which NOS in the following list fits that description?

   ❑ A. Windows 2000 Server
   ❑ B. Linux
   ❑ C. Novell NetWare
   ❑ D. Windows NT Server 4.0

3. On completing the installation of a new NOS, the administrator installs the applicable OEM drivers. After the OEM drivers have been added, she attempts to add the NOS patches to the installation only to be prompted to overwrite newer files. After following the prompts she reboots the system. Why does the system hang temporarily before finally coming up? (Select two.)

   ❑ A. Because the NOS patches should have been installed before the OEM drivers
   ❑ B. Because newer file versions were overwritten
   ❑ C. Because the hard drive is too small
   ❑ D. Because the OEM drivers did not load properly

4. A scheduled system service downtime has arrived and all servers are to be upgraded with a fresh NOS installation. Prior to beginning the upgrade, what is the most important step to take?

   ❑ A. The system restore function should be tested.
   ❑ B. All of the hard disk drives should be repartitioned.
   ❑ C. The latest driver and firmware updates should be obtained.
   ❑ D. The entire system should be backed up.

5. Why is it that a properly installed UPS cannot be recognized by the server?

   ❑ A. Configuration of the UPS software has not yet taken place.
   ❑ B. Charging of the UPS battery has not been completed.
   ❑ C. Although the UPS is installed properly, it is defective.
   ❑ D. Connections between the UPS and the server's power supply have not been completed.

6. When upgrading the NOS to a newer version, which of the following actions must be performed first?

   ❑ A. Keep a copy of the current NOS handy for reinstallation purposes in case problems occur.

   ❑ B. Make sure that the new NOS supports all of the peripheral devices on the server.

   ❑ C. First create a current backup, and then test the restore function.

   ❑ D. Make sure that the server board is compatible with the new NOS.

7. The first item installed on a server that will not be running SNMP should be which of the following?

   ❑ A. The software programs

   ❑ B. The latest service pack

   ❑ C. The OEM device drivers

   ❑ D. The NOS

8. The server industry considers USB and FireWire devices a security risk. Why is that?

   ❑ A. USB and FireWire devices possess hot-swapping capability.

   ❑ B. USB and FireWire devices have no security features built into them.

   ❑ C. USB and FireWire devices are easy to hack into.

   ❑ D. USB and FireWire devices are slow when compared to SCSI speeds.

Exam Prep Answers

1. Answer C is the correct answer. When a Unix server fails to boot properly, its top-level root directory is out of action, preventing anything else from working properly. In this situation, the Unix installation CD must be used to repair the damage. Answers A and B are incorrect because the Unix directory system is totally incompatible with either OS/2 or Windows 2000. Answer D is incorrect because the NetWare file structure is similar to that of Windows except that all directories can be named instead of having to use letter assignments for the drives.

2. Answer B is the correct answer. The Linux file system operates similarly to Unix in that only one top-level directory exists. That directory is represented by the symbol / (pronounced root). Windows systems use multiple top-level directories (C:, D:, and so on). Answer C is incorrect because the top-level directory in Novell NetWare is not referred to using /. As Windows operating systems, answers A and D are both incorrect.

3. Answers A and B are the correct answers. OEM drivers should never be installed before any applicable NOS patches have been loaded. In fact, newer NOS system files should never be overwritten with older versions. Answer C is incorrect because if this were true, warnings would have been given during the NOS installation. Answer D is incorrect because the OEM drivers did load properly. The faulty system booting resulted from those drivers being overwritten by older NOS patches.

4. Answer D is the correct answer. Because of the risks involved when upgrading a server NOS, a complete backup of the current system must be performed. This will permit a system restore to be undertaken if needed. Answer A is incorrect because the restore function is only useful after a current backup, not before. Answer B is incorrect because repartitioning will destroy any chances of performing a backup. Answer C is incorrect in that it is not the most important step at this point.

5. Answer A is the correct answer. Unless the UPS management software is properly configured, the server will not see the UPS as part of the system. Answer B is incorrect because a visual charging indication would be provided by properly configured UPS management software. Answer C is incorrect because the management software would identify and recognize a defective UPS. Answer D is incorrect because physically, the UPS is properly installed.

6. Answer C is the correct answer. Before a new NOS version is installed, a current backup and restore function must be performed. Although answers A and B are both important considerations, they are not the most important. Answer D is also subordinate to answer C.

7. Answer D is the correct answer. The order of installations for servers without SNMP should begin with the NOS. Answer B is incorrect because the latest service pack (with NOS patches) is always installed following the NOS installation. Answer C is incorrect because the OEM patches, containing the most recent device drivers, are installed following the NOS patches.

8. Answer A is the correct answer. Any storage device with hot-swapping capability poses a security risk in a server environment. A simple plug-in would provide immediate access to the server by a non-authorized individual. Answer B is incorrect because recent USB devices are equipped with formidable security features. Answer C is incorrect because the threat is through an unauthorized physical USB connection, rather than a network hack. Answer D is incorrect because data transfer speeds are not the determining factor when assessing security risks.

Preparing the Server
for Service

. . . .

Terms you'll need to understand:

✓ Simple Network Management Protocol (SNMP)
✓ Desktop Management Interface (DMI)
✓ Master Boot Record (MBR)
✓ Management Information Base (MIB)
✓ Network Management System (NMS)
✓ Managed devices
✓ Agents
✓ Traps
✓ Application Program Interface (API)
✓ Management Information Format (MIF)
✓ Intel Server Control (ISC)
✓ Backup window
✓ Application server monitoring
✓ Database monitoring
✓ Systems management
✓ Website monitoring
✓ Service management
✓ Application alerts
✓ Performance management
✓ Object identifiers (OIDs)
✓ Server Management Bus (SMB)
✓ Event logs and event viewers
✓ Audits

✓ Rescue mode
✓ GNOME
✓ Performance Monitor
✓ Server baseline
✓ System analysis
✓ Counters
✓ Bottlenecks
✓ Page file
✓ Virtual memory
✓ LogicalDisk
✓ PhysicalDisk
✓ Microsoft Management Console (MMC)
✓ Seek time
✓ Transfer rate
✓ Virtual Memory Manager (VMM)
✓ Overload
✓ Data loss
✓ Bandwidth on demand
✓ Redirector
✓ Routing and Remote Access Service (RRAS)
✓ Server Message Block (SMB)
✓ Autotuning
✓ Object monitor

- ✓ Saturation point
- ✓ Server farm
- ✓ Change management
- ✓ Authentication

- ✓ Kerberos
- ✓ Headless servers
- ✓ In-band and out-of-band management

Techniques you'll need to master:

- ✓ Installing various server system management service tools
- ✓ Using the Simple Network Management Protocol
- ✓ Accessing the Management Information Base (MIB)
- ✓ Communicating with the Network Management System (NMS)
- ✓ Understanding the DMI protocol architecture
- ✓ Implementing a server backup program
- ✓ Monitoring and logging server system performance
- ✓ Setting up event logs and using an event viewer
- ✓ Generating alert notifications
- ✓ Troubleshooting Linux systems through log files
- ✓ Performing and updating a server baseline
- ✓ Configuring performance monitors
- ✓ Conducting analysis of processor utilization measurements
- ✓ Optimizing the page file
- ✓ Recognizing disk bottlenecks
- ✓ Minimizing the debilitating effects of virtual memory on servers

- ✓ Identifying the need for larger amounts of server RAM
- ✓ Troubleshooting and avoiding network bottlenecks
- ✓ Enabling a server's autotuning capabilities
- ✓ Providing server system configuration documentation
- ✓ Obtaining hardware and software updates
- ✓ Recording accurate memory load measurements
- ✓ Recognizing network interface object monitors
- ✓ Examining server work queues
- ✓ Determining the server structure's saturation point
- ✓ Implementing a server management plan
- ✓ Installing server management software
- ✓ Improving server availability
- ✓ Creating a change management plan
- ✓ Developing a server network security plan
- ✓ Understanding cryptographic authentication for servers
- ✓ Managing server hardware remotely

Introduction

Server+ Exam Objective 3.6 states that the test taker should be able to install service tools such as SNMP, backup software, system monitoring agents, and event logs. To achieve this objective, you need to know and understand the following:

➤ The identity, purpose, and function of service tools

➤ How to set up SNMP

➤ How system monitoring software and management information bases (MIBs) are implemented on hardware

➤ The purpose of event logs

A variety of system management tools are available to manage a server. In addition to the management tools included in each operating system (OS), a variety of third-party tools are also available. Although there are a number of server management applications, they all typically use the same two network management protocols. These are called the *Simple Network Management Protocol (SNMP)* and the *Desktop Management Interface (DMI)*. The equipment's instrumentation design determines which protocol is used in a specific application.

Simple Network Management Protocol

SNMP is a network monitoring and management specification developed by the *Internet Engineering Task Force (IETF)* in the mid-1980s to provide standard, simplified, and extensible management of LAN-based TCP/IP devices, such as bridges, routers, hubs, switches, and a multitude of other network devices. Adopted by most TCP/IP device manufacturers as a primary or secondary management interface, SNMP is the most widely distributed TCP/IP network management protocol in use today.

Keep in mind that the order of operations at bootup differ somewhat for network servers running the SNMP protocol. In SNMP systems, the *Master Boot Record (MBR)* first points to the SNMP partition, and loads the SNMP utility before jumping to the NOS partition.

SNMP is a message-based protocol that generates notifications to alert server network administrators about detected situations such as overheating or component failures. Server management applications are based on the SNMP specification and are most often referred to as enterprise management consoles. SNMP agents are used in various types of network equipment, including routers, hubs, and servers, to collect information about network resources and events. The collected information is then stored in a database referred to as the *Management Information Base (MIB)*, which can be accessed and processed by the management console to produce alerts on a monitor, provide graphical analysis, or apply a corrective course of action to a remote server.

The server network SNMP model consists of three basic components:

➤ Managed devices—These are devices that contain an SNMP agent, collect and store information, and make it available to the NMS. Managed TCP/IP devices include (but are not limited to) bridges, routers, hubs, and switches.

➤ Agents—These are software modules that interpret information required by the NMS, translating this into an SNMP-compatible format for transferring it.

➤ Network Management System (NMS)—This is the software program running the applications that monitor and control managed server network devices through their SNMP agents. One or more NMS elements perform most of the work managing the SNMP network.

SNMP reduces the complexity of network management because it minimizes the resources required to support it. As a simple request/response protocol, its flexibility allows for the management of vendor-specific network equipment and components. It communicates with and receives alerts from the

TCP/IP network, and manages information between SNMP devices, agents, and the *Network Management System (NMS)*.

SNMP works as a client/server model, with the client being the network manager, and the server being the SNMP agent represented by the remote network device. SNMP applications run under the NMS and issue information queries about the configuration, status, and performance of associated TCP/IP network devices, or elements. Each element individually responds to the NMS requests/queries it receives.

Know what SNMP is used for.

Servers communicate with each other using port numbers that identify the processes to be performed on a currently transmitted message. For example, SNMP agents can be programmed to send various unsolicited reports, called *traps*, back to the NMS, using TCP port number 162. When specific network activities occur, these traps can be used to initiate preconfigured events such as automatic administrative notices, email alerts, or network configuration changes. Event communications are conducted using TCP port number 161.

Know which well-known TCP port is typically used by SNMP for communication.

Using the NMS bolsters the operation of the pre-established SNMP server "community." An SNMP community is defined as a logical group with relationships between an agent and one or more SNMP managers. For security purposes, an agent validates each NMS request before taking action by verifying that the requesting manager belongs to the SNMP community, and has the specific access privileges being exercised for that particular agent.

In spite of the widespread use of SNMP, it does contain important weaknesses. For one thing, it transfers data in a cleartext, ASCII format. For example, if intercepted by a sniffer, the community credentials would be completely exposed and exploitable. Experienced hackers can use this information to capture network data and take control of network devices. This is a well-known exploit.

Also, depending on the size of the deployment, SNMP can be a complicated protocol to implement, and transfers unnecessary version information with every SNMP message, wasting valuable bandwidth. However, NMS programs usually include additional resources to compensate for these shortcomings. In spite of its flaws, SNMP has become the most widely used enterprise management console for computer networking and will likely continue to be used for some time.

Know that SNMP transfers data in an ASCII format.

SNMP's wide deployment has justified the emergence of two updated versions. SNMPv2 expands the protocol and resolves some of the shortcomings of the original. For example, the SNMPv2 trap operation serves the same function as that used in SNMPv1, but uses a different message format and replaces the SNMPv1 trap. It also defines two new operations, one of which can efficiently retrieve large blocks of data. Another operation allows one NMS to send trap information to another NMS and to receive a suitable response. In SNMPv2, if an agent responding to a bulk data request cannot provide values for all the listed variables, it will provide at least partial results.

SNMPv3 provides additional security and remote configuration capabilities. Its architecture introduces improved measures for supporting message security, access control, and message processing. Unfortunately, because of the additions and extensions to the original SNMP, it probably should no longer be called "simple."

Desktop Management Interface

Originally, SNMP was intended to be a temporary standard and included many limitations that made it less useful than more recent server networking protocols. Recognizing the need for a better protocol, the *Desktop Management Task Force (DMTF)*, a consortium of hardware manufacturers led by Intel, produced the Desktop Management Interface (DMI) specification to replace SNMP. DMI has since become the most widely used client management standard. Many DMI-compliant networks and server devices currently exist, along with various systems to manage them.

However, improvements to the original SNMP standard, most notably SNMPv2 and SNMPv3, have resulted in a cooperative relationship developing between SNMP and DMI. SNMP frequently makes use of DMI agents in the gathering of necessary system information. DMI is a network management protocol. However, it is also classified as an Application Program (or Programming) Interface (API). An API is a set of routines, protocols, and tools used for building software applications. A good API makes it easier to develop a program by providing all the necessary building blocks a programmer needs. Most operating environments provide an API so that programmers can write consistent applications. All programs that use a common API have similar interfaces, making it easier for clients to learn new programs.

DMI collects information about a server network environment, such as what software and/or expansion boards are installed on various client machines. It's designed to be independent of specific operating systems or server platforms so that programs can make similar function calls when collecting information. This system independence is implemented by collecting data from *Management Information Format (MIF)* files, which are plain text files that contain information about software or hardware components.

DMI allows a central server to not only gather information about computers connected to the network, but also to configure them. Computers that comply with DMI are often thought of as managed. Essentially, DMI makes servers smarter by permitting them to report information about themselves.

Through DMI, the network can query each server or client to see what software and hardware it has. It then allows that information to be gathered and stored in an easily located directory, where clients can manage it using keywords. For example, if several clients are using IBM hardware, DMI collects information about that hardware and organizes it in a single directory. This prevents the necessity of hunting down information that might be stored in many different places.

SNMP/DMI Translations

The SNMP service must be installed at the administrator's workstation to facilitate the SNMP console, or viewer, and allow him or her to view various SNMP traps. In addition, the SNMP service must also be installed on servers that are managed by SNMP enterprise management consoles, including the *Intel Server Control (ISC)* management console. An example of this type of installation is shown in Figure 14.1.

Know when it is appropriate to use SNMP consoles to monitor a server from a remote location.

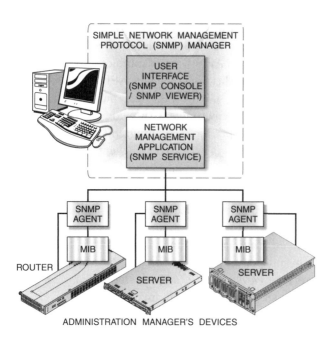

Figure 14.1 SNMP architecture.

The center of the DMI architecture is the DMI service provider, a system-resident program that oversees every DMI activity (see Figure 14.2). It collects data from the server's management instrumentation and consolidates it in the MIF database. Local or remote management application programs, which use SNMP, can access the collected data and apply control actions through the management interface. These programs include management tools capable of interrogating, tracking, listing, and changing the server's manageable objects. For example, if the system is configured to monitor the minimum/maximum preset temperatures of the server's processors, any deviation outside established ranges produces an "indication." This indication is applied to the remote management interface through the service provider. The installed management application provides the administrator with a number of predetermined "responses" that can be implemented based on the specified condition, ranging from logging the event to performing an emergency shutdown of the server.

DMI/SNMP translators are used to manage DMI-based server data from an SNMP-based workstation, converting the information back and forth between the two standards. Management requests from the SNMP workstation are converted to the DMI format, whereas DMI responses from the server are translated into SNMP format for processing and display. Keep in mind that these types of translators also manage SNMP-based server data from DMI-based workstations in networks using newer SNMP protocols.

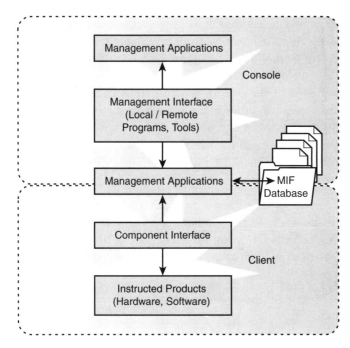

Figure 14.2   DMI protocol architecture.

Server Backup Software

The steps taken to protect essential business data must be equated with locking the front door, stashing valuables in a safe, and storing critical documents in a safe deposit box. Server data deserves more than mere UPS protection regardless of past system reliability. There are many backup software products from which to choose. Modern backup software is inexpensive, comparatively simple to use, and depending on the required solution, capable of being completely automated.

The only two types of server system administrators without backup are those who have already lost data, and those who will lose data.

Although data loss might be a simple annoyance to a residential user, to server-based business operators it amounts to negative productivity, degradation of customer relationships, and lost customers. Because customer and financial data is the lifeblood of any business (and can seldom be re-created from memory), it must be repeatedly backed up and protected. In the modern commercial climate, business data is the very foundation of a company's livelihood.

Most server operating systems come with backup utilities that support local backups with few frills. For systems that include multiple servers or workstations, each device might require its own separate backup media and operation. Such an approach also requires the independent management of each media device, as well as the backup tapes related to it. An additional drawback to using native backup utilities is their time-consuming operations, often characterized by backing up one file at a time, in series. Backing up large volumes of data could exceed the backup window for the server. The *backup window* is the period of time during which a server system is not operational due to ongoing backup procedures.

Backup solutions devised by third-party manufacturers who specialize in such software overcome many of the troubling aspects inherent with using native backup utilities. Although many products are available to improve backup speed, automation, and efficiency, the selected solution should minimally provide

➤ Backup for multiple servers and workstations to a single tape device

➤ Concurrent backups of multiple data streams from multiple devices

➤ Simplified interfacing for automated backup processes

➤ Backup of open files, for fully protected active databases

The ability to perform backup operations on an open database cannot be underestimated. This allows the database to be fully protected without having to shut down business-critical operations.

System Monitoring Agents

By implementing regularly scheduled performance monitoring on their servers, administrators can ensure that they always have the most recent information about how their client/server architectures are performing. Monitoring the server system's performance is an important part of maintaining your network's health. The data provided by monitoring tools helps the administrator to understand the effects being felt by the various system resources and the overall workload of the system. Usage pattern trends can be observed; the effects of system changes can be evaluated; and system performance bottlenecks can be diagnosed.

Performance monitoring for client/server systems is best implemented with an understanding of how and why such measurements are needed. Specific operating systems often require specific performance monitoring tools. To use such tools properly, it's important to know what types of data can be collected, and how. The accumulated data must also be interpreted correctly to acquire the necessary information about the system's overall condition.

The majority of today's server operating systems provide their own customized performance monitoring tools. However, third-party monitoring software can provide even more robust monitoring and control of these systems. Software that is designed to run various agent monitors across a server network can be run internally through the supervision of the server network administrator, or externally through the auspices of an external service provider. The performance monitoring tools available today are powerful and sophisticated, but no tool is useful if it is not used properly.

Proper server system monitoring provides accurate knowledge about the availability, performance, and responsiveness of the server. It allows server problems such as downtime and poor response time to be detected and repaired even before users are affected. Tasks that server system agent monitors should be equipped to handle include

➤ Application server monitoring—Web services and applications are monitored in real time.

➤ Database monitoring—The availability and flawless performance of databases in the network are critical. Events that affect database server performance include loss of high availability, unplanned growth of database size, improperly tuned buffer cache size, inability to handle all client connections, or abnormally long connection times.

➤ Systems management— Performance and event data should be archived for periodic evaluations of service-level compliance, and effective growth planning. Agents should track system load, disk utilization, memory utilization, and CPU utilization.

➤ Custom application management—Customized Java Management Extensions (JMXs) or SNMP monitors can be created to view management information on Java or SNMP applications.

➤ Website monitoring— Information provided includes the performance and availability of HTTP and HTTPS requests for the end user; webpage content validation; instant notifications for connectivity problems, slow load times, or content errors; time-specific performance reports; and webpage error message validation.

➤ Service management—The health and availability of various services are monitored, such as mail server, FTP, Telnet, SNMP, JMX, Web Server, and IIS.

➤ Application alerts—Application problems such as server downtime and delayed application response time are reported to the administrator.

➤ Performance management—Parameters that can be tracked include response times, resource availabilities, and resource utilizations. Real-time reports and graphs help to analyze application servers, databases, custom applications, services, and server systems for months at a time, without making major system changes.

A system monitoring agent for an enterprise must provide three generic, but essential, groups of services:

➤ Status indications concerning the installation, configuration, upgrade, repair, and retirement of software and servers

➤ Performance measurement, fault monitoring, and management feedback

➤ Resource usage metering for planning and billing purposes

MIBs are implemented on hardware through the use of *object identifiers (OIDs)*, which uniquely identify each specific piece of hardware being monitored. OID numbers are assigned to all monitored components depending on what the component is, and where it is located. After each device in the server system has been identified and logged into the MIB, its operating parameters can be tracked and recorded.

For example, the OID for a managed object such as a temperature probe might be `700.20`, whereas the OID for the location of the temperature probe embedded within some other device might be `700.20.1.8`. After it has been installed in the end device, the OID specified for the probe's location could be `1.3.6.1.4.1.674.10892.1.700.20.1.8`.

Most server boards are fitted with an independent management bus system called the *Server Management Bus (SMB)*. The management controller can use the independent pathways provided by this bus to monitor the temperatures of system processors and check the operations of other selected field-replaceable unit (FRU) components. Their correct identifications will be ensured through the use of the OIDs just described. The controller will send the monitored information back to the MIB for review by the administrator at the management console.

Event Logs

When things go wrong, it is critical to be able to accurately examine the system's performance and behavior. The main purpose for an *event log* is to continuously monitor and record a variety of events associated with the system, hardware, or installed applications so that the log is available to the administrator when troubleshooting the specified server system. These events include

➤ Resource usage

➤ Application errors

➤ System errors

➤ Selected audited events

➤ Security events

The event log itself is a file that contains cataloged entries of system occurrences that relate to the operating system or applications running on the system. Each entry includes information about the type of event, the date and time it occurred, the computer involved, and the client logged on at the time. Other useful information recorded includes an event ID, an event category, and the source of the event. Additional information concerning the event, and/or a link to this information might also be included.

Event Viewers

Event information can be monitored through the use of an event viewer specifically assigned to a local workstation or some remote network component.

Viewers divide recorded events into three specific types of logs:

➤ Application logs—Events associated with applications or programs. For example, a software application might record a file error in the application log. The application developer usually decides which events should be logged.

➤ System logs—Events associated with operating system components. For example, this type of log might record an entry when a system driver fails to load, or when the system does not locate a specified IP address. The OS developer decides which system events are logged.

➤ Security logs—Events associated with specific system components and applications. Security events often include valid/invalid login attempts as well as file creation, opening, and deletion activities. The system administrator is responsible for establishing which attributes will be monitored for security purposes, through use of an audit policy tool.

Event viewers can be accessed through any of the following types of software applets provided by the server's OS:

➤ Administrative tools

➤ Management console snap-ins

➤ Computer management tools

Figure 14.3 illustrates an example of an event from the DNS Server event log on a Windows Server 2003 domain controller.

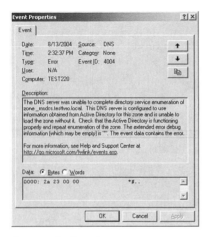

Figure 14.3 Event log entry.

Clicking on the event link opens the dialog box shown in Figure 14.4. The dates and times that the event occurred are displayed, in addition to other associated properties.

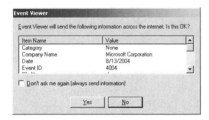

Figure 14.4 Event Viewer.

System and Application logs contain three distinctive event types, including

➤ Information events—Data that indicates the successful operation of a driver or application, such as the successful starting of the Windows Internet Naming Service (WINS)

➤ Warning events—Events that do not severely impact the system, but point to a possible future problem, such as an infection reported by an antivirus program

➤ Error events—Significant problems with an operation or service, such as a recorded error that details the failure of a network adapter to load

 Know where to check application error logs.

The Security log records the following events depending on which auditing protocol attribute is established by the administrator:

➤ Success audits—Records the successful completion of an event such as a user logging on successfully. These events are recorded if an audit policy permits audit enabling for this event.

➤ Failure audits—Records the unsuccessful completion of an event such as an unsuccessful logon attempt. These events are recorded if an audit policy is not enabled to capture the specified event type.

You can search for specific event types by using the Find option under the View menu on the toolbar. The following elements are searchable:

➤ Event types:

➤ Information

➤ Warning

➤ Error

➤ Success Audit

➤ Failure Audit

➤ Event Source—Process or resource that caused the event

➤ Category—Primarily used in the Security log to distinguish between logon and logoff, object access, and process tracking

➤ Event ID—Error number for the event; each program assigns its own error numbers

➤ User—Name of the user who was logged in when the event occurred

➤ Computer—Name of the computer that the event occurred on

➤ Description—More detailed information about the event

Although most clients are permitted to view application and system logs, only the administrator is normally allowed to view events posted to the security logs.

Manipulating Event Logs

Event logs can also be configured to limit their size as well as to define what action to take when the log file fills. These configurations can be made in the Properties sheet of the log to be modified. Each event log type (system, application, or security) can be assigned a unique maximum size and specific action to be taken when the log file is full. These actions include

➤ Overwriting events as required, also called *event log wrapping*

➤ Overwriting events older than a specified number of days, also a form of event log wrapping

➤ Not permitting event overwrites, requiring that the event log must be cleared manually

If the log becomes full under the "no overwrite" option, a warning message is displayed. The system can alternately be configured to automatically shut down when the log file is full.

In addition, event logs can be archived to keep a history of events. To archive a specific log, first select the log file, and then select the Save Log File As option. Options for saving the log files include

➤ Log file format (.evt)—Enables the specified events to be opened in an event viewer utility program

➤ Text file format (.txt)—Enables events to be viewed by any text viewing application

➤ Comma-separated format (.csv)—Enables events to be imported into database or spreadsheet applications

Performance Logs and Alerts

Most server system monitoring software is also capable of logging performance data and generating alert notifications when such data indicates the need for administrator intervention. Most current versions of server system monitoring software permit detailed configurations of performance logs and alert notifications for data from both local and remote servers and workstations.

These performance logs are configured so that their data can be viewed, copied, ported to other applications, or manipulated in much the same way as the event logs described earlier. Alerts can be set to issue messages whenever a counter falls outside its preset limits, and are available both during the capturing process, and after the data is collected. For example, an alert can be set up to notify the administrator if more than 90% of the hard disk space on a server is used. However, when counters are used in combination with alerts, they can normally be set for only one limit. For example the same counter cannot be used to issue an alert when the total processor usage exceeds 90% and when it falls below 50%.

Alerts can be formatted to

➤ Select the specific counters to track

➤ Define a threshold for the activity

➤ Specify the action to be taken if the threshold is exceeded

Actions commonly associated with alert notifications include

➤ Running a program

➤ Starting a log

➤ Sending a network message

Setting alert notifications in server software utilities usually involves

➤ Opening the alert utility program and specifying the Alerts option.

➤ Selecting a title for the new alert settings.

➤ Inputting a general description of the specified alert.

➤ Specifying to which server or workstation the new alert applies, its performance object, the specific counter(s) involved, the number of checks to perform, and add these parameters to its definition.

➤ Specifying the setting's threshold, sample interval, and selecting a password for the setting, if necessary.

➤ Checking the application event log for the alert just created.

➤ Selecting a specific alert message format, such as sending a network message, starting a performance data log, or running a specific program.

➤ Selecting and defining the schedule time frame and conditions for the new alert.

➤ Clicking the appropriate screen command to initiate the new alert notification function.

Linux Log Files

Linux provides what is known as a *rescue mode*. This mode allows you to boot to a minimal Linux environment entirely from a rescue-type diskette, CD-ROM, or other installation boot media, such as a USB flash device. Although rescue mode permits the system log files to be accessed on an improperly booting Linux server's hard drive, the information in these files can be accessed regardless of the machine's boot status.

Linux log files include information about the system installation parameters for the kernel, active services, and various applications. Most of the log files in Linux are located in the /var/log directory. When installation problems occur, these files are required for troubleshooting purposes. An examination of the /var/log directory will reveal a number of files that have numbers appended to their names. In order to limit the size of log files, they are rotated periodically according to these numbered assignments. How often these files are rotated is determined by the configuration settings held in the /etc/logrotate.conf file, which can be modified. By default, the applicable files are rotated every week with the most recent four weeks of historical logs retained.

Log files for Linux are created in plain text format, making them viewable from most available text editors such as emacs, or the vi editor.

As in other operating systems, all clients are permitted to access some of these log files, but the majority of them are viewable only by the system administrator, when logged in as the root. Viewing log files is eased somewhat by using the system's interactive Log Viewer graphical utility, launched from the desktop by selecting the panel's main menu button, and selecting System Tools/System Logs. Alternatively, the Log Viewer utility can be accessed by typing redhat-logviewer at the Linux shell prompt (for Red Hat Linux distributions). Other flavors of Linux will require slight variations of this command; check the local man pages for more information.

System information for Linux can be obtained using root-level commands, or through the use of the graphical interface GNOME System Monitor included with the system.

GNOME can be launched from the desktop by selecting the panel's main menu button, and selecting System Tools/System Monitor. From the Linux shell prompt within the X Window System, access GNOME by typing gnome-system-monitor and selecting the System Monitor tab.

The Linux installation includes additional utilities designed to monitor many of the same elements previously referenced for non-Linux operating systems. However, Linux documentation often indicates that when other operating systems are installed after Linux, the system may no longer be capable of booting to Linux because the Master Boot Record (MBR) containing the Linux GRUB or LILO boot loaders may be overwritten.

Performing Server Baselines

Server+ Exam Objective 3.7 states that the test taker should be able to perform a server baseline. To achieve this objective, you need to know and understand the following:

➤ Purposes and types of baselines:

> ➤ Processor utilization
>
> ➤ Page file
>
> ➤ Disk utilization
>
> ➤ Memory utilization
>
> ➤ Network utilization

➤ Conditions under which different baselines might be useful

➤ When baselines should be updated

Detailing every object and counter combination and what the expected or acceptable values should be provides information of limited value. This is mainly because each and every network is different in design as well as performance. Only a reliable and up-to-date baseline can help to determine what counter values are actually abnormal. Log files should be recorded for each major object on the server system, including memory, processor, system, network segment, network interface, LogicalDisk, and PhysicalDisk. These first log files should be used to create the original baseline. Each subsequent log collection can then be compared to the original baseline and significant deviations can be noted. The causes for any deviation should be tracked down and adjustments should be made, when possible, to return the system to its previously normal state. Otherwise, the new values must be accepted as normal.

Performance monitoring and tuning is not a one-time activity. It takes planning, preparatory work, and ongoing routine measurements. Skipping any step along the way can result in overlooking a critical network problem. Using a tool such as Performance Monitor can help to gather and display the pertinent data that can help diagnose what may be a problem. Your familiarity with the Performance Monitor tool and how it operates is key to detecting performance problems. However, the tool itself is not the solution. You must interpret the data and take appropriate action based on the results.

Baseline Purposes and Types

A server baseline is an initial measurement of how the server performs after all installations and configurations have been completed. Everything that is subsequently reconfigured can then be compared with the baseline. Noticeable slowdowns in system performance must also be baselined to justify any hardware or software upgrades that occur. When conducting a system analysis, it is important to know how things were running prior to a hardware change or software addition/upgrade. Only then can improvements in server performance be properly tracked.

Some feel that the ideal time to gather baseline statistical information is when server usage is at its lowest level, such as early in the morning or late at night. A more sensible approach for gathering reliable data is to take a series of measurements that span several days at different times. By using the averages for analysis, the results will be repeatable and reliable.

Performance monitors can be configured to record statistical measurements (counters) for a variety of system hardware and software components (objects). Each performance object has its own unique set of counters. Administrators can use performance monitors to

➤ Measure the processor utilization on the system

➤ Optimize page file memory management

➤ Monitor the utilization of various hard disk drives

➤ Track the utilization of system memory

➤ Estimate the amount of network traffic

The proper use of monitoring system information is the critical ingredient for server administration and maintenance and leads to an understanding about the system's workload and resource usage. Observable changes in server workload patterns establish resource usage trends to help justify whether or not to upgrade. Following an upgrade, comparative data is available for use in testing configurations and fine-tuning any changes. Any remaining problems can be diagnosed to pinpoint areas still requiring optimization.

Be able to describe what a server baseline is.

Processor Utilization Measurements

Bottlenecks do not magically appear during processor utilization measurements. They are not common on a server properly equipped to handle its client demands. Although locating processor bottlenecks is important, they are usually found after the performance analysis of processor utilization measurements, not before the analysis begins. A processor bottleneck is something to discover rather than to assume.

The biggest challenge when interpreting the results of these measurements is recognizing that a processor bottleneck exists at all. If measurements are conducted entirely during periods of low system utilization, a real problem bottleneck might simply be overlooked. At some point, counters specified for processor utilization measurements must be run during periods of peak server usage. Performance monitors can be set up to automatically begin and end their logging activities only during working hours. Logging periods of 24×7 are justified for larger organizations, whereas periods matching the 40-hour work week are suitable for smaller organizations. Likely bottlenecks include CPU-intensive applications, processes, drivers, and interrupts. Faulty hardware can cause excessive interrupts, as can IRQ conflicts between hardware devices. In addition, memory problems have a tricky way of hiding behind high processor use. Adding more RAM to a Windows Server 2003 system often results in dramatic drops in processor utilization times due to the reduction of page faults. Another processor load to avoid is the active screen savers that ship with various server-based OSes. Rather than using them to avoid screen burn, simply turn the monitor off when viewing is not required.

The following list describes several of the processor utilization measurement counters:

➤ Percent Processor Time—The percentage of an elapsed period that a processor is busy executing a non-idle thread. Idle threads are assigned to each processor to consume non-productive clock cycles. This counter might reach 100% during application launches or kernel-intensive operations, but if it remains above 90% for an extended period, suspect a CPU bottleneck. An instance of this counter can be assigned for each processor in the system.

➤ Percent of Interrupt Time—The percentage of elapsed time that the processor spends handling hardware interrupts. If this value is greater than 20% and continues to rise when compared to the server's baseline, a component within the server may be failing.

➤ Percent of Privileged Time—The percentage of processor time spent in Privileged Mode executing non-idle threads. If this value is greater than the percent value of the User Time counter, the applications running on the server might need to be tweaked to optimize overall performance. This statistic helps identify how much time a particular process spends executing in Privileged versus User Mode.

➤ Percent of User Time—The percentage of processor time spent in User Mode executing non-idle threads. If this value is greater than the percent value of the Privileged Time counter, the server's user/application process and the associated resources may need to be tweaked to optimize overall performance. This statistic helps identify how much time a particular process spends executing in User versus Privileged Mode.

➤ Interrupts Per Second—The number of device interrupts the processor is currently experiencing. A device interrupts the processor when it completes a task or requires attention. Normal thread execution is suspended during an interrupt, and the processor may switch to another, higher-priority thread. System clock interrupts are a constant on every system and create a continual base level of interrupt activity regardless of other system activities.

➤ Percent Total Processor Time—In multiprocessor systems only, this counter is used the same way as that for a single CPU counter. If any value remains consistently higher than 90%, at least one of the CPUs has a bottleneck.

Page File Optimization

Because server systems typically do not have more memory than needed, server system administrators must always be prepared to tweak the way in which the system uses its memory resources. It is essential to keep memory management in the forefront of one's thinking regarding the health of any client/server system.

For an Intel 386 or later processor, a program instruction can address up to 4GB of memory using its full 32 bits. However, few machines actually carry this much physical Random Access Memory (RAM). Instead, the machine hardware is designed to provide much of this 4GB address space as *virtual memory*. For systems running low on RAM, it's a good idea to optimize the page file. How much swap space is required depends on the amount of RAM installed and the programs being run. For a system that does not suffer from overloading, a good rule of thumb is 1.5 times the amount of system memory.

Because virtual memory use cannot be disabled, it's extremely important not to waste large amounts of RAM. If a system board were to be configured to use no page file space, serious RAM shortage problems would probably occur. This is because most programs ask for greater allocations of virtual memory space than they will ever use, often running into hundreds of megabytes. This addressing must be assigned to system resources, usually within the available page file space. If no page file space exists, these memory allocations are assigned to available RAM, locking it out from any other use! Properly optimizing a server's memory resources include the following techniques:

➤ Move the page file to a fast and dedicated hard disk that does not contain the system and boot partitions. Even so, leave a small amount on the C: drive; an initial size of 2 to 50MB is suitable for emergency use. Otherwise, the system might ignore the system settings and run as if no page file exists at all. Alternatively, the system might automatically create a large page file on the C: drive.

➤ Format the page file partition with NTFS and a 4KB cluster size, which is the default setting for an NTFS partition, and make its initial size at least 1.5 times larger than the amount of installed physical RAM. Under no circumstances should the page file be smaller than the amount of physical RAM installed on the system.

➤ Make the page file's initial size as big as the maximum allowed, if possible.

➤ Do not place multiple paging files on different partitions of the same physical disk drive.

➤ Use a RAID-0 (Stripe Set) array to store the page file, if available.

➤ Do not put a page file on a fault-tolerant drive, such as a mirrored RAID-1 volume, or a RAID-5 volume. Paging files do not require fault-tolerance. Some fault-tolerant systems suffer from slow data writes, as they write data to multiple locations.

➤ Special considerations for users of Windows XP and Fast User Switching include

➤ Making available space in the page file to "roll out" work for inactive users.

➤ Experimenting in a real situation to establish adequate page file sizing.

➤ Starting out with an initial page file size equal to half the size of RAM for each user logged in.

Disk Drive Utilization Parameters

Whereas page file size is an issue of memory or storage space, disk bottlenecks are directly related to the speed of read and write transactions. Adding new storage devices or removing unnecessary files can often resolve space issues. System performance suffers noticeably, however, when the disk subsystem cannot quickly process read and write requests. Server operating systems rely heavily on smoothly functioning disk access for processes such as virtual memory management.

The two objects used to measure disk performance are *LogicalDisk* and *PhysicalDisk*, which are enabled using the `diskperf` command. The LogicalDisk's counters focus on the logical volume constructions created through the Disk Administrator. The PhysicalDisk's counters focus on the physical drives themselves. If the `_Total` instance is used as a counter, you can examine the disk subsystem as a whole with either object. However, if you focus on components of the disk subsystem, the PhysicalDisk object is typically the best choice because performance varies by device, not by logical volume. As of Windows 2000, the Disk Administrator has been replaced with a *Microsoft Management Console (MMC)* snap-in, available through Computer Management. Its look and feel, however, should be familiar.

Most disk bottlenecks appear as sustained activity, with a consistent % Disk Time value of more than 85%. To be certain, this measurement should be combined with other symptoms. Look for an Avg. Disk Queue Length of 2 or greater, and/or the occurrence of hard paging more than five times per second. Before blaming the disk subsystem, memory, processor, and faulty application bottlenecks must be eliminated from the list of suspects. However, after a disk bottleneck has been determined, several actions can be taken to eliminate or reduce its effects on system performance. Within the parameters of reasonable cost, ease of implementation, and manageable system effects, the following steps should be implemented in the suggested order, to minimize changes to the entire system:

➤ Use a disk defragmenter utility to improve seek and read times.

➤ Remember to turn off `diskperf` whenever performance measuring is completed.

➤ Avoid using compression on files that are accessed often, such as any portion of the Winnt main directory tree, or the swap file.

➤ Exchange existing hard drives and drive controllers with faster models, whenever possible. Disk speed is a combination of two parameters—*seek time* and *transfer rate*. Seek time is the amount of time required for the drive to move the read heads one-third of the way across all cylinders. It is the average speed at which the drive can access any randomly placed data item.

➤ Don't settle for seek times slower than 10 milliseconds (ms), and, if possible, purchase drives with seek times of 5 ms or faster. The transfer rate is the maximum throughput the drive can sustain.

➤ Use a 32- or 64-bit bus mastering controller card.

➤ Upgrade from slower technologies such as IDE and SCSI to fast technologies such as UltraDMA or Wide Ultra SCSI.

➤ Use SCSI controller cards that support asynchronous I/O so that multiple drives can operate in parallel, improving the performance of stripe sets and multiple paging files.

➤ Install separate drives on individual controller cards, spreading read/write activities across multiple controllers and improving overall performance.

➤ Use RAID arrays to distribute drive load across multiple devices, or add more drives to an existing array. Remember that adding drives may require the breaking and rebuilding of a disk set that uses striping with parity.

➤ Use hardware RAID, instead of software RAID, to take advantage of PCI SCSI card solutions that perform RAID functions, and standalone, self-powered external RAID enclosures that attach to a SCSI bus.

➤ Use drives that transfer data at 40Mbps or better, and never settle for less than 10Mbps.

Memory Utilization Options

When server memory systems combine physical RAM with swap files on a hard drive to successfully manage more active memory than what is actually present as physical RAM, they use a *Virtual Memory Manager (VMM)* from within the OS kernel. Although transfers between RAM and disk memory pages are invisible to applications, the data transfers themselves cause time delays. Operating 10 to 100 times slower than RAM systems, disk memory transfers slow down the computer's data processing ability.

Older server systems that managed 4GB of physical RAM would have had more than enough memory for most applications had systems actually been configured with that much. Instead, applications and services often demanded more memory than available on a given system, although much less than the 4GB maximum. Virtual memory proved to be a debilitating condition for these servers. Fortunately, the effects of virtual memory on system performance can be minimized by considering two important memory-related issues:

➤ The speed of the physical RAM must be sufficient for the processor type and the required operational tasks.

➤ Enough physical RAM must be on board to maintain high server performance.

A bottleneck caused by slow memory can be resolved only by replacing the current memory with faster RAM chips. In most cases, this is a simple operation, provided that the board is not burdened with outdated buses or chip sets. However, if the server board or the computer system cannot be upgraded, the system limitations will persist until such time as the appropriate new components are provided.

Slow RAM is fairly easy to identify. Suspect a physical RAM bottleneck when the memory Pages Input/sec counter reading shows a value of 1 or less. This condition indicates that all memory usage is taking place within the physical RAM without the aid of a swap file. If the memory utilization of the hard disk systems and the processor remain low during heated system operations, the component with the least throughput will most certainly be the RAM.

More difficult to identify is the need for larger amounts of physical RAM. Suppose a server's virtual memory system is maintaining 4GB of address space for each of its virtual machines, and the address spaces allocated to each virtual machine are mapped to virtual memory. This virtual memory is a combination of physical RAM and space from the swap file, where memory is divided into 4KB chunks, called pages. Each time a process requests a page, the VMM determines where the page is located in virtual memory and moves it into the appropriate location, either to physical RAM for active pages, or to a hard disk for inactive pages. Moving these pages from one location to another is called *paging*.

When a process requests a page that is not currently located in its visible working set of pages within the physical RAM, a page fault is initiated. When a page fault occurs, the VMM locates and moves the appropriate page from its current location to where the process wants it. If the requested page must be moved from one physical RAM location to another, it's called a soft page fault and is quickly resolved. If the requested page must be moved from hard disk into physical RAM, it's called a hard page fault and directly affects system performance because the VMM forces the active process to wait until its requested memory page is moved from the slow disk system to a working set of physical RAM pages and becomes available. Server systems with greater amounts of RAM and larger addressing schemes use less virtual memory and therefore experience fewer memory utilization bottlenecks.

Network Utilization Strategy

Although slow or malfunctioning network interface cards (NICs) are often responsible for producing network bottlenecks, bottlenecks can also appear as a result of improper protocol configurations, equipment malfunctions, and poor network design. Network communication performance degradations can be attributed to conditions such as the following:

➤ Server overload—This condition occurs when a server or workstation is consistently operating at, or near, its maximum capacity. Under these conditions, network requests might not be adequately responded to. An overburdened server, or even a sluggish workstation, can cause network performance to slow, until such time as the faulty condition is corrected.

➤ Network overload—This condition frequently occurs on a network system that is consistently operating at, or near, its maximum capacity. Under these conditions, the network may not be properly suited to the size and traffic of the organization, until such time as the faulty condition is corrected by installing higher-speed networking hardware, or segmenting and routing the network differently.

➤ Data loss—This condition occurs on a network or an individual host due to faulty wiring, devices, or protocols. Under these conditions, data packets are not delivered properly, and normal communications will be interrupted until the faulty device or element is located and replaced.

Although a certain amount of data loss is to be expected, in most active networks, a data loss rate of over 5% should be examined. If the number of failed or corrupt packets increases sharply, a computer- or application-related problem is indicated. An examination of the network on a protocol-by-protocol basis may be required to determine the exact cause of the data loss. However, without a predetermined baseline to work with, it will be difficult to differentiate between a normal error level and a new problem. Object monitors capable of detecting general network-related problems include the following:

➤ Network Interface: Bytes Total/sec—Displays the amount of data transmitted to and from the NIC each second. This should be compared to the NIC's rated capacity. For high network workloads, if the maximum throughput is less than 75% of the expected value, a faulty NIC, a poorly configured server, a bad protocol, or a faulty network cable is indicated.

➤ Network Interface: Current Bandwidth—Displays the current NIC bandwidth, and is useful only on variable bandwidth devices. The value helps to determine if the *bandwidth-on-demand* feature is functioning properly.

➤ Network Interface: Output Queue Length—Displays the number of packets waiting to be processed by the NIC. The NIC is acting as a bottleneck if the average value is consistently greater than 2.

➤ Network Segment: % Network Utilization—Displays the percentage of available bandwidth actually being used for communications and data transmission. A value consistently greater than 85% indicates the use of network technology that is inadequate for the size and traffic of the network.

➤ Redirector—Manages network connections to other computers that have originated from the source computer.

➤ Redirector: Server Sessions Hung—Identifies active sessions that have timed out due to communications failures. Network communications problems are indicated if the value is 5 or more.

➤ Redirector: Current Commands—Indicates the number of requests queued for service. Either the network or the server is causing a bottleneck if this value stays above n, where n = twice the number of NICs in the server + 2.

➤ Current Commands—Displays the number of requests currently queued for service by the Redirector. If this value is greater than the quantity of network interface cards installed in the server, the server or the network is seriously restricting system performance.

➤ Server: Sessions Errored Out—Indicates the number of sessions terminated due to unexpected error conditions. This cumulative counter indicates network problems related to dropped server sessions. A network performance problem is indicated when this parameter exceeds 5 within a reasonable length of time, or if a significant count increase develops over time. The server must be rebooted to reset this counter to zero (0).

➤ Server: Work Item Shortages—Indicates the number of times a work item was not available for allocation to an incoming request. A potential performance bottleneck is indicated for a value of 3 or more, but adjusting the settings of the server's service properties might alleviate the problem.

Several specific actions can reduce or eliminate the effects of a bottleneck on system performance after a network bottleneck is determined or suspected. The goal is to change the system as little as possible within the parameters of reasonable cost, ease of implementation, and manageable effects on the overall system. The following actions are arranged in a suggested order of approach:

1. Install only those protocols actually used on the network.

2. Disable or uninstall all protocols and NICs not in use.

3. Bind the most commonly used, or fastest, network protocols first.

4. Add more RAM to the servers.

5. Use NICs at identical speeds throughout the network, or at least within each segment/subnet. Although server-focused NICs include special features such as I/O processors, expandable memory, and adjustable buffers, workstation NICs do not. Focus on using NICs that all communicate at the same speed because mixing speeds will cause the network to operate at the transfer rate of the slowest NIC.

6. Use a single vendor to reduce administration and software/driver management.

7. Use more than one NIC, with a routing solution, such as *Routing and Remote Access Service (RRAS)*.

8. Install 32- or 64-bit PCI bus-mastering NICs.

9. Segment the network, use multiple NICs in servers, or use routers to divide segments.

Establishing Conditions for Using Various Baselines

From their first days of operation, server systems begin handling increased demands from the attached clients. Sooner or later, server operations need to be evaluated and improved due to this inevitable growth. When these necessary evaluation periods arrive, the usefulness of properly selected baselines becomes readily apparent. After valuable performance data has been documented over a range of system loads and conditions, an initial performance baseline can be established.

To permit fine-tuning of the server for maximum performance, a comparative performance baseline must be established. This baseline helps to measure and compare performance variables across a variety of server components. When the server environment is upgraded or changed, an evaluation of how the changes affect server operations can be undertaken. Changes in server performance as more computers and users are added to the network can be compared to the baseline, permitting the establishment of optimum performance settings for the system. This establishes a measurable, concrete way of determining the effectiveness of system tuning. The following situations necessitate the performance of a baseline evaluation:

➤ After initial installation—After first setting up and configuring a server, the "initial" baseline must be completed, using no load on the server. This baseline measures the maximum throughput of the system. Its values will be compared with those from future baseline measurements to provide a reference point for measuring the effects of network load and system modifications on the server and to recognize future server problems when they occur.

➤ After attaching to a network load—A second baseline is established after attaching the server to a normal network load. A comparison between this baseline and the initial "no-load" baseline reveals the overall network load on the server. These results should be documented for comparisons with future server loads over time.

➤ A length of time after initial installation—After a specified length of time following the initial installation, another baseline measurement is taken and logged. Comparisons to previous baselines should assure administrators that the system is operating effectively. To provide optimum server performance, the system settings might be tweaked, if necessary.

➤ Periodically scheduled—After the normal operational baseline is established, the server undergoes periodically scheduled baseline measurements, and the results are documented in the baseline log. Periodic measurements are used to map ongoing system performance, and provide technicians with enough information to define the system's standard performance under normal load conditions. This information is also invaluable when troubleshooting future server problems.

➤ After replacing defective components—After replacing defective server components, an additional performance baseline measurement should be taken to ensure that replaced components were the ones actually causing the problem. If the baseline does not improve, the problem lies with another component or software configuration, and requires a continued troubleshooting process until the problem is resolved. Additional baseline measurements must be logged with each change. When component replacements are conducted using similar products, performance values will differ due to varying results from different manufacturers. Documenting this information is also important for future product selection.

➤ After an upgrade to the system—When upgrading the server, it's a good practice to perform a new baseline, and compare the results to the initial and previous baseline values. This ensures that the server deployment continues to meet established requirements. The baseline log reveals a quantifiable value when selecting and purchasing hardware to improve performance. Server upgrade designs must be capable of properly handling any future system needs. Comparing baseline values before and after an upgrade provides a trustworthy method for ensuring that all upgrade goals are met.

➤ When changes to the network occur—When significant changes to the network environment have been made, an additional baseline measurement should be taken to ensure that the network has not exceeded the capability of the server, and to determine if a server upgrade is required.

Know how to determine and when to perform the baseline evaluation of a server environment.

When the baseline information in the preceding list is being evaluated, certain information types should always be included in the data makeup. Several of these important parameters can be used to indicate situations in which a software component is impeding system operations. Specific software baseline counters that make periodic server evaluations of greater value include

➤ Blocking Requests Rejected

➤ Context Block Queue/sec

➤ Pool Non-paged Failures

➤ Pool Paged Failures

➤ Work Item Shortages

These counters can be used to indicate when the server is not keeping up with network demand. If these values continue to rise, the administrator will suspect that a server software component is bottlenecking the rest of the system. When hardware resources remain sufficient for the specified network, server configurations can be tweaked when client demands begin to overload the system's capabilities. To know when this point has been reached, include a *Blocking Requests Rejected* counter to report how many times client *Server Message Block (SMB)* requests have been denied. A *Context Block queue/sec* counter with average values of 20 or more can also indicate a server bottleneck.

SMBs are stored by the server; therefore, depending on how many work items have been programmed for the system, increasing the number of work items (within the limit of physical system resources) might reduce the frequency of delays associated with many concurrent users exhausting the existing supply. The values for paged and non-paged pool will indicate when insufficient memory resources are bottlenecking the server's activities. Non-paged pool relates to system memory, whereas paged pool relates to the page file.

When a server's *autotuning* capabilities are enabled, the number of work items increase automatically depending on the amount of system memory installed and the way in which the server has been optimized through the use of the Maximize Throughput option. The active value for work items fluctuates between the minimum and maximum number specified by `MaxWorkItems` and `InitWorkItems`, or some similar parameter depending on the server software being used.

Increasing software parameters such as the work items cannot improve performance if the network server is running too many services. Only services in the highest demand should even be loaded. Services such as databases, web servers, and mail servers should be moved to other machines.

Documenting the Configuration

Server+ Exam Objective 3.8 indicates that the test taker should also be able to document the configuration. To achieve this objective, you need to know, understand, and document the following:

➤ What components are in the box

➤ Where components are located in the box

➤ What updates have been applied

➤ Warranty information

➤ Baseline

➤ Server configuration information, such as BIOS information, RAID levels used, what drives were put into which arrays, and server network information

➤ Install date

Configuration documentation refers to written information that is directly related to the server, including server information collected by the installing technicians and the administrator, associated printed documents, reference storage disks, maintenance data, and a list of applicable resource websites. This documentation should be considered as critical as any piece of equipment making up the server system because it is required whenever server problems must be diagnosed or disaster recoveries must be initiated. Not only should this documentation be kept in electronic format, but hard-copy archives should also be maintained in a safe place. During server failures, it is critical that this vital information be retrieved quickly.

Documentation Contents

What makes server documentation so important to the well-being of the network is the nature of the information it contains. This information identifies what components are installed inside the server unit, including their exact locations and configuration.

Know what documents should be kept for troubleshooting purposes.

Hard-copy documents include the printed documentation that comes with software or hardware, whether as simple as a small pamphlet or as large as a complete product instruction manual. Electronic versions of the same documentation are often supplied with the product on CD-ROM, and might include the same information that was supplied in printed form. If so, the electronic versions of the documentation are often more up-to-date, as they typically include last-minute documentation revisions.

In most cases, the supplier's website has the most up-to-date product information available. This is the easiest and most economical way for the supplier to provide documentation and system driver updates to their customers.

However, although it is the most recent information, it might not be the most detailed. Some companies use the website only to give information on problems associated with the product, or modifications to the manual that was supplied in the original purchased package. Because each company handles documentation differently, it is necessary to research each product's documentation (electronic, hard copy, and web-based) to determine which is the latest and most detailed information available.

Warranty Information

Although most system components are supplied with separate warranties, systems purchased as part of a package are also warranted under specified conditions. All of these documents should be kept together to avoid the necessity of searching various locations when their examination becomes necessary.

Baseline Measurements

Before documenting the initial server baseline, the program used to record the measurements must be selected, as well as which measurements will actually be documented. For comparative purposes, all subsequent baselines must be consistent in both the process and the measurement tools used. Typical baseline measurements that should be documented are included here. However, unique situations may dictate that additional server measurements be performed for inclusion in the baseline. However, regardless of any special considerations, the role of the server is the most important baseline consideration.

Knowing the role of the server is the most important consideration when preparing to determine the baseline.

For server optimization, fine-tuning is most effective when the components listed in the next few sections are working at their maximum capabilities. The server cannot be considered prepared for service prior to recording the initial baseline measurements. To effectively document a server baseline, a minimum approach will consider including performance data for these components.

Be able to differentiate between important and unimportant baseline criteria.

Logical Disk

The following logical disk operations should be monitored and documented for the baseline:

➤ Percentage of disk time for disks containing the `Pagefile.sys`—If the percentage of disk time is over 10%, the available bytes are around 4MB, and pages/sec is high, the server is paging a significant number of memory requests to disk and is experiencing a memory bottleneck.

➤ Percentage of disk time for all other disks—If this value is above 80%, the disk response time may very well become unacceptable. This is an indicator that the following disk counters should be investigated:

   ➤ Average Disk Queue Length—If this value is greater than 2 for a single disk drive, and the percentage of disk time is high, the selected disk is becoming a bottleneck to the system.

   ➤ Current Disk Queue Length—If this value is greater than 2 for a single disk drive over a sustained period, and the percentage of disk time is high, the selected disk drive is becoming a bottleneck.

   ➤ Disk Transfers/sec—If this value is consistently over 80 for a single physical disk drive, and the average disk/sec transfer is less than acceptable, this disk drive is slowing down the overall system performance.

   ➤ Average Disk sec/Transfer—When the transfer/sec counter is consistently above 80 for a single disk drive, and the average disk sec/transfer has a value of greater than .3 seconds, the selected disk drive has become a bottleneck to the system.

   ➤ Disk Bytes/sec—This measurement is the rate at which bytes are transferred to or from the disk during write or read operations. Add up this counter's values for each disk drive attached to the same SCSI channel, and compare it to the throughput of the SCSI bus. If this summed value is close to 80% of the throughput for the SCSI bus, the SCSI bus itself is becoming a bottleneck.

Memory

Important object monitors for memory operations include

➤ Available Bytes—This value displays the size of the virtual memory currently on the Zeroed, Free, and Standby lists. If this value is near 4MB, Pages/sec is high, and the disk drive where the `Pagefile.sys` is located is busy, the server has a memory bottleneck.

➤ Pages/sec—This measurement is the number of pages read from or written to the disk to resolve memory references to pages that were not in memory at the time of the reference. High paging activity itself does not indicate a problem unless it is accompanied by a low Available Bytes counter and a high percentage of disk time on the paging file disks.

➤ Cache Bytes—This value represents the number of bytes of physical memory that are being used to cache pages of data for applications.

To take an accurate memory load measurement, the server should first be monitored under a "no-load" condition for a period of time using an acceptable performance monitoring tool, and the results should be properly documented. The performance monitoring tool should be configured to log all necessary information relevant to the specified server, such as physical RAM usage at bootup, and page reads to virtual memory, in addition to the available bytes, pages/sec, and cache bytes measurements noted in the preceding list. Be aware that a snapshot of the disk I/O will not be applicable under a no-load condition because there will be no disk activity without a load on the server. Disk I/O values should be monitored, however, for all measurements taken after the server is connected to the network.

Network Interface

Object monitors for the network interface include

➤ Output Queue Length—This value represents the length in packets of the output packet queue. If this is longer than 3 for sustained periods, delays are being experienced and the bottleneck in the selected network interface should be found and eliminated.

➤ Bytes Total/sec—This is the sum of Frame Bytes/sec and Datagram Bytes/sec. If this value is close to the maximum transfer rate for the network, and the output queue length is less than 3, the network is reducing system performance and the problem must be resolved.

➤ Current Bandwidth—This value is an estimate of the interface's current bandwidth in bits per second (bps). Use this value with the Bytes Total/sec counter to determine the estimated network utilization levels.

➤ Packets Outbound Errors—This is the number of outbound packets that could not be transmitted due to system errors. If this value is less than 1, the selected network interface is experiencing network problems, and has the potential to degrade system performance.

➤ Packets Received Errors—This value is the number of inbound packets that contained errors that prevented delivery to a higher-layer protocol. If this value is less than 1, the selected network interface is experiencing network problems, and has the potential to degrade system performance.

Server

Object monitors suitable for testing the network interface often include

➤ Pool Non-paged Failures—This value reflects the number of times allocations from the non-paged pool have failed. If this value is less than 1 on a regular basis, the physical memory is too small for the selected server application.

➤ Pool Paged Failures—This value reflects the number of times allocations from the paged pool have failed. If this value is less than 1 on a regular basis, either your physical memory is too small for the selected server application, or you need to increase the paging file size.

➤ Work Item Shortages—This value reflects the number of times a `Status_Data_Not_Accepted` error was denoted at receive indication time. When this occurs, it indicates that the server software is not allocating a sufficient value for `InitWorkItems` or `MaxWorkItems`, and the system requires tweaking to increase overall server performance.

Server Work Queues

A meaningful parameter related to the server is

➤ Queue Length—This measurement reflects the current length of the server work queue for a given processor. If the queue length is greater than 4, or if it is steadily increasing in value, with an associated level of total processor time greater than 90%, the processor is becoming a bottleneck.

Maximum Capacity of the Infrastructure

After a server is networked, monitoring should occur over an additional period of time to provide comparative system data. Continuously applying more load to the system and documenting additional baselines will determine the *saturation point* of the server's infrastructure. This is where the network actually slows down the server, and is useful for predicting when the server may outlive its usefulness, or require further upgrade. The saturation point is determined by monitoring the server's overall response time under varying conditions.

Response Time Measurement

Response time is the time from a client's work process request, to its returned result, from start to finish. It's measured at the client machine, and grows as demands on the server increase. When viewing a new page on a company intranet, the total response time would measure from the link click to the full page display on the client's monitor. Included would be the delays imposed by the network cabling, routers, and interface cards, and the server hardware, operating system, and software.

Server Configuration

Another type of documentation associated with server installations deals with when changes are made, who makes them, and what the results are. These documents generally exist in the form of schedules and logs that contain dated details of changes, upgrades, and events that occur during server lifetimes.

Install Date

Install date documentation indicates the original state of the server when first assembled, powered up, and placed online. Subsequent baseline documentation is not related directly to the conditions recorded as of the install date, except for comparison purposes.

Implementing the Server Management Plan

Server+ Exam Objective 3.9 states that the test taker should also be able to implement the server management plan for OS-dependent and OS-independent components. Plans typically include

➤ Server management software installation

➤ Availability

➤ Server change management requirements

➤ Security plan

➤ Remote management hardware

To achieve this objective, the test taker will need supporting knowledge that includes

➤ Purposes and function of server management tools

During the initial installation of a server-based network, or prior to updating an existing server system, the administrator or server technician needs to carefully review the company's management plan, which was drawn up as part of the original deployment strategy.

When a grouping of servers is used to service the Local Area Network (LAN), the term often used to describe this arrangement is a *server farm*. A properly designed server farm is often tied to a high-speed backbone, and all of these details are included in the plan. In fact, the more detailed the server management plan is, the more expensive the proposed system deployment tends to get, because the plan attempts to include every necessary component. However, the deployment of a server farm is always costly and time-consuming. A good server management plan helps to eliminate any waste of money or time.

One important consideration is the fact that all hardware and software being used in the server system will most likely need to be immediately checked for updates. This goes double for any driver installed, so it's wise to get in the habit of checking and updating everything, every time. For an existing system, remember to never install a driver, or any other type of software patch, on a live system without first running it through a test system. Although the quality of driver and software updates has increased much over the years, the responsibilities that come with the management of large server networks dictate the testing of any updates prior to installing them.

Server Management Software Services

Server management products tend to vary somewhat in the way in which they are installed. However, they typically provide similar services after their installations have been completed. These services include the following:

➤ Deployment of Applications

  ➤ Reports on clients' current hardware base, existing applications, versions, and the current service pack and/or hotfix status

  ➤ Software distributions to client machines

  ➤ Upgrades to previously deployed software packages by propagating only the source changes rather than the entire application

  ➤ Elevated rights assignments on the fly during package software installations

➤ Asset Management

  ➤ Generation of summary or detailed reports specifying which applications clients used, how long, and on which managed systems

  ➤ File-level software inventory searches

  ➤ Scans for detailed hardware inventory data

  ➤ Web-enabled reporting of hardware/software inventory, server status, and software deployment progress

➤ Security Patch Management

  ➤ Vulnerability identifications

  ➤ Patch deployment console wizards

  ➤ Vulnerability assessment and mitigation reports

➤ Mobility

  ➤ Remote detection of client network connection capacity

  ➤ Completion of partial client downloads

  ➤ Timed software package installations to client workstations

  ➤ Mobile operations through flexible site boundaries

➤ Windows Management Services Integration

  ➤ Targeting software packages according to the properties of both users and systems with Active Directory

  ➤ Basing site boundaries on Active Directory names, rather than on Internet Protocol (IP) subnets.

  ➤ Using built-in computer and local system accounts for all server functions

  ➤ Using status data for real-time information about current server and client processes.

  ➤ Troubleshooting clients from an administrator console when the client is present at the remote machine.

Improving Server Availability

The server system should be analyzed on a cost-benefit basis to determine the need to improve availability. Costs include the resources specifically allocated to the server, such as memory and processors. The benefits can be thought of in terms of the total percentage of time that the server is available to process requests. Systems that have higher availability requirements also seem to cost more to maintain an appropriate level of performance.

After it is determined that an improvement in availability is necessary, the administrator needs to be realistic. The cost required to maintain a 24/7 server availability level might be too great to sustain. This is where the cost-benefit analysis comes into play, and decisions must be made, such as whether a clustered or non-clustered system is required.

The highest state of availability is provided by clustered systems through the use of interconnected servers sharing central storage. System service can continue if one server fails because a secondary server immediately assumes the failed server's tasks. Specific hardware and software are required to realize a clustered server network design.

If one or more devices fail in a non-clustered system, its servers might not contain the required components to allow the system to maintain its availability. However, even though non-clustered servers cannot provide the consistent availability of a clustered environment, they do provide high availability through the use of fault-tolerant hardware components. The major benefit of a non-clustered server system is that it's considerably less expensive than a clustered one. The limited availability of cluster-aware applications is another benefit of choosing non-clustered systems. Although the majority of server applications now available are not cluster-specific, more are being marketed continually.

Making improvements to server availability requires both hardware and software evaluations. Hardware availability is concerned with maintaining consistent use of, and access to, the specified hardware component regardless of the operational condition of any single device. When one component fails, a backup component is poised to maintain the system's availability.

Software availability focuses on the consistent functional integrity of the operating system or an application. If some aspect of the operating system fails on one system, a backup system must take over the process. The functionality of software availability is not hardware dependent, except with regard to clustered systems.

When addressing server availability with hardware components, consider the following:

➤ RAID—Allows for continued hard drive access in cases of single drive failures, and increases the fault-tolerant capabilities in a drive array. Two common RAID levels are RAID 1 (mirroring) and RAID 5 (stripe with parity).

➤ Hot-plug hard drives—Drives that can be removed or added to a system while the system is still operating. This reduces system downtime by avoiding the need to remove power from the server.

➤ Hot-plug PCI cards—Cards that can be deactivated, allowing for removal and replacement of a PCI card while the system is in operation, similar to the situation involving hot-plug hard drives.

➤ Hot-plug power supplies—Provides redundant power to the server in cases of power supply failure. Two or more redundant power supplies are required to ensure zero downtime from power supply failures.

Although clustered systems have one or more of the previously listed hardware availability components, their primary benefit involves the way in which a secondary server assumes control of the cluster if the primary server fails. Software availability solutions are best achieved in a clustered system through the use of cluster-aware operating systems and applications that are designed to monitor system operations and move them to a secondary server, in the event of failure. In all cluster-aware situations, it is necessary to continuously evaluate the availability requirements of the system. As requirements change, the system should be reconfigured to accommodate them. When considering cluster-awareness, remember the following:

➤ Cluster-aware operating systems are specifically designed to support cluster hardware and provide fault tolerance in case of failure. Typical cluster OSes have two or more nodes with a virtual server encompassing the cluster, or group of nodes. As a client connects to the virtual server, the OS handles the routing of information to the appropriate node. If a node fails, the OS will reroute the information to the surviving node, while continuing to service the client seamlessly.

➤ Cluster-aware applications interact with the OS to determine node availability. When a node fails, the surviving node assumes control, and applications remain available.

Server Change Management Requirements

Documenting changes to the server environment is a necessary task that must be accomplished either manually or through a software tracking system. This is doubly important when changes taking place in the server system's infrastructure can be classified as either approved or unauthorized. Without consistent effort, many undocumented system or server changes could occur, including changes to operating systems, databases, applications, and network devices. Software tracking systems make keeping up with these changes somewhat easier. Still, there is no substitute for an active, comprehensive *change management* plan. Undocumented server network changes can inflict severe harm on an organization when a related problem is not corrected for quite some time.

To implement a living, functional change management environment, the following points are recommended:

➤ Simple beginnings—If changes are implemented slowly and steadily, sufficient time will be provided for them to take effect. Clients will have time to get used to changes, step by step. If the database is being evaluated, begin by creating some sensible guidelines about which changes would improve its operation. Forget about creating a master plan to solve all the problems, because it will never be implemented. Instead, create a small project plan that contains a sensible task list of things to accomplish, one task at a time. Adjust the plan as needed if something proves to be unworkable.

➤ Evaluate and tighten security—From a change control perspective, the security settings should be examined to determine how clients might be able to make undesired database changes. Look for clients who mistakenly have server access. Then examine the database roles with the aim of customizing them with limited access. The usual approach to security problems is to grant too much access—this practice should be reversed.

➤ Release scheduling—Do not make production changes on the fly, but rather on a controlled basis. If clients know when periodic changes are due, they can adjust their schedule accordingly. Although this does not preclude changes being made outside of scheduling norms, it does require a thorough explanation of why they can't wait until the scheduled release. At the risk of slowing down the development process where clients want changes invoked immediately, a controlled approach to release scheduling proves beneficial by removing the risk of making them in an unscheduled or undocumented manner.

➤ Communication and documentation—Clients must know what changes have been completed and what changes are planned. Although verbal communication is important in the short term, documentation is essential for long-term operations. Because people often hear what they want to hear rather than the entire story, providing them with written documentation facilitates later review. Documentation takes time to do properly, and should therefore not be delayed until the task becomes too difficult. Begin while the task is manageable and document through the entire process, rather than waiting until the very end. Also, gather meaningful feedback to ensure that the documentation communicates properly with others. Let clients know that the documentation is for their benefit, providing them with important information about change implementation.

➤ Duty assignments—Changes are more effective when clients know how a new process works and how it affects them personally. Documentation must define who is responsible for doing what, and should require various signature signoffs to verify that the targeted clients have read and understand it. When something goes wrong, documentation helps to establish the responsibilities for correcting the problem.

➤ Back-out plan—During server upgrades, reconfigurations, or expansions, always be able to back out if completed changes threaten continued server operations. This is important, even for changes as simple as restoring a backup. More complex back-out scripts could require a coordinated effort with other key groups, such as applications, engineering, and networking. Understand that a back-out plan is just as important as a roll-out plan. Hopefully, it will never be used. But if and when it's needed, it will be worth the time spent putting it together.

➤ Make processes repeatable—Regardless of the details, the management of server environments should involve processes that can be repeated for any number of scenarios. By reviewing past documents, processes, and emails, reusable documents for future projects can be created. This permits the recycling of past efforts and streamlines the task of creating repeatable processes and procedures.

➤ Involve others—Maintaining control over changes to a database, or any other part of the server system, requires a realistic assessment of what is required. Blaming technicians, developers, administrators, or clients is ridiculous if guidelines haven't been set. After the groundwork has been completed, others can be brought into the mix. Differentiate between the things that can be controlled personally, and those things someone else must be aware of and manage. Convincing others to change the way they do things requires the following:

  ➤ Examine past mistakes to determine how the new process will eliminate repeating them.

  ➤ Involve upper management so that someone with authority will champion the cause and take it to the next level.

  ➤ Find others who want change to get them to join in the effort to find a better way.

  ➤ Collaborate by talking to other people informally, getting feedback, and addressing their concerns.

Security Planning

The importance of developing a server network security plan cannot be overemphasized. Large server deployments might actually require more than one. If an organization spans the globe with server installations, a different plan might be required for each major location. Regardless of the company's size, having a server network security plan in place is vital. The minimal requirements for such a plan include

> Security group strategies—To plan the use of built-in universal, global, and local group types. Decide how the existing built-in groups and/or newly created groups will be used as the network security plan is formulated.

> Security group policies—Defined following the planning of an organization's group strategies. Policies must be formulated for active directory objects, file systems, the registry, system services, network accounts, local computers, event logs, and restricted groups. Each of these organizational items can be controlled through the use of group policy filters. Minimizing the number of group policies is an advantage because they must be downloaded to each computer during startup, and to each user profile during logon.

> Network logon and authentication strategies—Necessary for the organization, utilizing such strategies as *Kerberos* logon, Windows NT LAN Manager (NTLM) logon, smart card logon, or certificate mapping. The server software can operate in either mixed mode or native mode, depending on the organization's makeup, although NTLM might not be available in native mode.

> Strategies for information security—Includes the organization's public key infrastructure, use of the encrypting file system, authentication for remote access users, IPSec utilization, secure email, website security, and signed software code, if applicable.

To accurately identify the client making a server request, multi-user network systems traditionally verify identity by examining a login password. The identity information is recorded, and used to determine what operations are permitted to be performed. This password-based verification process, called *authentication*, is no longer suitable for use on commercial computer networks. Eavesdroppers can intercept passwords sent across the network and use them to impersonate the user. This vulnerability has been demonstrated through the use of planted password-collecting programs at various points on the Internet.

NTLM uses a challenge-response mechanism for authentication, in which clients are able to prove their identities without sending a password to the server. It consists of three messages, commonly referred to as *negotiation* (Type 1), *challenge* (Type 2), and authentication (Type 3). Although this protocol continues to be supported in Windows 2000, it has been replaced by Microsoft Kerberos as the current default authentication standard in Windows Server 2003. Kerberos uses authentication based on cryptography, so that an attacker listening to the network gains no information that would enable him or her to falsely claim another's identity. Kerberos is the most commonly used example of this type of authentication technology.

A checklist for creating an organization's network security plan should include answers for questions such as

➤ What universal groups are necessary?

➤ What global groups are necessary?

➤ How will we utilize the built-in local groups?

➤ What local groups are necessary?

➤ What filters are necessary for group policies?

➤ What policies are required for Active Directory objects?

➤ What policies are required for the file system?

➤ What policies are required for registries?

➤ What policies are required for system services?

➤ What policies are required for network accounts?

➤ What policies are required for local computers?

➤ What policies are required for event logs?

➤ What policies are required for restricted groups?

➤ How will we perform network logon and authentication?

➤ What approach do we take with smart cards?

➤ What approach do we take with certificate mapping?

➤ How do we implement Public Key Infrastructure (PKI)?

➤ How do we implement the Encrypting File System (EFS)?

➤ How will we provide authentication for remote access users?

➤ What approach do we take with IPSec?

➤ What approach do we take with secure email?

➤ How do we protect the website?

➤ How is code signing implemented?

After a server network security plan has been determined, it needs to be tested in a controlled lab environment to ensure that it meets the needs of the organization. This must be done before the changes are implemented in a production environment. Otherwise, the result could be a catastrophe, both to the organization and to the administrator's job security. Of course, the testing environment should realistically duplicate the organization's existing network, if possible. This allows the discovery of problems that might occur during an actual implementation of the upgrade, without risking company operations.

Managing Server Hardware Remotely

Before servers running specific server operating systems are deployed, you must determine how thoroughly the system administrators need to manage the server hardware remotely. Conventional management tools suffice in situations where only typical administrative tasks are performed over the network. When *headless servers* are involved—those that have no keyboard, video display, or mouse—the use of emergency management services might be necessary, along with additional hardware and software components to remotely bring servers having high availability requirements back into service, even when they are not accessible by means of the standard network connection.

When determining which servers must be managed remotely, consider the tradeoffs such as cost, convenience, and system availability. Evaluate both remote and local management, as well as *in-band* and *out-of-band* (OOB) management. With the introduction of Windows Server 2003, many server management tasks that previously could be accomplished only locally can now be performed remotely. In fact, with the exception of hardware installations, all server management tasks can be performed remotely using emergency management services along with the appropriate hardware and software tools. In addition, configuring certain servers for headless operation can result in significant cost savings. After a determination is made as to which servers to manage remotely, the proper tools and supporting components must be selected. Table 14.1 contrasts the use of in-band and out-of-band remote hardware management tasks.

Table 14.1 In-Band vs. Out-Of-Band Remote Server Management Tools

Operation State	Task Type Performed	Type of Tool Used
System powering on, off, or reset	Power up, power down, reset	Remote Desktop for Administration (out-of-band and in-band)
Firmware initializing	Configure firmware, troubleshoot, restart	Supporting firmware (out-of-band)
Operating system loading Services	Choose OS to start, troubleshoot	Emergency Management (out-of-band)
Text mode setup	Monitor, troubleshoot	Management Services (out-of-band)
GUI mode setup	Monitor, troubleshoot	Emergency Management Services (out-of-band)
OS fully functional	Monitor, troubleshoot, modify configuration settings	(in-band)
OS not responding on network	Troubleshoot, restart	Emergency Management Services (out-of-band)
Stop message occurred	Troubleshoot, restart	Emergency Management Services (out-of-band)
System extremely slow responding on network	Troubleshoot, restart	Emergency Management Services (out-of-band and in-band)

The in-band management method is the method of choice for managing servers accessed through standard connections. Conventional in-band management tools provide a broader range of functionality and greater security than that achieved using out-of-band management. This is because the security of in-band management techniques depends mostly on the individual management tool being used, whereas the security of out-of-band management depends mostly on the configuration of various out-of-band components. For example, out-of-band server configurations using remote serial connections depend on the security built into the modem. In fact, the sole legitimate use for out-of-band management is as a last resort when no other server access methods are possible. Accordingly, the use of out-of-band management is oriented toward bringing the server back into service so as to manage it with in-band tools.

Create a detailed list of all tools that will be required to manage specific tasks. These tasks can be as broad as managing a DHCP server, or as narrow as changing a server's static IP address. Include both in-band and out-of-band tasks, such as remotely installing the operating system, or powering up the computer. Remember that several different remote management tools can be used to perform the same task, so the list should include all the tools relating to each remote task to be performed.

If merely changing a configuration setting will perform a remote administration task, note this in the remote administration plan. For an environment that includes a mixture of OSes, look for tools that provide interoperability. The list should also include the out-of-band tools or components to be obtained or installed. Remember that remote administration can cause increased network traffic and decreased server performance, or create security vulnerabilities requiring the reconfiguration of the server network, the operating system, or the security settings. List each of these potential impacts, along with the specific steps planned to deal with them.

Exam Prep Questions

1. CPU temperatures and FRU component operations can be monitored by the management controller through which bus system?

   ❑ A. The server monitor bus
   ❑ B. The server management bus
   ❑ C. The baseboard management bus
   ❑ D. The controller management bus

2. Why is the SNMP protocol useful?

   ❑ A. It can communicate with a TCP/IP network and provide hardware alert notifications.
   ❑ B. It can be used to send alerts to a hub or router on a TCP/IP network.
   ❑ C. It can display and modify the IP-to-Physical address translation tables.
   ❑ D. It can disassemble a data packet before it is transmitted.

3. At what point in the system boot process is the SNMP utility loaded?

   ❑ A. Not until the administrator first presses the Enter key to run the monitoring program
   ❑ B. After the NOS is loaded onto the system
   ❑ C. Before the NOS is loaded onto the system
   ❑ D. After the last device driver has been loaded by the NOS.

4. What is the format that SNMP uses to transfer its data?

   ❑ A. ISO
   ❑ B. ANSI
   ❑ C. Unicode
   ❑ D. ASCII

5. What three basic components compose the SNMP model?

   ❑ A. Network management systems, managed devices, and agents
   ❑ B. Network management systems, agents, and nodes
   ❑ C. Agents, servers, and managed devices
   ❑ D. Managed devices, network management systems, and servers

6. Which of the following ports is the SNMP default?

   ❑ A. 25
   ❑ B. 161
   ❑ C. 170
   ❑ D. 110

7. When determining a server's baseline, what is the most important factor to consider?

- ❏ A. The operational role played by the network server
- ❏ B. The amount of data storage available on the server
- ❏ C. The amount of RAM installed on the server
- ❏ D. The number of clients being served by the network

8. When determining the server's baseline, which of the following factors is considered to be unimportant?

- ❏ A. The performance of the logical disk
- ❏ B. The ability of the server to effectively process its work queues
- ❏ C. The operational role played by the network server
- ❏ D. The operating system running on a client's computer

9. Which of the following baseline descriptions is most accurate?

- ❏ A. Only after changes in the network occur should a baseline measurement be taken.
- ❏ B. Using a baseline, hard disk performance can be measured and compared over a specified length of time.
- ❏ C. Performance variables across a variety of server components can be measured and compared using a baseline.
- ❏ D. The main reason for conducting a baseline is to measure the performance of the server's processor.

10. Under what conditions should the server first be monitored to secure an accurate memory load measurement?

- ❏ A. For a specified time period under no-load conditions
- ❏ B. For a specified time period under high-load conditions
- ❏ C. Only during a period of time when approximately 50% of the clients are using the server network
- ❏ D. For a specified time period under medium-load conditions

11. When testing server performance, which of the following would not be tested?

- ❏ A. The system memory
- ❏ B. The client/node network
- ❏ C. The application software
- ❏ D. The processors and associated components

12. What constitutes a bottleneck in a server system that executes a test task by consuming 0.3 seconds of processor time, 0.2 seconds for network access, and 0.6 seconds for disk access?

- ❏ A. The memory
- ❏ B. The disk drive
- ❏ C. The network
- ❏ D. The processor

13. The administrator is evaluating server baseline data for comparing parameters before and after the addition of four dozen networked clients. Given that the baseline peak usage comparisons in the following table indicate a noticeable drop in server performance, where does the problem lie and what is the solution?

Parameter	Before	After
Processor utilization	40%	45%
Network utilization	25%	30%
Memory paging	800 pages/sec	2700 pages/sec
Disk utilization	12%	7%

❑ A. Disk drive. Solution: Add more HDDs.
❑ B. Network. Solution: Install additional server NICs.
❑ C. Microprocessor. Solution: Add another CPU.
❑ D. Memory. Solution: Install more RAM.

14. Error logs perform the necessary tasks of recording and storing valuable troubleshooting data. How can the administrator check and examine this information?
❑ A. Using the event viewer
❑ B. Using the security log
❑ C. Using the computer viewer
❑ D. Using the system log

15. When determining which types of documentation to keep for troubleshooting purposes, which types should not be considered? (Select two.)
❑ A. Original purchase price logs
❑ B. Installation/configuration logs
❑ C. Hardware/software upgrade logs
❑ D. Fire detection logs

16. When discussing the subject of the SNMP, what is an MIB?
❑ A. An MIB is the Master Internet Boot program, which loads SNMP into memory.
❑ B. An MIB is the Management Interface Backup, which stores a copy of the NOS in logical memory.
❑ C. An MIB is the Management Information Base, which stores data collected from the SNMP agents.
❑ D. An MIB is the Master Intelligent Bus, which transfers ASCII text from SNMP agents to the processor.

17. What happens when SNMP is placed into a community configuration?

   ❏ A. The SNMP server network begins using Unicode instead of ASCII for its internal messaging.

   ❏ B. One or more SNMP managers form a logical group for the purpose of sharing their agent relationships.

   ❏ C. In the interest of security, an SNMP agent validates each NMS request following its related procedure.

   ❏ D. In response to hacker requests, a group of SNMP agents configure themselves to service them.

18. The administrator is connected to a remote machine when an application-specific error occurs. The remote machine's system and application error logs reveal no clues. What is the next logical step for the administrator to take?

   ❏ A. Report the problem to the service department.

   ❏ B. Reboot the remote server.

   ❏ C. Go on working as normal.

   ❏ D. Check the local machine's application error log file.

19. Which of the following management utilities is available with Windows 2000 Server and Server 2003?

   ❏ A. Microsoft Management Console

   ❏ B. Microsoft Console Monitor

   ❏ C. Microsoft Performance Monitor

   ❏ D. Microsoft Management Monitor

Exam Prep Answers

1. Answer B is the correct answer. The management controller communicates with the server board's other management components through the independent pathways of the Server Management Bus (SMB). Server board parameters such as CPU temperatures and FRU operations can be monitored. Answers A, C, and D are all fictitious bus names.

2. Answer A is the correct answer. The SNMP protocol can communicate with a TCP/IP network in such a way as to manage information between SNMP devices, SNMP agents, and the Network Management System (NMS). Answer B is incorrect because hubs and routers are not designed to take specified actions upon receiving alert notifications. Answer C is incorrect because the ARP utility is used to display IP-to-Physical address translation tables. Answer D is incorrect because disassembling a data packet prior to transmission would be useless.

3. Answer C is the correct answer. SNMP systems use the Master Boot Record (MBR) to point to the SNMP partition. Then the SNMP utility is loaded before the NOS. Answer A is incorrect because the boot process does not require the pressing of any keyboard keys. Answer B is incorrect because by the time the NOS is loaded onto the system, SNMP is already active. Answer D is incorrect because SNMP has already been loaded even before the NOS.

4. Answer D is the correct answer. The ASCII format is used by SNMP to conduct data transfers. Answer A is incorrect because ISO is merely the acronym for the International Organization for Standardization. Answer B is incorrect because ANSI is better known as the American National Standards Institute. Answer C is also incorrect. Although Unicode remains independent of platform, program, or language, it does provide a unique number for every character.

5. Answer A is the correct answer. The SNMP model consists of network management systems, managed devices, and agents. Answer B is incorrect because nodes are not basic components of the SNMP model. Answers C and D are incorrect because servers are not considered to be basic SNMP components.

6. Answer B is the correct answer. SNMP conducts its communication using the default port of 161. Answer A is incorrect because port 25 is used to transmit email with the Simple Mail Transfer Protocol (SMTP). Answer C is incorrect because network PostScript printers use port 170. Answer D is incorrect because the POP3 protocol uses port 110 to retrieve email.

7. Answer A is the correct answer. The server's baseline is determined mostly according to its role in the system. Answer D is incorrect because the initial baseline is usually performed prior to connecting the server to the network. Answer B is incorrect because server disk space is an important consideration for network operation, but it is not the most important baseline factor. Answer C is incorrect because a shortage of RAM would be an important factor to consider, but again, it is not the most important.

8. Answer D is the correct answer. When determining a server baseline, client computer operating systems are not important. Answer A is incorrect because the performance measurements for the logical disk are obviously important. Answer B is incorrect because the timely processing of server work queues is an extremely important baseline consideration. Answer C is incorrect because the role of the server is the most important baseline consideration.

9. Answer C is the correct answer. Baseline measurements permit performance comparisons across a variety of server component variables. Answer A is incorrect because the baseline documents the server's performance prior to any changes, and measurements taken after network changes are compared to the baseline. Answer B is also incorrect in that the baseline does much more than provide hard disk performance comparisons. Answer D is incorrect because processor performance is only a small part of baseline information.

10. Answer A is the correct answer. Following the beginning setup and configuration of a server, the "initial" baseline must be established under no-load conditions for measurements of maximum system throughput. These values will be compared with future baseline measurements to determine server network conditions. Answer B is incorrect because no-load conditions are specified. Answers C and D are incorrect because moderate network use does not provide the required no-load baseline conditions.

11. Answer C is the correct answer. When testing server performance, application software is not considered a valid testing component. Answer A is incorrect because system memory is always tested when evaluating server performance. Answer B is incorrect because client/node operations are targeted for performance testing. Answer D is incorrect because processors and associated components must be included in server performance testing.

12. Answer B is the correct answer. The selected disk drive should be considered a system bottleneck when the transfer/sec counter stays consistently above 80% for a single disk drive, and the average disk sec/transfer has a value of greater than 0.3 seconds. Answers C and D are incorrect because the consumed processor or network access times were within acceptable parameters. Answer A is incorrect because no memory operational parameters were provided for this test.

13. Answer D is the correct answer. No more than 2,000 pages per second should be accessed under maximum usage. Answer A is incorrect because disk drive utilization has decreased according to the new baseline. Answer B is incorrect because network utilization continues to be well within acceptable values. Answer C is incorrect because the percentage of processor utilization is well below 90%.

14. Answer A is the correct answer. In order to examine the information associated with the systems' hardware, software, and security events, the event viewer must be used. It directs the recording of event errors in application, system, and security logs. Answers B and D are incorrect because these logs are not directly readable. Instead, they serve as depositories for the data specified by the event viewer. Answer C is incorrect because no such viewer exists.

15. Answers A and D are the correct answers because they have nothing to do with server equipment troubleshooting. Answers B and C are incorrect because later troubleshooting scenarios will need to use documentation dealing with dates, personnel, installation results, configuration notes, and upgrades to either hardware or software.

16. Answer C is the correct answer. Answers A, B, and D are all based on fictitious items.

17. Answer B is the correct answer. Answer A is incorrect because SNMP messages are strictly ASCII in format. Answer C is incorrect because NMS request validation must occur prior to the requested action, not following it. Answer D is incorrect because community configurations are designed to prevent hacker operations, not to cooperate with them.

18. Answer D is the correct answer. When an application error occurs, it is normally logged only on the computer hosting the specific application. Answer A is incorrect because the administrator must be sure that he or she cannot correct the specified error before reporting it to the service department. Answer B is incorrect because the error cannot be investigated thoroughly by simply rebooting. Answer C is incorrect because a server error message must be noted and the underlying problem must be corrected.

19. Answer A is the correct answer. The latest versions of Server 2003 R2 use version 2.1 of the Microsoft Management Console. Answers B and D are fictitious. Answer C does not refer to a management tool but rather to a monitoring tool.

15.0—Upgrading the Basic System

Terms you'll need to understand:

- ✓ Emergency Repair Disk (ERD)
- ✓ Graphical User Interface (GUI)
- ✓ Repair Console
- ✓ Backups
- ✓ Archives
- ✓ Data copying
- ✓ Full vs. incremental backups
- ✓ Backup media
- ✓ Media pool
- ✓ Tape rotation and storage
- ✓ Backup schedules
- ✓ Autoloader
- ✓ Storage libraries
- ✓ Storage management databases
- ✓ System recovery
- ✓ Downtime schedules
- ✓ Stepping levels
- ✓ Upgrades
- ✓ Automatic termination
- ✓ Mounting
- ✓ Mount point
- ✓ Error-Correcting Code (ECC)
- ✓ Metal Oxide Semiconductor (MOS)
- ✓ Chip creep
- ✓ Earth, signal, and chassis ground
- ✓ Electromagnetic Interference (EMI)
- ✓ Firmware
- ✓ Field Replacement Unit (FRU)
- ✓ Sensor Data Record (SDR)
- ✓ Server Message Block (SMB)
- ✓ Baseboard Management Controller (BMC)
- ✓ Electrostatic Discharge (ESD)

Techniques you'll need to master:

✓ Determining when to perform a server upgrade

✓ Avoiding damage to system components

✓ Backing up server data

✓ Creating a current Emergency Repair Disk

✓ Differentiating between data copying and data backups

✓ Understanding various backup media

✓ Using a tape rotation backup plan

✓ Storing backup data wisely

✓ Managing storage libraries

✓ Performing a system recovery

✓ Verifying processor compatibility

✓ Adding a processor to the server

✓ Documenting a server upgrade

✓ Scheduling server system downtime

✓ Adding hard drives to a server system

✓ Examining RAID compatibility

✓ Maintaining current baselines

✓ Checking for proper SCSI terminations

✓ Matching hard drives and controllers

✓ Performing BIOS and firmware upgrades

✓ Implementing ESD best practices

✓ Using RAID management utility software

✓ Mounting drives in a Linux system

✓ Verifying memory compatibility for upgrading

✓ Handling MOS devices properly

✓ Differentiating between various types of grounds

Introduction

When a server system, including its related peripherals, requires an upgrade, the potential impact on the networked clients must be minimized. The administrator should plan, document, and execute the upgrade so as to provide the least amount of interruption. Each step in the upgrade plan should be clearly documented and organized into separate tasks. The following tasks are included:

➤ Provide documentation detailing exactly what is being upgraded, and how the upgrading process is intended to work.

➤ Identify all parts being ordered such as SCSI hard drives or IDE hard drives. To simplify future system troubleshooting chores, this information should verify that the purchased RAM is the correct type, and that parts being added to the system match the makes and models of existing network components. Order lists should be carefully checked to avoid ordering incorrect parts that would delay an upgrade while the correct parts are reordered.

➤ Ensure that each part is correct when upgrade parts arrive. Manufacturers often select substitute components or in some cases mistakenly ship the wrong part. Although substitute parts are acceptable for desktop machines, server systems are more susceptible to compatibility problems. Indicate on the original order document that the specified parts are for a server system and that prior consent is required for any substitutions.

➤ Schedule the upgrade when adequate company or service personnel will be available, so that the upgrade can be completed in the least possible amount of time. Success is more likely to occur if you plan and coordinate the upgrade with each individual affected. Productivity will take a nosedive if not enough personnel are available during the upgrade process. It might be necessary to assign backup personnel to critical activities in the event that primary personnel are called elsewhere while the upgrade is proceeding.

➤ Provide responsible personnel with the necessary tools and information. Ensure that enough room exists to perform the upgrade, and that all required tools are available. This includes making sure the necessary environmental disaster and ESD preventive measures are in place. Proper documentation forms should be available for use during the upgrade to record minor changes that occur during the work. Keep support information such as product keys and registrations available for all new software or related upgrades. When everything needed is readily available, the upgrade process can proceed with a minimal amount of downtime.

➤ Complete all documentation as soon as the upgrade is complete. Server network upgrade information is critical and must be documented, including all changes made throughout the upgrade process. This documentation becomes an important tool for effectively troubleshooting future system problems. Include extra copies as required and properly store the documentation. A working copy should be stored where company personnel can gain access to it in the future.

➤ Clean up the server area, and ensure that it is left in a safe and secure condition.

Scheduling Downtime

When any primary server activity or the entire server must be shut down, this action must be performed according to a previously circulated schedule that considers the following factors:

➤ The number of technicians available to do the required repairs

➤ The number of personnel hours that will be required to perform the server upgrade

➤ The hours when server use is at its peak

It is critical to provide a high level of system availability, even when upgrading or performing system maintenance.

Essential considerations when scheduling an upgrade include the day(s) of the week and the time of day that the upgrade activities will be performed. Although it might make sense to schedule an upgrade during the middle of the night or early in the morning to inconvenience the least number of clients, this choice can turn out to be unwise. These hours represent periods during which workers may not be capable of doing their best work. In spite of this, many commercial operations have no choice but to implement server network repairs during these hours. Under such conditions, all necessary personnel should be permitted to rest and properly prepare for the required work. Some businesses operate using 24-hour shifts, which makes it impossible to upgrade the server during non-peak hours. These operations require even greater care to schedule an upgrade during such a time, and in such a way, as to produce as little impact on productivity as possible.

Under these conditions, success is achieved only by planning and distributing annual or semiannual *downtime schedules* for all employees. These system update schedules must be provided repeatedly throughout the year, and reminder messages should be posted within a reasonable period of time shortly before the scheduled downtime. Clients can be conditioned to plan and schedule their activities around the scheduled downtime if the system maintenance schedule maintains a yearly time frame, such as every December.

 Know the correct order of steps needed to prepare for taking down a server.

The main idea behind this approach to scheduling server upgrades is that it becomes a predictable company activity. Keeping the organization well informed about server upgrade activities measurably reduces the stress on clients and minimizes the negative impact on overall company productivity. Only an emergency situation, such as a long-term power outage with short-term UPS backup, justifies issuing a 5- or 10-minute warning prior to system shutdown. Critical data and much productivity can be lost by commercial enterprises that do not provide proper server shutdown notice to their employees.

Never forget that the loss of power to a server always entails the possibility of losing valuable data. To prevent the possibility of this occurring, important precautions must be taken prior to the deliberate removal of server power. When a server must be taken down to perform required hardware/software upgrades, the following actions must be performed in a specific order:

1. Alert users

2. Take down applications

3. Perform backup procedures

4. Power down the server

5. Power down the peripherals

Performing Backups

Server+ Exam Objective 4.1 indicates that the test taker should be able to perform backups. Activities associated with this objective include

➤ Update the ERD/recovery disk, if applicable

➤ Verify backup

To achieve this objective, you need to know and understand the following:

➤ When full backups might be necessary

➤ How to select the appropriate type of backup:

   ➤ Differential

➤ Appended

➤ Copy

➤ Full

Determining the ideal time to perform a server upgrade can be a challenging task for any administrator. Although various server system components require periodic upgrades, when and how these upgrades are performed are critical decisions to make. Upgradeable items include the system's firmware, peripheral firmware, and various network operating system (NOS) components. Server+ technicians must be able to determine when a server needs to be upgraded, and how to find and install the necessary hardware components or software/firmware updates and patches.

However, before any upgrade process is undertaken, the data already being managed by the existing server system must be completely backed up. Unforeseen problems encountered during server upgrade activities have the potential for disaster, and disaster is what server administrators and technicians are paid to avoid! The main weapons used against such disasters are the *Emergency Repair Disk (ERD)* and a systematic backup program. As a server technician or system administrator, *never* make a system change until all of the system's data is completely backed up and verified!

Repair and Recovery Operations

When repairing a broken Windows server installation, an up-to-date ERD is critical. The ERD must be updated whenever server hardware is either added or removed or other significant changes are made to the system setup. To ensure this capability, the system must be configured to automatically record updated repair information. Unless this parameter is activated, only the server's initial installation information will remain stored on the ERD and/or its associated repair directory. Such information will be of little value six months or two years down the line. This is especially true when changes such as the addition of a hard drive, the replacement of a disk controller, or the addition/removal of a partition have occurred.

However, even if the ERD is not current, an up-to-date \winnt\repair directory can contain equivalent information. The rdisk /s- command automatically schedules updates of the files in this directory. The /s parameter instructs the repair disk to update the ERD and repair directory data. The minus sign prevents the repair disk utility from requesting a floppy disk to generate a new ERD while automatically updating the \winnt\repair directory. This technique only works if a server fails in a networked environment because the updated repair data can be later retrieved from the file server. For solo systems, ERDs should be kept current.

Because recent Windows server environments are too large to fit on a floppy disk, ERD capabilities have been removed. Instead, Windows 2000 uses a Repair Console, whereas Windows 2003 uses a Recovery Console to effect repairs on systems that no longer boot properly.

Other server OSes use proprietary repair formulas to achieve similar protections for their systems. Regardless of which system is used, the main concern is to keep recovery disks and files current, with information covering all of the latest updates and upgrades.

Backups, Archives, and Copies

The functional difference between creating data or application *backups* and making *archives* is negligible. Both backups and archives basically rely on the same technology and are stored on identical media. The main difference between the two is how long the data copies are retained. Normally, backup files are not retained as long as archived files. In addition, archived files are normally deleted from the primary disk or source storage media on which they originally resided.

There are differences between copying data and merely backing it up. *Data copying* is a manual, character-by-character, file-by-file, time-intensive process that requires the same quantities of storage media as do the original files. No attempt is made to determine if the previous copy has been changed in any way. The idea is to have a spare copy of the specified file located in some other directory, on another disk, or another medium, not necessarily as part of a backup program.

Alternatively, backing up data is much faster and more efficient than copying. Data backups take up less space on the storage media because of the possibility of creating incremental backups, rather than having to initiate a *full backup* each session. An *incremental backup* backs up only the files that have changed since the most recent backup was performed. This makes it easier and more cost-effective to undertake frequent backups of multiple versions of data.

In data backups, multiple copies are seldom kept for long periods of time. This approach to data protection often results in the availability of recent data resources, but without reliable copies of past versions. For example, if the tape containing this week's data was used to record over last week's data, it might not be possible to examine or restore a data file from last week, depending on whether it remains unchanged. A similar problem is encountered if you find that an important file on the latest data copy is corrupt.

Backup software often includes various backup solutions to streamline the backup process. One solution is to automatically copy application data into a single file that is not directly readable by its creating application. This file, which might also contain a backup of the creating application itself, is then compressed and protected with passwords or encryption to prevent unauthorized access. The backup file is copied to the selected media—a local hard disk, a remote hard disk, a CD, or a magnetic tape. All this action is performed by the backup software with one click of a mouse.

Backup Media

Storing data backups on the originating server hard drive is dangerous because if this drive fails, the original data will be lost along with the backups. Alternatively, using a remote hard drive limits the amount of data that can be backed up to the size of that hard drive. If multiple remote hard drives are used, the cost will increase over time as backed-up data volumes increase in size. More flexibility is offered through the use of CDs and DVDs as backup media because that additional media can be burned as needed without having to install new drives. However, CD or DVD backups are fairly slow and their capacity is comparatively small when the full backup demands of a commercial operation are considered. For these reasons, the *backup media* of choice for most business operations is tape. Tapes are removable, and because they are the largest-capacity removable media available, they can be used to back up enormous amounts of data. A single tape is capable of storing anywhere from 10 gigabytes to more than 600 gigabytes of data. Most importantly, writing data to tape is much faster than writing to any other removable media.

Each tape becomes part of the *media pool* used by resources as the target media for backups. The backup software ensures the efficient use of each tape by appending multiple backups to the tape until it's filled. Keeping track of what backup tapes contain which data is aided through the use of internal labels created on the tape by the backup software that correspond to external labels, such as barcodes that are physically embedded on each tape. The backup software maintains a database of all files backed up to each tape, the tape's used capacity, and its expiration date. The software can also determine if a tape has serious errors and if it should be removed from the media pool.

Tape rotation is an important aspect of any tape backup plan. If a large percentage of the company's backed-up data is on a single tape, and that tape fails, the data is lost. To avoid this unfortunate scenario, backup tapes should be rotated. For example, rather than using tape A for three consecutive weeks, use three tapes: "A" for the first week, "B" for the second, and "C" for the third. At the end of this three-week interval, reuse tape A for the fourth week, and so on. Having multiple backup tapes in the rotation will also become invaluable when specific data on the primary drive becomes corrupted or unusable. For the rotation just described, data from the previous three weeks will be available to repair or replace the problem data.

Tape storage is another important consideration for any backup plan. For maximum safety and protection, many companies store backup tapes at off-site locations. In situations where frequent access to backup tapes is required, select a backup software solution that permits the automatic creation of multiple copies of a single backup tape. This permits the storage of the most recent backups onsite, with the other copies stored offsite.

Backup Schedules

Decisions as to which files should be backed up and how often they should be backed up should be carefully made and dictated by how often that data changes, especially if it's considered critical to the operation of the business. In some cases, it might be necessary to conduct data backups several times each day, whereas in others, weekly backup procedures might be sufficient. Quality backup software often simplifies these important tasks through the use of program wizards that guide administrators through the process of creating realistic and functional *backup schedules*.

Backup schedules should be based on the need for the creation of either full backups or incremental backups. At the start of any backup program, the initial approach is to back up all business data and applications that have been earmarked for protection. This is performed through a process called full backup, which should be repeated periodically, generally on a monthly basis. In between the performance of full backups, incremental backups are conducted to protect data that has changed since the most recent full backup. Because incremental backups are smaller than full backups, they save time and reduce tape utilization.

The process of changing out and replacing backup tapes can also be streamlined through the use of a robotic device called an *autoloader*. Autoloaders operate with multiple-drive tape systems and are designed to automatically load and unload backup tapes from their attached *storage libraries*. Although autoloaders reduce the frequency with which backup tapes must be manually loaded into single-drive tape devices, the tape library requires even less frequent loading and unloading due to its use of multiple tape drives.

Backup Restorations and Recoveries

Backup files can be re-created on the original drive through the data restore function. Backup utility programs maintain catalogs, also called *storage management databases*, that contain an index of all files that have been backed up to tape—including the date and time of creation, file size, and the tape label designation. Individual files can be restored by reviewing this database, generally with an interface similar to the file trees common to Microsoft Windows Explorer, and double-clicking on the filenames. Data can be automatically restored or re-created to either primary storage or the original locations. Data can also be restored to an alternate location, or even restored under another name. The backup software indicates the appropriate tape for loading as indicated by the catalog. Remember, the more often data is backed up, the more versions there are to restore from.

There is always the possibility that a server platform will fail completely and require the initiation of a *system recovery*. A system recovery involves the repair and replacement of broken or malfunctioning hardware before reloading the OS. After the OS is functioning correctly, the backup software must be reloaded along with other required applications. The final step is to restore critical data from the backup tape(s). Various third-party solutions can be used to simplify the system recovery process through the use of bootable disks and/or disaster recovery tapes that contain OS software and a minimal version of the backup software to activate the system after the malfunctioning hardware has been repaired or replaced. With the system back in operation, the backup tapes can be used to restore the fully customized operating system, all applications, and all files originally associated with them.

Adding Processors

Server+ Exam Objective 4.2 states that the test taker should be able to add processors. Activities for this objective include

➤ On single-processor upgrade, verify compatibility

➤ Verify N+1 stepping

➤ Verify speed and cache matching

➤ Perform BIOS upgrade

➤ Perform OS upgrade to support multiprocessors

➤ Ensure proper ventilation

➤ Perform upgrade checklist, including:

➤ Locate/obtain latest drivers, OS update, software, and so on

➤ Review FAQs, instruction, facts, and issues

➤ Test and pilot

➤ Schedule downtime

➤ Implement ESD best practices

➤ Confirm that the upgrade has been recognized

➤ Review and baseline

➤ Document upgrade

To achieve this objective, you need to know and understand what it means to verify stepping.

Server boards normally have multiple processor slots. Administrators can choose to fill all, several, or only one of them through the use of special server board settings or by plugging in dummy adapters for the unused slots. The most effective method to upgrade the performance of a server is to populate these slots with multiple processors whenever possible.

However, several important considerations exist when selecting and installing multiple processors, including:

➤ Verifying processor compatibility—Check to make sure that all processors are the same brand and that they fit the identical socket. The production run of the processor should also be examined to ensure that it is within one level of the other processor(s) with which it will be joined. In the case of Intel processors, this is called a *stepping level*. For example, if you own a Pentium III 750 MHz processor that is a stepping 4, you should install only additional processors that are defined as stepping 3, 4, or 5. For optimal stability, it is advised that you install the same make, model, and clock speed for all processors. This includes using the same bus speed and multiplier, and the same cache size to ensure that there will be no speed difference between cache feeds. Refer to the server board manufacturer's manual or their online documentation for detailed information on their board and suggested processor compatibility.

➤ Performing BIOS upgrades—Server boards designed to use multiple processors are normally equipped with a multiple processor BIOS, which is sufficient for use with directly compatible processors. However, when performing a major upgrade that includes the installation of newer and faster processors, the BIOS is probably due for an upgrade or a change as well. In fact, a processor upgrade is always a good opportunity for also updating the server's BIOS. Updated BIOS programs are often developed by the board's manufacturer to permit the installation of faster processors as they come on the market.

➤ Verifying the upgrade—After a processor upgrade is performed, verify it by booting the system and carefully looking for error code reports. You must verify that the system recognizes the newly installed processor(s). Observing an automatic rerouting to the CMOS program does not necessarily mean that an error has been encountered. Instead, this is a normal procedure used during a system's initial reboot following the addition of another processor. The system will recognize the new processor(s) and provide corroborating information about it in the CMOS program, or its administrative tool package. This information verifies that the server board is recognizing all installed processors, and that all processors are working properly. The CMOS program also provides data on the actual processor speeds as well as the operation of the processor fans.

➤ Documenting the baseline—After performing a processor upgrade, create and document a new baseline using the techniques described in Chapter 14, "Preparing the Server for Service." For the initial baseline following an upgrade, ensure that there is no load (no users connected to the server) before testing the performance of a newly installed processor. Following the baseline measurements, compare the upgrade baseline to the previous measurements. If there doesn't seem to be any improvement, verify processor compatibility again. Fully optimize the system by checking for and resolving any bottlenecks.

Adding Hard Drives

Server+ Exam Objective 4.3 states that the test taker should be able to install hard drives. Activities related to this objective include the following:

➤ Verify that drives are the appropriate type

➤ Confirm SCSI termination and cabling

➤ For ATA/IDE drives, confirm cabling, master/slave, and potential cross-brand compatibility

➤ Verify connections on serial ATA drives

➤ Upgrade mass storage

➤ Make sure the RAID controller can support additions

➤ Add drives to the array

➤ Replace existing drives

➤ Integrate into storage solution and make it available to the operating system

➤ Perform upgrade checklist, including:

    ➤ Locate/obtain latest drivers, OS updates, and software

    ➤ Review FAQs, instruction, facts, and issues

    ➤ Test and pilot

    ➤ Schedule downtime

    ➤ Implement ESD best practices

    ➤ Confirm that the upgrade has been recognized

    ➤ Review and baseline

    ➤ Document upgrade

To achieve this objective, you need to know and understand the following:

➤ Available types of hard drive array additions and when they are appropriate:

    ➤ Expansions

    ➤ Extensions

➤ What "hot-swappable" means

➤ Difference between a RAID partition and an OS partition

➤ Importance and use of documentation such as maintenance logs and service logs

Adding a second hard drive to a personal computer system is a fairly simple procedure; not so for a server system. Several important points must be considered before making such changes to the server system, including verifying that the additional hard drives are of the appropriate type. You should also consider that SCSI drives must be fitted with proper cabling and terminations, whereas ATA/IDE drives must follow the master/slave ID conventions. Serial ATA drives must also be connected properly and RAID controllers must be capable of supporting any future additions that might be planned. Older hard disk drives might need to be replaced and additional drives might have to be incorporated into the existing arrays and storage solutions.

Scaling Up

The addition of hard drives is normally considered a "scaling up" operation. It might be necessary to install additional hard drives when changing from one type of RAID to another, when additional users are added to the network, or when the size of a primary database is increased. To minimize later troubleshooting efforts, always use the same make and model of hard drives currently in the system when installing additional units.

When integrating a new hard drive within an existing RAID implementation, a variety of issues must be examined and properly documented. RAID compatibility regarding both the type of drive and its associated connections must be ensured. In an IDE-based RAID system, the new hard drive must be configured as either a master or a slave, as applicable, and have the proper cabling. For instance, an ATA-133 drive requires an ATA 40 connector, 80-wire cable. An important concern for any new IDE hard drive is that jumpers on the new drive be set correctly. For example, if a jumper setting identifies the new drive as a second master drive, the system might not boot properly.

For RAID systems based on the SCSI format, each system component must have a unique identification number. In addition, the proper termination must exist at each end of the SCSI line, or chain. If you are primarily using external SCSI hard drives, the adapter itself will automatically implement termination. For all other instances, a termination resistor must be attached on the end of the SCSI cable. For custom SCSI terminations, refer to the component manufacturer's manual. SCSI RAID applications often utilize devices both inside and outside of the server box. Such a configuration might consist of an internal drive, the SCSI adapter, and an external drive. In this situation, the terminations would occur on one end of the internal cable and on the last external device, which satisfies the requirement for termination on both ends of the SCSI chain. SCSI terminations should always be re-evaluated every time a component is installed or removed. For example, when installing the first external SCSI component, remove the terminator from the adapter and install it on the newly installed external device. Because SCSI termination errors are common, always double-check the chain configuration after performing any modification.

One feature of newer SCSI technology is *automatic termination*. Following installation, the system detects modifications to the SCSI configuration and provides the required terminations to permit the system to operate properly. In addition, these intelligent systems are also capable of automatically assigning SCSI IDs as required, similar to the manner in which the Dynamic Host Control Protocol (DHCP) assigns Internet addresses for TCP/IP on the fly. However, when using these newer systems with servers, the best approach is to manually select the required device ID numbers to properly document each SCSI component's ID for future reference.

For strictly internal SCSI configurations, many of the latest internal SCSI cables provide a permanent terminator applied at the end of the cable. This means that for the proper configuration of SCSI devices, the types of cables and components being used should be examined carefully prior to installation.

Strict adherence to the following practices should result in successful scaling-up procedures for server systems:

1. Verify HDD compatibility—Before purchasing new hard drives, and certainly before performing any installation, verify the compatibility of the new drives with the drives already installed in the server. As closely as possible, match make, model, and size to ensure compatibility, limit troubleshooting problems, and ensure effective swap techniques when required. Ensure that the selected drives are of sufficient size to meet both current and future application plans.

2. Pre-plan the installation—Ensure that proper cabling is available to connect all required devices to the system according to the plan.

3. Identify storage devices—For SCSI systems, prepare the scheme for SCSI identification and termination ahead of time, and ensure the necessary supply of cabling and terminators. For IDE hard drive installations, ensure that the jumper(s) are correctly configured, and that the server board supports the type of IDE drive(s) being installed. For example, if a server board supports only ATA-66 drives, do not purchase ATA-100 drives without upgrading the server board as well.

4. Match devices and controllers—Be aware that when upgrading a SCSI component, both the SCSI controller and the attached devices can adapt to lower functionality when required. However, updated SCSI devices will only operate at the maximum performance level of the adapter in a system. Therefore, the SCSI host adapter might also require upgrading for maximum performance. Alternatively, updating the adapter (along with one or more devices) while continuing to run

some older SCSI devices will also result in less-than-optimal operations. Devices capable of operating at higher performance levels will attempt to do so, and slower devices will operate at their lower performance levels. The controller must slow down to work with the older devices and the operation of the entire SCSI system will be adversely affected.

 Be aware of how conducting partial upgrades on IDE and SCSI systems affects the performance of the devices involved and the drive system.

5. **Perform a BIOS upgrade**—A required BIOS upgrade is rare, but could occur when attempting to support a hard drive installation of a type or size that the current BIOS does not support. Information about the current BIOS hard drive support can be found in the server board's manual. The board manufacturer's website will also provide information about updated BIOS support for the specified hard drives. Updated BIOS software also includes a BIOS loader program, which can be downloaded together with the BIOS update. The BIOS loader program usually runs from a DOS command line and is responsible for loading the updated BIOS parameters into the programmable CMOS memory chip on the server board.

6. **Implement ESD best practices**—Proper ESD procedures must be used when handling a hard drive. These procedures include keeping the hard drive inside its antistatic bag until actual installation and wearing antistatic devices, such as grounded wrist or ankle straps, while installing a hard drive.

7. **Replace drives**—Hard drives that are not hot-swappable should be replaced after first turning off power to the server. The power cord should also be removed from ATX-type systems. Although these methods are similar to those used when adding a hard drive to a PC, a server requires that all previously installed software be reinstalled. If the hard drive containing the OS is replaced, the OS must be reinstalled along with any applicable updates, and system component drivers.

 It cannot be overemphasized that servers experiencing drive failures should be fitted with replacement drives of identical make, model, and size for compatibility and ease of swap procedures. The OS and the adapters being used must specifically support any drives being installed.

8. Add drives to an array—Adding one or more hard drives to an existing RAID array must be accomplished through the use of the existing RAID management utility software. This means that the hard drive integration process must occur while the server is up and running.

9. Verify the HDD upgrade—After the upgraded HDD has been physically installed, the server should be booted so that the Power-On Self Test (POST) can examine the configuration and indicate a valid connection. In a RAID system, the POST identifies the entire RAID architecture as a single large hard disk drive. If the new hard drive did not replace the OS drive, the system might see its presence as a "hot spare" drive. After the operating system is activated following the POST, the file manager can be used to see if the drive exists, how much space is allocated to it, and what the drive's file system structure looks like.

 Know that when the server boots up the POST, the server sees a RAID array of drives as one hard drive.

10. Document a new baseline—Following a hard drive upgrade, immediately perform and document a new baseline. Remember to conduct this baseline with no load and no users connected to the server. The performance of the new hard drive can be tested in Windows 2000 by using the Performance Monitor tool, for example. After the new baseline has been measured, it should be compared to the pre-upgrade documentation to look for improvements. In the event that improvements cannot be observed, it might be necessary to verify the new drive's compatibility once more. It might also be necessary to examine the system for bottlenecks being caused by the new hardware.

Mounting Linux Drives

When mounting drives in a UNIX/Linux OS environment, each partition is created to form a storage container that supports a single set of files and directories, or a file system. The root directory is the partition file system's top-level directory, which branches out like a tree through subdirectories that end in files. These individual file systems of partitions and disks can be merged into a single file system structure, where separate drive designations (A:\, C:\, D:\, and so on) do not exist.

The Linux OS tree structure can be distributed across multiple partitions or disks with directories and partitions linked to each other through a process called *mounting*. The process of mounting links the directory structures of the different partitions, connecting the disks with each other. Each partition or disk added to the structure has a separate directory within the main structure, called a *mount point*, which marks the beginning of its storage area. Various partitions and disks, including floppy and CD-ROM drives, mount to the system in different locations.

The system's root directory is where the first hard drive partition, called hda, mounts. Under the system root directory, other hard drive partitions are mounted to other directories, such as /diskapp, /opt, or /usr. Likewise, the floppy drive mounts to the subdirectory /mnt/floppy and the CD-ROM drive mounts to the subdirectory /mnt/cdrom. Remember that a mount point is the directory location under which any established file system can be accessed.

DOS utilizes separate floppy drive and hard drive file systems, which automatically assign the A: identity to the floppy drive, and C: to identify the first hard drive partition. Using the Linux file system, both of these systems can be merged into a single, large file system, with the floppy drive included under the directory of some other disk drive.

Copying a file to the floppy drive requires that the floppy's mount point location be specified in the command path. Suppose access is required to a file called myfile located in a subdirectory called /documents/newfiles on a CD-ROM. The / is the system root directory, whereas /mnt/cdrom is the CD-ROM's mount point. If the CD-ROM disk in the drive has its own root directory and directory structure, the complete path to the desired location could be /mnt/cdrom/documents/newfiles/myfile.

Although the task of mounting drive selections is usually accomplished when the OS is installed, these chores can also be performed using the mount command from the Linux command line, when logged in as the root user. The format for using this command calls for the name of the mount device followed by the name of the mount point, such as: mount /dev/cdrom /mnt/cdrom. If the Red Hat version of Linux is being used, the linuxconf utility can accomplish this function.

Increasing Memory

Server+ Exam Objective 4.4 states that the test taker should be able to increase memory. Supporting knowledge for this objective includes the following tasks:

➤ Verify hardware and OS support for capacity increase

➤ Verify that memory is on the hardware/vendor compatibility list

➤ Verify memory compatibility:

  ➤ Speed

  ➤ Brand

  ➤ Capacity

  ➤ EDO

  ➤ DDR

  ➤ RAMBUS

  ➤ ECC/non-ECC

  ➤ SDRAM/RDRAM

➤ Perform an upgrade checklist including:

  ➤ Locate/obtain latest drivers, OS updates, and software

  ➤ Review FAQs, instruction, facts, and issues

  ➤ Test and pilot

  ➤ Schedule downtime

  ➤ Implement ESD best practices

  ➤ Confirm that the upgrade has been recognized

  ➤ Review and baseline

  ➤ Document upgrade

➤ Verify that server and OS recognize the added memory

➤ Perform server optimization to make use of additional RAM (BIOS and OS level)

To achieve this objective, you need to know and understand the following:

➤ Number of pins on each type of memory

➤ How servers deal with memory pairings

➤ Importance and use of documentation such as maintenance logs and service logs

Increasing memory in a server system is similar to the process used to upgrade PC memory. For an administrator, the major difference is concern for the availability of the associated server to workers and clients. This is why the necessity for server downtime planning and scheduling is so important.

Steps to Memory Upgrading

Memory upgrades can proceed successfully when the appropriate steps are taken in the proper order.

1. Verify compatibility—Before actually installing the memory, consult the board's user manual to ensure that the server board supports the memory size, type, and configuration selected. Also check that the server board is not already loaded with the maximum amount of memory permitted. Verify that the additional memory is compatible with the memory currently installed. For example, do not install an additional stick of PC100-type memory when the currently installed memory is PC133. In fact, the normal approach is to use the same brand, type, and speed of memory in all related servers throughout the system. Because information about the memory type and speed is not normally indicated on the stick, a comparison of signal-to-clock Column Address Strobe (CAS) rates may be required. For example, when the current stick of memory displays a CAS3 marking, additions or replacements will require the same CAS3 marking to be compatible.

   The RAM used in modern server systems is traditionally *Error-Correcting Code (ECC)* RAM. ECC RAM can detect and often correct parity errors in the information processed, providing additional levels of data integrity. This extra bit of security work often results in lower overall performance levels than that achieved using non-ECC type RAM. However, because stability rather than performance is the most important concern for servers, the most common memory type used in modern server systems is registered ECC CAS2.

 When adding additional memory into a server, verify its compatibility with the existing memory and get the same make if possible.

2. Perform a BIOS upgrade—Memory issues rarely require a system's BIOS to be upgraded. One possible exception would be when an available BIOS upgrade permits a greater amount of system RAM to be installed. In addition, an updated BIOS might, on rare occasions,

correct a situation where the system refuses to recognize that compatible RAM is installed. These BIOS issues occur more often with desktop computers than in server environments.

3. Implement ESD best practices—Damage to sensitive RAM devices can be prevented by keeping them enclosed in their antistatic bags when not actually installed on a motherboard. Whenever handling them, be certain to wear the appropriate antistatic safety gear. It takes nothing more than a very small electromagnetic shock to seriously damage RAM memory.

4. Verify the upgrade—Carefully observe the memory test during the POST to verify that the server recognizes the latest memory upgrade. After the NOS has booted, it should also indicate a recognition of the latest memory installation.

5. Document the new baseline—After adding new memory to a server, testing and documenting a new baseline is mandatory. Follow the procedures mentioned in Chapter 14 to test and record the baseline performance of the system with the new memory installed. If necessary, run the system's memory-testing utility to document the results of the new memory installation and use the information provided to update the new baseline. Freeware programs, such as Sandro or Winbench, can be used to perform these types of tests. After the new baseline has been established, the results should be compared with the pre-upgrade documentation. Because various memory-testing software utilities produce slightly differing results, it's important to determine early on which software to use for current and future memory baseline tests.

Identifying Electrostatic Discharge

Upgrading a server system can also include taking additional precautions against the effects of *Electrostatic Discharge (ESD)*, which can irreparably damage IC components. The greatest care should be taken when installing or exchanging ICs in an effort to eliminate this danger. ESD is recognized as the most severe form of electromagnetic interference (EMI). Static charges ranging up to 25,000 volts can build up on the human body. These buildups can discharge very rapidly into an electrically grounded body or device, causing it to malfunction or permanently damaging it. The various devices used to construct computer equipment are particularly susceptible to damage from static discharge. In fact, ESD is the most damaging form of electrical interference associated with digital equipment.

The most common causes of ESD include

➤ People moving around electrical equipment

➤ Low humidity (hot and dry conditions)

➤ Improper equipment grounding

➤ Unshielded electrical or communications cables

➤ Poor electrical connections

➤ Moving machines

Everyone is familiar with demonstrations of static electricity, such as rubbing different materials together. The same phenomena occur when people move about, producing large amounts of electrostatic charge on their bodies as the clothes they are wearing rub together. The mere act of walking across carpeting can create charges in excess of 1,000 volts! Motors in electrical devices, such as vacuum cleaners and refrigerators, can also generate high levels of ESD.

Discharging to grounded conductive parts can occur whenever a static charge has attained a value near 10,000 volts. Even though ESD will not injure a human being, it will destroy certain electronic circuits. One high-voltage pulse can instantly burn out the inputs of many IC devices. Even when ESD damage does not immediately appear, the lives of exposed components will inevitably be reduced, leading to premature device failure. This is particularly true for electronic logic devices constructed from metal oxide semiconductor (MOS) materials. Server technicians must always be alert during periods of low humidity, when ESD is most likely to occur. Static charges can accumulate easily when the relative humidity goes below 50 percent. When the relative humidity remains above 50 percent, ESD rarely becomes a problem.

Why is it that the 25,000 volts present in VGA monitors can be lethal, but the 10,000 to 25,000 volts from ESD are not harmful to humans? Surprisingly to some, it is not the voltage that is the harmful parameter, but the associated amperage (current). Whereas the voltage associated with monitors and power supplies is capable of delivering many amps of current, amperage associated with ESD is rated at less than one thousandth of that value. Therefore, the 120Vac (volts alternating current) at one amp associated with a power supply unit can be lethal, whereas 25,000Vdc (volts direct current) at one microampere of current produced by ESD is not harmful.

Handling MOS and CMOS Memory Devices

When replacing *Metal Oxide Semiconductor (MOS)* devices, the existence of voltage spikes and static-electricity discharges can cause numerous problems. Complementary Metal Oxide Semiconductor (CMOS) devices are even more sensitive, with the static electricity present on a human body being sufficient to effectively destroy their inputs. MOS memory devices require a base current in order to function, which results in a net transfer loss from emitter to collector. Although the base current is small, it can quickly add up when gigabytes of RAM are involved. CMOS devices do not require this continuous base current to hold their memory states, and are therefore more efficient in spite of their increased sensitivity to static damage.

Reliable procedures have been developed to minimize the possibility of damaging MOS or CMOS devices through static shock during their handling and installation. To preclude such damage they are shipped in special conductive-plastic tubes, or trays, which can be retained for storage purposes. If possible, save the special antistatic bags used to ship PC boards containing static-sensitive devices. These bags are useful for storing and/or transporting integrated circuits (ICs) and other ESD-sensitive components. When such protective materials are not available, IC leads can be inserted into antistatic (conductive) foam, or even common aluminum foil. Materials similar to Styrofoam are not acceptable for this purpose, and can actually damage the components. When unsure of the static-handling properties of a given material, it should not be used to store MOS or CMOS components.

Professional server technicians employ a number of precautions when working on systems containing MOS or CMOS devices. One of these precautions is a grounding strap, placed around the wrists or ankle to ground the technician to the unit being serviced. The grounding strap prevents potential damage to the components being worked on by safely transferring any electrical static present in the technician's body to ground.

Because power cords to ATX-style server chassis are not plugged in while work is being conducted on their boards, antistatic grounding straps should be wired to a known good ground during use, rather than to any of the exposed metal interior of the case. This will discharge any static buildup on the repair technician to ground, rather than to the memory components on the server board.

On the other hand, keep in mind that an antistatic strap should never be worn while working on monitors, power-supply units, or other high-voltage components. Wrist straps do not offer any resistance in cases where large currents might be encountered, and the wearer could be seriously injured. Although some technicians have been known to wrap a copper wire around their wrist or ankle and connect the other end to the groundside of an electrical outlet, such a practice is unsafe and should never be employed.

An acceptable alternative is an antistatic mat composed of rubber or other antistatic materials, which permits the technician to work while standing. When working on server equipment around carpets or other major sources of ESD buildup, higher-end antistatic mats safely grounded to AC power outlets provide protection against damage to sensitive components. They also present the server technician with the safest possible working conditions.

Implementing ESD Best Practices

In addition to the procedures already described, the following precautions should also be kept in mind to avoid damaging static-sensitive devices and to minimize the chances of destructive static discharges:

➤ Touch an exposed part of the chassis, or the power-supply housing, before touching any components inside the system. Grounding oneself this way ensures that bodily static charges are transferred to ground before working with computers or other peripheral systems that contain a number of static sensitive devices. Keep in mind, however, that this technique is effective only when the power cord is directly attached between the system and a grounded outlet. Although a standard power cord's ground plug is the best tool for overcoming ESD problems, ATX-type equipment requires that the power cord be removed prior to working on the unit.

➤ Remember to remove ICs from their protective tubes or foam packages only when you are actually ready to install them. When boards or components containing static-sensitive devices are removed from a server, they should be placed on a conductive surface, such as a sheet of aluminum foil, to protect them from ESD.

➤ When removing a defective IC that is soldered onto a server board or replacing it with a new IC, use a soldering iron with a grounded tip. The replacement of computer ICs and peripherals that are socketed rather than soldered is greatly simplified.

➤ If it becomes necessary to replace a hard-soldered IC from a server board, it might be advantageous to install an appropriate IC socket before the chip. Keep in mind that a gradual deterioration of electrical contact between chips and sockets, referred to as *chip creep*, is an ongoing phenomenon for server boards. Chip creep occurs due to normal system operating vibrations and cycling temperatures. When handling a printed circuit board, remember to reseat any socket-mounted devices. Before removing ICs from their protective container, discharge any possible electrical static by touching the container to the power supply of the target server into which they are to be inserted.

➤ Be aware that solder-suckers used to remove solder from circuit boards and chips can cause high-static discharge. These discharges can damage electronic devices on the server board. To prevent this possibility, always use an antistatic version of the tool with MOS or CMOS devices.

➤ Remember that an antistatic spray or solution can be used to prevent static buildup on floors, carpets, desks, and computer equipment.

➤ Install static-free carpeting or antistatic floor mats in various work areas. Conductive tabletops and/or antistatic tablemats can also be used to keep static away from the targeted work area.

➤ Humidity levels in the work area can be controlled by use of a room humidifier. Keeping relative humidity levels in the work area above 50 percent helps to preclude ESD.

Signal and Earth Grounds

The term *ground* has often been a source of confusion for beginning technicians because it can be used to refer to a number of things. The original definition referred to the actual ground, and in electrical jargon was called *earth ground*. Laws governing the movement of electrical current along a conductor require the existence of a path for the current to return to its source. In both early telegraph systems and in modern power-transmission systems, the earth provides this return path, which is hypothetically considered to be an electrical reference point of absolute zero.

Alternatively, an actual conductor is used as a return path in most electronic circuits. This type of ground is referred to as a *signal ground*. For sophisticated electronic devices, a third type of ground is called *chassis* (or protective) *ground*. In general electronic language, ground refers to any point from which electrical measurements are referenced. Regardless of which type of ground is being referred to, ground continues to be the reference point from which electrical signals are measured. When troubleshooting server components, measurements referenced to ground are made from the chassis of the system unit.

Reference measurement tests are conducted on printed circuit boards using the signal ground point, which can usually be easily located on a circuit board full of ICs. Most DIP-style chips use the highest-numbered pin for the positive supply voltage, and the last pin on the chip's pin-1 side as the ground pin. However, because not all ICs use this pin for ground, the technician should carefully examine the ICs and connectors on the server board to determine which trace is being used for the ground foil. This trace should be used as the ground reference for all subsequent measurements.

In computer systems, effective grounding is an important consideration limiting the effects of *Electromagnetic Interference (EMI)*. If not properly dealt with, EMI distorts video images, interferes with radio and television reception, and corrupts floppy disk data. EMI can also result in signal loss through the use of improperly routed power and signal cables. For example, when signal cables and power cords are routed in close proximity, data signals may become distorted or unusable due to induced radiation from the power cord. EMI signals can be shunted away from logic circuitry and toward ground potential using effective grounding routes, thus preventing the disruption of normal network operations. Although EMI does not cause physical damage to components similar to ESD, it can compromise data integrity if not properly dealt with.

The extremely high electrical potential of a lightning strike is more than any computer can withstand, and a lightning strike could take a path through the computer equipment on its way to earth ground. Therefore, during electrical storms, many people turn off desktop PCs and disconnect them from the wall outlet to protect them from electrical damage. These computer systems are connected to the earth ground through the power cord, including all of its peripherals. Server systems cannot simply be turned off and unplugged, even during a dangerous lightning storm. They must be protected using reasonably thought-out scenarios. Think about what is being protected—*the data*! A direct hit will knock equipment out, without a doubt—at least in the short term. Therefore try implementing safeguards such as the following:

➤ Keep hard copies of all critical documentation—During the most critical time (while equipment is down and inoperative), gather hard-copy customer invoices for phone numbers and addresses. Having to make customers wait somewhat longer for information is better than having to tell them that the system is down.

➤ Make backup data tapes—A business that keeps all of its critical data on computer is totally dependent on the system. Make sure a viable backup program has been initiated as detailed previously. Keep at least weekly backups in a safe location, perhaps a bank vault for protection in the event of fire, flood, theft, or lightning strike. When the system is restarted, the data will be ready for reinstallation.

➤ Provide surge protection—It's not madness to consider investing a reasonable sum for surge protection for each computer together with an insurance policy for situations where lightning damage occurs despite all the steps you take to prevent it.

➤ Reconfigure the network—Complete protection against a direct lightning strike is a dream. However, a network wired together in a series arrangement with the server sitting at its far end invites unnecessary destruction of the entire string during a hit. An arrangement with the server being flanked by an even number of workstations on each side provides a shorter path for lightning to travel before hitting ground. A worst-case scenario would wipe out only half the network rather than all of it.

Upgrading BIOS and Firmware

Server+ Exam Objective 4.5 statesthat the test taker should be able to upgrade BIOS/firmware. Activities associated with this objective involve performing an upgrade checklist including:

➤ Locate/obtain latest drivers, OS update, software, and so on

➤ Review FAQs, instruction, facts, and issues

➤ Test and pilot

➤ Schedule downtime

➤ Implement ESD best practices

➤ Confirm that the upgrade has been recognized

➤ Review and baseline

➤ Document upgrade

To achieve this objective, you need to know and understand the following:

➤ When BIOS/firmware upgrades should be performed

➤ How to obtain the latest firmware

➤ Most hardware companies include self-installing installation applications for their components

➤ Implications of a failed firmware upgrade:

    ➤ Multi-BIOS systems

    ➤ Firmware recovery options available

    ➤ Backup flashing (when applicable)

    ➤ Failed flash implies inoperable device

➤ Issues surrounding multi-BIOS systems (how to properly upgrade, and so on)

➤ Need to follow manufacturer's flash instructions

➤ Importance and use of maintenance logs and service logs (documentation)

Although firmware functions in much the same way in servers as it does in personal computer systems, there is much more of it to keep track of. Most of the components that make up a server system are equipped with firmware of one type or another. This situation practically guarantees that the firmware will need to be upgraded from time to time for server applications. As with most upgrades, various considerations must be taken in the basic process of performing server firmware upgrades.

It cannot be stressed too firmly that in the server environment, the best approach taken is not to modify the server system just because a new update is available. A server that is performing an adequate job does not necessarily require an upgrade, and a careful determination must be made prior to undertaking one. Of course, when issues affecting network security are raised, or if the system is continually experiencing some recurring problem, an update might indeed become a necessary solution. This approach is viable not only for firmware updates, but also for system hardware updates. Remember, if the server is properly completing the tasks for which it was designed, *don't* modify it! Because server stability is valued more highly than increased performance, a stable system that is performing sufficiently does not justify the risk of trying to squeeze it for more. When performance is an issue, it might be more effective to wait for future technology.

Firmware update procedures usually require the use of specific utility software programs, and their installations must often be performed in a specific order. If this order is not followed, the existing firmware can be irreversibly damaged during the update process. Therefore, to ensure success, it is imperative to refer to the specific update procedure supplied by the manufacturer. Most system firmware updates and their accompanying update utility programs can be located and downloaded from the manufacturer's website.

Know when to install a firmware update.

Most server board manufacturers have equivalent utility programs for customized setups. Details about these programs can be found on their websites.

Exam Prep Questions

1. When should a firmware update be installed on a server?
   - ❏ A. Whenever problems might occur if updating is not done
   - ❏ B. During the next regularly scheduled maintenance
   - ❏ C. Immediately when available
   - ❏ D. Not less than 12 months following its release

2. When adding memory to a server, what should be done before purchasing?
   - ❏ A. Make certain that the RAM is ECC verified.
   - ❏ B. Make certain that the RAM matches the server board memory slot.
   - ❏ C. Verify the new RAM's compatibility with the existing RAM.
   - ❏ D. Use only RAM from the same manufacturer.

3. When installing additional memory to the server, which of the following precautions would not be a major consideration?
   - ❏ A. Performing a BIOS upgrade
   - ❏ B. Documenting a new baseline
   - ❏ C. Verifying memory compatibility
   - ❏ D. Implementing ESD best practices

4. Why should partial upgrades on either SCSI or IDE server systems be avoided?
   - ❏ A. Newer SCSI adapters will permit older SCSI devices to operate at higher speeds automatically.
   - ❏ B. System devices, including the specified hard drives could be adversely affected.
   - ❏ C. The operation of slower adapter cards is bypassed by enhanced system devices.
   - ❏ D. Enhanced system devices will operate at their highest capabilities at the expense of slower devices.

5. Which of the following scenarios would provide an appropriate reason for performing a server BIOS update?
   - ❏ A. When a new BIOS update is available from the manufacturer
   - ❏ B. When adding compatible processors to the server board
   - ❏ C. When adding peripheral devices to the server
   - ❏ D. After upgrading to newer and faster processors

6. A server previously running a single hard drive has been recently upgraded with an additional IDE drive. Why does this server now exhibit boot problems?

- ❏ A. The existing hard drive is an ATA-100 drives, but the new drive is an ATA-66.
- ❏ B. Compatibility does not exist between the OS and the new hard drive.
- ❏ C. An improper jumper setting exists on the new hard drive.
- ❏ D. The operating system is confused by having to deal with different brands of hard drives.

7. When downing a server for a hardware upgrade, in what order should these preparatory actions be done?

- ❏ A. Alert all users, deactivate applications, perform a complete backup, take down the server, and power down peripherals.
- ❏ B. Perform a complete backup, alert all users, deactivate applications, power down and disconnect peripherals, and take down the server.
- ❏ C. Alert all users, perform a complete backup, deactivate applications, and take down the server and peripherals simultaneously.
- ❏ D. Perform a complete backup, alert all users, deactivate applications, take down the server, and power down peripherals.

8. Regardless of how many drives there are in a RAID array, the server sees them all as one drive during which process?

- ❏ A. When mounting drives to the Linux root directory
- ❏ B. When the POST is executing
- ❏ C. When dealing with multiple operating systems
- ❏ D. When the operating system is booting

Exam Prep Answers

1. Answer B is the correct answer. When current network firmware is running a problem-free environment, any updates should be postponed until the next scheduled offline maintenance session. Answer A is incorrect because the risk of prematurely updating a properly functioning server system is considered to be greater than the anticipation of some future problem. Answer C is incorrect because a newly available firmware update is not as important as maintaining the continued operation of a properly functioning server. Answer D is incorrect because performing an update with year-old firmware would merely replace one obsolete firmware version with another.

2. Answer C is the correct answer. Compatibility between the current RAM and the RAM being added is the main requirement for working memory purchases. Answer A is not necessarily incorrect because in some cases a server system may be designed for use with non-ECC memory. If so, the use of ECC verified memory will not work. Answer B is an incorrect solution because incompatible memory may also fit the specified slot. Answer D is not necessarily correct because single manufacturers produce many different types of RAM, not all of which are compatible with a specified board.

3. Answer A is the correct answer. Server memory upgrading problems are rarely solved through the use of BIOS upgrades. However, answers B, C, and D are all major considerations when adding server board memory.

4. Answer B is the correct answer. Partial upgrades, such as the use of high-performance SCSI or IDE adapters, could adversely affect other system devices if the controller is forced to retard the entire system's operation. Answer A is incorrect because updating an adapter will not cause older devices to somehow operate at higher performance levels. They can only operate at speeds permitted by their controllers. Answer C is incorrect because enhanced system devices cannot some-how bypass their adapter attachments during operations. Answer D is incorrect because exactly the opposite is true. Older devices will continue to operate at their slower rates, regardless of how fast a controller may be. This will serve to slow down enhanced system devices.

5. Answer D is the correct answer. It will probably not be possible to ignore the need for a BIOS update when performing a major processor upgrade. Answer A is incorrect because a properly functioning server BIOS does not require an update regardless of availability. Answer B is incorrect because the existing BIOS will sufficiently serve additional processors that are directly compatible. Answer C is incorrect because the existing BIOS will automatically detect and configure any added peripheral devices.

6. Answer C is the correct answer. New hard drives are typically jumpered as masters. If the system sees two drives configured as masters, it will freeze. Configuring the new drive as a slave will prevent this problem. Answer A is incorrect because any server board supporting ATA-100 drives will have no trouble supporting ATA-66 drives. Answer B is incorrect because the OS already uses an IDE ATA drive successfully. Answer D is incorrect because the OS is capable of recognizing different hard drive makes and models.

7. Answer A is the correct answer. When a server hardware upgrade is due, users must first be notified about what is taking place and given enough time to complete their disengagements from the server. After

users have disconnected from the network, the server applications can then be deactivated to create a static backup state. Following a complete backup procedure, the server can be taken down. Finally, peripheral equipment can be powered down and disconnected. Answers B, C, and D do not list the proper order.

8. Answer B is the correct answer. During the POST the system sees the entire RAID architecture as a single large hard disk drive. Answer A is incorrect because the organization of the Linux operating system occurs following the POST. Answer C is incorrect because the POST is not concerned with how many operating systems may be set up on the server. Answer D is incorrect because the POST is completed before the OS boot process begins.

Upgrading Adapters and Peripherals

Terms you'll need to understand:

✓ BIOS upgrade
✓ Validated driver
✓ Beta driver
✓ Adapter verification
✓ Peripheral benchmark
✓ Volt-Amp (VA)

Techniques you'll need to master:

✓ Upgrading server adapters
✓ Ensuring adapter or peripheral compatibility
✓ Determining the need for server system, UPS, or adapter BIOS upgrades
✓ Obtaining the latest validated adapter, UPS, or peripheral drivers
✓ Implementing electrostatic discharge (ESD) best practices
✓ Verifying various adapter, UPS, and peripheral upgrades
✓ Checking server system resources
✓ Documenting baselines for every upgrade
✓ Performing necessary firmware upgrades
✓ Calculating required system UPS VA ratings

Introduction

Server+ Exam Objective 4.6 states that the test taker should be able to upgrade adapters such as NICs, SCSI cards, RAID controllers, and so on. Supporting knowledge for this objective includes performing backups and completing the adapter upgrade checklist, which consists of the following:

➤ Locating and obtaining latest drivers, OS updates, software, and so on

➤ Reviewing FAQs, instructions, facts, and issues

➤ Testing and piloting an upgraded system

➤ Scheduling downtime

➤ Implementing ESD best practices

➤ Confirming that the adapter upgrade has been recognized

➤ Reviewing and baselining

➤ Documenting the adapter upgrade

Additional supporting knowledge includes the following items:

➤ Available adapter bus types:

  ➤ PCI-X

  ➤ PCI–Express

  ➤ Hot-swap PCI

  ➤ PCI (bus architecture, bus speed)

  ➤ EISA

➤ Implementation of hot-swappable PCI in servers

➤ Implications on the array of changing RAID controller types

➤ Characteristics of SCSI:

  ➤ Levels

  ➤ Cabling

  ➤ Termination

  ➤ Signaling

➤ Importance and use of documentation including maintenance logs and service logs

Upgrading Server Adapter Cards

Most server adapter upgrades involve the installation of additional NICs, modems, RAID controllers, SCSI controllers, and other proprietary adapter cards. However, the same cautious approach previously stressed regarding server upgrading applies here. Server adapter upgrades should be undertaken only when a previously nonexistent function must be added to the server's capabilities. Continue to set stability and uptime as the main priorities in server operations and avoid knee-jerk temptations to upgrade adapters that are currently operating within acceptable parameters simply because an upgrade is available.

When preparing to upgrade a server adapter card, consider the information in the following sections carefully.

Verify Compatibility

When installing adapter cards, you must verify their compatibility with the server board, its adapter slot, and the other cards installed in the server. When upgrading a PCI card, make sure that the voltage is compatible with the available PCI slot. If the slot supports only 3.3 volts, the card being installed must also be rated at 3.3 volts. Cards that use 3.3 volts and those that use 5.0 volts are configured differently, so a 3.3v card will only fit in a 3.3v slot and 5v cards will only fit in a 5v slot. Dual-voltage PCI cards that support both 5 volts and 3.3 volts do not require any special considerations.

Remember that when adding additional network cards, they should be as identical as possible to those currently in the system to ensure compatibility. Difficult troubleshooting scenarios can occur when network cards with different transmission rates are used in the same server.

Know how to verify compatibility with adapter slots for sever boards.

Perform BIOS Upgrade

It is not necessary to update the system BIOS when upgrading adapter cards. However, some adapter cards contain proprietary BIOS programs that might require upgrading to ensure compatibility with other components in the server system. Although such a situation is rarely encountered throughout a career, a server technician should nevertheless be prepared for it. If any doubts exist, refer to the adapter manuals and the associated manufacturer's website for specific information.

 Know that system BIOS updating is not required when upgrading server adapter cards.

Obtain Latest Drivers

In most cases, the bundled drivers from the adapter's manufacturer include those required for use with the server's NOS. This is especially true when validated components are used. The driver on the CD-ROM or floppy disk supplied with the component is normally, but not always, the most recent "validated" driver available for the specified NOS at the time the adapter shipped. However, it's always a good idea to visit the manufacturer's website to check for a possible update.

Recall the warning about using beta drivers in a server environment. Although they might be available from the manufacturer's website, beta drivers have not yet been thoroughly tested by the manufacturer and therefore cannot be considered sufficiently stable for an NOS. This is why the driver is classified as "beta" rather than "validated." Again, stability is the primary concern for server applications.

Implement ESD Best Practices

Whenever an adapter is not actually being used, make sure it's enclosed in an antistatic bag to prevent accidental damage. Wear an antistatic device whenever handling the adapter to help protect its static sensitive components from damage due to small electromagnetic shocks.

Verify the Upgrade

Older adapter cards required jumper settings to be preset for these attributes; however, newer products use jumper-less BIOS programs instead. Modern plug-and-play operating systems normally preclude hardware conflicts by automatically setting up these adapter attributes. Verification strategies vary depending on the type of adapter involved.

Network Interface Cards

Several methods of NIC verification can be performed, such as checking to see if data is being transferred through the card across the network.

Error-checking commands available through the NOS can be executed to ensure that data is being sent and received without error. NIC performance across the network can be verified using its Ping resources, or through the use of a variety of utilities provided by third-party software manufacturers.

Modems

Similar to the way in which an NIC is verified, a new modem can be used to dial in to the server. The lights and/or sounds associated with the modem's activities can then be examined to verify modem activity. A successful server connection indicates that the modem is operating correctly. The modem's operating speed can be verified by connecting to a website containing various utilities to test the modem's actual upload and download bandwidth.

RAID Controllers

Diagnostic software is normally bundled with RAID controllers to perform operational checks. When these utility programs are not included with the RAID controller, the manufacturer's website can be searched, or a third-party website can be contacted to download an acceptable software tool. If necessary, the device manager within the NOS can be used to verify the proper operation of a RAID controller.

SCSI Controller

SCSI controller—Two verification methods can be used to verify that an upgraded SCSI Controller is working properly. The NOS device manager can be checked to see if the SCSI controller is recognized and is operating properly. The devices attached to the SCSI controller can also be examined to verify that they are detected and available to the NOS.

Proprietary Card

Proprietary card—Proprietary cards often require additional verifications and instructions to use them properly. The vendor's documentation and associated website should be examined, as necessary.

Check System Resources

Check the system resources of each upgraded adapter for proper operation and no existing conflicts. Be aware that changing one component's resource can cause a conflict with the settings of another component. As a final measure, check the resources of all active adapters, including those previously installed in the system.

Document the Baseline

Each time an adapter is upgraded, a new baseline should be run and documented. Follow the procedures outlined in Chapter 14, "Preparing the Server for Service," for documenting baselines with the new adapter installed. Baseline testing can be performed with utilities such as the Performance Monitor in Windows 2000, or third-party software such as Winbench, a freeware application. Following a new baseline measurement, look for improvements over the pre-upgrade baseline. If there are no improvements, you might need to reverify adapter compatibility or check for system bottlenecks caused by the new hardware.

Peripheral Devices

Server Exam Objective 4.7 states that the test taker should be able to upgrade internal and external peripheral devices such as disk drives, backup devices, optical devices, and KVM devices and verify appropriate system resources such as expansion slots and cards, IRQ, DMA, and SCSI IDs.

Activities involved with this objective include performing a peripheral device upgrade checklist, which consists of the following:

➤ Locating and obtaining the latest drivers, OS updates, software, and so on

➤ Reviewing FAQs, instructions, facts, and issues

➤ Testing and piloting an upgraded system

➤ Scheduling downtime

➤ Implementing ESD best practices

➤ Confirming that the peripheral device upgrade has been recognized

➤ Reviewing and baselining

➤ Documenting the peripheral upgrade

To achieve this objective, you need to know and understand the following:

➤ Potential effects on performance from adding devices

➤ Importance and use of maintenance logs and service logs (documentation)

➤ Validation via hardware compatibility lists, tips, documentation, and FAQs

Upgrading Server Peripherals

Peripherals suitable for upgrading include both internal and external devices that are already installed or being installed on the server system. Devices that come under this category include disk drives, backup devices, optical devices, printers, modems, and input devices such as keyboards and mice. In many cases, peripheral devices can be installed without rebooting the server. However, whenever the installation of a peripheral requires a system to be rebooted, it will be necessary to schedule server downtime to perform the upgrade.

When involved with server peripheral upgrade operations, carefully consider the information in the following section.

Verify Compatibility

Peripheral devices vary greatly in their configuration and use. Refer to the device's manual for information to ensure that the device will work properly and to verify the suitability of a particular device for use in a specified server system. Because external peripheral devices must connect to the server through its interface ports, you must also ensure that the proper port is available for the device to be installed. Common external interface ports include serial, parallel, USB, FireWire, and those provided by SCSI adapter cards.

Perform Firmware Upgrade

Occasionally, an update will be released for the peripheral device's firmware that provides features required by the server being upgraded. Prior to installing the peripheral, search the manufacturer's website for any such updates. The firmware's update tool will also have to be obtained from the manufacturer to apply the update.

Don't forget to inform network users ahead of time about the peripheral being upgraded and when it is scheduled to be temporarily out of service.

Obtain the Latest Peripheral Drivers

The drivers on the CD-ROM or floppy disk that comes with the peripheral device will normally include those required for use with the specific server NOS. Similar to drivers for NICs, these will include the most recent "validated" driver available for the specified OS at the time the peripheral shipped. If the peripheral device is not new, a quick check of the manufacturer's website may confirm the availability of a newer validated driver for download. Again, forget about using any beta drivers that might be available from the manufacturer's website. Think only about stability!

Implement ESD Best Practices

Because peripherals are often directly grounded through their power cords, they tend to be less sensitive to electrostatic damage. However, because peripherals are rather expensive, it's wise for the technician to be properly grounded before working with or on them.

Verify the Peripheral Upgrade

There are a variety of ways to test a peripheral upgrade depending on its configuration and use. For example, a printer can be tested by printing a manufacturer-supplied test page, printing a page from a client, or printing multiple print jobs to the queue. A Zip disk can be tested by first moving data onto the disk and then testing that data on another workstation.

Check System Resources

Because peripheral devices normally utilize the resources associated with the port through which they connect to the system, a properly functioning peripheral rarely requires a verification of its system resources.

Document the Peripheral Baseline

A new baseline associated with the peripheral should be run and documented immediately after its upgrade. Peripheral baselines are often achieved through the use of specific diagnostic tools supplied by the peripheral manufacturer, usually from a website. As with all baselines, the newest results should be compared with pre-upgrade baseline measurements to verify improved performance.

Benchmark measurement criteria vary between peripherals. Although an adequate printer test might include the number of pages printed per minute, a CD-RW device might be judged according to the amount of time it takes to create a particular CD. Packet analysis of the data transfer speed for a specifically sized file might be the most important benchmark for an external modem. The most important peripheral benchmark for any administrator is the one that confirms the value of the upgrade just performed. It should determine whether the factors driving the peripheral upgrade have been improved upon and borne out by the results of the latest baseline.

When the server requires upgrading that involves adding multiple devices or peripherals, each required device should be installed separately and tested thoroughly before moving on to the next component.

Uninterruptible Power Supplies

Server+ Exam Objective 4.10 indicates that the test taker should be able to upgrade the UPS. Activities associated with this objective include

➤ Performing firmware updates

➤ Making battery replacements and disposing of the battery

➤ Determining UPS physical requirements

➤ Determining the system load requirements

➤ Verifying whether the UPS supports hot-swap replacement

➤ Performing a UPS upgrade checklist, including

> ➤ Locating and obtaining the latest drivers, OS updates, software, and so on
>
> ➤ Reviewing FAQs, instructions, facts, and issues
>
> ➤ Testing and piloting an upgraded system
>
> ➤ Scheduling downtime
>
> ➤ Implementing ESD best practices
>
> ➤ Confirming that the UPS upgrade has been recognized
>
> ➤ Reviewing and baselining
>
> ➤ Documenting the UPS upgrade

To achieve this objective, you need to know and understand the following:

➤ UPS support for hot-swap battery replacement

➤ UPS support for smart cabling

➤ Which items can be upgraded on a UPS:

> ➤ UPS MIBs
>
> ➤ Management cards
>
> ➤ Management software

➤ Importance and use of maintenance logs and service logs (documentation)

Determining the Required Size of a UPS

When a given UPS device can no longer provide sufficient power to operate its assigned systems in the event of a power failure, it's time for an upgrade. This situation usually develops following the recent configuration of additional servers to the system. Whenever the load on a UPS increases, the amount of time it can keep its assigned servers up and running during a power failure is diminished. Eventually, the point is reached where not enough power is available to permit the servers to shut down properly, resulting in data that is either corrupted or lost altogether.

The required size of a UPS upgrade can be determined by first calculating the amount of Volt-Amps (VA) that the UPS is normally required to provide. Next, the time needed for an orderly shutdown of the system must be determined. The system must continue to operate for this length of time following a complete loss of power.

To calculate VA requirements, first convert all the system's power outputs into volt-amps. Each piece of server equipment has a sticker or information plate that lists the unit's load rating, given in amps, volt-amps, or watts. When the load rating is listed in amps, this value must be multiplied by the value of voltage used by the device. In the United States, most devices that plug into a wall receptacle operate at 60 cycles per second (cps) and 120 volts. The wall voltage and its associated cycles can vary in other countries. When the load rating is listed in watts, this value must be divided by 0.6 (or multiplied by 1.67). If a range of values is given for amperages, voltages, or volt-amps, always perform the necessary calculations using the highest value provided.

After all the system's individual VA power outputs have been calculated, they must be totaled to determine the combined total VA requirements of the UPS. Be sure to upgrade the system UPS to not only handle the current loads, but to support all loads being planned for future expansion. A good rule of thumb is to size the UPS at least 1.4 times larger than the minimum VA load calculation.

Know how to calculate the minimum size UPS VA rating for a server system.

Upgrading a UPS

Select a UPS with a volt-amp rating that matches the system's total calculated VA value to provide an estimated 10 minutes of backup power following a total failure. A UPS that provides half the calculated VA value will provide 5 minutes of system backup, whereas a UPS providing twice the calculated system VA value will run the system for approximately 20 minutes. After a UPS upgrade has been selected and procured, keep the information in the following sections in mind during its installation.

Obtain the Latest Drivers and Control Applications

The latest drivers and software updates issued for a given UPS can be located and downloaded by visiting the manufacturer's website. Again, do not use beta versions. Many software packages include autoupdating programs; however, these programs cannot always be relied on to select the latest updates applicable to a given system.

Implement ESD Best Practices

Even when handling a UPS, which is an enclosed system and not highly sensitive to electrostatic damage, it is still a good idea to wear a grounding strap. This is considered a wise precaution considering how expensive a UPS tends to be.

Verify Physical Compatibility

The only physical compatibility conflict that could possibly be encountered between a UPS and the server system is the lack of adequate space in which to install it. The interface between the unit's supporting software and the server system is the major consideration. The only way to verify if the UPS is working properly is to simulate a server power failure.

Document the Baseline

For proper baseline testing and documentation associated with the upgraded UPS, downtime has to be planned and scheduled to perform the associated tests. Clients and employees need to receive sufficient notification, and the downtime needs to be scheduled during periods of lower server usage. Plan for enough downtime to effectively test and retest the system until it can be ascertained that the UPS will handle a power outage properly. The baseline testing should include time tests that indicate the server's capacity to initiate a controlled shutdown when power to the building is suddenly interrupted.

Exam Prep Questions

1. A server system is operating a 30-watt hub, a 96-watt monitor, and a 450-watt power supply. The smallest UPS that could be expected to handle this system would be rated in how many VA?

   ❑ A. 1153
   ❑ B. 760
   ❑ C. 346
   ❑ D. 960

2. Which of the following upgrades might be required following an adapter card upgrade?

   ❑ A. A system BIOS upgrade
   ❑ B. A CMOS memory chip upgrade
   ❑ C. An adapter-specific BIOS upgrade
   ❑ D. A system processor upgrade

3. An existing 3.3v NIC must be newly upgraded. Because the PCI slot supports only 3.3v devices, which of the following NICs is suitable as an upgrade to the existing card?

   ❑ A. A dual-voltage 5v/3.3v NIC
   ❑ B. A 5v NIC
   ❑ C. A 3v NIC
   ❑ D. A dual-voltage 5v/3v NIC

4. A single Ethernet 10/100 switch is handling all data transfers for a server network configured with 10/100 NIC cards. Traffic is moving so slowly through the network that something must be done quickly to improve the network's performance. Which of the following solutions makes sense?

   ❑ A. Distribute a network use schedule among various network clients.
   ❑ B. Forbid more than two clients from simultaneously using the network.
   ❑ C. Install a Gigabit switch in place of the 10/100 Ethernet switch.
   ❑ D. Conduct the installation of an additional hub and three more NICs.

Exam Prep Answers

1. Answer D is the correct answer. The wattage of these components must be added together. Doing so results in a total of 576 watts. Then divide that by 0.6 and you get a total VA rating of 960. Therefore, the minimum VA rating for the specified system is 960 VA, making answers A, B, and C incorrect by process of elimination.

. . . .

2. Answer C is the correct answer. Because some adapter cards contain their own specific BIOS, a newly installed adapter card may require immediate BIOS upgrading to ensure its compatibility with other components already being used in the server system. Answer A is incorrect because adapter card upgrades rarely require a system BIOS upgrade. Answer B is incorrect for the same reason that answer A is incorrect. In addition to the current date and time information, the CMOS memory chip holds the system BIOS data. Answer D is incorrect because server adapter cards, if any, do not dictate which processor(s) is/are being used in the server.

3. Answer A is the correct answer. Because a dual 5v/3.3v NIC will work in PCI adapter slot voltages of either 5 or 3.3 volts, it is the logical choice. Answers B, C, and D do not include compatibility with a 3.3v PCI slot.

4. Answer C is the correct answer. Replacing the 10/100 Ethernet switch with the Gigabit switch will significantly improve network throughput, but not as much as also replacing the 10/100 NIC cards with Gigabit models. Answer A is incorrect because the effectiveness of the network would be severely compromised. Answer B is incorrect because it is impossible to implement and completely unacceptable. Answer D is incorrect because adding more NICs and a hub will only compound the problem.

17.0—Upgrading System Monitoring Agents and Service Tools

Terms you'll need to understand:

- ✓ Management bus
- ✓ Baseboard Management Controller (BMC)
- ✓ Watchdog timer
- ✓ Server Management Bus (SMB)
- ✓ Intelligent Management Bus (IMB)
- ✓ Intelligent Platform Management Bus (IPMB)
- ✓ Private Management Bus (PMB)
- ✓ Intelligent Chassis Management Bus (ICMB)
- ✓ Emergency Management Port (EMP)
- ✓ Inter-IC bus
- ✓ Secure mode signal
- ✓ Fault-resilient booting
- ✓ Simple Network Management Protocol (SNMP)
- ✓ Traps
- ✓ Common Information Model (CIM)
- ✓ Master Boot Record (MBR)
- ✓ Self-Monitoring Analysis Reporting Technology (SMART)
- ✓ System Setup Utility (SSU)
- ✓ Patch

Techniques you'll need to master:

✓ Understanding critical server parameters tracked and controlled by system monitoring agents

✓ Recognizing management controller components, ports, and buses

✓ Determining server board instrumentation

✓ Using a server's secure mode

✓ Configuring pager alerts for server administration

✓ Selecting appropriate server management components

✓ Dialing directly into the network interface with SNMP

✓ Adding SMART components to the system

✓ Upgrading various server tools

Introduction

Server+ Exam Objective 4.8 states that the test taker should be able to upgrade system monitoring agents. Activities associated with this objective include performing an upgrade checklist, which consists of the following:

➤ Locating and obtaining the latest drivers, OS updates, software, and so on

➤ Reviewing FAQs, instructions, facts, and issues

➤ Testing and piloting the upgrade

➤ Scheduling downtime

➤ Implementing electrostatic discharge (ESD) best practices

➤ Confirming that the upgrade has been recognized

➤ Reviewing and baselining

➤ Documenting the upgrade

To achieve this objective, you need to know and understand the following:

➤ Purposes and functions of the following management protocols:

　➤ Simple Network Management Protocol (SNMP)

　➤ Desktop Management Interface (DMI)

　➤ Intelligent Platform Management Interface (IPMI) 1.5 and 2.0

➤ Functions of monitoring agents

➤ Dependencies between SNMP and MIBs

➤ Importance and use of documentation such as maintenance logs and service logs

Modern server boards incorporate highly developed environmental monitoring and management systems. These systems include sensors that monitor important server board, chassis, and cabinet conditions and operations. In addition, special management buses and controller devices are incorporated on server boards that are not found in desktop computer systems. These devices pass monitoring and management information between each other (and from server to server) without impacting the server's normal processing buses or communication channels.

Although it's interesting to think about how various server systems automatically communicate with each other, the server network administrator is the one who really needs to know what's going on, especially when problems begin to occur. To that end, a Server+ technician needs to understand the critical parameters that are tracked and controlled, how those parameters are selectively monitored and recorded for future system analysis, and when the system monitoring agents themselves need to be upgraded or reconfigured.

The server system uses both hardware and software monitoring and management functions to provide the system administrator with enough data to determine if and when something in the system requires upgrading. Every proposed system change or upgrade must be justified by monitoring data that proves its necessity. Without this proof, the administrator will feel unjustified to risk making any changes.

Upgrades to system service tools may result in the purchase of additional hardware/software. However, a monitoring agent can be upgraded through the reorientation of the data it is designed to provide. This upgrading may not require the purchase of new equipment. Instead, it may require obtaining updated programming code for the reporting agent, so that more meaningful parameters can be observed.

Server Monitoring and Management

Server board environmental monitoring and management functions require coordination through the use of a special management controller device. This device manages the board's performance and environmental functions so that the system processors don't have to, which helps to increase the actual computing power of the server. The management controller device is called the *Baseboard Management Controller (BMC)* on Intel server boards, but similar components are called by other names by different manufacturers.

A management controller is a programmable intelligent device designed to perform its prescribed management functions independent of the system's main processors. It receives its power from the system's 5-volt standby power supply. On ATX server boards, this voltage is present even when the server unit is turned off, which enables the controller to continuously manage the system whether or not its host is running. A *watchdog timer* is built into the management controller to monitor the operation of the system processors. If no activity is detected for a predetermined length of time, the watchdog reboots the server to pre-empt hardware lockups that might adversely affect the server's availability.

As a rule, server boards can only perform those functions that are specifically permitted by the management controller chip.

The management controller uses a special set of management buses and ports to perform these various functions. On Intel server boards, these buses and ports include

➤ Server Management Bus (SMB)

➤ Intelligent Management Bus (IMB)

   ➤ Intelligent Platform Management Bus (IPMB)

   ➤ Intelligent Chassis Management Bus (ICMB)

➤ Private Management Bus (PMB)

➤ Emergency Management Port (EMP) interface

The following sections discuss each of these buses and ports in detail.

NOTE

Intel server boards feature all of the management buses mentioned in the preceding list; however, other server board designers might incorporate different management buses and features in their products. Although the names of these buses and features may differ, their capabilities and duties will be similar.

Server Management Bus

The s*erver management bus (SMB)* is a special system running through the server board that provides independent communication pathways between the management controller and the board's managed components. The SMB enables the controller to monitor the system processors' temperatures, and to check the operation of the server board's other field-replaceable units (FRUs).

Be aware that server boards include instrumentation to track and monitor temperatures associated with many areas of the server board, the chassis, and the server cabinet.

Intelligent Management Buses

The *Intelligent Management Bus (IMB)* is routed through the server board; however, it also provides an extension connector for routing throughout the chassis as well as to additional servers. The resulting inter-server communications enable the management of a cohesive system through the use of two different sections: the local Intelligent Platform Management Bus and the inter-chassis Intelligent Chassis Management Bus.

Intelligent Platform Management Bus

The *Intelligent Platform Management Bus (IPMB)* is the local serial bus running throughout the server chassis. It connects the server's major printed circuit boards together, and transfers system environmental monitoring, management control, and event information between the server board's monitoring and management devices. The IPMB also connects the management controller to non-volatile memory devices used to store important data such as system events, sensor data readings, and information about installed FRUs that must be available for recall and examination.

Intelligent Chassis Management Bus

On Intel server systems, the operation of the IPMB is extended to other servers and platforms through the use of the *Intelligent Chassis Management Bus (ICMB)*. The ICMB provides inter-chassis communications between different server platforms and peripherals, permitting them to exchange monitoring and platform management information. Similar to the management controller, the ICMB can remain active even when the server is turned off. This permits the management controllers from different platforms to continue to monitor and assess management data regardless of the system power conditions.

The ICMB is based on the Philips I2C bus specification, also known as the *Inter-IC bus*, which uses two lines to connect all of the system devices together. The flow of information is controlled through the use of simple request and grant commands, permitting any master device to exchange data with any slave device.

An example of an ICMB implementation is to connect the management controllers of two server systems with the chassis controllers of two peripheral systems. In this example, one server's ICMB would be primarily used to monitor the condition of chassis sensors, including the fans, the front panel, and the power supplies, through each chassis' management controller.

Private Management Buses

To handle the large quantity of server management data that is sampled and manipulated by the management controller, a proprietary memory storage structure is provided. Data movement in and out of this memory is accomplished through the use of a *Private Management Bus (PMB)*. This bus permits the management controller to monitor and grant access to its private storage area without interfering with normal system data. For example, temperature sensors might be set up to use the PMB to store digitized temperature information about the system in a variety of *Serial Electrically Erasable PROM (SEEPROM)* devices.

Emergency Management Ports

An *Emergency Management Port (EMP)* is a term used when one of the system's serial COM ports is configured to provide remote management that is independent of the server's operating system type. Remote system operations can include power up, power down, and reset. The EMP can also be used to remotely access event logs, sensor readings, and other customized server diagnostic tools.

Prevention of Monitoring Interruptions

Server boards provide front panel indicators and controls that are similar to those found in older AT and ATX desktop units. These front panel controls include the familiar Reset and Power buttons. However, when a server system is engaged in critical operations, the front panel controls can be disabled to prevent it from being manually shut down or reset.

Although the details vary for every combination of processor and keyboard controller, activating the server's secure mode requires that a specified key combination be pressed. This causes the keyboard controller to send a *secure mode signal* over the server management bus. The management controller then disables these front panel controls.

Fault-Resilient Booting Notifications

Many server boards include a *fault-resilient booting* feature to automatically reboot a single processor in a multi-processor system in the event that one of the processors locks up. The server board is able to reboot that processor while the other microprocessors carry the processing load. Fault-resilient booting is provided through a set of built-in BIOS and hardware support.

Although this feature permits a malfunctioning server to continue providing service, it does not solve the immediate problem. The server continues to be at risk and should be completely rebooted. Therefore, the administrator should configure one of the server's monitoring agents to send a paging alert whenever this type of event occurs.

Server Management Software Components

To achieve a high level of availability, the server must be reliable, redundant, and manageable. When problems occur on managed server boards, they must be recognized and reported. Server software management components are designed to implement a complete server monitoring solution. The following components are required to provide an effective proactive management and monitoring program:

➤ Monitoring software—Various server hardware and software operations are selected for tracking during the configuration of the monitoring software. The resulting problem information can be stored in a log file.

➤ Alarm/warning systems—Immediate warnings either in the form of an alert to the management console, or a page to the administrator, can be issued if and when the server system shows signs of failure.

➤ Remote management features—Administrators can dial into the server and check on its health from a remote location. Diagnostic logs can be reviewed remotely, and a failed server system can be powered on, powered off, or even rebooted to get it back up and running without waiting for a technician to arrive.

By using these critical software management components, administrators can proactively monitor and manage servers to optimize their availability. By providing system administrators with advance warnings before failures occur, server management software helps them to recognize and deal with problems before they become catastrophic and cost the company money or business.

Network Management Protocols

Various management protocols have been designed to provide system administrators with all the information necessary to keep a server network functioning properly without suffering dreaded downtime. When monitoring agents are doing a good job, enough information is available on a daily basis to know when to tweak the system, upgrade an aging or failing component, or perform an emergency backup.

If failures begin to occur that the administrator feels should have been preceded by timely warnings, it may be necessary to rethink how the existing monitoring agents have been configured and distributed. Regardless of the management protocol(s) being used, they will not be effective in the absence of well-designed agents. The purposes and functions of management protocols such as SNMP, DMI, and IPMI should be familiar to the Server+ technician in the establishment of meaningful monitoring agents. In addition, SMART systems are making it easier to identify failing hard drives or adapters before they cause system crashes.

Purposes and Functions of SNMP

The *Simple Network Management Protocol (SNMP)* was examined in a previous chapter. It runs underneath the installed operating system, and provides system management and reporting functions across the entire network. Administrators use SNMP to check server characteristics, and network activity, without actually going through the main network operating system. In this way, the administrator's management activities can be executed without locking up the NOS.

It should be obvious why the use of remote monitoring through the use of SNMP is more cost-effective than having a server technician on duty 24/7. Although a daily review of system event logs might reveal the existence of a problem after the fact, using this approach alone provides no advance warning before the problem adversely affects the system. System monitors should be capable of providing active notifications when parameters begin slipping. If they do not, the administrator is responsible for upgrading them.

The SNMP utility requires about 8MB of drive space and resides in its own partition on the hard drive. In these systems, the *Master Boot Record (MBR)* points to this SNMP partition and loads the utility before jumping to the NOS partition. This means that after it has initialized and started running in the background, SNMP actually loads the NOS. In the event of a problem on the server, SNMP sends an alarm paging the administrator about the situation. One drawback with SNMP is that in the event of a processor lockup, the SNMP software also locks up.

Know that SNMP is not automatically installed in Windows 2000 by default.

Purposes and Functions of the DMI

The *Desktop Management Interface (DMI)* was mentioned in a previous chapter in conjunction with making queries about each desktop, notebook, or server in the system to see what software and hardware it has. DMI generates a standard framework for managing and tracking these components, and workstation information such as drivers, peripherals, and operating systems can be easily collected and categorized. Recall that DMI was the first desktop management standard.

The DMI and the Internet-standard SNMP Network Management Framework (NMF) are widely deployed solutions to manage computer systems and network devices, respectively. Although these two frameworks are similar in concept and function, they are not inherently interoperable, even though they often coexist on the same system. When applications access management information using both frameworks, the interoperability gap between SNMP and DMI-based solutions must be bridged. This is accomplished through the use of the DMI-to-SNMP Mapping Specification.

Due to the rapid advancement of alternate Distributed Management Task Force (DMTF) technologies, such as the *Common Information Model (CIM)*, the DMTF recently defined an "End of Life" process for its Desktop Management Interface (DMI). The DMTF ended active development of new DMI standards on December 31, 2003, but it continued to provide bug fixes and specification errata for an additional 12 months, and email support for implementers and users was provided through March 31, 2005.

Be aware that the newer CIM is designed to provide a common definition of management information for systems, networks, applications, and services. It also allows for proprietary vendor extensions through the use of common definitions to enable the exchange of detailed management information between systems throughout an entire network. As time goes on, Server+ technicians will need to become familiar with the working of CIM.

Purposes and Functions of the IPMI

The *Intelligent Platform Management Interface (IPMI)* was introduced in 1998 as an embedded management specification for servers, storage devices, and other network equipment. It defines a common and secure interface for monitoring system hardware voltages, temperature, and fan speeds through the use of embedded sensors. It is designed to directly control system components such as power supplies and server blades, while permitting remote system management and the recovery of failed systems.

Server systems using IPMI contain firmware embedded in the Baseboard Management Controller (BMC) chip located on the server board or blade. Its management subsystem continues to operate regardless of the CPU or NOS status. This means that the system administrator through the management console can conduct access to the server using out-of-band operations over a LAN.

Information about internal server events such as open chassis or system reboot is recorded in the event log, while sensor hardware data is also saved for review. An inventory of system components, including FRUs, is also provided for inventory and/or service requirements. Because non-volatile memory is used to store this information, IPMI is crash-resistant and tamper-proof. Its relative independence from the server system makes the installation and configuration of agents unnecessary.

Self-Monitoring Analysis Reporting Technology

Because of the overall importance of keeping server operations going in spite of problems, adapter cards and hard drives designed specifically for server operations include *Self-Monitoring Analysis Reporting Technology (SMART)*. Similar to the monitoring technology incorporated into system boards, SMART technology signals administrators when problems occur related to hard disk drives. Devices such as Redundant Array of Independent Disks (RAID) adapters are capable of monitoring themselves because they are intelligent controllers with processors already built into them. This makes the addition of SMART functions possible.

The use of SMART technology allows the operating system to continue functioning normally without having to spend resources monitoring the adapter. If something goes wrong with a single hard drive, the disk array, or the RAID adapter, the SMART technology causes the adapter to issue an alarm, notifying the system administrator of potential problems before the operating system detects them. RAID adapters utilize a small light panel to display a sequence of lights. This light sequence is compared with the applicable status listing in order to pinpoint the exact problem.

Because a valid reason must exist prior to the opening of a server's case, a server or an adapter that is signaling the administrator about a problem helps to meet this requirement. In this way, SMART technology provides a type of preventative maintenance.

Upgrading Service Tools

Server+ Exam Objective 4.9 states that the test taker should be able to upgrade service tools such as diagnostic tools, EISA configurations, diagnostic partitions, system setup utilities (SSUs), and so on. Service tools covered in this objective include

➤ RAID utilities

➤ Small Computer System Interface (SCSI) utilities

➤ System configuration utilities

➤ External storage utilities

Activities related to this objective include performing an upgrade checklist, which consists of the following:

➤ Locating/obtaining latest drivers, OS updates, software, and so on

➤ Reviewing FAQs, instruction, facts and issues

➤ Testing and piloting

➤ Scheduling downtime

➤ Implementing ESD best practices

➤ Confirming that the upgrade has been recognized

➤ Reviewing and baselining

➤ Documenting the upgrade

To achieve this objective, you need to know and understand the following:

➤ Most utilities are vendor-specific

➤ The use of documentation such as maintenance logs and service logs is important

Service tools include those used to provide disk management, diagnostics, and the *System Setup Utility (SSU)*. When it becomes necessary to upgrade these tools, you should contact the software vendor for any updates that might be available. The vendor's web page might offer downloads of these updates, point to alternate suppliers of the operating system, or provide connections to third-party software developers.

SSUs are usually bundled with the server board, and are traditionally not specific to the operating system. Most SSUs allow the administrator to view the server's critical event logs and/or get information about installed Field-Replaceable Units (FRUs) and Single Data Rate (SDR) devices. To check for upgrades to the SSU, contact the server board manufacturer.

Network Operating System Upgrades

A good rule of thumb to remember when considering whether to upgrade operating systems on commercial servers is: if it's not broken, don't change it. In most server installations, upgrades of any kind are first considered at length, tested in a controlled setting, and then implemented. Operating system changes are questioned in even greater detail. However, there are times in the life cycle of servers and organizations when upgrades that involve changes to the operating system must be considered. Before performing an upgrade or a clean installation of an upgraded server NOS, a current backup copy of the existing system must be created. In addition, a test of the backup and restore function should be performed to confirm that the backup occurred correctly and ensure that it is possible to restore the system from the backup media. This is vitally important because any flaw in the backup and restore functions will leave the administrator with a poor chance of system recovery if the upgrade operation fails.

Be aware that when upgrading servers with a fresh installation of the latest NOS version, it is vital to create a current backup and test the restore function prior to proceeding with the upgrade.

Researching NOS Updates and Patches

After a network operating system has been in use for some period of time, various operational weaknesses inevitably are observed and reported to the manufacturer. These problems can be with the NOS itself, or with the way in which it interfaces with hardware products from various other manufacturers. Either way, updating the NOS can be an important undertaking in server environments.

The specific NOS being used dictates the proper methods of obtaining and installing server updates and security patches. NOS manufacturers generally provide patch and update information on their websites, along with instructions for successfully downloading the necessary files.

Be aware that vendors often make OS updates available that are not specifically related to the hardware problem currently being examined. Therefore, for each update, carefully research the available information to evaluate whether the update should be installed. Keep in mind that the installation of unnecessary or conflicting updates can increase the system's original stability problems. For example, if an update resolves only issues with specific server board models not used in company equipment, *do not* install that update! Installing unnecessary drivers can introduce new problems on top of old ones.

Locating Server NOS Updates and Patches

When an update, also known as a *patch*, becomes available, it consists of a collection of code that corrects a specific problem or set of problems that the specified NOS is known to have. Depending on the OS manufacturer, network operating systems are updated in different ways. The process of locating updates for most types of server NOSes is expedited by going directly to the appropriate vendor's website:

➤ UNIX—UNIX operating updates and their associated information can be found through the supplying vendor's website. For example, SCO OpenServer systems information can be located at http://www.sco.com. If the OS was purchased directly from Caldera, the selected website to visit would be http://www.caldera.com.

➤ Linux—Again, searching the supplying vendor's website is the best option for locating the appropriate updates for this operating system. With Linux, the searcher must also filter down to the distribution version being used to find the specific updates or security patches that apply. For example, for the RedHat distribution, the administrator should visit RedHat's official homepage at http://www.redhat.com, click on the Documents and Support button, and then click on the Errata button to access the area where RedHat locates all the applicable updates. After selecting the specific distribution version, such as 5.1, 6.1, 7.2, and so on, the administrator can locate the specific patch for the specific hardware being used. The appropriate patch is then downloaded, and the included instructions for deployment should be followed. Other versions of Linux have similar web locations for providing patches or updates.

➤ Windows—Updates for Windows server operating systems are some-what easier to locate. From the opening screen, click on the Start button, scroll up, and then click on the Windows Update button to automatically direct the system to the http://windowsupdate.com web-site. At that site, click on the Product Updates button to search for spe-cific critical updates that apply only to the server version being used.

➤ OS/2—Once again, to search for upgrades and patches for OS/2, visit the applicable vendor's website. For IBM's OS/2, this site is located at http://ps.software.ibm.com/pbin-usa-ps/getobj.pl?/pdocs-usa/softupd. html. At this site, the administrator can view critical information and download the latest updates for the IBM OS/2 operating system.

➤ Novell NetWare—To obtain the latest patches for the OS, applicable client installation files, and upgrades for Novell NetWare, visit their support website at http://support.novell.com/produpdate/patchlist.html.

Locating and Obtaining Device Drivers

To find specific device drivers, check the product manufacturer's vendor website and search the listings given for your specific server network operat-ing system. Information about the specific make and model of the device will be required. Although applicable device drivers are usually available directly through the website, in some instances update distributions are limited to disk formats that are sent through the mail. Information about this will be available on the vendor's website.

Timing a Server Update Installation

Determining the proper time and method for installing a specified server OS update is a critical and complicated undertaking that requires thorough research and careful planning. Any thoughtful network technician or server administrator understands how unwise it is to jeopardize a sufficiently oper-ating and stable system to install an unnecessary or poorly planned update. There are only two situations that justify the updating of the NOS:

➤ Security—The network operating system might require updating if a security flaw exists that makes the server system vulnerable. Careful research is required into the type of security issue involved, and whether the current use of the NOS requires that the update be performed. If the proposed security update involves areas of the OS that are not in active use by existing network operations, the system might not require the proposed modifications.

➤ Stability—When stability problems directly associated with the operat-ing system are periodically observed, available updates designed to resolve them must be seriously considered. One possible area of instability involves associated hardware or peripheral devices. If the problem cannot be resolved by updating or replacing the specified hardware, the NOS is the next logical candidate for examination.

NOS updates or patches should only be installed when the existing NOS cannot perform some necessary function. This includes patches that are designed to mitigate a critical security risk. Because server stability and uptime are an administrator's major priority, a security update designed to fix an Internet breach issue should never be installed on a server system that is not connected to the Internet. Such a modification can conceivably cause unwanted repercussions to occur in portions of the system that were previously operating properly, causing new system instability and/or downtime.

If server performance in an area targeted for improvement by a modification is currently sufficient, the risk to stability posed by installing the proposed modification cannot be justified. Having to explain that new network instability could have been avoided by simply leaving the system alone can easily prove embarrassing to an overzealous administrator.

However, after the decision to perform an upgrade has been made, the same notifications required during system maintenance activities are necessary here as well. The system administrator will be responsible for ensuring that all clients and employees know in advance when the server will be taken down for the upgrade, and approximately how long it will be down.

Service Tool Utility Upgrades

Upgrading a server's NOS software does not completely fulfill a system administrator's upgrade responsibilities. There are various utility programs that also deserve serious attention when the server network is scheduled for an overhaul. Among the candidates for consideration are utility programs designed for managing RAID systems, SCSI components, server system configurations, and external storage arrays.

RAID Utility Upgrades

Although a server system that receives its first RAID configuration can be thought of as being upgraded, most upgrades involve RAID systems that are already installed and are either being enlarged with more drives being added, or updated by patches or completely new versions having more features or capacity.

Of course, in order to introduce a RAID system to the server, the RAID controller must first be installed and configured. The setup software is usually contained within the controller and its manufacturer usually provides the necessary instructions on how to set the drives up, including any necessary jumpers or terminations.

In order to get to the RAID setup program, a key combination reported during the bootup process should be pressed. Depending on which configuration is selected, the program will finalize the controller's setup with the drives. These RAID drives can then be formatted and partitioned by a disk manager program for additional storage. The administrator may simply install a fresh copy of the NOS on the RAID drives for integration with the larger network.

After the RAID installation has been completed, the NOS will treat the new configuration just like a single, local hard drive. The new arrangement should be backed up as soon as possible, with the understanding that RAID mirroring will not protect against files being accidentally deleted. Files deleted from one mirrored drive are simultaneously deleted from all of them.

RAID utility programs can help to recover lost data when such accidents occur. For example, broken RAID 5 or RAID 0 arrays can be reconstructed in spite of missing block size or drive order RAID parameters. A utility can determine the correct values, and reconstruct a copy of the RAID either in an image file or on a physical drive.

An effective RAID utility is the administrator's best friend when data is lost because of accidental formats, file deletions, or virus attacks. The value of a tool capable of recovering and restoring deleted or damaged boot sectors or partitions cannot be underestimated. File recovery chores can often be eliminated through the use of RAID utility programs that restore damaged drives to their previous state.

RAID flash utilities permit the controller's setup routines to be upgraded, similar to the way in which server boards can have their BIOS programs updated. This permits the use of the existing RAID controller over several technological generations.

SCSI Utility Upgrades

Utility programs for SCSI systems perform such tasks as hard disk diagnostics, tape recorder firmware updates, formatting of external storage cartridges, and configuring of installed host adapters.

Hard disk diagnostic tests include sequential reads and writes, drive defect mapping, random reads and writes, drive profiling, optimizations, drive confidence, seeks, performances, bus loading, zoning, and high-speed data transfers. For example, the drive confidence tests can be employed to examine the drive's functionality through the writing of data patterns, executing random seeks, and starting/stopping the drive. Parameters that select the number of test passes, the data pattern, and the percentage of the disk to be tested can all be specified.

Tests for backup tape systems also include sequential reads and writes, as well as data integrity. Tape data contents are mapped and confirmed, and high-speed data transfer testing includes performance measurements. Diagnostic self-tests can be performed for specified products, such as Quantum DLT drives. Warm-up and media error rate testing can be specified for DDS drives manufactured by Exabyte.

Because the technical aspects of SCSI products change so often, leading manufacturers of SCSI utilities offer various services with their utility products by renewable contracts. These services include the latest upgrades, quarterly updates, new tests as they are developed, support for new interfaces, and explanations of new commands. Regardless of whether these changes encompass major upgrades or incremental changes, full technical support is usually provided.

Exam Prep Questions

1. The administrator learned that server access had become intolerably slow only when users began to complain. Which of the following server network monitoring scenarios would best serve the administrator?

   ❏ A. Hire on-duty server personnel for round-the-clock network monitoring and troubleshooting.

   ❏ B. Initiate SNMP to provide remote monitoring.

   ❏ C. Institute a daily review of system event logs.

   ❏ D. Make sure all system users have phone and pager numbers for the administrator.

2. SNMP uses which default port number?

   ❏ A. 161
   ❏ B. 110
   ❏ C. 80
   ❏ D. 21

3. What purpose does a RAID utility tool serve?

   ❏ A. It serves to make the active development of new DMI standards obsolete.

   ❏ B. It helps to correct periodic server system vulnerabilities from existing security flaws.

   ❏ C. It provides timely notifications to clients before scheduled server maintenance is performed.

   ❏ D. It permits the periodic upgrading of a RAID controller's setup routines.

4. Which of the following parameters can be examined solely by a backup tape system utility test?

   ❏ A. The sequential reads and writes of the heads
   ❏ B. The data defect mapping
   ❏ C. The data content mapping
   ❏ D. The performance of high-speed data transfers

Exam Prep Answers

1. Answer B is the correct answer. Remote system monitoring through the use of SNMP is the best solution. Answer A is incorrect because it is too expensive to employ 24-hour on-duty server repair personnel. Answer C is incorrect because serious server network damage can occur before a trouble warning from an event log is either read or understood. Answer D is incorrect because only a suicidal administrator would agree to such an arrangement.

2. Answer A is the correct answer. SNMP uses the default port 161. Answer B is incorrect because clients receive email through the standard port 110. Answer C is incorrect because the standard port used for web traffic is 80. Answer D is incorrect because network clients use standard port 21 to log in to and connect to FTP servers.

3. Answer D is the correct answer. As new features are developed, they can be downloaded into the existing RAID controller using the utility. Answer A is incorrect because there is no relationship between the RAID utility tool and the DMI standard. Answer B is incorrect because security flaws are corrected through NOS updates rather than through RAID utilities. Answer C is incorrect because the communications between the administrator and the client have nothing to do with the RAID utility.

4. Answer C is the correct answer. Tape drive testing includes the confirmation of mapped data contents. Answers A and D are incorrect because they specify tests that can be conducted on both hard drives and tape drives. Answer B is incorrect because hard disk drives require data defect mapping, rather than tape drives.

18.0—Proactive Maintenance

Terms you'll need to understand:

- ✓ Backup utilities
- ✓ Documentation
- ✓ Configuration
- ✓ System data
- ✓ Boot files
- ✓ Emergency Repair Disk (ERD)
- ✓ Automated System Recovery (ASR)
- ✓ Full backups
- ✓ Incremental backups
- ✓ Differential backups
- ✓ Selective backups
- ✓ Maintenance log
- ✓ SNMP thresholds
- ✓ Internal and external polling
- ✓ Poll interval
- ✓ Threshold value
- ✓ Mean Time Between Failure (MTBF)

Techniques you'll need to master:

- ✓ Recognizing the need for a full backup
- ✓ Storing backups safely

✓ Selecting the appropriate type of backup

✓ Performing and verifying the specified backups

✓ Updating the ERD

✓ Utilizing various file-compression techniques

✓ Using the ASR option

✓ Deciding between full, incremental, differential, or selective backups

✓ Using and keeping an up-to-date maintenance log

✓ Comparing pre-disaster and post-disaster baselines

✓ Testing new software

✓ Adjusting SNMP thresholds

✓ Differentiating between internal and external polling

✓ Performing the necessary server housekeeping

✓ Understanding cable management

✓ Following a server management plan

✓ Instituting change management functions

Introduction

Server+ Exam Objective 5.1 states that the test taker should be able to perform regular backups. Activities associated with this objective include

➤ Updating the Emergency Repair Disk (ERD) (if applicable)

➤ Verifying the specified backup

To achieve this objective, you need to know and understand the following:

➤ How to recognize when full backups might be necessary

➤ How to select the appropriate type of backup:

  ➤ Differential

  ➤ Appended

  ➤ Copy

  ➤ Full

➤ The importance and use of documentation such as maintenance logs and service logs

Backups protect server data in the event of system failure. Therefore, creating and safely storing backups is the most critical part of the server network disaster recovery process. If the server system is compromised because of an accident, theft, intentional sabotage, or natural disaster, the backups created from the system data will permit its complete restoration.

Performing Backups

Backup utility programs are available from a variety of sources. Server-based network operating system (NOS) software often includes backup programs that operate as integrated options, and third-party programs are routinely bundled with backup hardware devices. In addition, independent backup software packages that offer a number of powerful features can be purchased separately. Regardless of the source, server backup utilities enable an administrator to quickly create extended copies of critical files, file groups, or entire disk drives.

Prior to conducting an initial backup procedure you should ensure that the most up-to-date documentation for the backup hardware or software being used is on hand. Check the hardware or software supplier's website for the latest information.

Backing up the business-related files of most companies typically requires much more media than a single tape. More robust backup programs provide for the use of a series of tapes and utilize various file compression techniques to reduce the amount of space required to store the files. After data files have been compressed for storage, it is impossible to read or manipulate them in their original application. To be able to use them again, the files must be decompressed (expanded) and restored to their original file formats, if necessary.

Backing Up Files

All Microsoft Windows server operating systems provide a backup utility that is capable of backing up and restoring the system as required. You need to consider the following when creating backups with Windows NOSes:

➤ Backup operations can be performed using the System Backup utility or the Backup Wizard.

➤ An administrator's or a backup operator's authorization is required to back up or restore files.

➤ The backup utility is not always installed by default. Therefore, it might need to be selected during the initial operating system installation, or specifically installed at a later time.

➤ Windows backup utilities are not recommended for backing up Microsoft SQL Server files. SQL Server uses its own built-in backup utility to back up the maintained databases.

➤ If the program indicates that there is no unused media available when creating a backup tape, it might be necessary to use the Removable Storage utility to add the tape to the backup media pool.

The backup utility program is basically a graphical tool used to implement all backup operations on files located on the primary server as well as on any network computer that can be reached remotely. It can be scheduled to conduct automated backups for simplified data archiving and permits the backup and restoration of data and system files to a variety of storage media types, using either NTFS or FAT volume formats. When backing up an NTFS file system, the backup utility includes its special descriptive catalogs, metadata, and logging data information with the appropriate files.

Backing Up State of the System Data and System Boot Files

When performing server system backups, it's always a good idea to save information regarding the state of the operating system. If and when a total restoration of the server system is required, this data will ensure that the restored server will have all the settings required to run the network exactly as before. As such, the backup program usually includes a checkbox or a parameter selection to specify that the system state data be included each time a backup operation is performed. This instructs the backup utility program to preserve the system state data along with the other data selected for backup. Settings and information for all server system components and services are also included as part of the system state data backup.

System and file protection service catalog files are often backed up and restored as a single element, although some systems still permit the incremental backup and repair of operating system files. The administrator should configure the backup utility option to automatically include the system boot files when backing up the state of the system data.

Emergency Repair Disks and Automated System Recovery

In Windows 2000 Server, the *Emergency Repair Disk (ERD)* is a component of the Backup utility program. It is highly recommended that an ERD be created immediately following the server system's initial installation, or after a major system modification such as the installation of a service package or driver update. If the core server fails or refuses to boot, the ERD will allow the administrator to quickly restore the system's *configuration* information. For added protection from a destroyed or corrupted ERD, it's recommended to create and safely store a redundant copy of the system's latest ERD.

Unlike the Windows NT system, the Windows 2000 ERD does not contain a copy of the registry files. Instead, the initial installation registry files are copied to the `%SystemRoot%\Repair` folder, and can be installed as required to return the server computer to a usable state in the event of a failure. Subsequent backups of the system state data include copies of the modified registry to the `%SystemRoot%\Repair\Regback` folder. This allows corrupted or erased system registry files to be selectively repaired without performing a full-restore of the system state data.

In Windows Server 2003, the *Automated System Recovery (ASR)* option is used to recover the operating system in the event of a system failure. This approach basically replaces the ERD of previous Windows versions. Rather than backing up data, the ASR records a template of the server's disk configuration on a floppy disk. This disk is used during the recovery process in conjunction with the Backup tool to recall a portion of the Windows setup information.

Backup Methodologies

Modern backup utility programs provide for various methods of backup, depending on scheduling demands that exist at the company. Businesses that operate on a 24-hour basis do not provide numerous opportunities for performing lengthy full backups. At best, they will be performed at widely spaced intervals. The need to keep track of rapidly accumulating data, or data that changes quite frequently, necessitates the use of short, incremental backups on a daily basis. Instituting the necessary backup scheduling without causing painful conflicts throughout the server community requires a high level of administrative skill.

Know which backup type requires the least amount of time to perform and the least amount of effort to restore the system.

Full Backups

When running a full backup process, the entire contents of the subject disk, drive, or server are backed up including all directories, subdirectories, and files. Because every piece of information is copied, *full backups* require careful scheduling because they consume the most amount of time to perform compared with other types of backups. Many system administrators consider this well worth the effort because when failure strikes, a full backup enables a complete system restoration in the least amount of time.

Partial Backups

To conserve space on the selected backup storage device or media, and to quickly preserve continually changing data, *partial backups* are often performed in addition to regularly scheduled full backups. Partial data backup techniques are classified according to the following categories:

➤ An *incremental backup* operation backs up those files that have been either created or changed since the most recent backup was performed. Partial backups require the least amount of time to perform. However, they require the greatest amount of time to restore the system following a catastrophic failure. To restore a failed system through the use of incremental backup data, the most recent full backup must first be used. This is then followed with a sequential restoration using each incremental backup taken from the time the last full backup was performed.

➤ A *differential backup* examines each individual file to determine whether it has been altered since the performance of the most recent full backup. If no changes are detected in the individual file, it is not selected for a differential backup operation. If the examination determines that the file has been altered, it will be tagged for backup. This preliminary tagging operation actually saves time when using a periodic backup strategy. Depending on exactly when the need for a full system restoration arises, a combination of all three tape categories may or may not be required. One thing is certain: A full system restoration will have to begin with the most recent full backup. Because every altered file since the last full backup is included in a differential backup, it takes longer to execute than an incremental backup.

➤ When performing a *selective backup*, the administrator must manually browse through the server's disk tree structure and individually mark or tag various directories to be backed up. Following this laborious marking procedure, the marked directories and files are backed up in a single operation. Selective backup is not recommended for regular backups of an entire system. Not only is it extremely labor-intensive, it also risks the inadvertent exclusion of important data. Yet, it provides a method for preserving the installation status of a specified application prior to risking an upgrade or a change of configuration.

Maintenance Logging of Backup Schedules

As part of a complete backup procedure, up-to-date information about the backups performed on the server system should always be kept in an accompanying *maintenance log*. This data should include the dates of all backups performed, the types of backups performed, and the locations of all backup tapes or disks, both onsite and offsite. This information can save the company from total disaster if the system suffers some unforeseen catastrophe. In fact, a thoughtful system administrator might also ensure that a spare, up-to-date copy of the maintenance log is kept and stored in a safe location, different from the one where offsite data is located.

Creating and Using Baselines

Server+ Exam Objective 5.2 states that the test taker should be able to create a server baseline and compare performance.

Activities involved in this objective include:

➤ Making regular comparisons to the original baseline

➤ Verifying the specified backup

To achieve this objective, you need to know and understand the importance and use of documentation such as maintenance logs and service logs.

The importance of the creation and use of periodic baseline measurements has been covered in previous sections and does not need to be repeated here. In a well-planned server environment, a post-disaster baseline is performed immediately upon system restoration. Obviously, when disaster strikes and a complete restoration of the server is required, a favorable comparison of pre-disaster and post-disaster baselines can help to ease the worried mind of an administrator.

The best-case scenario shows identical results between the pre-disaster and post-disaster baselines. In rare circumstances, the post-disaster baseline might indicate an improvement, although this is highly unlikely unless some new equipment was inserted after the most recent pre-disaster baseline was taken. What you do not want to see is a post-disaster baseline that indicates server network performance substantially below pre-disaster values. When these indicators arise, it's time to look for server or network components that might have been damaged by whatever circumstances caused the original disaster. The baseline values themselves, upon close examination, can point directly to the source of the problem.

Such negative possibilities include

➤ Onboard server chips, connectors, or components malfunctioning

➤ Damaged cabling due to electrical or manual abuse

➤ Peripheral equipment operating inefficiently

➤ Physical hard drive or other server component damage

➤ Improperly configured network following a reconstruction

It is possible that whatever caused the original server failure also drove a borderline piece of equipment over the edge. If this is the case, repairing or replacing this component can result in an improved baseline measurement. Regardless of the circumstances, the post-disaster baseline must be performed, evaluated, approved, and documented.

Baselines are often used to help avoid disaster before it occurs. One example of this is the installation of new software packages. After management makes the decision for a company to begin using a new program, or to perform a major update of software that is already installed, the administrator needs to perform the task with appropriate care. Employees might have previously communicated their concern that the new software might slow down the network beyond reason or otherwise negatively impact the network.

Regardless of how popular the idea of a new software installation may or may not be, the logical approach for the administrator to take is to first install the new software on the test system that has been baselined. Next, a new baseline with the new software should be established. A comparison of pre-installation and post-installation baselines should indicate whether or not employee concerns are justified. If they are, various adjustments must be made until it can be reliably demonstrated that the new software will not slow the network down. Only then should the software be installed on the production network.

Adjusting SNMP Thresholds

Server+ Exam Objective 5.3 states that the test taker should be able to adjust *SNMP thresholds*. In conjunction with performing proactive system mainte-nance, important management information can be gathered by using SNMP to regularly poll various server and network devices.

The administrator, in collaboration with department heads, is responsible for determining where the critical areas of the server network are, and which devices will be polled. After these have been decided, the timing for activated devices must also be specified, which is typically referred to as the *poll inter-val*. The poll interval can be set for any length of time, such as once or twice daily, every hour, or every second. The point at which action is taken, called the *threshold value*, must also be determined. The threshold value can be either a binary value, or some point at which the number of data packets passing by a specific port falls below a predetermined level.

When selecting the poll interval, take into consideration the device's proces-sor, the amount of bandwidth consumed, and the value types being reported. For example, if reported values are five-minute averages, bandwidth would be wasted by polling them every three seconds. Examine the Management Information Base (MIB) surrounding the data being polled for timing values. At the risk of adding some congestion to the network, starting poll intervals can be fairly short until peak values and data trends are determined. They can then be reduced accordingly and without overlooking important infor-mation. Be sure to consider other events that might be happening on the net-work as the polling intervals are considered, so that backups, data loads, and routing updates do not coincide with them.

It's important to be able to monitor the limits of the server network and to configure the required alarm thresholds properly. For example, an adminis-trator might decide to set up an alarm threshold to trigger if the processor sustains a 70% utilization for a specific amount of time. This requirement could cause a problem if the alarm threshold is set too low.

Suppose SNMP is *polling* the status of a router interface and the interface suddenly goes down! The management system should be capable of detect-ing the polling status of the specified SNMP threshold. It should generate a report and/or signal to the administrator about what has happened, so that a timely resolution to the problem can be realized. For example, if a tempera-ture reading exceeds a preset SNMP threshold, a trap alert should be directed to an administrator's console, or to the enterprise console, reporting the situation accurately. A properly adjusted threshold will produce the desired result, whereas an improper threshold adjustment can result in a chaotic alert scenario.

For example, what would be the result of polling the asynchronous and serial server interfaces on an access server? As remote users dial in to an access server, normal behavioral activity for the interfaces will rise and fall accordingly. Depending on how the polling is set up, such a threshold might result in as many as three modem alerts being generated during an average 20-minute call. If this one modem produces approximately six alerts per hour, it could conceivably report up to 144 events each day. Taken to another level, a telecommunication server fitted with 1296 modems could produce up to 186,624 events every 24 hours! Clearly, SNMP thresholds must be adjusted sensibly so as to produce meaningful results. SNMP thresholds must be periodically adjusted to reliably report various performance threshold values that are used for error analysis. These thresholds can also be used to determine the frequency at which data is collected through polling. Various software tools are available that provide straightforward methods of setting and adjusting SNMP thresholds and reporting their violations in a timely manner. Whichever product is used, important SNMP thresholds to consider include both internal and external elements:

➤ Internal *polling* is typically used in conjunction with a daemon running a critical local network application.

➤ External *polling* is executed by the network management system, where specified data can be graphed and saved for later retrieval, or where administrative notifications can be generated when something goes wrong.

Some management systems permit proprietary scripts to be run to fine-tune the needs of the server network. The beauty of SNMP polling is that it permits server network administrators to keep mission-critical devices up and properly functioning, without having to hire individuals to continually monitor system servers, routers, workstations, and infrastructure.

Internal Polling

To an administrator who runs a large corporate server system, continually polling various network devices only to rediscover each time that all is well might seem like a waste of bandwidth—until the first time an important problem is discovered and corrected before any networkers begin logging complaints. During a 24-hour period, dozens of devices can be polled several thousand times each without detecting even one failure or weakness.

Internal polling is capable of providing the benefits of polling without the network bandwidth consumption normally associated with such monitoring. This is accomplished through the use of an agent that is already part of the device being managed. Because this type of polling is internal to the device being polled, no initiating data traffic is required between the agent and the system manager.

Although this discussion focuses on SNMP, an internal polling agent does not necessarily have to be an SNMP agent. Both hardware and software systems that do not specifically support SNMP can still be accurately monitored. What's required is the creation of an internal polling program (as a substitute for the external SNMP polling activity) that can be used to retrieve the status information generated by the device's internal agent. The polling program uses various hooks to extract the required information and then feed it into an SNMP trap. From the SNMP trap, the data is forwarded to the network management system.

 Know that internal polling provides the benefits of polling without its associated network bandwidth consumption.

Although timing intervals for internal polling can be widely spaced, the capability to detect a serious alarm condition must be provided regardless of the schedule. This is where the distinction between alarms and events becomes extremely important. Various alarms are tied to specified events. The events are created to perform specified action(s) when their attached alarms are activated. An alarm is triggered only when its threshold is met, calling its targeted event. The event can be programmed to perform any number of functions, such as sending SNMP traps, or recording error logs. Standard SNMP traps are usually preconfigured by the agent's manufacturer, and the administrator might not be able to adjust their thresholds.

External Polling

Polling internally is not always possible for various security, technical, or political reasons. Regardless of what the situation might be, if a server is fitted with SNMP, it can be polled externally from another server or an administrator's computer. Server networks are full of objects worth polling, and for some, the polling is critical to their continued good health. Large server systems can lend themselves well to distributed polling among several servers. External software polling engines can often be used to collect and display data graphically, and to save it for later retrieval and analysis.

Graphical data comes in handy when troubleshooting the network for specific problems. If the server administrator or the network manager begins getting calls from clients sitting at workstations that are exhibiting extremely slow connections, graphs similar to the one shown in Figure 18.1 can be used to check for routers having any unusually high traffic spikes. In this figure, the OpenView polling engine is used to graphically display the data for a specified node.

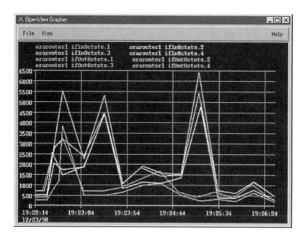

Figure 18.1 Graphing the specified polling data.

These types of graphs are useful for setting thresholds for alarms and other kinds of traps. Some preliminary time spent examining various graphs will provide guidance as to the network's behavior prior to setting critical thresholds and recording system baselines.

For example, an administrator will definitely want to be notified if a server's UPS battery is low, or if it has been returned to a full charge after use. This means that an alarm must be generated when the battery voltage falls below a specified percentage of full charge. After such an alarm has been noted, another alarm must be used to indicate when the battery is once again fully charged. A sensible threshold must be determined for this notification, but everything is merely guesswork without a valid baseline. Graphing the device's MIBs for a few days would provide the baseline information required to set realistic thresholds for the UPS. If these graphs reveal a normal charge of 94 to 97% for the UPS at rest, and a charge of 89% during its self-test routine, a fully charged threshold of 94% seems reasonable. An operating threshold of 85% also makes sense to provide adequate notification during battery use without generating useless alarms when the device is in self-test mode.

Housekeeping Duties

Server+ Exam Objective 5.4 states that the test taker should be able to perform physical housekeeping. Activities for this objective include making periodic checks for dust buildup and utilizing proper cable management techniques.

The environment, controlled or not, in which server equipment resides always affects its life span. Network administrators should continually remind themselves that electronic equipment, especially servers, should be protected from temperature extremes, surface dirt/grease accumulations, or dusty conditions. Regularly scheduled cleaning of a server's components along with periodic inspections of its surroundings undoubtedly increases the *Mean Time Between Failure (MTBF)* rates of most equipment, as well as its overall longevity.

Physical housekeeping around server equipment racks is much the same as with any computer equipment, except for the fact that there is more of it. One thing to be continually aware of is that a company's server equipment is usually off limits to the regular cleaning crews that often roam the halls during non-peak working hours. There is rarely enough trash generated in the server equipment room to justify such a security risk. That means that if the access to the equipment racks is limited to the administrator or to service personnel, they are responsible for the housekeeping duties.

Most rooms housing servers and their associated equipment are operated under controlled environments. The continuing efficient operation of this equipment usually requires clinical cleanliness and attention to detail. Servers, racks, power supplies, patch panels, printers, scanners, and telephones must not be permitted to gather dirt, dust, or grease. Cleaning duties extend to air conditioning units, furniture, interior glass, floors, and antistatic floor devices. Keep in mind that the cross-contamination of phones and keyboards is a major source of cross-contamination of bacteria between people. Even with the limited access often governing server rooms, unpleasant bacteria such as *Serratia rubidea*, *Shigella*, and *E. coli* can find their way in. Period cleaning of all server, telephone, and computer equipment is required to eliminate these unwelcome guests.

Unfortunately for server administrators, the need for security limits the possibility of training other employees to perform these somewhat time-consuming tasks. In addition, to ensure that these tasks are performed regularly, the administrator must formulate a realistic cleaning schedule to follow, at regular intervals:

➤ Daily—Checking the ventilator slots of all servers to be sure that nothing is obstructing them

➤ Weekly—Cleaning the exterior of all servers, along with any accompanying keyboards and monitors

➤ Monthly—Examining all fans for proper operation; running operational checks on all hard drives; checking all cabling for proper seating and attachment between the server and all peripheral equipment; using an air hose to blow accumulated dust out of server chassis and racks

Do not use volatile substances such as benzene, isopropyl alcohol, or paint thinners to clean plastic surfaces. The finish on these surfaces can be noticeably damaged. In addition, only fabrics approved for cleaning should be utilized. Common cleaning cloths such as household tissues, hand towels, and others leave behind fibers capable of clogging delicate mechanisms, and dyes contained on these products can dissolve in the cleaning solvent and transfer to the items being cleaned. Synthetic cloths can also be dissolved by certain solvents, creating the possibility of coating the surfaces being cleaned as the solvent evaporates.

Server Cases

Little preventative maintenance is required on the exterior of server cases, as they contain no moving or functioning parts. However, be aware that blank cover plates should always be installed in unused rear expansion slots to ensure that all possible gaps in the back of the case are covered. Otherwise, dust and debris will constantly be drawn into the interior of the case by the vacuum operation of the cooling fans(s) and disrupt the normal airflow patterns. This situation can eventually lead to the overheating of various components inside the case. Many servers contain built-in alarms that produce audible warnings if and when the processor overheats. The server BIOS settings should be examined periodically to ensure that this feature remains enabled. Another temperature sensor can be configured to produce an audible alarm if the interior of the server reaches an unacceptable temperature.

The more frequently a plastic or metal server cabinet is handled, the dirtier it will get. Static charges on its surfaces also attract dust. Therefore, an effective cleaning process must simultaneously remove the surface soil and reduce this static charge. To properly clean the exterior of a server case, try using one or more of the following:

➤ Soft, dry cloth

➤ Soft cloth moistened with water

➤ Manufacturer-approved cleaning kit

➤ Soft cloth moistened with a solution of water and a gentle, non-scratch household cleaner without ammonia

Although there is no need to turn off a server before cleaning its exterior surfaces, rigorous cleaning in the vicinity of its ventilation slots can require a temporary power-down. Never use spray cleaners when cleaning near these ventilation slots.

When it comes to the interior of the server case, an increased level of caution is required, including the necessity of performing a temporary shutdown of the unit. With all the components that are exposed when the server's exterior cover is removed, the approach taken to cleaning changes completely. The idea of using any type of liquid cleaning substances, including water, should be rejected. Most large server farms include compressed air systems running throughout the facility. To use the system, connect the portable air hoses to distributed valves that are located in close proximity to equipment racks. The end hose nozzles can be adjusted to regulate the force of the air being supplied to safely blow accumulated dust out and away from the racks, or from individually targeted server units. For smaller server systems, canisters of compressed air can be used to achieve the same results.

Know that the interior areas of racks and equipment should be dusted by using compressed air.

Server Mice

Although not as important a consideration as the server itself, the mouse can begin to malfunction as debris builds up on its ball or on its X and Y rollers. This debris can be a combination of skin debris, sweat, human hair, or environmental dust present on the mouse pad. Common symptoms of a dirty mouse include sluggish or random mouse pointer movement, which is caused by the trackball not making adequate contact with the X and Y rollers. Take the following steps to clean a mouse that is not operating properly:

1. Disconnect the mouse cable from the server. Normally, for a workstation mouse, you should power down the computer before doing this. However, it might not be possible to simply shut the server down to clean the mouse because of the negative effects on the network clients. If a KVM switch is used, it can be switched away from a critical server

before the mouse is serviced. Disconnecting the mouse is preferable to manipulating it on a live system, where accidentally activating a button can execute an unintended network command.

2. Next, flip the mouse upside-down and remove its trackball cover.

3. Remove the trackball by gently turning the mouse over and letting it fall into your hand.

4. Use a mild detergent with a soft cloth to gently clean the trackball, and then dry it with a clean, lint-free cloth.

5. After the ball itself is clean, use a lint-free cloth or similar material from a mouse-cleaning kit to remove dirt, grease, and dust from the internal rollers. Rotate the rollers during the cleaning process to cover their entire circumferences. The trackball compartment usually contains three rollers, two of which are used to trace horizontal and vertical movement. The third roller is used maintain trackball pressure against the other two.

6. After the rollers are clean, place the trackball back into its compartment and close its cover. It usually takes a quarter-turn twist to lock the cover into place.

7. The next step is to plug the mouse back into its appropriate interface on the server or KVM switch. This operation might not be as simple as when the mouse was unplugged. If the mouse is plugged into a PS/2 port, it will not be recognized by the system until after a reboot. A USB device is recognized as soon as it is plugged in. However, because of the security concerns surrounding the use of USB ports with servers, they are often not included on servers where security is a paramount objective. Therefore, the odds are that the server is using a PS/2 (or similar) arrangement and that it will have to be brought down, at least for a few minutes, to reconnect the mouse. After the mouse has been reconnected, reactivate the server. If a PS/2 KVM switch is used, only the switch has to be turned off momentarily to reconnect the mouse.

8. To ensure that the mouse functions correctly, move it along a clean, flat surface, such as on a mouse pad and check all of its functions.

Server Monitors

To avoid eyestrain when using a computer system for prolonged periods of time, the monitor screen should be kept clean and free of visual smears. Take the following steps to properly clean a monitor screen:

1. Turn off the power to the monitor. For server systems, the server should continue running.

2. Remove the monitor from its power source.

3. Use a soft, clean cloth to wipe dust off the monitor screen and cabinet.

4. When more than simple dusting is required, use an approved VDU screen cleaner. Wipe across the glass screen first horizontally, and then vertically, making sure to include the corners of the screen.

Do not allow still images to continuously remain on a monitor's screen for long periods of time. If this situation is not prevented, one of these images can become "burned" into the face of the picture tube. Remember to always either use the screen-saver software provided by the NOS, or configure the system to turn the monitor off automatically after a predetermined time period. Although newer CRTs are fairly immune to image burn-in problems, LCD screens are known to suffer from a form of image burn-in. When this burn-in is not permanent, it is referred to as image persistence. Image persistence can sometimes be removed over several days or weeks by displaying a white image on the screen for several hours each day.

As with server cabinets, do not use spray cleaners around the ventilation slots of a monitor. Malfunctions and high-voltage arcing will occur if these sprays are allowed to enter the monitor. Special antiglare coatings and mesh filters require cleaning with approved solutions and materials only. Sensitive plastic or polycarbonate front panels on notebook computer screens can easily be damaged using unsuitable cleaning materials. Therefore, always check the user manual before attempting to clean these screens.

Server Keyboards

Ensure that keyboards are not used in an environment where food and beverages are present, as spillage of these substances can cause the keyboard to malfunction and make it difficult to clean. Always power off the computer and disconnect the keyboard when cleaning the keys. Use the following procedure to clean the keyboard:

1. Grasp the keyboard at one end and face the keys slightly downward over a sheet of paper to catch any loose debris.

2. Use compressed air, a natural bristle brush, or a mini vacuum cleaner for keyboards to remove dust and debris that has settled between and under the keys. Move precisely down the length of the keyboard panel without missing any areas.

3. Clean the surface of the keyboard using an approved cleaning solution. It is not advisable to use foam cleaner on the keys, as the foaming action can lift dirt particles and deposit them in the key switches. Be careful! Unapproved cleaning solutions can actually erase the lettering off the key buttons.

Do not use an antistatic screen cleaner on a keyboard because it deposits a conductive film on the cleaned surfaces. If this film reaches into the key switches, the keyboard will malfunction. If a spray cleaner is used, first spray the cleaner onto a lint-free cloth. Then, use the cloth to do the cleaning. Avoid using household spray polishes containing silicone oil. Its conductive coating adversely affects the switch mechanisms.

Server Drives

Magnetic media devices, such as floppy disk drives and tape drives, require periodic cleaning of their recording heads. A cleaning product specifically designed for this task should be used, such as cleaning disks or cartridges. When these products are unavailable, you can use an approved cleaning pad, swab, or lint-free cloth. Avoid the use of cotton swabs, plain tissues, and similar household materials that leave fiber traces capable of clogging the read/write heads, causing data errors, or promoting excessive tape or head wear. Approved cleaning solutions are usually based on isopropyl alcohol, and require careful handling, because of its toxicity if inhaled or swallowed. Avoid the application of excessive pressure to the delicate read/write head assemblies during the cleaning process. Other than periodic cleaning, no other servicing of drive head components should be attempted.

Server Disks

Because of the normal abrasion that occurs between drive heads and the surface of floppy disks, the disks can eventually wear out. A simple precaution against the loss of data on these disks is to regularly copy important data from floppy disks onto new disks or media. Floppy disks must not be stored in dusty environments, extremely hot or cold areas, or near electromagnetic fields. Although CDs can be properly cleaned using lint-free cloths, they should be stored in their cases, and not exposed to temperature extremes or bending pressures.

Alternatively, hard disks are contained within a sealed unit and do not require manual cleaning. However, their data is still susceptible to being corrupted, and the files on the disk can become disorganized. After a system crash, temporary files left on the disk can fill up the free space, causing slow responses to system commands. Most operating systems provide a utility program to help find and fix these problems. Two well-known examples of these utilities provided with DOS and Windows OSes are SCANDISK and DEFRAG.

Server Power Supplies and Fans

Careful use of specially designed mini vacuum cleaners helps to remove dirt and dust deposits from around power supplies and fans. These deposits can reduce the lives of these units by reducing the airflow through them and causing their ambient temperature levels to rise above normal levels. Vacuum cleaners used around the home generate large amounts of static electricity and are dangerous for use near server equipment. Use only mini vacuum cleaners approved for the job of cleaning electronic equipment.

Dust and Trash Accumulation

Keep in mind that there is no way to know for sure what the housekeeping staff is doing unless someone is continually hanging around monitoring their activities. However, keeping a broom and a dustpan handy in the server room is not a breach of security, nor is it a disaster for the administrator to be tasked with sweeping the room. If and when the trash can is filled, it can be set outside the computer room door for collection by cleaning personnel.

It is important to carefully examine the contents of a trash can before setting it outside of the computer room for collection. Shred all printouts of sensitive information before throwing them away. This includes internal memos. Be aware that trash reveals much more than most people realize about themselves and about what goes on where they live and where they work. This is the main reason why paparazzi sift through the garbage cans of famous people. There are documented examples of corporate spying from trash inspection that gathered enough sensitive information to drive the targeted company out of business. In fact, when security professionals evaluate a specific corporation, the first thing they do is dig through the trashcans. Entire reports that were discarded because of simple formatting errors have been found. Passwords have been discovered written on scraps of paper. Other potentially damaging discoveries include "while you were out" messages complete with return phone numbers, valid documents tossed out with old file folders, and workable computer disks/tapes still containing useful data.

Be aware that background checks are routinely conducted by federal employers on those employees who have access to waste baskets and shredders at secure worksites. A detailed diagram of a network and its routers, including which ports were blocked and unblocked, should not be discarded in a company trash bin! All discarded paper documents should be routinely shredded and all magnetic media should be physically destroyed to make it useless to an enemy of the company. Server system administrators should never take the trashcan for granted.

Cable Management Duties

The ongoing, proper administration of a structured server cabling system is possible only through the detailed organization and identification of all lines and connections. Whereas international standards for the administration of premise cabling systems are applied with the understanding that changes must frequently occur during the life of a commercial building, cable management should provide options for continuous optimization. Equipment moves, rack additions, and personnel changes are much less disruptive when the network wiring infrastructure is simplified through the proper use of space, color coding, and accurate labeling.

Ongoing operations carried out by personnel who are not trained in the basics of good cable management can quickly transform a well-designed wiring closet into a nightmare of tangled and intertwined patch cords. Amazingly, the application of just a few simple housekeeping techniques can prevent such a situation from developing. Invariably, when proper cable management is neglected, so too is adequate recordkeeping. Although general housekeeping chores related to cable management are not nearly as comprehensive as those required for cable installation personnel, all moves, additions, or changes to cables, wire pairs, or port assignments should be documented on an ongoing basis.

One aspect of cable management that is often overlooked is the danger of tripping over a misplaced or carelessly deployed cable. Government studies of life-threatening risks from slips and trips indicate that many employee injuries occur because of cables routed improperly within walkways or without the use of cable management systems.

Although a properly installed cable plant will adhere to the management guidelines described earlier in this chapter, always be on the lookout for situations in which simple solutions can be implemented. For example:

➤ Are AC power cables kept separate from other cables? AC hum in audio circuits can be minimized by deploying AC cables at right angles to audio.

➤ Are the shortest possible cable lengths being used? Peripheral devices such as printers, modems, and scanners are often supplied with cables that are much too long. Clutter can be eliminated by using cables of correct lengths, rather than tolerating long cables dangling from equipment or coiled on the floor.

➤ Are cable ties and clips being used? The most cost-effective way to organize cables into related bundles is to use cable ties and cable clips, which are available in many colors and lengths.

➤ Would the use of split tubing help? Split tubing is flexible with a side split that permits various cable groups to be separated and then tucked inside.

➤ Is there a need to use a cable organizer? A cable organizer is a box or set of slotted guides that mounts on the server room wall or at a workstation, permitting cables to be wrapped and tucked inside.

➤ Are a power center and conditioner being used? Rack-mounted power conditioners eliminate much clutter by providing one central location for all AC cables to connect. Other power centers rest on the floor or mount on a wall, while providing surge protection and a convenient place to switch peripheral equipment on and off.

➤ Are USB peripherals used at workstations? Long runs of multiple cables can be eliminated through the use of USB keyboards, mice, printers, and scanners, which can plug into each other. USB or FireWire hubs can also serve to organize multiple connections.

➤ Is a wireless solution viable? It's unnecessary to eliminate cables if they are not used in the first place. Cabling can be seriously reduced through the use of wireless networks and peripherals, such as keyboards and mice.

Following the Server Management Plan

Server+ Exam Objective 5.5 states that the test taker should be able to monitor, maintain, and follow the server management and service plan. Activities associated with this objective include following the change management protocol. A server management and service plan includes courses of action spelled out for network administrators and all client levels to deal with various potential security risks. These risks include malicious hacks, viruses, hard disk crashes, and data corruption. The trouble areas for which preparation must be made include the following:

➤ Change passwords regularly—Change or create all required passwords immediately following the acquisition of a server system. This is especially critical for hosted systems, where default passwords are emailed using plain text. Even with totally internal systems, there is always the possibility that someone knows the current password who shouldn't have that information. Change all of the passwords again, remembering the following guidelines:

➤ Never use the same password for personal and administrative accounts. Be sure to differentiate between root or administrator accounts and normal employee accounts.

➤ Select fairly long and complex passwords that are difficult to guess, using combinations of letters, numbers, and punctuation. Do not select words from the dictionary, and count on regularly changing all passwords.

➤ Disable unused service ports—Where Internet service is available, security risks exist at a number of well-known service ports. If they remain open to the Internet, they pose a security risk to the company. Services such as HTTP and email might be required, but others are not. Services that should be disabled if not required include the following:

➤ Telnet, which is one of the biggest Internet security risks around. When Telnet is used for administration purposes, passwords can easily be stolen. Always disable Telnet and use secure shell (SSH) if necessary. SSH encrypts the traffic so that if it's intercepted in route, it will be protected.

➤ FTP, which is the second biggest Internet security weakness. If the FTP service is not needed, you should disable it. If it must be used, never include a root or administrator password with transfers, because FTP transmits the password in plain text for any snooper to see.

➤ Install a firewall for Internet protection—Firewalls are available in both software and hardware formats and allow the administrator to control which server ports, if any, are open to the Internet. They can also detect intrusion attempts.

➤ Install virus protection—Serious damage to a server system can occur because of virus infections. Most viruses are written for the Windows platform, making it particularly vulnerable. However, a number of worms are also released for Linux servers that can exploit security holes in common Linux services and cause them to crash. Administrators must run virus scans regularly, in addition to keeping antivirus programs updated frequently to protect against new viruses that are regularly released.

➤ Perform the latest firewall and virus software updates—Updates are continually released by software manufacturers to plug newly discovered security holes. Main software components should be updated regularly in systems exposed to Internet activity, including the web server, email server, firewall, and SSH server. This includes new servers that are added to the system over time. An administrator cannot assume that a host provider has provided the company with the latest update packages. Periodic upgrading for server security should be part of the overall approach to server networks that employ Internet services.

➤ Maintain current backups—Sooner or later, a serious problem will occur that causes data to be lost. If not a hacker attack, then an employee (or even the administrator) might type the magic command. Someone might pull the wrong plug, or the power company might experience a failure. Regardless of the cause, employees and customers will feel the same effect. When backups are maintained as outlined previously, the company will be back up and running in short order. Items that must be backed up include

   ➤ The contents of databases.

   ➤ Dynamic files, including traffic logs.

   ➤ Configuration files for all servers and software. This presupposes that all recently edited configuration files have been properly backed up.

   ➤ Customer profiles and working files. This protects both the customers and the company from serious errors or litigation.

➤ Monitor servers for security and hacks—A secure and working server will not remain so for long unless it is continually monitored for potential problems. The following are some monitoring tips:

   ➤ A number of services can be used to ping the company's web server to ensure the proper response, and alert the administrator through email or an alternate telephone line when an improper response is detected.

   ➤ A security auditing tool should be run regularly to check for hacking attempts. This utility is not perfect, but it can easily detect the vast majority of hacking attempts.

   ➤ Server logs should be examined regularly for unusual entries.

Administrators should spend several hours or more per week monitoring and securing the server against problems originating within and outside the company. Failure to do so can result in spending days, or even weeks, dealing with the resulting problems.

Changes on a server network often occur because the requirements for clients have changed. Other changes occur because a problem has arisen that must be dealt with. When these types of system changes are mandated, change management serves to help network inhabitants handle their effects by controlling the sending, retrieving, installing, and removing of change files at remote nodes, and by activating those nodes after the required changes have been accomplished. Although various network problems can be the motivating factors that cause necessary changes to be instituted, these changes themselves can cause problems for some clients. Change management attempts to minimize these types of problems by promoting orderly change and by tracking these changes for effect.

Exam Prep Questions

1. Where will the most recent backup software or hardware documentation be located?
   - ❑ A. In the accompanying printed hardware/software documentation
   - ❑ B. In hardware or software publications
   - ❑ C. In the accompanying electronic hardware/software documentation
   - ❑ D. On the website of the hardware or software supplier

2. The inside of a server case contains too much accumulated dust. Select one of the following substances to remove the dust safely.
   - ❑ A. Vacuum air
   - ❑ B. Compressed air
   - ❑ C. H_2O
   - ❑ D. Isopropyl alcohol

3. Differential backup tapes are recorded daily each afternoon. The most recent full tape server backup occurred at 5:30 a.m. Saturday morning, and the server subsequently crashed at 9:30 a.m. the following Thursday. In order to successfully restore this system, how many tapes will it take?
   - ❑ A. One
   - ❑ B. Three
   - ❑ C. Two
   - ❑ D. Four

4. Company employees are concerned that the proposed software application will cause the speed of the network to suffer. What approach should the administrator take?
   - ❑ A. Refuse to install the new program, based on the concerns of the affected employees.
   - ❑ B. Skip the baseline and install the new program as instructed by management.
   - ❑ C. Run an installation baseline on the company system and make the necessary observations and adjustments.
   - ❑ D. Run an installation baseline on a test system first and make the necessary observations and adjustments.

5. In a Windows server environment, what is the proper approach to accessing the Telnet service?
   - ❑ A. Click Start/Programs/Accessories/Command Prompt, type `telnet` and press Enter.
   - ❑ B. Click Start/Programs/Accessories/Accessibility/Accessibility Wizard and type `telnet`.
   - ❑ C. Click Start/Programs/Accessories/Entertainment/Windows Media Player, and click on Tools/Telnet.
   - ❑ D. Click Start/Programs/Accessories/Communications/HyperTerminal, type `telnet` and press Enter.

Exam Prep Answers

1. Answer D is the correct answer. As with most products, the website run by the manufacturer or vendor will always contain the most recent documentation. Answers A and C are incorrect because there is no way that the most up-to-date information will be contained within the product documentation, whether printed or electronic. Answer B is incorrect because a book or magazine cannot contain more up-to-date product information than that found on a website run by the manufacturer or vendor, unless the product is dated.

2. Answer B is the correct answer. Safely cleaning accumulated dust from inside the server, after the case is removed, requires the use of compressed air to blow it out. Answer A is incorrect because making physical contact with sensitive components using vacuum equipment risks damage to them. Answers C and D incorrectly risk the use of fluids near the circuitry, which should always be avoided.

3. Answer C is the correct answer. A full system restoration should be possible from the latest full and differential backups, requiring a maximum of two tapes. This would include Saturday's full backup and the most recent differential backup made on Wednesday afternoon. Answers A, B, and D are incorrect by process of elimination.

4. Answer D is the correct answer. To ensure against negatively impacting the employee workload, the administrator should install the new software on a test system and record a baseline. The effects of the new software on the system will then be better understood. Answer A is incorrect and will not be accepted by management. Answer B is incorrect because it places the company's commercial server network in jeopardy and represents improper system administration policy. Answer C is incorrect because any new software must first be properly tested to avoid possible damage to the company's server network.

5. Answer A is the correct answer. Because Telnet is a command-line function, the Windows command prompt must appear on the screen in order to use it. Answer B is incorrect because the Accessibility Wizard has nothing to do with Telnet. Answer C is incorrect because bidirectional communications is not a function of the Windows Media Player. Answer D is incorrect because HyperTerminal and Telnet are both terminal programs, but they are not interchangeable.

19.0—Environmental Issues

Terms you'll need to understand:

- ✓ Passwords
- ✓ Cracking
- ✓ Length, width, and depth
- ✓ Encryption
- ✓ One-time passwords
- ✓ Controlled access
- ✓ Environment

Techniques you'll need to master:

- ✓ Understanding various security levels
- ✓ Avoiding specific passwords and personal information
- ✓ Considering password length, width, and depth
- ✓ Limiting access to the server room and to backup tapes
- ✓ Establishing antitheft devices for server hardware
- ✓ Establishing secure password administration
- ✓ Securing the physical server environment
- ✓ Installing various server room, server chassis, and rack locks and alarms
- ✓ Determining server room access privileges
- ✓ Understanding limited and controlled access
- ✓ Dealing with server room waste and garbage
- ✓ Limiting access to backup tapes
- ✓ Knowing whom to contact for environmental problems
- ✓ Dealing with humidity and electrostatic discharge (ESD)
- ✓ Locating and using Class C fire extinguishers
- ✓ Securing a set of backup tapes offsite

Introduction

Server+ Exam Objective 6.1 states that the test taker should be able to recognize and report on physical security issues. Activities associated with this objective include

➤ Limiting access to the server room and to backup tapes

➤ Ensuring that physical locks exist on all doors

➤ Establishing antitheft devices for all hardware, including locked server racks

To achieve this objective, you need to know and understand the fundamentals of server security, such as the importance of physically securing a server.

The physical security of the server environment begins at the doors to the server room as well as the backup tape storage area. Various physical locking techniques are available for these thresholds, but access through the use of a key-only strategy may fall short. Keys notoriously fall into the wrong hands and although necessary, they should not be solely relied upon. Instead, they should be used in combination with password entry systems to further limit the possibility of unauthorized access.

Inside the server room or the separate tape storage area, antitheft and antitampering devices can be deployed to provide both audible and recordable warnings and observations during unauthorized activities.

Physical Security at the Entrance

Security measures in the server room can include locks on the server chassis, locks on the server room door, locks on the server rack, and installed server security software, but the first introduction to server network security for most employees occurs at the entrance to the server room itself. In addition to door keys, entrance passwords must be provided to server room employees by the administrator to enable them to successfully enter and exit the server room area, as duties require.

The password could be a word, a phrase, or a combination of miscellaneous characters that authenticates the employee's identity prior to the granting of server room access. Although passwords are less sophisticated and less expensive than alternate forms of authentication such as key cards, fingerprint IDs, and retinal scans, in combination with keylock access they provide a simple, effective method of protecting the server room from unwanted intrusion. Server room passwords should not be taken lightly because they are an important company defense against server network intrusion and the compromising of trade secrets, financial data, intellectual property, and customer lists.

As vital to system security as password components are, it is surprising how easily they can be cracked or broken. The process of determining an unknown password is called *cracking*, and it is frequently undertaken to gain unauthorized entrance to a system, network, or financial account. Although such an attack on an standalone password lock cannot be accomplished in a secured environment, server entrance passwords will nevertheless be changed frequently by the administrator.

Cracking works by making speedy comparisons between the targeted password and a large internal word list, a precompiled dictionary, or some other character combinations until a match is found. The best defense against this type of crack is to reset or change the password frequently.

Sniffer programs approach the password-nabbing task in a more technical way. They browse through raw network data and decipher its contents, essentially reading every keystroke sent out from a targeted machine, including network passwords unless strongly encrypted. A standalone server room password lock is immune to sniffer technology.

Keep in mind that there are numerous other ways for potential intruders to gather passwords. Many methods don't even require the use of sophisticated software. Potential intruders might browse through a server room employee's work area looking for self-reminder notes lurking under the keyboard or blatantly stuck to their monitor screens. Some have even called server room employees on their work phones claiming to be IT engineers performing legitimate work on the server system. If administrators create server room passwords using easily guessed personal information, the security of the server room could be compromised.

Password Basics

By knowing how password cracking is conducted, it becomes possible for the administrator to avoid certain pitfalls of password selection. Server room administrators should avoid using conventional words as passwords altogether. Proper nouns should also be left untouched, as should foreign words that are familiar to people of any language. Similarly, conventional words with numbers merely tacked onto their ends or with numbers substituted for similar-looking letters such as a zero for the letter O will not provide much password security. The same caution is recommended for using conventional words in reverse. How long can the word "krowten" hold off a determined server room intruder?

On the other hand, server room employees can quickly become frustrated when they can't remember the correct entrance passwords. Although the need to remember passwords is important, this requirement cannot be permitted to justify the incorporation of overly simple server room passwords. The administrator needs to avoid falling into this trap.

Password Specifics

For a password to be effective, it must possess a certain amount of complexity. Its *length, width, and depth* must be such as to thwart the efforts of the previously mentioned password-cracking techniques. The length of a password directly affects the ease with which it can be cracked. The longer the password is, the more difficult it will be to crack. It is generally recommended that passwords should consist of between six and nine characters. Passwords of five characters or less must be avoided. If permitted by the OS, longer passwords can be used, provided the employees or clients can remember them.

The width of a password relates to the number of different types of characters that can be incorporated, including those not belonging to the alphabet. Combinations of numbers, special characters, and uppercase and lowercase letters make passwords stronger, especially when an operating system considers uppercase and lowercase letters as completely different characters. Keep in mind that Windows operating systems do not always incorporate case sensitivity, and might not differentiate between characters such as "W" and "w". Passwords can contain control characters, alternate characters, and even spaces in some operating systems. Ideally, all the following character sets should be drawn from when the administrator selects passwords for the server room:

➤ Uppercase letters such as A, B, C

➤ Lowercase letters such as a, b, c

➤ Numerals such as 1, 2, 3

➤ Special characters such as $, ?, &

➤ Alternate characters such as µ, £, Æ

The depth of a password involves how difficult it is to guess its meaning. Although a good password should be easy to remember, it should nevertheless be difficult to guess. The meaning of a password should not be something that could be easily guessed or deducted through simple reasoning. One approach that seems to work well is to think in terms of phrases rather than simply words. Mnemonic phrases are often incorporated, allowing the creation of passwords that cannot be easily guessed, but yet do not need to be written down to be remembered. Mnemonic phrases can be spelled phonetically, using, for example, "UrmITygr!" instead of "You're my tiger!" Alternatively, the first letters in each word of a memorable phrase can be incorporated, such as "Ihnybtf," which is abbreviated from "I have not yet begun to fight!"

Another effective method is to choose a meaningful phrase that can be easily recalled. Then, the initials of some words in the phrase can be converted into alternate characters. For example, the number "4" could be substituted wherever the letter "f" is used.

Additional Password Security

The need for additional password security has become more recognized with the increased ease with which scam artists continue to steal them. Passwords have ultimately been gathered as easily as simply asking for them. Server room personnel should simply never talk about passwords with anyone, no matter how harmless or legitimate such conversation might seem.

Although standard password protection practices are often adequate to keep would-be intruders at bay, certain situations require a more sophisticated approach. In these cases, extra protection can be afforded through the use of *encryption* techniques and *one-time passwords (OTP)*. Encryption is the process of taking a standard password, and garbling it in such a way as to make it meaningless to sniffers, crackers, or other eavesdroppers. One-time passwords, such as those provided by S/key, are good only for one transaction. Although this security method is very reliable, it requires the server room employee to carry a list of server room passwords, a special password calculator, or a SecureCard password supply.

Server room employees can maximize password effectiveness through the practice of specific behavior patterns. These passwords should never be discussed with anyone other than known system administrators. Such discussions should be conducted in person, and never over the telephone or through email.

The act of writing down or storing passwords should be avoided when possible and carefully considered when not. Criminal hackers often obtain server room passwords by either searching through company trash or peeking over an unsuspecting employee's shoulder. This makes it extremely risky to write down these passwords on sticky notes pasted to monitors or stashed under keyboards. Although memorizing a password that is sufficiently complex is not the easiest task, it is the safest approach.

This is not to suggest that there is never a circumstance where a password can be written down. Although this practice is not recommended, it should be done with adequate forethought. A system administrator might be responsible for any number of periodically changing passwords for both the server room and the backup tape storage closet. Whatever written information he or she requires to do the job should be personally carried at all times. A photocopy might be stored at a safe alternate location, but this information must never reach a sticky note, email, or online file, even in an encrypted format.

Password Changes and Policies

Server room passwords must be changed on a regular basis to continue being effective. Online financial accounts require users to change passwords as often as once a month, whereas corporate network passwords are usually changed every three or four months. When it comes to server room password maintenance, administrators should use good judgment and avoid being lazy. Making password changes is a simple task when compared with the hassle and expense of dealing with severe cases of server room data theft.

Strong password policies are the building blocks of enhanced server room security for administrators. Password security requirements should be built into the organizational structure, with periodic changes and updates mandated. Server room employees must be continually reminded of the ease with which hackers can compromise the password system through personal interactions. This goes double for new employees who are being introduced to good password practices for the first time. The company password policy should be completely integrated into its security policy and server room employees must read and sign off on the policy several times each year.

Administrators should implement safeguards that ensure adequately strong password use on their systems. Administrators can prevent the reuse of passwords through the keeping of a password history, and except to the administrator, the server room door can be automatically locked for a specified period following three to five unsuccessful password attempts. Another good practice is to keep the number of company employees with server room passwords to a minimum. For many server room security systems, passwords are obviously only one piece of the puzzle. For enhanced server room protection in a controlled corporate environment, other pieces to the puzzle include

➤ General user education

➤ Good physical security

In situations where password control is the only available security method, the awareness of security risks and of password controls must be maximized.

Physical Security Inside the Server Room

Issues of security in a server environment include matters other than merely securing access to the server room. Providing security to both the server's immediate physical environment and to its related hardware is also high on the agenda. Providing a comprehensive security setting requires that network administrators have total control over their physical server environment. The administrator should have the responsibility of making the determination as to which personnel should have server room access.

To accomplish this, physical access to the servers must be strictly limited. Locks are usually installed on server room doors as well as on each individual server rack. This approach may even go so far as placing individual locks on each individual server chassis. In addition, alarms are often placed on servers, racks, and at various locations in the server room. Typical server security measures are illustrated in Figure 19.1.

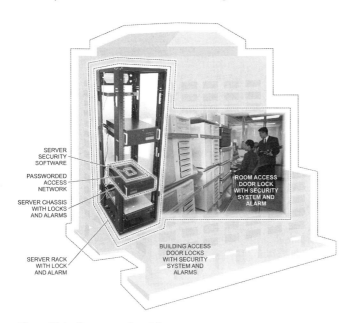

Figure 19.1 Server security points.

  Know the basic methods used to provide server security.

Evaluating server room security issues associated with physical equipment involves numerous items of interest, ranging from doors, server racks, server chassis, and KVM switches, to the danger of food and drinks left on the equipment. Whatever method is used to evaluate the security risks posed to the server room and its equipment, it's important to base that evaluation on the most imminent problem sources.

Various conditions and/or situations can pose potential threats to server room security. However, an unlocked server room door should always be considered as the most immediate threat for catastrophic server failure. Inside the server room, the further away you move from the door and toward the server chassis, the lower the threat from unlocked devices becomes. This is because a locked server room door prevents unauthorized personnel from even approaching, let alone accessing, the physical server equipment or any other unlocked devices.

Another area requiring strict control involves the presence of food or drink in the server room. There shouldn't be any! Accidents involving food and drink items risk causing severe damage to the company's network services, data, and equipment. Foodstuffs left in the server room can also attract rodents and other pests. They might decide to nibble on cables and equipment for dessert. One way to enforce this approach is to never permit a garbage can or waste receptacle to be placed in the server room. This helps discourage the bringing of food and drink items into the room. It also deters the possibility of tossing hard or soft data into a waste can without following proper disposal practices.

Controlled access can be activated and recorded by using a simple server room logbook for technicians and other employees to use. Make sure it contains columns for logging in and logging out and that it is used whenever anyone enters or leaves the server room.

Be able to identify the best type of physical access control for servers.

Backup Tape Access

The server administrator should also be concerned with limiting access to the backup tapes, whether they are stored in the server room or elsewhere. Often, backup tapes are stored in a separate room, which makes this room an important consideration in the overall physical security plan. Backup tapes usually contain all the valuable proprietary data that makes the company what it is. Anyone with access to those tapes can retrieve and misuse the company's privileged information. In addition to having doors with keylocks and/or password systems, rooms used to store the backup tapes should also use a sign-in/sign-out log to record and track the people entering and exiting.

Within the backup tape room itself, the tapes should be provided an extra level of protection such as being kept in a fireproof safe. In an ideal (and recommended) situation, two complete sets of backup tapes should be managed, one in the onsite safe, and the other at an offsite location. Fireproof safes are the most secure choices for the storage of backup tapes, for both the onsite and offsite locations. As an additional security measure, limit the number of employees who are informed where the backup tapes are stored, and are given access to the safe's key, or its unlocking combination.

Doors, Windows, and Locks

Administrators should ensure that physical locks exist on all doors to the rooms being used to house server equipment. The door to any server room should be of solid construction and capable of preventing anyone from gaining access without resorting to extraordinary measures. It should be lockable, preferably with a security pad that requires an entry code, key card, fingerprint ID, or other access control method to gain entrance. Its lock should also require a key, and the door must automatically lock whenever it closes. Inside button mechanisms that can be used to keep the door unlocked should not be used with server rooms. If the server room door is equipped with windows, they should be constructed from security glass embedded with wire designed to prevent access to the room by anyone deliberately breaking the glass.

Locks for Server Racks and Chassis

The server rack and the server chassis are the main lines of defense against the theft of physical server hardware components. In critical operations, the best practice is to spend a little more money to secure a rack cabinet with sensors capable of sending alert notifications whenever the rack cabinet is opened. The same notification system can also be configured to log these sensor signals for when and how long the rack cabinet door was open. The server's security system can also be configured to page and/or send related email notifications to network administrators or technicians.

Within the rack cabinet, each server chassis should also be equipped with locking front panels to prevent unauthorized access to the front panel controls and the server's drives, as shown in Figure 19.2. In addition, each server should have an intrusion alarm capable of sending an emergency page to the administrator when the server case or chassis is opened.

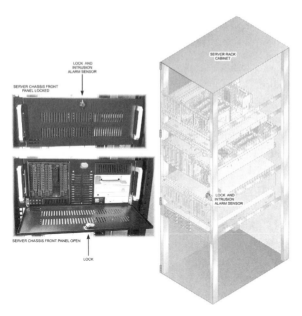

Figure 19.2 A locking chassis.

Be able to determine which physical security issue is most important in a server room.

Server Room Environmental Issues

Server+ Exam Objective 6.2 states that the test taker should be able to recognize and report on server room environmental issues, including

➤ Temperature

➤ Humidity

➤ ESD

➤ Power surges

➤ Backup generators

➤ Fire suppression

➤ Flood considerations

Environmental problems can be one of the most important areas of concern for server network administrators or service technicians. It's extremely important to carefully examine and evaluate the environmental conditions around the server room and the equipment on a daily basis. For example, the presence of dust on the equipment can indicate the intrusion of air sources other than those associated with the server room's access door. This dust translates to eventual equipment overheating. Discolored ceiling tiles can indicate the existence of some type of water leak, which can find its way into the server racks and cause network failure. Due to the potential server network equipment damage that environmental problems can cause, the administrator must ensure a speedy resolution to any problems that are discovered.

However, in most cases, the administrator or technician cannot personally do anything to immediately correct a threatening situation. Instead, the condition must be reported to the proper personnel for eventual resolution. The most important thing for the administrator to keep in mind is to whom reports concerning specific environmental issues should be directed. For example, if the server room loses power at the same time every day, this responsibility falls on the shoulders of maintenance personnel, or building owners. After those bearing direct responsibility for environmental issues in the building have been contacted, the administrator must ensure that all necessary actions to ensure the safety of server networking equipment are taken.

The designers of the CompTIA Server+ exam want to ensure that server technicians know whom to contact to effectively deal with any environmental problem. Searching for those responsible during an emergency wastes the company's money, and reveals a certain amount of negligence on the part of technicians or administrators.

Know whom to contact if the server room loses power at the same time every day.

Know the proper priorities for server environmental issues.

Table 19.1 includes several important server environmental issues that require attention, along with the specified personnel typically responsible for handling those types of problems.

Table 19.1 Environmental Issue Reporting	
Environmental Problem	**Personnel Typically Responsible**
Room at 110°F	Maintenance personnel or building superintendent
Drink left on top of server rack	System administrator
Garbage can in the room	System administrator
Power outages same time every day	Maintenance personnel or building superintendent
Water leak	Maintenance personnel or building superintendent
Missing filter on server room vent	Maintenance personnel
Unlocked server rack	System administrator

The term *environment* includes the server room, the servers, and all of the equipment surrounding them. A server network administrator must assume more responsibility than simply placing a computer in a server rack or on a desk and configuring it. They must also actively monitor and control the server room on a daily basis, perhaps even hourly. They must continually monitor everything from power and temperature, to personnel and procedures and quickly determine when environmental conditions are too far out of spec to be tolerated.

Know what environmental concerns are most critical for servers.

Temperature

Server equipment operates the most efficiently and effectively in a cooler room, rather than a hotter one. The cooler the server room is, the easier it is for chassis and rack fans to dissipate the heat generated by the components. The servers and their associated networks run under less stressful conditions when the processors are kept cool. The recommended operating temperatures of the processors being used in the servers should be common knowledge. If in doubt, consult the processor manufacturer's website. If these temperatures are exceeded, the server room environment should be carefully examined. This includes items directly affecting the chassis airflow, such as the location of the processor slots and the placement/design of the intake and exhaust vents. The size and style of the server chassis also have a major effect on airflow.

Know what can cause problems as far as the environment is concerned in the server room.

The temperature of the server room should be under the sole control of the system administrator. The authority to make adjustments to the air conditioning system, or to turn it on or off should not be granted to other personnel, such as the janitor or a guard. Inadvertently turning off the air conditioning can result in server room temperatures rising above 110°F, causing a server network crash. In a well-designed server installation, strategically located sensor alarms will initiate the necessary notifications to the system administrator through email messages, electronic paging, or highly audible signaling methods whenever server room temperatures push beyond their preset limits.

Humidity and Electrostatic Discharge

Although an ideal level of air conditioning helps to keep the server room and equipment chassis as cool as possible, it also provides the type of low humidity conditions that facilitate the gradual build-up of electrostatic charges. For this reason, the server room should also be reasonably humidified to reduce the likelihood of damaging electrostatic discharge (ESD) occurring. Remember that the human body can contain stored static voltages of up to 60,000 volts! This voltage is more than capable of damaging computer circuitry, in spite of the fact that ESD discharges result in currents of extremely low amperage.

Combining the use of a humidifier with the air conditioning system produces the exact opposite of the hot and dry conditions necessary for producing ESD and is the ideal solution to these twin server room environmental concerns. On the other hand, as important as it is for the server system administrators to maintain the server room in relatively cool and humid conditions, the humidity must not be allowed to reach the point where the servers build up condensation. Conditions should be kept just humid enough to prevent ESD.

Know what causes electrostatic discharge (ESD).

Dust facilitates electrical arcing and is another contributor to ESD. Therefore, a filtered air system is an important consideration in the prevention of electrical arcing around the server equipment. Dust also forms an insulating blanket on electrical circuits, causing them to overheat. Suitable airflow filters should be placed at various points in the air conditioning system to remove dust and other small particles from the server environment.

Fire Suppression

Fire suppression is another important consideration in server rooms due to the presence of so much sensitive electrical or electronic equipment. If a fire occurs in the server room, the idea of using water to extinguish it cannot be considered! Instead, every server room should be equipped with registered Class C (carbon dioxide) fire extinguishers. Carbon dioxide is recognized as the preferred fire-extinguishing medium for electrical fires by the National Fire Protection Association (NFPA) and by fire departments across the nation. Even if a server room fire is nonelectrical in nature, the preferred extinguishing medium would still be CO_2 rather than water. All personnel having access to the server room must know where these devices are located and be thoroughly trained in using them.

Flood Considerations

The susceptibility of electronic server equipment to water is a critical environmental consideration because a negative encounter with a water problem can shut down an entire enterprise. The idea of flooding usually conjures up thoughts of large rivers running over their banks and raging through homes and buildings. Although this is certainly one aspect of flooding to be concerned with, it can be successfully managed through the wise choice of where to set up business-related server operations. Other sources of flooding must also be considered in server environments. For example, a broken water pipe can flood an office or building located far from a flood plain. An improperly energized fire-suppression sprinkler system can also flood a server room.

The cost of completely protecting a server installation from the dangers of flooding is not economically feasible for most businesses. However, there are two precautions that can be taken to minimize the effects that flooding can have on server operations whether located in a flood plain, or elsewhere.

➤ Keep server operations out of basement areas and preferably on the higher levels of the building.

➤ Keep a set of backup tapes offsite and in a safe environment.

Exam Prep Questions

1. ESD is not caused by which of the following conditions?
   - ❏ A. Improper or non-existent grounding
   - ❏ B. Moderate to high humidity
   - ❏ C. People moving around
   - ❏ D. Unshielded cabling

2. When considering physical security for server rooms, which issue is the most important?
   - ❏ A. The installation of antitheft alarms
   - ❏ B. The monitoring of server room access
   - ❏ C. Keeping the server room door locked
   - ❏ D. Using sufficient complexity for all passwords

3. When considering server room security, which of the following considerations is least important?
   - ❏ A. Extreme temperatures
   - ❏ B. Faulty fire suppression system
   - ❏ C. Rodents
   - ❏ D. Environmental noise generation

4. Which of the following server room environmental problems would an administrator consider to be the most important?
   - ❏ A. Server cabinet doors kept unlocked
   - ❏ B. Spare parts being stored on the server room floor
   - ❏ C. Several trash cans located in the server room
   - ❏ D. Coffee cups sitting on top of the server rack

5. In an effort to rank various security issues being faced by the company, which one of the following concerns was considered to be least important to the administrator?
   - ❏ A. The absence of locks on the server chassis
   - ❏ B. The absence of locks on the server monitor
   - ❏ C. The absence of locks on the server racks
   - ❏ D. The absence of a lock on the server room door

6. When a severe environmental threat has been identified in the server room, what must the administrator now do?
   - ❏ A. Transfer all servers and associated equipment to another location.
   - ❏ B. Recognize that this is not an administration problem and wait for maintenance personnel to solve it.
   - ❏ C. Report the condition to the maintenance personnel or building superintendent for resolution.
   - ❏ D. Try to resolve the problem personally, although it is not considered a server administration responsibility.

7. When the server room vent is found to have a missing filter, which of the following company employees should the server system administrator contact?

❏ A. The maintenance personnel
❏ B. The immediate supervisor
❏ C. The safety inspector
❏ D. The building superintendent

8. From a security standpoint, which one of the following issues would be considered the most critical?

❏ A. Unclean floors
❏ B. Water cups on server equipment
❏ C. Air conditioning without proper venting
❏ D. Unlocked server cases and/or server room door(s)

9. Which of the following server room situations is of no environmental concern?

❏ A. Filters missing on vents
❏ B. Drinks near the server
❏ C. Low server room temperatures
❏ D. Warm server room temperatures

10. Which of the following environmental situations would be critical for a server room?

❏ A. Having a clean server room
❏ B. Server room temperatures above 110° F
❏ C. Having a cool server room
❏ D. Not having a garbage can in the server room

11. If the server room suffers a power outage each day at the same time, who is the first person that should be contacted?

❏ A. The maintenance personnel or building superintendent
❏ B. The computer technician(s)
❏ C. The system administrator
❏ D. The immediate supervisor

12. In order to decrease the risk of ESD, what would be the best possible server room conditions?

❏ A. Dry and hot
❏ B. Dry and humid
❏ C. Dry and cool
❏ D. Cool and humid

13. The server room is equipped with locks on the server room door, locks on the server rack, locks on the server chassis, and installed server security software. What additional server security measure should be provided?
    - ❏ A. Locks on server hard drives
    - ❏ B. Network access passwords
    - ❏ C. Network monitors
    - ❏ D. Locks on the server monitor

14. A server running security software with passwords is located in a server room fitted with door locks and rack locks. Which additional server security measures could be provided?
    - ❏ A. Server chassis locks
    - ❏ B. Server hard drive locks
    - ❏ C. Network monitors
    - ❏ D. Server monitor locks

15. In addition to placing alarms on the server machines, racks, and rooms, which of the following physical security measures would provide the best server security?
    - ❏ A. Locks on the server chassis, the server keyboard, and the monitors
    - ❏ B. Locks on the server chassis, the server rack, and on the server room door
    - ❏ C. Locks on the server room door, the server rack, and the server monitor
    - ❏ D. Locks on the server rack and the server chassis

16. The server room environment is severely endangered by which of the following situations?
    - ❏ A. Air filters missing from the HVAC vents
    - ❏ B. Dust accumulation in the corners of the server room
    - ❏ C. Active sprinklers located in the ceiling above the server
    - ❏ D. Bare concrete floors under the server racks

17. Information about recommended processor operating temperatures can be found at which of the following locations?
    - ❏ A. The computer company's hotline headquarters
    - ❏ B. The driver manufacturer's website
    - ❏ C. The computer company's website
    - ❏ D. The processor manufacturer's website

18. Server chassis airflow is not affected by which of the following factors?

☐ A. The location of the processor slots or sockets

☐ B. The speed of the microprocessor(s)

☐ C. The size and style of the server chassis

☐ D. The design and placement of intake and exhaust vents

19. Evidence that the server loses power nearly 10 minutes every Tuesday at the exact same time has been located in the UPS log files. Which of the following personnel should be notified about this situation?

☐ A. IS helpdesk personnel

☐ B. Building maintenance supervisor

☐ C. NOS technical support

☐ D. IT manager or administrator

20. What is the purpose for using a sniffer program?

☐ A. A sniffer permits the hacker to intercept and analyze data packets being transmitted over a server network.

☐ B. A sniffer permits the testing of a server workload. If problems occur, the sniffer alerts the administrator.

☐ C. A sniffer locates server network bottlenecks through various testing procedures.

☐ D. A sniffer is used to intercept only Novell data packets as they are transmitted over a server network.

Exam Prep Answers

1. Answer B is the correct answer. It is nearly impossible for ESD buildups to occur under highly humid conditions. Answer A is incorrect because improper grounding permits electrostatic charges to build up across various circuits and equipment types. Answer C is incorrect because the movement of people generates large quantities of static electricity. Answer D is incorrect because unshielded cables can prove susceptible to inductive and radiated coupling.

2. Answer C is the correct answer. The most important physical security issue for a server room is to keep the server room door locked. Answer A is incorrect because a company can be severely damaged by an intruder who steals nothing. Answer B is incorrect because monitoring an intrusion cannot immediately prevent whatever damage is being, or has already been, inflicted. Answer D is incorrect because whatever password protection the server room may have would be immediately compromised by an unlocked server room door.

3. Answer D is the correct answer. Although noise is a legitimate environmental concern, it is the one least likely to worry an administrator responsible for server room security. Answer A is incorrect because in a server environment, extremely high temperatures are considered a dangerous situation. Answer B is incorrect because major server room damage can occur through fire suppression equipment that is activated erroneously. Answer C is incorrect because severe problems can occur when rodents are permitted to chew through network cabling.

4. Answer A is the correct answer. The most immediate threat listed is the practice of keeping the server cabinet doors unlocked. Under these conditions, any number of negative scenarios could result in catastrophic system failure. Answer B is incorrect because the idea of storing spare parts on the floor of the server room doesn't sound good, but it's not the most important of the problems listed. Answer C is also incorrect only because an unlocked server room door is a more important concern. Answer D is incorrect although this problem also deserves attention. One coffee spill could destroy the target server.

5. Answer B is the correct answer. If other doors and cabinets are properly locked, keeping a server monitor unlocked will not endanger the server system. Answer A is incorrect because not having locks on a server chassis is an important security oversight. Answer C is incorrect because lockable server racks are pivotal in protecting from unauthorized entry. Answer D is incorrect because a lockable server room door is the most important security consideration.

6. Answer C is the correct answer. When an environmental problem is identified, even though it may be located in the server room, the situation must be reported to those personnel responsible for resolving it. Answer A is incorrect because it represents an impossible short-term task, especially for a large organization. Answer B is incorrect because ignoring the problem is not acceptable administrator behavior. Answer D is incorrect because tackling a job for which the administrator is not responsible may alienate managers and maintenance personnel.

7. Answer A is the correct answer. Maintenance personnel are typically responsible for such problems as missing filters from server room vents. Answer B is incorrect because it's certain that the server administrator's immediate supervisor will not be responsible for HVAC duties. Answer C is incorrect because the safety inspector will only verify what the administrator already knows. Answer D is incorrect because the building superintendent will, in all likelihood, not personally respond to this situation.

8. Answer D is the correct answer. Having unlocked server cases or server room doors is the most important security issue listed. Answer A is incorrect, although unclean floors can lead to other security concerns. Answer B is incorrect even though such a situation must be addressed at some point. Answer C is incorrect because the venting situation is not critical, but it is correctable and should be dealt with.

9. Answer C is the correct answer. Because of the damaging effects of heat, the server room and its components should be kept as cool as reasonably possible. Answer A is incorrect because keeping the server room dust-free is an important environmental consideration. The missing filter on the server room vent should be replaced as quickly as possible. Answer B is incorrect because having drinks anywhere near the server rack is a security violation. Answer D is incorrect because a warm server room would be immediate cause for the notification of the maintenance personnel.

10. Answer B is the correct answer. Server networks are highly susceptible to crashes at temperatures above 110°F. Answer A is incorrect because having a clean server room is always a good thing. Answer C is incorrect because having a cool server reduces the possibility of failures due to overheating. Answer D is incorrect because keeping garbage cans out of the server room is an important preventive measure. Personnel are discouraged from bringing in disallowed foodstuffs.

11. Answer A is the correct answer. Daily power losses at identical times are problems for which the maintenance personnel or the building superintendent are responsible. Answer B is incorrect because a computer technician cannot service an unpowered server. Answer C is incorrect because deciding on who should be contacted is the system administrator's responsibility. Answer D is incorrect because the immediate supervisor does not have the expertise or the authority to solve the problem.

12. Answer D is the correct answer. In order to keep the risk of ESD to a minimum, the server room should be kept cool and reasonably humidified. Answer A is incorrect because the optimal conditions for producing ESD are hot and dry. Answer B is incorrect because it is impossible to maintain dry and humid conditions simultaneously. Answer C is incorrect because even in a cool environment, dryness can still promote conditions suitable for ESD.

13. Answer B is the correct answer. The server already has security software installed. To use it properly, clients must be assigned passwords in order to log on to the network successfully. Answer A is incorrect because hard drive locks do not provide clients with the passwords they need to access the system. Answer C is incorrect because a network monitor does not help clients use the network. Answer D is incorrect because locking a server monitor does not help users to navigate the password protection being used by the server security software.

14. Answer A is the correct answer. The addition of individual server chassis locks would complete the security picture. Answer B is incorrect because it does not appreciably add to the existing server security. Answer C is incorrect because network monitors do not provide any additional security. Answer D is incorrect because locking the server monitor simply adds a security layer that is unneeded at this point.

15. Answer B is the correct answer. To provide hardware security, companies often install locks on the doors of the server rooms as well as on each individual server rack. They may also lock each server chassis. Answers A and C are incorrect because locking a monitor provides minimum security. Answer D is incorrect because it doesn't mention the server room door.

16. Answer C is the correct answer. If the sprinklers were accidentally activated, the server equipment would be ruined. Answer A is incorrect because a missing air filter will not severely endanger the server room environment, although it will limit the amount of dust filtering available. Answer B is incorrect because dust accumulation can become a hazard if permitted to grow unchecked, but it is not nearly as hazardous as the sprinkler situation. Answer D is incorrect because antistatic mats or flooring materials can be placed beneath the racks to provide insulation against electrostatic discharge.

17. Answer D is the correct answer. Recommended processor operating temperature information can be obtained from the manufacturer's website if its product brochure does not provide it. Answer B is incorrect because driver manufacturers are not concerned with processor parameters and are not set up to disseminate microprocessor data. Answer C is incorrect because the manufacturer of the computer would be more interested in providing server board, power supply, and server case data than processor details.

18. Answer B is the correct answer. As far as the airflow patterns across the server board and/or its associated components, the processor speed is irrelevant. Answer A is incorrect because the location of the processor will affect the chassis airflow, especially with regard to the placement of the processor fan. Answer C is incorrect because the

design of the server chassis will dictate the areas prone to heat buildup. Answer D is incorrect because the design and placement of air vents would directly affect the chassis airflow parameters.

19. Answer D is the correct answer. The IT manager or administrator, if one is available, is responsible for dealing with infrastructure support agencies such as the building maintenance supervisor, the power company, or the UPS manufacturer. Answer A is incorrect because help desk personnel specialize in providing help to clients in the use of the network or its tools, not in troubleshooting the problems of the network itself. Answer B is incorrect unless the position of IT manager does not exist at the company. Answer C is incorrect because the problem of power loss is not the responsibility of the NOS technical staff.

20. Answer A is the correct answer. Used for browsing through raw network data, sniffers permit hackers to decipher network contents and passwords. Answer B is incorrect because sniffer users do not want to contact the administrator for any reason. They do not even want the administrator to know they are there. Answer C is incorrect because a sniffer is not a network-testing tool. Answer D is incorrect, mainly because sniffers are not limited to use on Novell data packets.

20.0—Server Problem Determination

Terms you'll need to understand:

- ✓ Problem escalation
- ✓ Setup, startup, and operational problems
- ✓ Preventive maintenance
- ✓ Power-On Self-Test (POST) cards
- ✓ Basic and extended diagnostics
- ✓ Forced start
- ✓ Time Domain Reflectometers (TDRs)
- ✓ Optical Time Domain Reflectometers (OTDRs)
- ✓ Internet Control Message Protocol (ICMP)
- ✓ Wake-on-LAN
- ✓ Magic packet
- ✓ Hot, warm, and cold swapping

Techniques you'll need to master:

- ✓ Troubleshooting equipment failures
- ✓ Determining whether a problem is hardware- or software-related
- ✓ Identifying contact(s) responsible for problem resolution
- ✓ Using your senses to observe a problem
- ✓ Handling problem escalations
- ✓ Using server-related documentation
- ✓ Correcting improper upgrades
- ✓ Diagnosing and repairing server problems
- ✓ Observing problem indicators
- ✓ Examining the startup process
- ✓ Resolving hardware and software configuration problems
- ✓ Recognizing OS failures
- ✓ Using diagnostic tools and utilities
- ✓ Examining local network software
- ✓ Solving Wake-on-LAN problems
- ✓ Troubleshooting servers with FRUs

Introduction

Server+ Exam Objective 7.1 states that the test taker should be able to perform problem determinations. Activities associated with this objective include isolating a problem, for example:

➤ Determining whether the problem is hardware- or software-related

➤ Using questioning techniques to determine what, how, and when

➤ Identifying contact(s) responsible for problem resolution

➤ Using senses to observe problems such as the smell of smoke, unhooked cable, and so on

➤ Bringing it down to base

➤ Removing one component at a time

Troubleshooting equipment failures involves the application of a logical sequence of steps, leading to various possible paths. Most failures in electronic equipment are the result of a simple equipment problem or improper equipment settings. Careful observation, deductive reasoning, and an organized problem-solving approach usually lead to a successful troubleshooting experience.

An effective troubleshooting approach combines knowledge about correct equipment operations, good testing techniques, deductive reasoning skills, and proper documentation of the entire process. A general procedure for troubleshooting server-based equipment includes the following:

➤ Use valid questioning techniques during initial troubleshooting

➤ Identify the personnel responsible for specific problem resolutions

➤ Identify and refer to appropriate sources of technical documentation

➤ Observe the startup and operation of the system, when possible

➤ Use your senses to observe physical problem indicators

➤ Test the server system to determine its problem types

➤ Interpret error logs, operating system errors, health logs, and critical events

Information Gathering

The first step in the evaluation process is to interface with the personnel who are directly involved with the system problem.

Talk directly to the employee or client who originally reported the problem. During this discussion, important clues as to the origin of the problem can be gathered, because part of the troubleshooting process is to determine whether this user could be the problem source. Employ questioning techniques designed to identify the conditions under which the problem first appeared. Listen carefully to see if you can eliminate this person as a possible cause of the problem. He or she might have attempted to do something beyond the system's capabilities, or there might be a misunderstanding about how a specific aspect of the system functions.

Also collect information from other nearby employees. Determine whether other symptoms or error codes have been produced by the server board that could be used as troubleshooting clues. Try to determine the situations that existed just prior to the current failure.

Make a detailed, step-by-step review of any procedures that were recently performed on the system. If such procedures pose no additional risk of system damage, it might be helpful to repeat the procedure while observing the steps taken and their associated results. Gain an appropriate understanding of the suspect procedure along with the results it is designed to produce.

Handling Problem Escalations

Troubleshooting a specific problem often involves making an accurate determination as to which support personnel must be contacted. Server system environments often require the cooperation of various individuals who exercise jurisdiction over different operational areas. To identify the individuals qualified for resolving a specific problem, the primary responsibilities for each of these individuals must be thoroughly understood. You need to understand not only the core functions of a technician, the network administrator, and the IT administrator, but also where these functions overlap as well as the limits of their expertise. Problems that lie outside the immediate responsibilities of server network personnel must be referred to the proper individuals as well.

The troubleshooting technician, must determine the appropriate employees required to resolve the suspected problem after consulting with the operator or administrator and evaluating the primary characteristics of the problem. Common professional titles along with their associated responsibilities include

➤ Computer Technician—Hardware failures

➤ Network Administrator—Network configurations

➤ Help Desk—Simple operating system problems

➤ IT Administrator—Overall network and computer operations

➤ Landlord—Building maintenance and repair

Be aware that you might be included among the individuals associated with the area of the system experiencing the problem.

 Be able to troubleshoot problems that may have been caused by external sources, such as air conditioning and power availability problems.

A situation might occur that exceeds or lies outside of the expertise and job responsibilities of a given individual. When this occurs, it is vitally important to be able to quickly locate an individual in the company who is qualified to handle the problem. This activity is called *problem escalation* and results in the accurate referral of the problem to a person with the knowledge and responsibility to resolve it. The ability to quickly determine a person's depth of expertise is necessary to avoid a waste of time and effort in solving the immediate problem. Familiarity with various individuals and their assigned responsibilities will ease the burden of problem escalation when it inevitably occurs.

 From a given job level, know to whom problems should be referred when they exceed personal levels of expertise, or those of other employees.

Using Server-Related Documentation

After information about the problem has been gathered, the troubleshooting sequence next includes a careful review of the server system's documentation. Recall that this documentation contains the following information:

➤ Initial baseline data—The initial baseline that was recorded after the system's original setup and configuration should include no-load baseline performance data, baseline data under network load, and the initial performance-tuning data.

➤ Disaster recovery plan—The *disaster recovery plan* (sometimes referred to as a DR plan or DRP for short) should include a complete inventory of the components of each server and workstation in the system, and all associated software. It outlines the procedures for keeping each department functioning during network downtimes as well as data synchronization routines for network restorations.

➤ Baseline and upgrade documentation—Each system upgrade should also be documented. The details should include vendor and installation documentation associated with system maintenance, new or upgraded devices, system and peripheral BIOS upgrades, device drivers, Internet links to resource data and vendor websites, and upgrade performance baselines.

➤ Server equipment documentation—Server manufacturers publish specific procedures for troubleshooting their equipment. These policies and procedures include the manufacturer's repair policy, component-swapping procedures, and the procedures for reinitiating the system.

➤ Software and driver verifications—One major consideration in the successful use of hardware and software documentation is the verification that the latest versions are on hand, including those of any support software, and drivers, usually available from the vendor or manufacturing website.

The documentation package should also include logs indicating all activities conducted on the system, the personnel involved, and what operations occurred. Logs detailing the *preventive maintenance (PM)* that has been performed on the system should also be available. PM information includes the day and time the service was performed, routines performed, the associated conditions, and the ending outcomes. Server room in/out logs help to determine who accessed the server and when they accessed it. This information is useful when identifying the employees to be consulted.

The size and complexity of the organization determine the volume and type of the server documentation. Larger organizations might also include shift logs, maintenance logs, and guard duty logs as a part of their server room documentation.

Ongoing Documentation

It should be obvious that after the current troubleshooting scenario has resulted in a successful repair of the server network, ongoing documentation will be necessary. Time must always be taken to document every upgrade and/or problem, including all performance tests and their outcomes. In most organizations, routine documentation of server work is a requirement rather than a suggestion. Human memory is not a reliable documentation alternative, especially during stressful situations such as server downtime.

If a similar failure should occur in the future, the current documentation of tests and results will aid the next technician to find the cause of the problem. Accurately recorded information helps to prevent the need for taking repetitive, time-wasting steps, especially when more detailed tests or measurements are necessary.

Documenting Improper Upgrades or Configurations

Sometimes, in spite of your efforts to correctly prepare and implement an effective upgrade plan, improper upgrades or configuration modifications will occur. Although a well-documented plan usually precludes an improper upgrade, when something goes wrong, the upgrade plan also serves as a critical recovery element. A careful study of the plan should help to determine where to start the troubleshooting process to correct the associated problem(s).

Serious system problems can occur during the application of patches or updates to a server. During your interview with the system operator, find out if the system has recently undergone an update or system patch. It is a well-known fact that malfunctions can occur even in non-associated portions of the system as a result of the installation of system patches. This is the main reason why NOS updates or patches are recommended only when the NOS is not operating sufficiently for the application, and the update or patch is targeted to resolve the specific problem. The only other acceptable reason to apply an update is to resolve a critical security issue.

When a system upgrade is performed and a problem suddenly arises, an activity or component associated with the upgrade is most likely the cause. Try to pinpoint a specific procedure that was performed just before the problem arose, referring to the server's documentation if necessary. That procedure will most likely be the source of the problem. When operator error cannot be identified as the cause of the problem, focus on the system hardware involved and on the software being used.

System Evaluations

Attempts to start and test the system are also important aspects of the initial information-gathering process as you diagnose and repair problems associated with server equipment. An administrator can perform these actions on his or her own authority. A server technician can have the administrator or operator demonstrate. Carefully observe the system and document the results throughout this demonstration process. Combine your personal knowledgebase of system-specific information with the events that occur. As you evaluate a typical system, implement steps such as the following:

➤ Observe the startup of the system. Use your senses to look, listen, and smell for indications of physical problems, such as smoke, unusual noises, or disconnected cables that could explain a physical problem situation.

➤ Identify the problem as either hardware- or software-related. If the system is operational, test it thoroughly to determine whether the system's hardware or software is at fault. Also determine whether the problem is strictly a configuration issue, a component failure, or a combination of both.

➤ Ensure that the problem is not associated with a computer virus or other result of a malicious act of sabotage. Always be familiar with currently circulating viruses that could adversely affect the server. When a virus or other malicious code is discovered, take the appropriate steps to remove it and prevent its reintroduction into the system.

Be aware that additional problems unassociated with the current situation being investigated but potentially capable of causing future system failure might be discovered during the problem investigative process. If these additional discoveries are not causing current problems, document the situation and plan for a future fix. At this point, the most important task is to not change anything that might further aggravate or complicate the current troubleshooting mission. After the newly discovered situation is properly documented, resolve the current problem. The newly discovered problem can then be dealt with, or deferred for resolution during the next scheduled periodic maintenance or system shutdown.

Observing Problem Indicators

Be especially attentive during the startup process. Physical problems such as smoke, odors, unusual noises, and disconnected cables should be fairly easy to detect. Use your physical senses to

➤ Perform a visual inspection. If you are unfamiliar with the type of malfunction exhibited, conduct a careful visual inspection of the system, beginning with the outside. First, look for loose or disconnected cables or other connections and carefully observe the external front-panel lights. If no lights are displayed, check the power outlet, plugs, and power cords. All system power switches should also be examined to confirm their functionality, including the commercial power distribution system's fuses or circuit breakers.

➤ Listen to the system. Mechanical server components make various noises when they are failing. Power supplies and disk drives produce whining noises when their bearings begin to wear or dry out. Read/write heads striking the sides of their enclosure produce clicking or clunking noises as disk drives lose track of their logical geometries. Video cards, monitors, and modems produce high-pitched whines or squeals when they are misconfigured or their internal components begin to fail.

➤ Check for odors associated with the equipment. Failing electronic components often produce distinctive odors that tell technicians that a failure is occurring. In particular, check for the smell of overheating components.

Know which components make noise when they are failing and what types of noises they typically create.

Examining the Startup Process

A careful examination of the startup process can reveal a great deal about problems in a server system. Many possibilities can be either included or excluded by paying close attention during the bootup process. The following events should be observed, in order, during the cold boot of a working server system or a new system being powered up for the first time.

1. When power is applied, the power-supply fan activates.

2. The keyboard lights flash as the remaining system components are reset.

3. A BIOS message displays on the monitor.

4. A memory test flickers on the monitor.

5. The floppy disk drive access light comes on briefly.

6. The RAID controller BIOS information is displayed on screen briefly, if applicable.

7. If there is an IDE hard drive, its access light will come on briefly.

8. The system beeps, indicating that it has completed its power-on self-tests and the initialization process.

9. At this point, the operating system starts to boot up.

The floppy disk and/or CD-ROM drive access lights will come on briefly only if the CMOS is configured to check them during the boot process. At this point in the procedure, the BIOS is looking for additional instructions (boot information), first from the floppy drive, then the CD-ROM, and finally from the hard drive. It begins booting from the RAID array, or from the HDD, depending on how the server is set up.

In a defective server, some of these events, or possibly all, will not occur. By observing which step(s) fail and knowing which sections of the computer are involved in each step, the administrator can identify the problem area. If the system does not advance beyond a certain step, the component(s) involved in that step will be the first suspected.

For example, suppose that the server never makes it to step 2 after you've noticed the power-supply fan turning in step 1. The monitor will remain blank because the BIOS message is not displayed until step 3. There is no reason to suspect anything mentioned in the remaining steps as being wrong because something prior to the keyboard check is hanging the system. The one component called on to get us to step 2 is the processor. The server board's user manual will contain a section that details the various voltage settings and speed settings that can be adjusted through the use of jumpers. If these settings do not match the type and speed of the CPU being used, the server board will not function properly. Suppose a system failure occurs after step 3, but before the memory test in step 4 begins. At this point, a technician would not suspect a bad or failed floppy disk drive, because the floppy drive is not tested until after the memory test is completed.

By observing the number of listed steps completed by the system, you can eliminate various components as a possible cause depending on when the failure occurs. All components prior to the failure can be ignored as suspects. Subsystems associated with the successfully completed steps are probably working properly. Components that have yet to be successfully tested should receive attention, as should those directly associated with the exhibited symptoms.

Keep in mind that between steps 7 and 8, a server with a mixture of ATA and SCSI internal hard drives only reports the existence of the ATA drives during the power-on self-test (POST). However, the SCSI and RAID controllers are also mounted during the POST while the ATA drives are mounted. The respective controllers mount their individual disk drive volumes later.

After a suspect element has been located, and the problem resolution has been performed, you should document all actions taken. Then, the system should be rebooted to determine whether the system exhibits a problem at the same step as before. If it does, further investigation of the same element and/or its associated components is required. If the system fails at a later point in the boot process, resolve the associated problem by focusing the diagnosis on the current symptom exhibited. Eventually, the system should boot up without exhibiting errors because the system's boot problems will have been resolved. This systematic approach to troubleshooting and documenting the results is the strongest tool for resolving other server problems as well.

Resolving Hardware/Software/Configuration Problems

A functional server system is composed of two major elements, the system's hardware and its controlling software. Determining which element is the cause of a given problem is difficult because they are so closely related. Early server troubleshooting must determine whether the problem is due to a software glitch or a hardware failure.

Critical settings between hardware, software operating systems, and applications must accurately reflect the hardware installation. Configuration errors usually occur when the system is new or when new hardware or software is installed. An exception is when configuration information becomes corrupted through the occurrence of power surges, outages, improper system shutdowns, or computer viruses. Symptoms caused by computer viruses can often be confusing, and differ widely according to the type of damage they have been designed to inflict.

As mentioned previously, early indications of hardware-related problems can be observed during the system's boot process, when errors occur either before the audible beep following the POST, or prior to the OS booting up. Until then, only the BIOS and the basic system hardware are activated. After the beep, the OS and its accompanying support software are loaded. These pre-beep errors are grouped into two distinct categories, configuration errors and hardware errors, which are described in the following sections.

Configuration Errors

Configuration errors show up on first use of a new system or a new hardware option. Mismatches between the equipment installed and the programmed CMOS configuration are usually to blame. CMOS configuration settings can also disagree with the installed hardware's jumper or switch settings. You need to run the server's CMOS setup utility

➤ When the system is first constructed

➤ When the CMOS backup battery must be replaced

➤ When a new or different option is added to the system

Be prepared for configuration errors to occur whenever new hardware or software options are being installed. Although the addition of a hard drive, network card, or video display might require that the setup utility program be run on older servers or hardware, newer servers equipped with plug-and-play (PnP) capabilities often do not need to run the setup utility program.

Most modern server system BIOS and NOS programs employ PnP technology to detect newly installed hardware and automatically allocate the required system resources. However, in certain situations the PnP logic cannot resolve all of the system's resource requirements, and configuration errors can occur. These configuration problems might have to be resolved manually.

Configuration problems can also occur when certain application packages are first installed. Various parameters must be set by the administrator and established through the startup software in the ROM BIOS to match the program's capabilities with the actual system configuration. Setting these configuration parameters incorrectly can prevent the software from ever using the system's hardware properly, and corresponding errors will occur.

Peripheral hardware such as printers and scanners, usually contain some type of built-in self-diagnostics that produce coded error messages to identify the specific problem the device is experiencing. These error code messages are usually defined and explained in the device's user manual, along with information about what might cause the error code. Instructions for conducting specific tests to further isolate a specific problem might be given, along with various ways to remedy the situation. You can usually avoid troubling encounters with configuration errors by carefully following the manufacturer's installation instructions.

BIOS manufacturers also produce products that include proprietary error messages and beep codes. Some messages are fairly easy to interpret and relate to a specific problem, whereas others are cryptic in nature and require further clarification. The server board's installation or user's guide can help identify the specific error being reported. However, BIOS or server board manufacturers' websites are still the best place to verify the meaning or definition of a particular error message or beep code.

Be aware of the best places to check for information about error messages or beep codes.

Hardware Failures

When you are unable to locate a configuration problem during your troubleshooting efforts, a defective component is the most likely culprit. The most widely used method of hardware problem verification is to substitute a known good component (a field-replaceable unit or FRU for short) for the suspected bad one. Known as *FRU troubleshooting*, this process gets a bad component out of the system quickly. The use of hot-swap technology often permits the replacement without accumulating any server downtime.

Alternatives for isolating and correcting a hardware failure that manifests itself prior to system bootup depends on how much of the system remains operable. These alternatives include running a diagnostic program to rigorously test the system's components and using a POST diagnostic card to track down problems by reporting specific error codes. The diagnostic system software packages require that certain major blocks of the system be up and running. When not enough of the system is running to support other diagnostic tools, you can plug a POST card into one of the system's expansion slots and read the data moving through the various buses to help determine where the problems lie. Refer to "Using Diagnostic Tools and Utilities" later in this chapter.

Software Problems

After the POST beep sounds, the system locates and loads the operating system. Errors that occur between this beep and presentation of the operating system's user interface, such as the command prompt or GUI, generally have three possible causes:

➤ Hardware failure, such as a physical problem with the boot drive

➤ Corrupted or missing boot files

➤ Corrupted or missing operating system files

Server operating systems consist of large collections of complex programming code, which combine to control every primary operation of the server computer. The OS is required to perform basic tasks such as recognizing input from the keyboard, sending output to the display screen, keeping track of files and directories on the disk, and controlling peripheral disk drive and printer devices. Server operating systems are much more complex than those developed for use on desktop PCs or workstations. As with anything this complex, server operating systems will fail from time to time. Although there are potentially millions of problems that can occur within these complex software systems, the problems can be grouped into three basic areas. If you can isolate a particular software problem to one of these areas, the troubleshooting process becomes less complex:

➤ *Setup problems* occur during installation or upgrading. They typically involve the failure to successfully complete an original OS installation or upgrade operation. Setup problems that occur while upgrading the operating system can leave the system stranded between the older OS version and the upgraded one, which usually results in an unusable server system.

➤ *Startup problems* occur when the system is booting up. They usually produce conditions that prevent the system hardware and software from initializing or operating correctly. You can usually avoid these problems by buying and using only validated components during the server construction. However, startup problems can still occur in spite of making every effort in the selection of the components. These problems can usually be divided into two major groups:

➤ Hardware configuration problems

➤ OS bootup problems

➤ *Operational problems* occur during the normal course of operations after the system has booted up and is running. These problems can be divided into three main categories:

➤ Those that occur when performing normal application and file operations

➤ Those that occur when printing

➤ Those that occur when performing network functions

Using Diagnostic Tools and Utilities

Server+ Exam Objective 7.2 states that the test taker should be able to use diagnostic hardware tools and utilities. Activities associated with this objective include

➤ Perform shutdowns across the Microsoft Windows NT/2000/2003, Novell NetWare, UNIX, and Linux OSes

➤ Select the appropriate tool

➤ Use the selected tool effectively

➤ Replace defective hardware components as appropriate

➤ Identify defective FRUs and replace with correct part

➤ Interpret error logs, operating system errors, health logs, and critical events

➤ Successfully use documentation from previous technicians

➤ Locate and effectively use hot tips such as fixes, OS updates, E-support, web pages, CDs, and so on

➤ Gather resources to help solve the problem:

    ➤ Identify situations requiring a call for assistance

    ➤ Acquire appropriate documentation

To achieve this objective, you need to know and understand the following:

➤ Common diagnostic tools:

    ➤ PING

    ➤ IPCONFIG

    ➤ TRACEROUTE

    ➤ FDISK

    ➤ Basic hard disk tools

    ➤ TELNET

➤ NOS shutdown procedures:

    ➤ Novell NetWare

    ➤ Microsoft Windows NT/2000/2003

    ➤ UNIX/Linux

➤ Importance and use of documentation such as maintenance logs and service logs

Server administrators and technicians understand that they must find and resolve system problems quickly. The cost of downtime to a networked corporation is staggering. Fortunately, specific diagnostic tools are available that provide warnings as soon as server problems begin to develop. Rather than experiencing unscheduled system failures, these tools make it possible to address many server problems at regularly scheduled downtimes, helping to eliminate work-loss time. In the event that a server does fail, alternate tools have been created to help diagnose the problem and quickly return the system to service. These diagnostic tools are separated into hardware and software categories.

Hardware Diagnostic Tools

Hardware diagnostic tools often physically connect directly to the server or are used on the repair bench to run tests on suspected components. The following section explains how to use two different types of hardware diagnostic tools: POST cards and cable testers.

Using POST Cards

Because BIOS program chips do not contain an extensive set of onboard diagnostics, manufacturers have developed power-on self-test (POST) cards to assist in hardware troubleshooting of the server board. A *POST card* is a diagnostic expansion card that plugs into one of the board's expansion slots and is capable of testing the operation of the server system as it boots up. POST cards can be as simple as interrupt and DMA channel monitors, or as complex as full-fledged ROM BIOS diagnostic packages that carry out extensive system tests. They run on systems that appear dead or are incapable of reading from either a floppy or hard drive. The normal BIOS functions of the motherboard are replaced by firmware tests on the card. Various tests are carried out without the system having to use software diagnostics located on an inaccessible hard disk or floppy drive.

POST cards conduct tests similar to those performed by the server board's BIOS, in addition to more advanced routines. They report either fatal or nonfatal errors. Fatal errors cause the POST to discontinue any further system functions, and the card displays an error code that corresponds to the failed operation, which can be examined for further detail in the POST card's user manual. Nonfatal errors are noted, and the POST card continues through its initialization routine, activating as many additional system resources as possible. Carefully observing POST error codes and matching them with their corresponding timings allow you to determine at what point in the POST the error occurred, and which component is responsible.

Know where to look up the proper POST code error messages.

Basic POST cards are equipped with a set of light-emitting diodes (LEDs) that display coded error signals when a problem is encountered. Other cards produce beep codes along with seven-segment LED readouts of their error codes. One of the most recent POST products is shown in Figure 20.1. It contains advanced features that greatly improve the capabilities of contemporary POST card diagnostics.

Figure 20.1 A modern POST troubleshooting card.

After the server system clears the BIOS routines, the card assumes control over the system independent of the OS. The POST card in Figure 20.1 is not used simply for debugging purposes. Its features include the following:

➤ PCI specification testing

➤ Testing of PCI bus and all PCI slots

➤ Testing of all server board components, including:

   ➤ PCI local bus

   ➤ DMA page registers

   ➤ DMA controller

   ➤ Keyboard controller

   ➤ Interrupt controller

   ➤ CMOS RAM, and Realtime clock

   ➤ Timer/counter

   ➤ System RAM

➤ Testing of all peripherals, including:

   ➤ Keyboard

   ➤ Color video card

   ➤ Floppy drive(s)

   ➤ Hard drive(s)

   ➤ CD-ROM(s)

➤ Burning-in of new or repaired systems

➤ Detection of random errors through round-robin testing

➤ Certification of system as fully functional and error-free

Not all these time-consuming tests are automatic. Test parameters can be set to specify items for testing. For documentation purposes, test results can be printed out through the card's independent printer port. The card has its own video port for graphic analysis capabilities, which remains independent of the server's possibly malfunctioning video output. When in use, the card provides three different operational modes:

Know what a POST card is, when it should be used, and how it is used.

➤ *Basic diagnostics* mode runs automated tests on all system components following the BIOS routines. The card records all components that cannot be found, or are missing, skipping the corresponding tests and accurately recording what is and what is not tested. Failure is noted under the PASS/FAIL column and the specific area is identified within the SUBTEST RESULTS TABLE, for a detailed problem description.

➤ *Extended diagnostics* displays an option screen. When nothing is selected, the card defaults to burn-in mode and continually runs the specified tests until it is manually halted. Testing scripts can be set up to select which tests to run, and for how long.

➤ *Forced start* is a new approach to server board testing for systems that appear to be dead. It allows boards that fail to POST or that POST intermittently to be tested. To do this, the card self-initializes without assistance from the server board's BIOS. This mode can operate with a server configuration composed of merely a power supply and the CPU (no RAM or video card is required), and the POST card's video jack supplies the test data.

Using Cable Testers

Faulty cabling and/or connectors are the most frequent causes of hardware-related server network problems. Data communication cabling can often be adequately tested using specialized, hand-held devices such as inexpensive continuity testers, moderately priced data cabling testers, or more expensive *Time Domain Reflectometers (TDRs)*.

System LAN cards often contain internal cable testers that operate through the use of an activity LED on the card's back plate. This LED indicates if the network recognizes the card and its associated cabling, and flashes during network activity to demonstrate that the network cabling is functioning properly. LED indicators on system hubs, switches, and routers serve similar purposes.

Inexpensive continuity testers or digital multimeters (DMMs) can be utilized to check for broken cables or faulty connectors. Both ends of the cable must lie in close proximity to perform the testing, such as with short lengths of cable, or on longer lengths of cable that have not yet been installed. DMM tests are not practical on installed cable due to the costly removal and reinstallation that would be required.

However, a number of valuable tests can be performed on twisted pair and coaxial cables without having to remove them from their installed locations. These tests require more expensive cabling testers, which normally consist of a master test unit and a separate remote load unit, as illustrated in Figure 20.2.

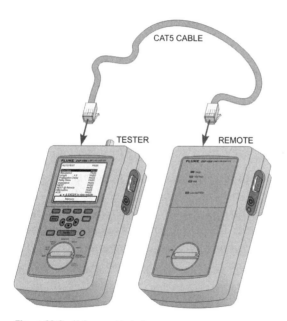

Figure 20.2 Using a cable tester.

The master unit is attached to one end of the cable and the remote load unit is attached to the other. The master sends test signal patterns through the cable, and reads them back from the load unit. These cable testers often feature both RJ-45 and BNC connectors for testing both cabling types. Problems with broken wires, crossed wires, shorted connections, and improperly paired connections can all be detected during twisted-pair cable testing.

When long lengths of installed cables must be tested, TDRs are the tools of choice. In addition to performing the previously described functions, they are sophisticated enough to pinpoint the exact distance to a break by transmitting signals along the cable and waiting for their reflections to return. The time that elapses between sending the signal and receiving its reflection is converted into a distance measurement. Similar test instruments, called *Optical Time Domain Reflectometers (OTDRs)*, have been developed to test fiber optic cable installations. A typical OTDR is shown in Figure 20.3.

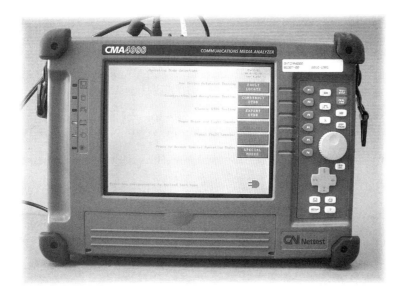

Figure 20.3   An Optical Time Domain Reflectometer.

Software Diagnostic Tools

Software diagnostic tools included with most NOS installation disks are extremely useful for checking and troubleshooting server hardware and software problems. They help to eliminate unnecessary troubleshooting and testing by quickly pinpointing a problem to a specific device or process.

However, there are also times when system software installation disks are required to overcome situations where the server's NOS has been damaged. For example, suppose the active primary NTFS partition for a Windows Server 2003 network operating system has somehow become corrupted. If the server no longer boots properly, its installation CD-ROM will be required to repair the damaged file(s) on the hard drive.

For less critical situations, the operating system's tool pack contains many powerful software diagnostic tools to help technicians and administrators manage and troubleshoot server system hardware components. The following diagnostic tool descriptions are related to the various Windows operating systems. General information is also provided about similar tools designed to work with other server and network operating systems, and about third-party diagnostic packages. Regardless of the operating system being used, OS diagnostic tools all perform similar functions.

TCP/IP Tools

When the TCP/IP suite is installed in Windows 2000 or Windows Server 2003, a number of TCP/IP troubleshooting tools are automatically installed as well. These TCP/IP utilities are entered, executed, and controlled from the command prompt. The Windows TCP/IP tools include the following:

➤ Address Resolution Protocol (ARP)—This utility enables the modification of IP-to-Physical (Ethernet) address-translation tables.

➤ File Transfer Protocol (FTP)—This utility enables the transfer of files to and from FTP servers.

➤ PING—This utility enables the verification of connections to remote hosts, or allows the testing of connections to the Internet.

➤ NETSTAT—This utility enables the display of current TCP/IP network connections and protocol statistics.

➤ NBTSTAT—A similar command to NETSTAT, this command performs the same function using NetBIOS over the TCP/IP connection.

➤ TRACERT—The Trace Route utility command enables the display of route and hop counts taken to a given destination. The route taken to a particular address can be set manually using the ROUTE command.

➤ IPCONFIG—This command-line utility determines the current TCP/IP configuration (MAC address, IP address, and subnet mask) of the local computer. It also may be used to request a new TCP/IP address from a DHCP server. IPCONFIG is available in both Windows 2000 and Windows Server 2003. Windows 9x did not support IPCONFIG. The IPCONFIG utility can be started with two important option switches: /renew and /release. These switches are used to release and update IP settings received from a DHCP server. The /all switch is used to view the TCP/IP settings for the network adapter cards that the local station is connected to.

➤ WINIPCFG—This Windows utility can also be used to quickly find the local computer's network address and other useful TCP/IP settings. It also allows the repair of network connection problems in certain situations.

Although all of these utilities are useful in isolating various TCP/IP problems, the most commonly used commands are PING and TRACERT. The PING command sends *Internet Control Message Protocol (ICMP)* packets to the selected remote location, and looks for echoed response packets. ICMP is a core protocol of the Internet protocol suite that is used by various NOSes to send error messages. Such messages can be used to indicate that a requested service is not available, or that a host or router could not be reached. The PING command waits for up to one second for each packet sent and then displays the data for the number of transmitted and received packets. In the absence of security routers specifically set up to reject it, PING can be used to test both the name and IP address of the remote node, and operates under various parameters that are set using switches.

The TRACERT utility traces the route taken by ICMP packets sent across the network. Routers along the path are instructed to return information to the inquiring system including the host name, IP address, and round-trip time for each path hop.

Know when to use the different TCP/IP tools, and how to troubleshoot TCP/IP connection errors.

When the Network settings for TCP/IP Properties are configured correctly, the current TCP/IP settings can be examined using the command line, IPCONFIG/ALL, or the WINIPCFG utility. Both of these utilities are capable of displaying the current IP settings of the local computer as a troubleshooting starting point. Then use the PING command to send test packets to other local computers. By using these tools, the viability of the network can quickly be determined.

NetWare TCP/IP Tools
NetWare contains its own set of TCP/IP utilities, similar to all the other major network operating systems. However, just because certain tools function identically in other NOSes, they are not necessarily named the same, nor are all tools included in each operating system. Several important TCP/IP tools included in the NetWare operating system are

➤ CONFIG—Displays a quick listing for a variety of the system's basic settings. It displays the uptime, network card settings, and a brief overview of the server layout from a tree structure perspective.

➤ INETCFG—Configures the network settings of the server.

➤ PING—This utility enables the verification of connections to remote hosts.

Linux TCP/IP Tools

Linux TCP/IP command-line utilities are nearly identical to those presented for Windows and Novell NetWare. However, they are case-sensitive. They include the following:

➤ ifconfig—This command is similar to the Windows IPCONFIG command. It displays the server's current network configuration, and permits changes to be made. Among some of the more useful things to configure are the gateway, DHCP server, subnet mask, and network mask assignments.

➤ ping—The ping command is used to determine how long a packet takes to reach the target and return to the host. It can be valuable to verify an actual Internet connection, or if there are unusually long packet delays.

➤ traceroute—Related to ping, traceroute lists the IP path that it takes to reach the targeted IP, and how long it takes to reach each jump. This can be useful to determine whether there are specific bottlenecks at a certain router.

➤ netstat—This command displays a number of various statistics about the host computer, including routing tables and IP addresses that are currently connected to the applicable workstation or server.

Be aware of the command to set the IP configuration in Linux.

Performing Server OS Shutdowns

A server should never simply be shut down as if it were a standalone unit, because in a server environment, there is the network to consider. Employees and clients depend on the servers to support their workstation operations. Therefore, other than for an emergency, notifications should be sent to all clients and employees prior to shutting down a server for any reason. This can be accomplished by sending them a network notification, an email message, or some other form of communication that specifies not only that the server will be down, but also the date, time, and for how long.

Employees and clients must be given enough notice to finish projects they are working on and store them before a shutdown occurs. Various departments might be required to coordinate their activities with the planned shut down process. For example, dissatisfaction will mount quickly if the server is shut down when the accounting department is running a company payroll operation.

 Know how to shut down different server operating systems and be aware of the precautions that must be taken when doing so.

Windows Server Shutdown

When performing a shutdown of Windows server operating systems, the Shut Down Windows dialog box is used to begin an orderly shutdown process. Alternatively, the Ctrl+Alt+Del keyboard combination can be used, followed by selecting the Shut Down option. Windows server operating systems employ utility programs to send appropriate console messages to network nodes indicating that the network is about to be shut down. These messages usually include a descending minute counter to keep track of exactly how much time remains before server shutdown.

NetWare Server Shutdown

Similar to the situation with Windows server operating systems, Novell NetWare systems must also be shut down in an orderly manner. Issue a down command at the system console, or from a command prompt, to shut down a NetWare server.

UNIX Server Shutdown

To initiate the operating system's shutdown process, UNIX-based servers must use the shutdown now command. Depending on the version of UNIX being used, different sets of options can be implemented according to the number of switches that are appended to the command. Common UNIX shutdown switches include: -F for fast shutdown, -h for halting the system in a prescribed time frame, and -r for automatically restarting the system after the shutdown operation has been completed. Because there are slight variations from one UNIX distribution to another, you might find it easier to view the server system's internal documentation for more information on how to operate the command. For specific UNIX version switch definitions, the man pages can be accessed by entering the man shutdown command at the command prompt. On man pages, you can find definitions of the switches available for the specific version of the UNIX operating system running on that server.

Be aware that all UNIX commands are case-sensitive, and the command line entries should always be lowercase.

Informing UNIX clients that the server will be shut down requires that a broadcast message be sent to all of them. To accomplish this, use the `wall` command, followed by the shutdown message appended to it. An example of this would read:

```
wall The server will be shut down for maintenance in 25
minutes. Please save your work and log off the network by
that time.
```

Logical switch syntax would be included with the `shutdown` command to specify the time when the command will stop the system, and to send a message to all network employees and clients notifying them that the system is being shut down. Of course, only someone with administrative authority (referred to as the root user) can execute a `shutdown` command on the server machine in a UNIX system.

Linux Server Shutdown

As a derivative of the UNIX operating system, Linux uses a `shutdown  now` command and procedure that are very similar to those in UNIX. As with the UNIX `shutdown` command, the Linux version also can also append various options to it, such as the `time` and `message` switches. The `time` switch stipulates the specific time at which the server will be shut down, and the `message` switch is used to append the specified warning text broadcasted to all logged employees and clients. For example, the command line might appear as the following:

```
shutdown -r 13:00 The server will shut down at 1:00pm. Please
log off the system before that time.
```

Differences between Linux and UNIX include the fact that the Linux `wall` command does not permit the direct appending of a warning message. Instead, it requires that the message be appended in the form of a text file, such as the following:

```
wall <filename>
```

Server Network Troubleshooting

The exact troubleshooting steps involved differ somewhat depending on whether a server network problem is related to a new installation or one that has previously been functioning properly. What does not differ, however, is the order of steps taken when attempting to isolate the problem. To determine where the problem lies:

1. Check the Network Interface Card (NIC).

2. Check the cabling and connectors.

3. Check the local networking software.

Checking NIC Adapters

Network adapter cards are usually bundled with a floppy or CD-ROM disk containing drivers and diagnostic utilities for that particular product. The administrator can quickly determine whether LAN hardware is functioning properly by first running these diagnostic utilities.

Checking Cables and Connectors

Because cabling accounts for the largest percentage of network installation problems, the administrator must verify that the proper cabling connections exist. This includes ensuring that all of the connectors are properly installed on the correct cable types. Terminations must be examined for correctness as well. The line testers described earlier in this chapter are the most efficient methods of testing the functionality of network cabling. With Unshielded Twisted Pair (UTP) cabling, simply unplug the cable from the adapter card and plug it into the tester. When testing coaxial cable, remember to unplug both ends of the cable from the network and install a terminating resistor at one end. The unterminated end of the cable should then be plugged into the tester, and the tests should be performed.

 Know the proper steps to troubleshoot an NIC.

Examining Local Network Software

When it is determined that the NICs are functioning properly and the network cables pass all their tests, only the local networking software remains to be examined. All server networks require the installation and configuration of specific protocols to effectively communicate between various nodes. These requirements must be verified to ensure that common protocols can be shared between all units. Nodes that do not have all the required protocols installed might not see other nodes, and other nodes might not see them. Obviously, nodes that do not see each other cannot communicate with each other. For these communications to occur, network users in a TCP/IP network must have the following three items configured correctly:

➤ A valid IP address

➤ A valid subnet mask

➤ A valid default gateway address

Clients who cannot see any other computers on the network are likely to be using improper IP addressing, which is a common problem associated with TCP/IP. Valid IP addresses are required, as well as valid subnet masks, in order to communicate with other clients or servers. When incorrect, invalid, or conflicting IP addressing is being used, only the local workstation will be visible and other network nodes will not be available.

LANs often use a DHCP server to dynamically assign IP addresses to their network clients. Addressing problems occur in TCP/IP networks when a local system looks for a DHCP server that is either not present or malfunctioning. Each segment of a large network requires its own DHCP server to properly assign its IP addresses. Otherwise, clients in that segment cannot see the network.

DHCP client computers installed on a network segment that is not using DHCP require manual configurations with static IP addressing. The TCP/IP properties must be properly configured for whichever version of Windows is being used. For example, in Windows 2000, the TCP/IP properties window is located under the Start/Settings/Network and Dialup Connections path. After opening the desired Local Area Connection, click the Properties button to set the required configuration.

One of the settings that must be correct for the network to be able to communicate with the local unit is the subnet mask. The subnet mask performs the same routing job as ZIP codes do for postal mail. An incorrectly set subnet mask will prevent the network routing system from correctly handling network mail packets to or from the misconfigured local node. As a result, that node will be invisible to the other network nodes.

An invalid address for the default gateway can also cause routing problems. This situation results in clients being able to see other local computers in the TCP/IP network, but not being able to see remote systems on other networks. When this situation is observed, the address listed in the TCP/IP properties for the default gateway should be checked for validity. The Net View command can be used to test the availability of the selected remote computer.

For example, suppose a server is configured with the IP address of 10.54.20.40, a subnet mask of 255.255.255.0, and a gateway address of 10.54.10.1. There are two specific reasons why this configuration would cause problems as soon as clients attempt to ping other servers' IP addresses. First of all, the Class C subnet mask for the local server is incorrect because it does not match the Class A IP address. It should be configured with the Class A subnet mask of 255.0.0.0. In addition, the gateway address is incorrect and will prevent the pinging of a computer on another network segment. It should carry an address of 10.54.20.1. Table 20.1 indicates how "classful" IP addresses are categorized through the identification of the patterns in the first octet of their 32-bit addresses.

Table 20.1	Address Ranges for Classful IP					
Class	First Octet	Lowest Value (binary)	Highest Value (binary)	Range (decimal)	Net/ Host Octets	Theoretical IP Address Range
Class A	0xxx xxxx	0000 0001	0111 1110	1 to 126	1 / 3	1.0.0.0 to 126.255.255.255
Class B	10xx xxxx	1000 0000	1011 1111	128 to 191	2 / 2	128.0.0.0 to 191.255.255.255
Class C	110x xxxx	1100 0000	1101 1111	192 to 223	3 / 1	192.0.0.0 to 223.255.255.255
Class D	1110 xxxx	1110 0000	1110 1111	224 to 239	—	224.0.0.0 to 239.255.255.255
Class E	1111 xxxx	1111 0000	1111 1111	240 to 255	—	240.0.0.0 to 255.255.255.255

Know how to recognize what problems can occur from not using the correct subnet mask.

Checking Wake-on-LAN Operations

Wake-on-LAN technology permits a remote server to be powered up from any local workstation across a network connection. Both the network adapter card and the system board must contain the technology for the Wake-on-LAN function. In addition, the two devices must be attached to each other through a Wake-on-LAN cable that terminates at each end with a 3-pin connector.

Even when the managed computer is turned off, its NIC remains active through the use of an alternate power source as it monitors network traffic for a special wake-up data packet, referred to as a *magic packet*. When the

NIC receives the magic packet from a remote source, it applies a system-reset signal to its system board, which in turn powers up the system to perform its assigned task. After the remote system has been restarted, it can be directed to scan for viruses, run a disk backup utility, automatically install software upgrades, and then return to its sleep mode. This allows administrators to save time by automating software installations and upgrades during off-hours, which increases end-user productivity by avoiding disruptions during work hours.

When problems associated with Wake-on-LAN network cards occur, you should first make certain that the Wake-on-LAN function is indeed available and properly configured in the system's CMOS. After the correct setup of the card is verified, it should be treated the same as any traditional network adapter arrangement. Because Wake-on-LAN cards are inexpensive, they are considered to be field-replaceable units. If a problem with the card itself is suspected, simply replace it with a known good card, and retest the system. Also examine the Wake-on-LAN cable running between the network adapter card and the server board. If this connection is not working, network activity will not be able to activate the remote server.

To perform remote troubleshooting for a Wake-on-LAN system, analyze the LAN's traffic to verify that the magic packets are reaching the NIC. Magic packets can be tested using a third computer that has a known good Wake-On-LAN NIC card installed.

Know what types of packets cause the Wake-On-LAN card to boot the remote system.

Checking Field-Replaceable Units

Computer repair technicians who focus on individual workstations or PCs achieve effective results by combining information gathering, symptom observation, and system knowledge with proven troubleshooting techniques. Although similar skills are applied to server problems, the need to keep server systems in continuous operation has led to the development of special redundant component designs to help to fulfill the demands of server network troubleshooting. These components are classified as *Field-Replaceable Units (FRUs)*.

Know what it means to hot-swap a drive.

A server computer's construction is designed to use many redundant components, including FRUs. Figure 20.4 illustrates a number of FRUs typically associated with servers. This approach permits the technician to isolate and exchange FRU components, when necessary, while keeping the server system in continuous operation. The way in which a failed or failing component is removed and replaced depends on the responsibilities of its server. When a defective component has been identified, the most effective way to repair or replace it must be chosen.

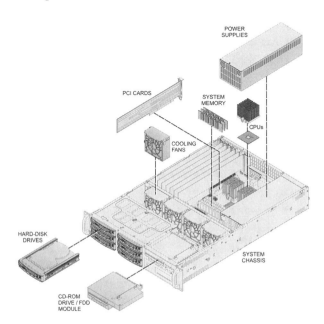

Figure 20.4 Various server FRUs.

Determine whether a defective FRU can be hot-swapped or warm-swapped, or must be cold-swapped. Cold-swapped FRUs require that the system be powered down and the power cord unplugged before the component exchange occurs. If the component can be hot-swapped, the server will not require any configuration changes prior to removing the original device and replacing it with another. Alternately, if the system permits, a warm-swappable FRU might merely require that the service for the device be turned off before the swapping can occur. This might require only that its device driver be temporarily shut down.

Know how to replace devices installed in hot-swappable PCI slots.

Users of consumer computer products are very familiar with the cold-swapping method of component exchange, where the specified computer must be completely turned off prior to replacing a defective component. In addition, units with ATX power supplies must have their power cords removed. This makes the use of cold-swapped components unacceptable when building server systems.

Exam Prep Questions

1. A server has just been assembled and is being powered for the first time. The technician observes the power light, hears the power supply fan begin to run, and detects the HDDs beginning to spin. If the monitor remains blank, which of the following statements identifies the actual problem?

   ❏ A. The jumpers related to the processor are set incorrectly on the server board.

   ❏ B. The server's power supply is malfunctioning.

   ❏ C. The correct network operating system drivers have not been loaded.

   ❏ D. The server board's BIOS needs to be upgraded.

2. Four internal hard drives have been installed in the server. However, the POST only indicates that two HDDs are installed. How can this be explained?

   ❏ A. Disks are configured in a RAID 1 mirrored array.

   ❏ B. Disks are configured in a RAID 0 striped array.

   ❏ C. Two of the drives are ATA and two of the drives are SCSI.

   ❏ D. Disks are configured in two separate RAID arrays.

3. During the IP configuration phase of a Linux server setup, the administrator types `ipconfig` without the desired results. What command should be typed instead?

   ❏ A. `inetcfg`

   ❏ B. `linuxconfig`

   ❏ C. `linuxcfg`

   ❏ D. `ifconfig`

4. An error message appears during the POST. What should the server technician do next to identify the suspect FRU?

   ❏ A. The NOS error codes should be carefully examined.

   ❏ B. The server board error codes should be carefully examined.

   ❏ C. The POST card should be installed and its error codes should be carefully examined.

   ❏ D. Various parts should be replaced until the bad device is finally located.

5. When troubleshooting and identifying a server hardware problem, what is the proper way to use a POST card?

   ❏ A. After installing the POST card, check the error code that appears in its software program.

   ❏ B. Use a serial cable to connect the POST card to the server and check the error code that appears in the software program.

   ❏ C. After installing the POST card, check the error code that appears on the card itself.

   ❏ D. Use a serial cable to connect the POST card to the server and check the error code that appears on the card.

6. Which of the documents in the following list should be safely stored for server system troubleshooting purposes? (Select two.)

❑ A. All server component purchase orders

❑ B. A listing of password changes

❑ C. Any logs related to system upgrades

❑ D. All installation and configuration data

7. What is the minimum amount of server documentation that should be preserved?

❑ A. Manufacturer's printed documents, baseline reference data, maintenance data logs, and applicable resource websites

❑ B. Maintenance data logs, manufacturer's printed documents, reference storage disks, and employee telephone numbers

❑ C. Associated printed documents, applicable resource websites, employee email addresses, and reference storage disks

❑ D. Baseline reference data, maintenance data logs, email configurations, and manufacturer's printed documents

8. For setting the IP configuration in a Linux server system, what TCP/IP utility should be selected to do the job?

❑ A. `vi config`

❑ B. `tracert`

❑ C. `ifconfig`

❑ D. `netstat`

9. Following the system-wide server installations of Wake-On-LAN cards, testing has demonstrated the inability to boot these servers remotely. Which of the possibilities in the following list could be the source of the problem?

❑ A. In a TCP/IP packet

❑ B. In a PXE packet

❑ C. In an SNMP packet

❑ D. In a magic packet

10. Following an emergency "server down" notification, the administrator determines that the problem requires a higher level of technical expertise. What is the next logical step to take in effecting a solution?

❑ A. Immediately contact the next person in the escalation plan.

❑ B. Dedicate all resources to solving the problem until it is successfully resolved.

❑ C. Recruit additional help from the available on-duty personnel.

❑ D. Issue immediate notifications to all clients that the server will be down indefinitely.

11. The domain examcram2.com has been configured on a server with a subnet mask of 255.255.0.0 and an IP address of 35.20.20.70. It operates behind a gateway using the address 35.20.15.1. After the configuration has been completed, it is impossible to ping other servers using their gateway IP address. What is wrong with this configuration? (Select two.)

   ❑ A. The hostname for the server is incorrect.
   ❑ B. The subnet mask is incorrect for the IP address being used for the server.
   ❑ C. DNS is configured on other servers and it must also be configured on the examcram2 server.
   ❑ D. The gateway address is incorrect and the target servers are on another network segment.

12. When a computer using an active primary NTFS partition refuses to boot properly, what is the required solution?

   ❑ A. The OS/2 Warp Server installation CD must be used to repair the problem.
   ❑ B. The NetWare installation CD must be used to repair the damage.
   ❑ C. The Windows Server 2003 installation CD must be used to repair the problem.
   ❑ D. The UNIX installation CD must be used to repair the damage.

13. Which of the following network troubleshooting utility tools use ICMP packets to perform their specified functions? (Select two.)

   ❑ A. nbtstat
   ❑ B. tracert
   ❑ C. netstat
   ❑ D. ping

14. The administrator must shut down a Novell NetWare server. What is the proper command syntax to use?

   ❑ A. At the console, click Shutdown Now.
   ❑ B. Press the Reset button.
   ❑ C. Press Ctrl+Alt+Del and then select Shut Down.
   ❑ D. At the console, type **down**.

15. The administrator is troubleshooting a Linux server network configuration. Which of the following commands should be used?

   ❑ A. tracert
   ❑ B. ipconfig
   ❑ C. ifconfig
   ❑ D. ping

16. Which one of the following operational strategies for preparing a server shutdown is incorrect?

- ❏ A. Provide accurate and current information about the date, time, and length of the proposed server shutdown.
- ❏ B. Delay any server shutdown activities until the current payroll services have been accomplished.
- ❏ C. Perform the server shutdown in exactly the same way that a stand-alone computer would be shut down.
- ❏ D. Send timely network notification messages to all of the affected employees and clients prior to shutdown.

17. The first regularly scheduled check of the server room indicates that none of the local computers can see the network, although no such problem existed during the previous evening's final check. In addition, work was performed on the AC system during swing shift according to the server room log. Which of the following statements properly relates these two events?

- ❏ A. Work was performed in close proximity to server equipment by personnel not normally given server room entry.
- ❏ B. Temperature sensitive server components were driven to failure by cooler-than-normal server room conditions.
- ❏ C. During the repair work, maintenance personnel indulged themselves with electronic games on the server computer.
- ❏ D. During the time in which the server room AC work was being performed, prolonged overheating led to server failure.

18. A server is unable to reconnect to the network following the installation of a new NIC. Running a set of diagnostic tests on the new NIC reveals no problems. Which one of the following troubleshooting steps is unnecessary?

- ❏ A. Checking the current cable connectors for proper operation
- ❏ B. Locating a known good NIC adapter and performing a swap
- ❏ C. Reviewing the configuration settings on the local networking software
- ❏ D. Performing continuity tests on the NIC cabling

Exam Prep Answers

1. Answer A is the correct answer. The server board is equipped with jumpers associated with the operation of the processor that offer a wide range of operating parameters. If they have not been set correctly, the system may freeze during the memory checks. Answer B is incorrect because the possibility of a bad power supply is highly unlikely given the fact that the power supply fan is running properly. Answer C is incorrect because the POST must complete successfully before the NOS drivers are activated. Answer D is incorrect because an outdated BIOS still permits its information to be displayed on the monitor.

2. Answer C is the correct answer. During the POST, only ATA drives are recognized and mounted. Although SCSI and RAID controllers are also mounted during the POST, the disk drive volumes themselves are not loaded until later. Therefore, answers A, B, and D are all incorrect.

3. Answer D is the correct answer. For Linux server configurations, the ifconfig utility should be used. Answer A is incorrect because inetcfg is a NetWare utility used for configuring the server network settings. Answers B and C are both incorrect because Linux does not use any such utility programs.

4. Answer B is the correct answer. Examining the server board error codes can usually identify any problems that occur during the POST. Answer A is incorrect because there are no such things as NOS error codes. Answer C is incorrect unless the server board error codes have already been checked. When the server board error codes offer no clear problem diagnosis, a POST card can be installed, the computer can be rebooted, and the POST card error codes can be examined. Answer D is incorrect because too much valuable time will be wasted.

5. Answer C is the correct answer. One of the helpful things about a POST card is that it can test hardware components without an operating system running. The POST card simply plugs into an available bus slot and the applicable error code is read directly from the card. Answer A is incorrect because the error code appears right on the card, not in a software program. Answer B and D are incorrect because the POST card does not connect to the server using a serial port.

6. Answers C and D are the correct answers. When the need for server system troubleshooting arises, all information related to its original installation and configuration, as well as past system upgrades, will be required. Answers A and B are incorrect because records of password changes or purchasing paperwork would not be required to perform system troubleshooting.

7. Answer A is the correct answer. Answer B is incorrect because employee telephone numbers are generally not stored on the server. Answers C and D are incorrect because essential server data does not include email configurations or addresses.

8. Answer C is the correct answer. The Linux `ifconfig` utility is similar to the Windows `ipconfig` utility, and it displays the specified computer's current network configuration. It also permits gateway, DHCP server, subnet mask, and network mask assignments by the administrator. Answer A is incorrect because `vi` is the UNIX/Linux test editor. Answer B is incorrect because `tracert` lists the path taken to locate an IP target, and the time between each jump. Answer D is incorrect because `netstat` displays host computer statistics such as routing tables and currently connected IP addresses.

9. Answer D is the correct answer. The magic packet provides the waking bootup command to a WOL adapter. If the Wake-on-LAN function is available, it must be properly configured in the system's CMOS. Answer A is incorrect, although TCP/IP packets could be used as a wide area transport device. Answer B is incorrect because although a Preboot eXecution Environment (PXE) packet is designed to bootstrap computers through a network interface card independent of available data storage devices or installed operating systems, it does not perform the actual function of the magic packet. Answer C is incorrect, although an SNMP packet would be used (in an SNMP server network) as a local network transport device.

10. Answer A is the correct answer. When a problem arises that cannot be solved by either the repair technician or the administrator, the escalation plan delineates when, how, and whom to contact. Answer B is incorrect because an unqualified technician will not solve the problem regardless of how much time is allowed. Answer C is incorrect because the available on-duty personnel would in all likelihood be no more qualified to solve the problem than the technician on duty. Answer D is incorrect because the administrator cannot be permitted to characterize server downtime as indefinite.

11. Answers B and D are the correct answers. The Class A IP address does not match the Class B subnet mask. An incorrect gateway address will prevent the pinging of a computer on another network segment. Answer A is incorrect because the direct ping of a valid IP address should not be susceptible to server hostname interference. Answer C is incorrect because DNS configurations do not affect direct ping operations.

12. Answer C is the correct answer. NTFS is used by the Windows Server 2003 network operating system. The installation CD for Windows Server 2003 will be required to repair the problem. Answer A is incorrect because the High Performance File System (HPFS) is used

exclusively by OS/2 Warp. Answer B is incorrect because the NetWare File System (NWFS) is used by Novell's NetWare server software. Answer D is incorrect because UNIX does not incorporate the NTFS file system.

13. Answers B and D are the correct answers. ICMP packets are required by both the `ping` and the `tracert` utilities in order to perform their specified functions. Answer A is incorrect because `nbtstat` displays current TCP/IP network connections and protocol statistics using NetBIOS without utilizing ICMP packets. Answer C is incorrect because `netstat` displays current TCP/IP network connections and protocol statistics using Windows without the use of ICMP packets.

14. Answer D is the correct answer. System and data integrity can be maintained during a Novell NetWare server shutdown by typing `down` shortly before removing power from its file server. Answer A is incorrect for a Novell NetWare server, but is appropriate for shutting down a UNIX or Linux server. Answer B is incorrect because pressing the Reset button on a server will ruin system and data integrity. Answer C is incorrect for a Novell NetWare server, but is appropriate for a server running Windows.

15. Answer C is the correct answer. The Linux `ifconfig` command is similar to the Windows `ipconfig` command. A Linux server's current network configuration can be manipulated using it. Answer A is incorrect because the path used to reach a targeted IP address is listed by the `tracert` command. Answer B is incorrect because `ipconfig` is not a legitimate Linux command. Answer D is incorrect because the `ping` command measures the transfer time of a packet to its target and back to the initiating host.

16. Answer C is the correct answer. The shutdown of company servers is much too important to be conducted without initiating company-wide notifications well ahead of time. Answers A, B, and D describe the necessary points to consider prior to conducting a properly scheduled server shutdown.

17. Answer A is the correct answer. Power to the server was unintentionally discontinued for a short period of time by the HVAC service personnel. An incomplete reset of the system occurred when the power was restored. Answer B is incorrect because server components are not susceptible to failure due to cooler room temperatures. Answer D is incorrect because in spite of the fact that the AC system required attention as late as the previous evening, all server operations were running smoothly. Answer C is incorrect for several reasons. First of

all, games are never installed onto network servers. In addition, KVM equipment in the server room is normally locked, precluding any possible accessibility. Finally, it assumes the maintenance workers are eager to lose their jobs.

18. Answer B is the correct answer. The new NIC has already passed diagnostic tests proving its operational status. Answer A is incorrect because the cable connectors could be causing the problem Answer C is incorrect because an incorrect configuration setting could prevent the network software from recognizing the new NIC. Answer D is incorrect because a broken or damaged cable would explain the current symptoms.

21.0—Troubleshooting Server Systems

Terms you'll need to understand:

- ✓ Optimal performance
- ✓ Primary Domain Controller (PDC)
- ✓ Backup Domain Controller (BDC)
- ✓ Self-tuning
- ✓ Memory bottleneck
- ✓ Throughput
- ✓ Page file
- ✓ Disk subsystem
- ✓ Network interface bottleneck
- ✓ Processor bottleneck
- ✓ Network redirector
- ✓ Server bottleneck
- ✓ Rescheduling
- ✓ Resource balancing

Techniques you'll need to master:

- ✓ Running server performance tools
- ✓ Comparing baseline results
- ✓ Optimizing server performance
- ✓ Diagnosing server network problems
- ✓ Making resource-balancing adjustments
- ✓ Maximizing server throughput
- ✓ Tweaking server memory
- ✓ Determining swap file size
- ✓ Dealing with bottlenecks
- ✓ Understanding how network redirectors function
- ✓ Handling and balancing server network resources

Introduction

Server+ Exam Objective 7.3 states that the test taker should be able to identify various system bottlenecks, including

➤ Processor operations

➤ Bus transfers

➤ Input/output operations, including

  ➤ Disk I/O

  ➤ Network I/O

  ➤ Memory I/O

One of the activities associated with this objective consists of running performance tools to compare results against the baseline.

Supporting knowledge includes how to run performance tools and make baseline comparisons of

➤ Processor utilization

➤ Page file

➤ Disk utilization

➤ Memory utilization

➤ Network utilization

Optimizing Server Performance

When the server system is capable of completing a task in the shortest amount of time possible, it is tuned to its *optimal performance*. Optimizing a server's performance often requires the rearrangement of system resources to ensure that any requested tasks are executed quickly, effectively, and completely. This means that the existing hardware and software must be configured to provide their best possible results. When the resource demands of the required tasks have been measured and analyzed, various changes can be made to the system in order to achieve optimal results in less time.

Before a given system can realize its optimal performance, the administrator must initially answer the following questions:

➤ Which tasks are considered the most important responsibilities for the system to perform?

➤ How should the server system be optimized: according to the speed with which a specific application or service operates, or according to the efficiency with which a particular hardware function is performed?

When the answers to these questions have been determined, subsequent performance measurements can be selected and interpreted with the aim of optimizing the system's performance according to how it will be used. These performance considerations may focus on the network server, the web server, the file server, or a server running the company's database applications. The needs of the organization will determine the server's operational priorities.

For example, if the company absolutely must service requests from clients as quickly and effectively as possible, the file server's performance would require the most careful attention. Any changes made to the file server's configuration could be compared to measurements taken previously to determine whether the overall performance of the file server has improved. The administrator will look for an improvement in the quantity of bytes transferred to all clients across the network in a given period of time.

Another example involves the desire to achieve optimal performance for a *Primary Domain Controller (PDC)*. The PDC must replicate a large database, containing numerous commercial accounts, to multiple *Backup Domain Controllers (BDCs)*. The optimal situation is to achieve quick and accurate synchronization of the database throughout its associated WAN, with a minimum of network traffic being generated. In order to achieve this, two primary measurements have to be obtained:

➤ The amount of time taken for changes to the database to be implemented across all domain controllers

➤ The overall volume of network traffic generated by the synchronization of the various controllers

When procedures have been implemented to optimize the system's performance, the next step is to determine whether the resulting performance meets the requirements of the company. The system may be tuned to its optimum potential, but may continue to offer insufficient capabilities in its current configuration to support its desired application. In such a situation, the system will require further upgrading of one or more of its components. Additional memory, more and larger disk drives, faster, multiple processor(s), or NIC port optimizations may be required.

Know how a particular server system is optimized to determine its suitability for the intended application.

Gathering Performance Data

Improving the performance of a server network is best achieved through

➤ Careful measurement and documentation

➤ Accurate interpretation of the results

➤ Appropriate modification of the application

➤ Repeated measurements, documentation, and comparisons

Although gathering data on system performance under a wide variety of circumstances provides the information upon which to base system adjustments, be aware that this data can also be misleading at times. The administrator or the technician must have a thorough understanding of what the system's configuration was at the time the data was collected. This is the only way that an accurate and complete analysis of the data can be achieved.

A full knowledge of all changes that have been made to the system is also necessary. All of the influences capable of affecting the system must be taken into account and researched along with the indicated problems. Keep in mind that problems can occur with one resource or in combination with several. Ongoing documentation permits the return to a previous configuration when specific changes do not correct the problem or alleviate the given symptom. Performance data can be helpful when setting up a database server. It can accurately indicate whether sufficient capacity exists to handle any additional future workload, or resource shortages will cause problems when additional clients are added to the system. It will also identify situations where multiple applications are competing for identical server resources. Sufficient performance for each application may require that one be moved to another server. Transient network problems are of short duration and rarely repeat on a regularly scheduled basis. This makes them particularly difficult to diagnose. The network can quickly be placed into a panic mode when numerous interrupts are suddenly generated by a malfunctioning application, or an NIC. As the processor attempts to handle all of the interrupts, the server's performance will be decimated and the network will be brought to a screeching halt! Transient network problems can be reliably indicated when monitoring a high number of network errors and interrupts being processed.

Variations in the way that clients use the server can be detected through scheduled monitoring of the server's performance. This will reveal when clients save and retrieve large files from the file server on a more frequent basis. The system administrator can then increase the overall system performance by modifying the server, as necessary. Appropriate remedial action can be taken before clients notice any reduced server performance by evaluating trends in the demand on server resources.

Achieving optimal system performance is a skill that develops over a period of time. When server OSes such as Windows 2000 Server or Server 2003 are being used, and the system has been certified, much of the optimization work has already been done. This is because these systems are *self-tuning*, which means that performance factors for the environment are automatically adjusted. Much of this functionality depends on whether only recommended hardware and drivers are installed. Performance might still be adversely affected through outside influences such as non-validated device drivers, massive network loads, or unique software applications. When additional services have been installed on a server system, accompanying documentation and registry parameters associated with those services can be examined for performance enhancement opportunities.

Documenting Suspected Bottlenecks

The word *bottleneck* is a term that refers to any phenomenon adversely affecting access to the server system's resources. It derives from a familiar phenomenon that occurs when a bottle, filled with the administrator's favorite beverage, is turned upside down. The width of the bottle's neck will determine the rate at which the liquid pours out of the bottle. Therefore, the neck of the bottle is its main limiting characteristic, because it prevents the liquid from pouring any faster. The neck of the bottle needs to be wider in order to pour the contents of the bottle more quickly.

The suspected bottleneck causing a particular performance problem must be thoroughly investigated and documented before making any changes that affect the system. When a well-planned approach to resolving bottlenecks is properly implemented, it includes the following process:

1. Discovering the bottleneck

2. Devising a problem resolution

3. Deploying a resolution to the bottleneck

4. Precluding a similar bottleneck from occurring again in the near future

To perform this process, the system resource responsible for the bottleneck must first be isolated. Next, the actual demands on that resource must be accurately determined. For example, suppose the system administrator discovers that while a specific task is being executed, the system processor is kept busy nearly 100% of the time. To immediately conclude that the system requires a faster processor would not be the correct approach. An investigation should first be undertaken to determine why the processor is under such strain. If the system's RAM is insufficient, the processor may be forced to handle the increased load by managing virtual memory. If the task being implemented invokes one or more other processes, these additional loads may be behaving in such a way as to dominate the processor's execution time.

The administrator or the service technician needs to have a true picture as to what is actually happening on the network at all times. By combining the use of performance monitoring tools with proper investigating techniques (including documentation), enough information can be gathered to allow for fine-tuning of any server system, and to ensure its operational readiness in support of its intended application.

Identifying Performance Bottlenecks

Specific counters and monitoring agents are used to detect bottlenecks in a server system and to measure a server system's performance. A simple strategy can be used to detect system performance bottlenecks by using the troubleshooting information already imparted.

 Keep in mind that the overall throughput for a client/server system depends on the slowest system element.

Usually, the slowest system element is automatically categorized as a system bottleneck. An evaluation of the performance monitoring results will reveal where the bottlenecks are occurring. Quite often, the bottleneck is the service or component using the highest volume of system resources. However, a resource-intensive application may also require heavy resource usage to normally accomplish its task, as shown in Figure 21.1. If the software operates properly, a resource-balancing adjustment may be necessary.

System bottlenecks increase the amount of time required to complete a task. The system resource exhibiting the bottleneck needs to be faster or larger in order to complete its assigned task more quickly. For example, if an assigned task employs several system resources, but uses the highest percentage of its time with the hard disk drive, the performance of the disk system is a limiting factor. If this suspicion is supported by the performance data, the bottleneck might be alleviated through the redistribution of the disk load, or through the installation of a faster hard disk. If client performance in a

Computer-Aided Design and Drafting (CADD) application is the main concern, bottlenecks associated with the lack of CPU speed no longer dominate system testing. Instead, CADD bottlenecks are currently associated with other system deficiencies, such as disk I/O operations and network traffic congestion, because of the application of multiple processors and faster-than-ever processors.

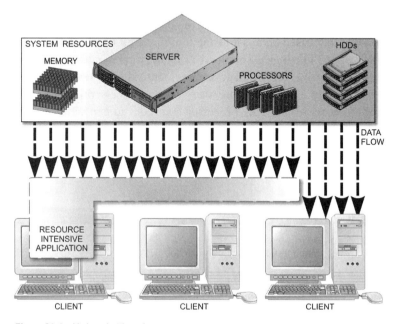

Figure 21.1 Various bottlenecks.

The most important performance parameter used with modern file server applications is *throughput*. A wide variety of possible hardware configurations and settings affects the average response time required by a file server to complete the tasks requested by its clients. Its throughput is directly affected by:

➤ CPU speed

➤ Memory available

➤ Memory access speed

➤ Disk I/O read/write speeds

➤ Network transfer rates

Detecting a system bottleneck is not the toughest task for an administrator to accomplish. The basic approach involves an examination of the amount of time taken by various system components to complete a task. The component that uses the most time to complete its portion of the task is the source of the bottleneck.

For example, imagine that for a given task, the performance monitoring tools determine that the system consumes 0.5 seconds of processor time, 0.1 second accessing the network, and 0.8 seconds accessing the disk drive. Another observation reveals that during most of the task's execution, the processor and network are sitting idle while waiting for the disk drive. It comes as no surprise to learn that based on this information, the bottleneck is determined to be the disk drive. The logical solution to this situation would be to install a faster drive. Following this installation, the identical task is repeated and monitored. The new results indicate that the disk access time has been reduced to 0.4 seconds, while the processor continues to consume 0.5 seconds. The bottleneck is now the processor. This tuning process is considered to be complete when the system has been adjusted to its optimum performance. Table 21.1 provides descriptions of various server bottleneck symptoms to be on the lookout for.

Table 21.1 Server System Bottlenecks	
Source Component	**Monitored Parameter Thresholds**
Memory	Available RAM less than 10MB; Memory paging greater than 20 pages/sec; Page file % Usage greater than 70; Non-paged memory pool over 30%
Processor(s)	% Processor time between 70-85%; System processor queue of 2 or more
Hard Drive(s)	Avg. Read Que Length of 2 or more; Avg. Write Que Length of 2 or more; % Disk time more than 50%
NIC(s)	Processor %DPC Time greater than 50%; %Net Utilization greater than 40%; Bytes Total/sec greater than 7MBps for 100Mbps cards, or 70MBps for 1000Mbps cards

Troubleshooting Bottlenecks

Not only can bottlenecks adversely affect a server system's performance, but they can ultimately be responsible for its complete functional failure. The performance monitoring tools mentioned previously are often needed to effectively troubleshoot server OS bottlenecks and identify which component(s) are to blame. We will now analyze some of the more significant server system devices and components for specific bottleneck issues. Because the

Windows Server 2003 OS allocates its virtual memory by using the `pagefile.sys` program tool, we will use it as an example. This is a significant issue because memory tweaking is an important part of the system administrator's responsibilities. The page-file swapping operation should always be optimized in a server system, especially one that runs low on RAM.

In determining how much swap space is required, the software programs used and the amount of RAM on the server board must be considered. For a system that is not overloaded, the rule of thumb is 1.5 times the amount of onboard system memory. Although virtual memory cannot be disabled, it can be set to zero. Doing so, however, wastes large amounts of RAM as various programs allocate much more virtual memory space (hundreds of megabytes) than they will ever need or use. When requested, these address allocations have to be assigned somewhere. If the page file is not set to zero, the system will assign the requested allocations to virtual memory. A page file set to zero will result in the assignment of program memory requests to RAM. When such an assignment occurs, that RAM is locked out from any actual system use. Even when certain programs are closed, the RAM they were using is often not returned to the memory pool. If enough RAM is locked out, a serious bottleneck is created.

Physical Disk Bottlenecks

Bottlenecks can exist due to mechanical or configuration deficiencies in hard disk operations. Important parameters that can be examined during a performance monitoring session include

➤ % Disk Time using `pagefile.sys`—A major concern associated with bottlenecks in a Windows 2000 or 2003 server system is a too-frequent accessing of `pagefile.sys` due to a shortage of installed system RAM. A memory bottleneck is indicated when the available memory is near 4MB, the % disk time for a disk using `pagefile.sys` is consistently over 10%, and the pages/sec value is unusually high. This indicates a physical memory bottleneck, rather than the logical disk.

➤ % Disk Time not using `pagefile.sys`—If this value is consistently above 60%, system bottlenecks will develop. Other system performance values should be examined in order to focus on the actual problem, such as

 ➤ Average Disk Queue Length—A high % disk time coupled with an average disk queue length greater than 2 indicates that the disk is a bottleneck.

➤ Average Disk sec/Transfer—If this value is over 0.3 seconds, and if the disk transfer/sec value is consistently over 80 transfers per second, the disk is a bottleneck.

➤ Current Disk Queue Length—This number includes all requests outstanding on the disk at the time the performance data is collected, plus all requests in service at that time. This is not an average over the time interval but rather an instantaneous value. Although this counter might reflect a transitory high or low queue length, a sustained load on the disk drive will likely result in a high reading. This difference between transitory and sustained values should average less than 2 for good performance. If this difference is 2 or higher over an extended period of time, the disk has become a bottleneck.

➤ Disk Bytes/sec—This value can be used to determine if the SCSI bus is a bottleneck. The sum of all disk bytes/sec drive values attached to a specific SCSI bus is compared to the throughput of the SCSI bus. If the sum is equal to 80% or more of the throughput, the SCSI bus is the bottleneck and will need to be upgraded for increased performance.

➤ Disk Transfers/sec—If this value is consistently over 80 transfers per second (a combination of reads and writes), then the disk is a bottleneck.

Important counters used to examine disk performance are included in Table 21.2.

Table 21.2 Disk Performance Counters

Performance Object	Counter	Description	Recommended Value
Logical Disk Physical Disk	Disk Transfers/sec	Measures the disk utilization; this value indicates the number of read/writes completed per second.	If the value consistently exceeds 80 transfers per second, it is often an indicator of a bottleneck.
	Disk Bytes/sec	Primary measurement of disk throughput; this is the rate at which bytes are transferred.	The higher the value, the better the disk drive performance.
Logical Disk Physical Disk	Average Disk sec/Transfer	This indicates how fast the data moves through the system, as the average time of each data transfer for both read/write requests.	A high value may indicate a large quantity of request retries due to disk failure of long disk queues.

(continued)

Table 21.2 Disk Performance Counters *(continued)*			
Performance Object	Counter	Description	Recommended Value
Logical Disk Physical Disk	Average Disk Bytes/Transfer	This is a measurement of the overall size of the I/O operation.	This is most efficient with large amounts of data transferred.
Logical Disk	% Free Space	Percentage of unallocated disk space.	

Resolving a *disk subsystem* bottleneck may involve moving labor-intensive processes to a different server and/or installing a faster disk subsystem. Here are some suggestions for using a page file with a server:

➤ Move the page file to another fast and dedicated hard disk and off the disk holding the system and boot partitions. However, leave a small amount on the C: drive as a precaution (between 2 and 50MB). This is done to prevent the system from ignoring the settings, in which case it may act as if there is no page file at all, or create a large one itself on the C: drive.

➤ Wherever the page file is placed, be sure to format its partition with NTFS, with a 4KB cluster size.

➤ Never create a page file that is smaller than the amount of physical RAM actually installed. An initial size of at least 1.5 times as large as the amount of physical RAM should be adequate.

➤ If in doubt about how big the page file should be, make its initial size as big as the maximum size allowed.

➤ Multiple paging files should not be placed on different partitions within the same physical disk drive.

➤ When the server is equipped with a RAID 0 striped set array, use this array to store the page file.

➤ Because paging files do not need fault tolerance, do not place a page file on a fault-tolerant drive, such as a mirrored RAID 1 or a RAID 5 volume, which write data to multiple locations. These fault-tolerant systems suffer from slow data writes.

Memory Bottlenecks

Because paging with Windows 2000 Server and Windows Server 2003 involves the use of virtual memory when not enough RAM is available, fixed-size blocks of data are moving from RAM to a paging file on the hard disk.

Overuse of the disk subsystem occurs when this paging becomes excessive, making the disk appear as a resource bottleneck. A few of the important parameters used to spot *memory bottlenecks* include:

➤ Available Bytes—If this counter value is approaching 4MB, the memory has become a bottleneck. The counter itself is counting in bytes, rather than megabytes. If the disk containing the page file reports a high percentage of disk time, a memory bottleneck is easier to identify.

➤ Pages/sec—Pages refer to discrete amounts of the page file reads from or writes to the hard disk. A bottleneck is not necessarily indicated when this parameter exhibits a high value by itself. If its high reading is also accompanied by a low available bytes memory reading, and a consistent % disk time measurement of 10%, or greater, for a disk using `pagefile.sys`, the memory has become a bottleneck.

Table 21.3 reveals the most common indicators of memory bottlenecks.

Table 21.3   Memory Activity Counters

Counter	Description	Recommended Value
Pages/sec	This is the number of requested pages not immediately available in RAM.	A high rate indicates excessive reading from the disk page file is occurring.
Available bytes	This number indicates how much RAM is available after working sets and cache.	Available bytes should not stay consistently below the system-defined threshold. If this value is low, more memory is needed.
Paging File/% Usage	This value indicates the percentage of the maximum page file used.	A consistently high value requires additional RAM, or a larger page-file size.
Paging File/% Usage Peak	This value indicates the value of peak paging file usage.	A consistently high value requires additional RAM, or a larger page-file size.

Network Interface Bottlenecks

The overall responsiveness of a server network is affected by network performance. The System Monitor performance analysis tool can be used to monitor network activity. The Network Monitor packet analysis tool can also be used to discover *network interface bottlenecks*. Parameters of interest include

➤ Bytes Total/sec—When the network is consistently being utilized at its maximum transfer rate, suspect that the network interface device is a bottleneck.

➤ Current Bandwidth—The maximum transfer rate of the network can be determined from this value. Together with the bytes total/sec parameter, network throughput bottlenecks can be identified.

➤ Output Queue Length—If the length of the output packet queue (in packets) is longer than 2, delays are being experienced. The responsible bottleneck should be located and eliminated, if possible.

➤ Packets Received Errors—The specified device/interface is having problems if during monitoring, it is receiving a much higher number of packets received errors than during an average operation.

A network bottleneck is indicated when the network interface is consistently saturated. The administrator should consider offloading network applications to other servers when this situation develops. Other possible solutions include the installation of a faster network adapter, or placing the physical network on a subnet in order to reduce the overall workload per physical segment. Objects and counters described in Table 21.4 can be analyzed using the System Monitor tool.

Table 21.4	Objects and Counters to Analyze		
Object	**Counters**	**Description**	**Recommended Value**
Transmission Control Protocol (TCP)	Segments Received/sec Segments Retransmitted/sec Segments/sec Segments Sent/sec	These counters indicate traffic at the transport layer.	High values indicate a high number of open Internet ports.
Internet Protocol (IP)	Datagrams Forwarded/sec Datagrams Received/sec Datagrams/sec Datagrams Sent/sec	These counters indicate traffic at the network layer.	High values indicate a large amount of Internet traffic.
Network Interface	Bytes Total/sec	This counter monitors performance of the network adapter.	A high value indicates a large number of successful transfers.

(continued)

Table 21.4 **Objects and Counters to Analyze** *(continued)*			
Object	**Counters**	**Description**	**Recommended Value**
Network Interface	Packets Outbound Discarded	This counter is used to determine network saturation.	A consistently increasing value indicates a network is too busy.
Network Interface	Output Queue Length	This counter is used to determine the length of an output packet.	The value should remain consistently low.

Processor Bottlenecks

Values measured at the processor can also indicate current or future problems. Counters that may be useful in preventing or revealing *processor bottlenecks* include

➤ % Interrupt Time—During the sample interval, this counter measures the percentage of time the processor has spent receiving and servicing hardware interrupts. The activity of devices that generate interrupts, such as system clocks, mice, disk drivers, data communication lines, and network interface cards is indirectly indicated by this value. These devices interrupt the processor when they have completed a task or require attention. During these interrupts, normal thread execution is suspended. The system clock alone, which normally interrupts the processor every 10 milliseconds, creates a background of interrupt activity. The average busy time is displayed as a percentage of the sample time by this counter. If this value is high, the processor is interrupted more often than normal. Peripheral devices should be examined for unusual amounts of activity.

➤ % Processor Time—This counter can determine how much of the processor's capabilities is being tapped. If processor times are seen approaching 100% when only system services are running, the processor is likely already running at maximum capacity. If any additional applications begin running, a bottleneck problem would most likely occur, either immediately or in the near future.

➤ Queue Length—When the queue length is consistently greater than 4, or if there is an increase in the queue length along with a processor time that is greater than 90%, the processor has become a bottleneck.

Table 21.5 identifies several important processor values that can be analyzed using System Monitor.

Table 21.5	Analyzing Processor Values		
Object	**Counter**	**Description**	**Recommended Value**
Processor	% Processor Time	This is the percentage of time the processor is busy processing a non-idle thread.	Should not consistently exceed 80%.
Processor	% Privileged Time	This is the percentage of non-idle and non-user time spent processing.	Should not consistently exceed 80%.
Processor	% User Time	This is the percentage of non-idle and non-privileged time spent processing.	Should not consistently exceed 80%.
System	Processor Queue Length	This is the number of threads waiting for the processor.	Should be consistently less than two.

Network Redirector Bottlenecks

A *network redirector* is a File System Driver (FSD) that functions as a client in a network I/O operation by sending I/O requests to specified servers and processing the related responses. From a server in a network I/O operation, a network redirector receives I/O requests from other servers and/or clients, and processes those requests. The redirector performs all of the low-level interaction with the server for resolving a filename provided by the application with its resource location on the remote server. Client applications use the redirector to access and manipulate resources on remote servers just as if they were actually located on the local server. An important redirector parameter is

Current Commands—A count of the requests sent to the network redirector and processed during the sampling period is called the server's current commands parameter. If the current commands value is larger than the number of network adapter cards installed in the monitored server, a bottleneck exists at the server.

Server Bottlenecks

Two important counters can be used to determine when physical RAM or page file allocations require upgrading or reconfiguring in order to avoid *server bottlenecks*.

➤ Pool Nonpaged Failures—This counter displays the number of times memory allocations from a nonpaged pool have failed. If this value is consistently greater than 1, the server, in all likelihood, has a memory bottleneck.

➤ Pool Paged Failures—When allocations from the paged pool begin to fail consistently, the server's physical memory or paging file is too small and requires attention.

For each of the bottlenecks, know how to look at a baseline for troubleshooting and know where the bottleneck exists.

When analyzing bottlenecks, you need to know how to determine what condition is indicated by the information gathered through different system monitoring tools.

Server Resource Handling

Depending on how a server is being used, demands on its resources will fluctuate radically at various times of the day. For example, the end of an accounting period will undoubtedly usher in the heaviest demand on a company's accounting application server. The file server that contains drawings for a CADD engineering department will see its heaviest usage during normal and extended work hours closely approaching the deadline for getting an important project review package to a client on schedule. The beginning of the workday will signal a spike in usage for a logon server, as clients board the system. The heaviest demands on print servers typically occur during late morning and late afternoon periods.

Task Rescheduling

The overall load on a server can be greatly moderated by *rescheduling* specific activities from peak traffic periods to alternate times. If possible, the best approach is to schedule non-critical tasks that compete with primary applications to non-peak hours. Administrators can determine the best times to schedule these activities through the use of ongoing performance monitoring documentation. For example, it's fairly obvious that a processor-intensive batch job, requiring the compiling and printing of an extensive image library, would not be scheduled to run on a domain controller at 8:00 a.m. on a workday. This is the time when most users are logging on to the system, and the server is busy processing their authentications. A winning approach to this situation would be either to shift such labor-intensive activities to hours when the server has a surplus of available resources, or to reallocate this work to a server not burdened with such critical demand.

Resource Balancing and Distribution

Another way to avoid bottlenecks and optimize the performance of a server/client network system is to employ the process of *resource balancing*. Resource balancing can be achieved through the thoughtful distribution of hardware, I/O, software, and data demands. A server system's overall performance will naturally be enhanced when these resources are distributed as evenly as possible across the system's resources.

The implementation of resource balancing requires the sensible balancing of speed and temperature variations across multiple processors, the thoughtful allotment of PCI cards across multiple available server buses, the equal distribution of data across disks and partitions, and the division of client network load equally across multiple NICs.

Exam Prep Questions

1. A Windows Server 2003 server is examined by the system administrator. Using System Monitor, the administrator notices an abnormally high rate of activity in the disk subsystem. Although the normal conclusion to draw from this evidence is that a bottleneck exists in the disk subsystem, what other parameter check can be made to verify this diagnosis?
   - ❏ A. Network utilization
   - ❏ B. Processor utilization
   - ❏ C. Video system
   - ❏ D. Memory paging

2. A commercial server system is running much too slow following the addition of a dozen client nodes. Running a baseline comparison between the before and after parameters, the following results are observed:

Process	Before	After
Disk drive utilization	10%	8%
Memory paging	1000 pps	3000 pps
Network utilization	25%	40%
Microprocessor utilization	50%	60%

How can the server's unacceptable drop in performance be corrected?
   - ❏ A. Correct the disk drive bottleneck by installing a faster disk subsystem.
   - ❏ B. Correct the memory bottleneck by increasing the page file size, or by installing more RAM.
   - ❏ C. Correct the network bottleneck by transferring various network applications to another server.
   - ❏ D. Correct the processor bottleneck by adding another processor.

Exam Prep Answers

1. Answer D is the correct answer. When not enough RAM is available, paging with Windows uses virtual memory, where a paging file is created on the hard disk of fixed-size data blocks from RAM. Excessive paging results in the overuse of the disk subsystem, and makes the disk look like a resource bottleneck. Answer A is incorrect because the parameters such as Bytes Total/sec, Current Bandwidth, Output Queue Length, and Packets Received Errors do not adequately test

the disk subsystem. Answer B is incorrect because in order to suspect the processor as a bottleneck, the % Interrupt Time would have to be abnormally high. Answer C is incorrect because the video system must be working properly in order to use the System Monitor.

2. Answer B is the correct answer. The baseline comparisons indicate that a bottleneck is occurring in the server's memory paging process. Answer A is incorrect because the disk drive utilization decreased. Answer C is incorrect because the network utilization parameter is nowhere near its saturation point. Answer D is incorrect because the processor's utilization percentage is only slightly higher than before the node additions.

22.0—Disaster Recovery

Terms you'll need to understand:

- ✓ Disaster Recovery Plan (DRP)
- ✓ In-chassis and system redundancy
- ✓ Point of failure
- ✓ Backups
- ✓ Helical scan
- ✓ Quarter-Inch Cartridge (QIC)
- ✓ Digital Audio Tape (DAT)
- ✓ Error-Correcting Code (ECC)
- ✓ Cyclic Redundancy Check (CRC)
- ✓ Data Transfer Rate (DTR)
- ✓ Digital Audio Tape (DAT)
- ✓ Digital Data Storage (DDS)

- ✓ Advanced Intelligent Tape (AIT)
- ✓ Memory-In-Cassette (MIC)
- ✓ Advanced Digital Recording (ADR)
- ✓ Digital Linear Tape (DLT)
- ✓ Super Digital Linear Tape (SDLT)
- ✓ Linear Tape-Open (LTO)
- ✓ Tape libraries and arrays
- ✓ Hierarchical Storage Management (HSM)
- ✓ Policy repository
- ✓ Grandfather-father-son backup rotation
- ✓ Remote Storage Service (RSS)
- ✓ Hot sites, warm sites, and cold sites

Techniques you'll need to master:

- ✓ Planning for a disaster recovery
- ✓ Introducing the disaster recovery plan (DRP)
- ✓ Identifying points of failure
- ✓ Documenting and updating the DRP
- ✓ Scheduling a disaster recovery drill
- ✓ Performing an actual disaster recovery
- ✓ Understanding backup hardware and media
- ✓ Differentiating between various tape backup technologies, systems, and standards

- ✓ Implementing robotic data tape storage solutions
- ✓ Incorporating server network policy statements
- ✓ Determining backup schedules and rotations
- ✓ Recognizing when differential, incremental, full, and/or unscheduled backups are appropriate
- ✓ Extending disk space through alternate backup methods
- ✓ Storing backups offsite

Introduction

Server+ Exam Objective 8.1 states that the test taker should be able to read and follow the DRP. Activities surrounding the DRP include

➤ Finding, reading, and implementing the recovery plan

➤ Confirming and using offsite storage for backup

➤ Participating in the testing of the DRP

To achieve this objective, you need to know and understand the following:

➤ The need for redundancy for hard drives, power supplies, fans, NICs, processors, and UPSes

➤ The ability to read and comprehend a DRP

➤ The various types of backup hardware and media

  ➤ DAT

  ➤ SDAT

  ➤ DLT

  ➤ Super DLT

  ➤ Optical backup device

  ➤ AIT

  ➤ LTO

  ➤ Disk to disk

  ➤ Libraries vs. stand-alones

➤ The types of backup and restoration schemes

➤ The concept of hot, cold and warm sites

A critical element in the management and administration of a server network is the preparation for disaster recovery. Lost data translates into system downtime, wasted production, customer dissatisfaction, and a reduction in company earnings. Although preventive measures are always the preferred tool to use against possible disaster, they cannot guarantee that system recovery will never be necessary. The disaster recovery process should be designed to restore all or part of the server system in the event of a critical failure caused by accident, theft, intentional sabotage, or a naturally occurring disaster. In the event of that inevitable failure, a sufficient *disaster recovery plan*

(DRP) must be in place, consisting of all the necessary elements for an expeditious restoration of the system with no data loss. The most important elements of successfully recovering from a disaster include planning, system redundancy, security, and scheduled backup.

Documenting the Disaster Recovery Plan

One of the most important aspects of a DRP is the creation and distribution of a printed copy of the plan itself. By planning for the worst possible data security scenario, the company and its employees will be prepared to recover from any server failure or system disaster that might occur.

Know that the most important part of a DRP is having the plan printed out and stored in a safe place.

The plan itself is the first and foremost factor in preparing for a successful disaster recovery. It should include a complete inventory of all the components that make up each network in the system, as well as all components that make up each server and workstation. This includes all associated software that needs to be restored. This inventory should be prioritized; it should list which systems are most critical to the company's operation, meaning that they must be restored first. These priorities are most easily identified by considering how valuable the data is on each system. The monetary and productive cost to the company in the event of server failure should be determined. Most often, these studies reveal that the labor and hardware costs associated with planning, preventive maintenance, redundancy, security, and data backup are less than the inevitable financial loss due to a major server system failure. As such, the DRP should be formulated side by side with the planning for the original server network scheme, prior to any installation work.

Know when to create a DRP.

Provisions and procedures for recovery from various types of data loss and system failure should be included in the DRP, including natural disasters, electricity-related failures, or server shutdowns. Situations that might require detailed recovery scenarios include floods, fires, power outages, viruses, sabotage, or hacking. When the DRP properly addresses the obvious reasons for its implementation and completely outlines all necessary steps to be taken, server downtime will be greatly minimized when it becomes necessary to actually use the plan.

This plan should also include reliable methods by which each department can continue to function productively during those periods when networks are down. A means to successfully synchronize and integrate newly generated data when the infrastructure is restored must also be formulated. The administrator is responsible for ensuring that all department heads are aware of the plan and are capable of implementing it if and when necessary.

Updating the Plan

As critical as it might be, any DRP will quickly become obsolete if it is not updated periodically. The plan itself should detail procedures for how and when it will be updated, stored, and preserved. The following supporting documentation is usually bundled with a DRP:

➤ A copy of the official DRP

➤ An inventory of the DRP documentation package components

➤ Contact information for all individuals on the disaster recovery team

➤ Hardware and software listings associated with the server, and copies of the applicable information manuals

➤ Copies of critical software and hardware drivers

➤ Location information for primary and offsite backup data packages

➤ Baseline metric data for both recent and original measurements

➤ All other critical plan elements

DRP documentation should be duplicated in hardcopy and immediately available onsite. Copies should also be stored with all offsite system data backups. These copies must also be continually revised as the plan is updated.

Be aware that DRP documentation should be stored offsite in addition to backup tapes.

Testing the Plan

Testing a DRP within the company's actual working environment can be difficult; however, a disaster recovery drill should be scheduled yearly. The difficulties involved with implementing a DRP are not fully understood without experience. Exercising the disaster recovery system will reinforce the importance of performing timely and consistent backups so that data recoveries are always possible.

Various strategies can be developed to test the plan without actually shutting down the server. To become familiar with the critical elements, members of the disaster recovery team should study the plan and dry-run portions of it throughout the year. By doing so, they will reveal, consider, and correct various weaknesses in the plan, and new features might be added as required. Although even the most thoughtful plans can have weaknesses, a consistently rehearsed and edited plan will serve to minimize them.

DRPs are often tested by actually performing the necessary data restorations to the appropriate servers. These tests are critically important because data restorations must be performed correctly. For example, mail server data must not accidentally be restored to a designated file server. The confusion in distinguishing servers will be compounded by performance problems with servers handling data for which they are not properly configured. Therefore, a method for identifying and marking specific types of data for its intended destination server must be considered in the design stage of the DRP. You must ensure that each backup tape is marked with appropriate dates and server IDs for that backup. To ensure that data and hardware matches, the server case itself should also be labeled with its individual server ID.

When testing the plan, the administrator must make sure it functions properly, and that all personnel are aware of their individual roles. Areas of the plan deserving review include the following:

➤ Make sure that the documentation is usable and that components can be located easily.

➤ Test the notification procedures, so that there is always a reliable means to contact personnel when the server goes down. For example, if the company's e-commerce site is down, those supervisors will need to be informed. Ensure that current phone numbers for these personnel are on hand, for all times of the day and night.

➤ Verify that the location and identity of all spare components or servers listed in the plan are correct.

> ➤ Make sure that the telephone numbers for all equipment vendors and manufacturers are available and correct.

> ➤ Check all support contracts and ensure that phone numbers are available for any that are still in effect.

Backup tapes should be tested at least once a month, or as often as once a week for more critical servers. The administrator should perform a full restore test at least once a quarter. This restore testing should be performed by restoring the data to a different folder than its original location to ensure that the backup contains all necessary data without being contaminated by pre-existing files.

Large enterprises conduct periodic testing of full disaster recovery plans. To maintain business continuity while testing the recovery plan, they often bring a commercial hot-site facility online as a systems backup. This facility has a complete backup of the company's online data and can provide business continuity during the time that the main site is down for testing. This arrangement provides a real-time testing environment for the company's IT staff in the knowledge and execution of the DRP. Hot-site facilities are discussed later in this chapter, in the section "Offsite Storage Planning."

After the test has been completed, the results might indicate that more planning or troubleshooting is required. For example, if data was accidentally restored to an email server that should have been restored to the file server, the DRP must be examined carefully to determine what went wrong. Then it will need to be edited and rerun to ensure that the problem has been eliminated.

Know what to do when testing the restore function results in data being restored to the wrong servers.

Implementing the Plan

In the event of an actual disaster, several steps must be followed, in sequential order, to ensure that the data will be restored to the correct locations, and that the actual cause of the failure is found:

1. Discover what caused the server to go down.

2. Determine how to perform the necessary repair.

3. Identify any failed components.

4. Match failed components to existing good components.

5. Implement the DRP.

The DRP should provide enough documentation and test results to permit the full restoration of the company's data. After the DRP has been implemented, the network should be returned to normal operation.

System Redundancy Planning

To maintain network resources, extra hardware is often devoted to the express purpose of immediately replacing any failing device. This practice is known as *redundancy*. The addition of backup power supplies, hard drives, and network cards provides *in-chassis redundancy*. The process of increasing the number of servers in the system implements *system redundancy*. The placement of additional servers helps to prevent a single malfunction from causing network failure. The loss of any server network element that can potentially cause the shutdown of a critical process makes the location of that element a *point of failure*. For example, if the only email server in the system were to malfunction, it would be considered as a point of failure. The company employees would be unable to send and receive email until the service was restored. This scenario can be avoided by the strategic deployment of redundant components and servers.

Know how to avoid single points of failure in server networks.

Offsite Storage Planning

System redundancy must also take the data into consideration. Remember that even though new hardware can be purchased, new buildings can be built, and new personnel can be hired, the company's data cannot be purchased at any price if it is lost. The success or failure of any DRP depends to a large degree on how and where the various server backups are stored. Many options are available.

Storing backups at a separate location within the building might preserve the data in the event of an accident or other destructive event in the server room. However, this data would still be in significant peril during a building-wide or area-wide disaster. Therefore, the odds of company data surviving a catastrophe are greatly increased when multiple copies of the data exist and at least one backup copy is securely stored offsite. In fact, the ideal backup storage scenario is for two sets of each backup to be made, with one stored onsite allowing immediate access in case of a localized system failure, and the other stored offsite to ensure survival in case of a major disaster such as a flood, fire, hurricane, or earthquake.

Another necessity, in addition to an offsite backup of company data, is a spare tape drive and cable to ensure that the recovery of lost data can be quickly facilitated in a disaster. It's also a good idea to keep copies of essential applications stored offsite as well, including the NOS. Finally, any backup plan must take into consideration the periodic backup of remote storage tapes themselves to allow data recovery from the backups in the event that the original remote storage tapes become lost or corrupted.

In addition to storing duplicate system backup tapes in a simple offsite lockbox, there are several types of active offsite storage backup facilities to consider using:

➤ Hot sites—These are sites where the backup facility has continuous access to the server, either directly or remotely, allowing ongoing mirror operations of the primary server to be conducted. The replication speeds of these operations depend mostly on the distance that separates the hot site from the primary site. These types of systems are frequently employed to allow access to the server's data by outside clients, especially in the case of lengthy troubleshooting sessions at the primary server site, or in the event of catastrophic failure there. The offsite facility could also be used to store historical backup data for periodic access if it becomes needed.

➤ Cold sites—These sites are not continuously connected to the primary server, but are periodically connected according to a prearranged schedule, for the purpose of copying the backup data. For small businesses, this is the most common type of remote backup system used. The cold site's equipment is used only to perform backup or restore functions in these cases.

Backup facilities may be located within the same geographical area in which the server is operating, or they may be located hundreds of miles away. Disaster recovery technology is evolving rapidly, and many of those agencies that have incorporated cold sites into their backup strategies have been in the process of upgrading to *warm sites*. Warm sites are not continuously connected in the way hot sites are, but they are equipped with wide-area networking and other basic communications assets. They can be implemented using commercial or even free software and are typically used to protect information classified as important. An optimal warm-site implementation is much easier to manage than a hot site, although it is more susceptible to increased data loss. The elimination of proprietary software licenses at both the primary and warm site makes its operation significantly less expensive.

Backup Hardware and Media

Although server system *backups* are usually performed by copying the entire contents of system hard drives to backup tapes, other methods of backup can be used as well, provided the time spent using them can be justified. Some administrators have been known to simply replicate the contents of every hard drive in the system onto other hard drives capable of being plugged directly in if any of the original drives fail. This approach, though fast, is an extremely expensive one.

At the opposite end of the cost spectrum, backups can also be created using older equipment and media, when such storage requirements are mandated due to budget restraints. This approach requires maintaining or storing older equipment and its associated operational software to ensure the future retrieval of the data. When this backup method is used, details outlining the exact steps to be taken to successfully retrieve data must be included in the organization's customized DRP.

In a worst-case scenario, requirements might dictate that a separate computer be maintained and equipped with legacy operating system and equipment to ensure the possible recovery of archived data. In a pinch, this arrangement could be used to provide successful server data recoveries from DVD-ROM, CD-ROM, or even (gasp) floppy disks. Certainly, a system administrator would be extremely nervous to realize that the survival of the company rested on the successful recovery of data stored on thousands of fragile floppy disks!

Tape Drive Backup Systems

Modern server hardware backup systems usually rely on tape drives, which are currently the most cost-effective and durable devices on the market. Backup tape systems utilize small magnetic tape cartridges (see Figure 22.1) capable of storing large amounts of data in either a raw or compressed format.

Figure 22.1 A backup tape cartridge.

However, in spite of their cost effectiveness, backup tape cartridges are slow when restoring only a small quantity of data. Unlike the random access capabilities of disk drives, most tape drives store and retrieve information linearly. This often requires scanning an entire tape to locate a small amount of required data. For this reason, tape drives are never used for online data storage, where speedy data retrieval is imperative. They are most effective in backing up extremely large amounts of data and application programs. Backups of application programming permit the restoration of software systems with their applications ready to execute, making system reconfigurations unnecessary.

Backup electronic storage requirements have dramatically increased because more servers are increasingly dedicated to data-intensive, mission-critical applications. As a result, tape drive technology has been steadily adapting to provide higher capacity, increased performance, and improved data integrity solutions. The result is the emergence of a new generation of tape drive technology along with a hierarchical class of tape storage management, where server system backups can be reliably conducted without the intervention of manual commands.

Quarter-Inch Cartridge Tape Backup Systems
A QIC looks similar to an audiocassette tape cartridge, with two reels to spool data and a built-in drive belt. A metal capstan rod projects from the drive motor and pinches the magnetic tape against a rubber drive wheel. The QIC format appears similar in construction to that shown in Figure 22.2.

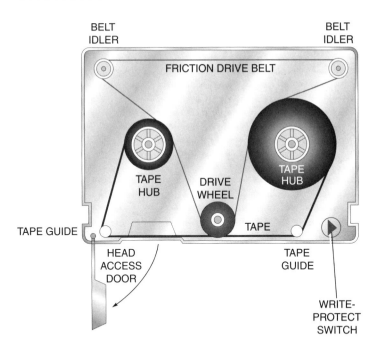

Figure 22.2   A quarter-inch tape cartridge.

Data is written to parallel tracks running along the length of the tape using a linear recording technique, and the number of tracks determines the data capacity of the tape. During a backup operation, the directory information is loaded into the system's RAM, along with the files to be backed up. As these two sets of data are sent to the tape drive controller, a header containing its directory information prefaces each file.

The tape moves past the stationary read/write heads between 100 to 125 inches per second in record mode. Standard drives and formats use heads that read/write data in straight lines, one track at a time. Drive performance can be dramatically improved by adding more read/write heads. QIC read/write heads are depicted in Figure 22.3.

Just below the middle of the tape is where the first track is written. The direction of tape travel reverses as the tape reaches one of its ends and the head repositions to the next outside track. The complete directory of backed-up files is usually listed at the beginning of track 0.

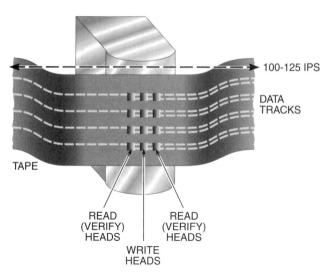

Figure 22.3 QIC read/write heads.

In the mid-1990s, QIC cartridges began providing greatly increased data capacities through lengthening and widening of the tape. Table 22.1 reports the native capacities for the most commonly used QIC formats.

Table 22.1 QIC Standard Most Commonly Used Formats				
Specification	Tracks	0.25-inch	Long Tape	0.315-inch
QIC-80	28/36	80MB	400MB	500MB
QIC-3010	40/50	340MB	n/a	420MB
QIC-3020	40/50	670MB	n/a	840MB
QIC-3080	60/77	1.18GB	1.6GB	2GB
QIC-3095	72	n/a	4GB	2GB

The main weakness with the QIC format is the incompatibility between all of its existing standards.

Travan Tape Backup Systems

The Travan specification provides rational backward compatibility with earlier QIC standards, offering a number of high-capacity formats. Rugged high-quality QIC/Travan cartridges are more expensive than DAT cartridges. However, tape drive hardware is reduced through the use of built-in tape alignment and tensioning elements in the cartridges.

Travan drives have been standardized by the QIC consortium, and are backward compatible with previous QIC standards. They are capable of reading from and writing to older QIC tapes, as well as current high-capacity Travan tapes. Travan cartridges look much like QIC cartridges, and Travan tape drives are sometimes able to read certain types of QIC tapes. Table 22.2 displays the characteristics of various Travan tape and drive formats.

Table 22.2	Characteristics of Travan Tapes and Drives				
Parameter	TR-1	TR-2	TR-3	TR-4	TR-5
Capacity:					
Native	400MB	800MB	1.6GB	4GB	10GB
Compressed	800MB	1.6GB	3.2GB	8GB	20GB
DTR:					
Minimum	62.5KBps	62.5KBps	125KBps	60MB/min	60MB/min
Maximum	125KBps	125KBps	250KBps	70MB/min	110MB/min
Tracks	36	50	50	72	108
Data Density	14,700 ftpi	22,125 ftpi	44,250 ftpi	50,800 ftpi	50,800 ftpi
Compatibility	QIC-80 (R/W) QIC-40 (R only)	QIC-3010 (R/W) QIC-80 (R only)	QIC-3010 (R/W) QIC-3020 (R only)	QIC-3080 (R/W) QIC-3095 (R only)	QIC-3220 (R/W) TR-4 (R only)

* ftpi = flux transitions per inch

Digital Audio Tape Backup Systems

The *Digital Audio Tape (DAT)* format has gained public acceptance in the realm of data storage. The ability to back up large amounts of data onto small tape cartridges is a tribute to the unique design of the DAT tape drive.

DAT drives also use a helical scanning recording system, with a cylinder head that is slightly tilted to permit the data to be placed on the tape at a slightly offset angle, as depicted in Figure 22.4. The cylinder head spins at 2,000 RPM, while the tape is moved less than one inch per second in a direction opposite to that of the spinning cylinder. The effect is the same as if the tape were moving at 150 inches per second, and the linear space required for the data is minimized by the angled recording technique.

Additional data information is recorded over the stripes of the first data group using a second write head. An opposite polarity encoding method positions this second recording at a different angle to the first, permitting the DAT drive to record huge amounts of data with reliable integrity.

DAT drive restore operations require that the entire directory of the tape first be read by the backup software. Next, the tape is wound to the appropriate location and the targeted contents are read into the controller's buffer. Data that has been verified as correct is then written to the hard disk.

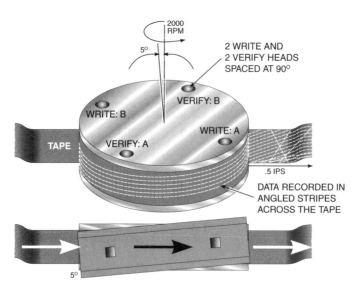

Figure 22.4 A DAT drive recording scheme.

The most popular data storage format used with DAT is called *Digital Data Storage (DDS)*. Various DDS standards are listed in Table 22.3 along with related technical information, and are designed to be backward compatible.

Table 22.3 Current and Proposed DDS Standards		
Standard	**Capacity**	**Maximum DTR**
DDS	2GB	55KBps
DDS-1	2/4GB	0.55/1.1MBps
DDS-2	4/8GB	0.55/1.1MBps
DDS-3	12/24GB	1.1/2.2MBps
DDS-4	20/40GB	2.4/4.8MBps
DDS-5/DAT-72	36/72GB	3.5/7.0MBps
DDS-6/DAT-140	80/160GB	5.0/10.0MBps
*DDS-7/DAT-240	160/320GB	8.0/16.0MBps

*due for release on 2007

One thing to keep in mind is that DAT drives are only compatible with SCSI interfaces, and although they offer large capacities, they retail at nearly twice the price of QIC drives. However, their higher costs reflect the increased usability of their tape cartridges.

Know which tape formats will maximize the storage of a DAT drive.

Tape Backup Systems Using 8MM Technology

Originally designed for the video industry, 8mm tape technology is increasingly used in the IT market as a reliable data storage method. Although very similar to DAT, 8mm provides greater storage capacities using helical scan technology. There are three major 8mm protocols being utilized today: Standard 8mm, Mammoth, and Advance Intelligent Tape (AIT). These 8mm protocols use different compression algorithms and drive technologies, but their basic function is identical. The key features of current 8mm tape cartridge protocols are summarized in Table 22.4.

Table 22.4 Features of Various 8mm Protocols			
Protocol	**Capacity**	**Interface**	**Maximum DTR**
Standard 8mm	3.5/7.0GB	SCSI	32MB/min
Standard 8mm	5.0/10.0GB	SCSI	60MB/min
Standard 8mm	7.0/14.0GB	SCSI	60MB/min
Standard 8mm	7.0/14.0GB	SCSI	120MB/min
Mammoth	20/40GB	SCSI	360MB/min
Mammoth-2	60/150GB	Ultra2/LVD SCSI	720MB/min
Mammoth-2 Fiber	60/150GB	Fiber Channel	1800MB/min
AIT-1	25/50GB	SCSI	360MB/min

Mammoth 8MM Technology

The *Mammoth* tape drive technology was introduced in 1996 as a more reliable 8mm standard containing 40% fewer parts than previous 8mm drives. This improves the tape drive's reliability by reducing the tape wear and tension variations. Exabyte Corporation built their Mammoth tape decks out of solid aluminum castings, providing the rigidity required to perform the heavier workloads demanded by data backup operations. The internal workings of the drive were protected from dust and contamination, and heat was directed away from the tape path.

Mammoth drives are designed without capstans and do not cause damage to the tape edges during repositioning. This supports the use of *Advanced Metal Evaporated (AME)* recording media, which is thinner and more sensitive than previous media types. This data-grade tape will store large amounts of data per cartridge, while its anti-corrosive properties permit a 30-year archival rating.

The Fibre Channel version of the Mammoth-2 8mm protocol standard offered an increased native DTR of 30MBps. The introduction of the Mammoth protocol changed the way in which tape backup was previously viewed, making it more favorably comparable to magnetic disk backup techniques.

Advanced Intelligent 8MM Tape Technology

The first multisourced 8mm tape standard targeted at the midrange server market was *Advanced Intelligent Tape (AIT)*. Introduced in 1996, AIT provided the combination of exceptional data integrity, speed, and capacity through the use of stronger, thinner, more stable tape media. Server-level tape technology now included advanced head designs, higher levels of circuit integration, and a unique *Memory-In-Cassette (MIC)* feature resulting in a multi-gigabyte, high-performance, low-error tape drive system.

As drive firmware, the MIC estimates how far to fast-forward or rewind, eliminating the need to read individual address ID markers on a moving tape. The motors slow down as the target zone approaches, and sensors read the ID markers for fine positioning. These search speeds exceed the tape drive's normal read/write capabilities by up to 150 times! AIT is perfect for server backup systems running robot applications with tape libraries.

When AME media technology is combined with AIT, data integrity is considerably improved. The construction process for AME tape includes the application of two additional layers: a backcoat, applied to the substrate to reduce friction with Mammoth drive components, and a lubrication layer tops the *Recording Surface Protective Coating (RSPC)* layer to improve durability, as shown in Figure 22.5. In addition to improved durability, the hardness and anti-corrosive properties of the RSPC coating reduce tape wear and its resulting debris accumulations, allowing the media to achieve a 30-year archival rating, and withstand 20,000 passes.

Higher signal outputs than normally provided by conventional tape systems were made possible by Sony's superior *Hyper Metal Laminate Head (HMLH)* technology for use in AIT-2 drives. This development enabled a 50% increase in data recording density. With advanced data security coming to the 3 1/2-inch tape form factor, protection against inadvertent or malicious deletion/alteration of data made this format particularly suited for the archival of financial, securities, insurance, medical, and government data.

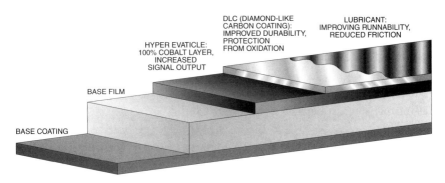

Figure 22.5   Layers of AME tape.

The AIT family of data tape compression formats is compared in Table 22.5.

Table 22.5   AIT Formats

Parameter	AIT-1	AIT-3	AIT-3	S-AIT
Native Capacity	35GB	50GB	100GB	500GB
Compressed Capacity	90GB	130GB	260GB	1300GB
Native DTR	4MBps	6MBps	12MBps	30MBps
Compressed DTR	10MBps	15.6MBps	31.2MBps	78MBps
Form Factor	3 1/2-inch	3 1/2-inch	3 1/2-inch	5 1/2-inch
Media Type	8mm AME	8mm AME	8mm AME	1/2-inch AME

Advanced Digital Recording

The unique ability to simultaneously read or write eight tracks of data is incorporated with *Advanced Digital Recording (ADR)* data tape technology. This approach enables the delivery of impressive transfer rates at relatively low speeds, providing minimal tape wear. ADR's continuous monitoring technique, called *full tape servo*, helps to precisely reposition the tape in the event it moves up or down even the slightest amount and results in an extremely high track density for 8mm tape. The combination of full tape servo and multi-channel recording make ADR tape drives an outstanding data reliability specification. Merely one unreadable bit in every 1,019 recorded bits is a common bit error rate (BER), making ADR drives 10,000 times more reliable than hard disk drives.

Data can be recorded twice as efficiently as with traditional tape drives due to ADR's advanced media-defect-mapping technique, which allows the drive to map defective areas of the media and to avoid writing data to these locations. This permits ADR to handle these media defects in a single pass.

Future enhancements to the ADR standard may see it outgrowing its original concept as an 8mm solution with increased potential for wider and longer media applications.

Digital Linear Tape Backup Systems

Using half-inch wide metal particle tapes that are 60% wider than 8mm recording media, *Digital Linear Tape (DLT)* drives record their data in serpentine patterns on parallel tracks. By using a technique called *Symmetric Phase Recording (SPR)*, as many as 208 tracks can be recorded by angling the data onto adjacent tracks in a herringbone pattern. In this way, SPR eliminates the need for using guard bands, and permits greater track density.

What makes the DLT drive unique is the design of its *Head Guide Assembly (HGA)*. The HGA is a patented boomerang-shaped aluminum plate, fitted with six large bearing-mounted rollers, as shown in Figure 22.6.

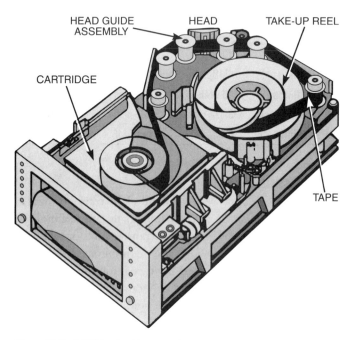

Figure 22.6 A DLT head guide assembly.

The tape's leader strip is pulled out of the cartridge by the DLT guide system. The leader strip is threaded around the head guide assembly in a smooth arc, and then gently wrapped around the drive's take-up reel. As with most helical scan systems, the rollers guide the tape, without pulling it, to ensure that the recorded side never touches the guides and to minimize tape wear. The life of a DLT drive's recording head is specified at 30,000 hours, compared to 2,000 hours for those used with 8mm helical scan devices.

In order to optimize performance over a wide range of host data rates, DLT technology incorporates a highly effective adaptive cache-buffering feature. This gives the tape drive the ability to adjust its tracking to the data rate of the host system for maximum tape throughput. This is important because if the transfer rate of a tape drive exceeds that of the host, the tape mechanism will be forced to frequently stop and reposition, thus degrading system performance. By monitoring the host system and dynamically adjusting cache-buffering operations to match its data rate, repositioning delays are minimized and throughput is improved.

Near-line applications that manipulate images must frequently search for files and append or restore data. The time required to do this is an important measurement for tape drives. DLT technology minimizes the time required to perform these searches by locating a file mark index at the logical end of the tape, which lists the tape segment address of each file. The drive consults the index for the address of the specified file, "steps" to the track containing the file, and performs a high-speed streaming search. Any file in a 20GB DLT tape can be located in an average of 45 seconds. Several common DLT formats are listed in Table 22.6.

Table 22.6 Some More Common DLT Formats		
Type	Disk Space Native/Compressed	Data Transfer Bandwidth
DLT 2000	15GBs/30GBs	2.5MB/sec
DLT 4000	20GBs/40GBs	3.0MB/sec
DLT 1	40GBs/80GBs	6.0MB/sec
DLT VS80	40GBs/80GBs	6.0MB/sec
DLT 7000	35GBs/70GBs	10MB/sec
DLT 8000	40GBs/80GBs	12MB/sec
DLT VS160	80GBs/160GBs	16MB/sec

Super Digital Linear Tape

Super Digital Linear Tape (SDLT) formats increase the capacity and the transfer rates of the DLT standard, while maintaining backward compatibility with earlier DLT standards. However, SuperDLT drives far exceed the 35GB native capacity of the DLT 7000 format. They use a combination of optical and magnetic recording techniques called *Laser Guided Magnetic Recording (LGMR)* to precisely align the recording heads. LGMR incorporates *Pivoting Optical Servo (POS)* technology to reduce sensitivity to external influences and incorporate high track densities for use with high-duty cycle applications. The need for formatting the tape is eliminated, decreasing the cost of manufacturing and increasing user convenience. The optical servo operates on the media's formerly unused backside, gaining 10 to 20% more recording surface capacity for actual data.

Highly efficient recording densities are encoded through an advanced technology called *Partial Response Maximum Likelihood (PRML)*. Normally associated with hard disk drives, this technique further increases data capacity and boosts its transfer rates. Several SDLT standards are included in Table 22.7.

Table 22.7 Various SuperDLT Standards					
Parameter	SDLT 220	SDLT 320	SDLT 640	SDLT 1280	SDLT 2400
Native Capacity	110GB	160GB	320GB	640GB	1.2TB
Compressed Capacity	220GB	320GB	640GB	1.28TB	2.4TB
Native DTR	11MBps	16MBps	32MBps	50+MBps	100+MBps
Compressed DTR	22MBps	32MBps	64MBps	100+MBps	200+MBps
Interfaces	Ultra2 SCSI LVD HVD	Ultra2 SCSI Ultra160 SCSI	Ultra320 SCSI Fibre Channel	To be determined	To be determined

Linear Tape-Open Backup Systems

The *Linear Tape-Open (LTO)* tape technology has resulted in the development of the Ultrium format-compliant tape drives, which are designed to be extremely fast, reliable, and optimized for high capacity. LTO's beginning specifications include a maximum native mode transfer rate of 15MBps with an accompanying media capacity of 100GB.

The reliability of LTO technology surpasses that of other tape technologies, including DLT and DAT. For example, LTO head life has been engineered for 60,000 hours as compared to 30,000 hours for DLT 1 and DLT 7000. Multiple component redundancy also ensures that LTO tape drives will meet the increasing demands of server backup systems.

Although LTO technology is not backward-compatible with DLT, it offers impressive performance and capacity improvements. Table 22.8 provides comparative specifications for the LTO Ultrium against various DLT technologies.

Table 22.8 LTO and DLT Tape Technology Comparisons

Feature	DLT 4000	DLT 7000	DLT 8000	SDLT	DLT 1	LTO Ultrium
MTBF @ 100% duty cycle	200,000 hrs	250,000 hrs	250,000 hrs	250,000 hrs	200,000 hrs	250,000 hrs
Capacity (native)	20GB	35GB	40GB	100GB	40GB	100GB
Capacity (compressed)	40GB	70GB	80GB	200GB	80GB	200GB
Transfer Rate (native)	1.5MBps	5.0MBps	6.0MBps	11.0MBps	3MBps	15MBps
Transfer Rate (compressed)	3.0MBps	10.0MBps	12.0MBps	22.0MBps	6MBps	30MBps
Read Compatibility	DLT 2000	DLT 4000	DLT 4000 DLT 7000	DLT4000 DLT 7000 DLT 8000 DLT 1	DLT 4000	LTO Ultrium Open Format
Head Life	10,000 hrs	30, 000 hrs	30,000 hrs	30,000	30,000 hrs	60,000 hours

Robotic Applications for Data Tape Storage

Automated solutions for data tape storage applications provide the speed, capacity, and reliability options needed to protect shared network data. Among the recently emerging storage solutions are tape libraries, tape arrays, and hierarchical storage management applications.

Tape Libraries

Storing, retrieving, reading, and writing multiple magnetic tape cartridges are all activities that can be performed through the use of a high-capacity *tape library*. In addition to the heavy demands already placed on servers, they must also handle the automated access and control functions for nearline data storage, such as tape libraries. Tape libraries incorporate two important pieces of hardware, one being the tape drive itself. The other is a robotic autoloader, which provides the required tape cartridge capacity by picking up the tape cartridges from within its built-in storage racks, loading them into the drive as required or directed by the backup software, removing them when they fill with data, and storing them until they are needed.

Even small tape libraries can utilize several tape drives to handle simultaneous reading and writing chores and control operations for anywhere from several cartridges up to several hundred. Large systems can be composed of hundreds of tape drives and store several thousand cartridges. Although tape library devices are not as fast as online hard disks, they do have their data readily available at all times, and are therefore referred to as "near-line" devices.

Tape Arrays

Tape arrays have become an extremely practical solution for midrange storage requirements. The platform is based on RAID technology borrowed from hard disk subsystems. Unlike the slow sequential access operations that take place on a single device, tape arrays utilize special controllers that can stripe data across multiple tape drives in parallel. In addition, most tape arrays can be configured with a parity drive to provide extra fault tolerance. However, the use of a parity drive decreases the system's overall throughput.

Hierarchical Storage Management

When an administrator is seeking to minimize storage costs while simultaneously optimizing system performance, he or she may opt for the *Hierarchical Storage Management (HSM)* application. This approach combines multiple storage media such as magnetic disks, optical disks, and tape into a single logical unit. As such, its data can be automatically and transparently migrated between the various media based on its access frequency. HSM is more frequently used in the distributed network of an enterprise, although it can be implemented on a standalone system.

This management occurs in a way that uses storage devices economically. The administrator does not need to be aware of every file manipulation being carried out between the system and the backup storage media. Different types of storage media are represented in the hierarchy, with each type representing a different level of cost and retrieval speed. When called for, HSM determines whether the access methods require the use of RAID, optical storage, and/or tape. For example, as a file ages in an archive, it can be automatically moved to a slower but less expensive form of storage.

HSM is actually a policy-based file management system whereby a formal set of statements are used to define the allocation of network resources among clients such as individual users, departments, servers, or applications. These network resources can be allocated according to time of day, client authorization priorities, resource availability, and network traffic variations. After the administrator determines what the policy statements will be, they are stored inside the network management software's *policy repository*. During network operation, the policies are retrieved and used by the HSM software to make storage decisions about when to back up or archive files and migrate them from one form of backup storage to another.

The *Remote Storage Service (RSS)* feature of the HSM system for Windows 2000 Server and Windows Server 2003 allows disk space to be extended on the server even though additional hard drives are not installed on the system. Instead, infrequently used programs and data are moved to slower storage devices, such as tape drives, CD-RW, or DVD-RW. The RSS function is used to help the system maintain the appearance of this data being present online, and retrieving the data from the slower devices when requested by a client. Space is reclaimed from the server without creating a noticeable network inconvenience.

The RSS utility is not a substitute for regularly scheduled system backups, but serves as an additional layer of protection in the overall backup plan. The RSS function is a Microsoft Management Console (MMC) snap-in that is part of the Microsoft hierarchical storage management system depicted in Figure 22.7.

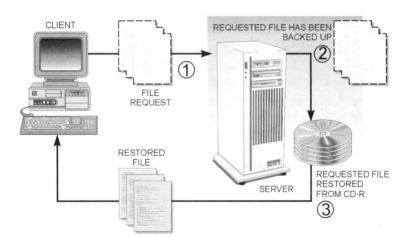

Figure 22.7   The Microsoft hierarchical storage management system.

The HSM software, as established by the administrator's policy, automatically governs how often different kinds of files are copied to a backup storage device, and which type of device is used. For example, older files that are not frequently accessed are automatically moved to less expensive storage.

Backup Scheduling Considerations

Backup scheduling must take into account what types of backups must be performed and when they must be performed. These considerations must ensure that an acceptable level of recovery will be possible if and when a system failure occurs. The following questions must be adequately answered when setting up a backup methodology:

➤ How critical is the data being backed up?

➤ Can the company tolerate losing the financial records created over the past 24 hours?

➤ Which server systems are critical enough to deserve first reinstatement?

➤ How far back should system settings be retained?

➤ How far back must backups go to recover the specified files?

➤ During normal operation, how long can servers remain offline while backups are performed?

Another critical element in determining a backup schedule is the amount of time it will take. Although the quickest and most complete system recovery is made possible through the performance of a full system backup, the amount of server downtime required to perform it could be expensive. The company must be able to afford to halt productivity during the time necessary to perform a full system backup. When backing up a small server system that is measured in megabytes, server downtime might not be an issue. However, a system database measured in multiple gigabytes or terabytes can adversely affect overall company productivity during a full server backup.

When determining the company's backup methodology, considerations must include not only when to perform these backups, but what form of media rotation will be used.

Backup Rotation Schemes

After the administrator is convinced that the company's backup plan is sufficiently robust to ensure the initial recovery of the server system, he or she must then determine under what conditions the retrieval of historical copies of company data will be activated. The historical timeframe under which company data can be retrieved is determined by the backup media rotation method employed. Numerous media rotation methods are available, with each one having its own timeframe of available data to recover.

Grandfather-Father-Son

One of the most common backup media rotation methods used today is called the *grandfather-father-son*, as shown in Figure 22.8. Notice that the backup tapes are divided into three different groupings: the grandfather for monthly backups, the father for weekly backups, and the son for daily backups.

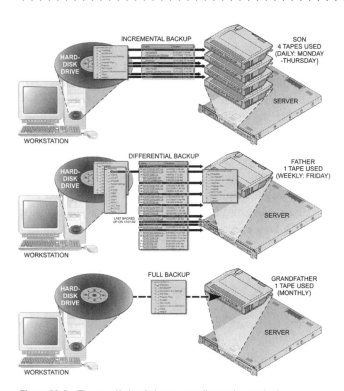

Figure 22.8 The grandfather-father-son media rotation method.

The typical daily son backup group uses four tapes, one for the weekdays of Monday, Tuesday, Wednesday, and Thursday. These backups are typically made using the incremental backup method. The weekly father backup is performed each Friday, and uses one tape per week with the differential backup method. The next subsequent daily backups reuse the corresponding son tapes. At the end of the month, one tape is used to run the grandfather backup, which is a full system backup. The specific needs of the company determine whether these tapes are stored in an ongoing historical backup library, or reused in a rotation scheme for future backups.

 | Know how many tapes are required to restore using a grandfather-father-son backup implementation.

Full Daily

A basic backup scheme can be implemented whereby a full copy of every file is backed up to a new tape each evening. In this scenario, the expense of the tape media alone is enough to force an administrator into adopting some form of tape rotation schedule. Even though these are full backups, the Monday through Thursday tapes might be recycled each week, and the Friday tapes would be stored without rotation for one year. If an annual restoration scheme is considered to be overkill, a 30-day protection system can be implemented through the use of four different sets of Monday-through-Thursday tapes. Having multiple sets of tapes would prevent short-lived files from being lost completely by the end of the week.

When every backup tape in the system contains a full backup, the possibility of restoring the system to a specific date would require locating the tape that was used for backup on the night in question. A failure of this particular tape media would not spell disaster because the data would still be available using a tape from the set going a day or so forward or backward.

Although the restoration scenario of a full daily backup regimen is simplified, its cost is quite substantial. The administrator will be required to devote considerable amounts of time to the tasks of using different tapes each backup session, maintaining the tape backup hardware, managing the growing tape library, and performing the necessary file restorations. Costs associated with this implementation would include the tape drive(s), their maintenance requirements, and all of the required tape media. In order to protect data that is located on a client machine not equipped with a tape drive, running the required backup will undoubtedly impact the operation of other network services.

Progressive Incremental

One type of backup software takes the incremental storage backup approach deeper than others. Originally developed by IBM, the Tivoli Storage Manager (TSM) uses only the incremental approach to conducting server system backups. Its initial backup assumes an incremental format even though every file is included, similar to a full backup. Each subsequent evening, backups involve only the files that have changed since the most recent backup session (normally the one conducted the previous night). TSM is intelligent enough to send only as many or as few bytes across the network as have changed since the previous backup.

In addition to conserving large amounts of storage space on the tape, when compared to periodic full backups, progressive incremental backup software provides these additional capabilities:

➤ Consolidation of tape hardware

➤ Policy-based management

➤ Database management techniques for all data

➤ Automatic reclamation of tape space

➤ Simplified arranging of offsite data

➤ Database and application plug-ins

➤ Automatic tape changes

File restorations keyed to specific dates are initiated through requests to the TSM server. The server locates the requested data from within its storage pools, mounts the appropriate media, and transfers a copy of the data back to the requesting client. This is all accomplished without any human intervention.

Windows Removable Storage

The Windows Removable Storage utility is another tool that provides system administrators with a variety of storage options. It is located in the Computer Management section, as shown in Figure 22.9. This tool permits the removable media devices attached to the server to be set up, shared, and managed by either Windows or third-party backup applications. The Removable Storage utility helps to track and identify all backup media being used, and facilitates the mounting of the media requested by the backup application. Keeping track of the actual data written or retrieved from the media is the responsibility of the backup application itself.

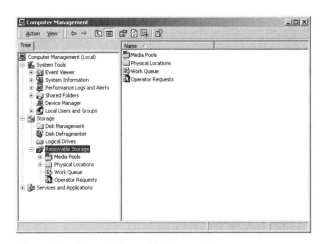

Figure 22.9   Microsoft Removable Storage utility.

Exam Prep Questions

1. The server's backup system uses a DAT tape drive capable of storing 24GB of data. In order to utilize its maximum storage capability, which backup tape format should be selected?

   ❑ A. DDS-24

   ❑ B. DDS-3

   ❑ C. DDS-2

   ❑ D. DDS-1

2. What should be the highest priority for any network server installation or operation?

   ❑ A. Having printed copies of the disaster recovery plan available

   ❑ B. Meeting the scheduling needs of the payroll department

   ❑ C. Establishing a dependable remote monitoring system for all servers

   ❑ D. Providing for the safe storage of system backup tapes

3. When considering minimum offsite storage, what other items besides a complete set of backup tapes and a copy of the disaster recovery plan should be included? (Select two.)

   ❑ A. Backup copies of NOS software

   ❑ B. A spare tape drive and interface cable

   ❑ C. Backup copies of critical application software and related drivers

   ❑ D. An ample supply of blank tapes

4. Disaster recovery plans should be tested periodically. What corrective measures must be taken when various servers end up containing data belonging to others?

   ❑ A. Each server should be fitted with a different tape drive type, along with matching tapes.

   ❑ B. Backup tapes should be stored with the server to which their data belongs.

   ❑ C. As long as the servers are identical, it doesn't matter which data is restored to which server.

   ❑ D. All backup tapes should be labeled with the correct backup date and server ID.

5. A grandfather-father-son backup implementation has been used at a large company for some time. If the need were to arise for restoring the server system to its identical state of five months past, what would be the maximum number of tapes required for this task?

   ❑ A. One tape

   ❑ B. Two tapes

   ❑ C. Four tapes

   ❑ D. Six tapes

6. What is considered to be the proper time for formulating the disaster recovery plan?
   - ❏ A. When it first becomes apparent that a server system backup has failed
   - ❏ B. Immediately following the first signs of trouble with the server system backup capabilities
   - ❏ C. During the initial planning, prior to beginning the server system's construction
   - ❏ D. Immediately following the server system's successful installation

7. In order to achieve the maximum amount of storage possible using a DAT tape backup system, which of the following formats should be selected?
   - ❏ A. Travan
   - ❏ B. QIC
   - ❏ C. DSS
   - ❏ D. DDS

8. What is the most important duty for any server network administrator?
   - ❏ A. The purchase of a secondary storage device
   - ❏ B. Providing each department with a "downtime" duty list
   - ❏ C. The creation of a viable disaster recovery plan
   - ❏ D. The installation of a network monitoring system

9. After a suitable disaster recovery plan has been formulated, how should it be disseminated and protected?
   - ❏ A. A printed copy of the disaster recovery plan should be stored in a known safe place or places.
   - ❏ B. A copy of the disaster recovery plan should be stored on the server's primary hard drive.
   - ❏ C. A copy of the disaster recovery plan should be stored on the server's secondary hard drive.
   - ❏ D. A printed copy of the disaster recovery plan should be stored with all the sales receipts for server network equipment.

10. Within a 24-hour period after having performed a full backup, the next daily backup is designed to consume the least amount of time. What category of backup would that be?
    - ❏ A. A differential backup
    - ❏ B. A selective backup
    - ❏ C. An incremental backup
    - ❏ D. A full backup

11. In the grandfather-father-son backup implementation, which of the following correctly identifies the number of tapes required for each category?
    - ❑ A. Grandfather = 1, father = 1, son = 1
    - ❑ B. Grandfather = 4, father = 1, son = 1
    - ❑ C. Grandfather = 1, father = 4, son = 1
    - ❑ D. Grandfather = 1, father = 1, son = 4

12. The most valuable data the company has was transferred to a secondary storage device as backup. What is the most sensible storage location for this backup device?
    - ❑ A. In the case, next to the server's master hard drive
    - ❑ B. Offsite, in a secured location
    - ❑ C. Onsite, in a room other than the server room
    - ❑ D. In the company safe, located near the office

13. What is the most recently devised active offsite storage strategy?
    - ❑ A. Hot sites
    - ❑ B. Cold sites
    - ❑ C. Warm sites
    - ❑ D. Medium sites

14. Which backup method takes the longest amount of time to perform but can quickly and fully restore a server system?
    - ❑ A. A full backup
    - ❑ B. A differential backup
    - ❑ C. An incremental backup
    - ❑ D. A selective backup

15. Offsite storage must include what type of documentation, in addition to the set of server backup tapes?
    - ❑ A. The server user manual
    - ❑ B. The application user manuals
    - ❑ C. The installation instructions for various drivers
    - ❑ D. The disaster recovery plan

16. A small insurance agency with a limited budget requires an affordable disaster recovery scenario. What type of offsite protection fits their requirements?
    - ❑ A. Connection to a third-party cold site
    - ❑ B. Connection to a hot site with continuous server connectivity
    - ❑ C. Connection to a third-party hot site
    - ❑ D. Access to an offsite lockbox for storing system backup tapes

17. The administrator is instituting a backup strategy that will quickly restore company data in the event of a disaster. Which of the following solutions makes the most sense?

    ❏ A. Conducting full backups each Friday, and differentials Monday through Thursday

    ❏ B. Conducting differential backups on Friday, and incrementals on Monday through Thursday

    ❏ C. Conducting incremental backups on Friday, and differentials on Monday through Thursday

    ❏ D. Conducting full backups on the last day of each month, differentials on Friday, and incrementals Monday through Thursday

18. Which of the following is a legitimate feature of tape arrays?

    ❏ A. The simultaneous handling of writing and reading chores

    ❏ B. The striping of data across multiple, parallel tape drives

    ❏ C. The reading, writing, storing, and retrieving of multiple magnetic tape cartridges

    ❏ D. The backing up of multiple servers on one type of recording media

19. Shortly following the replacement of a DAT drive with a new DLT drive, the system crashes. A recent set of DAT backup tapes is still available, but not DLT tapes. How should the administrator handle this situation?

    ❏ A. Another DLT tape drive should be added to the system immediately.

    ❏ B. The available DAT tapes should be used to restore the system with the new DLT drive.

    ❏ C. The DAT drive should be reinstalled temporarily to restore the system using the DAT tapes.

    ❏ D. A restoration should be conducted using a DAT/DLT data converter cartridge.

20. LTO Ultrium and DLT drives enjoy which of the compatibilities in the following list?

    ❏ A. LTO units read DLT 7000, DLT 8000, and SDLT tapes.

    ❏ B. The DLT 8000 reads LTO tapes.

    ❏ C. LTO units read SDLT tapes.

    ❏ D. None.

Exam Prep Answers

1. Answer B is the correct answer. A DDS-3 DAT tape is capable of storing up to 24GB of data, but only if compressed mode is used. Answer A is incorrect because a DDS-24 tape format is fictional. Answer C is incorrect because compressed mode operations would provide only

8GB of maximum storage on a DDS-2 formatted backup tape. Answer D is incorrect because compressed mode operations would provide only 4GB of maximum storage on a DDS-1 formatted backup tape.

2. Answer A is the correct answer. No network server installation should be permitted to begin operations without having printed copies of the disaster recovery plan available to all interested parties. Answer B is incorrect, although the needs of the payroll department are a priority consideration. Answer C is incorrect, although the server administrator would consider this a high priority task. Answer D is incorrect, although the backup tapes could be second in importance only to the disaster recovery plan itself.

3. Answers A and C are the correct answers. At a minimum, backup copies of the network operating system, as well as critical application software and drivers, should be included at the offsite storage location. Answer B is incorrect only because the question is considering minimum offsite storage, which does not include a spare tape drive. Answer D is incorrect because nothing can be restored from blank tapes.

4. Answer D is the correct answer. To ensure that backups are restored to their original servers, mark each backup tape with the correct date and the ID of the server being backed up. The server ID should also be clearly labeled on each server case. Answer A is incorrect because the administration of system backups would be complicated beyond reason. Answer B is incorrect because common sense dictates that backup tapes are stored at separate locations from where their source servers reside. Answer C is incorrect because identical server hardware often operates using extremely different configurations.

5. Answer A is the correct answer. Provided that the tape backup plan can reach that far back, locate the grandfather tape of five months past and perform a complete system restore. Answers B, C, and D are incorrect by the process of elimination.

6. Answer C is the correct answer. Prior to the beginning stages of the server system's construction, the disaster recovery plan should already have been created and recorded. Although answer D is better than answers A or B, the plan's creation still occurs much too late in the server network's creation process. Its implementation will prove to be much more difficult to implement successfully than it would have been at the beginning. Answers A and B are both incorrect and represent situations where the creation of a comprehensive disaster recovery plan would be practically impossible to implement.

7. Answer D is the correct answer. When using a DAT tape backup system, the Digital Data Storage (DDS) standard is the most widely used format. Answer A is incorrect, although Travan drives do outperform the original QIC format. Answer B is incorrect because QIC drives fall considerably short of DDS storage capacities and are also often incompatible with each other. However, they do not hold as much data as DDS drives. Answer C is incorrect because DSS is a fictional tape drive standard.

8. Answer C is the correct answer. This could be a difficult assignment depending on how long the current server network has been in operation, and whether any disaster recovery plan has already been formulated. Answer A is incorrect, although secondary storage devices are an absolute necessity for data backup chores. Answer B is incorrect, although it's an important consideration to be able to use server downtime productively. Answer D is a good idea for server network troubleshooting purposes. However, such considerations remain subordinate to the disaster recovery plan itself.

9. Answer A is the correct answer. Regardless of what type of catastrophe occurs, a copy of the disaster recovery plan must survive. This may require the simultaneous utilization of both onsite and offsite storage locations for copies of the disaster recovery plan. Answers B and C are incorrect because during an emergency, the failure of the server containing these hard drives could potentially prevent timely access to the plan. Answer D is incorrect because a simple office fire could potentially destroy the disaster recovery plan along with its accompanying receipts.

10. Answer C is the correct answer. Daily backups taking the least amount of time are called "incremental." Answer A is incorrect because a differential backup is performed on a weekly basis, rather than daily. Answer B is incorrect because a backup type called "selective" does not exist. Answer D is incorrect because a monthly full backup was performed within the preceding 24 hours.

11. Answer D is the correct answer. Daily son backups use different tapes on Monday, Tuesday, Wednesday, and Thursday, whereas the grandfather and father categories both require the use of one tape. Answer A is incorrect because the son category was assigned only one tape. Answer B is incorrect because grandfather status was assigned to four tapes. Answer C is incorrect because father status was assigned to four tapes.

12. Answer B is the correct answer. In the event of catastrophic occurrences at the company's main location, onsite storage of secondary storage devices will not adequately protect valuable company data. Answer A is incorrect because it ties the data's survival to the survival of the server. Answers C and D are incorrect because they also limit the data's protection to the well-being of the main site.

13. Answer C is the correct answer. Warm sites are a recent offsite storage strategy that is growing, but has not yet become a common industry phenomenon. Answers A and B are incorrect because these offsite storage facilities are the most common storage strategies. Answer D is incorrect because "medium" offsite storage sites do not exist.

14. Answer A is the correct answer. Although a full backup takes the longest amount of time to perform, a server system can be restored quickly from a full backup tape. Answers B and C are incorrect because full restorations are beyond the capabilities of either differential or incremental backups. Answer D is incorrect because "selective" backup types do not exist.

15. Answer D is the correct answer. A copy of the disaster recovery plan is the most important type of offsite documentation that should accompany a set of server backup tapes. Answer A is incorrect because having a copy of the server user manual stored offsite is not an imperative requirement. Answer B is incorrect because most application manuals can be located on manufacturers' websites if they are somehow misplaced. Answer C is incorrect because most third-party driver programs are bundled with installation instructions. Other system drivers are usually installed automatically by the NOS as needed.

16. Answer A is the correct answer. Third-party cold sites are the most common type of remote backup system used by small businesses. Answer B is incorrect because continuous server connectivity is beyond the budget of such a small company. Answer C is incorrect because this alternative is still too costly and the company is too small to require this level of service. Answer D is incorrect because an offsite backup storage lockbox does not qualify as a disaster recovery site. Having duplicate system backup tapes is a good idea, however.

17. Answer D is the correct answer. This scenario uses all three backup formats in the most complete way. Answer A is incorrect, although such a backup schedule would be capable of fully restoring the server. Following a disaster, however, an inordinate amount of time will be

required to perform the restoration. Answers B and C are incorrect because no full backups are performed. Under these strategies, the ability to perform a quick restore will not be provided.

18. Answer B is the correct answer. Striping of data across multiple tape drives in parallel is a legitimate feature of tape arrays. Answer A is incorrect because simultaneous reading and writing capabilities are a feature of tape libraries, rather than tape arrays. Answers C and D are also legitimate benefits of tape library use, rather than tape arrays.

19. Answer C is the correct answer. Temporarily reinstalling the DAT drive will allow the restoration of the system from the older DAT tapes. Following the restoration, the DLT drive should be used to perform a new backup on DLT tape. Answer A is incorrect because adding another DLT drive cannot help to restore the system. Answer B is incorrect because of the incompatibility that exists between DAT and DLT tapes and drives. Answer D is incorrect because DAT/DLT converter cartridges do not exist.

20. Answer D is the correct answer. No compatibilities exist between LTO Ultrium and DLT tape drives regardless of the fact that some specifications for SDLT tape drives match up with those for LTO units. Therefore, answers A, B, and C are all incorrect by the process of elimination.

Practice Exam 1

Now it's time to put the knowledge you've learned from reading this book to the test! Write down your answers to the following questions on a separate sheet of paper. You will be able to take this sample test multiple times this way. After you answer all of the questions, compare your answers with the correct answers in Chapter 24, "Answers to Practice Exam 1." The answer keys for both tests immediately follow each Practice Exam chapter.

Try to take no longer than 90 minutes for each exam. When you can correctly answer at least 90% of the 80 practice questions (72) in each Practice Exam, you are ready to start using the PrepLogic Practice Exams CD-ROM at the back of this *Exam Cram 2*. Using the Practice Exams for this Exam Cram 2, along with the PrepLogic Practice Exams, you can prepare yourself well for the actual Server+ certification exam. Good luck!

Exam Questions

1. In a multi-tiered server system, which tier is typically used to store large pools of information for other server tiers?

   ❑ A. Back-end servers

   ❑ B. Front-end servers

   ❑ C. Mid-tier servers

   ❑ D. Web-tier servers

2. You just received your components to build the server and you realize that one of the adapter cards is not the correct one you ordered. It is a substitute adapter card that should work fine. What should you do?

   ❑ A. Test the adapter card to make sure it works, and then start to build the server.

   ❑ B. Download the latest validated drivers for the adapter card, and then start to build the server.

   ❑ C. Verify on the Internet that the adapter card is compatible, and then start to build the server.

   ❑ D. Return it for a replacement of the initial item ordered.

3. You need to connect eight servers to a disk drive array with 250 HDDs. What technology is best suited to support this array?

   ❑ A. Ultra ATA-3

   ❑ B. Ultra320 SCSI-3

   ❑ C. Fibre Channel

   ❑ D. IEEE 1394

4. Which of the following server applications is considered the most vital?

   ❑ A. System monitoring software

   ❑ B. Backup software

   ❑ C. Antivirus software

   ❑ D. SNMP software

5. Which of the following is *not* important when determining the baseline?

   ❑ A. The role of the server

   ❑ B. The client computer's operating system

   ❑ C. The logical disk

   ❑ D. The size of the server work queues

6. Which of the following is the most important environmental security issue in a server room?

   ❑ A. Password complexity

   ❑ B. Locked server room doors

   ❑ C. Room access monitoring

   ❑ D. Antitheft alarms

7. You just installed Wake-On-LAN cards into your servers. You try to test this function, but it fails to remotely boot the servers. Where could the problem be located?

   ❑ A. TCP/IP packet
   ❑ B. SNMP packet
   ❑ C. PXE packet
   ❑ D. Magic packet

8. Which tape format maximizes the storage of a DAT drive?

   ❑ A. QIC
   ❑ B. Travan
   ❑ C. DSS
   ❑ D. DDS

9. The network administrator wants secure remote server access. What protocols should be used?

   ❑ A. STP over UTP
   ❑ B. L2TP over IPSec
   ❑ C. WWW over ISP
   ❑ D. FTP over HTTP

10. What is the difference between disk mirroring and disk duplexing?

   ❑ A. Disk mirroring uses one controller for both drives and disk duplexing uses one controller for each drive.
   ❑ B. Disk mirroring uses a minimum of three drives and disk duplexing uses two.
   ❑ C. Disk duplexing uses one controller for both drives and disk mirroring uses one controller for each drive.
   ❑ D. Disk mirroring strips data and disk duplexing shares data parity disks.

11. What TCP/IP utility would you use to set the IP configuration in Linux?

   ❑ A. `netstat`
   ❑ B. `tracert`
   ❑ C. `ifconfig`
   ❑ D. `vi config`

12. Which step would you implement first when installing multiple devices on the server?

   ❑ A. Verify compatibility
   ❑ B. Check system resources
   ❑ C. Implement ESD best practices
   ❑ D. Perform firmware upgrade

13. Which of the following best describes a baseline?
    - ❏ A. A baseline measures and compares performance variables across a variety of server components.
    - ❏ B. A baseline measures the performance of the server's processor.
    - ❏ C. A baseline measures and compares hard disk performance over a length of time.
    - ❏ D. A baseline measures the server's performance after changes in the network occur.

14. Which of the following are causes of ESD?
    - I. Low humidity
    - II. Unshielded cables
    - III. Improper grounding
    - IV. People moving around
    - ❏ A. I
    - ❏ B. II, III
    - ❏ C. I, III
    - ❏ D. I, II, III, IV

15. Which of the following is the best place to store a disaster recovery plan?
    - ❏ A. Print out a copy of the disaster recovery plan and store it in a safe place.
    - ❏ B. Save a copy of the disaster recovery plan to the primary hard drive.
    - ❏ C. Save a copy of the disaster recovery plan to the secondary hard drive.
    - ❏ D. Print out a copy of the disaster recovery plan and store it with all the other files dealing with the network configuration.

16. A problem has occurred when writing files to the "/" partition. Now the computer won't boot. What software is needed to fix the problem?
    - ❏ A. UNIX installation CD
    - ❏ B. Netware installation CD
    - ❏ C. OS/2 installation CD
    - ❏ D. Windows 2000 installation CD

17. What is the difference between the availability needs of a front-end server when compared to a back-end server?
    - ❏ A. There is no difference.
    - ❏ B. Availability needs for a front-end server can be variable, but they always are high for a back-end server.
    - ❏ C. A back-end server has greater availability needs.
    - ❏ D. A front-end server has greater availability needs.

18. What is the formula for determining the best UPS size and type for a new server?
    - ❑ A. Volts * Amps
    - ❑ B. Ohms + Amps
    - ❑ C. Amps – Volts
    - ❑ D. Volts + Amps

19. Which of the following network operating systems uses only one top-level directory represented by the symbol "/"?
    - ❑ A. Novell NetWare
    - ❑ B. Linux
    - ❑ C. Windows 2000 Server
    - ❑ D. Windows NT Server 4.0

20. Which of the following performance-monitoring utilities is available with Windows 2000 Server?
    - ❑ A. Microsoft Management Monitor
    - ❑ B. Microsoft Performance Monitor
    - ❑ C. Microsoft Console Monitor
    - ❑ D. Microsoft Management Console

21. What type of backup tape format should be used to get the maximum storage out of a 24GB DAT drive?
    - ❑ A. DDS-1
    - ❑ B. DDS-2
    - ❑ C. DDS-3
    - ❑ D. DDS-24

22. How many devices can be connected to a two-channel SCSI-3 RAID 5 controller?
    - ❑ A. 45
    - ❑ B. 40
    - ❑ C. 30
    - ❑ D. 55

23. After a server technician conducts a server installation, he notices that although the server successfully boots to the NOS, not all the RAM is being recognized. What did the technician fail to do?
    - ❑ A. Configure the memory in CMOS
    - ❑ B. Verify memory compatibility
    - ❑ C. Install the latest patch for the NOS
    - ❑ D. Update the motherboard BIOS

24. When testing a disaster recovery plan, you notice that some of the servers were restored with other servers' data. What can be done to fix this problem?

 ❏ A. Store the backup tape with the server to which it belongs.

 ❏ B. Label each backup tape with the appropriate date and server ID.

 ❏ C. Use different types of backup tape drives for each different server.

 ❏ D. If the servers are identical, it does not matter.

25. If multiple RAID components fail, what will happen to the data on the drives?

 ❏ A. The data will be backed up.

 ❏ B. The data on the drives will be lost.

 ❏ C. The drive will need to be corrupted.

 ❏ D. The volume continues to function and the data is still there.

26. How is it possible to run multiple operating systems using the same host bus adapter?

 ❏ A. By removing an HBA from one server and installing it in another

 ❏ B. By configuring a server for multiple OSes using the HBA manufacturer's drivers

 ❏ C. By networking the host bus adapter to a server running a different OS

 ❏ D. By reformatting the server's hard drive with a different OS

27. What devices would not be connected with a crossover cable?

 ❏ A. Devices running in a two-workstation network

 ❏ B. Devices connected to an Ethernet network

 ❏ C. Two switches connected to each other

 ❏ D. Two servers connected to each other

28. When configuring a redundant server system, how should the redundant parts be tested?

 ❏ A. They cannot be tested.

 ❏ B. Simulate a fault on the original server.

 ❏ C. Pull them out of the system and test them on a test bench.

 ❏ D. Pull them out of the system and test them with another system.

29. Which of the following is an advantage of a two-node cluster?

 ❏ A. Single points of failure are eliminated.

 ❏ B. The number of single-point failures are increased.

 ❏ C. Data can be downloaded twice as fast.

 ❏ D. Virus attacks are virtually eliminated.

30. What is the minimum number of computers required to configure a clustered server environment?
    - ❏ A. 2
    - ❏ B. 3
    - ❏ C. 4
    - ❏ D. 8

31. When selecting a UPS, what is the most important feature to consider?
    - ❏ A. Volt-ampere rating
    - ❏ B. Wattage rating
    - ❏ C. UPS battery type
    - ❏ D. Ampere-hour rating

32. Which of the following conditions can cause the server to recognize only one processor instead of multiple processors?
    - ❏ A. Not adding additional VRMs
    - ❏ B. Not reconfiguring the operating system to use multiple processors
    - ❏ C. Mismatched processor speeds
    - ❏ D. Not adding terminator resistor packs in the empty processor sockets or slots

33. Which of the following is an essential step when upgrading the NOS to a newer version?
    - ❏ A. Make sure the server board is compatible with the new NOS.
    - ❏ B. Create a current backup and test the restore function.
    - ❏ C. Make sure the new NOS supports all the peripheral devices on the server.
    - ❏ D. Have a copy of the current NOS handy to reinstall in case problems occur.

34. Which of the following component(s) would you *not* test when testing the server's performance?
    - ❏ A. The processors and associated components
    - ❏ B. System memory
    - ❏ C. Application software
    - ❏ D. Client load/network

35. A problem occurred on the active primary NTFS partition, and now the computer won't boot. What is needed to fix it?
    - ❏ A. UNIX installation CD
    - ❏ B. OS/2 Warp Server installation CD
    - ❏ C. NetWare installation CD
    - ❏ D. Server 2003 installation CD

36. When should you update the server's BIOS?
    - ❏ A. When adding additional directly compatible processors
    - ❏ B. After upgrading to newer faster processors
    - ❏ C. When a new BIOS update is available from the manufacturer
    - ❏ D. When adding additional peripheral devices to the server

37. When is the SNMP utility loaded onto the system?
    - ❏ A. When the administrator runs the monitoring program.
    - ❏ B. Before the NOS is loaded onto the system.
    - ❏ C. After the NOS is loaded onto the system.
    - ❏ D. It is the last program loaded on the bootup.

38. At what voltage(s) can a Universal 32-bit PCI card operate? (Select all correct answers.)
    - ❏ A. 3V
    - ❏ B. 5V
    - ❏ C. 4V
    - ❏ D. 3.3V

39. One of the drives in a RAID-5 disk array fails. Shutting down the server is not an option. What should you do?
    - ❏ A. Uninstall the associated driver and swap the drive with a good hard drive.
    - ❏ B. Shut down the server and then swap the bad drive with a good one.
    - ❏ C. Hot-swap the drive with a good hard drive.
    - ❏ D. Reinstall the associated driver for the bad drive.

40. Which of the following is an advantage of using the NOS drivers for peripheral devices?
    - ❏ A. The NOS drivers work better than drivers supplied by the manufacturer.
    - ❏ B. The drivers supplied with the NOS are more compatible than the drivers that are supplied from the manufacturer.
    - ❏ C. The NOS drivers are more up-to-date than drivers supplied by the manufacturer.
    - ❏ D. If you no longer have the drivers supplied by the manufacturer, you can use the drivers that come with the NOS.

41. Which of the following should you consider when determining whether or not to upgrade the server?
    - ❏ A. Whether the new server software supports the older server hardware
    - ❏ B. Whether a new server costs less than the older server
    - ❏ C. Whether the new server will be able to be repurposed in the future
    - ❏ D. Whether the new server meets the current service levels

42. Your last full backup was yesterday. Your boss wants you to back up the system today. What kind of backup would you choose to back up the system in the least amount of time?
    - ❑ A. Incremental backup
    - ❑ B. Full backup
    - ❑ C. Differential backup
    - ❑ D. Selective backup

43. What type of server provides a wide variety of services such as e-mail, file, print, and web services?
    - ❑ A. Application server
    - ❑ B. Mid-tier server
    - ❑ C. Back-end server
    - ❑ D. General-purpose server

44. A technician is installing a server and has checked all the proposed components against the hardware compatibility list for the NOS. After building the server, he can't get the NIC to work. What should have been included in the technician's pre-installation check?
    - ❑ A. Check the OEM hardware computability list
    - ❑ B. Plan the system resource designations
    - ❑ C. Locate and obtain the latest OEM drivers
    - ❑ D. Verify the UTP cable

45. You have two drives using a RAID 1 array. Drive A is 4GB in size and Drive B is 5GB in size. If Drive A has 2GB of data on it, how much available space does Drive B have?
    - ❑ A. 4GB
    - ❑ B. 2GB
    - ❑ C. 1GB
    - ❑ D. 3GB

46. What type of connector is used with CAT5 cabling?
    - ❑ A. RJ-45
    - ❑ B. RJ-11
    - ❑ C. RJ-12
    - ❑ D. RJ-35

47. Where should you check for the latest list of hardware that is compatible with Windows 2000 Server?
    - ❑ A. The Windows Catalog on Microsoft's website
    - ❑ B. Microsoft's Windows Update page
    - ❑ C. A hardware compatibility list on the Internet
    - ❑ D. The server manufacturer's website

48. Why are USB and FireWire devices considered a security risk in the server industry?
    - ❏ A. Because they are easy to hack into
    - ❏ B. Because they are slow compared to SCSI
    - ❏ C. Because they have no security features built into them
    - ❏ D. Because of their hot-swapping capability

49. A technician is trying to set the IP configuration in Linux and typed `ipconfig` with no result. What should be typed instead?
    - ❏ A. `linuxcfg`
    - ❏ B. `inetcfg`
    - ❏ C. `ifconfig`
    - ❏ D. `linuxconfig`

50. Where is the best place to look when checking the hardware compatibility for a network operating system?
    - ❏ A. NOS installation CD
    - ❏ B. NOS vendor website
    - ❏ C. Hardware vendor website
    - ❏ D. Hardware installation CD

51. Which of the following RAID systems protects against two drives failing at the same time?
    - ❏ A. RAID 5+3
    - ❏ B. RAID 1+0
    - ❏ C. RAID 5
    - ❏ D. RAID 4

52. You are trying to make a server more fault-tolerant. Which of the following components should you install?
    - ❏ A. A larger power supply
    - ❏ B. An additional stick of RAM
    - ❏ C. An additional floppy drive
    - ❏ D. A redundant NIC

53. What benefit is derived from having redundant NICs installed on the server?
    - ❏ A. If one card fails, the other will keep the network available.
    - ❏ B. The server will be capable of faster speeds.
    - ❏ C. There will be less traffic on the server.
    - ❏ D. There will be less data loss when transferring packets to client computers.

54. What documents should be kept for hardware troubleshooting purposes?

    I. Installation and configuration information

    II. Upgrade log

    III. Password changes

    IV. Component purchase orders

    ❑ A. I, II, III

    ❑ B. I, II

    ❑ C. II, III, IV

    ❑ D. III, IV

55. What is the term used to designate processor revisions?

    ❑ A. Level

    ❑ B. New type

    ❑ C. Stepping level

    ❑ D. Production revision

56. You have five 4GB drives in a RAID 5 array. What is your total available disk space?

    ❑ A. 16GB

    ❑ B. 20GB

    ❑ C. 25GB

    ❑ D. 30GB

57. What is the most important factor in determining the baseline for your server?

    ❑ A. The number of users on the network

    ❑ B. The available disk space on the server

    ❑ C. The role of the server in the network

    ❑ D. The amount of memory installed

58. You have decided to update the driver for your network adapter card. Where is the best place to obtain the latest validated driver?

    ❑ A. Microsoft's HCL website

    ❑ B. The network adapter card manufacturer's website

    ❑ C. Any driver site on the Internet

    ❑ D. The operating system's driver download site

59. What technology enables individual PCI slots to be powered on and off independently and allows PCI adapters to be added or removed without having to power down the computer system?

    ❑ A. Hot-sock PCI

    ❑ B. Hot NMOS PCI

    ❑ C. Hot-Plug PCI

    ❑ D. Hot PMOS PCI

60. A company installs a new server. It stops communicating with the SCSI drives after six hours. After a reboot, it appears fine. What is the most likely cause?
    - ❑ A. Power fault
    - ❑ B. NOS drivers needed updating
    - ❑ C. Nothing
    - ❑ D. Drives terminated incorrectly

61. Which of the following best describes fault tolerance?
    - ❑ A. Improving the capability of a server
    - ❑ B. Using multiple components to increase the server's productivity
    - ❑ C. Making sure you have backups of all the company's valuable data
    - ❑ D. Use of a component or components that continue to work with no loss of data or downtime when one component fails

62. What is the height of a 1U server chassis?
    - ❑ A. 1.75 inches
    - ❑ B. 1.55 inches
    - ❑ C. 1.70 inches
    - ❑ D. 1.65 inches

63. When should a disaster recovery plan be created?
    - ❑ A. Before the construction of the server
    - ❑ B. Right after successful installation
    - ❑ C. At the first sign of trouble
    - ❑ D. When a backup fails

64. What does CSMA/CD stand for?
    - ❑ A. Carrier Sense Multiple Access with CAT6 Detection
    - ❑ B. Carrier Sense Monolithic Access with Carrier Detection
    - ❑ C. Carrier Sense Multiple Access with Collision Detection
    - ❑ D. Carrier Sense Monolithic Access with CAT6 Detection

65. You want to upgrade a server by installing an external SCSI tape drive. The system currently has a SCSI card and an internal SCSI hard drive. At bootup, the system fails to recognize the new tape drive. What can be done to solve this problem?
    - ❑ A. Disable termination on the SCSI controller card
    - ❑ B. Disable termination on the tape drive
    - ❑ C. Enable termination on the internal hard drive
    - ❑ D. Enable termination on the SCSI controller card

66. During POST, a technician notices an error message. To determine which FRU is going bad, the technician should do which of the following?

❏ A. Check the NOS error codes

❏ B. Replace the parts until he or she finds the bad one

❏ C. Check the POST card error codes

❏ D. Check the motherboard error codes

67. What is the total bandwidth for a PCI slot that incorporates a 64-bit PCI bus operating at a clock speed of 66MHz?

❏ A. 264 MBps

❏ B. 512 MBps

❏ C. 528 MBps

❏ D. 545 MBps

68. A faulty NIC has been replaced in a hot-swap/hot-plug PCI system. The system does not recognize the replacement NIC. What is the first troubleshooting step to perform?

❏ A. Check to be sure that the hot-swap PCI slot has been reactivated.

❏ B. Configure the NIC to transmit both LAN and storage communications.

❏ C. Assume that the replacement NIC is also faulty.

❏ D. Configure a software bridge with Windows.

69. In most cases, where can you find the most up-to-date documentation related to your system's software or hardware?

❏ A. With the electronic documentation accompanying the hardware or software

❏ B. With the printed documentation accompanying the hardware or software

❏ C. In books dealing with hardware or software

❏ D. On the supplier's website

70. An additional microprocessor is installed on a server running an SMP-capable NOS. After the system boots, it fails to recognize the new CPU. Which of the following is most likely to solve the problem?

❏ A. Replace the bad CPU

❏ B. Configure the NOS for SMP

❏ C. Upgrade the BIOS

❏ D. Increase the stepping of the CPU

71. What is symmetrical multi-processing?

   □ A. Dividing tasks up between multiple processors and executing them one at a time

   □ B. Having multiple processors on a server board

   □ C. Dividing tasks into multiple threads for processing on multiple micro-processors and running these threads at the same time other threads are being executed

   □ D. Having multiple processors on a server board and multiple NOSes on the server to boot up to

72. After looking at a UPS log file, you notice that the server room loses power for about 10 minutes at the same time every Friday. Who should be notified?

   □ A. IT manager or administrator

   □ B. IT help desk

   □ C. IS help desk

   □ D. NOS technical support

73. After you verify component delivery, what should be your next step for proper server assembly?

   □ A. Obtain latest validated drivers

   □ B. Start the assembly of the server

   □ C. Prepare the chassis

   □ D. Install the server board

74. Which of the following actions should be done to all server components before installation to ensure hardware reliability?

   □ A. Nothing

   □ B. Individual testing

   □ C. Validation

   □ D. Testing with the processor

75. An intranet web server is failing to meet the performance needs of your corporation. This server has an SMP-capable NOS and motherboard. The motherboard is currently configured to use a Pentium III 1GHz microprocessor, and is using the maximum amount of RAM that the board will allow. Which of the following scaling options should be implemented first?

   □ A. Install faster memory.

   □ B. Upgrade the CPU to a Pentium 4.

   □ C. Install another Pentium III 1GHz CPU.

   □ D. Build an identical server to help carry the load.

76. Which of the following should always be performed when making changes on the server?
    - ❏ A. Power down the server before testing it.
    - ❏ B. Retest and document after each and every change on the server.
    - ❏ C. Perform all changes on the server at once before testing.
    - ❏ D. Test the server only before each change is performed.

77. You get a call because a server is down. After arriving, you find that the problem is beyond your technical expertise. What should you do?
    - ❏ A. Get the closest co-worker to help you.
    - ❏ B. Contact the next person in the escalation plan.
    - ❏ C. Tell the user that the server will be down for 24 hours.
    - ❏ D. Continue working on it until it is fixed.

78. What advantages do clustering services provide? (Select all correct answers.)
    - ❏ A. Data is continuously available.
    - ❏ B. RAM downtime is decreased.
    - ❏ C. Single points of failure are eliminated.
    - ❏ D. Data failure due to electrostatic discharge is eliminated

79. Which of the following CDs would you use to repair NTFS5 boot partition problems?
    - ❏ A. Windows Server 2003 CD
    - ❏ B. Windows NT Server CD
    - ❏ C. Windows 98 CD
    - ❏ D. Windows NT 4.0 CD

80. Which of the following best identifies the major difference between NAS and SAN?
    - ❏ A. System cost
    - ❏ B. Drive identification scheme
    - ❏ C. Data addressing scheme
    - ❏ D. System speed

Answers to Practice Exam 1

Answer Key

1. A	**17.** B	**33.** B
2. D	**18.** A	**34.** C
3. C	**19.** B	**35.** D
4. C	**20.** D	**36.** B
5. B	**21.** C	**37.** B
6. B	**22.** C	**38.** B, D
7. D	**23.** B	**39.** C
8. D	**24.** B	**40.** D
9. B	**25.** B	**41.** A
10. A	**26.** B	**42.** A
11. C	**27.** B	**43.** D
12. A	**28.** B	**44.** C
13. A	**29.** A	**45.** D
14. D	**30.** A	**46.** A
15. A	**31.** A	**47.** A
16. A	**32.** B	**48.** D

49. C	**60.** D	**71.** C
50. B	**61.** D	**72.** A
51. B	**62.** A	**73.** A
52. D	**63.** A	**74.** C
53. A	**64.** C	**75.** C
54. B	**65.** A	**76.** B
55. C	**66.** D	**77.** B
56. A	**67.** C	**78.** A, C
57. C	**68.** A	**79.** A
58. B	**69.** D	**80.** C
59. C	**70.** B	

Answers to Exam Questions

1. Answer A is the correct answer. The large pools of information used by the front-end and mid-tier servers are stored in the back-end servers. Answer B is incorrect because a front-end server is configured to perform one function, or a multiple of related functions, that are not necessarily related to the storage of large pools of data. Answer C is incorrect because mid-tier servers are designed to pass information between front-end and back-end servers. Answer D is incorrect because there is no such thing as a web-tier server.

2. Answer D is the correct answer. Even if the substitute components are compatible, they should not be installed. Instead, they should be returned and replaced with the initial components ordered. Answers A, B, and C are all incorrect because the system was originally designed with the specified adapter in mind. The compatibility or incompatibility of the substitute is irrelevant to the installing technician.

3. Answer C is the correct answer. Fibre Channel is an external bus that allows tens, hundreds, and thousands of devices such as disk drives to be arrayed. Fibre Channel can transmit data at up to 2Gbps using fiber-optic cable. Answer A is incorrect because Ultra ATA-3 supports only mid-range server storage. Answer B is incorrect because Ultra320 SCSI-3 technology is not robust enough to handle the proposed problem. Answer D is incorrect because FireWire (IEEE 1394) has a maximum data transfer rate of only 400Mbps and is a less optimal choice.

4. Answer C is the correct answer. For a server with a properly configured RAID 5 array, antivirus software is the most vital for system security and reliability. A network server has a significantly greater need for antivirus software than a typical computer. Answer A is incorrect because without protection from virus infections, system monitoring software will simply monitor an infected, failing system. Answer B is incorrect because backing up an infected system gains nothing. Answer D is incorrect because management of an infected server network is an administrator's worst nightmare.

5. Answer B is the correct answer. When determining a server baseline, client computer operating systems are not important. Answers C and D are incorrect because performance measurements for the logical disk, server work queues, memory, network interfaces, processors, and redirector are important. Answer A is incorrect because the most important consideration is the role of the server.

6. Answer B is the correct answer. The most important thing you can do to ensure proper security is make certain that your server room door is locked at all times, and that access to the room is controlled. Answer A is incorrect because passwords will not protect an unlocked server room. Answer C is incorrect because monitoring access to the server room does not necessarily prevent unauthorized access. Answer D is incorrect because antitheft alarms can only establish that server room security has already been compromised.

7. Answer D is the correct answer. Although answers A, B, and C have something to do with administering the remote booting of a server, a magic packet is the name used to describe the function that gives the bootup command to a WOL adapter. Answer A is incorrect because TCP/IP packets are involved with transferring fragmented messages, and then reassembling them on any type of computer platform or software. Answer B is incorrect because an SNMP packet would be used (in an SNMP server network) as strictly a local network transport device. Answer C is incorrect because although a Preboot eXecution Environment (PXE) packet is designed to bootstrap computers through a network interface card, it does not perform the actual function of the magic packet.

8. Answer D is the correct answer. The most popular format for DAT today in terms of data storage is the Digital Data Storage standard. DDS-4 has a maximum capacity of 40GB. Answer A is incorrect because the maximum data storage available with a QIC drive is 4GB. Answer B is incorrect because the maximum data storage available with Travan drive is 20GB. Answer C is incorrect because there is no such storage drive standard as DSS.

9. Answer B is the correct answer. Whereas L2TP provides per-user authentication and dynamic address allocation, IPSec provides secure encryption and data confidentiality. Answer A is incorrect because STP and UTP are types of twisted-pair cabling, not network protocols. Answer C is incorrect because WWW and ISP are merely acronyms for World Wide Web and Internet service provider. Answer D is incorrect because neither the FTP nor the HTTP protocols can provide secure remote server access.

10. Answer A is the correct answer. Disk mirroring uses one controller for both drives, whereas disk duplexing uses one controller for each drive. If the controller fails with disk mirroring, both hard drives will fail. Disk duplexing eliminates the controller as a point of failure by having a controller for each drive. Answers B, C, and D are all incorrect through the process of elimination.

11. Answer C is correct. `ifconfig` is similar to the `ipconfig` command in Windows. It shows you the current network configuration of your computer, and enables you to make changes, such as the assignment of a gateway, the DHCP server, the subnet mask, and the network mask. Answer A is incorrect because the `netstat` command displays a number of statistics about the host computer. Answer B is incorrect because `tracert` lists the IP jump path to reach the targeted IP, and the time taken to reach each jump. Answer D is incorrect because `vi` is the Unix/Linux test editor.

12. Answer A is the correct answer. The proper procedure to install multiple devices on the server is (1) verify compatibility, (2) perform the firmware upgrade, (3) check system resources, and (4) implement ESD best practices.

13. Answer A is the correct answer. A baseline measures and compares performance variables across a variety of server components. Answer B is incorrect because processor performance is only a small part of baseline information. Answer C is also incorrect because the baseline does much more than provide hard disk performance comparisons. Answer D is incorrect because the baseline documents the server's performance prior to any subsequent changes. All measurements taken after network changes are compared to the baseline.

14. Answer D is the correct answer. Factors that can cause the buildup of an excessive electrostatic charge include high temperature, low humidity, people moving around, high-friction surfaces (carpets), unshielded cables, and improper grounding.

15. Answer A is the correct answer. Printing a hard copy of the disaster recovery plan and storing it in a safe place is the best way to ensure that it can be easily found when it is needed. Answers B and C are incorrect because saving a copy of the disaster recovery plan to the primary or secondary hard drive is not a good idea. These drives could fail and the plan would not be retrievable. Answer D is incorrect because storing a hard copy of the disaster recovery with all other files dealing with the network configuration can make it difficult to find when it is needed.

16. Answer A is the correct answer. The UNIX file system structure uses the "/" symbol to define the top-level root directory of the file system. If the top-level directory is out of action, nothing else will operate properly. The UNIX installation CD must be used to repair whatever damage has occurred. Answer B is incorrect because the NetWare file structure is similar to Windows except that all directories can be named instead of having to use drive letter assignments. Answers C and D are incorrect because OS/2 and Windows 2000 are both totally incompatible with the Unix directory system.

17. Answer B is the correct answer. To achieve availability, back-end servers utilize multiple power supplies, hot-swappable PCI slots, and a RAID array of hard disks, as well as multiple PCI cards of the same type for added fault tolerance. Front-end servers use failover servers that automatically begin operations when the other server goes down. When front-end servers are used to run critical applications, most large businesses achieve their high availability ratings by implementing failover servers. In the event of a critical server failure, the network can switch over to the failover machine.

18. Answer A is the correct answer. To calculate the load of your UPS that is normally rated in volt-amperes (VA), multiply the voltage number by the amps to derive the VA. Answers B, C, and D are all incorrect because performing additions and/or subtractions with these parameters provides no useful information.

19. Answer B is the correct answer. The Linux file system works differently from the Windows-based file system. Whereas the Windows system has multiple top-level directories (C:, D:, and so on), the Linux file system has only one top level directory, which is represented by the symbol "/" (pronounced root). Answer A is incorrect because the NetWare file structure permits all directories to be named rather than using drive letter assignments.

20. Answer D is the correct answer. With Windows 2000, the Disk Administrator has been replaced with the Microsoft Management Console (MMC) snap-in, available through Computer Management. Answers A and C are fictitious. Answer B refers to a monitoring tool rather than a management tool.

21. Answer C is the correct answer. Of these tapes, only a DDS-3 DAT tape can store up to 24GB of data in compressed mode. Answer A is incorrect because DDS-1 can store a maximum of only 4GB. Answer B is incorrect because DDS-2 can store a maximum of only 8GB. Answer D is incorrect because DDS-24 does not exist.

22. Answer C is the correct answer. The number of SCSI devices that can be connected to a two-channel SCSI-3 RAID 5 controller is calculated by multiplying the number of channels by the number of devices that each channel can handle. Each channel of the controller will accommodate 15 devices, therefore 2 * 15 = 30.

23. Answer B is the correct answer. RAM that is verified as approved by the hardware and the NOS compatibility list does not need to be configured, as suggested in answer A. Answer C is incorrect because installing NOS patches will not cause the system to recognize incompatible RAM. Answer D is incorrect because updating the BIOS cannot alter the physical RAM requirements of the board.

24. Answer B is the correct answer. Whenever you perform a server backup, make certain that you mark each tape with appropriate date and server ID for that backup. You should also label the server case itself with the server ID. Answer A is incorrect because backup tapes should be stored at separate locations from the servers containing their data. Answer C is incorrect because this approach would hopelessly complicate the administration of system backups. Answer D is incorrect because even identical servers may be configured somewhat differently from each other.

25. Answer B is the correct answer. Data on drives is lost when multiple RAID components fail, so answers A, C, and D are incorrect.

26. Answer B is the correct answer. Major HBA manufacturers bundle a number of software drivers with their products that make it possible to configure the server with a number of operating systems. Answer A is incorrect because the work involved would not be worth the outcome. Answer C is incorrect because an HBA only runs an OS installed on its own server. Answer D is incorrect for the same reason answer A is incorrect.

27. Answer B is correct. Ethernet devices require straight-through connections. Answers A, C, and D reflect situations where a crossover cable can be used. A crossover cable permits the connection of two devices without the need for extra hardware. This is useful when necessary to connect two switches or hubs together, or when connecting two servers or workstations together without the use of a hub or switch.

28. Answer B is the correct answer. The best way to test a redundant system is to create a situation where it must perform as intended. Answer A is incorrect because all parts of a server system can be tested in one way or another. Answer C is incorrect because test bench results do not prove that system operations will be successful. Answer D is incorrect because components that work in one system may not work properly in another.

29. Answer A is the correct answer. One of many advantages for a two-node cluster is that all single points of failure are eliminated. If one fails, the other takes over. Answer B is incorrect because having a two-node cluster doubles the number of possibilities for single points of failure, but it does not necessarily guarantee that more will occur. That is not an advantage. Answers C and D are incorrect because the cluster does not directly relate to data download speeds, nor does it eliminate the possibility of virus attacks.

30. Answer A is the correct answer. A cluster can be composed of two or more computers or servers that act as one and are managed as one. Therefore, a minimum of two servers is required when planning for the creation of a cluster. Answers B, C, and D are incorrect by the process of elimination.

31. Answer A is the correct answer. When selecting a UPS, the most important feature to be aware of is the volt-ampere (VA) rating. It should be higher than required by the computer system. Answer B is incorrect because UPS ratings are not provided in values of power. Answer C is incorrect because the batteries simply contribute to the VA rating. Answer D is incorrect because an ampere-hour rating is not a valid feature of a UPS.

32. Answer B is the correct answer. Although the NOS is capable of running multiprocessor systems using Symmetrical Multi-Processing (SMP), it must be configured to do so. Simply adding another processor to the motherboard without properly configuring the NOS can result in the system ignoring the additional processor altogether. Answer A is incorrect because a voltage regulator module (VRM) is a small module that installs on a motherboard to regulate the voltage fed to the microprocessor. Answer C is incorrect because mismatched processor speeds may instead cause board damage. Answer D is incorrect because terminator resistor packs designed for installation in empty processor slots will not cause the server to miscalculate the correct number of installed processors.

33. Answer B is the correct answer. Creating a current backup and testing the restore function is vital when upgrading servers with a fresh installation of the new version of the NOS. Answer A is incorrect because an NOS upgrade is basically to add more features to the existing system. Answer C is incorrect because an upgrade would obviously support all devices supported by the previous NOS version, and then some. Answer D is a good idea but it is an incorrect answer because being able to back up the entire system as currently configured is better than reinstalling the NOS.

34. Answer C is the correct answer. Application software is not considered a valid component when testing the server's performance. Answers A, B, and D are incorrect because the processors, associated components, system memory, and client/node network are tested.

35. Answer D is the correct answer. The Windows Server 2003 network operating system is designed to use NTFS. Answer A is incorrect because UNIX also uses its own proprietary file system. Answer B is incorrect because OS/2 Warp uses the High Performance File System (HPFS). Answer C is incorrect because Novell's NetWare software uses the NetWare File System (NWFS).

36. Answer B is the correct answer. For major upgrades, such as installing newer and faster processors, the BIOS may have to be changed. Answer A is incorrect because the BIOS should be sufficient when using directly compatible processors. Answer C is incorrect because the availability of a BIOS update must not dictate when a properly functioning server's BIOS will be changed. Answer D is incorrect because the BIOS detects and configures additional peripheral devices automatically.

37. Answer B is the correct answer. In systems that run SNMP, the Master Boot Record (MBR) points to the SNMP partition, and loads the SNMP utility before it jumps to the network operating system partition. Therefore, answers A, C, and D are incorrect through the process of elimination.

38. Answers B and D are correct. Universal PCI cards are keyed so that they will fit into either type of slot. These cards can detect the correct voltage through special voltage-in sensing pins. Answers A and C are incorrect because PCI signalling voltages do not include either 3V or 4V systems.

39. Answer C is the correct answer. Hot-swap technology permits server administrators to insert or remove various PCI cards and/or device modules from within a host system without having to first shut down the system's power. Answer A is incorrect because devices and controllers that support hot-swap technology automatically load and unload associated drivers. Answer B is incorrect because shutting down the server is not an option. Answer D is incorrect because reinstalling the driver for the bad drive will not solve the problem.

40. Answer D is the correct answer. When the new version or upgrade of the NOS is installed, it should automatically install its own drivers for the devices it detects. In most cases, these drivers are the best choice for the installed devices because they have been tested to work with the operating system and should provide the least amount of problems. Answers A, B, and C are incorrect because NOS drivers do not necessarily work better nor are they typically more up-to-date or compatible than drivers supplied by the manufacturer. However, if you no longer have the latest drivers from the manufacturer, the second best choice is to use the drivers that come with the NOS.

41. Answer A is the correct answer. When determining the need for a server upgrade, there are several questions to ask: (1) Does the existing server meet the current service levels required? (2) Will a newer server be cost-effective and increase the productivity and efficiency level for the customer? (3) Does newer server software support the older server hardware? Answer B is incorrect because the cost of a new server will in all likelihood be greater than that of the old server. Answer C is incorrect because the future purpose of the server is not as important as what the current requirements are. Answer D is incorrect because any upgrade must not only meet current service levels, but also exceed them.

42. Answer A is the correct answer. An *incremental backup* backs up only files that have changed since the most recent backup was performed. Because incremental backups are smaller than full backups, they save time and reduce tape utilization. Answer B is incorrect because a full backup takes the greatest amount of time to perform. Answer C is incorrect because a differential backup procedure must take the time to examine each individual file. Answer D is incorrect because the administrator must manually browse through the server's disk tree structure, taking a great amount of time.

43. Answer D is the correct answer. As its name implies, a general-purpose server is intended to provide a wide variety of services such as handling departmental e-mail or providing file, print, and web services. Answer A is incorrect because application servers manage application programs running between client computers and the organization's database. Answer B is incorrect because mid-tier servers are used to process and relay information between front-end and back-end servers. Answer C is incorrect because a back-end server is large, expensive, and used to store vast volumes of data in archive and data farms.

44. Answer C is the correct answer. When doing an installation, the technician should always use the latest drivers for the system's devices. Answer A is incorrect because there is no such thing as a hardware computability list. Answer B is incorrect because having the latest OEM drivers will make system resource planning more meaningful. Answer D is incorrect because disconnected UTP cables should have been detected during a visual inspection before powering the system.

45. Answer D is the correct answer. RAID 1 uses disk mirroring, in which duplicate information is stored on both drives. Answers A, B, and C are incorrect through the process of elimination.

46. Answer A is the correct answer. CAT5 UTP network cabling is terminated in an eight-pin RJ-45 plug. Answer B is incorrect because RJ-11 connectors are fitted with six pins (four wired). Answer C is incorrect because RJ-12 connectors are fitted with six pins, and all of them are wired. Answer D is incorrect because RJ-35 connectors are rarely used, if ever.

47. Answer A is the correct answer. To check for the latest list of compatible hardware with Windows 2000 Server, go to the Windows Catalog on Microsoft's website. Although Microsoft used to rely heavily on a hardware compatibility list to identify compatible equipment for their operating systems, their comprehensive reference is now called the Windows Catalog. Answer B is incorrect because the Windows Update page is concerned with updating various Microsoft products, which may or may not include additional hardware drivers for added compatibility. Answer C is incorrect because other hardware compatibility lists might not relate to Windows 2000 Server. Answer D is incorrect although the manufacturers of server equipment will certainly claim compatibility with everything.

48. Answer D is the correct answer. Their hot-swapping capability makes them undesirable in the server environment. You would not want an unauthorized person to be able to plug in a USB or FireWire device and gain immediate access to your server. Answers A and C are incorrect because USB and FireWire devices do contain protection against unauthorized use, while motherboards fitted with USB and FireWire ports employ built-in anti-hacking protection. Answer B is incorrect because the speed of a device does not determine whether it is a security risk or not.

49. Answer C is the correct answer. When configuring the network for a Linux server you should use the `ifconfig` utility. Answers A and D are incorrect because there are no such utility programs in Linux. Answer B is incorrect because `inetcfg` is a NetWare utility that configures the network settings of the server.

50. Answer B is the correct answer. Always check the hardware compatibility list on the network operating system vendor's website to make sure that all the hardware for the network server is on the list. Some vendors might have alternative names for the HCL. Answer A is incorrect, although the NOS installation CD might mention certain products that are known to have specific problems with the NOS. Answers C and D are incorrect because hardware vendors do not deliberately publish information detrimental to the sale of their products.

51. Answer B is the correct answer. The RAID 1+0 combination applies RAID 1 first after splitting the eight drives into four sets of two drives each. Each set is individually mirrored with duplicate information and RAID 0 is applied by individually striping across all four sets. Answers A, C, and D are incorrect by the process of elimination.

52. Answer D is the correct answer. A redundant NIC allows the server to maintain a network connection even if one of the NICs fails. Answers A and B are incorrect because a larger power supply and more memory will not improve the fault-tolerance status of the server. Answer C is incorrect because a floppy drive is usually irrelevant to maintaining a network connection.

53. Answer A is the correct answer. Redundant NICs are used to provide fault tolerance for the network connection. If one card fails, the other will keep the network available. Answers B and C are incorrect because the presence of redundant NICs is unrelated to a server's speed capabilities or the amount of server data traffic. Answer D is incorrect because the continued availability of the network does not guarantee a reduction in data loss.

54. Answer B is the correct answer. A record of password changes or purchasing paperwork is not required to do server system troubleshooting.

55. Answer C is the correct answer. Normally, processor manufacturers issue minor revisions to their devices over their manufacturing life cycle. These revisions are called *stepping levels*, and are identified by special numbers printed on the body of the device. Answer A is incorrect because the word "level" by itself could refer to anything. Answers B and D are both incorrect generic terms, which could be used to describe any type of device or product change.

56. Answer A is the correct answer. The total disk space of a RAID 5 array is the number of drives minus 1, multiplied by the individual drive size. Therefore, (5-1) * 4 GB = 16 GB. Answers B, C, and D are incorrect by the process of elimination.

57. Answer C is the correct answer. The most important factor in determining the server's baseline is the role it will play in the system. Answer A is incorrect because the initial baseline is usually performed prior to connecting the server to the network. Answer B is incorrect because server disk space is an important consideration for network operation, but it is not the most important baseline factor. Answer D is incorrect for the same reason with memory as for answer B with disk space.

58. Answer B is the correct answer. To obtain the latest validated driver, go to the network adapter card manufacturer's website. Download the latest confirmed gold driver. Do not use a beta driver, even if it is released later than the newest gold driver. Answer A is incorrect because neither the HCL nor the appropriate Windows Catalog is related to supplying drivers. Answer C is incorrect, especially when looking for the latest drivers. Answer D is incorrect because even if the OS manufacturer can provide some drivers, they will most likely not be the latest versions.

59. Answer C is the correct answer. Hot-Plug PCI is a standard containing special hardware that enables individual PCI slots to be powered on and off independently. This allows PCI adapters to be added or removed without having to power down the computer system. Answer A is incorrect because no such thing as hot-sock PCI exists. Answer B is incorrect because no such type of PCI standard as hot NMOS exists. Answer D is incorrect because no such type of PCI standard as hot PMOS exists.

60. Answer D is the correct answer. Improper termination of a SCSI system can result in intermittent and unpredictable failures. Answer A is incorrect because a power problem would result in many more symptoms besides the ones described. Answer B is incorrect because NOS drivers do not base their SCSI operations on time limits. Answer C is incorrect because a server should not normally require a reboot every six hours.

61. Answer D is the correct answer. Fault tolerance protects the server network by having the two components work in tandem. If one fails, the other will continue and no loss of data or service will be incurred. Answer A does not specify how the server's capability would be improved, even though providing fault tolerance would definitely be one way to improve it. Increased productivity is certainly a good thing, but if the server goes down, productivity stops, so answer B is also incorrect. Answer C is incorrect although making backups is important. Data backups do not protect against server system downtime.

62. Answer A is the correct answer. The Unit, or simply designated as "U", is the common unit of measurement in rack systems. A U is 1.75 inches high and is considered the smallest unit that can be placed into a rack. Therefore, answers B, C, and D are incorrect.

63. Answer A is the correct answer. You should make a disaster recovery plan even before you begin construction of your servers. Therefore, answers B, C, and D are all incorrect.

64. Answer C is the correct answer. CSMA/CD stands for Carrier Sense Multiple Access with Collision Detection. Answers A, B, and D are all incorrect by the process of elimination.

65. Answer A is the correct answer. Every SCSI channel must be terminated at both ends. The current setup has the termination at the controller (SCSI ID 0) and the internal drive (SCSI ID 7). To extend the channel to the external device, the SCSI controller's terminator must be disabled. Most new SCSI adapters do this automatically. Answer B is incorrect because the tape drive is the only external SCSI device and must be terminated. Answer C is incorrect because the internal SCSI drive is already terminated. Answer D is incorrect because termination on the SCSI controller card must now be disabled.

66. Answer D is the correct answer. If there is a problem during POST, you should first check the motherboard error codes. If this does not present a clear diagnosis, you should consider installing a POST card, rebooting the computer and reading the error codes off the POST card. Answer A is incorrect because system error codes are generally concerned with OS problems rather than hardware problems. Answer B is incorrect because too much valuable time will be wasted finding the problem FRU. Answer C is incorrect because no POST card has yet been installed.

67. Answer C is the correct answer. The latest PCI slot incorporates a 64-bit PCI bus operating at a clock speed of 66 MHz. This increases the total bandwidth of the bus up to 528 MBps. 66 MHz * 8 Bps = 528 MBps. Answers A, B, and D are all incorrect by the process of elimination.

68. Answer A is the correct answer. The technician will initially switch off the power to the slot containing the faulty NIC prior to unplugging it. After the replacement NIC is securely inserted and tightened, the power switch to the slot is turned back on. Answer B is incorrect because it would be impossible to configure any hardware not recognized by the system. Answer C is incorrect because a server technician never assumes that a component is faulty without further testing. Answer D is incorrect because the question did not indicate that the NIC was being used for bridging purposes.

69. Answer D is the correct answer. Although it is sometimes necessary to research each product's documentation (electronic, hardcopy, and web-based) to determine which is the latest and most detailed information available, in most cases, the supplier's website will have the most up-to-date product information. Answers A and B are incorrect because neither the electronic or printed documentation will contain the most up-to-date information. Answer C is incorrect because books dealing with hardware or software will most likely not have the most up-to-date documentation because they are not frequently updated.

70. Answer B is the correct answer. Although both answer C and answer D might be necessary in some situations, the most likely cause of the problem is that the NOS is not properly configured to provide SMP support. Answer A is incorrect because no proof has yet been provided that one of the CPUs is bad.

71. Answer C is the correct answer. A thread is a section of a program that can be time-sliced by the operating system to run at the same time when other threads are executed in a symmetrical multiprocessing operation. Answer A is incorrect because there is nothing to be gained by executing threads one at a time. Simply having multiple processors on a server board and/or multiple bootable NOSes does not ensure SMP operation. Therefore answers B and D are not correct.

72. Answer A is the correct answer. It is the job of the IT manager or administrator to deal with infrastructure support agencies such as the building super, the power company, or the UPS manufacturer. Answer B is incorrect because the help desk is meant to help users with work-station-related problems. Answer C is incorrect because an "IS help desk" is a fictitious idea. Answer D is incorrect because NOS technical support personnel are not necessarily qualified to work on power-related problems.

73. Answer A is the correct answer. To properly assemble your server, you must verify component delivery first and then obtain latest validated drivers before preparing the chassis (answer C) and the server board for assembly. Installing the server board (answer D) comes next.

74. Answer C is the correct answer. To ensure hardware component reliability, all server components should be validated before installation. Therefore, answers A, B, and D are incorrect.

75. Answer C is the correct answer. A server fitted with an SMP-capable motherboard that has only a single CPU will have an open ZIF socket. Adding an additional CPU will permit the server system to be significantly scaled up. Answer A is incorrect because installing faster memory will not help the existing CPU process more data. Answer B is incorrect because a motherboard designed to use a Pentium III CPU is incompatible with the P4 CPU. Answer D would not be a cost-effective solution.

76. Answer B is the correct answer. When making changes on a server, always: (1) perform only one change at a time; (2) check all available monitoring and event logs after each test; and (3) retest after each and every change.

77. Answer B is the correct answer. The escalation plan is created by man-agement to delineate when, how, and whom to contact in cases where the technician cannot solve a particular problem. Answer A is incor-rect because there is no assurance that the closest co-worker is any more qualified to fix the problem than the first technician. Answer C is incorrect because server downtime is not an acceptable option. Answer D is incorrect because continued work risks damage to the network.

78. Answers A and C are the correct answers. Clustering provides a way of configuring storage so that data can be continuously available at all times. Clustering also eliminates single points of failure because if one PC (or server) fails, another will take over and deliver the requested data. Answer B is incorrect because RAM memory is either good or bad. If bad RAM must be replaced, the machine on which it resides must be powered down for service regardless of where in the cluster it is located. Answer D is incorrect because data failure due to ESD is always a possibility. However, clustering can protect against the complete loss of that data.

79. Answer A is the correct answer. The NTFS5 file system is the primary file system type used by Windows 2000 Server and the Windows Server 2003. Answer B is incorrect because early versions of Windows NT used NTFS version 1.0. Answer C is incorrect because Windows 98 was only capable (with some trickery) of using NTFS version 1.0. Answer D is incorrect because the NTFS4 version is used in Windows NT 4.0.

80. Answer C is the correct answer. NAS hardware devices are assigned their own IP addresses, making them accessible by clients through a server acting as a gateway to the data. The architecture of a SAN works to make all included storage devices available to all servers, but the stored data does not reside directly on any of the network servers. Answer A is incorrect because although NAS is a less expensive solution than SAN, this difference is not major. Answer B is incorrect because drive identification, although done differently, is not the main concern with these data structures; retrieving the desired data is. Answer D is incorrect because although SAN data transfers take place across fast Fibre Channel systems, NAS systems are not that much slower.

Practice Exam 2

1. What server type is normally used for data farm and archive server operations?
   - ❑ A. Front-end servers
   - ❑ B. Mid-tier servers
   - ❑ C. Back-end servers
   - ❑ D. Appliance servers

2. You have installed five 2U server chassis on a full rack. How many inches do you have left in your rack?
   - ❑ A. 50 inches
   - ❑ B. 56 inches
   - ❑ C. 60 inches
   - ❑ D. 65 inches

3. What is the Simple Network Management Protocol used for?
   - ❑ A. To disassemble a packet before it is sent
   - ❑ B. To display and modify the IP-to-Physical address translation tables
   - ❑ C. To communicate with and receive alerts from a TCP/IP network
   - ❑ D. To send alerts to a hub or router on a TCP/IP network

4. A device has power connected but is not in active service. It operates as a standby, ready-to-go component. What is it called?
   - ❑ A. Hot-swappable
   - ❑ B. Warm-swappable
   - ❑ C. Hot spare
   - ❑ D. Hot-plugged device

5. Server management components designed to implement a complete server management solution do not include which of the following?

❑ A. Monitoring software

❑ B. Alarm/warning systems

❑ C. Networked games

❑ D. Remote management features

6. A technician is reporting environmental issues with the server room. Which of the following problems should be considered the most important?

❑ A. Unlocked server cabinet

❑ B. Coffee cup on top of the server rack

❑ C. Trash cans in server room

❑ D. Spare parts on the floor of the server room

7. To what directory does the floppy drive usually mount in a Linux operating system?

❑ A. `/dev/fd0`

❑ B. `/mnt/floppy`

❑ C. `\dev\fd0`

❑ D. `\mnt\floppy`

8. Which of the following is the best policy for storing the disaster recovery plan?

❑ A. Print out a copy of the disaster recovery plan and store it in a safe place.

❑ B. Save a copy of the disaster recovery plan to the primary hard drive.

❑ C. Save a copy of the disaster recovery plan to the secondary hard drive.

❑ D. Print out a copy of the disaster recovery plan and store it with the other documentation dealing with the network configuration.

9. Which of the following servers can potentially be configured to host more than one site?

❑ A. Terminal server

❑ B. Database server

❑ C. Proxy server

❑ D. Web server

10. Which of the following procedures should you *not* follow when moving a full server rack?

❑ A. Make sure you unplug the components before moving the rack.

❑ B. Remove the components before moving the rack.

❑ C. Move the server rack to its new destination without removing its components.

❑ D. Clear everything in your path before moving the rack.

11. SNMP transfers data in what format?

   ❑ A. ASCII
   ❑ B. Unicode
   ❑ C. ANSI
   ❑ D. ISO

12. Valuable company data has just been backed up to a secondary storage device. Where should it be stored?

   ❑ A. Offsite in a secure location
   ❑ B. In a separate room
   ❑ C. On the hard drive
   ❑ D. In a secure place in the building

13. Which backup method restores the system faster, but takes more time and space to perform the actual backups?

   ❑ A. Incremental backup
   ❑ B. Selective backup
   ❑ C. Weekly backup
   ❑ D. Differential backup

14. Which of the following situations presents the most important security issue?

   ❑ A. Not having proper venting on the air-conditioning system
   ❑ B. Not locking the server case and server room door
   ❑ C. Not having clean floors
   ❑ D. Having a cup of water near the server

15. What problem can occur when RAM compatibility is not checked?

   ❑ A. The system might not boot.
   ❑ B. The server board might fry.
   ❑ C. The RAM on the server board might be destroyed.
   ❑ D. The NOS might become corrupted.

16. Which of the following application servers acts as an intermediary between a workstation user and the Internet by caching frequently visited websites to save bandwidth?

   ❑ A. Mail server
   ❑ B. Proxy server
   ❑ C. News server
   ❑ D. Terminal server

17. Which of the following should be stored offsite in addition to a set of backup tapes?

  ❑ A. Driver documentation

  ❑ B. Copy of the server user manual

  ❑ C. Copy of the logical disk user manual

  ❑ D. Copy of the disaster recovery plan

18. Which of the following types of servers is designed to assist network navigation by resolving TCP/IP names to IP addresses?

  ❑ A. DNS server

  ❑ B. SNA server

  ❑ C. Mail server

  ❑ D. NAT server

19. When purchasing a UPS, what should be the most important specification to consider?

  ❑ A. Watts

  ❑ B. Volt-Amps

  ❑ C. Downtime

  ❑ D. Clamping voltage

20. The SNMP model consists of what three basic components?

  ❑ A. Managed Devices, Network Management Systems, Servers

  ❑ B. Network Management Systems, Managed Devices, Agents

  ❑ C. Network Management Systems, Managed Devices, Nodes

  ❑ D. Agents, Servers, Managed Devices

21. In which tier environment are blade servers best suited for deployment?

  ❑ A. Tier 3, as a database server

  ❑ B. Tier 0, as an edge server

  ❑ C. Tier 4, as a back-end server

  ❑ D. Tier 1, as a front-end server

22. Which of the following should you consider when adding additional memory to the server?

  ❑ A. Using sticks having different CAS types

  ❑ B. Upgrading the server board's BIOS

  ❑ C. Verifying whether the NOS is capable of handling the additional memory

  ❑ D. Verifying whether the added memory is compatible with the existing memory

23. A half rack is available for mounting three 2U server chassis and four 1U chassis. How many available Us remain after these chassis are installed?

    ❏ A. 5 Us
    ❏ B. 11 Us
    ❏ C. 22 Us
    ❏ D. 33 Us

24. A company wants its employees to be able to work with a new software application, but the affected users are concerned that the installation of the new program will slow the system down. How should the server administrator handle this concern?

    ❏ A. Run an installation baseline on the test system first and then perform the necessary observations and adjustments.
    ❏ B. Run an installation baseline on the company system and then perform the necessary observations and adjustments.
    ❏ C. Refuse to install the new program, based on the concerns of the affected employees.
    ❏ D. Skip the baseline and install the new program as instructed by management.

25. After recognizing a server room environmental issue, what should the administrator's next step be?

    ❏ A. Try to resolve the problem.
    ❏ B. Move the servers to another room.
    ❏ C. Report the condition to the maintenance personnel or building superintendent for resolution.
    ❏ D. Do nothing because it is not the administrator's problem. This is a problem for maintenance personnel.

26. Which of the following uses would be suitable for a blade server?

    ❏ A. Back-end system for web hosting
    ❏ B. Middle-end email reader
    ❏ C. Edge server system counter
    ❏ D. Front-end system for web hosting

27. Which of the following are 64-bit operating systems? (Select all correct answers.)

    ❏ A. Panther
    ❏ B. Redhat Linux
    ❏ C. Windows Server 2003
    ❏ D. Windows 98

28. How many tapes are required for each category in the grandfather-father-son backup implementation?
    - ❑ A. Grandfather = 4, father = 1, son = 1
    - ❑ B. Grandfather = 1, father = 1, son = 4
    - ❑ C. Grandfather = 1, father = 4, son = 1
    - ❑ D. Grandfather = 1, father = 1, son = 1

29. Which of the following statements best describes scalability?
    - ❑ A. The ability to add more users to the system
    - ❑ B. The ease with which a system or component can be modified to resolve a problem associated with additional loading
    - ❑ C. The ease with which additional server boards and processors can be added to the system to increase network performance
    - ❑ D. The ability to reduce problems with a server when adding additional users to the system

30. When moving a large server rack from one office or floor level to another, what is the proper order of events?
    - ❑ A. Remove all components, create an accurate rack wiring diagram, move the rack, rewire components, and then replace components.
    - ❑ B. Rewire the components, create an accurate rack wiring diagram, remove all components, and then move the rack.
    - ❑ C. Create an accurate rack wiring diagram, replace components, remove all components, move the rack, and then rewire components.
    - ❑ D. Create an accurate rack wiring diagram, remove all components, move the rack, replace components, and then rewire components.

31. What kind of server is a viable alternative to using email for transferring extremely large files?
    - ❑ A. FTP server
    - ❑ B. Web server
    - ❑ C. Application server
    - ❑ D. Terminal server

32. A company just added 50 users to their network. Comparing the baseline for peak usage both before and after the additions (shown in the following table) indicates that the performance of the server has dropped below its predefined tolerance level. Where does the problem lie and how can it be resolved?

Parameter	Before	After
Microprocessor utilization	50%	60%
Network utilization	25%	40%
Memory paging	1000 pages/sec	3000 pages/sec
Disk drive utilization	10%	8%

- ❏ A. Microprocessor. Solution: Add another CPU.
- ❏ B. Disk drive. Solution: Add more HDDs.
- ❏ C. Memory. Solution: Install more RAM.
- ❏ D. Network. Solution: Install an additional NIC.

33. A technician is attempting to upgrade the RAM for a server. After placing the RAM in his own workstation and verifying that it is functional, he installs the RAM in the server and discovers that the RAM does not work. What is the most likely problem with this RAM?
- ❏ A. The RAM is defective.
- ❏ B. The RAM is DDR-2, and the server supports DDR.
- ❏ C. The RAM is not ECC-compatible.
- ❏ D. The RAM is designed for faster operations.

34. Which of the following actions must be taken when replacing devices in a hot-swappable PCI slot?
- ❏ A. Turn off the service for the device before swapping the device.
- ❏ B. Completely turn off the computer before swapping any device.
- ❏ C. Simply remove the original device and replace it with another.
- ❏ D. Reinstall the driver first; then swap the specified device.

35. When discussing the subject of RAM volatility, which of the following is true?
- ❏ A. All data stored in RAM is lost when power is discontinued.
- ❏ B. When power is discontinued, DRAM loses its data, but SRAM does not.
- ❏ C. When power is discontinued, SRAM loses its data, but DRAM does not.
- ❏ D. All data stored in RAM is saved when power is discontinued.

36. The most recent full tape backup of a server occurred at 1:00 a.m. Sunday morning, and differential backup tapes were recorded every day at their specified p.m. time periods. At 9:30 a.m. on Tuesday, the server crashed. How many tapes are required to restore the system?

   ❑ A. One
   ❑ B. Two
   ❑ C. Three
   ❑ D. Four

37. DDR-SDRAM is a form of SDRAM that can do which of the following?

   ❑ A. Transfer data on both the leading and falling edges of each clock cycle.
   ❑ B. Transfer data on the leading edge of each clock cycle.
   ❑ C. Transfer data on the falling edge of each clock cycle.
   ❑ D. Transfer data only during the most stable portion of each clock cycle.

38. A system consumed 0.4 seconds of processor time, 0.3 seconds accessing the network, and 0.5 seconds accessing the disk drive to execute a task. Where is the bottleneck in this network?

   ❑ A. The processor
   ❑ B. The memory
   ❑ C. The network
   ❑ D. The disk drive

39. Which type of memory is normally reserved for local, temporary data storage by the microprocessor?

   ❑ A. Buffered memory
   ❑ B. Video memory
   ❑ C. Cache memory
   ❑ D. Registered memory

40. What are the two most common types of active offsite storage facilities in use today?

   ❑ A. Hot sites/warm sites
   ❑ B. Cold sites/hot sites
   ❑ C. Cold sites/warm sites
   ❑ D. Hot sites/medium sites

41. When using a three-channel SCSI-3 RAID 5 controller, what is the maximum number of disk drives you can use in the array?

   ❑ A. 47
   ❑ B. 45
   ❑ C. 23
   ❑ D. 21

42. A KVM is a switchbox through which multiple servers are interfaced using a single _____.
    - ❏ A. Keypad, vacuum, and monitor
    - ❏ B. Keylock, VCR, and mouse
    - ❏ C. Keyswitch, video, and monitor
    - ❏ D. Keyboard, monitor, and mouse

43. Which of the following protocols should you use to monitor a server from a remote location?
    - ❏ A. TCP/IP
    - ❏ B. NetBEUI
    - ❏ C. SNMP
    - ❏ D. IPX/SPX

44. A hard drive is replaced with a new one while the server system is running. What is this procedure called?
    - ❏ A. Swapping
    - ❏ B. Cold swapping
    - ❏ C. Warm swapping
    - ❏ D. Hot swapping

45. What was the bus size and bus speed of the first SCSI standard?
    - ❏ A. 8 bits/5MHz
    - ❏ B. 8 bits/7MHz
    - ❏ C. 16 bits/7MHz
    - ❏ D. 16 bits/5MHz

46. Which of the following substances can safely be used to clean accumulated dust from inside a server case?
    - ❏ A. Isopropyl alcohol
    - ❏ B. Water
    - ❏ C. Vacuum air
    - ❏ D. Compressed air

47. Which of the following describe a SATA signal connector? (Select all correct answers.)
    - ❏ A. It consists of seven lines in a single row.
    - ❏ B. It is seven-eighths of an inch wide.
    - ❏ C. It is half an inch wide.
    - ❏ D. It consists of 15 lines in two rows.

48. What is a sniffer used for?

   ❏ A. Intercepting and analyzing packets as they are transmitted over a network
   ❏ B. Blocking Novell data packets as they are transmitted over a network
   ❏ C. Testing the network to indicate where bottlenecks are located
   ❏ D. Probing a network to indicate the location of ports that can be hacked

49. A newly formatted DAT tape works properly in a new tape drive. However, when it is placed in an older tape drive, error messages result. What could be the problem?

   ❏ A. The tape is broken.
   ❏ B. The tape is write-protected.
   ❏ C. New tapes do not work with older tape drives.
   ❏ D. The read/record format of the older tape drive is not compatible with the new tape drive.

50. What Fibre Channel port is used to link to either a single F port or N port using a switch on a point-to-point connection?

   ❏ A. FL port
   ❏ B. E port
   ❏ C. N port
   ❏ D. SS port

51. What is the difference between UTP and STP networking cable?

   ❏ A. STP cable contains an additional layer of insulation surrounding the four-pair wire bundle.
   ❏ B. STP cable contains an additional foil shield surrounding the four-pair wire bundle.
   ❏ C. UTP cable contains an additional layer of insulation surrounding the four-pair wire bundle.
   ❏ D. UTP cable contains an additional foil shield surrounding the four-pair wire bundle.

52. At a minimum, what server information should be documented?

   ❏ A. Associated printed documents, reference storage disks, maintenance data, and applicable resource websites
   ❏ B. Reference storage disks, maintenance data, email configuration, and server manufacturer information
   ❏ C. Maintenance data, server manufacturer information, reference storage disks, and a list of employee telephone numbers
   ❏ D. Associated printed documents, applicable resource websites, employee email addresses, and reference storage disks

53. Which of the following parameters need to match when adding additional processors to a server system?

   ❏ A. Stepping numbers, processor speeds, server board, and the maximum number of processors installed

   ❏ B. Processor speeds, stepping numbers, and PCI slots

   ❏ C. Stepping numbers, server board manufacturers, and processor speeds

   ❏ D. Processor speeds, server board manufacturers, and PCI slots

54. A customer has four 18GB SCSI drives in a hardware-based mirror array. He wants a proposed solution that will give him a final capacity of 126GB, using the same size drives. What solution would accomplish this while keeping redundancy?

   ❏ A. Add 3 drives using RAID 5.

   ❏ B. Add 3 drives using RAID 0+1.

   ❏ C. Add 10 drives using RAID 5+1.

   ❏ D. Add 10 drives using RAID 1+0.

55. The server was running normally when observed last night. However, its performance is greatly diminished today. A check of the most recent event recorded in the server room log reveals a late-night cleaning by the maintenance crew. What is the most probable source of the problem?

   ❏ A. External

   ❏ B. Software

   ❏ C. Hardware

   ❏ D. Configuration

56. What is the minimum number of drives necessary to operate a RAID 5 array?

   ❏ A. 1

   ❏ B. 2

   ❏ C. 3

   ❏ D. 4

57. An employee at the help desk is experiencing serious network failures. Who should this employee contact first?

   ❏ A. The company computer technician

   ❏ B. The network administrator

   ❏ C. The landlord

   ❏ D. The IT administrator

58. Which of the following is one of the advantages of having a server rack?

   ❏ A. Not having multiple cooling fans

   ❏ B. Having a high-friction chassis

   ❏ C. Having low-friction rails for easy access

   ❏ D. Not needing to worry about environmental conditions

59. What is the default port used by SNMP?

   ❏ A. 110

   ❏ B. 170

   ❏ C. 161

   ❏ D. 25

60. When adding an additional Intel microprocessor to an SMP-capable motherboard, which CPU characteristics should match the original processor?

   ❏ A. Family, model, stepping

   ❏ B. Make, model, clock speed

   ❏ C. Front-side bus speed, multiplier, cache size

   ❏ D. Internal clock speed, multiplier, cache size

61. Which two components produce a whining noise when their bearings start to wear?

   ❏ A. Modem and power supply

   ❏ B. Soundcard and disk drive

   ❏ C. Disk drive and power supply

   ❏ D. Video card and disk drive

62. What type of RAID is RAID 4?

   ❏ A. Independent data disks with distributed parity blocks

   ❏ B. Independent data disks with shared parity disk

   ❏ C. Parallel transfer with parity striping

   ❏ D. Data striping with error recovery

63. You need to reroute some cables, which will require moving a server rack. What is the best method for moving an established server rack?

   ❏ A. Remove all equipment from the rack and move it to the new location.

   ❏ B. Raise the feet, lower the wheels, and then roll to a new location.

   ❏ C. Place the server on a gurney and move it to the new location.

   ❏ D. Take the heavy components off the rack and move it with the light equipment to the new location.

64. Which of the following is one of the best places to check when you receive an error message or beep code in the BIOS?

❑ A. NOS installation media
❑ B. Server board manufacturer's website
❑ C. Server user manual
❑ D. BIOS manufacturer's website

65. What technology allows a server administrator to insert or remove PCI cards and device modules from a host system while the power is still on?

❑ A. PCI hot switch
❑ B. PCI cold plug
❑ C. PCI hot exchange
❑ D. PCI hot swap

66. What does a KVM switch do?

❑ A. Enables the operation of multiple servers using the same keyboard, mouse, and monitor.
❑ B. Enables you to power down multiple servers on the network.
❑ C. Allows you to disable banks of memory to test memory problems.
❑ D. Allows you to use the same RAM on different machines.

67. Which of the following steps is *not* necessary when troubleshooting an NIC?

❑ A. Check the LED lights on the NIC.
❑ B. Check the driver for the NIC.
❑ C. Check the server board manufacturer's website for the latest driver.
❑ D. Make sure the cable from the NIC to the hub is working properly.

68. When setting up a server with SNMP, which of the following should be installed first?

❑ A. The NOS
❑ B. OEM patches
❑ C. The service partition
❑ D. Device drivers

69. A UPS is properly installed and connected to a server. After bootup, the server cannot recognize the UPS. What is the most likely problem?

❑ A. UPS battery is not charged.
❑ B. UPS is defective.
❑ C. UPS is not connected to the power supply.
❑ D. UPS software is not configured.

70. Which of the following is a good example of a procedure that can be implemented across the network to reduce the potential for introduction of viruses or other malicious code?

- ❑ A. Allow all file types to be propagated via email to facilitate person-to-person data transfers.

- ❑ B. Ignore Internet browser security settings so that users can access an unrestricted range of content.

- ❑ C. Disable antivirus settings on the firewall to lower the risk of software conflicts.

- ❑ D. Use only official shrink-wrapped software products from a reputable source.

71. Which of the following is not a recognized type of server?

- ❑ A. General-purpose server
- ❑ B. Resource-balancing server
- ❑ C. Back-end server
- ❑ D. Appliance server

72. What Linux command line is used to find a specific command's purpose?

- ❑ A. man
- ❑ B. vi
- ❑ C. pico
- ❑ D. ls

73. Which of the following documentation types should be kept for troubleshooting purposes? (Select all correct answers.)

- ❑ A. Original purchase price logs
- ❑ B. Installation/configuration logs
- ❑ C. Hardware/software upgrade logs
- ❑ D. Fire detection logs

74. Which of the following is *not* a valid ESD best practice?

- ❑ A. Apply antistatic sprays or solutions to floors, carpets, desks, and computer equipment.
- ❑ B. Install static-free carpeting or an antistatic floor mat in the work area.
- ❑ C. Use a room humidifier to control the humidity level in the work.
- ❑ D. Install antiglare covers on all monitors.

75. Which of the following is not a Windows 2000 Control Panel object?

- ❑ A. Network and Dial-up Connections
- ❑ B. ConsoleOne
- ❑ C. Users and Passwords
- ❑ D. Phone and Modem Options

76. Why is failover important?
    - ❑ A. To protect against virus software
    - ❑ B. To protect against RAM failures
    - ❑ C. To provide for continuous system availability
    - ❑ D. To protect against power surges

77. Why are USB and FireWire devices considered a security risk in the server industry?
    - ❑ A. Because they are easy to hack into
    - ❑ B. Because of their hot-swapping capability
    - ❑ C. Because they are slow compared to SCSI speeds
    - ❑ D. Because they have no security features built into them

78. Which of the following statements reflects a basic rule about upgrading system peripheral firmware?
    - ❑ A. When the server system is sufficiently performing the tasks for which it was designed, don't modify it.
    - ❑ B. Never upgrade, because all server systems are secure and stable enough after their first installation.
    - ❑ C. Always upgrade whenever possible to stay as technologically superior as possible.
    - ❑ D. Upgrade the system peripheral firmware once a year to prevent gradual system obsolescence.

79. Which of the following is the cause of most hardware-related network problems?
    - ❑ A. RAM
    - ❑ B. Microprocessors
    - ❑ C. Faulty cabling and connectors
    - ❑ D. Hard drive failures

80. Which of the following types of servers are capable of caching client requests? (Select all correct answers.)
    - ❑ A. DNS server
    - ❑ B. Proxy server
    - ❑ C. DHCP server
    - ❑ D. RAS server

Answers to Practice Exam 2

Answer Key

1. C	**17.** D	**33.** C
2. B	**18.** A	**34.** C
3. C	**19.** B	**35.** A
4. C	**20.** B	**36.** B
5. C	**21.** D	**37.** A
6. A	**22.** D	**38.** D
7. B	**23.** B	**39.** C
8. A	**24.** A	**40.** B
9. D	**25.** C	**41.** B
10. C	**26.** D	**42.** D
11. A	**27.** B, C	**43.** C
12. A	**28.** B	**44.** D
13. D	**29.** B	**45.** A
14. B	**30.** D	**46.** D
15. A	**31.** A	**47.** A, C
16. B	**32.** C	**48.** A

49. D	**60.** A	**71.** B
50. C	**61.** C	**72.** A
51. B	**62.** B	**73.** B, C
52. A	**63.** A	**74.** D
53. A	**64.** D	**75.** B
54. D	**65.** D	**76.** C
55. A	**66.** A	**77.** B
56. C	**67.** C	**78.** A
57. B	68. C	**79.** C
58. C	**69.** D	**80.** A, B
59. C	**70.** D	

Answers to Exam Questions

1. Answer C is the correct answer. Back-end servers typically are large, expensive units used to store vast volumes of data in archives and data farms. A typical back-end server used in a data warehouse operation can have 30 or more disk drives connected to it. Answer A is incorrect because front-end servers are configured to perform one or more functions not related to data farm and archive server operations. Answer B is incorrect because mid-tier servers are designed to pass information between front-end and back-end servers. Answer D is incorrect because appliance servers provide a single service such as web serving or multi-services such as providing Internet caching and firewall protection.

2. Answer B is the correct answer. Rack mount cases and other rack mount components are measured in terms of Us, and typically come in 1U, 2U, 4U, or 5U sizes. The height of one U is equal to 1.75 inches. If the height of a full rack is 42U, its overall height equals 42×1.75, or 73.5 inches. Five 2U server chassis equal 10×1.75, or 17.5 inches. The rack would still have 32×1.75, or 56 inches of mounting space remaining. Therefore, answers A, C, and D are incorrect.

3. Answer C is the correct answer. It is a simple request/response protocol that communicates with and receives alerts from a TCP/IP network. It manages information between SNMP-managed devices, SNMP agents, and the Network Management System (NMS). Answer

A is incorrect because packets are not disassembled prior to transmission. Answer B is incorrect because the IP-to-Physical address translation tables are displayed using the ARP utility. Answer D is incorrect because hubs and routers are concerned with message distribution, not with taking action upon receiving an alert.

4. Answer C is the correct answer. The term hot spare refers to a standby drive that sits idle in an array until a drive in the array fails. The hot spare then automatically assumes the role of the failed drive. Answer A is incorrect because the term hot-swappable describes a device that can be inserted or removed from a host system without having to shut down the system's power. Answer B is incorrect because the term warm-swappable does not exist. Answer D is incorrect because a hot-plugged device is a PCI adapter that plugs into a PCI slot enabled by Hot Plug PCI technology. The slot can be powered on and off independently so that the entire system does not have to be powered down.

5. Answer C is the correct answer. Although computer games are fun for home networks, they do not provide useful software management in a server environment, and are not permitted. On the other hand, answers A, B, and D do represent necessary functions of a proactive server management program.

6. Answer A is the correct answer. An unlocked server cabinet is the most immediate threat because it has the greatest potential for catastrophic failure of the system. Answers B, C, and D are all legitimate environmental issues for a server room. However, none of them are as important as an unlocked server cabinet.

7. Answer B is the correct answer. In a Linux operating system, the floppy drive mounts to the `/mnt/floppy` subdirectory. Answer A is incorrect because the directory information is erroneous. Answers C and D are both incorrect because both the directory information and the formatting are erroneous.

8. Answer A is the correct answer. Printing a hard copy of the disaster recovery plan and storing it in a safe place is the best way to ensure that it can be easily found when it is needed. Answers B and C are incorrect because saving a copy of the disaster recovery plan to the primary or secondary hard drive is not a good idea—if these drives fail, the plan will not be retrievable. Answer D is incorrect because storing a hard copy of the disaster recovery plan with other network documentation makes it harder to locate in the event of an emergency.

9. Answer D is the correct answer. A web server hosts web pages for intranet and/or Internet access. It can host more than one site depending on its underlying operating system. Answer A is incorrect because management services are special tools and protocols used for remote system management by administrators. Answer B is incorrect because although messaging services provide the capability to send instant messages throughout the network, they have nothing to do with hosting web pages. Answer C is incorrect because although proxy servers act as the intermediary between a workstation and the Internet and can cache frequently visited websites, they do not act as web hosts.

10. Answer C is the correct answer. Server racks are not designed to be moved with components mounted in them. Be sure the rack is empty while moving it and then install (or reinstall) the components later. This will prevent damage from occurring to the components installed in the rack. Answers A, B, and D are all recommended practices.

11. Answer A is the correct answer. SNMP transfers data in an ASCII format. Answer B is incorrect because Unicode provides a unique number for every character, independent of platform, program, or language. Answer C is incorrect because ANSI is the acronym for the American National Standards Institute, rather than the data transfer format for SNMP. Answer D is incorrect because ISO is the acronym for the International Organization for Standardization, and not a format for SNMP data.

12. Answer A is the correct answer. For maximum safety and protection, many companies store backup tapes at offsite locations. Answers B and D are incorrect because placing backup media in a separate room or a secure place in the building does not protect it from a catastrophe that affects the entire building. Answer C is incorrect because backing up the data to a hard drive limits its security to the well-being of that hard drive.

13. Answer D is the correct answer. A differential backup can help restore a system more quickly because only it and the most recent full backup are required. Answer A is incorrect because an incremental backup takes the least amount of time to perform. Answer B is incorrect because a selective backup takes the most amount of time to perform, but it usually consumes the least amount of space. Answer C is incorrect because weekly backups can be performed using any of the three recognized methods, although they are usually configured as full backups.

14. Answer B is the correct answer. Areas of the server system that contain the company's most valuable data should be kept more secure than areas containing public knowledge. Answers A, C, and D are all legitimate security and environmental issues for a server room. However, none of them are as important as an unlocked server case and server room door.

15. Answer A is the correct answer. The system might not boot correctly. Prior to installation, always verify that the correct RAM is being used for the system being installed. Answer B is incorrect because the server board is in no danger. Answer C is incorrect because the technician will not be able to insert the incorrect RAM into its designated slot(s). Answer D is incorrect because neither the operation nor the non-operation of system RAM can corrupt the NOS.

16. Answer B is the correct answer. Although similar to firewalls, proxy servers act as the intermediary between a workstation and the Internet. To save bandwidth, they can also cache frequently visited websites. Answer A is incorrect because mail servers have nothing to do with caching web pages. Answer C is incorrect because news servers receive, store, and distribute strictly news articles to and from newsgroups on a specific network or on the Internet. Answer D is incorrect because terminal servers are primarily used to answer modem-based phone calls and complete connections to the requested node(s).

17. Answer D is the correct answer. A copy of the disaster recovery plan should always be kept at a safe, offsite location. Answer A is incorrect because driver documentation is available from multiple sources. Answer B is incorrect because the server user manual is not considered critical documentation. Answer C is incorrect because there is no such thing as a logical disk user manual.

18. Answer A is the correct answer. A Domain Name System (DNS) server is designed to resolve TCP/IP names to IP addresses. The DNS server contains mappings between TCP/IP names, such as www.microsoft.com, and TCP/IP addresses, such as 207.45.4.12. Answer B is incorrect because an SNA server allows client access to mainframe (IBM) and mid-range data facilities, and also permits print facilities to be located on the host computer. Answer C is incorrect because an email server is used to receive and store email messages in private mailboxes. Answer D is incorrect because network address translation (NAT) servers work as the gateway to the Internet.

19. Answer B is the correct answer. The most important specification to consider when purchasing a UPS is its power rating, which is measured in Volt-Amps (VA). The power rating indicates whether the unit has the required capacity to support all servers in case of a power outage. Answer A is incorrect because although watts are a measurement of power, this is not the parameter used to rate a UPS. Answer C is incorrect because no vendor would consider using downtime as a product spec. Answer D is incorrect because clamping voltage relates to surge protection rather than to the operation of a UPS.

20. Answer B is the correct answer. The SNMP model consists of Network Management Systems (NMS), managed devices, and agents. Answers A, C, and D are incorrect because servers and nodes are not considered to be basic components of the SNMP model.

21. Answer D is the correct answer. Blade servers are best suited for Tier 1 environments as a front-end system for service delivery networks such as web hosting, email, directory services, firewalls, and network management. Answer A is incorrect because blade servers have performance, heat-generation, and cost-efficiency problems that make them unsuitable for more demanding Tier 2 or Tier 3 operations. Answer B is incorrect because there is no such thing as Tier 0. Answer C is incorrect because no such thing as a Tier 4 environment exists in server networks.

22. Answer D is the correct answer. When adding additional memory to the server, verify that the memory being installed is compatible with the memory already installed on the server board. Answer A is incorrect because if the type and speed of the memory stick are not indicated, the CAS rates must be identical. Answer B is incorrect because a BIOS upgrade is performed only to permit a greater amount of system RAM to be installed or on the rare occasion when the system refuses to recognize that compatible RAM is installed. Answer C is incorrect because the amount of installed system RAM does not depend on the NOS.

23. Answer B is the correct answer. The height of one U is equal to 1.75 inches. Therefore, if the height of a full rack is 42U, its overall height equals 42×1.75, or 73.5 inches. Therefore, a half rack would equal 36.75 inches. Three 2U server chassis equal 6×1.75, or 10.5 inches. Four 1U server chassis equal 4×1.75, or 7 inches. The rack would still have 36.75–17.5, or 19.25 inches of mounting space remaining. Dividing 19.25 by 1.75 gives you a remaining rack space of 11U. Therefore, answers A, C, and D are incorrect.

24. Answer A is the correct answer. The administrator must carry out the wishes of management in a way that does not impact the ability of employees to do their work. The best approach is to install the new software on the test system first and take a baseline to demonstrate what effect, good or bad, the new software might have on the system. Answer B is incorrect because the company system is placed in jeopardy without prior testing of the new software. Answer C is incorrect, unless the administrator wants to lose his or her job. Answer D is incorrect because no legitimate excuse exists for administrators of commercial server networks to skip a baseline measurement prior to making major changes to the system.

25. Answer C is the correct answer. When environmental problems are found, the administrator or technician must report the condition to the proper persons for resolution. This means that answers A and B are incorrect. Answer D is incorrect because it suggests that ignoring the problem is acceptable behavior for the administrator.

26. Answer D is the correct answer. Because web hosting is a Tier 1 operation, and blade servers are best suited for Tier 1 environments, web hosting seems to be a good job for a blade server. Answer A is incorrect because a blade server is not powerful enough to assume back-end responsibilities. Answer B is incorrect because there is no such server category as middle-end. Answer C is incorrect because an edge server is used to cache and/or mirror multimedia content that is otherwise stored on the web.

27. Answers B and C are the correct answers. Various 64-bit software and retail OS packages, such as Redhat Linux and Windows Server 2003, make 64-bit computing an attractive solution for business and home use. Answer A is incorrect because Panther is a 32-bit OS. Answer D is incorrect because Windows 98 is a 16/32-bit hybrid OS.

28. Answer B is the correct answer. Answer A is incorrect because only one grandfather tape should be used and four son backup tapes are required. Answer C is incorrect because only one father tape should be used, and four son backup tapes are required. Answer D is incorrect because four son tapes are required.

29. Answer B is the correct answer. Scalability is the ease with which a network system or component can be modified to resolve problems associated with additional loading. Answer A is incorrect because adding additional users to a system with poor scalability only compounds problems. Although increasing network performance is also a good thing, scalability is directly related to handling increasing network load rather than its existing performance, so answer C is also incorrect. Answer D is incorrect because additional users can always be added to a network regardless of scalability.

30. Answer D is the correct answer. The proper order of events for moving a large server rack from one office or floor level to another is to create an accurate rack wiring diagram, remove all components, move the rack to its new location, replace all components, and finally rewire components. Answers A and B are incorrect because the wiring diagram was not created first. Answer C is incorrect because components cannot be replaced before they are removed.

31. Answer A is the correct answer. A File Transfer Protocol (FTP) server is specifically designed to transfer large files, whereas email is specifically designed to handle short messages. Answer B is incorrect because a web server hosts web pages for intranet and/or Internet access. Answer C is incorrect because an application server provides a single service, such as web serving, or multi-services such as providing Internet caching and firewall protection. Answer D is incorrect because a terminal server allows serial line devices to connect to the network, with basic arrangements permitting access only to dumb terminals via modems and telephone lines.

32. Answer C is the correct answer. Generally, the number of pages accessed should be less than 2,000 per second. Answer A is incorrect because the processor utilization time is below 90 percent. Answer B is incorrect because the new baseline shows that disk drive utilization has actually dropped. Answer D is incorrect because the increased network utilization is within acceptable parameters.

33. Answer C is correct. ECC and non-ECC RAM do not work together. If the RAM were defective, it would not work in the workstation computer, so answer A is incorrect. If the RAM were DDR-2, it could not have been physically installed, so answer B is incorrect. Even if the RAM were capable of working in a faster system, it would still operate properly at a lower speed, so answer D is incorrect.

34. Answer C is the correct answer. Special circuitry, built into hot-swappable PCI slots, permits power to be selectively disabled to the specified slot without cutting power to the server. The suspected PCI card can then be exchanged while the server is still running the network. Answer A is incorrect because no device services need to be turned off before performing a hot swap. Answer B is incorrect because the server continues to run during the swap. Answer D is incorrect because no drivers need to be reinstalled during a hot swap.

35. Answer A is the correct answer. If power to the computer is disrupted, all data stored in RAM devices will be lost. This means that answers B, C, and D are all incorrect. Neither SRAM nor DRAM can retain data when power is discontinued.

36. Answer B is the correct answer. When the need for a full system restoration arises, copies of the most recent full and differential backups are required. In this situation, two tapes are required to restore the system, including Sunday's full backup and the most recent differential backup made on Monday afternoon. Answer A is obviously incorrect. Answers C and D are both incorrect unless incremental backups rather than differential backups had been recorded on a daily basis.

37. Answer A is the correct answer. DDR-SDRAM can transfer data on both the leading and falling edges of each clock cycle. This means that answers B, C, and D are all incorrect.

38. Answer D is the correct answer. When the transfer/sec counter is consistently above 80 for a single disk drive and the average disk sec/transfer has a value of greater than 0.3 seconds, the selected disk drive has become a bottleneck to the system. Answers A and C are incorrect because the times consumed by the processor or network access were within acceptable parameters. Answer B is incorrect because no parameters were provided for memory operations.

39. Answer C is the correct answer. A small, fast section of SRAM, called cache memory, is normally reserved for local, temporary data storage by the microprocessor. Answer A is incorrect because buffered memory electronically isolates the user data within a temporary and protective data storage area. Answer B is incorrect because video memory is stored in a separate memory area from microprocessor use. Answer D is incorrect because registered and buffered memory types are considered to be synonymous.

40. Answer B is the correct answer. Answer A is incorrect because traditional offsite storage facilities are categorized as either cold sites or hot sites. Answer C is incorrect because warm sites are a recent strategy and not yet a common industry phenomenon. Answer D is incorrect because there is no such offsite storage strategy as medium sites.

41. Answer B is the correct answer. The number of SCSI devices that can be connected to a three-channel SCSI-3 RAID 5 controller is 45 (3×15 = 45). This is because each channel of the controller can accommodate 15 devices. This means that answers A, C, and D are all incorrect.

42. Answer D is the correct answer. When several servers are housed in a single cabinet, only one monitor, one keyboard, and one mouse are typically used. A KVM switch is used to share these resources among the various servers in the rack. Answer A is incorrect because no keyboard or mouse is mentioned. Answer B is incorrect because no keyboard or monitor is mentioned. Answer C is incorrect because no keyboard or mouse is mentioned.

43. Answer C is the correct answer. To facilitate the SNMP console, or viewer, the SNMP service must be installed at the administrator's workstation, from where he or she can view various SNMP traps. Answers A, B, and D are incorrect because they are communications protocols used to ensure communications between all servers and clients, whereas SNMP is a network management protocol used to provide standard, simplified, and extensible management of LAN-based TCP/IP devices.

44. Answer D is the correct answer. Hot-swap technology allows server administrators to insert or remove cards, cables, PC boards, drives, and modules from a host system without shutting the power off. Answer A is incorrect because merely swapping any component in a running server system could cause severe damage. Answer B is incorrect because cold swapping requires that the system be powered down and the power cord unplugged before the component exchange occurs. Answer C is incorrect because no mention was made of first shutting down services prior to the swap, which is required for a warm swap.

45. Answer A is the correct answer. SCSI-1 has a data bus width of 8 bits with the maximum speed of 5MBps. Answer B is incorrect because SCSI-1 does not operate at a speed of 7MBps. Answers C and D are incorrect because SCSI-1 uses an 8-bit bus.

46. Answer D is the correct answer. After the server case is removed, the only safe cleaning method for removing accumulated dust is to blow it out with compressed air. Answers A and B are incorrect because they erroneously risk the use of fluids near the circuitry. Answer C is incorrect because the use of ESD-producing vacuum equipment risks making physical contact with, and/or damaging electrical discharge to, sensitive components.

47. Answers A and C are the correct answers. The SATA signal connector is half an inch wide and directly connects four signal wires and three ground lines to the receiving terminal in a single row. Answers B and D are incorrect because the SATA power connector is a 7/8-inch wide, 15-pin, single-row arrangement.

48. Answer A is the correct answer. Sniffers can browse through raw network data and decipher its contents by essentially reading every keystroke sent out from a targeted machine, including network passwords. Answer B is incorrect because sniffers do not block data packets, and they are not limited to Novell systems. Answer C is incorrect because a sniffer is not a testing utility. Answer D is incorrect because the mere presence of a sniffer on the network means that it has already been compromised.

49. Answer D is the correct answer. The recognized format on the older tape drive is not compatible with the new tape drive's recording format. Answer A is incorrect because the tape works perfectly in the new drive. Answer B is incorrect because write protection does not prevent the tape from being inserted into other drives and played back properly. Answer C is incorrect because new tapes are purposely manufactured to operate properly with a wide range of new and older hardware.

50. Answer C is the correct answer. Using a switch on a point-to-point connection, an N port is linked to either a single F port or an N port. Answer A is incorrect because an FL (FabricLoop) port located on a switch allows the switch to engage in an arbitrated loop. Answer B is incorrect because an E (Expansion) port is used for connecting one switch to another. Answer D is incorrect because there is no such thing as an SS port.

51. Answer B is the correct answer. UTP contains four pairs of individually insulated wires, whereas STP cable is similar except that it contains an additional foil shield surrounding the four-pair wire bundle. Answers A and C are incorrect because neither STP nor UTP cable contains an extra layer of insulation. Answer D is incorrect because UTP cable does not contain a foil shield surrounding the four-pair wire bundle.

52. Answer A is the correct answer. Configuration documentation refers to the written information directly related to the server, including server information collected by the installing technicians and the administrator, associated printed documents, reference storage disks, maintenance data, and a list of applicable resource websites. This documentation is required whenever server problems must be diagnosed or disaster recoveries must be initiated. Answer B is incorrect because the email configuration and server manufacturer information are not critical resources. Answers C and D are incorrect because lists of employee telephone numbers and email addresses are not much help in the event of a server failure.

53. Answer A is the correct answer. When adding additional processors to a server system, the processor must be within one stepping level of the other processor(s). For optimal stability, the same make, model, and clock speed should be selected for all of the processors. This includes the use of identical bus speeds, multipliers, and cache sizes to ensure that there will be no speed differences between cache feeds. Answers B and D are incorrect because the PCI slots are irrelevant to matching processors. Answer C is incorrect because the server board manufacturer has nothing to do with matching processor parameters.

54. Answer D is the correct answer. To reach a capacity of 126GB, seven 18GB hard drives are required. To ensure proper redundancy, these drives should be mirrored. This results in an RAID 1+0 array of 14 HDDs with 126GB of storage capacity. Accordingly, answers A, B, and C are incorrect.

55. Answer A is the correct answer. Because the only logged event is the cleaning episode, the most probable problem source of those suggested would be of external origin, such as a plug being inadvertently disconnected during cleaning activities. Answers B and D are not plausible because the server system itself was previously running normally. Answer C would be possible, but unlikely unless a piece of hardware suddenly failed without previous warning.

56. Answer C is the correct answer. To obtain redundancy, RAID 5 arrays require an extra drive. Therefore, the minimum number of RAID 5 drives required for proper operation is three, making answers B and D incorrect. Answer A is incorrect because an array requires more than one drive.

57. Answer B is the correct answer. Help desk workers are qualified to help solve simple operating system problems, but not serious network failures. For these situations, the network administrator must be contacted. Answer A is incorrect because a computer technician cannot undertake any work on the problem without authority from the administrator. Answer C is incorrect because the landlord is not responsible for maintaining the network infrastructure. Answer D is incorrect because the IT administrator's duties involve the overall administration of the network rather than troubleshooting details. However, the network administrator would contact this person if it became necessary.

58. Answer C is the correct answer. Rack equipment chassis slide smoothly in and out on low-friction rails for easy access. Answer A is incorrect because depending on a server rack's design and job, not

having multiple cooling fans can become a fatal flaw. Answer B is incorrect because server racks are normally designed with low-friction features. Answer D is incorrect because environmental conditions are always a concern when using server racks.

59. Answer C is the correct answer. The default port used by SNMP is port 161, which is typically used for communication. Answer A is incorrect because port 110 is used by the POP3 protocol to retrieve email. Answer B is incorrect because port 170 is reserved for network PostScript printer use. Answer D is incorrect because port 25 is used to transmit email with the Simple Mail Transfer Protocol (SMTP).

60. Answer A is the correct answer. The simplest method for matching Intel SMP processors is to match family, model, and stepping. Answer B is incorrect because the make (Intel) is already known. Answers C and D are incorrect because none of the important match characteristics are listed.

61. Answer C is the correct answer. Both a disk drive and a power supply fan are equipped with motor bearings. Answer A is incorrect because a modem does not contain bearings. Answer B is incorrect because a sound card does not contain bearings. Answer D is incorrect because a video card does not require any bearings to perform its function.

62. Answer B is the correct answer. RAID 4 uses independent data disks along with a shared parity disk. Because the controller interleaves sectors across the drives in the array, it creates the appearance of one very large drive. Although the RAID 4 format can be used for larger arrays, it is generally reserved for use with smaller ones. Answer A is incorrect because distributed parity blocks are a feature of RAID 5. Answer C is incorrect because parallel transfer with parity striping is a feature of RAID 3. Answer D is incorrect because data striping with error recovery is a feature of RAID 2.

63. Answer A is the correct answer. The one drawback to a server rack is that when it is fully filled, it can weigh well over 200 kilos. To move the rack from one location to another, the network server and its components must be removed before the rack is moved and then reinstalled after the rack has been moved. Answers B and C are incorrect because the rack is moved before removing its equipment. Answer D is incorrect because even the light equipment must be removed before the rack is moved.

64. Answer D is the correct answer. The BIOS manufacturer's website should contain the specified information regarding BIOS error messages or beep codes for the version being used. Answer A is incorrect because the troubleshooting information provided by the NOS media will relate to the network operating system rather than BIOS hardware or firmware operations. Answer B is incorrect, although this choice might be second best if the server board manufacturer includes BIOS information for its products. Answer C is incorrect because it is not the best place to check, although it too might contain some useful information in an emergency.

65. Answer D is the correct answer. Hot-swap technology allows server administrators to insert or remove PCI cards and device modules from a host system without shutting the power off. Answers A, B, and C are incorrect because there are no such things as PCI hot-switch, cold-plug, or hot-exchange technology.

66. Answer A is the correct answer. A Keyboard Video Mouse (KVM) switch enables you to operate multiple servers using the same keyboard, mouse, and monitor. Answer B is incorrect because powering down multiple network servers spells disaster. Answer C is incorrect because KVM switches do not disable memory banks. Answer D is incorrect because server RAM is used only by the specific machine in which it is installed.

67. Answer C is the correct answer. The server board manufacturer's website will probably not be concerned with providing drivers for third-party NICs. Answer A is incorrect because the NIC's LEDs can be used to help determine the trouble. Answer B is incorrect because checking the NIC's driver might reveal that an updated version is available or that the one currently being used is incorrect. Answer D is incorrect because a faulty cable running from the NIC to the hub is a legitimate troubleshooting concern.

68. Answer C is the correct answer. For management purposes, the service partition should first be created and configured on a small portion of the primary hard drive. After the service partition is successfully installed, the NOS (answer A) can be installed on the drive's remaining portions, followed by the OEM patches (answer B) or the latest service pack. Finally, the most recent device drivers (answer D) are installed.

69. Answer D is the correct answer. In this case, the most common problem is that the UPS management software is not properly configured. Answer A is incorrect because an uncharged battery should not prevent the server from recognizing the presence of the UPS. Answer B is incorrect because there is as yet no proof that the UPS is defective. Answer C is incorrect because the UPS has been properly installed and connected.

70. Answer D is the correct answer. Using shrink-wrapped software lowers the possibility that it has been tampered with since being manufactured. Answers A and B are incorrect because unrestricted file movement increases the likelihood of network virus infections. Answer C is incorrect because firewall virus checking is essential in the battle against network virus infection.

71. Answer B is the correct answer. Servers can be divided into three major types and defined by the primary applications they are designed to perform. These are general-purpose servers, appliance servers, and multi-tier servers. The multi-tier server category can also be subdivided into three groups, which are front-end servers, mid-tier servers, and back-end servers. This means that answers A, C, and D are incorrect.

72. Answer A is the correct answer. The man command followed by the specific command returns information about the purpose of the command. Answer B is incorrect because vi is the command to activate the Linux default text editor. Answer C is incorrect because typing pico on a Linux screen activates a simplified text editor. Answer D is incorrect because the ls command is used to display a listing of all current files and directories on a Linux system.

73. Answers B and C are the correct answers. Documentation dealing with when installations, configurations, and hardware/software upgrades were performed, who performed them, and what the results were should be kept for later troubleshooting purposes. Answers A and D list documentation that has nothing to do with server equipment troubleshooting.

74. Answer D is the correct answer. The installation of antiglare covers is not a valid ESD best practice. Answer A is incorrect because using antistatic spray or solution is a valid ESD best practice. Answer B is incorrect because the installation of static-free carpeting or antistatic floor mats in various work areas is also valid. Answer C is incorrect because controlling humidity levels in the work area is an ESD best practice.

75. Answer B is the correct answer. ConsoleOne is an administration tool used to manage NetWare server resources. Answers A, C, and D are all program objects in the Windows Control Panel.

76. Answer C is the correct answer. Server systems relying on continuous availability use failover as an important fault-tolerant function to enable additional network servers to assume the duties of a failed server. Answer A is incorrect because failover is not related to antivirus software operations. Answers B and D are incorrect because they represent protection against conditions that could cause a server to fail, whereas failover operations keep the system running in spite of those failures.

77. Answer B is the correct answer. Their hot-swapping capability makes them undesirable in the server environment. Unauthorized individuals could possibly plug in a USB or FireWire device and gain immediate access to the server. Answer A is incorrect because the focus is not on hacking into USB/FireWire devices; rather it is on using USB/FireWire devices to hack into the server. Answer C is accurate but incorrect because the speed of USB/FireWire devices is not what makes them a security risk. Answer D is incorrect because USB/FireWire devices do have security features built into them, although these features do not in any way enhance server security.

78. Answer A is the correct answer. A server system that is performing its intended function should be left alone. Answer B is incorrect because upgrading is a periodic requirement of all server systems, sooner or later. Answer C is incorrect because if the specified peripheral is functioning effectively, it is best to refrain from performing an upgrade until normally scheduled maintenance. Answer D is incorrect because a firmware update should be considered only when the system and the peripheral are showing signs of instability.

79. Answer C is the correct answer. Most hardware failures in electronic networking equipment turn out to be the results of faulty cabling and connectors or improper equipment settings. Answer A is incorrect because RAM problems are generally confined to shortages rather than bad chips. Answer B is incorrect because processor problems usually relate to the available processor's power rather than its failure. Answer D is incorrect because although hard drives fail from time to time, they are not the leading cause of network problems.

80. Answers A and B are the correct answers. A proxy server and a DNS server are both capable of holding onto client requests until they are again needed. However, a DNS server can hold the request only for a limited amount of time. Answer C is incorrect because a DHCP server is used to maintain a group of IP addresses for temporary assignments to the governed workstations. Answer D is incorrect because an RAS server is used to allow a client to dial in to a computer from a remote site.

Need to Know More?

Chapter 1

Havens, Paul, and Jason Ho. *Server+ Certification Concepts & Practices*. Kennewick, WA: Marcraft International Corporation, 2004. (This textbook covers the basics of server hardware components, network operating systems, server designs and configurations, NOS installations, server upgrading, server administration and maintenance, and common server system problem troubleshooting.)

http://www.rackable.com/products/dsheet_pdfs/
Rackable%20Systems%20S3116-NAS%20Server.pdf

http://eracks.com/products/Firewall%20Servers/
config?sku=DMZ&session=00903110077830899

http://www.toptentshirts.com/articles/
article_2004_08_16_0003.php

http://www.pcworld.com/news/article/
0%2Caid%2C106763%2C00.asp

http://www.w3.org/AudioVideo/9610_Workshop/paper14/
paper14.html

Chapter 2

Bird, Drew, and Mike Harwood. *Server+ Exam Prep*. Scottsdale, AZ: The Coriolis Group, 2001. (This textbook covers the basics of server network environments, network fundamentals, server hardware, server storage devices, server installations, server designs and configurations, NOS installations, server configurations, server maintenance, server upgrades, fault tolerance, disaster recovery, operating system basics, network management, and network troubleshooting.)

 Welsh, Matt, Lar Kaufman, Terry Dawson, and Matthias Kalle Dalheimer. *Running Linux, 4th Edition*. Sebastopol, CA: O'Reilly and Associates, 2002. (This book delves deeper into installation, configuring the windowing system, system administration, and networking. A solid foundation text for any Linux user, the book also includes additional resources for dealing with special requirements imposed by hardware, advanced applications, and emerging technologies.)

 http://www.linktionary.com/f/failover.html

 http://www.microsoft.com/windows2000/technologies/clustering/

 http://en.wikipedia.org/wiki/Scalability

 http://lcic.org/ha.html

 http://www.geocities.com/Paris/Musee/2712/tfcc.html

 http://www.webopedia.com/TERM/f/fault_tolerance.html

Chapter 3

 Bigelow, Stephen. *All-In-One Server+ Certification*. Berkeley, CA: Osborne/McGraw-Hill, 2001. (This textbook covers the basics of server installation, configuration, upgrading, preventive maintenance, environmental issues, disaster recovery, restoring, and troubleshooting.)

 Pfister, Gregory F. *In Search of Clusters, 2nd Edition*. Upper Saddle River, NJ: Prentice Hall PTR, 1997. (This is an excellent book for those studying computer architecture, or anyone considering purchasing a server-based system. Depending on specific needs, cluster-based systems may be more appropriate than a single large computer system or a symmetric multiprocessor system. This book gives you the critical information necessary to make an informed decision.)

 http://www.tldp.org/HOWTO/SMP-HOWTO.html

http://www.freebsd.org/smp/

 http://www.microsoft.com/windowsserver2003/default.mspx

Chapter 4

 Kay, Trevor. *Server+ Certification Bible*. New York: Hungry Minds, Inc. 2001. (This textbook covers multiple server types, server installation procedures, configuration and upgrading, advanced hardware issues, proactive maintenance, network cabling and connecting, troubleshooting, SCSI, multiple CPUs, and RAID.)

 http://rambus. org/story/

 http://rambus.com

 http://www.microsoft.com/whdc/hcl/default.mspx

Chapter 5

 Wilen, Adam, and Schade, Justin. *Introduction to PCI Express*. Santa Clara, CA: Intel Press 2005. (This book offers an introduction to PCI Express, a new I/O technology for desktop, mobile, server and communications platforms designed to allow increasing levels of computer system performance. Hardware and software developers will discover how to employ PCI Express technology to overcome the practical performance limits of existing multi-drop, parallel bus technology.)

 Chevance, Rene. *Server Architectures*. Burlington, MA: Digital Press. 2004. (This book presents and compares various options for systems architecture from two separate points of view. One point of view is that of the information technology decision-maker who must choose a solution matching company business requirements. The second point of view is that of the systems architect who finds himself between the rock of changes in hardware and software technologies and the hard place of changing business needs.)

 http://www. windowsitpro.com/Windows/Article/ArticleID/7292/7292.html

http://www.networkmagazine.com/article/NMG20000724S0005

 http://www.mycableshop.com/techarticles/busarchitectures.htm

 http://www.computerworld.com/printthis/
2005/0,4814,100559,00.html

Chapter 6

 Field, Gary, Peter Ridge, et al.. *The Book of SCSI*. New York: No
Starch Press. 2000. (This updated second edition of *The Book of SCSI*
provides down-to-earth instructions for installing, implementing,
utilizing, and maintaining SCSI on a PC. Accessible to readers at all
levels, this is the standard reference for anyone working with or
maintaining a SCSI system. It includes complete coverage of
SCSI-3 and all its latest features.)

 Columbus, Louis. *Exploring the World of SCSI*, San Jose, CA: Prompt
Publications. 2000. (This book helps the server user get the most
from peripheral devices, including scanners, printers, external
drives, and more. It focuses equally well on the needs of hobbyists
and PC enthusiasts, as well as system administrators. This work
includes valuable information about logical unit numbers (LUNs),
termination, bus mastering, caching, RAID, and configuring SCSI
systems. It also provides diagrams, descriptions, information
sources, and guidance on implementing SCSI-based solutions.)

 http://wks.uts. ohio-state.edu/sysadm_course/html/
sysadm-201.html

 http://www.storagereview.com/guide2000/ref/hdd/if/scsi/
protLVD.html

 http://www.findarticles.com/p/articles/mi_m0BRZ/is_6_21/
ai_77610586

 http://www.ppc.com/modules/knowledgecenter/
storagetechnology.pdf

 http://www.paralan.com/lvdarticle.html

Chapter 7

 Schmidt, Joseph Friedhelm. *The SCSI Bus and IDE Interface*. New York: Addison-Wesley, 1999. (This book is a very informative but specialized text for the hardware engineer building interfaces to these buses or the programmer implementing device drivers. It describes terminology, commands, and protocols of both SCSI and IDE interfaces. Coverage includes peripheral core technologies and device models, testing SCSI targets, and SCSI-3 standard documentation (all SCSI material has been adapted and updated to reflect the new SCSI-3 standard documentation). The disk contains the source code for the program examples and a SCSI monitor tool for testing and troubleshooting SCSI devices.)

 Rosenthal, Morris. *Computer Repair With Diagnostic Flowcharts*. La Vergne, TN: Lightning Source, Inc., 2003. (This unique book presents a visual approach to troubleshooting computer hardware problems from boot failure to poor performance.)

 http://www.seagate. com/content/docs/pdf/whitepaper/ D2c_tech_paper_intc-stx_sata_ncq.pdf

 http://www.schelto.com/SFP/SFF/sff.htm

 http://leuksman. com/pages/Ultra-DMA_HOWTO

 http://www.nwfusion.com/details/6350.html

 http://members.iweb.net.au/~pstorr/pcbook/book4/eide.htm

 http://techrepublic.com.com/5100-6255-1041753.html

 http://www.pcmech.com/show/harddrive/78/

Chapter 8

 Naik, Dilip C. *Inside Windows Storage*, Boston, MA: Addison-Wesley 2003. (This book provides a comprehensive look at new and emerging Microsoft storage technologies. The text begins with an overview of the enterprise storage industry and Windows Server architecture, including the Windows NT I/O subsystem. With that foundation in place, readers explore the ins and outs of current Windows offerings, upcoming Windows server releases, and third-party products.)

Toigo, Jon William. *Holy Grail of Data Storage Management*, Brookfield, CT: Rothstein Associates Inc. 2000. (This book documents current trends in storage technology and shows IT executives exactly how to plan a comprehensive strategy for maximizing the availability, performance, and cost-effectiveness of enterprise storage.)

 http://www.lsilogic. com/

 http://www.ofb.net/~jheiss/raid10/

 http://arstechnica. com/paedia/r/raid-1.html

 http://en.wikipedia.org/wiki/
Redundant_array_of_independent_disks

 http://www.ostenfeld.dk/~jakob/Software-RAID.HOWTO/
Software-RAID.HOWTO-2.html

Chapter 9

 Troppens, ULF, Rainer Erkens, and Wolfgang Mueller. *Storage Networks Explained*, Hoboken, NJ: John Wiley & Sons, Inc. 2004. (This book explains how to use storage networks to fix malfunctioning business processes, covering the technologies as well as applications. It provides basic application information that is key for systems administrators, database administrators and managers who need to know about the networking aspects of their systems, as well as systems architects, network managers, information management directors and decision makers.)

 Clark, Thomas. *IP SANS*, Boston, MA: Addison-Wesley Professional 2001. (This guide offers an overview of new IP technologies, focusing on practical implementations. It explains existing data access paradigms and recent innovations of IP-based SANs. Discussing basic architecture and products alongside management strategies, the book provides general instruction for meeting increased storage needs. IP storage and related vendors are listed. A glossary is included.)

 Farley, Marc. *Building Storage Networks*, Columbus, OH: Osborne/McGraw-Hill 2001. (This book gives information professionals the basic skills needed to understand modern storage technologies. The author argues that the common storage types SAN and NAS are two different manifestations of a common set of principles, which all professionals should understand no matter which solution they implement.)

 http://www.networkmagazine.com/shared/article/
showArticle.jhtml?articleId=8702597&classroom=

 http://www.cptech. com/index.jsp?tnAction=cto&articleId=13

 http://www.smallbusinesscomputing. com/webmaster/article.php/
2197291

 http://www.mskl.de/CONTENT/63/san-tutorial.pdf

Chapter 10

 Deuby, Sean. *Windows 2000 Server: Planning and Migration*, New York: Macmillan Technical Publishing 1999. (Full of practical advice for the designer of large-scale NT networks, this book provides tips and design techniques gained by the author from years of personal experience as an NT architect of large corporations with global NT networks. This book can quickly save the NT professional thousands of dollars and hundreds of hours. Content includes how to balance the design of an NT 4.0 network between ease of administration, distributed security, and ease of migration to Windows 2000.)

 Redmond, Tony. *Microsoft Exchange Server 2003*, Burlington, MA: Digital Press 2004. (This updated version provides thorough coverage of implementation, migration, and management issues for Exchange 2000 and 2003, all backed up by best practices developed by Hewlett-Packard. It's a clear, to-the-point source of information filled with sound practical advice. Whether you are new to Exchange or upgrading an existing Exchange system, this detailed guide can help to tap all the power, performance, and features of Exchange 2003.)

 http://www.sun.com/products-n-solutions/hardware/docs/html/
816-2481-13/app_external_devices.html

 http://www.powercom-ups.com/products/ups.htm

 http://www.cisco.com/univercd/cc/td/doc/product/software/
ios120/120newft/120t/120t1/l2tpt.htm

http://www.microsoft. com/whdc/hcl/default.mspx

 http://www.sun.com/products-n-solutions/hardware/docs/html/
816-1613-14/Chapter4.html

Chapter 11

 Boswell, William. *Inside Windows Server 2003*, Boston, MA:
Addison-Wesley Professional 2003. (This book guides you through
the complexities of installing, configuring, and managing a
Windows Server 2003 system. Thousands of practical tips, recommendations, diagnostic aids, and troubleshooting techniques based
on actual deployments and migrations help you set up and maintain
a high-performance, reliable, and secure server that meets or
exceeds the needs of its users.)

 Missbach, Michael, Hoffman, Uwe M. *SAP Hardware Solutions*,
Upper Saddle River, NJ: Prentice Hall 2000. (The book includes
detailed coverage of disaster recovery, including sophisticated zero-
down-time backup and remote database mirror solutions; clustering
and automated failover for high availability; and requirements for
client PCs, printers, and output management systems. The book's
extensive section on networking covers everything from network
architectures and IP address structures to the physical components
of a SAP network, including innovative high-availability approaches
to cabling infrastructures.)

 http://www20.tomshardware. com/howto/20040319/
server-05.html

 http://support.intel.com/support/motherboards/server/srcu31a/
sb/CS-012432.htm

 http://publib.boulder. ibm.com/infocenter/iseries/v5r3/ic2924/
index.htm?info/rzahghardware.htm

 http://www.microsoft.com/technet/prodtechnol/
windowsserver2003/library/ServerHelp/
2798643f-427a-4d26-b510-d7a4a4d3a95c.mspx

 http://www.faqs.org/docs/Linux-HOWTO/
Network-Install-HOWTO.html

 http://h30097.www3.hp.com/docs/cluster_doc/cluster_15/
TCR_HWCFG/CHHRDWRC.HTM

Chapter 12

 Held, Gilbert. *Server Management*, Boca Raton, FL: Auerbach Publications 2000. (This book contains concentrated information explaining the specific server management technologies. It includes multi-chapter information on selecting an NOS or server platform upgrade or migration/conversion. Included are guidelines for problem identification and resolution in server-specific areas. Particularly useful for troubleshooting are the case-study chapters supplying examples from common situations, such as selecting a processor type for a particular server application, new NOS design considerations, and disk drive array level selection.)

 Robb, Drew. *Server Disk Management in a Windows Environment*, Boca Raton, FL: Auerbach Publications 2003. (This book explains the basic elements of disks and disk architectures, and explores how to successfully manage and maintain functionality within a Windows environment. The author focuses on critical issues that are often ignored by other books on this subject, issues including disk quotas, fragmentation, optimization, hard drive reliability, asset management, software deployment, and system forensics.)

 http://www.serverwatch.com/tutorials/article.php/3500916

 http://www.openxtra. co.uk/articles/

 http://mcpmag. com/features/article.asp?EditorialsID=278

 http://searchwinsystems.techtarget.com/originalContent/ 0,289142,sid68_gci1091974,00.html?bucket=NEWS

 http://www.wown. com/articles_tutorials/ File_Server_Windows_2003.html

 http://www.microsoft.com/windowsserver2003/community/ centers/management/default.mspx

Chapter 13

 Shinder, Thomas W. and Martin Grasdal. *Configuring ISA Server 2004*, Cambridge, MA: Syngress Publishing 2004. (This book provides step-by-step instructions for installing Internet Security and Acceleration (ISA) Server 2004 in common networking scenarios, taking into account different network configurations, business models, and ISA Server roles. The authors compare ISA Server 2004 with other firewall solutions, and explain how to create firewall access policies, publish network services to the Internet, protect remote access and VPN connections, and make best use of the server's web caching.)

 Minasi, Mark and Christa Anderson et al. *Mastering Windows Server 2003*, Alameda, CA: Sybex Inc. 2003. (This book provides the most comprehensive coverage of Microsoft Windows Server 2003. It describes how to plan, configure and install your network, maintain it for optimum performance, and troubleshoot if necessary.)

 http://www.deslock.com/deslockp_tour.php?page=10

 http://www.usbgear.com/USB-Encryption.html

 http://labmice.techtarget.com/articles/usbflashdrives.htm

 http://www. yolinux.com/TUTORIALS/ LinuxTutorialWebSiteConfig.html

 http://support. microsoft.com/kb/816042

 http://www. windowsitpro.com/Article/ArticleID/41403/ 41403.html

Chapter 14

 Mauro, Douglas, and Kevin J. Schmidt. *Essential SNMP*, Cambridge, MA: O'Reilly 2001.

 Perkins, David T., and Evan McGinnis. *Understanding SNMP MIBs*, Indianapolis, IN: Prentice Hall PTR 1996.

 http://www. redhat.com/

 http:// www.symantec.com/

 http://www. execsoft.com/

Chapter 15

 Habraken, Joe. *Installing Windows Server 2003*, Indianapolis, IN: Sams Publishing 2003.

 Morimoto, Rand, Kenton Gardinier, Michael Noel, and Omar Droubi. *Microsoft Windows Server 2003 Unleashed, 2nd Edition*, Indianapolis, IN: Sams Publishing 2004.

 Crawford, Sharon, Charlie Russel, and Jason Gerend. *Microsoft Windows Server 2003 Administrator's Companion*, Redmond, WA: Microsoft Press 2003.

 http://www.microsoft. com/technet/prodtechnol/exchange/55/deploy/upgrade2000.mspx

 http://www.microsoft.com/technet/prodtechnol/exchange/2003/upgrade.mspx

 http://www.novell.com/documentation/oes/index.html?page=/documentation/oes/cluster_admin/data/al3oeqd.html

 http://www.it-enquirer.com/main/ite/more/upgrading_mysql/

 http://windows.about.com/cs/beforeyoubuy/a/aa030601a.htm

 http://www.microsoft.com/windowsserver2003/evaluation/whyupgrade/win2k/w2ktows03-2.mspx

http://www.samspublishing. com/articles/article.asp?p=174154&seqNum=3

Chapter 16

 Mueller, Scott. *Upgrading and Repairing Servers*, Indianapolis, IN: Que Publishing 2005.

 Tulloch, Mitch. *Windows Server Hacks*, Cambridge, MA: O'Reilly Media, Inc. 2004.

 Morimoto, Rand. *Microsoft Windows Server 2003 Unleashed*, Indianapolis, IN: Sams Publishing 2003.

 http://www1.us.dell. com/content/topics/global.aspx/power/en/ps4q00_pirich?c=us&cs=04&l=en&s=bsd

http://www-132.ibm.com/content/search/
computer_accessories.html

 http://www.daileyint.com/hmdpc/handtoc.htm

 http://www.nksd.net/schools/nkhs/staff/jim_viner/A+/
IT%201%20presentations/ITE-I-PPTs/ITE-I-ch08.ppt

 http://www.techsupportalert.com/search/e1721.pdf

 http://news.managingautomation.com/news/264/1520

 http://www.storagesearch.com/news2000oct-4.html

 http://download.microsoft.com/download/e/b/a/
eba1050f-a31d-436b-9281-92cdfeae4b45/dchct. doc

Chapter 17

 Minasi, Mark, and Christa Anderson. *Mastering Windows Server 2003*, Alameda, CA: Sybex Inc. 2003.

 Williams, Jason, and Peter Clegg. *Expanding Choice: Moving to Linux and Open Source with Novell Open Enterprise Server*, Provo, UT: Novell Press 2005.

 Morimoto, Rand. *Microsoft Windows Server 2003 Insider Solutions*, Indianapolis, IN: Sams Publishing 2003.

 http:// www.microsoft.com/windowsserver2003/upgrading/nt4/
upgradeassistance/default.mspx

 http://www.windowsdevcenter.com/pub/a/windows/2004/07/27/
print_server.html

 http://h18013.www1.hp.com/products/servers/management/
hpsim/upgrade-ent.html

 http://www.sun.com/software/products/appsrvr/migration/

 http:// www.intel.com/design/servers/ism/

Chapter 18

 Larson, Eric and Brian Stephens. *Administrating Web Servers, Security, and Maintenance*, Indianapolis, IN: Prentice Hall PTR 1999.

 London, Susan Sage, and James Chellis, et al. *MCSE Windows Server 2003 Network Infrastructure Planning and Maintenance Study Guide*, Alameda, CA: Sybex Inc. 2003.

 Microsoft Windows Server 2003 Delta Guide, Indianapolis, IN: Que Publishing 2003.

 http://www.mic-inc.com/school/serverplus/

 http://www.vtc.com/products/server-plus.htm

 http://www.32learn.com/server-plus.php

 http://www. microsoft.com/smserver/techinfo/administration/20/
recovery/default.asp

Chapter 19

 Desai, Anil. *MCSE/MCSA Windows Server 2003 Environment Study Guide*, Emeryville, CA: McGraw-Hill/Osborne Media 2003.

 Rampling, Blair. *Windows Server 2003 Security Bible*, Indianapolis, IN: Wiley Publishing, Inc. 2003.

 http://www. windowsecurity.com/articles/
Windows-2000-2003-Server-Physical-Security-Part1.html

 http://www.windowsecurity.com/articles/
Physical-Security-Primer-Part2.html

 http://www-106.ibm.com/developerworks/library/s-crack

 http://www-128.ibm.com/developerworks/security/library/
s-pass.html

 http://techrepublic.com.com/5100-6329-5054057-3.html#

http://www. samspublishing.com/articles/
article.asp?p=102178&seqNum=4&rl=1

Chapter 20

 Friedman, Mark and Odysseas Pentakalos. *Windows 2000 Performance Guide*, Cambridge, MA: O'Reilly Media, Inc. 2002.

 Sugano, Alan. *The Real-World Network Troubleshooting Manual*, Hingham, MA: Charles River Media, Inc. 2005.

 http://teamapproach. ca/trouble/

 http://www.awprofessional.com/articles/article.asp?p=99969&seqNum=4&rl=1

 http://www.beaglesoft.com/clwacliservertroublemain.htm

 http://teamapproach.ca/trouble/DNS.htm

 http://www.novell.com/documentation/oes/index.html?page=/documentation/oes/sos__enu/data/hlgnvvum.html

 http://members.tripod.com/exworthy/hardware.htm

Chapter 21

 Young, Terry R. *Windows Server Troubleshooting*, Ottawa, CA: Team Approach Limited 2003.

 Microsoft Windows Server Team. *Windows Server 2003 Resource Kit*, Redmond, WA: Microsoft Corporation 2005.

 http://techprep.mv. cc.il.us:8082/netware/Service/html_7/LAN-CH7.html

 http://www.microsoft.com/technet/prodtechnol/exchange/guides/TrblshtE2k3Perf/a6509466-4091-4fa5-a538-47dd118ebb5a.mspx

 http://www.windowsitlibrary.com/Content/141/13/1.html

 http://teamapproach.ca/trouble/MemoryCounters.htm

 http://www-128.ibm.com/developerworks/lotus/library/app-troubleshooting1/

 http://www.techworld.com/features/index.cfm?fuseaction=displayfeatures&featureid=1462&page=1&pagepos=3

Chapter 22

 Erbschloe, Michael. *Guide to Disaster Recovery*. Boston, MA: Thompson Learning Inc. 2003.

 Toigo, Jon William. *Disaster Recovery Planning*. Upper Saddle River, NJ: Prentice-Hall 2002.

 http://www.petri.co.il/disaster_recovery.htm

 http://labmice.techtarget.com/disaster.htm

CD Contents and Installation Instructions

The CD features an innovative practice test engine powered by MeasureUp™, giving you yet another effective tool to assess your readiness for the exam.

Multiple Test Modes

MeasureUp practice tests are available in Study, Certification, Custom, Adaptive, Missed Question, and Non-Duplicate question modes.

Study Mode

Tests administered in Study Mode allow you to request the correct answer(s) and explanation to each question during the test. These tests are not timed. You can modify the testing environment *during* the test by selecting the Options button.

Certification Mode

Tests administered in Certification Mode closely simulate the actual testing environment you will encounter when taking a certification exam. These tests do not allow you to request the answer(s) and/or explanation to each question until after the exam.

Custom Mode

Custom Mode allows you to specify your preferred testing environment. Use this mode to specify the objectives you want to include in your test, the timer length, and other test properties. You can also modify the testing environment *during* the test by selecting the Options button.

Adaptive Mode

Tests administered in Adaptive Mode closely simulate the actual testing environment you will encounter taking an Adaptive exam. After answering a question, you are not allowed to go back, you are only allowed to move forward during the exam.

Missed Question Mode

Missed Question Mode allows you to take a test containing only the questions you have missed previously.

Non-Duplicate Mode

Non-Duplicate Mode allows you to take a test containing only questions not displayed previously.

Question Types

The practice question types simulate the real exam experience. For a complete description of each question type, please visit:

```
http://www.microsoft.com/learning/mcpexams/faq/innovations.asp
```

➤ Create A Tree Type

➤ Select and Place

➤ Drop and Connect

➤ Build List

➤ Reorder List

➤ Build and Reorder List

➤ Single Hotspot

➤ Multiple Hotspots

➤ Live Screen

➤ Command-Line

➤ Hot Area

Random Questions and Order of Answers

This feature helps you learn the material without memorizing questions and answers. Each time you take a practice test, the questions and answers appear in a different randomized order.

Detailed Explanations of Correct and Incorrect Answers

You'll receive automatic feedback on all correct and incorrect answers. The detailed answer explanations are a superb learning tool in their own right.

Attention to Exam Objectives

MeasureUp practice tests are designed to appropriately balance the questions over each technical area covered by a specific exam.

Installing the CD

The minimum system requirements for the CD-ROM are:

➤ Windows 95, 98, ME, NT4, 2000, or XP

➤ 7 Mb disk space for testing engine

➤ An average of 1 Mb disk space for each test

To install the CD-ROM, follow these instructions:

If you need technical support, please contact MeasureUp at 678-356-5050 or email support@measureup.com. Additionally, you'll find Frequently Asked Questions (FAQ) at www.measureup.com.

1. Close all applications before beginning this installation.

2. Insert the CD into your CD-ROM drive. If the setup starts automatically, go to step 6. If the setup does not start automatically, continue with step 3.

3. From the Start menu, select Run.

4. Click Browse to locate the MeasureUp CD. In the Browse dialog box, from the Look In drop-down list, select the CD-ROM drive.

5. In the Browse dialog box, double-click on Setup.exe. In the Run dialog box, click OK to begin the installation.

6. On the Welcome Screen, click MeasureUp Practice Questions to begin installation.

7. Follow the Certification Prep Wizard by clicking "Next."

8. To agree to the Software License Agreement, click Yes.

9. On the Choose Destination Location screen, click Next to install the software to C:\Program Files\Certification Preparation.

NOTE

If you cannot locate MeasureUp Practice Tests through the Start menu, see the section later in this Appendix entitled, "Creating a Shortcut to the MeasureUp Practice Tests."

10. On the Setup Type screen, select Typical Setup. Click Next to continue.

11. In the Select Program Folder screen you can name the program folder your tests will be in. To select the default simply click next and the installation will continue.

12. After the installation is complete, verify that Yes, I want to restart my computer now is selected. If you select No, I will restart my computer later, you will not be able to use the program until you restart your computer.

13. Click Finish.

14. After restarting your computer, choose Start, Programs, MeasureUp, MeasureUp Practice Tests.

15. On the MeasureUp Welcome Screen, click Create User Profile.

16. In the User Profile dialog box, complete the mandatory fields and click Create Profile.

17. Select the practice test you want to access and click Start Test.

Creating a Shortcut to the MeasureUp Practice Tests

To create a shortcut to the MeasureUp Practice Tests, follow these steps.

1. Right-click on your Desktop.

2. From the shortcut menu select New, Shortcut.

3. Browse to C:\Program Files\MeasureUp Practice Tests and select the MeasureUpCertification.exe or Localware.exe file.

4. Click OK.

5. Click Next.

6. Rename the shortcut MeasureUp.

7. Click Finish.

After you have completed Step 7, use the MeasureUp shortcut on your Desktop to access the MeasureUp products you ordered.

Installing the CD-ROM for MeasureUp Microsoft Office Specialist (MOS) Test Engines

If this book covers the Microsoft Office Specialist (MOS) certification, please follow these instructions:

1. Follow steps 1 through 15 in the section in this Appendix entitled, "CD-ROM Installation Instructions." A dialog displays. Click Yes to install the MeasureUp DSA Engine.

2. On the Welcome screen, click Next.

3. On the Choose Destination Location screen, click Next to install the software to C:\Program Files\MeasureUp\DSA Engine.

4. On the Select Program Folder screen, verify that the Program Folder is MeasureUp DSA Engine, and click Next.

5. On the Start Copying Files screen, click Next.

6. Verify that Yes, I want to restart my computer now, is selected. If you select No, I will restart my computer later, you will not be able to use the program until you restart your computer.

7. Click Finish.

8. After restarting the computer, choose Start, Programs, MeasureUp DSA Engine, Launch.

9. Select a Test Bank and Mode, and click Launch Test.

MeasureUp Microsoft Office Specialist products offer multiple Test Banks. Each Test Bank measures the same skills, but uses a different assessment document and different task wording to minimize memorization.

Certification Mode assessments closely simulate the actual testing environment of the certification exam. Certification Mode assessments are timed, the tasks are randomized, and the task solution is not available.

Study Mode assessments allow you to request the correct solution to each task during the test. Study Mode assessments are not timed, and they allow the examinee to retake questions.

Technical Support

If you encounter problems with the MeasureUp test engine on the CD-ROM, please contact MeasureUp at 678-356-5050 or email support@ measureup.com. Technical support hours are from 8 a.m. to 5 p.m. EST Monday through Friday. Additionally, you'll find Frequently Asked Questions (FAQ) at www.measureup.com.

If you'd like to purchase additional MeasureUp products, telephone 678-356-5050 or 800-649-1MUP (1687) or visit www.measureup.com.

Glossary

access control   Security precautions that protect network users from Internet intruders, or prevent intruders from gaining access to locally networked files that are considered beyond their class of permissions.

Active Directory   A Microsoft technology that enables applications to find, use, and manage user names, network printers, and permissions in a distributed computing environment.

active termination   The practice of adding voltage regulators to the resistors of a passively terminated Small Computer System Interface (SCSI) bus to allow for more reliable and consistent termination. Active termination is the minimum required for any of the faster-speed single-ended SCSI buses.

Address Resolution Protocol (ARP)   This utility enables you to view or modify IP-to-Ethernet address-translation tables.

agents   Small software modules that perform well-defined tasks in the background while other applications and services run in the foreground.

appliance server   Server designed to provide a specific single service, such as web serving, or to deliver a predefined set of services, such as providing Internet caching and firewall protection. This type of server is usually treated as a field-replaceable unit, so if it crashes, it is simply replaced by a comparable unit as quickly as possible. No attempt is made to repair the unit in the network.

application server   Server configured to run programs that can be accessed by multiple users, and can be implemented for handling large information databases. Also called an *appserver*, this machine runs program software that manages all of the application programs running between client computers and the organization's database.

Asymmetrical Multiprocessing (ASMP) A processing system that designates one processor to run system-oriented tasks and another processor to perform user-oriented tasks, such as running applications.

audits The collections and/or periodic reviews of audit policy data, including security events such as valid/invalid login attempts, file creations, openings, or deletions.

authentication The process of identifying an individual as who they claim to be. This process is normally based on user names and passwords.

automatic termination Newer SCSI technology permitting system configuration modifications to be automatically detected and properly terminated, for continued proper system operations.

autotuning Server capability permitting an automatic increase in the number of allowable work items depending on the amount of system memory installed and the way in which the server has been optimized.

availability A measure of the amount of time a company requires the resources shared by the server to be available on the network. It is expressed as a percentage of the time that the server is expected to keep its resource available. The availability level set by the company directly impacts the way the network is designed in terms of components selected for use in the server and the level of redundancy built into the server and the network.

backbone The main physical data bus, or cable, that connects all of the nodes in a large server network.

back-end servers Powerful servers that act as data warehouses that store large pools of information for the other server tiers. The back-end server tier typically includes servers designed for use as archive servers and data farms.

backup software Software utilities that enable users to quickly create copies of files, groups of files, or an entire disk drive. This operation is normally performed to create backup copies of important information, for use in the event that the drive crashes or the disk becomes corrupt. The Backup and Restore functions can be used to back up and retrieve one or more files to another disk.

Baseboard Management Controller (BMC) Intel integrated circuit (IC) device that is part of their server board chipsets. This device coordinates the various server management functions by taking over the responsibility for managing the server's performance and environmental functions from the system's processors. In doing so, it frees them up for additional processing functions that increase the actual computing power of the server.

baseline Server performance measurement initially used to establish maximum performance settings on a variety of components in the server. These measurements should be performed each time the server is altered and the outcomes should be compared to the previous baseline measurement to verify the effects of the alterations on system performance.

bridge A device used to reduce network traffic by filtering Data Link layer frames. A bridge examines MAC addresses to determine whether the frame should be sent on to another portion of a network, or if it should remain in the portion of the network where it originated.

buffers Temporary storage areas used to store data before being transferred to or from a device.

bus snooping A method of preventing access to outdated system memory from some other system device before it is correctly updated. To do this, memory addresses placed on the system bus by other devices are monitored by the processor.

business continuity plan An orderly and planned approach to dealing with any number of unpredictable events ahead of time, so that the temporary loss of critical server data or an important customer service is not permitted to destroy a company's reputation or operational viability.

cable tester Instrument used to test communication cables for continuity and proper configuration. These instruments typically consist of a master unit and a remote feedback unit. The remote feedback unit is responsible for returning signals generated by the master portion of the test instrument.

cache server A special server is used to store files. A cache server that's related to Internet applications will store website information for sites that users have recently visited.

client/server network Network in which workstations or clients operate in conjunction with a master file server computer that controls security and provides services management for the network.

clients Workstations that operate in conjunction with a master file server that controls the operation of the network.

clustering A way of configuring server storage so that the data can be continuously available, such as having a cluster of two or more servers acting and being managed as one.

cold site A location where the backup facility is not always connected to the server. Instead the backup facility only connects to the server for some set amount of time. This is the type of backup that is implemented in most small businesses with the backup machine only being used when performing a backup or restore function.

cold swapping   Device swapping that requires the computer to be completely turned off (and, for ATX-powered units, the power cord removed) before removing and replacing the defective part.

collaboration services   Services that enable multiple users to communicate in text and graphical environments. An example of this is Microsoft's NetMeeting, which possesses a whiteboard application that enables the user to both communicate in a text chat box, and to draw diagrams using the whiteboard.

Common Internet File System (CIFS)   A protocol standard that defines remote file access among millions of computers running simultaneously. Various computer platforms can be used to share files without requiring new software installations.

database servers   A specialized server utilized to store and sort through data in response to client queries. These server types are necessary for organizations that must manage large quantities of data.

data warehouse   A computer storage system that is designed to hold a wide variety of data. This normally involves combining information from many different databases from across an entire organization. Businesses use these storage structures to track business conditions at any single point in time.

decryption   The process of recovering information from encrypted data.

DHCP server   A dedicated server using the DHCP protocol to assign IP addresses to hosts or workstations on the network. When an address assignment is not used for a specified period of time, the DHCP server may assign its IP address to another machine.

differential backup   Data backup technique in which the backup utility examines each file to determine whether it has changed since the last full backup was performed. If not, the file is bypassed. If the file has been altered, however, it will be backed up. This option is a valuable time-saving feature in a periodic backup strategy. To restore the system, you need a copy of the last full backup and the last differential backup.

Digital Audio Tape (DAT) Recording format used in tape backup systems that borrows helical scan techniques from videotape recording to write large blocks of information in a small length of tape. The system uses a dual, read-after-write recording head to place data on the tape at angles.

Digital Data Storage (DDS) The industry standard for digital audiotape formats. These types of tapes can store up to 40GB of compressed data, depending on the data format used. There are currently six kinds of DDS: DDS-1 through DDS-6, with DDS-7 slated for release in 2007.

Digital Linear Tape (DLT)
Digital tape drive format that uses multiple parallel tracks and high-speed data-streaming techniques to provide fast backup operations with capacities in excess of 160GB. These tape drives provide reliable, high-speed, high-capacity tape backup functions and tend to be faster than most other types of tape drives, achieving transfer rates of 16.0MBps.

Direct Attached Storage (DAS)
A storage device, or array, that is directly attached to the host system. This is still the most common method of storing data for computer systems.

disaster recovery plan   A written list of all steps needed to recover data after a failure, taking into account various scenarios, written under the guideline that the server downtime should be minimized whenever possible.

disk duplexing   The practice of duplicating data in separate volumes on two hard disks. Each hard disk is controlled by its own controller.

DNS server   A server that determines Internet Protocol (IP) numeric addresses from domain names presented in a convenient, readable form. Even DHCP IP address assignments must be updated in the DNS server.

domain controller   A server that has been configured to decide who has access to which network resources.

Domain Name System (DNS)
A database organizational structure whereby higher-level Internet servers keep track of assigned domain names and their corresponding IP addresses for systems on levels under them.

drive arrays   A collection of multiple disk drives operating under the direction of a single controller for the purpose of providing fault tolerance. Data files are written on the disks in ways that improve the performance and reliability of the disk drive subsystem, as well as to provide detection and corrective actions for damaged files.

dual-level RAID   Multiple hardware RAID arrays, referred to as RAID 0+1 or RAID 10 and RAID 0+5 or RAID 50, and grouped into a single array or parity group. In dual-level RAID configurations, the controller firmware stripes two or more hardware arrays into a single array, achieving a balance between the increased data availability inherent in RAID 1 and RAID 5 and the increased read performance inherent in RAID 0 (disk striping).

dual looping   A networking arrangement that permits Fibre Channel drives to be simultaneously connected to two separate server environments.

Emergency Management Port (EMP)   Normally one of the system's serial COM ports, which is used to provide remote management that is independent of the server's operating system.

encryption   A process of hiding the content of data packets so that the information in the packet will remain confidential and unchanged.

Error-Correcting Code (ECC) Also called Error Checking and Correction. File transfer protocols that detect bit-level errors, recalculate the error code, and repair the defective bit in a bit stream without shutting down the system.

expander connection manager (ECM)   A component internal to a SCSI expander that accepts status data from the destination expander and path requests from the source expander and sends arbitration confirmations to the source expander and forwarding instructions to the ECR.

expander connection router (ECR)   A component internal to a SCSI expander that forwards transmit indicators from the source expander to the destination expander. It also forwards status responses from the destination expander to the confirmation inputs of the source expander.

failover servers   Servers that include a service that causes them to take over the processing duties of another server in their cluster if it crashes or goes offline.

fault-resilient booting   A feature on server boards that can reboot a locked processor in a multiprocessor system, while the other microprocessor(s) carry the processing load.

fault tolerance   A term used to describe the ability of a system to maintain normal system operations in the face of component failures.

Fax servers   Communications devices that operate through the telephone infrastructure, capable of quickly transporting required documents electronically. The authenticity of printed faxes as legal and official documents is commonly recognized.

Fibre Channel over IP (FCIP) A revolutionary protocol that functionally integrates a number of geographically remote storage networks without changing a SAN's basic structure.

Fibre Channel Standard (FCS) A flow control protocol that uses a look-ahead, sliding-window scheme and provides a guaranteed data delivery capability to transport multiple existing protocols, including IP and SCSI.

Fibre Channel Tunneling Another name for FCIP that translates control codes and data into IP packets for transmission between geographically distant Fibre Channel SANs, used only in conjunction with Fibre Channel technology.

firewalls   Hardware or software methods of blocking unauthorized outside users from accessing a private internal network. These protective services can be implemented in the form of hardware or software.

firewall servers Servers that control the connections between two networks, often acting as a gateway to the Internet. They protect the network by implementing access control to block unwanted traffic, while allowing acceptable communications between the networks.

FireWire Also known as the IEEE-1394 bus, this specification provides a very fast I/O bus standard designed to support the high bandwidth requirements of real-time audio/visual equipment. The IEEE-1394 standard employs streaming data transfer techniques to support data transfer rates up to 400Mbps. A single FireWire connection can be used to connect up to 63 external devices.

five 9's Server industry standard for availability that signifies that the resource is available 99.999% of the time.

Forced Perfect Termination (FPT) An advanced form of active termination in which diode clamps are added to the receiver circuitry to force the termination to the correct voltage.

front-end servers Servers designed to perform a single function or multiple functions that are related. These servers function as mail servers, proxy servers, firewalls, and web servers. Unlike appliance servers, front-end servers pull information from the network's mid-tier and back-end servers.

FTP server A server that a client can contact in order to transfer files by means of the File Transfer Protocol (FTP) over a TCP/IP network.

full backup Type of backup operation in which the entire contents of the designated disk are backed up to a different location or media. This includes directory and subdirectory listings along with their contents. This backup method requires the most time each day to back up, but it also requires the least time to restore the system after a failure.

gateway An interface or mechanism that stands between different types of networks or protocols and provides access from one system to another. It's a special-purpose device that performs protocol conversions.

Gigabit Interface Converter (GBIC) A transceiver that converts serial electric signals to serial optical signals and vice versa. In networking, a GBIC is used to interface a fiber optic system with an Ethernet system, such as Fibre Channel and Gigabit Ethernet.

group An administrative gathering of users that can be administered uniformly. In establishing groups, the administrator can assign permissions or restrictions to the entire body. The value of using groups lies in the time saved by being able to apply common rights to several users instead of applying them one by one.

hardware disk array Multiple hard disks that provide data storage with a high degree of operational availability, performance, and fault tolerance.

hardware stability Measurement derived by testing server boards for compatibility with particular memory, add-in cards, and peripherals.

Hierarchical Storage Management (HSM) A Windows storage management component that enables the offloading of seldom-used data to selected backup media.

High Performance Parallel Interface (HIPPI) A standard technology for physically connecting devices over short distances at high speeds. Basic HIPPI transfers 32 bits in parallel for a data transfer speed of 0.8Gbps. Wide HIPPI transfers 64 bits in parallel to yield 1.6Gbps and newer HIPPI standards are under development that support rates of 6.4Gbps.

High Speed Serial Data Connector (HSSDC) Also called Fibre Channel Style 2, a 9-pin connector type for copper Fibre Channel cabling that provides reliable connectivity up to 75 meters.

High-Voltage Differential (HVD) Signaling systems that run on 5 volts DC. SCSI-1 buses originally used high-voltage differentials.

hot plugging Feature of server boards that enables many of their components to be replaced while they are still running.

hot sites A location where the backup system is continuously joined to a server through either a local or remote connection (that is, this could be a backup facility a hundred miles away).

hot spare Any component that is connected to the server and has power applied but does not actively participate in processes until one of the regular components fails. During this time, the hot spare is continuously being fed information so that it can automatically operate as soon as a unit fails.

hot-swap components Components that can be manually exchanged out of a system while the server is still performing normal operations.

identical shared disks A strategy whereby data consistency is ensured through the connecting of servers to various identical shared disks for rapid recovery in a failover situation.

IEEE-1394 bus Also known as FireWire. A fast I/O bus standard designed to support the high bandwidth requirements of real-time audio/visual equipment. The IEEE-1394 standard employs streaming data-transfer techniques to support data transfer rates up to 400Mbps. A single FireWire connection can be used to connect up to 63 external devices.

`ifconfig`   A Linux TCP/IP command similar to the `ipconfig` command in Windows. It displays the current network configuration of the specified node and allows changes to be made. Among some of the more useful things to configure include gateway, DHCP server, subnet mask, and network mask assignments.

in-band management   The preferred management method for servers accessed through standard connections. Conventional in-band management tools provide a broader range of functionality and greater security than that achieved using out-of-band management techniques, especially with regard to security.

incremental backups   Data backup technique in which the system backs up those files that have been created or changed since the last backup. Restoring the system from an incremental backup requires the use of the last full backup and each incremental backup taken since then. However, this method requires the least amount of time to back up the system but the most amount of time to restore it.

`inetcfg`   A NetWare TCP/IP configuration utility for network settings.

Intel Server Control (ISC)   An SNMP enterprise management console provided by the Intel Corporation.

Intelligent Chassis Management Bus (ICMB)   A bus that provides interchassis communications between different server platforms and peripheral chassis. This bus allows them to exchange management information.

Intelligent Management Bus (IMB)   A special bus that runs through the server board and can be extended throughout the chassis as well as to other servers. This bus enables different servers to communicate with each other so that they can be managed in a consistent manner.

Intelligent Platform Management Bus (IPMB)   A serial bus that connects the server's major PC boards together. It is responsible for transferring monitoring, management control, and system event information between the server board's management devices.

Internet Control Message Protocol (ICMP)   A core protocol of the Internet protocol suite. ICMP is used by various NOSes to send error messages, which can be used to indicate that a requested service is not available, or that a host or router could not be reached.

Internet Fibre Channel Protocol (iFCP)   A Fibre Channel protocol that delivers FC traffic over TCP/IP between various iFCP gateways, replacing the FC transport level with the IP network transport. Traffic running between FC devices is routed and switched with TCP/IP only.

Internet Information Services (IIS)   Or Internet Information Server. A Microsoft file and web application server, or service, that can be used on a local area network (LAN), a wide area network (WAN), or the Internet.

Internet SCSI (iSCSI)   An IP-based technology for connecting data storage devices and facilities across a network and distributing data using SCSI commands over IP networks.

IP addresses   32-bit numbers, expressed in a dotted decimal format, that make up the source and destination addresses of an IP packet.

`ipconfig`   A TCP/IP networking utility that can be used to determine the IP address of a local machine.

Keyboard Video Mouse (KVM) switch   Mechanism for switching one set of video monitor, keyboard, and mouse so that these peripherals can be selectively connected to multiple server units. The input and output functions are routed to the systems and the monitor through a selector switch.

load balancing   The even distribution of network processes among the nodes of a peer-to-peer LAN.

logical disk   A set of consecutively addressed disk blocks as part of a single virtual disk to physical disk mapping. Logical disks are used in some array implementations as constituents of logical volumes or partitions, and are normally not visible to the host environment, except during array configuration operations.

Low-Voltage Differential (LVD)   A SCSI signaling technique that operates on 3-volt logic levels instead of older TTL-compatible 5-volt logic levels. By employing LVD technology, the Ultra2 SCSI specification doubled the data throughput of the 8-bit SCSI bus. In addition, the presence of the LVD technology permitted the maximum cable length specification to increase to 12 meters.

mail server   A host server that holds email messages for clients. The client (the program used to retrieve the email) connects to the mail server and retrieves any messages that are waiting for the specified client.

manageability   In the interest of business continuance, the collective processes of server network storage, configuration, optimization, and administration. This includes data backup and recovery duties.

managed device   A network device containing an SNMP agent. Managed devices collect and store information, making it available to the Network Management System (NMS). Managed TCP/IP devices include bridges, routers, hubs, and switches.

managed server boards   Server boards that are designed to recognize and store information in a log file when problems arise. The server board can be configured to send alerts to a management console or send a page to an administrator by use of a modem.

management controller   Server board chipset component that coordinates the various server management functions. It does this by taking over responsibility for managing the server's performance and environmental functions from the system's processors. In doing so, it frees them up for additional processing functions that increase the actual computing power of the server.

management services   Special tools and protocols (such as SNMP) for remote management, usually for scripting. These protocols enable a system to notify the administrator of a network of specified changes/scenarios that are affecting the server, like increased internal temperature.

Massively Parallel Processing (MPP)   A derivative of SMP, whereby tightly coupled processors reside within one machine, providing scalability far beyond basic SMP solutions. As more processors are introduced, MPP performance increases almost uniformly.

metadata   Metadata provides information about the content, quality, condition, and other characteristics of some specified data.

Microsoft Management Console (MMC)   A collection of Windows manageability features existing as "snap-in" applets that can be added to the operating system through the MMC.

mid-tier servers   Servers that pass information between the front-end and back-end server tiers. This tier typically includes file servers, mail servers, database servers, and web servers.

mirrored drive array   A RAID fault-tolerance method in which an exact copy of all data is written to two separate disks at the same time.

mount points   A specified beginning and end point where a partition or disk has an allocated amount of space to store its data.

mounting   In a Linux/UNIX-based operating system, the process in which directories and partitions can be integrated into one tree structure.

multiprocessing The simultaneous execution of instructions by multiple processors within a single computer.

multithreading Similar to multitasking; the simultaneous performance of two or more tasks by a single computer, where the tasks are components or "threads" of a single application, rather than belonging to separate programs.

multitiered servers Using specialized servers to perform specific functions by organizing groups of servers into a tiered structure to optimize the use of different types of servers that perform related functions.

NAS server A server arrangement that effectively moves storage out from behind the file server, and puts it directly on the transport network using an NIC to transmit both LAN and storage communications. This permits any network user with access rights to directly access stored NAS data.

nbtstat A network troubleshooting command that displays the current TCP/IP network connections and protocol statistics using NetBIOS over TCP/IP.

nearline storage Data that is not online but is capable of being accessed and placed online within 15 seconds. Archived data is typically kept in nearline storage status.

netstat A network troubleshooting command that displays the current TCP/IP network connections and protocol statistics.

network A group of computers and peripherals connected together so that data may be exchanged between them.

Network Attached Storage (NAS) A storage arrangement whereby storage devices are accessed over a network, rather than over direct connections to a server. Multiple users share the same storage space simultaneously, minimizing the overhead through centralized hard disk management.

network availability The amount of time that network services are available: $A = (TB - TD)/T$ where A = availability; TB = time the network is busy; TD = time the network is down; and T = total time the network is available.

Network File System (NFS) A method of making a remote file system accessible on the local system. From a user's perspective, an NFS-mounted file system is indistinguishable from a file system on a directly attached disk drive.

Network Interface Card (NIC) A hardware adapter card that contains a transceiver for sending and receiving data frames on and off a network, as well as the Data Link layer hardware needed to format the sending bits and to decipher received frames.

Network Load Balancing (NLB)
A system that enables incoming network traffic to be handled by multiple servers, while giving the appearance that only one server is handling network traffic, resulting in balance.

Network Management System (NMS)   A system that runs the applications that monitor and control the managed devices through their SNMP agents. One or more NMS elements perform the majority of the work required to properly manage the SNMP network.

offline storage   The storage of digital data outside of the network in daily use, such as on backup tapes. This data is typically only accessible through the offline storage system, rather than the network.

online storage   The storage of digital data on devices that are included in the total system configuration. This data is fully accessible information on the network in daily use.

Optical Time Domain Reflectometer (OTDR)   An instrument that characterizes fiber cable loss by measuring the backscatter and reflection of injected light as a function of time. It is useful for estimating attenuation and for locating splices, connections, anomalies, and breaks.

out-of-band management   A server management strategy using remote serial connections and depending on the security built into the modem. It is used primarily as a last resort when no other server access methods are possible. Its usefulness is oriented toward bringing the server back into service for subsequent management with in-band tools.

passive termination   The simplest and least reliable mode of termination. It uses resistors to terminate the bus, similar to the way terminators are used on coaxial Ethernet networks. Passive termination is acceptable for short, low-speed SCSI-1 buses but is not suitable for modern SCSI buses.

physical disk   This term is sometimes used to distinguish between a logical disk, and a real (physical) disk.

ping   A network troubleshooting utility that is used to verify connections to remote hosts. The `ping` command sends Internet Control Message Protocol (ICMP) packets to a remote location and then waits for echoed response packets to be returned. The command will wait for up to one second for each packet sent and then display the number of transmitted and received packets. The command can be used to test both the name and IP address of the remote unit. A number of switches can be used to set parameters for the ping operation.

private storage bus A structure on a server board that permits the management controller to monitor and grant access to its private storage devices. Devices can use the private bus to store information about the system. This information is digitized and stored in a variety of Serial Electrically Erasable PROM devices.

proxy servers Servers that act as intermediaries between clients and the Internet. They can also cache frequently visited websites to save Internet bandwidth and increase access speed by allowing the internal network to access them locally from the proxy server.

rack-mount chassis A box-like container that houses different types of rack mount server components. The chassis is the rough equivalent of the desktop system unit case. Rack mount chassis are normally mounted on sliding rails and possess easy access mechanisms to provide easy access to internal components.

rack-mounted components Server components designed to be housed in special rack-mount cabinets that are primarily designed to provide service personnel with efficient access to systems so that they can get in and fix problems that may occur on the server.

RAS server A server dedicated to taking care of RAS clients who are not connected to a LAN, but do require remote access to it.

redundancy The practice of devoting extra hardware to maintain network resources. It is one form of fault tolerance commonly designed into server systems. Redundancy may be created inside the chassis with backup power supplies, hard drives, and network cards, or it may be created by adding more servers to the network so that more than one machine will be serving the resources.

Redundant Array of Independent Disks (RAID) Formerly known as Redundant Array of Inexpensive Disks, a data storage system that uses multiple hard drives to increase storage capacity and improve performance. Some variations configure the drives in a manner to improve performance, while other levels concentrate on data security.

redundant component A component that works in tandem so that if one fails, the other will still be working and no loss of data or service will be incurred.

reliability A determination of how dependable a server component or system is at all times.

Remote Storage Service (RSS) The Windows Hierarchical Storage Management system function that enables users to move infrequently used programs and data to slower storage devices, such as tape or CD-R, while maintaining the appearance of the data being present. When the server receives a request from a user for a file that has been offloaded, it retrieves the data from the storage device and ships it to the user. This frees up space on the server without creating an inconvenience when users need to access these files. This function is established through the Microsoft Management Console interface.

Routing and Remote Access Service (RRAS)   A Windows software routing and remote access feature capable of combining Remote Access Service (RAS) and multiprotocol routing. Additional capabilities include support for packet filter, demand dial, and Open Shortest Path First (OSPF) routing.

SAN server   A server that is part of a large-scale enterprise server storage system of attached disk array controllers and tape libraries, including data protection and retrieval functions. SAN servers access their data using low-level block storage methods.

selective backup   A methodology of backing up a system in which the operator moves through the tree structure of the disk while marking, or tagging, directories and files to be backed up. After all the desired directories/files have been marked, they are backed up in a single operation. This form of backup is very labor-intensive and may inadvertently miss saving important data.

Self-Monitoring Analysis Reporting Technology (SMART)   Technology that is built into drives and adapters to signal administrators when problems occur. It enables devices, such as RAID adapters, to monitor themselves. SMART functions are made possible by the fact that intelligent controllers already have processors built into them.

Serial Attached SCSI (SAS)   A data transfer technology that eliminates the headaches associated with clocking and skew compensation in parallel SCSI systems. Capable of providing the high data rates and greater bandwidths required by modern networks, SAS devices transmit data over larger geographic distances than parallel SCSI devices.

Serial Storage Architecture (SSA)   A high-speed method of connecting disk, tape, and CD-ROM drives, printers, scanners, and other devices to a server.

server chassis   An enclosure to specifically house server components in a server environment.

Server Management Bus (SMB)   A special management bus system that runs through the server board to provide independent pathways for the management controller to communicate with the board's other management components.

server management controller
An IC device that is part of the
server board's chipset. This device
coordinates the various server management functions by taking over
the responsibility for managing the
server's performance and environmental functions from the system's
processors. In doing so, it frees
them up for additional processing
functions that increase the actual
computing power of the server.
(See **Baseboard Management
Controller [BMC]**.)

Server Message Block (SMB)　A
network protocol mainly applied to
share files, printers, serial ports,
and miscellaneous communications
between nodes on a Windows-
based network OS.

service partition　A partition that
hosts diagnostic agents and tests
necessary to support the operating
system. This partition also supports
a redirection of a text-based console over supported communication paths, such as modems and
network cards. The service partition is a DOS-based operating
system that is configured with
TCP/IP, PPP, and FTP protocols.

**Simple Network Management
Protocol (SNMP)**　This protocol
is a network management specification developed to provide standard,
simplified, and extensible management of LAN-based internetwork-
ing products such as bridges,
routers, and wiring concentrators.
This protocol provides for centralized, robust, interoperable network

management, along with the flexibility to handle the management of
vendor-specific information.

SNA server　A communications
type of server that allows client
access to mainframe (IBM) and
midrange data facilities. The SNA
server also permits print facilities
to be located on the host computer.

sniffer　A program that analyzes
packets as they move across the
network. These utilities can be
used to check for malformed packets, and also to make sure that
packets are reaching the correct
locations. They can also examine
the data inside the packets, to see if
data is being correctly received
from the right sources.

software RAID　A type of RAID
array that is established and configured using the server's main
processors instead of a separate
intelligent controller to keep track
of the data in the array. Although
this may seem like an inexpensive
way to get a RAID array on your
server, software RAID inevitably
slows the performance of the
server.

standby UPS　A type of UPS system that monitors the power input
line and waits for a significant variation to occur. The batteries in
these units are held out of the
power loop and draw only enough
current from the AC source to stay
fully charged.

stepping levels   The production run of an Intel processor. For multiprocessor server boards, all CPUs should be within one stepping level of all other processors on the board. For optimal stability, it is recommended that the same make, model, and clock speed be selected for all installed processors.

Storage Area Network (SAN)
A specialized high-speed fiber optic Storage Area Network that extracts data from the servers without using the bandwidth of the main network. These networks are connected to the back-end servers and pull the data up to the main network.

striped array   A type of drive array that operates its drives in parallel so that they can deliver data to the controller in a parallel format. If the controller is simultaneously handling 8 bits of data from eight drives, the system will see the speed of the transfer as being eight times faster.

subnet mask   The decimal number 255 is used to hide, or mask, the network portion of the IP address while still showing the host portions of the address. The default subnet mask for Class A IP addresses is 255.0.0.0. Class B is 255.255.0.0, and Class C is 255.255.255.0.

symmetric multiprocessing. A multiprocessor architecture in which all processors are identical, share memory, work in parallel with each other, and execute both user code and operating system code.

system policies   Settings used to establish guidelines that restrict user access to the options in the Control Panel and desktop. They also allow an administrator to customize the desktop and configure network settings.

System Setup Utility (SSU)   A software server setup program that is usually bundled with the server board, and is traditionally not specific to any operating system. It permits the administrator to view the server's critical event logs, and/or get information about installed FRUs and SDR devices that may be installed.

tape backup   The most common method used for backing up hard drive data on a server or client.

tape rotation and storage   A backup strategy whereby the latest data, as well as the entire server operation, is always available on backup tape in the event of a catastrophic failure of the server system.

task   A unit of measurement in operating systems to allocate processing power. Programs are split into tasks. Tasks, in turn, can be split into threads.

TCP/IP   The language of the Internet. This protocol suite calls for data to be grouped together, in bundles, called network packets. The TCP/IP packet is designed primarily to permit messages to be fragmented, and then reassembled, no matter what type of computer platform or software is being used. All information must move across the Internet in this format.

Telnet server   A server used to enable remote users to connect in such a way that their monitors will display information as if they were directly connected to the server. To utilize a Telnet server, the client computer must have a Telnet client installed on it.

threads   Sections of programming that can be time-sliced by the operating system to run at the same time that other threads are being executed.

throughput   A general term describing the ratio of frame header to user data contained in the frame. High throughput indicates that a network is operating with high efficiency, and is calculated by this formula: $TP = C/T$ where TP = throughput; C = the number of messages sent; and T = the total time of the transmission.

trace route (tracert)   A network troubleshooting utility that displays the route, and a hop count, taken to a given destination.

Unit (U)   A standard unit of measurement for rack-mount server cases and components. A U is 1.75 inches high and is considered the smallest unit that can be placed into a rack. The server case may be any size but will come in a multiple of the U size.

UPS clustering   UPS redundancy technique that involves packing several similar components into a frame to increase power in two KVA or four KVA increments.

UPS mirroring   UPS redundancy technique that enables customers to use the UPS components in a manner similar to disk mirroring for redundancy.

validated components   A special class of components that have been thoroughly tested to work together and to work with specific operating systems, including testing for thermal considerations.

validation   The process of testing server boards and components for both hardware and software stability under given configurations.

virus   A man-made program or section of code that causes an unexpected, usually negative, computer event. It can replicate automatically and spread through a computer system, local network, across the Internet, or through infected floppy disks.

Volt-Amperes (VA) Rating   A rating that indicates the capability of the UPS system to deliver both voltage (V) and current (A) to the computer, simultaneously. This rating differs from the device's wattage rating, and the two should not be used interchangeably.

wake-on-LAN   Operation in which the system automatically boots through an NIC to a remote network server across the network.

warm spare   A spare hard disk or other storage system that is installed in the server, and also has power applied to it, but does not spin, thereby reducing wear and tear on the device while it is not participating in system activities.

warm swap component   Any type of component that can be manually exchanged in a system while the server is suspended, but power is still on.

watchdog timer   A feature built into management controllers that monitors the operation of the system processors, and when there is no activity for a predetermined length of time, reboots the server.

wattage rating   The wattage power rating of a device is a factor of multiplying the voltage and current use, at any particular time, to arrive at a power consumption value. This rating differs from the device's VA power rating, and the two should not be used interchangeably.

web server   A server that hosts web pages and uses the HTTP protocol to send HTML and other file types to clients.

web services   Any sort of applications or communications carried out over the web via open, public standards.

WINS server   A server running the Windows Internet Naming Service software, which coverts NetBIOS names to IP addresses.

Index

B

How can we make this index more useful? Email us at indexes@quepublishing.com

How can we make this index more useful? Email us at indexes@quepublishing.com

service packs, 308-309
setting time for, 430-431
upgrading, 428-431
Novell NetWare
patches, downloading from website, 430
updates, downloading from website, 430
NT LAN Manager, authentication, 359
challenge-response mechanisms, 360
NWFusion.com, 649

O

object identifiers (OIDs), system agent
monitors, 326
object monitors
counters, 341-342
network-related problems, detection of,
341-343
offline data storage, 177
offsite storage facilities
cold sites, 550
hot sites, 550
warm sites, 550
Ohio State University website, 648
On-Line Transaction Processing (OLTP),
server clustering, 41
on-when-needed UPS, 259-260
online data storage, 177
online interactives (UPS), mission-critical
applications, 236
OpenXtra.com, server management
resources, 653
operating systems
multiprocessing support, 62
multitasking support
OS/2, 62
Unix, 62
upgrading, 428
operational problems, troubleshooting, 497
operator errors, server failure percentages,
37
Optical Time Domain Reflectometers
(OTDRs), cable testers, 502
optimizing server performance, 524-525
Originator, Fibre Channel port mechanism,
210
OS (operating systems), server installation
plans
compatibility, 228-229
RAM requirements, 228
OS-specific modules (OSMs), Intelligent
I/O (I2O), 134

OS/2
multiprocessing support, 62
patches, downloading from website, 430
updates, downloading from website, 430
out-of-band (asymmetrical) virtualization,
advantages/disadvantages, 283-284
out-of-band ESCON (Enterprise Systems
Connection), 285-287
out-of-band server management, 361-363
overvoltage conditions, 231-233

P

P-cable connectors (SCSI), 153
page file optimization, 336-338
Paralan.com, 648
parity blocks, RAID 5 level, 188
partial backups, 442-443
differential type, 442
incremental type, 442
selective type, 443
passive terminations (SCSI), 156
passwords
administrator safeguards, 468
change frequency, 458, 468
complexity of, 466-467
encryption measures, 467-468
one-time use, 467-468
physical security
administrator safeguards, 468
change frequency, 468
cracking, 465
effectiveness of, 466-467
encryption measures, 467-468
entrance of server room, 464
one-time use, 467-468
selection criteria, 465-466
sniffing, 465
RAS servers, hacker attacks, 22
selection criteria, 458
patch cables
reversed, 239
straight-through, 239
patches
Network Operating System (NOS)
updates, 308-309
NOSs
downloading from websites, 429
locating, 429-430
researching, 428-429

How can we make this index more useful? Email us at indexes@quepublishing.com

S

BTU heat generation, UPS
   operations, 236
case-types
   blade server centers, 7-8
   pedestals, 4-6
   rack-mounts, 4-6
communication protocols
   AppleTalk, 302
   IPX/SPX, 302
   NetBEUI, 302
   TCP/IP, 302
components, improper grounding, 252
counters, 351
device upgrades, exam prep questions,
   414-415
DHCP
   dynamic IP addressing, 25
   IP address assignments, 25
external peripherals
   cable types, FireWire, 304-305
   cable types, Serial ATA, 306-307
   cable types, USB, 305-306
   UPS systems, configuring, 302-303
failures
   financial impacts, 37
   hardware versus operator errors, 37

fax
   function of, 23
   hardware options, 24
   software-based, 24
file
   function of, 23
   large client/server environments, 23
FTP
   accessing, 18
   software downloads, 18
   versus email servers for file
      attachments, 18
gateways, 16-17
general-purpose, 8
   processor types, 9
   RAM requirements, 9
   redundancy capabilities, 8-9
   typical environments, 8
installation plans, 227
   blade servers, 240
   cabling, category 3, 238
   cabling, category 5e, 238
   cabling, category 6, 238
   cabling, coaxial, 239
   cabling, connectors, 240
   cabling, crossover, 239
   cabling, fiber-optic, 240
   cabling, patch, 239
   cabling, Shielded Twisted Pair
      (STP), 238-239
   cabling, Unshielded Twisted Pair
      (UTP), 238-239
   client verification, 227
   desk servers, 240
   domain naming conventions,
      237-238
   hardware compatibility, BIOS
      updates, 229
   hardware compatibility, driver
      updates, 229-230
   hardware compatibility, hard drives,
      230
   hardware compatibility, power source
      variations, 231-237
   network protocols, 237
   OS compatibility, 228-229
   rackmount servers, 240
   racks, 240
installations
   blower fans, 253
   cabling, 263-265

How can we make this index more useful? Email us at indexes@quepublishing.com

How can we make this index more useful? Email us at indexes@quepublishing.com

The logo of the CompTIA Authorized Quality Curriculum (CAQC) progr and the status of this or other training material as "Authorized" under the CompTIA Authorized Quality Curriculum program signifies that, in CompTIA's opinion, such training material covers the content of CompTIA related certification exam.

The contents of this training material were created for the CompTIA Serve exam covering CompTIA certification objectives that were current as of February 14, 2005.

CompTIA has not reviewed or approved the accuracy of the contents of thi training material and specifically disclaims any warranties of merchantability or fitness for a particular purpose. CompTIA makes no guarantee concernir the success of persons using any such "Authorized" or other training materi in order to prepare for any CompTIA certification exam.

How to become CompTIA certified:

This training material can help you prepare for and pass a related CompTL certification exam or exams. In order to achieve CompTIA certification, you must register for and pass a CompTIA certification exam or exams.

In order to become CompTIA certified, you must:

➤ Select a certification exam provider. For more information please visit http://www.comptia.org/certification/general_information/ exam_locations.aspx

➤ Register for and schedule a time to take the CompTIA certification exam(s) at a convenient location.

➤ Read and sign the Candidate Agreement, which will be presented at the time of the exam(s). The text of the Candidate Agreement can be found at http://www.comptia.org/certification/general_information/ candidate_agreement.aspx.

➤ Take and pass the CompTIA certification exam(s).

For more information about CompTIA's certifications, such as its industry acceptance, benefits or program news, please visit www.comptia.org/ certification

CompTIA is a not-for-profit information technology (IT) trade association. CompTIA's certifications are designed by subject matter experts from across the IT industry. Each CompTIA certification is vendor-neutral, covers multi ple technologies and requires demonstration of skills and knowledge widely sought after by the IT industry.

To contact CompTIA with any questions or comments, please call (1) (630) 678 8300 or email questions@comptia.org.